The Kelloggs

The Kelloggs

THE BATTLING BROTHERS OF BATTLE CREEK

Howard Markel

PANTHEON BOOKS, NEW YORK

Library of Congress Cataloging-in-Publication Data
Name: Markel, Howard, author.
Title: The Kelloggs : the battling brothers of Battle Creek / Howard Markel.
Description: First edition. New York : Pantheon Books, 2017
Identifiers: LCCN 2016053946 (print). LCCN 2016054724 (ebook).
ISBN 9780307907271 (hardcover : alk. paper). ISBN 9780307907288 (ebook).
Subjects: LCSH: Kellogg, John Harvey, 1852–1943. Kellogg, W. K. (Will Keith), 1860–
1951. Battle Creek Sanitarium (Battle Creek, Mich.)—History. Kellogg Toasted Corn
Flake Company—History. Kellogg Company—History. Physicians—Michigan—
Biography. Industrialists—Michigan—Biography. Battle Creek (Mich.)—Biography.
Classification: LCC F574.B2 M36 2017 (print). LCC F574.B2 (ebook).
DDC 977.4/22—dc23.
LC record available at lccn.loc.gov/2016053946

www.pantheonbooks.com

Case art: (front) front cover of brochure for the Battle Creek Sanitarium, circa 1928,
courtesy of the University of Michigan Center for the History of Medicine;
(back) advertisement for Kellogg's Corn Flakes appearing in *The Literary Digest,*
August 2, 1919, courtesy of the University of Michigan Center
for the History of Medicine

Lettering on jacket front by Nick Misani
Front-of-jacket images: (bottom left) *J. H. Kellogg.* Bain Collection, Library of
Congress, Washington, D.C.; (bottom right) *W. K. Kellogg.* Bettmann/Getty Images
Jacket design by Janet Hansen

Printed in the United States of America
First Edition

2   4   6   8   9   7   5   3   1

Again, for my girls,
Sammy and Bess,
the "true golden gold" lights and loves of my life

He that withholdeth corn, the people shall curse him: but blessing shall be upon the head of him that selleth it.

—Proverbs 11:26

Contents

Author's Note

BECAUSE THERE ARE SO MANY Kelloggs in this book who have the same first name, "John," I refer to John Harvey Kellogg in the text as "John," while I add the middle names of his father, John Preston, his nephew, John Leonard, and his grand-nephew, John Leonard Jr., or "Junior," when referring to them respectively. John and Will's mother and John Preston Kellogg's second wife was named Ann Janette Stanley Kellogg; John Preston's first wife was Mary Ann Call Kellogg. To keep these two women straight in the reader's mind, I have referred to each by their first and middle names, Mary Ann and Ann Janette, respectively.

Introduction

THE CAIN AND ABEL OF AMERICA'S HEARTLAND

THIS MORNING, MORE THAN 350 million people devoured a bowl of Kellogg's Corn Flakes.[1] Hundreds of millions more started their day with a cornucopia of crunchy, and frequently sugar-laden, flaked, popped, puffed grains. While perusing the cereal box, peering over the bowl, and gripping a spoonful of the stuff, few of these sleepy diners know that *two* men created those famously crispy, golden flakes of corn. John Harvey and Will Keith Kellogg were brothers from the Michigan hamlet of Battle Creek. Together, they introduced and mass-marketed the concept of "wellness." And in so doing, they changed how the world eats breakfast.

John and Will began their ascent into the pantheon of American history by building the Battle Creek Sanitarium, a once world-famous medical center, spa, and grand hotel. For more than half a century, "the San" attracted droves of people actively pursuing health and well-being. The brothers also developed a successful medical publishing house, an exercise machine and electrical "sunbath" firm, cooking, medical, and nursing schools, an undergraduate college, and sundry other profitable health product companies. Yet throughout these endeavors and for most of their lives, the "Kellogg boys" hated each other's guts.

From the late nineteenth century to World War II, John—the elder by eight years—was one of America's most beloved physicians. His books were worldwide best-sellers. The advice he dispensed in these volumes, lectures, and his magazine, *Good Health* ("the oldest health magazine in

The Battle Creek Sanitarium, circa 1915

the world—established 1866"), was followed by millions, including some of the most prominent celebrities of the day.[2] In 1921, his "lifesaving" research on digestion and diet was nominated for the Nobel Prize for Medicine or Physiology.[3] Eleven years later, a 1932 poll ranked him second on a list of twenty-five important American luminaries and lauded him as "the noblest man" in the United States; only Herbert Hoover ranked higher (a status that would drastically change for the beleaguered president).[4]

During this same period, Will became one of the world's most successful industrialists. In 1906, he founded the Battle Creek Toasted Corn Flake Company, the original name of the Kellogg Company, which today enjoys more than $13 billion a year in net sales of breakfast cereals, snacks, and other manufactured foods in 180 nations around the globe.[5] With cunning and élan, Will Kellogg revolutionized the mass production of food, invested a fortune to advertise his wares to the public, and as a result made an even bigger fortune. When he was done amassing his wealth, he created the charitable means to give it away to those most in need of help and support.

John Harvey Kellogg in his heyday, circa 1915

W. K. Kellogg, at his Arabian horse ranch in
Pomona, California, circa 1925

Behind all these triumphs the Kelloggs' filial relations were a mess. For decades John and Will fought, litigated, and plotted against one another with a passion more akin to grand opera than the kinship of brothers. Born the sons of two early votaries of the Seventh-day Adventist Church, a denomination predicting the imminent end of the world and the Second Coming of Jesus Christ, they were unable to contain the destruction wrought by their long-running quarrel. In their dotage, each brother came to regret their feud's acidic effects even if they were never able to reach a peaceful resolution. In light of their incredible success, how could things have gone so horribly wrong between them?

At age eighty-nine, John decided he had had enough of the hot and cold war. On September 8, 1941, he sat down, unscrewed his fountain pen, and searched his soul to compose a letter to his long-estranged sibling. The result was a heartfelt expression of apology for all the fights and slights that characterized their every discourse over eight decades. It was a glowing appreciation of Will's phenomenal accomplishments. In the months that followed, John must have wondered why his brother never acknowledged, let alone responded to, this literary equivalent of an olive branch.

We do know that the doctor's attempt at rapprochement failed miserably during their last face-to-face meeting. In early October 1942, John invited the cereal mogul to his home hoping for financial assistance to pull his Sanitarium out of the quicksand of bankruptcy, an embarrassment brought on by overexpansion, the Great Depression, and the advent of World War II. The tête-à-tête lasted more than five hours and was anything but civil. Will had heard John's mea culpas too many times to put much stock in promises of brotherly concord. Every interaction the two brothers attempted rapidly fell into the rut of past fights and was warped by the corrosive dynamics of emotional pain, hostility, and resentment. Will walked into the doctor's parlor anticipating—and then finding—a packet of annoyance and aggravation. Almost as soon as he left, the eighty-two-year-old Will began a whispering campaign attacking his brother's mental acuity. Worse, he plotted with members of the Seventh-day Adventist Church (which originally owned the Sanitarium and, in 1907, excommunicated John) to buy the facility for its own imperial plans.[6]

ON DECEMBER 14, 1943, the doctor died. He was ninety-one years and nine months old, only eight years and three months shy of his goal of living to be one hundred. The following morning, his body was transported to the Andrew C. Hebble Funeral Home on Main Street. Once there, the mortuary staff embalmed, tonsured, and dressed the doctor in his standard uniform: an all-white three-piece suit, with matching shirt, tie, socks, and shoes, made to measure by Marshall Field and Company of Chicago. The doctor wore this flamboyant ensemble during much of his professional life. He claimed it was "impossible to wear a garment two hours without soiling it."[7] The white suits allowed him to identify contact with dirt of any kind and, upon such discovery, change into a new suit of fresh white clothing.

John's mahogany and silk-lined coffin was taken to the Sanitarium where it was placed atop a carnation-lined bier on the stage of its cavernous auditorium and surrounded by an honor guard of his former nurses. In the aisles was a long line of patients, friends, and admirers, each clutch-

The December 15, 1943, issue of The Battle Creek Enquirer
and News *Announcing Dr. Kellogg's Death*

ing a long printed pamphlet reproducing the condolence telegrams sent by hundreds of prominent writers, industrialists, journalists, former U.S. presidents, physicians, politicians, academics, scientists, and world leaders who could not attend the ceremony.[8] Some mourners were better at holding back their tears than others; all of them wanted to pay their last respects to the man they reverentially referred to as "Doctor."

Once the service drew to a close, and after the pallbearers lugged the casket into Mr. Hebble's black Cadillac hearse, a phalanx of automobiles made its way down the hill from where the Sanitarium was perched.[9] The procession passed an enormous billboard proclaiming in two-foot-tall letters: "GET BETTER IN BATTLE CREEK." If any of the car radios were turned on during the doctor's last ride, they probably played the dulcet tones of Battle Creek's premier radio station, W-E-L-L. (The original call letters of that broadcast station, incidentally, were W-K-B-P, or "We Keep Breakfast Popular.")[10]

The funeral cortege finally wound into the Oak Hill Cemetery, the town's most distinguished burial ground. Here were the remains of Sojourner Truth, the former slave and author, and Ellen White, the founding prophetess of the Seventh-day Adventist Church. Nearby was the famously rich C. W. Post, whose popular Postum "cereal coffee," Grape-Nuts, and Post Toasties was the nucleus of what became the massive General Foods Corporation. The Kellogg brothers despised Charley Post, a former Sanitarium patient, because Post acquired his millions only after "borrowing" some of their most popular recipes. Legend has it that Post was buried under seven feet of concrete to prevent grave robbers from stealing his corpse; and yet he remains easy to find because his mausoleum is the largest monument in the cemetery.[11] John opted, instead, for a simple stone, upon which was carved his name and years on earth. He rests, hopefully in peace, next to his beloved wife, Ella Eaton Kellogg, who died of colon cancer in 1920.[12]

CONSPICUOUSLY ABSENT from the memorial proceedings was Will Kellogg. He was across the continent, in Palm Springs, California, convalescing from a recent illness. From the distance of more than two thousand miles, his anger at John simmered and spluttered even as his elder brother's casket was being lowered into the ground. Sadly, no amount of Will's riches could purchase a healing opportunity for forgiveness.[13]

In 1906, at the age of forty-six and after serving twenty-two and one half years as the Battle Creek Sanitarium's business manager without official title, Will exploded out from under his brother's yoke. Complaining that the doctor "was a czar and a law unto himself, ignoring his associates and subordinates," Will decided he had had enough of being John's right hand.[14] He was, however, docile enough to ask his older brother for permission to start up his own corn flakes cereal company. John consented only after Will proffered a sizable tribute of money and stock in the nascent firm. In return, the elder brother aggravated and harassed Will long after he was finally able to completely buy John out of the business. Undaunted, Will described the certainty with which he decided to strike out on his own, "I sort of feel it in my bones."[15] A mere three years later, Will's company was producing 120,000 cases of Corn Flakes a day.[16]

It was precisely when Will's business began to soar that John attempted to destroy his success by setting in motion a series of lawsuits lasting more than a decade. The doctor's antagonistic actions did more than just taunt or anger Will. John's nasty maneuvers forced Will to litigate all the way to the Michigan State Supreme Court over the issue of which brother held the claim over their greatest creation and the commercial rights to use the family name. John insisted he was the originator of flaked cereal (he was) and the more widely known of the two (he was). Will just as forcefully argued that he was the Kellogg who perfected the recipe for Corn Flakes (he did), legally bought the doctor's rights to the cereal (he did), and because he so widely and effectively advertised the brand name of Kellogg in connection with his cereals, he and his company deserved the commercial rights to the family surname (in the end, he was right).

After the contentious legal battle was decided in Will's favor, the brothers rarely spoke to each other if they could possibly avoid it, and when they did things often became bitter, fast. Their tempestuous relationship was a battle royal over primacy, credit, and respect. The Kellogg brothers shared so much and yet resented one another so deeply. Their beloved sister Emma described it best as she observed, "The Kellogg women are amenable, but the Kellogg men can be *mean*."[17]

Will was a major player in an entirely new industry centered on the transformation of foods from their natural state into cooked, shaped, chemically manipulated, mass-manufactured products. During his lifetime, his name appeared on billions of boxes of Corn Flakes, Rice Krispies, All-Bran, Bran Krumbles, Pep, Corn-Soya Shreds, and similar products. After his death, in 1951, his company successfully pushed glucose-loaded concoctions such as Kellogg's Sugar Frosted Flakes, Sugar Smacks, Froot Loops, Cocoa-Krispies, Pop-Tarts, Frosted Mini-Wheats, and Apple Jacks and, later, Eggo frozen waffles, Special K, Nutri-Grain breakfast bars, cookies, crackers, drinks, potato chips, veggie burgers, and a long list of other processed foods. Many of these food products are nutritious and convenient; others played a role in fueling the current obesity epidemic among children and adults. Regardless of the precise ingredients filling the Kellogg Company's horn of plenty, Will's crunchy, toasted grain concoctions comprise the most consumed breakfasts in the history of humankind.

In a pun reluctantly intended, Will Kellogg's accomplishments are ingrained in our national fiber, as Bing Crosby crooned in the opening refrain of a song he recorded in 1968, "What's more American than Corn Flakes?"[18] By all measures, except for his own, Will's life constitutes a classic American success story. Sadly, no matter how much he achieved, Will could never squelch the relentless, inner voice. It was a voice that tormented him with what would appear to objective observers as an absurd notion: the belief that he was nothing more than his older brother's lackey.

IT COULD NOT HAVE BEEN easy being John Harvey Kellogg's little brother. Even as boys, it was understood that John was their mother's favorite child and the family's brightest star while Will was considered to be slow, at best. Young John was so brilliant that the leaders of the Seventh-day Adventist Church groomed him to preach its health reform gospel. As adults, the doctor was a famous and respected visionary long before Will ever dreamed of becoming a food manufacturer. Dr. Kellogg exuded waves of charisma, good cheer, eloquence, showmanship, and clinical reassurance. He possessed an encyclopedic intellect, an oceanic ego, and a volcanic temperament. Too often, he unleashed withering torrents of sarcasm against anyone who disagreed with him. John's drive and industry were truly breathtaking but he was an impossible boss, unwilling to accept excuses or failures from his employees and adamantly opposed to delegating a micron of his authority. His religious counselor, the Seventh-day Adventist prophetess Ellen White, once reproached him: "there is with you a love of supremacy whether you see it or not."[19]

As a young man, the five-foot-four medical dynamo embarked upon a self-appointed mission from God to make the world healthier. Always overcompensating for his small physical stature, John was a member of just about every prestigious medical, scientific, and public health association in the United States. Dr. Kellogg knew and interacted with nearly every prominent doctor and medical scientist of his era.[20] Several medical professors and social reformers derided Dr. Kellogg's bombastic personality behind his back but they always took his telephone calls and answered his letters. He began his clinical practice when medicine was just starting to evolve from a murky craft based on religious beliefs, antiquated theories, quackery, and outright mumbo jumbo. By the time he died, in 1943, the field was a bona fide scientific enterprise demanding the accrual and expenditure of enormous amounts of money in the development of new hospitals, medical schools, research laboratories, breakthrough discoveries, technological advances, and the promise of miraculous cures.

Today's medical consumer might consider some of Dr. Kellogg's theories to be quaint, if not outright wacky. A latter-day Nostradamus, many more of his medical predictions and prescriptions are now widely accepted. Without doubt, his most lasting contribution to American society was encouraging the active pursuit of wellness, the now commonplace concept of being healthy in mind, body, and spirit in order to promote longevity and even prevent illness. Wellness was not yet a word in the American lexicon when John prescribed such practices; instead, he called it "biologic living." Regardless of its name, Dr. Kellogg presciently warned his patients against sedentary lifestyles, meat[21], tobacco,[22] sugar[23], caffeine, alcohol, and overeating. Long before the medical profession caught up with him, he described obesity "not just as a mere inconvenience or a deterrent to physical attractiveness but a definite health hazard."[24]

Throughout his career, the doctor advocated regular, vigorous exercise, massage therapy, fresh air, spirituality, laughter, a worry-free demeanor, the reduction or elimination of stress, plenty of sleep, and, much to the deterioration of his posthumous reputation, an avowed allegiance to sexual abstinence (excepting for procreation) and a ban against masturbation. More to his credit, John abjured drugs and advised patients to drink plenty of pure, clean, unadulterated water. As early as 1875, for example, Dr. Kellogg was warning his patients about the dangers of lead poisoning from consuming water supplied through lead pipes.[25]

It was another set of pipes—the alimentary canal with its streams and rivulets—that most concerned the doctor. The son of a broom manufacturer, Dr. Kellogg was obsessed with bodily cleanliness, both external and internal. In his never-ending battle against constipation, he developed fiber and bran products guaranteed to produce four to five odorless bowel movements a day, just like the gorillas he studied in zoos around the world.[26] On the other end of the equation, the doctor's paramount prescriptions centered on diets consisting of grains, nuts, fruits, vegetables, yogurt, and soy milk. The goal of these carefully measured meals was to improve one's overall health, aid digestion, guard against overeating and obesity, and repopulate the intestinal flora with beneficial rather than potentially pathogenic microbes.

Dr. Kellogg originally derived many of his ideas from a prescribed set of Seventh-day Adventist Christian beliefs on health reform. No doctor, John modestly posited, ever healed patients on his own. A benevolent Creator and a willingness to obey His laws of natural, wholesome living made for the best medicine, or as the doctor often said, "It is a good thing for a sick man to have faith in God."[27] That said, John was a pack rat of the many medical concepts he appropriated and embellished from the greatest scientific minds of his era. Always bending, shaping, and shoehorning these discoveries into his faith and worldview, the doctor applied the latest findings in microbiology, physiology, surgery, nutrition, pathology, eugenics, genetics, and chemistry, to name but a few of the scientific fields he followed in his exhaustive and multilingual reading, to underpin his greatest creation, the Battle Creek Sanitarium. As he pursued this eclectic approach, the doctor helped lead the charge for a thorough cleansing of the grime and sickness that characterized late-nineteenth-century America.

JOHN HARVEY KELLOGG often told audiences how he first conceived the idea of ready-to-eat breakfast cereals in 1875, while still an impoverished medical student at New York City's Bellevue Hospital Medical College. Short on time to prepare a hot bowl of porridge, he began a search for palatable concoctions of wheat, oats, and corn for a fast, cheap, and nutritious meal. The result, some twenty years later, was the creation of "flaked cereals." This story, of course, is much more complicated and John required a great deal of help in the process.

Two decades later, his shy brother Will worked right beside him, during many long nights in the kitchen, seeking their culinary quest. They rolled out endless sheets of dough to find the precise configuration of ingredients, cookery, machinery, and toasting. John was so busy strutting his medical stuff that Will had to assume the time-consuming task of perfecting their cereal by mixing up batch after batch of failed attempts of "flaking" grain. Stewing in resentment, the younger brother labored for over five years before emerging with a bowl of Corn Flakes. John's bossiness, however, reflected more than dominance between a physician and staff member. There was a streak of cruelty that ran through their relationship and would ultimately pull the brotherly bonds asunder.

As children, John terrorized the smaller Will with stinging rebukes, mean-spirited practical jokes, tattling, and harsh beatings from which he never fully recovered. As adults their conflicts ceased to be physical; nevertheless, the psychological warfare continued. While making his rounds across the Sanitarium's vast campus, Dr. Kellogg often rode his bicycle from building to building while insisting that his brother, pad and paper in hand, jog alongside him recording his every creative thought. At other times, the doctor demanded that Will accompany him into the bathroom, à la Lyndon Johnson, so as not to waste any time even as he defecated.[28]

Indeed, when it came to relations with his "little brother," the doctor was too often an overbearing oaf, given to histrionic behavior, impulsivity, boastfulness, and, in the words of one scientist, "irresponsible emotionalism."[29] If John Harvey Kellogg fell in love with an idea no matter how far-fetched or lacking in evidence it may have been, that notion quickly became something he carried out to wide promotion. For the multitude of readers and patients who hung on to his every word, the doctor could do no wrong. Still, there were many times when his enthusiasm and outright exaggerations took him too far out on the limb of scientific progress, only to be sawed off by a more judicious member of the medical establishment. Such grandstanding behavior irritated the far more precise Will, a man who "would not make an extreme statement or take an extreme position until he had controlled and corroborated evidence."[30]

WILL WAS, IN FACT, a serious student of the emerging "science" of business, whether he was publishing his brother's books and magazines, running the Battle Creek Sanitarium, or manufacturing cereal. He methodically analyzed, applied, and adopted efficiency techniques and business systems espoused by the best commercial gurus of the day. For nearly a quarter of a century, while John enacted one scene after another of fraternal dominance, the quiet, stolid Will was doing far more than merely taking orders. He was preparing to become a renowned captain of industry. Just as Henry Ford was figuring out the economies of scale to sell the millions of automobiles rolling off his vaunted assembly line, Will Kellogg revolutionized the administration of the modern medical center and, later, the mass production and marketing of "manufactured food."[31] Many of the industrial best practices he helped develop remain familiar parts of our daily landscape and lives.

Soon after establishing his company, Will tirelessly convinced American grocers to carry his products and consumers to relish his cereals. Echoing his brother by heralding breakfast as "the most important meal of the day," Will made the hectic mornings of beleaguered mothers and dads so much easier by providing a quick, convenient, healthy, nutritious breakfast they could simply pour out of a box and into a bowl.[32] He was an early adopter of the newly created field of mass advertising and invested millions of dollars in a never-ending barrage of colorful and attractive advertisements, slogans and jingles, cartoon characters, and, when radio, and later, television, took the nation by storm, entertaining shows and commercials. He was quick to recognize and target youngsters as the demographic group most likely to hunger for his products. Over the years, many billions of children gleefully sang the catchy tune "K-E-Double L-O-Double-Good, Kellogg's Best to You!" as they hunted for the prized coloring books and toys he so cleverly placed in his cereal boxes.

Will Kellogg, of course, benefited by creating his business at the dawn of the twentieth century when huge corporations and interstate commerce began to boom and nationally known brands first gained favor with the American public. He became the "Corn Flake King" during the synchronous rise of urban populations, better living and nutritional conditions, and a national system of transportation, first by rail and later by highways, which allowed for the rapid delivery of a constant stream of raw grain into his factories and cases of cereal out of them. He capitalized on the widespread distribution of his food products, thanks to the development and rise of self-serve grocery stores and supermarkets, and the nationwide delivery of clean, safe, fresh, nutritious, pasteurized milk—the essential accoutrement to any bowl of cereal.

Yet there was far more to Will Kellogg's genius than mere timing or the willingness to adopt new business methods. As he labored to create the means to process corn and, later, rice, wheat bran, and even soybeans into ready-to-eat cereals, Will Kellogg refused to be satisfied with the status quo. The boss's charge was to always improve on what the company produced. He encouraged his employees to develop ever more sophisticated means of packaging to keep his cereals fresh and toasty whether on the grocery shelf or in the kitchen cabinet. He worked indefatigably to insure that his factories were safe, hospitable, and fiscally sound workplaces. Like many industrial magnates of his era, Will was fervently anti-union, but he was also sincerely concerned about and loyal to his workers. During the Great Depression, for example, Will split the factory's three 8-hour work shifts into four 6-hour lengths of time to keep more employees on the payroll.[33]

In 1906, Will announced himself to the American public with a facsimile of his signature on every box of the "original" Kellogg's Corn Flakes. It was initially devised as a means of thwarting the dozens of copycat companies stealing ideas and sales from his cereal business. (Parenthetically, Will's signature looked a lot like John's, who, when they were partners, refused to sign the cereal boxes lest it damage his hard-won medical reputation.) Above Will's signature was the solemn promise that the box's contents were tasty, crisp, fresh, nutritious and, most importantly, genuine. This pledge, backed by better and better means of quality control, was essential to building a long-standing, trustworthy, and profitable relationship with the American public.

Three decades later, in 1936, W. K. Kellogg's signature was famous enough to warrant lampooning in a *New Yorker* cartoon drawn by the magazine's founding cartoonist, Rea Irvin. In it, a bald, bespectacled, black-suited and plump Will is sitting at an enormous desk, pen in hand, meeting with one of his underlings. Directly behind him is a wall of stacked Kellogg's Corn Flakes boxes. The caption accompanying the cartoon, "Historic Moments in the Annals of American Industry: An efficiency engineer discovers that printing will save Mr. Kellogg from having to sign his name on each of the Corn Flakes boxes."[34] Will, of course, already knew and did just that; nevertheless, the joke managed to tickle *New Yorker* readers. Today, an artist's rendition of Will's signature—the

*Food industrialist W. K. Kellogg portrayed in a
1936* New Yorker *cartoon. The cartoon's caption
reads "Historic Moments in the Annals of American
Industry: An efficiency engineer discovers that
printing will save Mr. Kellogg from having to sign
his name on each of the Corn Flakes boxes."*

familiar red script "Kellogg's"—appears on virtually every product his
company manufactures. It is a scribble almost as famous as another
iconic American scrawl, "Walt Disney."

John built his medical kingdom upon the foundation of his personality, ideas, and vitality. It was a realm he dreamed would last forever even
though it effectively ended with his funeral. Will died a little more than
eight years later and, despite their differences, was buried only a few
dozen feet away at the Oak Hill Cemetery. Nevertheless, it was Will, the
lonely, unloved, unappreciated little brother, who achieved immortality
on his own terms. The company he founded remains a multinational
behemoth of food production. The charitable foundation he endowed is
one of the largest in the world and continues to work for the welfare of

children, families, and communities. When uttering the name "Kellogg" today, it is, undoubtedly, Will's industry we recall.

Unfortunately, the recorded evidence Will left behind is far less voluble when compared to the hundreds of boxes of papers, writings, letters, and scrapbooks the doctor bequeathed to three universities.[35] "W.K.," as he is still referred to in hushed, reverential tones along the halls of his foundation, wanted no such snooping. Although he authorized a writer named Horace B. Powell to write his biography, Will died four years before it was published. His company and foundation, zealously protective of their beneficent founder's memory, had final editorial say over what went into the finished copy. There are many frank insights that the cagey tycoon and his proxies did allow to be published even if this corporate biography primarily represents only what Will was willing to reveal to the world, no more and no less. His final will and testament decreed that his diaries, letters, photographs, and papers be safely placed within the W. K. Kellogg Foundation's archives. Lovingly preserved and indexed, Will controls them even from the grave. Will's will dictates that these materials cannot be reviewed, let alone quoted or reproduced, without contractual permission of his $8 billion foundation. Presently, if one is granted access to his papers, every page of any book using those materials must be approved, and potentially redacted before publication by representatives of the W. K. Kellogg Foundation. The foundation's lawyers politely warn each historian that the publication of any unsanctioned quotation (or what the foundation considers to be undesirable descriptions of Will Kellogg) emerging from such an archival review may well result in legal action. I fully understand their intent to honor their founder's wishes but these are conditions no serious historian can sanction. As problematic as these restrictions may be, however, I was fortunate to discover a trove of W. K. Kellogg materials quietly reposing in other archives and libraries, including long-ignored reams of legal depositions and testimony transcripts, letters, advertising copy, business ledgers, interviews, a wide number of superb historical articles and books, and forgotten photographs and advertisements long in the public domain, as well as a wonderful, privately printed memoir of

Main Street, Battle Creek, Michigan, circa 1900

him, written by his grandson Norman Williamson Jr. This latter volume is especially important not only because the author knew his subject so well but also because Williamson makes extensive use of and liberally quotes from Will's now restricted diaries. Taken *in toto,* then, the available materials afford a fascinating, albeit incomplete, glimpse into the life, work, words, and mind of a fascinating and tight-lipped man.[36]

RELEGATING THE Kellogg brothers' long, internecine warfare as a nasty sibling rivalry trivializes and obscures their epic drive, ambition, and genius. Each brother spurred the other on to greater heights and many of their achievements were symbiotic, even if they were not always able to acknowledge that fact. Nor can their productive lives be explained merely as a contrary response to growing up in a religious culture predicting the imminent end of the world and fiery destruction of most of its inhabitants. Their childhoods were equally shaped by the harsh realities and grand promises of settling on the frontier. From adolescence into adulthood, they witnessed the authority of religious faith supplanted by an even more authoritative, modern science. During their professional careers, they became key historical actors in what Henry Luce characterized as "the American century."[37] Indeed, the lives and times of the Kellogg brothers afford a superb window through which we can view vast changes in social mores, belief systems, lifestyles, diets, health, science, medicine, public health, philanthropy, education, business, mass advertising, and food manufacturing as they evolved in the United States from the Civil War up to World War II.

In recent years, too many novelists, journalists, and screenwriters have lampooned and ridiculed John Harvey Kellogg's unconventional theories while virtually ignoring Will Keith Kellogg. Such disregard delivers a resounding disservice to the historical record. John and Will's supreme achievement was to dream up and deliver the American pursuit of wellness. This quest focused on health, physical exercise, nutrition, moderation and, above all, balance in how we maintain our bodies, how much and what we eat and the consistency, color, volume, texture and even the smell of what we excrete.

At the same time, John and Will Kellogg suffered a tragic, emotional imbalance, if not outright constipation, in their relationships with each other and their loved ones. Personal strife aside, John and Will Kellogg were magnificent showmen, resolute empire builders, and unwavering visionaries. Eccentric, perhaps, but just as their Michigan-reared peers Henry Ford and Thomas Edison ruled over vast realms of automobiles and electricity, the Kellogg brothers set forth a veritable fountain of fitness and, in the process, became industrial kings of health.

And it all happened in Battle Creek.

PART I

"Michigan Fever"

Covered wagon headed west, circa 1835

I

"Go West, Young Man"

I N THE SPRING OF 1834, two black horses pulled a heavy covered
wagon along a narrow byway headed out of Hadley, Massachusetts.
The picturesque Yankee village built along the Connecticut River was
incorporated in 1661 by a disgruntled group of families who had previously settled in the Puritan communities of Hartford and Wethersfield,
Connecticut.[1] Central to life in this community was an arduous existence and the daily struggle against the temptations of evil, fortified by a
deep religious faith.[2]

The rhythmic clip-clopping of the horses' hooves was almost hypno-
tizing. Mile after mile, a twenty-seven-year-old farmer named John Preston Kellogg ignored such sounds and paid close attention to the muddy,
rutted road he was negotiating. He had precious cargo aboard: his wife of
three years, the twenty-three-year-old Mary Ann Call Kellogg, and their
two small sons, a two-year-old named Merritt Gardner and the couple's
newborn infant, Smith Moses.[3] With each step the two horses took in
a westerly direction, the Kellogg family traveled further away from the
only home they knew for a new life in the great Northwest Territory.

As an adult, John Harvey Kellogg boasted he was a descendant of William the Conqueror on his father's side and the New England Puritans
on his mother's side.[4] Regardless of exact provenances, it can be safely
stated that the Kelloggs constituted an old American family. Their forebears emigrated from Essex County in Great Britain sometime between
1633 and 1644, settling first in what is today Farmington, Connecticut,
and then moving on to Hadley, Massachusetts, in 1663, where they could

Hadley, Massachusetts, on the Connecticut River

practice their Christian faith as they saw fit. Despite many legends as to how the family acquired the surname Kellogg, most preferred to tell a tale beginning with the line, "In ancient times, after a severe storm at sea, there was a foundling taken from the keel of a wrecked vessel off the coast of Wales." The foundling spoke a language that the Welsh people did not understand, but they nevertheless adopted him as one of their own. John's forebears reportedly named the foundling "Keel-logg" because he was discovered lashed to a boat's keel constructed of logs.[5]

It was not a search for salvation that inspired John Preston and Mary Ann Kellogg to leave their familial home of six generations for the wild, wooded frontier. It was the reality of a bleak future in Hadley. John Preston's father, Josiah, was saddled with debt brought on by ill-timed real estate investments and poor crop production. As a result, John Preston faced a difficult life of subsistence farming on a rented patch of New England's nutrient-poor soil. Ambition, courage, and an economic calculation for a better life on earth spurred the Kelloggs to "Go West."

A YEAR BEFORE Mr. Kellogg and his family trekked into the woods of the Michigan Territory, in 1833, he made an exploratory trip to a thriving village of French fur traders nestled along the western shore of Lake Michigan. The settlers named the town Shikaakwa, a word appropriated from the Native Americans, describing the pungent wild onions growing along the river flowing into the great lake.[6] We now know it as Chicago. The available land did little to inspire John Preston to uproot his kin. The soil was poor and sandy, interrupted by swampy stretches teeming with mosquitoes (and malaria). Worse, in John Preston's eyes, was the glaring lack of Christian morals among the settlers. The unsavory life he witnessed there led him to search the far more bucolic Michigan Territory.

Between 1807 and 1842, the U.S. government made a series of forced "treaties" with the Ottawa, Chippewa, Wyandot, and Potawatomi Native American tribes living in the region to acquire the lower and upper peninsulas of Michigan, thus opening up a vast space of land for settlement.[7] Captivated by promises of abundant timber and fertile farm land, selling at $1.25 (about $36.40 in 2016) per acre,[8] Mr. Kellogg may have even sung one of the most popular "emigrant songs" of the day while preparing his family for their migration: "With little prudence any man can soon get rich in Michigan."[9]

Travel by horse and wagon in the 1830s was no easy matter even though the first stop on the journey, Albany, was a mere ninety-six miles away. The roads between Hadley and Albany were often impassable depending upon weather, fallen trees, and many other natural obstacles. Too often, the Kelloggs had to get out of the wagon, with Mary Ann carrying the baby, Smith, and Mr. Kellogg leading his other son, Merritt, and the horses on foot, until the ground became firm enough to carry the weight of the fully loaded wagon. This exhausting leg of the trip lasted nearly a week. Mrs. Kellogg prepared most of the family's meals over an open fire. The four Kelloggs slept either on the wagon or, if it rained, under it. They evacuated their bowels and bladders with hurried trips into the brush. Bathing was simply postponed.

Albany was the Kelloggs' first way station because it served as the eastern terminus of the grandest, and in terms of national growth, most important thoroughfare of early nineteenth century America: the Erie Canal.[10] Nicknamed the "artificial river," the 363-mile waterway was a monumental feat of civil engineering. It cost roughly $50 million to build and another $30 million to repair and maintain (an investment that would be worth at least $1.97 billion in 2016 dollars).[11] People of many nationalities congregated at Albany, New York, to embark upon a long, wavy ride that went up- and downhill, depending on the topography through which it cut, passing by dense forests and burgeoning towns. Passengers and freight were transported on specially built boats pulled by a team of horses and a width narrow enough to accommodate the uniformly fifteen-foot width of the Canal. It took seven days or more to get from Albany to Buffalo, New York.

The more comfortable packet boats transported thirty to fifty travelers, carried no freight, and were about sixty to seventy feet in length. Three horses or mules pulled these vessels at a clip of about four miles per hour. On board was a cabin that included a kitchen for the preparation of meals, a library, a separate area for the women, and a playroom for the children. The heartiest passengers lounged on top of the cabin's roof to enjoy the view.[12] For more budget-conscious travelers, like the Kelloggs, there was a line of far less accommodating, eighty-foot passenger boats.[13] These vessels moved more slowly because they carried many more passengers, heavy loads of cargo, and were pulled by only two horses. Passengers brought cookware, food, bedding, and a tarpaulin in case of inclement weather.[14] If the travel writer Frances Trollope (mother of British novelist Anthony Trollope) is to be believed, it was anything but luxurious. In 1832, she complained, "I can hardly imagine any motive

Erie Canal boats, circa 1826

of convenience powerful enough to induce me again to imprison myself in a canal boat under ordinary circumstances."[15]

COMFORTABLE OR NO, when the Kellogg family disembarked at the canal's western end, Buffalo, they rushed to purchase overpriced food and four tickets to travel by steamship across Lake Erie to Detroit. Unlike the placid calm of the canal, this form of travel was no pleasure cruise. Fed by the Detroit River and drained by the Niagara River into the Falls and, eventually, Lake Ontario, Lake Erie is the shallowest and warmest of the Great Lakes. Despite its small size and depth, the micro-climates comprising the lake yield treacherous thunderstorms and powerful windy conditions where fierce waves can spring up unexpectedly, wreaking havoc on even the most stable of vessels.

The Kelloggs began their four-day lake voyage by boarding one of eleven boats traveling each day between Buffalo and Detroit. Cabin class fares were priced at $18 and $7 for steerage (roughly $425 and $184, respectively, in 2016 dollars). The Kelloggs elected the economy of steerage but even these discounted tickets represented a deep dent in their savings. Nevertheless, it was the fastest and surest way to make the trip into the Michigan Territory.

Their steamship traversed Lake Erie and then aligned itself into a large channel that opened up into the Detroit River. The Kellogg family must have been excited when they first laid eyes on "the brick walls and glittering spires" of Detroit, a city that boasted a deep-water port and some five thousand inhabitants.[16] Further along was what appeared to be an infinite strip of "ribbon farms" along the river's edge, replete with barns and windmills. These farms extended two to three miles inland but were only 250 feet wide each for ease in plowing straight lines with relatively few turns for the farmers' heavy oxen. Beyond was an unparalleled "view of the untrimmed forest, where the deer roamed, and wild beasts prowled frequently to the very barn-yards."[17]

Only a year before the Kelloggs landed in Detroit, the town was decimated by a cholera epidemic, which first struck the Eastern Seaboard and then fanned out across the continent along travel routes such as the Erie Canal line and points north and west.[18] By 1834, Detroit had recov-

ered from its contagious crisis, several skirmishes between the French
settlers and local Native Americans, and more intense battles between
the nascent United States and Great Britain to become a bustling hub
town and port.

Long after the fur trade of the eighteenth century collapsed because
of the slaughter of too many furry creatures but well before the mining
of northern Michigan's rich supply of copper and iron ore, the state's
most plentiful natural resource was timber. This abundance would rapidly change thanks to an ecologically reckless deforesting of the state. By
the 1870s, the massacre of the Michigan pine forests provided much of
the nation's wooden fencing, the 184 million ties needed to build more
than 71,000 miles of railroads crisscrossing the United States, and every
year during this period more than 50 million cords of wood, or 600,000
acres of forest, to heat American homes. These astonishing figures do
not begin to account for the 1.2 million acres of forest cleared each year
between 1860 and 1870 to make room for human settlement and to build
tens of thousands of houses across the treeless prairie to the west. The
denuding of the Michigan forest continued through most of the nineteenth century, and in 1897 some 160 billion board feet (a piece of wood
measuring one foot square and one inch in thickness) of Michigan pine
was cut down. If laid end to end and side to side, this knotty cache would
yield a "wooden floor" covering the entire surface of Michigan "with
enough left over to cover Rhode Island," and plenty more to spare.[19] At
the opening of the twentieth century, the Michigan forests were largely
exhausted and the timber industry funding Detroit's original plutocracy
moved westward.[20]

Along Detroit's riverfront were trading posts, businesses, stables, inns,
general stores, saloons, and eating establishments all catering to the pioneering travelers. Mr. Kellogg sold his team of horses in Albany before
alighting onto the canal boat. That sale provided him with enough
money to replace his Hadley-reared beasts of burden and buy a used
wooden wagon, some farming tools, an iron pot, an ax, a rifle, a small
amount of seed for crops, and several days' worth of flour and salt. After
completing these transactions, the Kelloggs headed sixty miles northwest for the Saginaw Valley. The arduous path consisted of a single post
road, crudely cut through hills, swamps, and seemingly impassable
streams bridged by loose logs always ready to roll, slip, and slide. On

either side of the road, Merritt Kellogg recalled as an adult, was a wall of "high, dark woods."[21]

As with virtually every migrant, John Preston knew someone in the place where he wanted to settle. A neighbor from Hadley named Lansing Dickinson wrote to Mr. Kellogg about the homestead he had claimed near the modern-day city of Flint. Mr. Kellogg was originally offered an opportunity to purchase eighty acres of land for $2,000 (about $57,100 in 2016), in what much later became Flint's downtown district. Instead, he filed a claim on 320 acres of "equally as good" land, for the price of $400 (or $11,400 in 2016), two miles north of what was then known as Dickinson's Settlement. John Preston was hardly alone in his desire to homestead in the region. During the early 1830s, the sale of public lands in the Michigan Territory was so great that people referred to it as "Michigan Fever."[22] In 1833, land sales in Michigan made up more than one tenth of the federal government's total income; by 1835, these sales constituted one seventh of the U.S. government's net revenue, and the following year, 1836, the peak of the Michigan land boom, it comprised one fifth of the federal receipts.[23]

After unloading the family wagon, Mr. Kellogg began the work of erecting a one-room log cabin and establishing a farm. His first task was to clear the land and cut down hundreds of thick, tall trees with many swings of an ax (the far more efficient crosscut saw did not exist until the 1870s). He used the hard maple and oak trees as fuel for cooking and heating, constructing the log walls of their new home, and some crude furniture. Many more trees were felled because they interfered with his farming plans. In all, Mr. Kellogg cleared and burned a mass of timber equaling more than ten thousand cords of wood.[24] From his perspective, and those of his generation, there were plenty more trees left standing.

Once his land was cleared, John Preston planted corn, oats, wheat, rye, barley, and buckwheat to feed his family. Supplementing these grains were trades with neighboring farmers for bushels of potatoes, beans, turnips, and other produce. When food was scarce, Mr. Kellogg went out hunting for wild game. The rifle that killed these ducks, geese, turkeys, and deer for food was also used as protection against wild bears as well as in occasional clashes with the Ojibwe (Chippewa), Potawatomi, and Odawa (Ottawa) Native American tribes who had long lived in the vicinity. It was a hard life where both Mr. and Mrs. Kellogg worked from dawn until dusk. When darkness came, they were so exhausted that they found it easy to fall asleep. Even if they wanted to stay awake after dark, there was little to do, save conversation. There was no artificial light except for the candles Mrs. Kellogg made as just one of her difficult, daily household chores, a list that ranged from weaving and dying cloth to tailoring, dressmaking, the tanning of skins into leather, shoemaking, and harness making, in addition to cooking, cleaning, and raising and schooling her two young boys.[25]

The winters on the Michigan frontier were brutally cold, with wood-burning fires as the only source of heat. One contemporary observer bemoaned: "No word is too harsh to express the utter discomfort of such days, which have all the gloom of the winter without any of its delights."[26] The climate made their original one-room cabin, sans fireplace, uninhabitable and before long Mr. Kellogg felled many more trees to construct a more spacious (eighteen feet by twenty-four feet) log house with a parlor, sitting room, and dining room–kitchen on the first floor and above it two small bedrooms.[27] Alongside it, he erected a stable for the horses he acquired in Detroit and two cows he bought from the Dickinsons. A crisis emerged shortly after one of the horses died. Mr. Kellogg replaced it with a well-matched team he purchased in Flint for an excellent price only to learn from the local constable that the horses had been stolen from a farm in Ohio. The loss of both the money and the animals made for a very tenuous existence in the months that followed.

Setbacks aside, John Preston Kellogg managed to improve his family's lot in life. The first year, he fenced his land using split rails requiring chopping down hundreds of trees and not a single nail. The second year, he built a brick oven in which to bake their bread. The following spring, Mr. Kellogg and several other men erected a large frame barn, constructed of heavy, hand-hewn hickory. Such barn raisings were cheerful, communal affairs attracting the neighboring farmers and their families. The women cooked plenty of good food, the children played all kinds of games, and the barn raisers often passed around a jug of whiskey or hard cider. Imagine the disappointment when the Kelloggs announced they abstained from alcohol and would not be serving the traditional

"Building the Log-Cabin" and "Laying the Fence"
(published in 1874 but depicts a scene around 1835)

libations. According to family lore, the thirsty men eventually simmered down and "bellied up" when Mrs. Kellogg served a platter of her delectable spiced doughnuts.[28]

BEYOND HARD WORK and few comforts, pioneer families like the Kelloggs were constantly threatened by a slew of life-threatening illnesses and injuries. The family's collective medical history, then, serves as an illustration of the many dangers of life on the frontier. Homing in on as to why the lives were so fragile, however, first requires a brief explanation of health and disease during an era when the average life span of an American was pitifully short; most men lived 38.7 years and women 40.9 years.[29]

To begin, the state of medical care in America of 1834 was abysmal. Doctors were scarce in the Michigan Territory and disease was rampant. Even as late as 1850, there were fewer than 4,000 doctors, or 240 per 100,000 settlers, practicing along the entire frontier. Indeed, many settlers were warned in verse to avoid the place entirely: "Don't go to Michigan, that land of ills; the word means ague, fever and chills."[30] Those desiring a medical career during this era typically worked for a few years under a practicing physician, in the form of an apprenticeship; some of them took a smattering of formal lectures, even though no one school of thought, from allopathic and homeopathic to the botanical and eclectic, was considered more or less qualified than the next. They were all equally bad.[31] There existed few effective medications, and surgery, still without the benefits of anesthesia let alone sterile technique, was a most perilous and painful pursuit.[32] The best of these doctors did little or nothing in the form of intervention but such watchful healers were few and far between.

Most Americans at this time believed health and disease existed within a dynamic equilibrium between one's physical constitution and the environment in which he or she lived. Taking a page from Hippocrates, a person's health relied upon a symmetry of four bodily humors (black bile, yellow bile, phlegm, and blood) and what entered or affected the body, including diet, the air, lifestyle influences, and even the weather. Disturbances in this delicate balance resulted in disease. For example, a troubled state of mind often yielded an upset stomach just as the upset stomach could cause a disturbance of the psyche. Muscle tone and the circulatory function of arteries and veins was thought to be related to both local lesions, such as swollen limbs, and systemic ills, such as "dropsy" or congestive heart failure. And because there existed no means to peer into the body while a patient was alive, physicians tended to focus on what came out of the body—urine, sweat, phlegm, and stool—for their diagnostic process.[33]

A great deal of the early nineteenth-century physician's efforts was directed at pinpointing what imbalances existed, making a prognosis in terms of whether or not the patient would survive the illness in question, and prescribing chemical agents and herbs that supposedly increased or decreased the flow of the deficient or excessive humors, respectively. In reality, many of these drugs simply induced people to vomit, urinate, or defecate in staggeringly dangerous amounts. These physicians also prescribed toxic doses of mercury—or calomel—soporific doses of opium for pain, and strychnine and arsenic to "stimulate" weakened hearts.[34] For inflammations, they often removed what was perceived to be excesses of blood by means of bloodletting. The actual results were far less sanguine in that draining massive amounts of blood only made a sick person sicker. All these interventions ran counter to Hippocrates' sage advice (and one that John Harvey Kellogg would later echo): "*Vis medicatrix naturae* (Nature is the healer of disease)."[35] Little wonder then that many Americans avoided doctors at all costs and simply treated themselves.[36]

ONE OF THE MOST common conditions demanding medical attention on the frontier was the act of delivering a baby. The main reason for such fruitful reproduction, beyond the paucity of effective contraception, was the fact that these pioneering families needed many children to help eke out a living from the land. Soon after settling in Michigan, in 1836, Mary Ann Kellogg gave birth to another son, Albert; two years later, 1838, a daughter named Julia Elvira was born; and in 1840 she delivered a second daughter, Martha.

Typically assisted by other women settlers not always adept at midwifery, the act of giving birth on the frontier was fraught with complications and, too often, death. A trip through an old graveyard filled with those who died in the early nineteenth century reveals headstone after headstone announcing the premature death of infants and young children, often alongside their mothers who died during or soon after childbirth. Data on infant mortality rates in the United States for 1830 to 1840 are sparsely recorded but as early as 1850 the infant mortality rate for white babies was 216.8 per 1,000 live births per year and 340 per 1,000 live births for African American babies.[37] By 1870, that key measure of a community's health declined to a still problematic rate of 175.5 deaths per 1,000 white babies. Data on U.S. maternal mortality is even sparser during the nineteenth century, but as late as 1910, a far cry from life on the frontier, 6.9 mothers died per 1,000 births. The risk of a woman dying during childbirth increased markedly with each successive pregnancy and delivery. Using historical estimates from developed nations at this time, such as England, the maternal mortality rate in Michigan during the 1840s was at least double the 1910 figure and probably a good deal greater.[38]

Moreover, the ruggedness of pioneer life failed to afford new mothers much time to recover from childbirth. These young women were locked into a seemingly unending cycle of pregnancy and delivery, followed by a few months of nursing the new infant and caring for the rest of the family, before the whole process began again, leaving many women depleted,

exhausted, and in poor health while still in their twenties.[39] Mary Ann
Kellogg was an excellent example of this tragic life cycle. The combination of her unending household chores, the births of five children over
eight years, poor nutrition, and what turned out to be a galloping case of
consumption robbed her of youth and starkly numbered her days.

LONG BEFORE Mary Ann's tuberculosis declared itself victorious, it
was Mr. Kellogg who experienced the family's most serious health threat.
In the spring of 1838, he developed eye irritation and redness, which
progressed to severe inflammation. The rims of his eyes and his eyelids
swelled and turned beefy-red, and soon he complained of excessive tearing and blurred vision.[40] At this far remove, it is impossible to make a
definitive retrospective diagnosis but given the severity of the ailment,
the length of his symptoms, the prevalence of infectious eye disease and
poor hand washing and sanitation practices along the frontier, Mr. Kellogg was probably stricken with trachoma. No mere pink eye; for 75
percent of those infected, trachoma resulted in a slow and inexorable loss
of vision, much like the closing of a window shade as the eyeball becomes
a wasted battleground between the human being and the microbe. It
was also quite contagious. When an infected person rubs his or her eyes
(something we all do many times a day) and then touches or shakes
hands with another, the infected person places the uninfected person at
risk for contracting trachoma.[41]

In the Michigan Territory of the 1830s, a family's principal breadwin-
ner becoming sightless signaled a calamity of stunning magnitude. How
would the Kellogg farm continue to provide food and income if John
Preston could not see where to plant his crops or raise his livestock? How
would they travel unless Mrs. Kellogg learned to master their team of
horses? Who would protect the family from danger? What help could
they expect from a tiny community of striving pioneers who already had
their hands full bringing food to their own tables and working their own
struggling farms?

Against John Preston's wishes, Mary Ann contacted a doctor from
Flint to come and examine her husband. The doctor prescribed "counter-
irritation," a therapy designed to "correct" severe inflammation in one
part of the body by creating a source of inflammation somewhere else

on the patient's body. The prescriptive logic was that the new irritation would draw away the bad humors causing the inflammation, redistribute and equilibrate it, and thus restore humoral balance. There were several harsh chemical and physical means to induce counter-irritation but a favorite method in early nineteenth century America was the "fly blister." Finding a suitable spot on the back of Mr. Kellogg's neck, the doctor applied an unhealthy dose of finely ground "Spanish Fly," which is actually derived from an emerald-green beetle. The beetle's body produces a substance called cantharidin, a chemical so irritating to human skin that, even when applied in small doses, it rapidly raises an angry red and fluid-filled blister.

John Preston's doctor also prescribed the purgative calomel, or mercury chloride. He was given such a high dose that within days he was drooling like a rabid dog, unable to swallow the copious saliva he produced because his lips, gums, and tongue were so swollen. More alarming, his hair and teeth began falling out and he was constantly running to evacuate copious runny, emerald green stools. His doctor interpreted these symptoms as a clear sign that the calomel was working by increasing the bile flow of a "congested liver"; today, this constellation of symptoms would be easily recognized as acute mercury poisoning.[42] None of these treatments helped and it was entirely possible they worsened Mr. Kellogg's condition. Fortunately, the patriarch's immune system was stronger than both the infection and the doctor's treatment regimen. After several months of agony, John Preston's eyes somehow emerged intact and healthy.

Nevertheless, John Preston's infirmity could not have occurred at a worse time for the family. Described as a cautious man loath to part with a hard-earned dollar, Mr. Kellogg was inexplicably persuaded to subscribe to a "solid investment" that proved nearly disastrous. A year before he took ill, in 1837, two friends and neighbors, Charles Haskell and Warner Lake, convinced Mr. Kellogg to sign a promissory note for $500 (about $13,100 in 2016) and a surety on their notes to establish the Bank of Genesee. Underfunded and poorly managed, the bank failed within a year, saddling Mr. Kellogg with $500 worth of personal debt, half of the investment share of his now bankrupt friend Warren Lake, and a banker's fee of an additional 10 percent interest. This financial burden drained his pocketbook for the next ten years.

———

ONLY A FEW YEARS LATER, Mary Ann's tuberculosis recrudesced with a vengeance. The Romans called it *consumare,* or consumption, from the Latin words "to eat up" or "to devour." Indeed, this is precisely what active tuberculosis does; it consumes its victim with a passionate and incisive energy, inexorably devouring the structure of the lungs and other critical body organs, but typically not until its progeny have had the opportunity to travel to the lungs of another human being to begin the same destructive process again.[43] The microbe that causes tuberculosis, *Mycobacterium tuberculosis,* was not discovered until 1882, and in the early nineteenth century the very notion that a microscopic, living entity could fell a human being was laughable. Instead, the most commonly subscribed theory at this time was that tuberculosis was caused by a weak constitution and an imbalance of the humors.

Mary Ann was likely infected with tuberculosis long before she ever got to Michigan but during the last four years of her life, 1837–1841, she experienced the disease at its worst. She may have also infected her husband and neighbors in the process. Her symptoms began with exhaustion, not an uncommon complaint for any hardworking pioneer woman. Soon enough, she experienced night sweats severe enough to drench her bed clothing along with unpredictable and scorching fevers. She became so incapacitated during the last four months of her life that she instructed her husband to hire Ann Janette Stanley, a teenaged daughter of a blacksmith living in nearby Threadville, to help maintain the household and look after her five young children while the mother awaited a painful, bloody, and suffocating death.

Near the end of Mary Ann's life, the local physician took to dosing her with a daily inhalation of the fumes of camphor and iodine resin placed on a shovel of hot coals. The doctor put the smoky, hot shovel near her nose and mouth and exhorted her to breathe as deeply as her injured lungs allowed.[44] The smelly medication was thought to relieve chest tightness and coughing. Such palliative measures, if they worked at all, were certainly no match for the deadly tuberculosis microbes and on September 16, 1841, Mary Ann experienced a severe lung hemorrhage. When she regained consciousness, she instructed her husband, "Go to Ann Stanley, I want her and no one else."[45] Unfortunately, Ann Janette

Stanley was working as a schoolteacher some twenty miles away in a new settlement called Shiawassee and could not leave her post until the end of the term. Over the next eleven days, Mary Ann experienced daily lung hemorrhages, growing weaker and weaker because of the copious loss of bright red blood. On September 27, Mary Ann Kellogg died. She was a few days short of turning thirty.

Mr. Kellogg, like many a young widower on the frontier, knew that a mate had to be found quickly in order to protect his family and livelihood. Five weeks after Mary Ann's funeral, John Preston hired a "very large and strong" sixteen-year-old girl named Miss Trickey to care for the home and children. As "the winter advanced," the teenager began to neglect these tasks. John Preston berated the girl for her poor work but instead of improving her efforts, Miss Trickey packed up her belongings and went home.[46] It was around this point when John Preston recalled his late wife's dying advice about Ann Janette Stanley.

The thirty-five-year-old John Preston managed to win the young woman over and they married the following March. Ann Janette Stanley was only eighteen years of age.[47] Decades later, Merritt recalled the events of March 29, 1842, when he witnessed his father hitch up his team of horses. Before leaving John Preston told his eldest son, "I expect to bring someone home with me when I return." Just before dusk on the same day, Smith heard the rattling noise of wheels and hoofbeats on the rough road leading to their log cabin. When the boy peered out the window, he saw his father's wagon approaching. Smith exclaimed, "Father has come and he has got a woman in the wagon with him." The Kellogg children ran out to welcome their father and were overjoyed to see that the woman was their beloved friend, Ann Janette Stanley. Merritt told Ann Janette, "I am awfully glad to see you." Ann Janette replied, "So am I. I am glad to see you, Merritt, and you, Smith, and you, Albert, and you, Julia." The young woman then picked up the toddler Martha, kissed her lovingly, and noted how much she had grown since last holding her. As he alighted from the wagon, John Preston decreed, "Children, you must not call her Ann. You must call her mother for she is your mother now." Merritt asked Ann Janette if this was, indeed, the case. She gently replied, "I have come to be a mother to you all." She reaffirmed her solemn promise with a kiss on the cheek of each of John Preston's children. After unloading the wagon of her possessions, Ann Janette asked Mer-

ritt, "If you build a fire, I will get some supper." Merritt later admitted it
was the best possible solution to an awful set of circumstances and Ann
Janette loved Mary Ann's children as if they were her own.[48]

DURING THE WINTER of 1844, John Preston's health was again seriously jeopardized. This time it was not a microbe calling but, instead, the
errant swing of an ax while he was fencing in eighty acres of land to pasture his burgeoning collection of cows and oxen. Again we turn to Merritt
Kellogg for a recollection of the events on the bitter cold January day he
was walking home from school, down the section line road.[49] Alarmed to
find blood in the snow near where he had last seen Mr. Kellogg chopping
wood, Merritt followed a bloody trail of scarlet red foot tracks leading all
the way to the front of their home. At the door's threshold, he found his
pale, drawn, and nearly moribund father lying on the floor with a foot
leaking out a pool of blood. Ann Janette struggled to stop the flow with
ice-cold water and a rag acting as a makeshift tourniquet. Frightened but
resolute, Mrs. Kellogg ordered her twelve-year-old stepson, "Merritt, go
to Hartland Center [a village near the Kellogg farm] for Dr. Clark. Go
as fast as you can. I fear your father will bleed to death." Before embark-
ing on the four-mile journey by horseback, Merritt—a future physician
himself—suggested that his mother "bind his foot as tight as you can."

Merritt made a mad dash through farmland and a dense wooded forest, where only hatchet-blazed trees marked the trail, never stopping or
slowing until he got to Hartland Center. The boy eventually found Clark
and ordered, "Doctor, come with me quick. My father has cut his foot
and is bleeding to death." By the time Merritt and the doctor arrived,
Mrs. Kellogg had managed to stop the bleeding with the makeshift tourniquet. Upon removing the bandage, everyone in the room was horrified
at what they saw: a gash three and a half inches on the top side of the foot
and an exit wound on the sole of the foot measuring three quarters of an
inch. The ax had cut completely through John Preston's foot.

Dr. Clark, very likely the same one who nearly killed Mr. Kellogg with
the fly blisters and calomel a few years earlier, was not exactly a skillful
surgeon. Clark decided to bind a piece of soft, spongy leather to the
wound. The physician asked if there was a shoemaker in the area and
was quickly told there was none. Still faint from his massive blood loss,

Mr. Kellogg labored to speak and eventually whispered that he owned a piece of sole leather he was saving for a new pair of shoes. Merritt knew where to find the leather and ran up the stairs to get it while the doctor manipulated the clots on the wound, causing the foot to bleed even more. Yet instead of searching for the severed blood vessels and ligating, or tying them off, he simply sewed up the entire wound, covered it with the shoe leather, followed by the application of a layer of bandages. He instructed Mrs. Kellogg to clean the wound daily with castile soap.

No thanks to Dr. Clark, the wound took nearly two months to heal, a miracle given that the wound was closed with a germ-ridden piece of leather and without the aid of antibiotics or modern surgical or wound care. Mr. Kellogg was left with a huge, painful scar of angry red granulation tissue, what nineteenth-century doctors called "proud flesh," and the foot swelled up and ached with the least provocation. Decades later, Dr. Merritt Kellogg concluded "had the doctor let it alone, as Mother fixed it, it would have healed in a month. By "Mother," of course, Merritt meant Ann Janette Stanley Kellogg.

2

The Chosen One

ANN JANETTE REARED five small children grieving the loss of their mother all the while she delivered another eleven babies to the Kellogg brood. Between 1843 and 1866, she gave birth to Mary Ann (1843–1858), Laura Evelyn (1845–1916), Emma Frances (1847, who died before her second birthday in 1849), Emma (1850–1892), John Harvey (1852–1943), Preston (1854, who died at age one year and two months in 1855), Ella (1856–1858, who also died before her second birthday), Preston Stanley (1858–1930), Will Keith (1860–1951), Clara Belle (1863–1951), and Hester Ann, or "Hettie" (1866–1930).[1] Death was a constant specter looming over the Kellogg home and the collective mourning over these losses was often overwhelming. Inexplicable deadly epidemics, often interpreted as visitations from an angry God, struck on an almost annual basis. John Preston and the late Mary Ann's two daughters (Julia, age thirteen, and Martha, age twelve) both died of infectious maladies in 1852, in addition to four more of Ann Janette's children who died between 1849 and 1858.

The death of Will's sister Emma Frances, in 1849, was especially haunting. The local physician insisted that the child was suffering from worms while Ann Janette argued the problem was in the baby's chest, which explained Emma's labored breathing. After the child's death, her mother insisted on an autopsy, an extremely rare event along the frontier, and her diagnosis of pneumonia was proven correct.[2] For the rest of her life, Ann Janette believed a better doctor might have saved Emma Frances's life.

The children of Ann Janette and John Preston Kellogg. Left to right:
Preston Stanley (age 8), Emma (16), Will Keith (6), Clara Belle (seated, 3),
John Harvey (standing behind Clara Belle, 14), and Laura (21).
The photograph was taken in 1866, just before the birth of Hester Ann.

Her distrust of "regular doctors" only grew stronger with each childhood death in the family. Their feckless ways inspired Ann Janette's interest in "water cures," or hydrotherapy. For example, in 1850 a measles outbreak struck the whole family, which made each child terribly ill but took no lives, thanks to Ann Janette's round-the-clock nursing and the application of cold water wraps to ease their scorching fevers. She made certain to pass on her faith in water's healing powers to her children, especially John Harvey Kellogg.[3]

On the farm, Ann Janette encouraged her husband to raise sheep to produce a steady supply of wool yarn for the family as well as to sell and pay off John Preston's bad bank debts. Mr. Kellogg promptly purchased fifty sheep from a dealer in the East. The flock multiplied even faster than his family. He scrounged together the money to buy Ann Janette a new spinning wheel and loom so she could weave and make clothing for the growing Kellogg clan during four very different climates. Within months of the animals' arrival, Ann Janette was making yards of wool cloth. Using butternut bark to dye some of the wool brown, and yellow oak bark to dye the rest yellow, she fashioned smart suits for her husband

and sons and dresses and petticoats for her and her daughters. Crafting each outfit with a minimum of waste, Ann Janette made sure to have enough wool left over to sell.[4]

In 1842, a neighbor's son approached Mr. Kellogg with a proposition. The son had established a profitable 160-acre farm twenty-two miles away in the settlement of Tyrone, a village consisting of a small grist-mill, a general store, a blacksmith, a schoolhouse, and eight families. Another twenty-five farming families lived within a six-mile radius. The Tyrone farm boasted a large frame house with a living room, parlor, two bedrooms, and an enormous brick fireplace that could be used for both cooking and warmth. There was also an attached stable for six cows, an open pasture for livestock, and a deep well for drawing water.[5] The neighbor's son was willing to trade down, farm for farm, because his parents' spread was adjacent to John Preston Kellogg's homestead. The Kelloggs eagerly accepted the deal and looked forward to a fresh start and a much better home and farm.[6]

THE VILLAGE OF Tyrone proved hospitable and devout. Eager to establish a permanent place of worship, the families living there invited the Kelloggs to become charter members of the Hartland Center Congregational Church. Given John Preston's and Ann Janette's propensity to work hard and pray harder, this was a request they accepted with alacrity. A deep Christian faith played a fundamental role in the lives of the entire Kellogg family. Every Sunday, during his first few years in Michigan, John Preston traveled two miles south to Flint for a Baptist church service. On one Sunday, he underwent a public baptism and was immersed in the Flint River. Mr. Kellogg also built a family altar where he and Mary Ann, and after her death Ann Janette, led the children in daily Bible readings and morning and evening prayers. After the family moved to Tyrone, the children attended Hartland's Sabbath school every Sunday, following a formal church service.

The principles of honesty, kindness toward one's fellows, hard work, and forgiving the trespasses of others were demonstrated by example rather than preached or otherwise drilled into the children's heads. Occasionally flawed by a streak of stubbornness, a character trait both John and Will inherited, Mr. Kellogg maintained a peaceful, austere, and, above all, God-fearing home. As his eldest son, Merritt, later recalled:

> The first 20 years of my life was spent under my father's roof, and during all those years, I never heard of his telling an obscene or vulgar story, or using unbecoming language. I never saw him angry, I never knew him to call any of us children reproachful names. . . . I never heard [Ann Janette] complain of a hard lot, a hard row to hoe, or of being tired, or sick, of the job that she had undertaken, nor did I ever see her manifest anger or impatience toward one of the children or to father.[7]

More earthly, Ann Janette told John Preston about an article she had read in the *Farmer's Almanac* extolling the agricultural advantages of growing red clover, instead of the more popular and common "redtop," or timothy grass. Red clover had the double benefit of serving as an excellent source of hay for feeding the sheep, horses, and other livestock as well as significantly improving the fertility of the soil. This dual use made red clover seeds extremely valuable. On the vanguard of a farming trend, the Kelloggs found a third source of income: selling red clover seeds they harvested from their crops to other farmers.

By the following spring, Mr. Kellogg was raising apples and peaches, currants, and vegetables, in addition to the red clover. His sheep were so prized that he sold each animal for $5 (or $150 in 2016), a healthy increase from what he paid, $1.50 (about $45 in 2016). With the daily churning of butter from the farm's two milk cows, eggs provided by a brood of chickens, and the soap and candles Ann made from the tallow of their slaughtered livestock, she expanded the household accounts in ways that once seemed unreachable.[8] Each successive season, John Preston became more adept at managing the soil and livestock so that his farm produced multiple harvests each year: clover seed and hay in the winter, wool and mutton in July, wheat during the months of August through October, and fattened pigs for slaughter in November and December.

Within a few years, Mr. Kellogg operated the most profitable farm in the county. He paid off his banking debts, added a spacious kitchen and woodshed to their farmhouse, and purchased both a two-seater wagon for the spring and a double bobsled replete with sleigh bells for winter riding. John Preston and Ann Janette shared their success by giving a nearby widow a spinning wheel so that she might generate some income and forgiving a debt of $250 (about $8,250 in 2016) from Warner Lake, the former partner, who was still insolvent after the Genesee bank investment fiasco.[9]

WHEN JOHN HARVEY KELLOGG was born on February 26, 1852, the family still lived in Tyrone. Like many Americans in the early to mid-nineteenth century, the Kelloggs actively participated in what became known as the Second Great Awakening, a period when many preachers took to traveling from town to town in New England, New York, and westward, announcing that they were "God's chosen people in the redemption of the world."[10] The most popular evangelists held rousing, emotional revival meetings, spread the Gospel, and promised that the Second Coming of their Lord, Jesus Christ, was imminent.

A key actor in this movement was a Baptist preacher named William Miller. Based on his study of the Holy Scriptures, especially the books of Daniel and Revelation, Reverend Miller predicted a simultaneously apocalyptic and miraculous happening, the Second Advent, sometime between March 21, 1843, and March 21, 1844. After that prediction failed to occur, Reverend Miller retreated to recalibrate his biblical timeline. In August of 1844, at a camp meeting in Exeter, New Hampshire, a preacher named Samuel Snow announced that from studying the Jewish calendar his calculations pointed to October 22, 1844, which coincided with Yom Kippur, the Jewish Day of Atonement.[11] A wide swath of the denizens of upstate New York, Connecticut, New Hampshire, Vermont, and Massachusetts awaited something that never happened. The earth continued to rotate on its axis and revolve around the sun. The inhabitants of the "Burnt-over District" returned, as Henry Thoreau famously wrote a decade later, to living "lives of quiet desperation."[12]

Reverend Miller's incorrect predictions came to be known as the "Great Disappointment." A large number of his followers, the so-called Millerites, abandoned the cause as they struggled to reclaim the earthly possessions they had given away in preparation for ascending to heaven. That said, this movement did attract many others who continued to

In 1831, William Miller began preaching in Vermont on the Second Coming of Christ, which by 1844 came to be known as the "Great Disappointment."

believe that a utopian life was possible if one bound his or her actions and thoughts with the teachings of Christ. Moreover, these devout followers fervently believed in the imminence of the Second Coming even as they debated over when that might occur.

The religious group that came to play the major role in the Kelloggs' lives was led by Ellen Harmon, a former Millerite, and her soon-to-be husband, a Sabbatarian Baptist minister, James White. Although the Whites avoided setting a specific date, they preached that an apocalyptic end of the world was fast-approaching and, when it did come to pass, only the most devout Christians would ascend to heaven. Like many of their neighbors, the Kelloggs prayed that the Advent would remake a deeply flawed society into one that mirrored heaven; that the lives of wayward Americans would be transformed and saved; and the nation would rid itself of the social evils of poverty, drunkenness, unequal access to education, ill treatment of women, and, that most peculiar of institutions, slavery.[13]

In the summer of 1852, a neighbor named Merritt E. Cornell impressed John Preston with his interpretation of the new religious movement unfolding in upstate New York, led by Harmon and White, and spreading its faith westward. Growing increasingly dissatisfied with the mode of Christianity he had been practicing in Tyrone, John Preston joined

Cornell for a series of prayer meetings in nearby Jackson. Before the meetings ended, the patriarch fell under the influence of Joseph Bates, a charismatic preacher and former sea captain traveling through Michigan with the goal of recruiting others to join a new denomination that became known as Seventh-day Adventism. The first portion of the denomination's name was because its followers celebrated the Sabbath on Saturdays, as the ancient Hebrews did in the Old Testament. After several more prayer meetings, the Kellogg family sold their farm and followed an Adventist congregation just beginning to sprout and praise Jesus in Jackson. There, John Preston opened his first broom factory alongside a store to sell his wares. It was a trade he imported from his hometown of Hadley, Massachusetts, where the broomcorn manufacturing industry began in 1798.[14]

In 1854, the Whites and many of their Adventist followers decided to leave New York and base their operations in Battle Creek. Two years later, in 1856, Mr. Kellogg moved his family to Battle Creek as well—and there they stayed.[15] A full and financially supportive member of his church, Mr. Kellogg raised or contributed critical capital beginning in 1854 when he donated $200 (about $5,820 in 2016) to purchase the first of many large tents the Adventist clergy used for holding outdoor prayer meet-

Ellen and James White, and others, leading a Seventh-day Adventist camp meeting in Eagle Lake, Minnesota, circa 1875

ings.[16] In the winter of 1855–1856, he and three other donors contributed $1,200 (about $33,900 in 2016) to relocate the Seventh-day Adventist Church's publishing arm, the Review and Herald Company, from Rochester, New York, to Battle Creek.[17] In addition to a biweekly newspaper, *The Advent Review and Sabbath Herald,* the firm published Bible tracts, church doctrines, sermons, magazines, newsletters, health reform magazines, and other materials sold by subscription to the growing congregation of Seventh-day Adventists across the nation. In the infancy of mass printed media, these publications allowed for communication with the denomination's far-flung followers. They were essential to its growth and sense of community. More pragmatically, the subscriptions and book fees generated revenue for the Church.

Once established in Battle Creek, John Preston added political and civic activities to his religious obligations. Initially a Whig, John Preston disapproved of William Henry Harrison's somewhat alcoholic "Log cabins and hard cider" presidential campaign. An early supporter of the abolitionist cause, John Preston was almost certainly in attendance at one of the earliest mass meetings of the Republican Party, a gathering of more than ten thousand voters near Jackson, Michigan, on July 6, 1854.

According to family accounts, John Preston and Ann Janette's opposition to slavery led them to become "station agents" on the "Michigan Central Line" of the Underground Railroad. In the years before the Civil War, the Kelloggs facilitated the passage of several runaway slaves as they escaped through Michigan to Canada and freedom. They, like all the underground conductors, took considerable risk especially after passage of the Fugitive Slave Act of 1850, which carried a penalty of six months imprisonment and a $1,000 fine (about $31,300 in 2016), for helping runaway slaves.[18] Many brave Michiganders thumbed their proverbial noses at the federal statute.[19] One Battle Creek conductor, Charles E. Barnes, described the station as one "conducted with the greatest secrecy . . . the work was done gratuitously and without price. It was all out of sympathy for the escaped slaves and from principle. We were working for humanity."[20] Others insist that Battle Creek's Underground Railroad, while wonderfully humanitarian, was a poorly kept secret: "the sentiments of the inhabitants were such that slaves could have been escorted through the town to the accompaniment of a brass band and a hallelujah chorus without fear of arrest."[21]

Ann Janette Kellogg (age 46) and
John Preston Kellogg (age 63), circa 1870

Nevertheless, Ann Janette's and John Preston's brave acts of charity made lasting impressions on their children. Late in his life, Merritt recalled how impressed he was by the kindness and sympathy his parents offered to the fugitives they aided and how they "took as much pains" to help these runaways as they did for "white folks." To come full circle, years later in 1883, one of Dr. John Harvey Kellogg's patients was Sojourner Truth. She moved to Battle Creek in 1860, the same year Will was born. At the end of her life, the abolitionist, author, women's rights activist, and former slave developed skin ulcers on her legs that would not heal despite heroic medical efforts by Dr. Kellogg, including, as he claimed in 1932, a skin graft using his own skin, which produced "a ring of white skin around the colored woman's limb."[22] Weakened by infection and relentless pain, she died in Battle Creek at the age of eighty-six on November 26, 1883. At the time, her funeral was reported to be the largest ever held in the town.[23]

COMPARED TO THE OTHER strapping Kellogg children, John was the "runt of the litter." His parents worried that the little boy was so sickly he would never reach adulthood. Given the family's medical history, Ann Janette developed a fierce overprotectiveness for the child. She constantly contrived ways to keep John indoors, safely away from the roughhousing of the other boys in town. John Preston, on the other hand, distanced himself from his son and had little faith in John's survival. Before he died of consumption in 1881 at the age of seventy-three, Mr. Kellogg pleaded with Ellen White to look after his twenty-nine-year-old son. Twenty-seven years later, while speaking to a group of San volunteers on September 2, 1908, John discussed his father's parting words: "He said to me, 'John, if I had known you were going to amount to anything, I would have taken more pains with you.' "[24]

John Preston and Ann Janette had several other tangible reasons to be concerned about their son's survival beyond the fact that he was small for his age. While still a child, John contracted pulmonary tuberculosis, then one of the most common causes of death for children and young adults in the United States. John's body managed to immunologically sequester his lung infection, which he most likely contracted from his father, who, most likely, contracted it from his first wife, Mary Ann. The future doctor continued to have serious lung problems, intermittently, for the remainder of his life, including life-threatening relapses of tuberculosis during his adolescence and again from 1918 to 1919. In 1935, John told H. C. Sherman, the distinguished nutritional chemist at Columbia University, "I lost my left lung before I was 20 years of age from tuberculosis. There is no motion in my left side when breathing. This has been something of a handicap to me, but I have managed to carry on and am still at work."[25]

Young John also suffered from several gastrointestinal disorders, which were only exacerbated by a steady diet of fried meats, overcooked grains and potatoes simmering in fatty gravy, and a youthful predilection for the sugary treats distributed by his mother at the completion of a day's chores. At age twelve, John developed a bloody colitis severe enough to scar his colon with adhesions. This condition led to frequent bouts of constipation and he eventually developed hemorrhoids from straining so much at stool. Before John was fifteen, he experienced one of the most painful, chronic maladies known to man, an anal fissure, which is, literally, a tear in that highly sensitive spot. After incurring this injury, the mere passage of a bowel movement felt like barbed wire scraping against his rectum and anus. The rest of the day (and night), his nether region either throbbed with pain or burned like fire. And because the fragile tissue of the rectum is so poorly supplied with blood, his fissure took months to heal but would easily reopen upon the next bout of constipation or evacuation of a hard stool, only to begin the cycle of bleeding, barbed-wire-like pain, and nonstop burning, itching, and throbbing all over again. It hardly takes a degree in psychology to suggest these chronic conditions contributed to his subsequent obsession with "colon hygiene," the consumption of bowel-friendly foods, and his advocacy (and practice) of the frequent evacuation of soft, unthreatening bowel movements.

As a child, John exhibited many of the character traits that would mark his entire life. To begin, he loved the spotlight and he quickly learned how to play the violin, organ, and piano, which helped make him a popular guest at events and gatherings.[26] He also demonstrated a deeply held sense of responsibility, righteousness, and a genuine ambition to do good for others. The boy's tenacity was far greater than his small frame or physical health suggested and others underestimated his resolve at their peril. At age four, John asked if he could accompany his father and half-brother Merritt on an errand. Skeptical of the boy's stamina and unwilling to be slowed down on what was certain to be a long jaunt, Mr. Kellogg agreed on the condition John keep up with their pace. During the journey, the toddler tripped and fell headlong into a patch of mud. Before his older brother and father could turn around and extricate him from the potentially embarrassing tumble, the little boy lifted himself up from the muck. Cleaning himself off, John beamed a big smile and exclaimed, "I did that on purpose!"

Despite John's obvious intelligence and desire to "learn things," his parents were less than eager to enroll him in school. So convinced of the looming return of Jesus Christ and the end of the world, many adult members of the Seventh-day Adventists saw little need to "overeducate" their children. This belief, combined with John's relatively poor health, led to a rather spotty lesson plan beyond Ann's insistence that he be taught to read and write. When John finally did enter grammar school at age ten, he quickly outpaced his peers and became a voracious consumer of history, chemistry, botany, and astronomy. Adept at mathematics, he sailed through his multiplication tables, long division, square roots, algebra, and the rudiments of geometry. He mastered shorthand and German and devoured the works of Pope, Swift, Addison, Hume, Johnson, and Franklin, all of whose writings he could quote with great accuracy throughout his long life.[27]

John's avid reading and need for attention also served as fuel for a somewhat wild imagination. He became well known about town for spinning elaborate yarns of heroic encounters with wild animals and how he emerged victorious from a series of dangerous but imaginary scrapes. When his mother confronted the boy with his public fibbing, John quickly owned up to it, explaining, "Satan made me." Demonstrating impeccable timing, he added, "Mother, I wish God would kill Satan."[28]

A steady diet of fire-and-brimstone sermons along with the lessons he learned in Sabbath School led the boy to become preoccupied with discerning good from evil. During many class sessions, the children were shown images of terrifying beasts predicted to descend upon earth come the Judgment Day. At one class, his teacher informed the youngsters that only 144,000 souls would be saved on the "Day of Reckoning." After a cursory calculation of how many people were living at the time, John wept in despair that he would never be good enough to be selected and saved. All these fatalistic and frightening lessons would have been unsettling for any young mind but especially for a boy who was as imaginative, thoughtful, and impressionable as John. In his later years, the doctor recalled, "When I was a boy anything that was fun was regarded as wicked."[29]

John was, however, blessed with an inquiring mind and he had the courage to challenge the lessons he was being taught. While reviewing the opening lines of Genesis, his teachers told him that God had created the universe and everything in it and that all of His creations were good. The boy mulled things over before asking, "If God made everything, did he also make Satan?" The teacher admitted that God did create Satan. "Johnny," as he was called, queried, "If God made everything good, why didn't he make Satan good?" Stumped by his pupil, the teacher abruptly dismissed the class and sent them all home for dinner. The following week, little Johnny was assigned to another class.[30]

John was especially hard on himself when he thought he had committed a sin. Some seventy-five years after the event, with tears in his eyes, John told an associate about the time he spied a robin resting on a log. The boy was armed with a rawhide whip, which he used to lead cows to the water trough. He decided to see "how near I can come to it" and flicked his whip at the robin. With perfect aim, the whip hit the bird's head causing it to fall over dead. Young John was stricken with a lingering remorse: "I sobbed and sobbed and on my knees I promised God I would never kill another thing as long as I lived, and I have not. I even walk around the cockroaches." So committed to this pledge, he maintained a large menagerie, ranging from dogs and wolves to exotic birds, on the San's grounds.[31]

When he was nine years old, John asked his mother to assign him some of the household chores, just like his other brothers and sisters. Ann Janette instructed him to tend to the milk cows, fill up the woodbin, and help her prepare meals and make soap. This he did and because it often involved working with his mother, the two became especially close. When John turned eleven, Mr. Kellogg insisted the boy earn his keep in a more substantial way. John told his father, "If you will pay me for what I do for you, I will pay you for what you do for me." John Preston took his son at his word and from that moment on, John proudly recalled later in life, he made his own way in the world.[32]

Mr. Kellogg assigned young John to a ten-hour shift on the broom factory floor sorting broomcorn. The boy's manual dexterity was such that he was soon able to process as much broomcorn and put together brooms as quickly as the adult men working for his father. John assessed the inequity in compensation, when compared to the other workers, and cheekily demanded their full wage of $2 per day (about $38.90 in 2016). John Preston paid him the full amount, knowing a bargain when he saw it. Unfortunately, the long hours hunched over the workbench making brooms resulted in John's becoming somewhat "round-shouldered." John counteracted this postural damage by sleeping on the hard floor; both the condition and treatment helped spark his later research on the importance of proper carriage, posture, sitting, and standing.

A few years before the son joined his father's firm, John Preston built a makeshift candy counter to attract the sweet teeth and, more importantly, the pennies of the town's children. Several times a day, John dipped into its stores for licorice and sour balls to satiate his love of sugar, a desire he would conquer as an adult and warn against to his legion of patients.[33] Consequently, the adult John knew from whereof he spoke when he warned his patients to avoid the consumption of sugar because "there are people who are actually candy inebriates."[34]

No fan of backbreaking manual labor, John committed to performing only "hard jobs that were worthwhile," meaning those that required the ingenuity of his mind rather than the sweat of his brow. One afternoon he told his mother of these intentions but iterated he would not likely satisfy her wish that he study medicine. He recounted his spying through the window of a friend who was undergoing minor surgery on the kitchen table. The sight of blood so sickened him that he was determined to become "anything but a doctor." Not long after his confession, he passed his mother's bedroom and overheard her praying. The boy quietly entered, sidled next to his mother, and nestled in the crook of her bent arm. Ann Janette reached down with her other hand and touched John's head, praying that her favorite son dedicate his life to God, for the greatest benefit of humanity. It was a formative moment that the child recalled, embellished, and treasured for the remainder of his days. Despite his many faults and foibles, flaws that would only become more aggressive and detrimental in the years to come, there was always a deep vein of Christian spirit and service that ran through most everything John ever did.[35]

AN EQUALLY IMPORTANT childhood influence was John's relationship with Ellen and James White, the spiritual leaders of the Seventh-day Adventists. Ellen was a self-proclaimed prophetess with a remarkably large following that continues to the present day. She told her followers that she experienced many "visions" from God. These episodes and their spiritual import were promptly recorded, interpreted, set into type, printed as "testimonies," and distributed to her co-religionists. Not a few retrospective diagnosticians have suggested her "visions" shared great similarity with the symptoms of epilepsy. Mrs. White insisted, and many others believe, these spells—be they neurologically, psychologically, or theologically derived—were supernatural and constituted a true line of communication with God.[36]

From the distance of more than a century and a half, it is fascinating to note how many of Ellen White's experiences of the religious variety were connected to personal health. Her Seventh-day Adventist theology was remarkable for its emphasis on a sound body and a slate of hygienic habits, to maintain one's physical, mental and spiritual health, and sexual purity. When it came to diet, Ellen found great import in a passage from Genesis (1:29): "And God said, 'Behold, I have given you every herb bearing seed, which is upon the face of all the earth, and every tree, in the which is the fruit of a tree yielding seed; to you it shall be for meat.'" She strictly interpreted this as God's order to consume a grain and vegetarian diet. She further preached that Seventh-day Adventists must abstain not only from eating meat but also tobacco, coffee, tea, and, of course, alcohol. She warned against indulging in the excitatory influences of greasy, fried fare, spicy condiments, and pickled foods; overeating; drugs of any kind; binding corsets, wigs, and tight dresses. Such evils, she taught, led to the morally and physically destructive "self vice" of masturbation and the less lonely vice of excessive sexual intercourse.[37]

An Elder in the Church, James White was president of the Church's Review and Herald Publishing Company and Ellen's husband. Impressed by John's intellect, spirit, and drive, James groomed John for a key role in the Seventh-day Adventist Church. Imagine how awe-inspiring for a twelve-year-old boy to be selected for glory by the de facto head of his church. White hired John as *The Advent Review and Sabbath Herald*'s "printer's devil," the now forgotten name for an apprenticeship to printers and publishers in the days of typesetting by hand and cumbersome, noisy printing presses. There, like many other American printer's devils who went on to greatness, including Thomas Jefferson, Benjamin Franklin, Mark Twain, Walt Whitman, and Lyndon Johnson, John mixed up batches of ink, filled paste pots, retrieved individual letters of type to set, and proofread the not always finished printed copy. He was swimming in a river of words and took to it with glee.

John reviewed news stories about church members and events. He edited sermons, health advice, and the transcripts of Ellen's testimonies of her visions with the Creator. While proofing the pages of so many other writers, John discovered his own talent for composing clear and balanced sentences, filled with rich explanatory metaphors and allusions. At sixteen, he was editing and shaping the church's monthly health advice magazine, *The Health Reformer.* One perk of the job was being a frequent dinner guest at the Whites'. On many winter evenings, after a long day of meeting deadlines in the printing plant, he spent the night there, as well. In late adolescence John became a vegetarian, because the Whites told him abstaining from "flesh-eating" helped young men grow a few inches. His commitment to a meatless diet was lifelong even if his height topped out at a mere five-foot-four.

THERE WERE SEVERAL practical reasons, beyond those described in Ellen White's ministry, that inspired John's interest in dietary matters. One historian of foodways has characterized this moment of culinary history as the era of "the great American stomach ache."[38] In 1858, Walt Whitman described indigestion as "the great American evil."[39] A cursory review of the mid-nineteenth-century American diet on the "civilized" Eastern Seaboard, within the nation's interior, and on the frontier explains why one of the most common medical complaints of the day was dyspepsia, a nineteenth-century catchall term for a medley of flatulence, constipation, diarrhea, heartburn, and "upset stomach."

Poor or rich, Americans of this era simply overate. Worse, their diet consisted of huge amounts of animal fat, salt, and sugar. Well-to-do Americans routinely ate large, midday "dinners," or luncheon, consisting of two or three main courses, served with creamed vegetables, heavy (and fatty) gravies, cheese, bread and butter, pitchers of whole milk, and a dessert such as fruit pie or a pudding. At the evening supper, there might be three meat entrées on the bill of fare, a longer list of side dishes, and many more caloric desserts. On the Atlantic coast, there was often fresh seafood, even if frying was the preparation of choice, unless it was shellfish, which tended to be steamed or boiled. During the harsh winter months, when fishing proved difficult if not impossible, many ate codfish that was dried, salted, and stocked in barrels, reconstituted with water, and boiled.

In the backwoods of Michigan, settlers consumed great quantities of cured pork and, if they could afford it, beef preserved in wet brines. For supper, the matriarch typically fried up a hunk of one or both of these salty meats in a great amount of oil or leftover fat. If the meat was too lean to produce enough fat for frying, the dry and stringy cut was boiled and served with a flour-and-butter-based gravy. On special occasions there might be beef tongue, veal, mutton, or any number of game animals shot, killed, and dressed that day. Molasses and cane syrup, typically stored in hogsheads, added another huge source of calories and a sweet taste to the savory. Fresh produce was often in short supply, depending on the time of the year and the family's financial situation, even among those who farmed. This situation necessitated the canning, pickling, jellying, and preserving of vegetables and fruits. To make up for the de-flavorizing nature of these early attempts at food processing, most meals were accompanied by a variety of spicy condiments and lots of pepper and salt.[40]

The American breakfast was especially problematic in terms of fat content and indigestion. For much of the nineteenth century, many early morning repasts included filling, starchy potatoes, fried in the congealed fat from last night's dinner. As a source of protein, cured and heavily salted meats, such as ham or bacon, were fried up as well. Filling as these meals were, the staggeringly high salt content made one quite thirsty and eager for a drink—a situation not lost on the saloonkeepers of every town in America who routinely opened for business in the morning. Others ate a meatless breakfast, including whole milk or heavy cream and boiled rice, often flavored with syrup. Some ate brown bread, milk-toast, and graham crackers to fill their bellies. The most conscientious of mothers awoke at the crack of dawn in order to stand over a hot wood-burning stove for hours on end cooking and stirring gruels, or mush, made of barley, cracked wheat, or oats. Almost all of these meals were washed down with seemingly bottomless cups of coffee, tea, or cocoa.[41]

One wag inappropriately cracked that "Michiganders would eat anything, even a boiled Indian."[42] While nowhere close to the cannibalistic, John's half-brother Merritt recalled that his family's diet was hardly light or salubrious: "our morning meal was invariably hot pancakes with bacon fat and molasses; our dinner was, in part, of pork cooked in some of the various ways, fried, baked or boiled."[43] Confirming his half-brother's memories, John told a rapt San audience, "When I was a boy we knew nothing about diet. . . . The American people eat less than one half as much per capita as they did in those days." Dr. Kellogg went on to describe his favorite boyhood dish, "I thought there was nothing more delicious than an oxtail, which had been turned to a rich brown in the oven."[44] With menus like this, it is easy to see why the family's patriarch, John Preston Kellogg, complained of a bout of chronic diarrhea that lasted more than a decade.[45]

3

New Brooms Sweep Clean

T HE BOOKSHELVES in the Whites' library bulged with volumes on Christian theology, health, child rearing, diet, sexuality, and physiology. John had ready access to them all and voraciously read his way through their collection. Among the many early- to mid-nineteenth-century American medical theorists who influenced him were William A. Alcott, James Caleb Jackson, Russell Trall, and Sylvester Graham. Each of these men was blessed with a literary gift for explaining anatomy, physiology, and hygiene through the prism of Christian theology.[1] Their books sold well, went through several editions, and were read by a wide and varied American audience. Unlike the "regular" or orthodox doctors of the era, these health reformers taught that toxic drugs, savage blood-letting, and painful cupping were best avoided. Theological explanations aside, their most enduring prescriptions for health and diet are famil-iar, reasonable, and even admirable by twenty-first-century standards. Not surprisingly, Ellen White gobbled up and appropriated all of these experts' religio-medical theories for her ministry. She called her version "health reform."[2]

Undoubtedly, the most influential health reformer of this era was Sylvester Graham (1794–1851), a fiery Presbyterian minister, temperance advocate, health zealot, and self-proclaimed "Christian physiologist." Graham was the cofounder (with the "Christian physician," William A. Alcott) of the American Physiological Society, an academic organization that continues to advance the field to this very day, albeit in a far more scientific manner than its earliest iteration. In 1850, he helped found

Sylvester Graham, the health reformer and "Christian physiologist"

the American Vegetarian Society (with the hydrotherapy expert Russell Trall and others). Graham is best recalled, however, as the inventor of the graham cracker.

Long before millions began chomping on those delightfully crisp, thin wafers, Graham conjured up what he called "Graham Gems." The main ingredients were whole grain wheat flour (which contained the most nutritious part of the wheat berry, often discarded in the manufacture of white flour) and some water. He baked this batter into small, hard, crunchy "nuggets," using a cast iron "gem pan" he invented and sold by the thousands.[3] His lectures were eagerly attended by a legion of devoted followers known as Grahamites and delivered along the church circuits, to YMCA chapters, and at civic auditoriums across the United States.

In his orations Mr. Graham stressed the importance of personal and sexual cleanliness through daily baths and vows of abstinence against sexual activity of any kind (especially masturbation, or "Self-Pollution"). Given their double duty as both reproductive and urinary tract organs, he described the penis and the vagina as the human body's sewer. His treatment for sexual impurity was a meatless diet of vegetables, whole wheat "Graham bread," and the moderate consumption of eggs, cheese, and milk. This regimen, he insisted, blocked impure thoughts and drowned out the siren call to masturbate.[4] Graham further lectured about the evils of alcohol, which not only destroyed families but could also lead to tuberculosis, cholera, and insanity. Graham saw himself as a modern-day savior and worked hard to convince the adults attending his lectures to adopt his health teachings and pass them on to their children. Physical health meant physical purity and because the body was intertwined with the soul, Graham argued, his prescriptions helped eliminate evil, promoted the greater good in human society, and pleased God.[5]

Not satisfied to merely read medical texts or set the latest Ellen White sermon into type, the teenaged John began composing his own editorials on health matters for the Seventh-day Adventist publications, thus marking the opening leaves of a prolific career as a writer. Within the crucible of these exciting influences, John explored how he might be of the most service to God and humanity. On many nights, he snuck out of the house, through his bedroom window, for long walks along the empty streets of Battle Creek. He always seemed to wind up at the Review and Herald Press building, then the tallest and largest structure in town. Letting himself in through a side door, John breezed past the enormous press room and scaled several flights of steps to reach the rooftop. Once there, he stood and gazed at the surrounding town, homes, and countryside. He imagined the heaven above him. He dreamed big dreams. Some evenings he sat near a chimney, pencil and pad in hand, composing baroque poems dedicated to the moon and stars, the divine creator, and his ambitious hopes to better mankind. Expressing his thoughts in verse was a literary hobby he indulged in for the rest of his life. Yet it was a daytime reverie that presaged the next step in his career path:

> One day while working in the broom factory, I stopped for lunch and sat down on the steps at the back of the building, with my head in my hands thinking about the future . . . and I had a vision. I saw a road winding up a hill, where stood a schoolhouse. There were groups of children coming along the road—ragged, unkempt, pitiful children—going towards the schoolhouse. I saw myself standing in the doorway of the schoolhouse, beckoning the children to come in. I knew at that instant that I had found my life work. It was to help children. Some of the faces of those children were so deeply impressed upon my mind that I often found myself looking for them in later years.[6]

Whether it was in the classroom or, more informally, with youngsters at Sabbath School sessions, John loved teaching. It satisfied his need to control and command the attention of an audience. Moreover, it served as a productive outlet to expand and share his rapidly growing knowledge base. He mastered the available texts on pedagogy and progressive education and found novel ways to put these techniques to use. His father, John Preston, suggested he help educate his younger siblings. John began with geography and used a stick and the "soft dirt" of his father's garden to draw maps, enchanting his brothers and sisters with stories of far-off lands. He increased the enrollment of this casual course by inviting some of the neighboring children. Soon after, he took to tutoring younger boys on everything from the rudiments of reading to mathematics.

At sixteen, John lived and taught for a term in the district school of Hastings, Michigan (about twenty-five miles from his family home), where he supervised forty students at differing levels of learning. He reported to the schoolhouse at the break of dawn to build a fire and stoke the furnace. His workday included a full day of teaching responsibilities, often lasting until late in the evening. He could not rest until he finished grading his pupils' tests, prepared the next day's lesson plan, and, because he had not yet graduated from high school, study it enough to stay ahead of his students. For these efforts, he received free room and board and a monthly stipend of $30 (about $515 in 2016).

A flare-up of tuberculosis delayed John taking the teacher's training course at Michigan State Normal College in Ypsilanti until he was twenty. During the interregnum, he completed his high school work, did occasional stints at the *Review and Herald,* sold brooms for his father, and, mostly, convalesced. When John did matriculate into the Normal College, he quickly moved to the head of his class. John astounded his professors by passing the mathematics examination without even taking the course.[7] Restricted to a budget of 6 cents per day (about $1.20 in 2016), he lived in Ypsilanti "like a monk," dining only on a small daily allotment of vegetables, nuts, fruits, and Graham bread. In 1872, he graduated as a bona fide schoolteacher.

THAT SAME YEAR, James and Ellen White conspired to delicately steer John's ambitions toward medicine.[8] The Whites had more than mentorship in mind. They were worried about the paltry success of their Western Health Reform Institute in Battle Creek, which at this stage was little more than a boardinghouse offering water cures and teaching the Seventh-day Adventist health regimen to visiting coreligionists. The doctors in attendance were buffoons, poorly trained, and not exactly inspirational. To bolster the medical staff at the Western Institute with more qualified physicians, the Whites sent John and two of their sons, Edson and Willie, and a young Adventist acolyte named Jennie Trembley

Ellen, Willie, James, and Edson White, circa 1860s

for a six-month course at Russell Trall's Hygeio Therapeutic College in Florence, New Jersey. Trall was the editor of Ann Janette Kellogg's favorite health periodical, *The Water Cure Journal,* and centered his practice on hydropathy, which involved consuming huge volumes of water and the application of hot and cold water-soaked wraps, ostensibly to rid the body of toxins and inflammation.[9] The forty-year-old Dr. Merritt Kellogg was selected to serve as a chaperone. He attended Trall's school for six months in the winter of 1867, and saw the trip as an opportunity to gain some additional medical training.[10]

It was Merritt, incidentally, who convinced the Whites to form an alliance with Trall and his odd little school, even if the New Jersey hydropath was considered to be an outsider in the Seventh-day Adventist community. After completing his first set of coursework at the Trall Hygeio Therapeutic College in 1867, Merritt returned to Battle Creek. He assured the Whites of the compatibility between Dr. Trall's medical theories and Ellen's visions of health reform. Equally important to this pitch, Merritt demonstrated that his commitment to Adventism was neither diluted by his travels east nor challenged by his "secular" education, giving his endorsement of Trall even more credibility.

In May of 1868, the Whites invited Dr. Trall to Battle Creek to lecture at the all-important annual General Conference meeting. According to one "unreliable" witness, who wrote about the events more than

Russell T. Trall, John Harvey Kellogg's
first medical professor

thirty-five years later, Ellen declined to attend Trall's lectures. She did consent to daily carriage rides with the physician, during which she discussed her "visions" with God on "hygiene, disease and its causes, the effects of medicine, etc." Dr. Trall assured Mrs. White "that her ideas were all in the strictest harmony with physiology and hygiene, and that on many of the subjects she went deeper than he ever had."[11]

Not long after his Battle Creek pilgrimage, Dr. Trall became a regular contributor to *The Health Reformer,* an arrangement that helped both the Adventist publication, which was enriched by running an interesting and well-known medical author, and Trall, for which it was a perfect and wide-reaching forum that presented his work to many new readers. In 1872, for example, the Adventist-run Office of the Health Reformer published one of Trall's most prescient publications, *An Essay on Tobacco-Using.* In it, Dr. Trall warned not only against the many physical, mental, and moral dangers of smoking tobacco but also the dangers for those exposed to the exhaled smoke, or what we today refer to as "second hand smoking":

A person has no more right to pollute the air which all must breathe alike with tobacco smoke, than he has to poison it with the fomites of yellow fever, or the infection of small-pox. . . . My neighbor will no more be allowed to spit tobacco-juice in my house, or blow smoke into my face, than he will be permitted to strike me with felonious intent, or stab me with malice *prepense*.[12]

At its height of operations, the Trall Hygeio Therapeutic College was connected to the Trall Hygeian Home, a small-scale version of what would become John's Battle Creek Sanitarium. Invalids came to take "the water cure," enjoy long walks on the beautiful grounds overlooking the Delaware River, ride horses, sail and rowboat, chop wood and clear brush, garden, and, on Dr. Trall's advice, spin wool, "one of the best possible exercises for women."[13] Patients were encouraged to take control of their health by practicing personal hygiene, vegetarian diets, and vigorous exercise, or as Trall called it, the "movement cure." Dr. Trall lectured to his patients on all these matters, drawing from his many books, such as *The Scientific Basis of Vegetarianism* and *The Complete Gymnasium*.[14]

When it came to sexuality, however, Dr. Trall did not hew to the draconian theories espoused by Ellen White or Graham and his ilk. Instead,

The Trall Hygeian Home and Hygeio Therapeutic College

he appreciated sexual activity as both critical for procreation and, as long as it was conducted within the confines of marriage, a pleasurable experience. In his advice tome, *Sexual Physiology and Hygiene,* he advised, "Surely, if sexual intercourse is worth doing at all, it is worth doing well."[15] There were limits, especially for women who spoiled themselves and their husbands by having sex too often. "I have had patients," Trall warned, "who had for years indulged in sexual intercourse as often as once in twenty-four hours, and some who have indulged still oftener. Of course, the result was premature decay and, in many cases, permanent invalidism." In the same book, he recommended contraceptive methods to avoid unwanted pregnancies and protect the health of women who were at risk of dying prematurely because of bearing too many children. The physician also argued passionately about "the right of a woman to her own person." Sexual intercourse was "under all circumstances, for the female to accept or refuse, and not for the male to dictate or enforce."[16]

Sexual congress aside, by the time John arrived to the Trall College in the fall of 1872, the place was shabby, poorly attended by patients and students, and facing extinction because of an oncoming wave of reform in American medical education. The great Dr. Trall, the same explicator of disease whom John had so often read with delight and translated into hot type, was old, tired, and no longer an inspiring teacher. Enrollment had dropped from a high of fifty students per term to fewer than twenty.[17] Merritt later recalled that the curriculum consisted of a few lectures on water therapy and vegetarianism delivered by a wobbly and distracted Dr. Trall. There was also a course on physiology and hygiene delivered by a woman doctor named Harmon who "seemed to be quite thoroughly acquainted with the subject." Miss Harmon most impressed Merritt with her clothes. She wore a "health reform dress of her own device" consisting of a cutaway men's dress coat that, in the front, resembled a woman's dress, and "men's trousers" underneath.[18]

The Kelloggs, the White boys, and Jennie Trembley spent their days in a stuffy, overheated classroom. They took their meals and slumbered at night in an adjoining boardinghouse run by Mrs. Trall. Merritt complained of being served "wormy" dried fruit, "which we had to examine very carefully before eating," Graham flour mush, bread, and boiled potatoes without butter, salt, sugar, pepper, vinegar, or condiments of any kind. On special occasions, the half-brothers scrambled to a grocer in the nearby village and bought themselves a fresh apple or two; if especially lucky, they found an orange or a lemon.[19]

On many winter evenings, Merritt and John escaped outdoors for some much needed recreation. They enjoyed skating on the frozen Delaware River, which lay a mere fifty feet below the bluff on which the school stood, and often glided two miles downriver where William Penn first settled and farmed after his arrival to America. Once there, they drank a replenishing dose of "pure, sweet water" from the well Mr. Penn had dug, rested a short while, and then turned around to skate back to the Trall boardinghouse. On other occasions, the young men congregated with their fellow students in the dining room to trade tales and sing songs. Things became especially raucous when they all joyously danced to the accompaniment of John's violin. His signature tune was one of the greatest hits of early-nineteenth-century American popular music, "Turkey in the Straw." Although John enjoyed being the center of attention while playing music to an audience, he worried about the possibility of committing, or at least encouraging, a sin. He confessed to Merritt, "I don't know what my sister Emma would say if she knew I had played for a dance." Merritt managed to convince his younger half-sibling that dancing with ladies was perfectly wholesome if conducted as a form of physical exercise.[20]

As with so many proprietary medical schools of this era, the education offered at the Trall Institute was patently inadequate. Decades later, Merritt allowed that the proper training of doctors was not the college's primary goal: "Dr. Trall did not conduct a medical school for his health but for the money there was in it." Short on teachers, the hydrotherapist enlisted Merritt to lecture on human anatomy during the twenty-week period the Battle Creek contingent was in attendance. In return, Dr. Trall arranged for a weekly $10 discount on their room and board (about $200 in 2016). When the students complained there was no course in chemistry, John volunteered to apply the lessons he learned at Michigan State Normal College and instruct the others. Matters became testy, however, when John turned to the new field of organic chemistry,

whereupon the old man shut the course down.[21] To describe the contretemps briefly, organic chemistry sought to explain the chemical and
physical actions underpinning every human and animal physiological
mechanism. Dr. Trall heatedly objected to such notions, countering that
a God-given (and driven) vital force controlled all of the inner workings
of the body. The relationship between the aging teacher and his ambitious and overly bright student deteriorated with each passing day. A few
years later, in 1875, John had his revenge when he assumed the editorship
of *The Health Reformer.* Once in the chair, John began to criticize Trall's
diatribes against the medical profession. Eventually, he convinced James
White to drop Trall's column, depriving the hydrotherapist of a powerful
pulpit.[22]

Academic battles aside, John exhibited a scholarly intensity at the Trall
College that would characterize the rest of his professional career. As
Merritt recalled in 1916:

> During all this time, my brother was the most studious person in
> the institution. He and I occupied the same study room, the same
> sleeping room, and the same bed. At eight or nine o'clock in the
> evening, after having had our recreation, we would study together
> until ten or eleven o'clock, then I would retire. My brother would
> continue his study till two or three o'clock in the morning, then
> he would retire, and I would get up and resume my studies until
> time for breakfast. Between us, we kept the stove in our study room
> red hot all winter long, as hard coal was cheap and we had plenty
> of it.[23]

John left New Jersey in the spring of 1873, clutching a large, calligra-
phied diploma bearing Dr. Trall's greetings and awarding him the title
of medical doctor. Deep down, however, he knew the certificate meant
little and, if anything, made him a potential danger to those seeking his
medical advice. In later years, John made it a point of pride that he never
included the Trall degree on his *Curriculum Vitae* or his annual entries
in *Who's Who.* Ellen and James White's "scholarship program" for the
four young Adventists was about as successful as a stomped-on soufflé.
Neither of the White boys demonstrated much aptitude for medicine
despite their mother's hopes that they would become physicians.[24] Jen-

nie Trembley returned to Battle Creek and married an Adventist doctor named D. B. Richards in July of 1874. She resumed her editorial tasks in December of 1880 but soon after "was taken suddenly and violently sick from cold, which resulted in typhoid pneumonia" and her ultimate demise.[25] Only John would pursue a medical career.

By THE TIME he returned to Battle Creek, John grasped that American medicine was in a state of flux and, in order to practice at the level his ambitions demanded, he required a better education. James White agreed, knowing that the Western Health Reform Institute would only succeed if staffed by doctors who understood the denomination's health reform philosophy and mastered the evolving science of medicine. Not wanting the young man to veer too far from familiar environs, however, White suggested that John matriculate into the two-year course at the University of Michigan in nearby Ann Arbor.

Slightly smaller than Battle Creek (population, 7,363) and eighty miles due east, Ann Arbor had only 5,838 inhabitants, not counting the more than 1,200 college students in residence during the school year.[26] Unfortunately, John was to be as discontented with the medicine taught in Ann Arbor as he was in New Jersey. During the 1870s, some of the Michigan faculty members agitated to improve the educational standards. They were summarily turned down by the dean, who worried that setting the bar too high might encourage prospective students to apply elsewhere where a medical degree could be more easily obtained.[27] This concern extended to the rudimentary entrance examination, which was written to be simple enough for most grammar school graduates to pass. It consisted of questions about American geography and government and a few general questions about the candidate's previous work experiences and the name of the medical preceptor they planned to study under after their didactic work was completed in Ann Arbor.[28]

During the fall of 1873 through the spring of 1874, when John sat in the University of Michigan lecture halls, the curriculum he undertook was little different from that of most other "regular" or allopathic medical colleges in the United States: a six-to-nine-month course of lectures and demonstrations in anatomy, chemistry, physiology, pathology, and *materia medica* (the memorization of hundreds of prescriptions of commonly used drugs ranging from mercury and arsenic to strychnine and ipecac). During the second year of medical school, the students were required to sit through an exact repeat of these lectures, followed by a four-or-more-year apprenticeship under a practicing physician, an experience that varied heavily depending on the quality of the doctor the student selected. The senior physician John proposed to study under for this purpose was his half-brother, Merritt Kellogg.

The University of Michigan Medical School, circa 1866. Students who registered last had to contend with the worst seats in the lecture amphitheater, way high up and in the back.

In class, John was disgruntled and bored largely because of the protocol of seating assignments. The Michigan Medical School calendar
clearly stated, "seats in the lecture rooms are assigned by selection to
students in the order of registration on the Steward's books, and each
student is expected to occupy during the session such seat as he may
select. The graduating class, by courtesy, are allowed the privilege of the
seats nearest the operating table and lecture desk."[29] John came very late
to the party by registering for classes on October 16. As a result, he was
exiled to seat number 336, way high up in the auditorium, far away from
the patients and out of earshot of the lecturer's voice.[30]

When it came to interesting patients, there was not much to see in
Ann Arbor. Victor C. Vaughan, a classmate and, later, the longtime dean
of the University of Michigan Medical School, complained that in the
1870s the "University Hospital" was "nothing more than a receiving
home, in which patients brought in for the clinics could be kept before
and after presentation to the class. There were no wards and no operating or dressing rooms, no place where students might receive bedside
instruction."[31] The lack of a big, busy university hospital was frustrat-
ing to the professors and students alike. The university's long distance
from the more populous Detroit translated into a dearth of patients to
treat and use for teaching purposes. Ann Arbor medicine was a perfect
example of the axiomatic quandary Dr. William Osler presented to his
students at the Johns Hopkins Medical School: "To study the phenomenon of disease without books is to sail an uncharted sea, while to study
books without patients is not to go to sea at all."[32]

The lectures young John enjoyed best were delivered by Alonzo Palmer,
a brilliant professor of pathology, *materia medica,* and the practice of
medicine, a former Civil War surgeon, and a founder of the Michigan
State Medical Society. Professor Palmer was a devout Episcopalian and,
like John's Adventist mentors, an avowed enemy of all things alcoholic,
nicotinic, or caffeinated. Equally important, Palmer looked askance at
the many toxic drugs doctors then prescribed and, instead, suggested far
gentler therapies including regular bathing, personal hygiene, exercise,
and adequate amounts of sleep and rest. Palmer recommended the consumption of lots of vegetables and Graham flour–based breads to relieve
constipation, much to the ridicule of his more aggressive colleagues at
Michigan, many of whom prescribed powerful laxatives and insisted that

children fed a purely vegetarian diet were bound to get ill since "man could not live on vegetables alone."[33]

Despite his childhood aversion to blood, John also took a shining to a dashing young Canadian surgeon named Donald Maclean. Dr. Maclean trained in Edinburgh under the surgical reformer James Syme and was an early adherent to Joseph Lister's methods of antiseptic surgery. According to Victor Vaughan, Dr. Maclean "was the beau ideal of the young men on the benches [the medical students]."[34] During the course of his seventeen-year tenure at Michigan, Maclean came to be resented and shunned by many of his faculty colleagues. He was derided as a troublemaker who too frequently urged the students to leave bucolic Ann Arbor and seek training in a major urban center such as Detroit or Chicago, where he believed they could more reliably find the wealth of clinical experience they sorely needed.[35]

Dr. Maclean was not the only teacher in Ann Arbor who stressed the importance of seeking professional training in a large city. Two of his other professors had strong connections to New York City. Most American physicians considered New York to be the nation's medical Parnassus because of the size of its population, the number of hospitals and physicians practicing there, and a dedicated culture of medical progress. One of John's teachers, the anatomist Corydon L. Ford, spent the fall and winter terms in Ann Arbor but every spring and summer he taught anatomy and physiology at Long Island College Hospital. John's obstetrics and gynecology professor, Edward Swift Dunster, had a similar arrangement between Michigan and Long Island and, eventually, moved on to teach at Bellevue Hospital Medical College.

There exists no documentary evidence of exactly why John Harvey Kellogg abandoned the two-year course at the University of Michigan halfway through, but it seems likely that being forced to watch the classroom exercises from a distance, the insufficient patient census, and the urging of one or more of his professors all contributed to his decision to attend a large urban medical school connected to a big, busy hospital.[36]

John completed the winter 1874 term at Michigan and in spring returned to Battle Creek for an advanced course in shorthand. He applied these skills at the side of Elder White during the annual Seventh-day Adventist conference.[37] In between the sessions, John informed James and Ellen White about the poor quality of his medical education. The

Whites listened and were prepared to invest more resources in John, who had already proved his natural aptitude to be far beyond that of his half-brother Merritt or the White boys. James White asked the young man where he might go if he had the money.

Realizing a long sojourn to the vaunted medical schools of Vienna, Berlin, or Paris was not a viable option, John repeated the advice he likely received from his Michigan professors: the best place to study medicine in America was New York City's Bellevue Hospital Medical College. The Whites prayed on this question and returned to John with a united front of opposition against his "going out into the world." They worried about John's getting caught in the sticky web of sin and urban temptation that was New York City. They spent hours trying to convince him to pick another school. John held his ground and pledged that his head would not be turned by such wicked doings. According to the doctor's secretary, August Bloese, "the last thing John heard when he boarded the train was the old gentleman [James White] exhorting him to give up this danger-ous project and to remain safe at home within the field."[38] Bloese's ver-sion rings less than true; shortly after the 4th of July holiday, the Whites agreed to lend John the monumental sum of $1,000 (or $21,400 in 2016) so that he could matriculate into Bellevue that fall. At the end of August, the twenty-two-year-old John Harvey Kellogg boarded a powerful loco-motive train bound for the biggest and, to many God-fearing folks, most iniquitous city in the Union. He was about to begin the medical adven-ture that launched his career.

"WILLIE," as the Kelloggs' youngest son was then known, experienced a far less meteoric childhood and adolescence. Eight years younger than "everybody's favorite," John, Will was not considered to be bright, viva-cious, sociable, or much fun. The boy was truly unhappy. He despised his nickname Willie and never cared for the more formal William Keith. Will found his name to be so grating that at the age of thirty-eight he legally changed it to Will Keith.

One of the few things that did tickle him as a little boy was think-ing about and calculating numbers and figures. Born his father's seventh son, on the seventh day of the week (Saturday) and the seventh day of the month (April 7, 1860) and with a surname containing seven letters,

Will had a lifelong affinity for the number seven. As an adult, he reserved hotel rooms only on the seventh floor and he made sure his automobiles' license plates always ended with the number seven. The great "good luck and fortune" he was to derive from his birth order and the resultant numerology would not be evident for several decades to come but it was a superstition he held dear. As he told his grandson John Leonard Kellogg Jr., "If one seven is good, seven sevens ought to be better. Who can fail to make a success in anything with a combination of seven times seven in the family?"[39]

"Lucky sevens" aside, almost every other childhood memory Will articulated as an adult, which if collected *in seriatim* might fill two or three typewritten pages at best, is enveloped in a cloud of melancholy. Will never felt smart enough, loved enough, or even worthy enough to deserve much of a future. Diffident but desperate for attention, he was too socially awkward to know how to ask for it, let alone find it. As a result, young Will felt deprived of positive attention from either of his parents. Years later, when dedicating his fortune to making the "lives of little children happier, healthier and more promising for their adult years," Will poignantly reflected that as a boy "I never learned to play."[40]

Will did become the center of his parents' attention when he developed the fevers, chills, and aches of malaria. Will's was hardly a rare case. Malaria was a major health threat to Americans living in the Deep South all the way up to Michigan, Illinois, and Minnesota because of the enormous population of female *Anopheles* mosquitoes, too many swampy, stagnant pools of water, and the ubiquity of two of the most common causative parasitic malarial organisms, *Plasmodium falciparum* and *Plasmodium vivax*. Between 1861 and 1866, for example, more than one million Union soldiers were diagnosed with malaria.[41]

Decades later, Will recalled the stress of imbibing copious amounts of water, enduring his mother's applications of ice-cold compresses to alleviate the burning fevers, and hot water wraps for the chills, followed by daily prayer sessions and huge doses of quinine:

> The entire state of Michigan was known for its malaria. I had several spells of this miserable disease. I would have a chill, then a high fever, and the next day I would skip the chill and fever and would occasionally feel fairly well. The use of quinine was known at that

time in the form of a black substance that looked very much like stick licorice. Pellets were made from this product and the horrible bitter-tasting stuff was administered to me in applesauce. Capsules had not been devised. They did not administer this medicine until after several months of chills and fever. I lost much weight and also my ruddy complexion. My skin was a yellow, bilious color. My tongue was coated continuously and I had no appetite.[42]

Although Will eventually recovered, John insured that his daily childhood life was a living hell. The elder son used his guile and storytelling skills to tattle on Will's every indiscretion, knowing that his stern father would transform them into mountainous sins and mete out a swift punishment.[43] Worse, John surreptitiously administered a daily barrage of verbal humiliation accompanied by painful punches, shoves, and a hundred other abuses. Hardly surprising, Will much preferred the company of his sisters or the docile and sweet Preston Stanley, his other older brother by two years, to any and all contact with John. This inclination only increased as the decades passed. Always careful not to criticize the doctor publicly, the adult Will politely described their childhood relationship with a telling anecdote about their sharing of a bed as boys: "I have vivid recollections of John warming his cold feet by placing same on my back, not conducive to sleeping well."[44]

Will's father always seemed disappointed with the stroppy boy. John Preston Kellogg repeatedly told his wife that teaching Will to read was a waste of time. This conclusion was based on more than just the patriarch's belief that the end of the world was at hand. Especially damaging to the boy's fragile psyche was the father's insistence that Will was intellectually lacking and destined to become a burden to the family unless he learned some vocational skills. Fortunately, Ann refused to accept her husband's edict and insisted that Will enter the Battle Creek No. 3 Ward School, at eight, and two years later an Adventist, sectarian "select" school. Will's recollections of his brief schooling consisted of a smattering of elementary mathematics and a steady diet of lessons on reading, morality, and character as spelled out in the poems, short stories, and pictures of the *McGuffey Eclectic Readers,* which enjoyed a huge popularity, influence, and use in schoolhouses across America between 1830 and 1900.[45]

Will's teachers reinforced John Preston's harsh assessment, especially when compared to his stellar older brother. In the classroom, Will was dutiful but "dull" and his formal education ended at the age of thirteen. A major cause of his so-called dullness, incidentally, was not discovered until years later: he was terribly nearsighted. Will discussed this sorry situation many times during his working life:

> When I was a boy in school, the teacher thought I was dim-witted because I had difficulty reading what was on the blackboard. I was twenty years old before I myself found out what was the matter: I was nearsighted. A proper medical examination would have settled that the day I entered school. Since then, I have often thought of what science can do for underprivileged children if they can be taken in hand at the proper time.[46]

Like many men who succeeded despite poor educational attainment, as an adult Will overcompensated by becoming a voracious reader of books on history and the occasional novel. Although he was famous for eschewing casual conversation, when he did speak, he was articulate, interesting, and "had a nice command of the English language," which allowed him to coin phrases, make astute observations, and utter the occasional witticism.[47] One friend later compared Will to President Calvin Coolidge, "who had two languages, the language of statesmanship and the language of the country store on a Saturday afternoon."[48]

Whether real or perceptual, the experience of being the slowest kid in the classroom had a corrosive effect on Will's development. From childhood and throughout his adulthood, he wore an expressionless face that rarely revealed his thinking or feelings, a trait that later baffled his business associates who complained behind his back that he was cold. His school chum Frank Belden later recalled that unlike the other boys in school, Will never suffered a beating from their sadistic schoolmaster: "Will K. was into meanness just as much as the others but he had such a poker face that the teacher never blamed him for some of the pranks."[49] Yet in a very real sense Will's lifelong guarded nature may have been a manifestation of his insecurity. He desperately wanted to be loved but was, as his biographer Horace Powell observed, "reluctant to form close relationships because of the fear of losing them. He moved cautiously among his fellow men, anticipating rebuffs and ready for the fight or the flight."[50]

Beyond his horribly blurred vision and the resultant inability to read the facial expressions of his peers, Will's tight-lipped expression might also be explained by his precarious dental health. In an era before fluoride treatments and modern dentistry, Will developed multiple cavities and, before he was twenty, lost most of his teeth. His smile was marred by a not so charming, toothless grin. In later life, Will occasionally entertained his youngest grandchildren by "slipping [his dentures] from their moorings with his tongue." Once he had the means to give away his vast fortune, however, the bespectacled and dentured Will insisted that children's dental and eye care be among the major foci of his beneficent W. K. Kellogg Foundation.[51]

AT AGE SIX, Will began working in his father's broom factory, first after school and later full-time. As his brothers before him, Will sorted straw and broomcorn for the manufacture of sweeping sticks six days a week, excluding the Saturday Sabbath. During the mid to late nineteenth century, the enforced labor of children was hardly restricted to the clothing factories, textile mills, and hundreds of other manufacturing firms along the Eastern Seaboard. In big cities and small towns across the United States, adults who ran large companies, parents responsible for farm harvests, and small business owners routinely enlisted the help of children, much to the detriment of these youngsters' physical and mental development. Will, like each of his older brothers, was one of millions of American children forced into the workplace, exposed to potential injuries, and cheated out of a complete education and childhood for the pennies he earned to help support his family.[52]

Will's boring and repetitive work at his father's factory was punctuated by only one joyful event, which occurred when he was eight. After an uncharacteristic campaign by Will consisting of much begging and pleading, John Preston grudgingly allowed the love-starved boy to accompany him on a forty-mile train ride to sell brooms in Allegan, Michigan. Some eighty years later, Will precisely recollected the sights he saw, the people he met, and the one-on-one conversations he had with his father. It was an occasion of parental monopoly that was monumentally special to a boy living with so many sisters and brothers who seemed to outshine him on a daily basis, his perception of parental neglect, and an Adventist faith that held the end of all time was soon approaching.

Clear to anyone observing this youngster, however, was a steady work ethic and growing competence for business affairs. In terms of broom making, Will quickly became even more adept than John at sorting out broomcorn, separating the seed from the brush, selecting the proper strands and wiring them together to make the sweeping portion of the broom. He also developed great skill in quickly sharpening the handles and driving them into the broom, nailing them down, and trimming off the edges to make a finished and attractive product. During a typical twelve-hour shift, Will took 5 cents (or about $1 in 2016) worth of materials plus a dime's worth of his hourly wage (about $2 in 2016) to produce enough brooms to clear 25 cents (roughly $5 in 2016) in profit.

Before he was twelve, Will mastered the art of supervising the work of

Will Kellogg, age 15, selling his father's brooms in St. Charles, Michigan, April 7, 1875

"six or eight" other boys (including his older brother Preston). At fourteen, he went on the road to sell brooms. By the age of sixteen, Will supported himself with a weekly paycheck of $18 (about $411 in 2016) and acquired significant experience in production, sales, and management even if his hard work was rarely acknowledged by his father. Decades later, Will complained, "My father was not active in the business, due to a broken hip, and while the business was conducted in the name of J. P. Kellogg and Son (Dr. J.H. being the son), I do not recall father being in the factory to any extent after his surgery."[53]

In addition to working at the broom factory, Will performed many other tedious chores. Armed with a hoe, a spade, and a youthful spine, every spring and summer Will tilled the soil, growing vegetables on the vacant lots his father owned. The backbreaking work of weeding and planting never left Will's memory, even in old age. "Before daylight in the summertime," he recalled, "we boys were routed out of bed to weed berries and vegetables, or to root, bunch, and wash onions and lettuce for the local market. I cannot say I enjoyed weeding the onions and other vegetable beds." During the harvest that coincided with his ninth year of life, Will estimated that he "pulled and topped three hundred and fifty bushels of Bermuda [onions]."[54]

Perhaps the most memorable episode of Will's childhood centered on Old Spot, the family's swaybacked, speckled horse, a steed reputedly of Arabian heritage. John Preston assigned Will the task of tending, washing, and feeding the nag. The Kellogg children loved Old Spot because he was gentle, smart enough to do all sorts of horsey tricks, and fun to ride along the dusty, unpaved streets of Battle Creek. They mischievously pulled at his tail to get his attention, and, after the local farrier trimmed and balanced the animal's hooves, played games with his old, discarded horseshoes. Will was especially proud of an equestrian trick he mastered that never failed to impress the neighborhood children. He would ride Old Spot while hanging upside down, underneath the horse's belly. That is until the fateful day when Will returned from school to learn that his father had sold the horse. Heartbroken but unable to demonstrate a hint of emotion, Will promised himself that someday he would own a stable of Arabian steeds. It was a pledge he would make come true. In 1925, Will established the W. K. Kellogg Ranch in sunny Pomona, California, which became one of the world's finest Arabian horse farms.

At times, the boy fantasized about escaping the family broom business and becoming a doctor like Merritt and John or, perhaps, finding wealth through a business of his own choosing. Such dreams seemed futile every time he was called to return to the mind-numbing task of making still more brooms. Nowhere is this despair better expressed than in a photograph taken of him in 1875, after his father promoted him to become the firm's principal sales agent. The picture depicts Will during a sales trip to St. Charles, Michigan, a village near Saginaw. Upon alighting from the train, Will spied a local photographer's shop and, with the impulse of a teenaged boy, decided to have his portrait taken. Dressed in an ill-fitting vested black suit and a derby that sat on the back of his head, Will posed with one hand in his vest pocket and the other holding a bundle of four brooms. It is his face that best reflects the state of his mind.[55] Nearly a century and a half after the photographic plate was exposed to the light, one cannot help but be saddened by the image of a young man with little hope, even less joy, and a weary resignation of many uneventful years of drudgery ahead.

4

Long-Distance Learning

T HE ELEGANT DR. AUSTIN FLINT began his daily hospital
rounds precisely at 12:00 noon. At 11:59 a.m., his eager "house
pupils" listened for the click-clacking of his boots down the corridor,
knowing a moment later would welcome the entry of a large man with
an overwhelming pair of muttonchop whiskers, sparse silvery-white hair
combed over a patch of baldness, hazel eyes so piercing that they tres-
passed his gold spectacles and proceeded directly to whoever or whatever
was in his gaze, and a booming voice exuding confidence. Dr. Flint always
carried his black leather "doctor's bag," whether he was in his clinic, his
private office, or along the halls of the many hospitals he attended. The
battered satchel was filled to the brim with the tools of his trade, from
rubber mallets and pleximeters (small ivory plates to contain the blow
of the mallet when eliciting a reflex movement) to hypodermic syringes
and vials of morphine. More important to the young interns and medical students straining to hear his every word, Dr. Flint was the author
of one of the leading American medical textbooks of the late nineteenth
century. Between 1865 and 1888, more than 75,000 medical students purchased, clutched, and memorized six successive editions of his *Treatise on
the Principles and Practice of Medicine.*[1]

Dr. Flint was, perhaps, the most prominent teacher in a high-powered
faculty at John's third (and last) medical school, the Bellevue Hospital
Medical College. The school was founded in 1861 and attached to the
largest and oldest public hospital in America. In its day, Bellevue was
the premier institution of its kind in North America. The distinctive

Austin Flint, MD, circa 1880s

feature of a Bellevue medical education was its application of "a system almost universal in Great Britain," which had "the advantage of combining clinical with didactic teaching during the entire collegiate course of the student."[2] Today, such a combination seems intuitively obvious, although it was not until the early twentieth century when the troika of lectures, books, and clinical teaching on hospital wards was finally embraced by all American medical schools as a better means of building doctors.

Attending the Bellevue Hospital Medical College did not come cheap. John's tuition for the first session amounted to about $155 (or $3,320 in 2016) and, because of an extra charge for graduation, $175 (or $3,750 in 2016) for the second session.[3] The Bellevue bursar was quick to inform every student that these levies covered all matriculation fees, dissection laboratory costs, graduation fees, and a full slate of tickets for the professors' lectures.[4] Such dear expenses were only the launching point in the mad dash to obtain a Bellevue MD. There were also the steep admission costs for after-class "quizzes," led by select professors to help students prepare for their oral examinations and to obtain references for future work opportunities. The quizzes were not included in the formal tuition but they signified an important percentage of the medical school professors' annual salaries. The price tag for such after-hours "cram sessions" was more than twice the fees charged for the regular term. And, of course, there were the expenses of living in the costly city of New York. When John sent his bills back to Battle Creek for James White, the Elder likely shook his head in dismay at the mounting expenses it took to train his protégé.

THERE WERE SEVERAL REASONS why so many of the nation's most ambitious physicians coveted the opportunity to work at Bellevue. The hospital offered an endless river of what doctors then euphemistically termed "clinical material"—impoverished and vulnerable "public ward" patients whose bodies and conditions helped teach generations of students how to become doctors. By the time John walked Bellevue's hospital wards, thousands of desperate New Yorkers sought entry into its doors every year and filled its more than 1,200 beds each night. Situated at the foot of Kips Bay on the East River, its pastoral name was derived from the farm that once stood in its place. By the 1860s, Bellevue's long, bed-filled wards, affording little privacy or dignity, were a human potage reeking of poor hygiene and filth. Those patients looking outside the hospital windows were wise to leave them shut because the East River was the stopping place for much of Manhattan's raw sewage, via a jumble of pipes and shovels, making it a stream that positively stank.[5]

When John Harvey Kellogg first crossed the wrought iron gates of the hospital's imposing red brick portal, he entered the largest physical plant devoted to health care in the United States. Its campus spanned from East 26th Street to 30th Street and was bounded by First Avenue and the East River; it included dozens of interlocking pavilions of differing styles and heights, containing a beehive of charity wards, laboratories, surgical suites, psychiatry units, and the "dead-house," or morgue, where countless autopsies were conducted to figure out exactly what caused the deaths of so many Bellevue patients.

The conduct of so many postmortem examinations reflected the state of medical care at the time. In 1876, for example, 5,165 patients were admitted. Only 4,313 lived long enough to be discharged, meaning 16.5 percent of those admitted to Bellevue did not leave alive. Many families failed to claim the remains of a loved one because they did not have the money for a funeral, a situation that forced the City of New York to handle such rites in a perfunctory manner. Moored alongside the dock serving the hospital was a funeral ferry that transported the unclaimed dead up the East River to potter's field on Hart Island.[6]

In retrospect, it is easy to see why so many died at Bellevue. Beyond the paucity of medicines or effective treatments available at the time, there was also the very real risk of succumbing to the surgeon's scalpel. Even if a patient did manage to get off the operating table while still drawing breath, the grimy hospital wards, attended by doctors and nurses who rarely washed their hands or changed out of blood-stained clothing, all but guaranteed contracting overwhelming infections such as erysipelas and pyemia, or what we now understand to be bacterially mediated forms of blood poisoning.[7] When John matriculated into

Bellevue Medical, the most medically prudent decision a patient could make was not to seek care in a big hospital and, instead, stay at home under the watchful eye of a relative, hoping and praying that nature and time would heal one's wounds.

Nevertheless, from morning to late at night, year after year, the sick and needy *did* come to Bellevue, pounding on the hospital's doors and begging for admission. The majority were the urban poor, immigrants, "lunatics," the chronically and acutely ill, and the mentally or physically broken, all of them without the means to pay for their hospital stay. Those in most desperate need of attention were rapidly transported there in horse-drawn ambulances, thanks to another marvel of modern technology—the telegraph. Twenty-four hours a day, seven days a week, an operator at Bellevue received calls through an independent telegraph wire that connected every New York City police precinct with the hospital. In the busy accident room, or what we today would call the emergency room, doctors attended those in the building trades who spent their days transforming Manhattan from a colonial village into a modern Gotham until they encountered a serious mishap or fall. Above the tables on which these battered patients were placed, a sign painted on the wall

Interior of the Bellevue Hospital central courtyard, 1893

suggested the chances of recuperation. It read, in six-inch-high black letters, "PREPARE TO MEET YOUR GOD."[8]

Unlike today's pristine, high-rise, and profitable temples of medicine, most nineteenth-century American hospitals were primarily charitable affairs.[9] The wealthy trustees running and funding these hospitals, rather than the doctors, made the final decisions of who would be admitted each night and who would be turned away. They often based their judgment on a moral compass rather than the triage of illness. Sinners and social outcasts—drunks, criminals, prostitutes, unwed mothers, and other members of the "undeserving poor"—understood there was little chance of attention even when suffering from the most dire of medical conditions.

Although Bellevue was a public municipal hospital, the politics and decisions of the New York City Board of Commissioners of Public Charity could be just as byzantine and judgmental, if not more so, as the hospitals run by private charities or churches. Despite the best efforts of a cadre of crusading doctors struggling to pull the profession out of the mire of antiquity, many hospital trustees focused on improving the unhealthy living environments and spiritual ways of patients. Equally problematic, too many hospital trustees still considered the new-fangled tools, therapeutics, and surgical operations secondary to the whole "charitable enterprise."[10]

EACH DAY during his rounds, Dr. Flint dispensed a slew of clinical pearls that his students resolutely committed to memory. Flint's great gift was an uncanny ability to synthesize all the data, signs, and symptoms he gathered while on his hospital rounds and then relate them to the latest discoveries being made in clinical medicine. Walking down the open wards, Dr. Flint bowed at each bedside and courteously greeted patients assigned to his care, regardless of their social station or mental status. He explored the luster of their eyes, reached into their mouths to examine the coating of their tongues, and thumped on their chests and bellies to fathom the hidden processes brewing within their bodies.

The most exciting moment of these displays of clinical legerdemain occurred when Dr. Flint reached into one of the pockets of his splendid waistcoat and pulled out a set of two ivory earpieces connected to metal tubing converging in a hollow ball meant to amplify sound and attached to a conical, or bell, chest piece. Called the stethoscope (from the Greek roots *stethos,* or chest, and *skopein,* to look at or to observe), it was invented in 1819 by a French doctor named René Théophile Hyacinthe Laënnec. The device allowed doctors to peer into the body of a patient's chest by means of auscultation (from the Latin *auscultare,* "to listen").[11] So adept was Dr. Flint at using the stethoscope that he discovered and reported a low rumble heard at the apex of the heart, signifying aortic valve regurgitation and which still carries the eponym "the Austin Flint murmur."[12]

Dr. Flint exhibited an unending allegiance to the future of science, even if it challenged or overthrew dogma that doctors held dear for centuries. As a successful textbook author, he kept scrupulously abreast of the latest advances in medicine. In practice, he avoided the dangerous medications of the day, opting instead for nature-based therapies, a concept known as "therapeutic nihilism." As a teacher, he drilled into his students a strict code of ethical conduct and new discoveries on the infectious nature of many deadly and all too common diseases.[13] A knowledge-hungry John Harvey Kellogg attached himself to Austin Flint like a suction cup on a ceramic-tiled wall.[14]

Dr. Flint's services cost a great deal of money. John paid an additional $500 (about $10,700 in 2016) in order to study physical diagnosis privately under Flint and his associate, Edward G. Janeway, a brilliant physician who created Bellevue's system of medical charts so that the clinical symptoms of those patients who died in the hospital could be better correlated to their autopsy results.[15] Walking the wards with these learned men on a daily basis was a medical student's dream come true. Before Dr. Flint arrived each noon, Janeway polled the medical students and internes to help select the most interesting and complex cases for presentation to the chief. Other times they drew patient cases from Flint's private practice or his charitable rounds for the city's Bureau of Medical and Surgical Relief for Out-Door Poor.[16] Dr. Janeway would then direct the medical students to elicit the patients' histories, examine their ailing bodies, and report back what they had found and what they believed to be the best course of action. By evening, John reliably amazed them all with his natural aptitude for clinical diagnosis and rational, therapeutic solutions. When evaluating John for his "report card," Dr. Janeway remarked, "Young Kellogg from Battle Creek, Michigan, is the brightest student I have."[17]

TWO OTHER CLINICAL luminaries who made a lasting impression on John were the genitourinary surgeons William H. Van Buren and Edward Keyes. Each year, they presented a series of simultaneously titillating and repulsive lectures detailing the work of "the venereal department . . . [which was] extremely rich in cases illustrating all forms of specific diseases, and in this respect is second to none other in the world."[18] The same year John learned about the many health risks of sexual activity, 1874, Dr. Frederic R. Sturgis, a surgeon at the city's charity hospital on Blackwell's Island, reported before the American Public Health Association that at least 50,450 New Yorkers (5.4 percent of the total population of 942,292) suffered from syphilis. This number underestimated the true incidence because it was based only on those residing in the city and not the thousands of unreported sailors, soldiers, and merchant marines who came to New York every day, all eager for fun and highly susceptible to syphilis, gonorrhea, and other venereal diseases. These relatively incurable, hugely debilitating, rampant, and morally suspect illnesses remained a significant public health problem during Dr. Kellogg's entire career. By 1895, 1 out of every 20 Americans, 3,445,000 men and women, were infected with syphilis. In 1937, the incidence doubled; 1 out of every 10 Americans suffered from the "great pox."[19]

In Ann Arbor and New York, John listened to lectures on venereal diseases. His student notebook entries for March 13, 1874, ominously list every disgusting symptom of gonorrhea (which John refers to as "the clap") and syphilis—from the creamy yellow-green, purulent discharges and severe pain in "making water" seen in the former malady to the raging systemic infections, skin rashes, cardiac damage, and insanity seen in those infected with the latter. The extant treatments included direct injections of burning silver nitrate into the urethra and massive doses of mercury and iodides. As he recorded these prescriptions, John astutely observed, "sometimes the cure is worse than the disease."[20] Leafing through his yellowed and frayed notebooks, one can almost feel John's revulsion transform into a lifetime edifice of strict sexual abstinence.

Although John favored the teachings of an obstetrician named

Edmund Randolph Peaslee, Dr. Fordyce Barker, a flamboyant professor of midwifery and diseases of women, also impressed him. Barker lectured to John's class on puerperal disease, or childbed fever, one of the leading causes of maternal mortality during the eighteenth and nineteenth centuries. Professor Barker taught them the work of Harvard's Oliver Wendell Holmes Sr. and Ignaz Semmelweis of Vienna. Both men independently made the contagious connection between the rising incidence of childbed fever and the fatuous obstetricians who moved freely between the delivery room and the autopsy suite, delivering babies in one room and practicing pelvic examinations on cadavers in another. Over two summers, Dr. Barker "select[ed], fus[ed] and ma[de] homogenous" a collection of his Bellevue lecture notes on "the puerperal diseases." They were published in 1874, while John was still sitting in his clinical amphitheater. On the page or at the lectern, Barker taught that the disease was "transmitted by the physician from one patient to another" and all doctors must vigorously wash their hands as "the greatest precaution to guard against so terrible a calamity."[21]

The most lasting and significant professional relationship John made during his Bellevue days was with Stephen Smith. A surgeon, public health reformer, and an early proponent of the antiseptic surgical techniques prescribed by Joseph Lister, Dr. Smith unleashed a tornado of modern surgical techniques that rippled widely across his admiring medical students at Bellevue and beyond. Internationally respected, Smith was a founder of the American Public Health Association and a prominent member of virtually every major local, state, and national public health board.[22] John often "rounded" with Dr. Smith during his weekly trips to the city's contagious disease ward (mostly smallpox) on nearby Blackwell's Island.[23] In his later life, John pointed with pride to the time he served on the Michigan State Board of Health from 1878 to 1891 and, then again, from 1911 to 1917. It was Stephen Smith, he reliably recounted, who first inspired him to take a strong interest in the newly emerging field of public health and introduced him to the basic language of vital statistics while studying the infant mortality rates of New York City.

In the outpatient clinics, John learned the practical tasks of how to set a broken leg, deliver a baby, quarantine a household, and treat pneumonia, heart attacks, cirrhosis, and the infectious diseases of childhood.

Along Bellevue's famous insanity ward, he studied women and men mad with mania, depression, and alcohol and opium abuse.[24] When it came to applying the lancet to "scarify," or bleed, a patient, for a variety of maladies, John noted that while "the question of blood letting is important to consider, it is now a remedy scarcely ever employed by many physicians. Some don't ever use it, don't have the means for doing it." The medical student also jotted down an anecdote Dr. Flint relayed about a colleague "who bled and bled a patient with peritonitis and yet the patient died."[25]

LECTURES, patient rounds, "quizzes," and studying occupied the entirety of John's days and much of his nights. There was little time to carve out for rest. Money was scarce and John subsisted on an extremely limited budget, having spent most of the money the Whites lent him for tuition and course fees. He lived in the attic of a cheap lodging house on East 28th Street and Third Avenue, which was then a rather shabby and impoverished neighborhood. His landlady provided no board. Each term, John went down to one of the warehouse markets off the foul-smelling East River and purchased one barrel of apples and a second one filled with graham crackers. For every meal, he consumed "two apples and seven crackers." He gleefully wrote to his parents that his dietary choice cost a mere 16 cents a day (about $3.43 in 2016) and was so nutritious he had gained seventeen pounds![26] On the days after completing a tough set of examinations, John would treat himself to a roasted potato purchased from a street vendor near the hospital.

The most important meal he ever consumed during his medical student years occurred on the afternoon a grocer sold him a package of "steam cooked" oatmeal. John was disappointed to discover that this "new" preparation was almost as time-consuming as cooking any other hot grain cereal. Nevertheless, it was a finding that proved to be a watershed moment in John's creative life. Decades later, he recalled this moment as the birth of prepared cereals: "It . . . occurred to me that it should be possible to purchase cereals at [the grocery store] already cooked and ready to eat and I considered different ways in which this might be done."[27]

On the other end of his alimentary tract, the house's sanitary facilities could not have pleased the fastidious John. He had weekly access to a washtub ("filled" with a few pitchers of lukewarm water and not drained until each resident in the house had his bath) and when nature called he endured long lines to a communal privy in the alley behind the building. According to the 1867 New York City Tenement House Law, the ratio of tenants to privies was "at least one to every 20 occupants," but the lines must have seemed longer when John stood in them.[28] "Night soil" removers only occasionally rinsed the privies out and, by all accounts, the stench emanating from a tenement house's privy was truly "sickening."[29]

GRADUATES OF BELLEVUE were required to present signed certificates attesting to attendance of two terms of the predetermined curriculum (e.g., anatomy, *materia medica,* chemistry, physiology, the theory and practice of medicine, surgery, and obstetrics). An equally steep requirement was the composition of "an acceptable thesis composed by, and in the handwriting of, the candidate."[30] Unlike many of his classmates who wrote lengthy reviews of a particular illness or drug, John's dissertation asked the far broader question "What Is Disease?" It serves as a superb glimpse into the mind of a young man who would go on to author more than fifty medical books and edit a monthly health magazine for more than half a century. John's thoughtful, declarative sentences take the reader on a long journey into the history of disease concepts across Western civilization, beginning with Antiquity and extending all the way to the decade after the Civil War. Disease, he argued, resulted from a derangement of the body's natural functions and represented "an effort of nature to rid itself of obnoxious encumbrances." John insisted that the physician must discard toxic drugs and the lancet to become a guide who helps the patient naturally resolve that derangement and return to a proper state of health.[31] What remains so interesting about John's doctoral thesis is that it articulates a theory of medicine he would burnish to a high sheen for the remainder of his career. Specifically, he dedicated himself to the prevention of disease long before it had an opportunity to cause serious harm. The damaged body, John elegantly wrote, could be repaired and disease entirely avoided or, at least, attenuated by living within a carefully considered set of dietary and physical rules.

Gathering the mandatory "proper testimonials of character" was probably the most time-consuming requirement for graduating from Bellevue. Such letters of recommendation were only to be dispensed upon "three years' pupilage, after eighteen years of age, with a *regular physician in good standing.*"[32] The italics of emphasis were part of Bellevue's boilerplate medical school catalog and the descriptor "regular" was neither casual nor expansive; it had a specific and strict meaning. Only those doctors studying at allopathic, or "regularly-organized medical colleges," were qualified to teach Bellevue students. "The tickets and diplomas of Eclectic, Homeopathic, or Botanic Colleges, or colleges devoted to any peculiar system of medicine are considered irregular." Students were further warned that preceptors who "advertise or violate in any way the code of ethics adopted by the profession, will not be received under any circumstance, even if the preceptors be regular graduates in Medicine."[33]

Three years of service must have seemed like an eternity to the young medical student and neither time nor the huge amount of money it represented were commodities John had at his disposal. Even though he divested himself of the diploma he earned at Russell Trall's Hygeio Therapeutic College, he did have one occasion to use this connection to his professional advantage. Despite the Bellevue Medical College's clearly written requirements for training only under specific types of physicians, John took the huge risk of choosing a Brooklyn-based doctor named O. T. Lines to endorse his apprenticeship certificates.[34]

The young man from Battle Creek met Dr. Lines two years earlier, while still a student at Trall's makeshift medical school. Hardly what the good Doctors Flint or Janeway would deem a "regular" physician, Dr. Lines was a full-throated, practicing homeopath and hydropath. John may have excelled in his coursework but he, nevertheless, defied Bellevue's strict rules by completing his all-important clinical preceptorship with an "irregular" physician. Some have argued this lapse as a function of the poor supervision by the Bellevue medical faculty; others might cynically suggest that, like many medical students past and present, John opportunistically cut a few corners to get on with his medical career.

THE PLOY WORKED. On the cold, blustery afternoon of February 25, 1875, there was John lined up with the rest of his class for a grand com-

mencement ceremony held at the New York Academy of Music. Located
on 14th Street and Irving Place, the Academy boasted a four-thousand-seat
auditorium, one of the largest in the city. Two decades old, *The New York
Times* once declared the hall to be an acoustical "triumph."[35]

Promptly at 3:00 p.m., the New York Philharmonic Society began
blasting Wagner's "Kaiser March," conducted by the German-born cel-
list and conductor Carl Bergmann, who in 1852 first introduced American audiences to Wagner's work.[36] A committed alcoholic, the Maestro
was well into his cups as the commencement commenced. Despite his
chemical impairment, once the grandiose march wound down, he woo-
zily lifted his baton to signal the orchestra to segue into Meyerbeer's
dramatic *"Conjuration et Bénédiction des poignards"* from the fourth act
of the hugely popular 1836 opera *Les Huguenots.* The opening notes of
the Meyerbeer served as the cue for John and his other 192 classmates to
make their processional entrance.[37] Waiting on the stage, poised to swear
the students into the profession, was a receiving line of the faculty; the
former governor and U.S. senator of New York Edwin D. Morgan; the
graduation speaker, Judge John R. Brady; and an assortment of clergymen, all of them gussied up in their best frock coats and black silk cravats
tightly wound around starched and sharply pointed, wing-tipped collars.

Caps and gowns were not yet part of the medical school graduation
ritual in 1875. Instead, the graduates wore somber black morning coats.
John, eager to appear as well groomed as his fellows, saved up until he
had enough to buy new togs. The woolen suit was made to measure and
the tailor promised it would be ready in time for the big day. After pick-
ing it up, an exuberant John left the haberdashery shop and dashed home
with glee. Once there, he carefully hung the new suit up in the tiny,
makeshift "closet" in his room, which was actually a bar jammed into a
corner covered by a curtain.

The night before the ceremony, a crisis struck that ruined John's plans.
Returning home, after one last nostalgic tour of the hospital, he disrobed
and got himself ready to sleep. As he hung up the threadbare and frayed
suit coat that was his daily uniform for the past two years, he discovered
his new garment had been stolen. No description of the sensation of
his sinking stomach survives but it must have been palpable, especially
since the young man had neither the capital nor the time to replace the
loss. Forced to wear his old suit, he realized shortly before receiving his

diploma that there was a gaping hole in the seat of his battle-worn pants. Fleet of mind, John slowed down his march up to the stage so that the graduate behind him was close enough to block his exposure problem.[38]

An hour later, the newly minted Doctor Kellogg proudly walked out of the Academy of Music, diploma in hand, to the stirring chords of Strauss's "Egyptian March." He then joined his comrades for a boisterous and celebratory banquet. Later that evening, after a meaty dinner that must have repelled the abstemious young man, John wrote to William C. White, the son of Ellen and James White, a boyhood friend and a fellow traveler to the Trall College, "I was one of the 193 graduates who were sworn into the profession to make 'regular kills.' . . . I feel more than 50 lb. bigger since getting a certain piece of sheepskin about two feet square. It's a bona-fide sheep too, by the way, none of your bogus paper concerns like the [Trall] hygeio-therapeutic document."[39]

AFTER GRADUATION, John spent several weeks in the reading rooms of the Astor Library, the forerunner to today's New York Public Library, as well as the Cooper Union and New York Academy of Medicine libraries. There, he pored over the latest medical texts, including a newly collected set of papers echoing his favorite physiological popularizer, Sylvester Graham. Writing home to William White, John recounted how he hoped to apply these lessons to his nascent medical practice: "I find he left some very fine 'nuggets' and I am gathering them up. I leave the smelting and coining until I get home."[40]

John's most intriguing postgraduate medical adventure was his enrollment in a private course on electrotherapeutics conducted by George Miller Beard.[41] Dr. Beard was one of the nation's most respected experts on "nervous diseases," or mental illness, in the pre-Freudian era and served as an expert witness in defense of Charles Guiteau, the man who murdered President James Garfield in 1881.[42]

Dr. Beard coined the term "neurasthenia," or "American nervousness," to describe the condition he most often diagnosed among his many wealthy, jangled, and overwrought patients. This syndrome was marked by fatigue, exhaustion, depression, headaches, dyspepsia, insomnia, psychogenic paralysis, painful neuralgias, and even bouts of hysteria. Beard hypothesized that the neurasthenic had dissipated his or her "nerve force" by engaging in all sorts of stressful or untoward activities, such as masturbation, illicit sex, gambling, excessive work, and over-worrying, as opposed to pursuing "finer and spiritual things." In his 1881 treatise *American Nervousness,* Beard eloquently compared the ancient but placid Greeks to the harried, modern American: "the modern differ from the ancient civilizations mainly in five elements—steam power, the periodical press, the telegraph, the sciences and the mental activity of women. When civilization, plus these five factors, invades any nation, it must carry nervousness and nervous diseases with it."[43]

Whether these patients suffered from clinical depression, chronic fatigue syndrome, fibromyalgia, or some other entity is difficult to gauge, especially in light of the chronological blockade against interviewing and examining Dr. Beard or his patients. What is clear is that these patients were suffering and desperate for a plan of action, no matter how remote the chance of a "cure" might be. Given the "invalids," worried but well, and psychologically damaged patients Dr. Kellogg would soon be attending at the Battle Creek Sanitarium, George Beard was the perfect guide into this poorly understood but all too common byway of American medical practice. That said, as medical historian Charles Rosenberg once described Dr. Beard, he was "careless, visionary, uncritical, and ambitious to a degree which compromised his ability as a scientist."[44] In the years to come, this appraisal might be easily applied to the often overenthusiastic John Harvey Kellogg.

When John studied under Beard, the senior physician was experimenting with the therapeutic uses of electricity and was "shocking" his willing patients with low-voltage waves from the brass leads of a galvanic battery. Dr. Beard made loud public claims that his patients responded well to the treatment and published an influential medical monograph on the topic.[45] John did not record how much he paid Dr. Beard for the tutorial privilege but the fee was likely similar to what Drs. Flint and Janeway charged. Whatever the cost, John convinced the Whites that it was worth the expense. Throughout his career, Dr. Kellogg applied a variety of electrotherapies of his own design for treating neurasthenia, hysteria, depression, and many other psychogenic disorders.[46]

By the time John returned to Battle Creek in late June of 1875, his mentors were eager to appoint him medical director of the Western Institute. The physicians working there, however, blew a strong gust of resentment aimed at John's favored status with the Whites. John, too, had reservations about running a health institute bound by the strictures of religious beliefs alone and was eager to test out the newer scientific principles he learned at Bellevue. He told the Whites he wanted to devote his time to conducting research, writing, and advancing medical knowledge and turned down their initial offer.

By 1876, it was clear the Western Institute required a drastic change if it was going to succeed in the manner the Whites envisioned. Throughout the winter and spring of that year, John served as the secretary of the institute's board of directors, sat in on their meetings, and engaged in several conversations with James and Ellen White; Uriah Smith, the editor of the *Advent Review and Sabbath Herald;* and Professor Sidney Brownsberger, the president of the Adventist Battle Creek College.[47] These exercises helped John sharpen his vision for placing the health reform institute on a more modern footing. His sponsors, even more impressed by the diminutive doctor's abilities, redoubled their efforts to get him to direct the place.[48] John understood both his debt to the Whites and their expectation that he would apply his expensive medical education to the Adventist health reform cause, but the young man still needed more time before fully committing.

Specifically, he wanted to take one more trip back east to visit the United States International, or Centennial, Exhibition of 1876 (in honor of the hundredth anniversary of the signing of the Declaration of Independence), where "never before in the history of mankind have the civilized nations contributed such a display of their peculiar treasures."[49] It was the first world's fair to be held in the United States, at Philadelphia's Fairmount Park along the banks of the Schuylkill River, and was designed both to impress and announce America's dominance in modern technology and industry. The Whites agreed to this pre-employment sabbatical provided that following the exhibition John visit Wilmington, Delaware. There, he was to be the guest of a married team of Adventist doctors named Pusey and Mary Heald, who ran a water cure clinic called the Healds' Hygeian Home.[50]

BEYOND THE SHEER FUN of it, John attended the World's Fair of 1876 to help staff Dr. Stephen Smith's health exhibit for the International

Temperance Conference, from June 13 to 16. In this capacity, he prepared pamphlets and exhibit cards warning fairgoers about the many health risks of imbibing.[51] Fortunately, his temperance work did not occupy too much time, leaving him with plenty more to explore the fair.[52]

As he wandered through the buildings and exhibits of the exposition, John made certain to avoid the vast Brewer's Hall, which offered up cold draughts of beer, ale, porter, and stout from around the globe. He was equally quick to sidestep the sumptuous French and Italian wine exhibits and the many food booths serving up fresh, hot (and greasy) waffles, funnel cakes, frankfurters, cotton candy, and ice cream sundaes. He did, however, thrill to the sight of the completed copper arm holding the torch of Liberty, a limb of the famous statue that was France's gift to the United States on the occasion of its hundredth birthday. He perused the enormous displays of artwork, from oil paintings and sculptures to exotic fine art to jewelry. And, considering his love of gadgets, he was mesmerized by the exhibition featuring Alexander Graham Bell's miraculous new invention called the telephone (from the Greek for "distant voice"), the original John Bull steam locomotive, the Remington Typographic Machine, or typewriter (a machine he would never master during his prolific writing career), and a giant printing press that could put out 35,000 copies of a neatly folded broadsheet newspaper in only an hour.[53]

Young Dr. Kellogg focused most intently on the medical displays at the fair. One of them was a stunning painting unceremoniously hung behind the United States War Department's specially constructed full-sized modern "military post" hospital ward. The picture was an eight feet by six feet portrait of surgeon Samuel Gross by the Philadelphia Realist painter Thomas Eakins.[54] Now considered an American masterpiece, it is mandatory to note the Exhibition's Art Gallery committee rejected *The Gross Clinic* on the grounds that Eakins's vivid image of a surgical operation was too gory and offensive for the average fairgoer.[55] Other "health exhibits" John passed by included those sponsored by the manufacturers of "Pine Tree Tar Cordial," a patented panacea for coughs, colds, consumption, and sore throats, equipment manufacturers displaying the finest microscopes from Germany, surgical instruments made of British steel, the newest artificial legs, hernia belts and other prosthet-

*The U.S. Post Hospital exhibit at the Centennial Exhibition ("World's Fair")
of 1876 in Philadelphia*

ics, and others demonstrating a huge array of allopathic, botanical, and
homeopathic medical products.

John spent most of his time, however, taking notes at an elaborate
demonstration booth mounted by the G. M. Zander Medico-Gymnastic
Company of Stockholm. Gustav Zander was a doctor and a gymnastics
teacher at both the University of Stockholm and at his own medico-
gymnastic institute. The Zander Company designed and sold all types
of exercise machines "by means of which the several muscles, tendons,
and ligaments of the body can, in due sequence, be brought into play, so
gradually and so delicately as to render the exercise perfectly safe, even
for the most confirmed invalid, or the most delicate child."[56] One of Dr.
Zander's most popular machines was a leather-clad cylinder equipped
with a saddle, which was set upon a contraption with wooden legs and
springs. The device essentially mimicked the bucking and cantering of
a horse with none of the hassles of tending to a live beast. After a trip
to Sweden in 1883, and again in 1886, Dr. Kellogg purchased several of
Zander's "exercise machines" to equip his gymnasium at the San, which
he tinkered with and redesigned for American use.[57]

BACK IN BATTLE CREEK, Ann Janette Kellogg glowed with pride over John's adventures on the busy wards of Bellevue Hospital. As exciting as the young medico's exploits were for the majority of the Kellogg family, however, the fifteen-year-old Will silently ground his teeth in resentment over his mother's favoritism. Unfortunately, Ann Janette dispensed maternal nourishment in as sparing a manner as Bumble the Beadle distributed bowls of gruel to Oliver Twist. It was, as one family friend noted, a home where "everything was so serious." Her style of mothering was not the best fit for a child who was so in need of affection. One of the Kellogg children recalled as an adult, "If we could get Mother to laugh, we could get anything out of her, but it was not very easy to get her to laugh."[58] Uriah Smith, a close friend of the family, described her as remarkable, vigorous, and indomitable, "a glance from her piercing eyes was sufficient to bring the most rebellious child speedily to terms . . . some might have mistaken her reticence and dignity of character and bearing for coldness of disposition, but those who came near to her knew her to be an uncommonly generous and exceedingly tender-hearted person."[59] Will's authorized biographer Horace Powell described her more succinctly, "Unfortunately for young Will, Ann Janette Kellogg was not a mother who wasted love."[60]

Resigned to toiling away as the traveling salesman for John Preston's broom works, Will's life consisted of long, dusty train trips, nights spent sleeping in bedbug-ridden cheap hotels, and horrendous meals gobbled in haste before jumping onto the next train. The roadwork was so unattractive and lonely that he longed to return to making brooms in Battle Creek and living in his cold but competent mother's home.

At sixteen, Will temporarily moved to nearby Kalamazoo to help out at his half-brother Albert's broom firm, which Albert had all but run into the ground long before Will arrived. The little brother attempted to teach his older sibling how to recognize when the broomcorn jobbers were foisting off inferior materials. He gave him tips on inspecting each three-hundred-pound bale for "size, straightness, color," and double-checking the quality by scraping the "seed from the brush by drawing it through a hoe with comb-like teeth, mounted on a bench." Displaying a patience far beyond his youth, Will sat for hours in Albert's shop, "with a ball of string on the floor between his feet as he wrapped the twine around and around the brush and tied each broom by hand" in order to insure every broom was well made and satisfactory to their discerning customers.[61] Will even helped Albert organize a team of younger workers to perform these intensive labors so that the brothers could keep their hands clean and their heads focused on managing the shop.[62] A disinterested Albert failed to see the point of all these broom-making lessons and, instead, let Will take on the responsibilities of running the business while he sat in the back office, laughing and chatting it up with friends or reading the newspapers.

Will shook his head in disbelief at his brother's behavior. He knew, from hard experience and his father's demanding expectations, that one had to ignore the pain of the chaff settling in one's eyes or the "fell of broomcorn itch on sweaty skin" and get the job done. It was during this awful, perspiration-ridden work that he first displayed his outsized talent for management. Indeed, these early examples of Will's attention to every step of the manufacturing process, no matter what he was manufacturing, informed his entire career.

Will's strong streak of resentment finally bubbled over when Albert refused to pay the several weeks back wages he had earned. The business was so precarious that Albert offered to unload it to Will in lieu of monetary compensation. Instead, Will hoisted his heavy trunk onto Albert's front porch and demanded room and board with his half-sibling's family until the bill was paid. Albert's wife would have none of it and ordered him to pay the morose, prickly boy his money, with the stipulation that Will move back to Battle Creek and his father's broom factory.[63]

Will at age 18 or 19. A tintype taken in Dallas sometime between 1878 and 1879.

OVERLAPPING WITH John's return to Battle Creek was Will's first big adventure away from Battle Creek. In December 1878, Will made a sojourn to Dallas, Texas, the home to a small but growing Seventh-day Adventist community. In the spring of that year, James White partnered with George H. King, an Adventist acolyte, to open a broom factory in Dallas. Brooms, Ellen White decreed, made for a cleaner and healthier house; a healthier house meant healthier parishioners honoring the bodies the Creator gave them. Consequently, broom manufacturing epitomized a somewhat symbolic sacrament to the Adventist health reform movement. Financially speaking, expanding the broom business beyond Michigan represented a significant windfall to the Adventist Church's coffers.

Six months into the venture, the Texas factory was on a direct path to bankruptcy. King wrote a letter begging Elder James for assistance. White replied by post advising Mr. King "to hire one of the Kellogg boys to show you how to make brooms."[64] A determined King entrained to Michigan and interviewed a number of young men from Battle Creek, including Will's older, gentler brother, Preston Kellogg. By the end of the day, King had hired the best man for the job, the eighteen-year-old Will.

Eager to make good in a venture he briefly fantasized about claiming for his own, Will was disappointed the second he stepped off the platform at the Dallas train station. In a diary he kept during this period of his life, Will confessed:

> I left in December when the weather was below zero and the ground covered with snow, and I had great expectations with reference to the wonderful climate of the South. The day after my arrival, what was known as a "Texas Norther" arrived and there were several inches of snow on the ground.[65]

Will pined for the comfort and familiarity of Battle Creek, a place farther away in his mind than the thousand miles marked by the railway line between Michigan and Texas. While shivering in the unseasonably frigid Dallas weather, Will dutifully documented every cold he caught, the poorly heated room he rented with a colleague identified only as "Willson," the infestations of bedbugs and fleas who kept him "company," the makeshift meals he prepared for himself, and the lonely work he endured.

In search of some sense of belonging and recreation, he joined Dallas's Seventh-day Adventist community and began attending their church-sponsored activities. For example, on January 18, 1879, Will used the teenage slang of the day to record the fun he had at a church sing and splitting the bill for refreshments at the after party: "Had a fly time, all dutch." Later that month, he attended church singing school, taught children at Sabbath school, and was even introduced to a young woman, identified only as "Miss Cole."[66]

Back to business, things were entirely another matter. In his diary, Will described the difficulties of working both in King's factory and in the field where the broomcorn was grown. Like most teenaged boys on a job, Will complained about the incompetence of his boss. George King "does not act much like a man of business," he griped, "he is fearful slow and don't work any himself."[67] Will's workdays began at dawn and lasted until well after dark. His health was not "robust," he endured a number of

Will (standing) and his roommate, "Willson," while he was working at the King broom factory in Dallas, Texas, circa 1879

dental problems and teeth extractions, and he appears rather gaunt in photographs taken of him at the time.[68]

In late January, Will told his parents about a letter he received from James and Ellen White remarking on how pleased they were with his work. The Whites also announced an upcoming visit to Texas and hinted about plans to start another broom factory in Denison, about seventy-five miles north of Dallas. Displaying his lifelong sensitivity, on February 14, he told his parents about the day the Whites finally arrived in Dallas: "I worked at sorting [brooms] this forenoon and bunched and cleaned up this afternoon and labeled . . . Elder White and wife came from Denison this evening by team. Elder didn't know me. He didn't speak." The following day, a Saturday Sabbath, Will ate breakfast, put on his best clothes, and went to church only to experience another slight: "Mrs. White preached this forenoon. She spoke to me after the meeting and so did the Elder. He didn't know me. He spoke *of* me in the meeting and so did Mrs. White" (the emphasis in italics is Will's).[69]

In addition to these disappointments, Will hated the dirty, unkempt town of Dallas where "the sewers . . . all run out in the open air, some along the streets and some under the sidewalks." "Down by the central market," he reported in his diary, "there is a fearful stench comes up from under the sidewalk. I should think they would have the fever if they don't clean up."[70] He was further irritated by King's constant requests for money to help shore up his fledgling firm. Will complained on May 13, "King wanted me to sign a note. I wouldn't."[71] By early August, it was clear that King's firm was anything but and the workers revolted. "There has been a whole posse in after their pay," Will wrote. "Sent to the Elder after some money last Monday but it didn't come."[72]

Most of Mr. King's broom-making workers were young men and regardless of the church they attended were bound to indulge in boisterous high jinks. One evening Will visited a flea-bitten animal circus, with "electric lights," and on another he attended a production of Gilbert and Sullivan's warhorse operetta *H.M.S. Pinafore*. Such activities were sinful enough to cause his parents to shake their heads in disapproval. Matters only became worse after Will took charge of the payroll on August 11 and he scraped together $250 (roughly $6,120 in 2016) to pay the broom cutters a fraction of their owed wages. Before nightfall, many of them spent their newfound cash on liquor and fun. Will reported having to clean up after a fellow named Smith who "got into the jug last Friday night." A few weeks later he complained that he "had a fearful time with Thom Alison. He was drunker than a fool. Came near having some trouble. Had to take some beer with him." On September 10, these alcohol-related antics led to a formal reprimand from the church: "They had a meeting at the church today. Had my name up for treating some of the hands to beer. Also Bates for drinking it." The churchly rebukes may have been well earned, considering Will's diary confession of October 28: "Don't feel very well today. We had a fearful time last night. I am going to swear off and am not going around any more."[73]

Hangover-induced repentances aside, Will's shenanigans and the terrible working conditions worried Ann Janette back home: "Got a letter from Mother. She is afraid I will get killed or have the fever."[74] Apparently, Will's Texas adventure proved intoxicating enough and he rarely, if ever, took a drink for the remainder of his long life even though he was hardly as temperance-minded as John Harvey and Ella Kellogg. Late in his life Will confessed to his grandson Norman Jr. that "Uncle Doc [John Harvey Kellogg] was death on alcohol. . . . I have since learned that alcoholic beverages in moderation might make social occasions more enjoyable. It's too late for me to start but I don't object to those who do imbibe so long as they do it in moderation."[75]

There were, however, many other letters from Battle Creek that made Will's Texas exodus far more tolerable. All year, Will engaged in a lengthy correspondence with "the girl next door," Elmirah (Ella) Osborn Davis, the daughter of Obadiah Davis, the town's grocer. On the days she received a missive from Will, Miss Davis promptly wrote back the news from Battle Creek. Her notes were cheerful and encouraging. Some of them were illustrated with drawings, which Will deemed "the bossiest of pictures . . . just splendid."[76] It was during this period when Will gave Ella his lifelong nickname for her, "Puss."

The pull to Michigan proved too strong and Will finally gave in to the homesickness for his family, familiar sights, and a stirring heart for Miss Davis. By November 29, 1879, Will Keith Kellogg was back in Battle Creek: "I hardly knew the girls [his sisters], they had grown so. Folks were all glad to see me and I to see them. I saw Puss and she made me go home with her." He concluded his diary on the last day of the year, "Happy New Year is coming and the old one is going as fast as it can. Goodbye to 1879, also to this diary."[77]

THE NEW YEAR, 1880, meant far more than a fond goodbye to his drudgery in Dallas and his diary; it welcomed three momentous moves that shaped the remainder of Will's life. The first was his decision to enroll in the Parson's Business College in Kalamazoo. No grove of academe, Parson's was a for-profit institute offering three- to twelve-month courses in the basic skills needed to conduct a business. Tuition started at $28 (or $669 in 2016) for three months all the way to $75 (about $1,790 in 2016) "for the highly recommended 12-month program." Will had little patience to sit through a year's worth of lectures and lessons. Nor did he look forward to twelve months of commuting the twenty-mile distance between Kalamazoo and Battle Creek. Such rides took a fast horse about three hours to run but bridging the distance was mandatory because Will was not welcome to stay at his brother Albert's home, and lodging in Kalamazoo was too prohibitive. Like many an impoverished student, Will was forced to commute to school and live with his parents. Consequently, he told William Parsons, "the big, red-headed Irishman" who ran the school, that he desired a thorough business education but he could not afford an entire year's tuition acquiring it. Instead, the determined Will proposed an accelerated course over a period of ninety days. Impressed by Will's evident resolve, Parsons replied, "You take this seat right next to my desk, work like hell, and any time you want to know something or to have more lessons piled upon you, just say the word."[78]

By the end of three months, Will qualified as a "bookkeeper and accountant." The young man left Kalamazoo armed with an ornately handwritten certificate signed by Mr. Parsons and dated May 16, 1880, attesting that Will had completed a course in the "following branches of bookkeeping: Single and Double Entry, Wholesale and Retail, Manufacturing, Banking, Commercial Calculations, Business Correspondence, and making out commercial papers, including deeds and mortgages." Parsons also gave Will a strong endorsement letter, declaring "during his course of study he has always conducted himself as a gentleman and I can cheerfully recommend him to the business community."[79]

The second important pursuit was of Ella "Puss" Osborn Davis, a small woman, five-foot-four, and "not so much shy as absorbed in her work and thoughts." Will's frequent visits to the Davis home included chaperoned evenings of sitting and chatting on the front porch, playing games, and singing old hymns such as "Marching Through Georgia" in an out-of-tune voice, while Ella plunked them out on her father's even more out-of-tune piano. Will's crush of infatuation turned into love and in the autumn of 1880 he proposed marriage. The nuptials took place on November 3 at the Adventist Tabernacle Church. Flush with the $1,500 (or $35,800 in 2016) Will had squirreled away from his broom work, the couple made a down payment on a small home on Champion Street, close by the Kelloggs' and the Davises' family homes. One relative, who temporarily lived with Puss and Will Kellogg, described her as "a good housekeeper and her home and family meant everything to her . . . she wasn't the kind who came and put her arms around you, but she did the necessary things for your comfort."[80] Ella would serve as Will's supporting helpmeet for the next thirty-two years, even if he did not always have the time or inclination to show her the attention she craved.

Puss Davis and Will Kellogg, 1880

When it came to religion, Will was never as devout or enthusiastic about Adventism as his brother or parents, even at this early point in his life. He rarely went to church, except for weddings and funerals. During the early years of their marriage, he and Puss kept the Saturday Sabbath, and restricted themselves to a vegetarian and grain diet. As time passed, Ella began to serve meat and fowl for dinner and, soon enough, Will openly consumed oysters, much to his brother's disgust.[81] For most of his life, Will eschewed the *verboten* sugar, coffee, and tea, and instead preferred drinking tall glasses of buttermilk. He was, however, known to occasionally satisfy his sweet tooth with a spoonful of clover honey and, on especially indulgent moments, a chocolate soda or, better still, a chocolate bar.[82]

Yet every night before retiring, Will recited the Lord's Prayer followed by a request to remain humble and "blessings and security" for his family's health and welfare. His longtime friend, the Adventist minister and religious radio show broadcaster H. M. S. Richards, insisted that Will "believed in prayer, in God, and in Christ. He had a very complete knowledge of the Bible and of the intricate prophecies uncomprehended by many persons."[83] Late in his life, there were moments where Will questioned his faith, such as when he asked the Nobel Prize–winning physicist Robert Millikan, "In your study of science, do you not feel there is a pattern or a guiding force?" Millikan is said to have replied, "There is no other answer."[84] As the historian Brian Wilson noted, "It might be better said that business, and then philanthropy, became the younger Kellogg's true religion."[85]

Will made his third and most momentous life decision by seeking a stable job near his home. The biggest industry in town was his older brother's transformation of the Western Health Reform Institute into the Battle Creek Sanitarium. John had enough on his hands in creating this medical mecca and desperately needed someone he could both dominate and trust to put the enterprise on a sound business basis. That someone was the twenty-year-old Will K. Kellogg. In April 1880, John hired Will as manager of his publishing and food businesses at a salary of $9 (about $215 in 2016) a week, with the veiled promise for steady and equitable advancement at the San. Although the arrangement did not turn out to be nearly as equitable as Will would have liked, the Kellogg brothers were about to begin a nearly twenty-five-year adventure of medical conquest and destructive fraternal battle, all in the name of Health.

PART II

An Empire of Wellness

The cover of Dr. Kellogg's monthly magazine, Good
Health, *February 1917—"The Best Remedy for 'the Blues'"*

5

Building the San

I N THE LATE SUMMER OF 1876, John walked into New York City's cavernous Grand Central Terminal and bought a train ticket that would take him home to Battle Creek. Soon after making his purchase, he boarded "the fastest train on the American continent," Cornelius Vanderbilt's New York Central Line Limited. The locomotive was a sleek, all parlor and sleeper car train that traveled at 35 or more miles per hour along "the only 4 track railroad in the world all laid with steel rails."

John could not afford the added price of a sleeping berth so he was forced to sit upright in the parlor car for much of the twenty-two-hour ride (including multiple stops along the way). To counteract any physical discomfort, he got out of his seat every hour or so to stretch his short, powerful legs and walk up and down the long line of passenger cars. The only two cars he did not enter were the smoking car, constantly blue with cigar and pipe fumes, and the dining car, where for a hefty fee the famous Vanderbilt fare was served to passengers. Smoking, of course, was not an option and whenever John grew hungry, he pulled into his coat pocket for a handy traveling meal of his own design: apples, Graham flour gems, and a bag of assorted nuts—cashews (his favorite), pecans, walnuts, and peanuts.

John sped through Albany and west to Buffalo, reading, writing, and thinking about the medical practice he was about to launch. From upstate New York, the train chugged along the southern border of Lake Erie and through Cleveland on a virtually flat "water level route," which made the ride far more comfortable than other trains restricted to mountainous or

Young Dr. Kellogg (age 24), circa 1876

hilly railways. The locomotive ultimately merged onto the tracks of the Michigan Central line. During a brief stopover at the Detroit station, John quickly ducked out of the train to purchase a pack of the local newspapers for distraction and to calm his excitement as the train carried him the remaining 123 miles west and home to Battle Creek.[1]

Years later, John recalled a conversation he had with a Battle Creek medical colleague, soon after his return home from New York, about the wisdom of establishing a practice in the sleepy little town. The other doctor beseeched John to join him in search of bigger and better opportunities. "Dr. Kellogg," the medico announced, "I am going to leave to-morrow for Washington. Battle Creek is only a small country town and I will never amount to much if I stay here. Why don't you go to New York or Chicago where you can really make a name for yourself? You will be buried here and never have the opportunity to do great things." Dr. Kellogg replied, "I am not interested in making a name for myself. But I want to be of human service. I think I can be of more service in Battle Creek than anywhere else, so I will remain here. I think you are making a mistake in going away. You have my best wishes for your success."[2]

Beyond the desire to be of "human service," there was his debt to Ellen and James White, the patrons of his superb medical education. Mrs. White began promoting health as a major part of her ministry as early as June 6, 1863. At a Friday evening Sabbath welcoming service in Otsego, Michigan, she reported a forty-five-minute vision she had on "the great subject of Health Reform."[3] Over the next few years, she developed a doctrine on hygiene, diet, and chastity enveloped within the teachings of Christ. Her canon of health found even greater clarity while preaching on Christmas Eve 1865 in Rochester, New York. There, Ellen vividly described a vision in which God emphasized the importance of a life in harmony with dietary and lifestyle principles designed to stay well and prevent disease.[4] The following spring, on May 20, 1866, "Sister" White formally presented her ideas to the 3,500 Adventists comprising the denomination's governing body, or General Conference. She was so convincing that the members unanimously voted to create an institute of health reform. It was at this moment that the Battle Creek Sanitarium was born and, to a large extent, John's concept of disease prevention and "wellness."[5]

One of Ellen's most enthusiastic supporters in this endeavor was the broom maker John Preston Kellogg. In August of 1866, John Preston spearheaded a call for contributions. Each donor, he suggested, would "purchase" stock in the proposed health reform institute. Although every "investor" was accorded a vote in determining the institute's progress, it

The original Western Health Reform Institute, circa 1867

was understood that the capital and accrued dividends were charitable gifts to the Church and would be reinvested for the institute's future growth.

THE ORIGINAL "articles of incorporation" for the Western Health Reform Institute of Battle Creek, Michigan, restricted membership only to those who kept "the commandments of God and the faith of Jesus Christ," an expression that Adventists typically used to describe themselves during this period. Its stockholders openly declared their allegiance to the wisdom and counsel of Ellen White and their meetings were held as part of the denomination's annual General Conference during the summer Michigan camp gathering. The Western's founders fully intended the institute to be a center of natural healing methods based upon Christian, and more specifically Adventist, religious principles.[6] After signing the incorporation documents, John Preston announced his gift of $500 (or $7,690 in 2016). To those still sitting on their hands and worrying about the burden of maintaining such an ambitious enterprise, John Preston declared, "This is what I think of it. The $500 is a seed to start the institution, sink or swim."[7]

The Western Health Reform Institute officially opened its doors for business on September 5, 1867. Situated on an eight-acre plot of land west of the town's main streets, the original facility was a two-story wooden structure, attached to an old home donated by one of the church members. During the first decade of its existence, fewer than two thousand patients (or a monthly census of about sixteen) were treated there. The patient rooms were sparsely furnished, dank with mold, heated with temperamental wood-burning stoves, and lit by flickering oil lamps. The doctors there emphasized the healing powers of water, and the therapeutic action occurred in three treatment rooms outfitted with wooden bathtubs. Water was provided by a windmill that pumped water from the Kalamazoo River into an elevated water tank, which supplied patients with thrice-daily baths, water sprays, and wet pack treatments. When there was little wind or a drought in the creek, water became scarce and the reuse of bath water between patients was poorly tolerated. One "garrulous old lady" went as far as to complain, "We are all being dipped in the same gravy."[8]

The medical staff doctors at the Western Institute were neither distinguished nor friendly. For example, Ellen described one of them, "Doctor B," as rude, easily discouraged, overly sensitive, and prone to displaying a "quick impulsive temper."[9] The patients tended to ignore the doctors' sanctimonious lectures on disease and prescriptions of rigorous exercise.[10] Others rebelled at orders to wear loose-fitting suits and dresses so as not to impede drawing in breath or intestinal movements necessary for the proper digestion of food. Entertainment was hard to come by, especially after the medical staff banned them from playing checkers or engaging in levity of any kind. Perhaps the worst part of staying at the Western Institute was the food. Three times a day, the kitchen staff served up bland and mushy mixtures of boiled grains, roasted nuts, and stewed fruits. All of these problems resulted in few people willing to spend their money recuperating in Battle Creek. Those who visited rarely returned. By 1869, the institute's debts added up to more than $13,000 (about $233,000 in 2016), leading Ellen White to observe: "It was at this discouraging point that my husband decided in his mind that the Institute property must be sold to pay the debts, and the balance, after the payment of the debts, be refunded to the stockholders in proportion to the amount of the stock each held."[11]

As a last effort before closing the place down, James White asked the business-minded John Preston Kellogg to put it on a firmer financial footing. John Preston accepted White's challenge with one stipulation: his son John would serve as his deputy. In the late spring and early summer of 1876, the board of directors argued for eight weeks before emerging with a renewed determination to bring "discipline and order" to the Health Reform Institute. Each member agreed the institute needed a vibrant, effective physician at the helm. The answer resided in the compact body of John Harvey Kellogg, MD.[12]

JOHN WAS CONVINCED to take the helm only after James White promised him a free hand in reorganizing the institute on a scientific basis, without interference from the Adventist Church. Water therapy and grain-based diets were important, to be sure, but Dr. Kellogg was determined to incorporate the "rational medicine" he had learned at Bellevue. "The rational physician," Dr. Kellogg later wrote in *The Medi-*

*Western Health Reform Institute, in 1876, when John Harvey Kellogg
became its medical director*

cal Missionary, applies "all of hygio-therapy and all the good of every
other system known or possible."[13] This was John's first step in aligning
the doings at Battle Creek with the elite of the American medical profession. It was a transformation later lauded by Dr. Henry Hurd, the
superintendent of the Johns Hopkins Hospital, for "having converted
into a scientific institution an establishment founded on a vision."[14] The
Whites could not yet see it but John's insistence on independence was
a harbinger of the wedge that ultimately developed between an increasingly confident Dr. Kellogg and his micromanaging coreligionists.

John began his tenure as the institute's director on October 1, 1876,
for an agreed-upon one-year trial. The day he assumed command, there
were twenty patients. Only eight of them were paying for services and
six others left with the outgoing director, Dr. William Russell, who abandoned Battle Creek to open a water cure clinic in Ann Arbor. There was
also the matter of the institute's mounting debt and a treasurer-keeper of
the purse who happened to be his demanding father, John Preston. Years
later, when recalling his early days as the Western's physician-in-chief,
Dr. Kellogg said, "I was just a lad of 24 . . . so great did the task before

me seem that the only thing I can remember was a prayer I offered many times a day and for weeks following, 'Help me Lord' . . . [and I was determined to] succeed to justify the Whites' confidence in me or die in [the] attempt."[15] After his first year as medical director, John agreed to stay permanently. In 1921, he told a reporter, "I gradually became more and more entangled in the work and find myself still with it."[16]

When he assumed command of the institute, John looked so youthful that he felt compelled to grow a mustache and beard to appear more authoritative. What resulted turned out to be *frumbierding*, the Old English term for the patchy, wispy, "peach-fuzz" facial hair of a young man. John kept those whiskers for the remainder of his life and they matured and filled out with the rest of him; his beard became positively bushy and his mustache curled on both ends, both thrusting their way out of his face as if they each had a trajectory of their own. In his final years, he trimmed them back a bit but his facial hair remained one of the most prominent features of his beaming, energetic face.[17]

As AN AGENT OF CHANGE, the doctor threatened his more orthodox medical colleagues. For example, in the summer of 1877, as virtually every doctor did when starting a practice in the United States during this era, he joined the local medical society. In Battle Creek, that group was the Calhoun County Medical Society. Seven years later, in 1885, the Medical Society entertained damaging allegations that John was violating the American Medical Association's code of ethics by advertising his services, writing slanderous critiques of the medical profession, undermining the confidence patients had in their doctors, and deliberately misquoting eminent physicians in his published work. The worst charge, however, was that Dr. Kellogg practiced "irregular" medicine, an especially laughable offense given the state of American medicine combined with the fact that the most dangerous therapies, such as bloodletting, the prescription of toxic drugs, and cupping and blistering, were still tools of many an "orthodox" medical practitioner.[18] John's "water cures" may not have cured, per se, but they, at least, caused no harm.[19]

As with many professional disputes, there was much more behind these allegations than an ethical violation. In fact, an aggrieved enemy of John's, William J. Fairfield, was responsible for setting the whole event in motion. Fairfield formerly worked for John, but the two men passionately hated each other and Dr. Fairfield resigned in a huff only to establish a competing health institute in Battle Creek. Unlike John's burgeoning venture, however, Fairfield's failed miserably and soon closed. Thereafter, Fairfield was consumed by the need for revenge against his former boss.[20]

On December 7, 1885, Dr. Fairfield successfully petitioned for a set of hearings before the entire medical society. From January to June of 1886, the trial proceeded in fits and starts mainly because the busy practitioners involved had far more pressing business. In his defense, John argued that it was the Sanitarium, not he, taking out the advertisements in question, which meant he did not personally break the AMA ethical code. This explanation was somewhat disingenuous given that most of these advertisements at the time (and well into the first decades of the twentieth century) ended with the tagline "J. H. Kellogg, M.D., Medical Director."[21] He apologized and backpedaled on the many articles and books he wrote espousing "irregular" medical theories and criticizing the "heroic" and toxic therapies then in vogue. He told his colleagues that after acquiring more clinical experience and seasoning, he now had the opportunity to revise many of his most offensive opinions. Moreover, he adroitly reasoned, his very membership in the Calhoun County Medical Society spoke of his allegiance to "regular" orthodox medicine as taught and practiced at the best medical schools in the United States.

Only twelve members came to the trial's final session, including John. The group decided to vote on Fairfield's charges by secret ballot and, if necessary, take the next steps, up to and including censure and expulsion from the medical society. Some of these doctors were uncomfortable standing in judgment over a colleague; others were eager to fill out their ballot and get on with their medical practice. Dr. Fairfield must have been outraged when the foreman reported that the results were evenly split at 6 to 6. According to the Medical Society's by-laws, a majority of votes was required for any type of censure or action. The disciplinary committee had no choice but to dismiss the charges with prejudice. Ironically, it was John Harvey Kellogg who filled out the tying ballot, one that protected him from a professional embarrassment his fledgling career might never have withstood.[22]

ASSERTING HIS DOMINANCE over an ever-increasing staff and increasingly complex array of clinics, treatment rooms, laboratories, and dining and living facilities, John transitioned from a one-man band to a symphony orchestra conductor who ruled with an iron baton. Those who challenged John's authority were not likely to last long in his employ. He was the undisputed majordomo. When the Adventist Elders asked if he needed some help from a trusted colleague, such as his half-brother Merritt, the doctor dismissed their request and replied, "I find it difficult to carry a fraction of a burden and leave the rest. If I have any responsibility in a matter, I somehow cannot avoid feeling a burden of the whole."[23] Similarly, if the Sanitarium board gave him a directive he did not like, he simply ignored or dismissed it out of hand. Throughout his career, John interpreted every bit of constructive criticism as an insult or a plot to undermine his work. Those expecting an apology or admission of error from the ever-imperious John had to wait a very long time, indeed.

Dr. Kellogg's first major move was to change the name of the institution. Always the talented wordsmith, he coined a new one to describe his vision: *Sanitarium.* On September 15, 1910, Dr. Kellogg told the audience packed into the San's parlor how he discarded the original name of Health Reform Institute:

> I didn't like the name because I had already had enough experience in the world to know that people didn't like to be reformed; they liked to be informed and taught, but they didn't like to be reformed. So I thought I would get rid of that phrase, Health Reform Institute. Our journal now called *Good Health* was then called the *Health Reformer.* I changed the name of the journal for the same reason. . . . Well, I was casting about for a name, and I found the word "sanatorium" in the dictionary defined as . . . a health resort for invalid soldiers; so I changed the word "sanatorium" to "sanitarium." We didn't want the institution to be looked upon as a health resort; I wanted it to be . . . something different from what existed before, and a place where people would cultivate health in every possible way by every means afforded by medical science and by modern hygiene.[24]

It was a perfect word created long before now familiar medical "brand names," such as the Mayo Clinic or the Johns Hopkins Hospital, were introduced into the American vernacular. From the onset of his career, John Harvey Kellogg understood the need to establish and widely advertise a temple of health, healing, and well-being. He knew that this institution had to be attractive, modern, luxurious, and a worthwhile destination for those wealthy enough to seek such commodities. Thus, he had to invent the Battle Creek Sanitarium.

To satisfy his evolving ambitions, Dr. Kellogg needed more money, which meant convincing the Whites to invest in a new and bigger Sanitarium. After John retired all but $3,000 (or $70,000 in 2016) of the institute's debt, James White took the matter up with Ellen, who subsequently had a dream in which the Lord authorized such a plan. The next morning, James embarked upon a fund-raising campaign to cover the proposed costs.[25] The goals the Adventist Elders set out for themselves in 1877 were nothing if not transformative. The new Sanitarium, they declared, was "to wield a mighty influence in the world, and to be a powerful means of breaking down the old, pernicious autocracy of empirical practice and of encouraging sanitary reform."[26]

A beautiful new structure opened in the spring of 1878 but John remained unsatisfied. The doctor informed his board that he needed an additional $50,000 (about $1.19 million in 2016) for a new wing to house his latest treatment modalities and deluxe patient suites. The board members were hesitant to commit to still more debt, given the poor return on investment they had previously seen with the Health Reform Institute. Some went as far as to call the expansion plan "John's Folly." Ellen White, who was already concerned about the doctor's unquenchable ambition, publicly expressed her strong disapproval. The "financial embarrassment" brought on by the new building, she fumed, "called into active exercise all of Dr. Kellogg's scheming and planning to gather means to lessen the heavy debt. This has caused him great care and labor, and has nearly cost his life." Ellen further chastised John for having converted her beloved health institute into a "grand hotel."[27]

Mrs. White's charges were perfectly aimed at John's psychological buttons and the young physician did not take these goads terribly well. Unfortunately, James White was the one man who reliably tempered the fraught and emotional relationship between Ellen and John. Hardly robust, especially after suffering a stroke in 1865, James developed a mysterious fever in the summer of 1881 and despite all of Dr. Kellogg's medical ministrations, he died on August 6. Yet even this important relationship grew strained during Elder White's final year of life, when John grew increasingly suspicious of James White's strong influence and maneuvered to force the old man off the Sanitarium board. While taking care of James White during his last months, the two men were said to have reconciled but Ellen never forgot or forgave John's hostile actions.[28]

The doctor had little time to mourn his former mentor's demise. He was too busy raising money for his expanding empire. Legend has it that John came up with a perfect Seventh-day Adventist rationale by having the Sanitarium apply for a twenty-year bank loan. The doctor convinced his all-Adventist board of directors to approve his request by arguing that the Advent of Jesus Christ's imminent return to earth would occur long before the bank loan would ever come due.[29] The truth is far more mundane. Dr. Kellogg organized a separate "stock company" for raising additional funds with the contractual promise to Ellen White and the Elders that the Sanitarium, not the Church, would be responsible for all of its debts. His financial entreaties hardly ended there. In the mid-1880s, he sold a few acres of the San's grounds to build a charity hospital. Finding the inspiration for this expansion far more pleasing to her Christian sensibilities, Sister White acquiesced and the Sanitarium board followed suit.[30]

IN FACT, John never stopped improving the San. The entire complex was based on his careful study of the architectural plans of some of the most famous hospitals in the world. The main building was constructed of wood and covered by a brick veneer. It was five stories tall and the first three floors boasted long wraparound, iron-railed, open-air verandas to provide ample access to fresh air and sunshine. At the complex's center was an expanse of suites devoted to hydrotherapy, featuring Turkish, Russian, and fifty other types of baths. Every patient's room was gas-lit, directly supplied with hot and cold water, and centrally heated by means of a $10,000 (about $239,000 in 2016) ultramodern furnace system. There were nearly a "half mile of glassed-in halls" and acres of rolling, manicured lawns replete with fountains. Thanks to multiple standpipes

The Battle Creek Sanitarium, circa 1880

and fire hoses at the ready, along with the Adventist ban against smoking, the doctor insisted that the risk of a fire was "nonexistent," a boast that would later prove to be monumentally wrong.[31]

John installed an expensive electric dynamo in 1884 to replace the gas lighting and power his electric light baths and electrotherapeutic medical treatments. That same year, he added a plush six-story patient wing on the south end of the Sanitarium to accommodate the growing number of paying patients; two years later, he added a similar wing to the north side of the original building. In 1886, he established a nursery and a kindergarten so that patients who brought along their children could fully participate in all the activities.[32] The children, incidentally, were "not required to follow the Sanitarium health regimen, but elementary principles of healthy living were introduced in the nursery when possible."[33] He erected a modern five-story hospital building in 1888, complete with sparkling white-tiled and arc-lamp-lit operating rooms, special facilities for those patients needing more intensive medical care, and a suite of laboratories to analyze every possible bodily fluid and each patient's caloric intake. Two years later, in 1890, John built a one-thousand-seat auditorium for lectures, entertainments, and concerts. Thus, in a span of only fourteen years, the Sanitarium's physical plant evolved from a two-story converted home into a massive, beautiful, and luxurious medical center; it was so grand that it employed over one thousand people, cared for seven to ten thousand patients each year, farmed over four hundred acres of land to grow the vegetables, fruit, and dairy products his guests consumed daily, and operated a canning and food manufacturing facility, laundry, charity hospital, creamery, and a resort comprised of twenty cottages (reserved for the most wealthy of the worried well) overlooking Goguac Lake.[34]

At the center of Dr. Kellogg's "university of health" was the Sanitarium's dining room. Most of man's maladies, Dr. Kellogg repeatedly insisted, were a result of poor diet—"too much food and not the right kind of it." The doctor taught his patients that "you are what you eat," mentally, spiritually, and physically. In its earliest days, however, Dr. Kellogg's Sanitarium offered a far different menu than the varied vegetarian and grain-based fare it later made so famous. Throughout the 1880s, meat was still served for those choosing to dine at the "liberal table." At the "conservative table," one could still tuck into a beefsteak or roast chicken but there was no coffee and tea during or after the meal. At the "radical table," all of these "flesh foods" were forbidden in lieu of stewed vegetables, crunchy crudité, salt-free broths and jellies, and whole grains, which were boiled and bubbled into tasteless bowls of mush or baked into crunchy hard rolls and biscuits. There was no shortage of San patients lining up to eat at the "radical table" because this was where Dr. Kellogg regularly dined. The price one paid for enjoying erudite conversations with the charismatic physician was to eat the same foods he ate. By the mid-1880s, John banished tea, coffee, and all condiments, but it was not until 1900 that Ellen White finally granted the doctor permission to permanently ban meat from the premises.[35]

THE MONEY TO PAY for all these improvements remained a troubling concern to the Adventist churchmen, as did John's growing power among the fold. Much of the revenues John generated for the San came from his clinical activities and medical procedures. To increase his bottom line further, Dr. Kellogg decreed that his staff members be paid minimal amounts of money in exchange for room, board, and the experience of working at the San. Amazingly enough, an army of the Adventist faithful accepted this penurious arrangement for virtually the entire period Dr. Kellogg ran the place. Yet no set amount of money was enough to transform John's endless rolls of blueprints into bricks and mortar. The Sanitarium's debt increased with every new idea, piece of equipment, or hospital wing the doctor demanded, much to his board's discontent.

At this point in his career, John must have sensed that a break with the Whites and the Seventh-day Adventists was inevitable. His ambitions were so large and his patience far too limited for his timid partners, most of whom he considered unimaginative and unqualified to appropriately judge his medical goals. This troubling dynamic led John to embark on what became one of the most contentious but clever legal maneuvers of his career. As with all nonprofit corporations in Michigan during the late nineteenth century, the Battle Creek Sanitarium was required by law to operate under a state charter limited to a lifetime of thirty years. The San's charter expired in April of 1897. Recognizing the risks to his medical empire, John convinced the "stockholders" of the Western Health Reform Institute's original corporation (all of them Adventist church members) to oppose any separation or breakup of the San's assets. When the charter did expire, a court order logically made John, as the institution's medical director and superintendent, the receiver. The following year, a new Michigan Sanitarium and Benevolent Association was incorporated with every word of the new charter carefully written by Dr. Kellogg. Soon after, a public auction was held to sell the "old corporation's" physical plant, and because there were no other bidders besides the new association, Dr. Kellogg purchased the entire place for the exact amount of the San's outstanding bank loans.[36]

The doctor hedged his bet by neatly tucking into the charter's boilerplate a description of the San as a "nonprofit and benevolent corporation." This meant that the new Michigan Sanitarium and Benevolent Association was required by state law to be nondenominational rather than a Seventh-day Adventist venture. Some of the Adventist stockholders balked at this new configuration but Dr. Kellogg convinced them it was to their benefit since it allowed the San to continue grossly underpaying the staff and would yield significant tax savings on any profits accrued. Such fiscal advantages were critical to keeping the Sanitarium's ledgers in the black. If the Seventh-day Adventists chose to buy the Sanitarium outright and run it as a for-profit institution, he argued, they could never manage to fund the nonsubsidized employee payroll, let alone pay the state tax bills.

John veered toward the disingenuous as he explained that the new legal phraseology simply meant that if the "new" Sanitarium was "to be conducted as a medical institution, that it may have the advantages of the statutes of the state; as a hospital it must be carried on as an undenominational institution. It cannot give benefits to a certain class, but must be for the benefit of any who are sick. The institution may support any work it chooses with the earnings of the Association, but cannot discriminate against anyone because of his beliefs."[37] Dr. Kellogg's explanation carried the day and the stockholders unanimously consented to the plan. These explanations, however, obscured John's tactics of consolidation. In 1905, he confessed to a close colleague that he had anticipated a break from the Adventists for more than a decade, which was why he so adamantly insisted that the San was a "private, distinct independent corporation."[38]

WITHOUT FEAR OF CONTRADICTION, the most important move John made in insuring the Sanitarium's success began in 1880 when he hired Will as his assistant. Balding and already plump, Will hid his bulbous nose with a toothbrush bristle of a mustache, which he would not shave until after he successfully started his own cereal company. Preternaturally shy, his highly observant eyes hid quietly underneath thick-lensed round spectacles. Will's looks mattered little to John, who knew him to be completely trustworthy and in possession of a drive and business savvy that complemented the doctor's unparalleled clinical creativity.

One of Will's earliest administrative assignments at the Sanitarium was to run the doctor's publishing house, alternatively called the Modern Medicine Publishing Company, the Health Publishing Company, and the Good Health Publishing Company. Unlike virtually every other major publishing operation in America, the doctor's firm only had one major author to publish: John Harvey Kellogg. Preferring to dictate

John dictating to Will at the San, circa 1890

his medical wisdom, John hired and maintained a rotating staff of four or more secretaries. All of them, primarily men, were on call for work, no matter what time of day, to record his every thought. A typical day's dictation often lasted four to five hours and the doctor would ramble on at around two hundred words per minute as the written pages stacked up higher and higher until there were enough to be bound into his latest book or treatise. John's dictation sessions frequently lasted well into the early hours of the morning because "3:00 to 4:00 am were his best working hours," without regard to how grueling these marathons were for those who worked for him. The doctor's longest literary sitting lasted over twenty hours, all the while one attendant massaged his temples and another placed bags of ice on top of his head to keep him stimulated as he dictated "for hours" on the open porch of his home during the dead of night to a "benumbed secretary."[39]

When traveling across the country by train for lecture tours and medical meetings, the doctor was always accompanied by at least two stenographers who each kept a bag packed at the ready. They were armed with reams of pads and packs of newly sharpened pencils so that every word the doctor dictated along the journey was properly recorded. Upon completion of the dictation of the article, chapter, or lecture John was composing, the stenographer jumped off the train at the first convenient stop and traveled back to Battle Creek to type up the notes so they were in perfect order upon the doctor's return.

Will had little to do with the composition, editing, or really any of the creative work that went into producing John's many books and the dozens of issues of medical magazines he put out each year (with titles such as *Good Health, Health and Temperance Beacon, Modern Medicine Journal, Bacteriological World, Modern Medicine and Bacteriological Review, Health Reformer, Medical Missionary,* and the *Bulletin of the Battle Creek Sanitarium Hospital and Laboratory of Hygiene,* as well as his weekly newsletter and monthly magazine directed at patients, the *Sanitarium News* and the *Battle Creek Idea*). Instead, Will was the one who saw to it that every book, magazine, and pamphlet the doctor wrote or edited was properly printed and that the proofs were checked and double-checked to remove any typographical or factual errors. He supervised the bindery men to insure that no page was stapled or sewn out of order. Once bound, the finished copies were gently placed in wood crates filled with soft, curled wood shavings known as excelsior to prevent any damage during delivery. Clipboard and inventory in hand, Will made certain that every crate was correctly sealed, addressed, and stamped with the necessary postage and shipped by train to the subscribing library, university, medical institution, or individual reader. Will kept systematic records so each subscription was recorded and every payment deposited. It is doubtful that any one of Dr. Kellogg's millions of readers thought much about Will's fastidious labors as they pried open the coveted parcels from Battle Creek and eagerly consumed the doctor's latest medical sermon. That is, no one contemplated these issues until something went wrong, such as a delay in delivery, a problem with the U.S. Post Office or the freight train companies, and a dozen other potential snafus that plague any mail order business. When these problems did arise, upset readers often wrote scathing letters of complaint that landed on Will's desk. After investigating these grievances, Will corrected the problem by sending out a new book and a letter of apology that very day. Today, such practices would be called "customer service." Will referred to them as "good business."

Within months of watching his younger brother perform these tasks so efficiently, it became clear that the more responsibilities John gave Will, the better things ran. As a result, John appointed Will the general manager of a family of other businesses that included a health food company and equipment companies producing sun lamps, exercise machines, sanitary supplies, and clothing.[40]

ALL OF THESE DEMANDING JOBS, however, were secondary to what ultimately became his main role: administering the massive and complex Battle Creek Sanitarium. Will managed the San's payroll, paid the bills to all of the vendors and suppliers on time, handled every guest's complaint, real or perceived, and calmly allayed the financial worries of the charity patients, always treating them fairly and with respect. On occasion, he was an unwilling undertaker who arranged the funerals for those who died while being treated at the Sanitarium, all the way down to selecting the deceased's casket. Many times, Will trekked into the woods surrounding the San to find confused or addled patients who came to the San only to wander away off the grounds.[41] Every afternoon, he read, replied to, and frequently signed his brother's name on some 60 to 120 pieces of mail regarding San business. In the evenings, he operated the hot, smoky lantern-slide projector for his brother's lectures.

Perhaps most demeaning, Will was forced into the service of the doctor's personal valet, shining his white shoes, trimming and shaping his beard each morning with a straight razor, and following John into the bathroom to take ever more dictation while the doctor unloaded one of his four to five daily bowel movements into the toilet. Less disgusting but equally cruel, John humiliated Will by demanding that he follow him about the Sanitarium campus jotting down his latest order to be executed to perfection. An all too familiar sight was the overweight Will jogging, huffing, puffing, and writing down memoranda, while John pedaled his "high-wheeler" bicycle in full view of the guests and staff.

On days when he felt particularly sanguine about his work, Will referred to himself as the San's "bookkeeper, cashier, packing and shipping clerk, errand boy, and general utility man." When trapped in the muck of melancholia, a mood that became more frequent with each passing year, Will groused he was nothing more than "J. H.'s flunkey."[42]

Expressing his oppression in body language, an "austere" Will walked the halls in a stiff, halting manner, according to one Sanitarium physician, "just like he had swallowed a ramrod."[43]

Will somehow took John's verbal and psychic abuse with quiet dignity, much to the detriment of his self-esteem. Yet as good as he was at performing his thankless tasks, it was a constant struggle to keep up with, let alone please, his dynamic brother. With the slightest slip, lapse in judgment, or merely the perception of something that irked his demanding boss, Will suffered the wrath of the doctor's biting tongue. In later years, long after he left his brother's oppressive employ, Will complained that during the entire time he worked at the Sanitarium he never held an official title—a vice presidency, perhaps, or even a junior partnership that he could point out to others with a sense of pride and accomplishment. Nonetheless, Will wore many important hats at the San and he wore them all well. Titled or not, he was the San's "fixer-in-chief" of virtually every problem that arose on any given day at a large facility with hundreds of patients and employees. Most important, he served as buffer for his preoccupied brother. When the doctor's rough edges inadvertently (and invariably) insulted a patient or staff member, it was Will who upholstered the matter over with a layer of diplomacy and tact.

As a wealthy industrialist who presided over a multimillion-dollar corporation and worked terribly hard doing it, Will bitterly recalled his years at the San as some of the most difficult of his life:

> Dr. Kellogg was a prodigious worker. He worked long hours and was not only willing but insisted that others work with him. . . . One year I kept a record of the number of hours I was on duty for the sanitarium. This record shows that one week I was on duty 120 hours. . . . Saturday was the rest day at the sanitarium. However, I was expected to open the heavy mail on that day as on other days in order to have the porter meet the trains on which patients might be arriving, since some of them might require an ambulance.[44]

Amazingly, Will labored at the San for more than seven years before the doctor granted him his first two-week vacation. "For many years," Will recalled, "we worked on Christmas and New Year's Day and were also on duty the Fourth of July."[45] Whenever Will meekly asked for some time off from his busy work schedule so that he might spend a few hours with his growing family, Dr. Kellogg said "No!" and derided Will as a "loafer."[46]

Perhaps the best example of John's tyranny was the night in 1894 when the doctor kept his brother waiting around the Sanitarium offices "on call," while John entertained a valued guest well into the early hours of the next morning. Will's task was to escort the guest back to the train station after the meeting had concluded, while Puss patiently waited for his return home. As each hour passed and Will failed to show up, she fretted over what might have possibly happened to her absent husband. The beleaguered younger brother was not to finish his escorting role until after the break of dawn only to return to the Sanitarium to begin a new day's work. In his diary that night, Will angrily wrote, "Puss came up to the office about half past seven to see why I didn't come home. She was so scairt [sic] that she cried."[47]

Making matters worse, Will was poorly paid. He started in 1880 at a mere $9 a week (or $215 in 2016), a sum that barely made ends meet for his growing household. After three and a half years of service, John begrudgingly gave Will a dollar-a-week raise and, a few weeks later, offered an additional $3 per week if Will would feed, water, and clean up after the doctor's horse (or $317 in 2016). Unlike his successful brother who wore brilliant white, custom-made suits, Will wore the same inexpensive blue serge sack suit day after day, which eventually became so worn out that the seat of his pants and the jacket's elbows were almost as shiny as a polished coin. And with each new child in the Will Kellogg home, the paychecks were stretched even thinner.

At one point, Will grew so desperate for funds to pay his mortgage and put food on the table, he informed his brother of his plan to sell whatever he owned in Battle Creek and move his family west. Carolyn Geisel, a physician who worked for years at the Sanitarium, described the doctor's influence as "practically hypnotic."[48] John used these powers time and again on his younger brother and almost every time he did Will capitulated, accepted another small raise in salary, and remained in the family business. Will's salary gradually increased over the next decade, thanks to a series of structured deals where John granted him a percentage of the profits generated by the publishing business and, later, the sales of their food products. Yet even with these new sources of income, it took him thirteen years before he was free from debt and could pay off the mortgage on his house.

Although John may have demeaned him on a daily basis, Will was widely respected by his employees as a "just man and an efficient straw boss."[49] As one of John's junior doctors recalled years after Will left his brother's employ, "The helpers around the San held this united opinion: if you want anything done, go to W.K. He will listen to your story and he will give you an answer and the answer will be perfectly fair and it will be accomplished as he says."[50] Will held these important personnel meetings in hallways and stairwells because he did not have his own office until 1890, a decade after he joined the Sanitarium's staff. The chamber

THE BATTLE CREEK SANITARIUM AND FAMILY.

The San's "Staff and Family," 1897

he finally commanded was little more than a cramped and dingy storage room, off in a remote corner of the first floor of the hospital. The tiny window was "darkened by a veranda," which prevented the entry of a single, warming ray of sunlight. Regardless of where he conducted his business, the enormous staff of doctors, nurses, orderlies, maids, cooks, clerks, laundresses, waiters, boiler operators, carpenters, plumbers, and groundskeepers, not to mention the patients, constantly besieged Will with favors, requests, and adjudication of the intrigues, battles, and political skirmishes that occur in every workplace. With his typical efficiency and attention to detail, the dutiful Will kept records of each of these meetings and their resolution or progress. For example, in 1890 he noted, "I kept account of the people who called on me one evening after 5:00 and they numbered thirty-three."[51]

If one were searching for a training ground on how to run a major international corporation, such as the Kellogg cereal company, one could hardly have done better than to apprentice for and assume command of John's medical kingdom. It is just that the psychological costs charged to the account of Will's fragile ego were much higher than most of us would be willing to pay. Few people said it loudly, at least in the doctor's presence, but it was widely accepted that the Sanitarium prospered because of two Kelloggs, not one. The doctor was the San's showman and carnival barker while Will kept the place running smoothly and served as a brake to his brother's tendency to make poor and costly business decisions. The real pity, as we delve into the guarded, inner life of Will Kellogg, is that he was never able to fully appreciate that he was, in fact, remarkable. An insightful description of Will's state of mind during this period, and for many years thereafter, was the melancholy diary entry he wrote for September 27, 1884:

"I feel kind of blue. Am afraid that I will always be a poor man the way things look now."[52]

6

"What's More American than Corn Flakes?"

I T IS IMPOSSIBLE FOR SOMEONE born after World War I to appreciate the stunning sensation ready-to-eat breakfast cereals created at the beginning of the twentieth century. Long before that event, many American housewives prepared hot cereals from grains such as oats, barley, buckwheat, and corn. Bowls of this thick or thin mess, depending upon one's budget, were alternatively called "porridge," "gruel," or "mush." It required hours of boiling and cooking to soften up the grain, meaning the cook had to awaken quite early before she could serve it to her family. Other common breakfasts of this era, as noted earlier, were comprised of salt pork products, gravies, syrup, hot milk, and boiled coffee. These meals, too, required a great deal of work and time, especially in the days when stoves were powered by wood fires that had to be lit and tended. None, then or now, are desirable chores upon arising from a deep slumber, a hard night of insomnia, or, especially, after taking care of one's younger (and all too awake) children.

Oats, in the form of "oatmeal," first emerged as a popular and faster option for a hot, healthy, filling grain breakfast in 1875. The "father" of this now familiar cereal was Henry Parsons Crowell, an evangelical Christian businessman from Cleveland. Casting about for a milling company to launch, Crowell was impressed by the methods of an irascible German American miller named Ferdinand Schumacher. With machinery Schumacher designed himself, oat kernels were cracked into tiny cubes and, thus, easier to boil and soften. Even with this preparation, however, many customers still complained that the preparation time for the new "cracked oats" product was not all that faster than the older methods. Crowell also had difficulties developing an affordable way to ramp up Schumacher's inefficient "oat-cracking" machinery. Everything changed, however, when one of Crowell's employees, William Heston, rigged a series of rollers and blades for cutting the oats so that they could be far more easily milled, rolled, and packaged. The greatest feature of Crowell's oatmeal, beyond its nutritional value, was that it required far less time to cook than traditional porridge.[1]

By 1883, Crowell was successfully producing his rolled oats (often in bitter competition with Ferdinand Schumacher) at a mill in Ravenna, Ohio, thirty-five miles outside of Cleveland. Working with several other millers in Ohio, he organized the Consolidated Oatmeal Company in 1887. As a means of promoting the firm's integrity and the product's healthy qualities, Crowell named his product "Quaker Oats." He also innovated the practice of selling his cereal in individual packages, rather than the older method of sending barrels of the stuff to full-service grocers who would then dole out the amount a customer requested. The sales of his red, round, sealed, and hygienic two-pound canisters, featuring a reassuring "Quaker Man" on the label, were terrific.[2] Oatmeal soon became a popular breakfast option; but even with Crowell's new "rolled oat" process, preparing it was hardly "instant" by today's microwave standards. Consequently, making oatmeal during this period still signified a time burden for millions of women who had more than enough menial tasks to complete every morning in addition to making the family breakfast.

IT WAS AT THIS POINT when the Kellogg brothers made their entrée into the breakfast business. Unfortunately, telling this story is difficult because so many conflicting narrative strands have convoluted it. There is John's version and, of course, a slightly different version from Will on how, beginning in the 1880s, they discovered a process that converted wheat dough into flakes. John's wife, Ella, also insists she played a seminal role in the proceedings. And there exist accounts by a few early Sanitarium employees who claimed minor roles as well. We must also factor in versions of the Kelloggs' chief rivals, who were just as eager to

Battle Creek Health Foods advertisement, 1897

create and control the highly profitable ready-to-eat cereal manufacturing industry. The most interesting competitor was Henry Perky, who invented Shredded Wheat. The Kellogg brothers' most unlikable foe was Charles W. Post, who made bundles of cash after stealing and manufacturing many of the doctor's and Will's most successful recipes. And then there are the reams of conflicting secondary historical and journalistic accounts. As a result, recounting and accommodating all the multiple "histories" of the origins of Kellogg's Corn Flakes is neither a simple nor a linear task.

What is not in dispute is the germinating idea behind the whole enterprise. While still a busy medical student at Bellevue, John was frustrated with the time and effort it took to prepare a nourishing, inexpensive hot breakfast out of whole grains. Making mushes of oats, barley, or wheat just took too long to accommodate his busy schedule of lectures, hospital rounds, and cramming pages of medical knowledge into his brain. Years later, John described his "Eureka moment" in great detail:

> As a boy of 14 years old I became very much interested in a scientific way of eating; read books thereon and resolved to adopt and follow during my lifetime a scientific or biologic diet. When a student in normal school I made experiments to ascertain the cost of living; was paying my way through school, rented a room, paid the landlady for cooking for me but I furnished foods for myself, [and] made an observation that it cost me six cents a day for a period of three months; I continued these experiments and others as to the cost of a biologic diet; later in New York as a medical student in 1874 I rented a room and boarded myself, purchasing raw materials and prepared it. One day I found in the market a package of food, oatmeal labeled "steam cooked." However, I found it as raw as any. That brought me to think it important to prepare cooked foods to be bought at market in packages, ready for immediate use and I resolved to give that consideration.[3]

Beyond convenience or affordability, John's long search for a ready-to-eat, "already cooked" cereal centered on his clinical studies of the disabled gastrointestinal system, which he so often treated among his many patients at the San. The doctor sought "to displace the half-cooked, pasty, dyspepsia-producing breakfast mush" with a healthier whole grain version that stimulated and aided the digestive process.[4] Digestibility rather than profitability was John's main concern in the development of flaked cereals. This focus placed Dr. Kellogg in the center of a scientific revolution then occurring in understanding the gastrointestinal system. Indeed, at the turn of the twentieth century, gastroenterology was a field as productive and intellectually exciting as the burgeoning fields of bacteriology and surgery. Such enthusiasm for the vague and testy workings of the gut was hardly confined to the scientific literature. In a society beleaguered by upset stomachs and constipation, large numbers of people, on both sides of the Atlantic, followed the progress then being made in gastrointestinal research and consumed a long list of best-selling books and magazine articles on the topic.[5]

SHORTLY AFTER MAN'S first bowel movement, if not soon before, humans became curious about the set of circumstances we call digestion. Yet for more than 2,500 years of recorded history, no one really knew how this process worked. Some of the best scientific minds from Antiquity to the nineteenth century asked questions they could not come close to answering even as they encountered evidence of the way we eat and eliminate every day. Why did we become hungry at predictable intervals? What happened to the food we bit, chewed, and swallowed after it traveled down the gullet and into the stomach? How did we extract the nutrients from the food we eat, affording us energy and vigor, and then transform those meals into the smelly, brown feces we pushed out of our rectums? And how did all of these machinations coordinate themselves into a concerted set of events?

The textbooks John read during his medical school days in the 1870s presented a hodgepodge of digestive theories, none of them satisfactory. This confusion would not be clarified until well after the scientific grounding of physiology (the study of how the organs in the body work), which was just beginning to emerge in Germany, Russia, Great Britain, France, and, ultimately, North America. Precisely when John began his medical practice, science had advanced to the point where a cadre of cutting-edge researchers posited that every physiological mechanism of our organs and cells was based on a series of specific, reproducible chemical and physical reactions. Accompanying such innovative thinking was the development of an arsenal of experimental, chemical, surgical, and imaging technologies to actually observe, measure, and record the mouth, esophagus, stomach, small intestines, liver, pancreas, colon, and rectum in action.[6]

Dr. Kellogg was an admirer of many explorers of the gastrointestinal tract, but two in particular caught his eye. The first was his Michigan predecessor, William Beaumont, a U.S. Army physician stationed on Mackinaw Island near the headquarters of John Jacob Astor's American Fur Trading Company.[7] A horrible accident that occurred during the summer of 1822 elevated Dr. Beaumont to medical immortality. While waiting in line at the American Fur Trading company store, a

French Canadian fur trapper named Alexis St. Martin was shot under his left breast. The gory results were a few shattered ribs and a gaping hole through which a part of his lung and stomach protruded. Thanks to Beaumont's quick-witted ministrations, St. Martin survived the event but was left with a large fistula, an unhealed hole or passage that led directly into his stomach.

Dr. Beaumont cared for St. Martin over the next two years but the wound only partially healed. St. Martin was miserable and refused any attempts by Beaumont to try and suture the hole shut. May 30, 1823, marks the date when this odd medical complication (and Alexis's refusal for further surgical manipulation) changed everything about our knowledge of the gastrointestinal tract. It was then that Dr. Beaumont introduced a cathartic (a drug that speeds up the evacuation of the bowels) via a glass funnel through St. Martin's fistula and into his stomach, "as never medicine was administered to man since the creation of the world." What the army surgeon realized was that by peering into the window that was St. Martin's fistula, he had access to a living, working stomach.

Over the next decade, Beaumont used St. Martin's fistula to administer all sorts of foods followed by analyses of the gastric fluids and chyme (the pulpy mass created by the stomach's wavelike motion and digestive juices) he extracted. The result was his 1833 treatise, *Experiments and Observations of the Gastric Juice and the Physiology of Digestion.* By 1850, Beaumont enjoyed the status of being the first American-born medical scientist to achieve international renown. No less an authority than the French physiologist Claude Bernard credited the "backwoods" army doctor with initiating "a new era in the study of this important organ and those associated with it." In Beaumont's wake, across Europe, North America, and beyond, physiologists searched for individuals with similar fistulas or created them, experimentally, in animals so as to elucidate the digestive process.[8]

The other great "gut man" John Harvey Kellogg revered was Ivan Pavlov of St. Petersburg, Russia, whose work on the physiology of digestion won him the Nobel Prize for Medicine or Physiology in 1904. Drs. Kellogg and Pavlov visited the other's laboratory and maintained a lengthy written correspondence. Advancing the peephole Alexis St. Martin's gunshot wound afforded Dr. Beaumont more than fifty years earlier, Pavlov developed several new surgical procedures to construct gastric fistulae augmented by a biological pouch of sorts, which allowed him to sample and analyze gastric juices during a battery of experimental digestive conditions endured by his famous dogs. Emerging from what one historian called his "physiology factory," the Russian genius elaborated how, at different points, the digestive tract secreted hydrochloric acid and specific chemicals in the form of enzymes, which accelerated specific chemical reactions, and how the secretion of specific hormones sent messages to distant parts of the gut to absorb key nutrients and eliminate the waste.[9]

One of Pavlov's many interests was the function of salivary glands and the autonomic nervous system controlling their secretions, especially when anticipating a meal. His most famous salivary studies, of course, were centered on the "conditioned reflexes" of dogs.[10] Many other experiments demonstrated that saliva was far more than a means of lubrication for the mouth. The three pairs of salivary glands (parotid, submaxillary, and sublingual), for example, secrete an enzyme called amylase, which sets in motion a chemical reaction called hydrolysis, the breaking down of complex starch molecules into simple sugars.

Ivan Pavlov (far left) visits John Harvey Kellogg for a stay at the San in 1923. Left to right: Pavlov, John Harvey Kellogg, unidentified San staff member, and V. N. Boldyreff (director of the Battle Creek Sanitarium's gastrointestinal laboratory and former associate of Pavlov's).

John applied both Beaumont's and Pavlov's work (as well as that of many other scientists exploring the salivary glands and digestive juices) in treating his dyspeptic, constipated, and otherwise gut-challenged patients. For decades, Dr. Kellogg emphasized the importance of chewing one's food thoroughly and allowing it to be well mixed with saliva and amylase for sound digestion. We now know that while salivary amylase certainly helps begin the digestive process, the pancreas secretes the lion's share of this digestive enzyme to break down complex carbohydrates once the meal leaves the stomach and enters the small intestine. Nevertheless, it was the hope of harnessing the digestive powers of spit (and the amylase it contained) that initially powered Dr. Kellogg's quest for a palatable, baked, grain-based "health food" that was "easy on the digestion."[11]

Dr. Kellogg took these ideas a few steps further by hypothesizing that the digestive process could be helped along if grains were precooked and predigested before they even entered the patient's mouth. In the process of baking grain-based dough, he discovered that intense heat broke down the starch content into the simple sugar dextrose. He called this baking process dextrinization. As the twentieth century progressed, John's dextrinization theory fell by the wayside even if many of the breakfast cereals he did create, and Will's cereal company later "sugared up," are, in fact, easy to digest. Ironically, today most nutritionists, obesity experts, and physicians argue that the easy digestibility Dr. Kellogg emphasized and worked so hard to achieve is not such a good thing. Specifically, in most processed cereals, the bran and germ of the grain has been removed. These concoctions of broken-down grain and sugar do rapidly digest in the mouth, often before it gets to the stomach, and the result is a sudden spike in one's blood sugar, followed by an increase in insulin (the hormone that enables cells to take up glucose) being secreted by the pancreas into the blood. A few hours after consuming this breakfast, however, one experiences a "crash" in blood sugar (thanks to the over-secretion of insulin), which translates into a loss of energy and a ravenous hunger for an early lunch. High-fiber cereals like oatmeal (and other whole grain preparations with a carbohydrate-to-fiber ratio of less than 10:1), on the other hand, are digested more slowly. Those who eat them report feeling "more full" for longer periods of time and, thus, have far better appetite control when compared to those who consume a bowl of Kellogg's Corn Flakes.[12]

IN THE LATE 1870S, Sanitarium guests aroused their salivary glands by starting their meals with a double-baked hunk of zwieback bread (from the German for *zwei,* two, and *backen,* to bake). Zwieback was served dry, without butter, water, or milk to stimulate the salivary glands to secrete more amylase. Unfortunately, most patients hated the dry, tasteless zwieback biscuits. According to San lore, a broken tooth forced Dr. Kellogg back to the laboratory. One morning, a woman marched into his office and complained that she had broken her dentures while following the doctor's orders to munch on the rock-hard zwieback. As Dr. Kellogg recalled in 1917, "My prescription broke one woman's false teeth she claimed, and she said she thought I ought to pay her $10.00 for them. I did not really know whether she was quite serious about it or not but she looked rather serious. At any rate, it occurred to me it would be good to have a food that would not break teeth."[13]

Sometime in 1877, the doctor began preparing dough consisting of wheat (a low-fat grain) and oats and corn (high-fat grains). He baked the dough at high temperatures for long periods to thoroughly "dextrinize" the grains' starch molecules. After taking the loaves out of the oven, he cooled them, sliced them up, forced the slices through a sieve, and, finally, served the oven-baked crumbs in the dining room, much to the delight of the jaw-weary zwieback eaters. John initially called the new product Granula and it was the first drum major in a parade of foods John created in the years that followed.

Granula soon became a San favorite and Will Kellogg set up a tiny store near the dining room where patients could buy boxes of it so they might take a bit of the Sanitarium home with them. Sensing there was more money to be made, Will used his book business know-how to institute a small mail order company allowing San alumni to continue their Kellogg diets long after they left Battle Creek. Myopically, the San's board of directors saw no future in these crumbly pieces of toast, or any other of the doctor's "health foods," and refused to finance Dr. Kellogg's request for the equipment he needed to manufacture his culinary creations. As a result, John incorporated his own Battle Creek Sanitarium Health Food Company and gave Will a 25 percent interest in the new firm, provided he ran it in his typically efficient manner, which, of course, he did. By 1883, John used his own money to build an experimental food kitchen in the basement of the San, where he would be able to study the effects of cooking on certain foods and develop new products.

Unfortunately, the Danville, New York, physician James Jackson had already developed his own ready-to-eat cereal, also called Granula, and he did not appreciate what he saw as the culinary equivalent of plagiarism. Dr. Jackson was well regarded by many Adventists who had visited his spa (including Ellen White). He was also a prolific author who wrote many essays for the *Advent Review and Sabbath Herald* on proper dress, fresh air, diet, water cures, and other health topics. Most of these articles were read, and some set into type, by a much younger John Harvey Kellogg.[14] Thus, it was highly likely that John read or heard about and even tasted Dr. Jackson's cereal. The Kellogg brothers argued that their product was different in that Jackson's "Granula" consisted only of wheat, while the San's mixture contained wheat, corn, and oats and was baked for a much longer period of time. Notwithstanding, in 1881 Dr. Jackson instructed his lawyers to sue Dr. Kellogg, forcing John to quickly rename his product "Granola," which he sold to his Sanitarium guests at 12 and then 15 cents a pound. By 1889, Will was manufacturing, shipping, and selling two tons of "Sanitarium Foods Granola" every week.[15]

Granola spurred John and Will on to want to create an even better "dextrinized" cereal.[16] Great ideas, however, are often conceived by more than one person, typically around the same time, and that was certainly the case when it came to developing ready-to-eat cereals. The Kellogg brothers' most formidable competitor was an odd attorney named Henry D. Perky. His tinkering with raw wheat and a complex series of rolling machines exploded into the boxed sensation that came to be known as Shredded Wheat.

BORN ON A hardscrabble farm in Holmes County, Ohio, in 1843, Henry Perky was the embodiment of the Horatio Alger "rags to riches" stories. He spent one year at the Bryant, Stratton, and Felton's Business and Telegraphic College in Cleveland, learning bookkeeping and

Henry Perky, inventor of Shredded Wheat,
circa 1890s

accounting before taking jobs as a clerk in a dry goods store and then as a schoolteacher in nearby Akron. Perky soon grew weary of trying to control unruly students and left to run a general store, where he learned the grocery trade. On slow days, he read law books. In his twenties, he moved west to Nebraska, where he passed the bar examination on his first try and, at age twenty-five, was elected to the Nebraska State Senate.

Henry Perky pursued many business opportunities, including a failed effort to manufacture cylindrical steel railway cars, but his most important venture began while defending a client bilked out of a considerable amount of money. Perky discovered that the debtor had fled by night to Colorado and he followed that man to Denver where he successfully collected his client's cash. Long a sufferer of dyspepsia, Henry found Denver's oxygen-thin but fresh mountain air soothing to his stomach and moved there in 1880, where he worked as the general counsel for Union Pacific Railroad.[17] Perky's chronic indigestion inspired him to read widely on the emerging sciences of nutrition and gastroenterology. When prominent lecturers on the workings of the gut passed through town, Perky was always in attendance armed with a pad and scribbled notes and questions. By the early 1890s, he was experimenting with Graham's wheat flour to concoct an easily digestible, wheat-based health food.

Perky quickly learned that boiling wheat dough into a pliable form and baking it into bits of crunchy cereal was no simple matter. He began by pushing the dough through a sieve to make doughy-wheat threads that he could later toast; but he only succeeded in clogging the sieve and making a mess. On the advice of a machinist with the improbable name of William Henry Ford, Perky put together a set of heavy, "mating," or "male and female," rollers. One of the rollers had V-shaped grooves and the other one was smooth.[18] In its finished version, the machine featured a steel comb that removed the rolled-out dough, which the rollers had fashioned into "threads," much like a pasta machine only the diameter of these wheat "noodles" was far smaller. The threads were shaped into a golden "spool" of wheat, folded into the iconic shredded wheat biscuit, and subsequently baked. Perky put the biscuits in an oven at a low heat for several hours but not long enough for the dough to be fully dextrinized, à la Kellogg. On August 1, 1893, he was awarded a U.S. patent (No. 502,378) for his wheat-shredding machine, the first of more than forty patents he would receive for his cereal-making creations.

The original Shredded Wheat biscuits Perky produced were moist and almost grasslike in texture. Perky peddled early versions of his Shredded Wheat to local health food dealers and grocers, and eventually featured it in meals he served up in a "vegetarian health food" restaurant he opened in Denver. He also enlisted some local bakers to make his product, but sales remained negligible. More problematic, his under-baked wheat pillows tended to become moldy in a matter of days. This easy spoilage led to his shift in manufacturing and selling wheat-shredding machines for homemakers to use in their own kitchens, through his side firm, the Cereal Machine Company. The idea was to enable housewives to make just enough shredded wheat for what they needed that day, as both a breakfast cereal and a binding agent for many other recipes, thus avoiding any waste.

DURING THE WINTER OF 1893–1894, one of Dr. Kellogg's dyspepsia patients told him about the new wheat cereal being made in Denver and how it helped allay her many digestive troubles. Describing the product as "little whole wheat mattresses," she gave John a few boxes for his own experimentation. Dr. Kellogg organized an early version of a focus group of San patients to determine if the "wheaty filaments" helped their digestion. While the wheat pillows appeared to be easily tolerated, the participants complained they were "tasteless, difficult to chew," and "like eating a whisk broom."[19]

While traveling in the West for a lecture tour in the spring of 1894, John made a point of stopping over for a few days in Denver. Once there, he visited Perky's vegetarian health food restaurant. The two men quickly developed a rapport over their mutual interests and, as the doctor later told Will, "he showed me his device and explained his process." Perky promised to send one of his machines to Battle Creek but, apparently, he had second thoughts about such generosity and the machine never arrived, a perceived slight that initiated John's lifelong grudge against Perky.[20]

The breakdown in their collaboration became complete after John offered to buy the entire enterprise for approximately $100,000 (or $2.48 million in 2016). The details are murky at this point but in many accounts the doctor seems to have hesitated about the purchase and either rescinded the offer or tried to low-ball Perky with a smaller amount of money. Either way, Perky had great confidence in the value of what he created and John's indecisiveness led to his exit from the deal. Rightly criticized as a terrible businessman, one of John's greatest flaws in his commercial dealings was a Hamlet-like tendency of vacillation and altering his course "with the caprice of a March wind."[21] Whatever actually transpired, Dr. Kellogg long regretted not snapping up Perky's fledgling firm. Years later, he told a friend: "The greatest business mistake I ever made was in not buying Shredded Wheat when it was offered at a reasonable price."[22]

In one sense, the victor in these failed negotiations was Henry Perky. As the two men traded ideas about baking grain cereals, Dr. Kellogg instructed Mr. Perky about the critical importance of dextrinization and how to achieve it using his long and hot baking methods. Perky adopted Dr. Kellogg's advice and, at the very least, the dextrinization process helped make Shredded Wheat far more tasty and crunchy than the earlier moist, strawlike version; it also, likely, improved the product's digestibility. Shredded Wheat soon became one of the most popular ready-to-eat cereals on the market. By 1901, Perky's company was so profitable that he moved to Niagara Falls (after establishing factories in Boston and Worcester, Massachusetts), where he built an ultramodern factory glowingly described in colorful advertisements as a "Palace of Light" and a "Conservatory of Food."[23] Perky's business model was buttressed by the more than fifty grain elevators in Buffalo and the Niagara Falls Power Company, which provided cheap electricity from its "Cathedral of Power," designed by famed American architect Stanford White and built by industrialist George H. Westinghouse. The power plant harnessed the energy of the Niagara River and converted it into the alternating current developed by Nikola Tesla, much to the consternation of the Wizard of Menlo Park, and staunch supporter of direct current, Thomas Edison.[24]

Perky invited the droves of American and Canadian honeymooners coming to the Falls directly after pledging "I do" for free tours of his factory. For decades, millions of newlyweds breakfasted on gratis samples of Perky's crunchy "wheat pillows," liberally handed out as they exited the tour. The majority of them purchased several larger boxes at the factory's

Shredded Wheat factory in Niagara Falls

store. At the end of their honeymoons, the newlyweds began their new households with fond memories of their time in Niagara Falls. Thanks to Perky, they also had the catchy slogan, "Shredded Wheat. It's All in the Shreds," floating about in their heads and the actual cereal floating in bowls of milk at their breakfast table.[25]

In the longer run, John and Will ultimately won the battle over Shredded Wheat. John consoled his disappointed younger brother after the failure of the Shredded Wheat deal by characterizing it as a new opportunity for greatness on their own terms. "We'll invent a better food," he vowed.[26] Perky's success convinced the brothers that there was a market for their culinary ambition and pushed them to redouble their efforts by creating and perfecting the far superior, and ultimately far more popular, ready-to-eat flaked cereals.

Thirty-four years later Will Kellogg enjoyed an even sweeter plate of revenge. In 1912, Perky's patent on Shredded Wheat expired and Will, by now a successful cereal man, began manufacturing his own version of the "wheat pillows." The "new" cereal, backed by his capable team of advertising men, salesmen, and a loyal American public eager to buy the Kellogg brand, became an instant hit. Perky was displeased, to say the least, and threatened a lawsuit. An obscure accord was reached between the two firms in 1919 and Will temporarily backed off on producing his shredded wheat product. As Will grew more successful, however, he increasingly enjoyed engaging in the business version of cockfights to maintain his company's supremacy in the cereal industry. Consequently, in 1927 he ordered the Kellogg Company to enter the shredded wheat market in full force by duplicating (and improving) Perky's process. More provocative, he sold identically shaped and tasting biscuits, brazenly labeled "Kellogg's Shredded Wheat."

By 1930, the National Biscuit Company (Nabisco) had purchased Perky's company; two years later, Nabisco, no small shakes itself as a powerful corporation, decided to sue America's largest cereal company over "unfair competition." Citing brand-name infringement and that the Kellogg Company appropriated their product's distinctive biscuit shape, the case went all the way to the United States Supreme Court. In a 7–2 decision, written by Associate Justice Louis Brandeis in 1938, the Court ruled in favor of Will Kellogg's cereal company. The shape, the Court determined, was fairly generic and not protected by any patent, let alone

Ella Kellogg, wife of John Harvey, with some of their adopted children

an expired one. The name "shredded wheat" was deemed to be equally generic, descriptive, and represented "truth in labeling," long before that became a commonplace phrase. It was a double victory for Will.[27] His company made a mint off a highly profitable product that should have been his all along had not John's indecision bungled the deal to purchase Perky's Shredded Wheat outright in 1894.[28]

THE UNSUNG HERO in the corn flake story is John's devoted wife, Ella Eaton Kellogg.[29] She was nearly an equal partner in the Kellogg health empire and the undisputed mistress of their grand Queen Anne home replete with turrets, a wraparound porch, twenty rooms, including bathrooms with the most modern conveniences in indoor plumbing (of course), an office for the doctor and his on-call stenographer, as well as a small laboratory and an indoor gymnasium. Outside were nine acres of grounds, with a greenhouse for growing vegetables, and groves of trees, a small apple orchard, a playground, and an elaborate and fragrant flower garden.

"The Residence," as it was called, was five blocks west of the San on leafy Manchester Street.[30] Ella kept the house immaculately clean, even with forty-two children living in the house at different points of time, at least seven of whom were formally adopted and all of whom were home schooled by Ella and a teacher named Mary Lamson. Decades later, Lamson recalled how much Dr. Kellogg loved these children. He would frequently "romp and roll [with the children] on the floor" as a means of relaxation before going off to the operating room.[31] Four of the brood were Mexican (one of whom became a physician and another a dentist), at least seven were African American, and another Puerto Rican. There existed a strict set of rules and deportment in the Residence. Ella made certain each child understood the importance of loyalty to the family, the health principles they practiced, and her cardinal rule, "If a member of the household sees or hears (in other words, knows) of misdemeanors on the part of other members of the household, it shall be their care not to speak of the matter to others who do not know of it, but to go to the offender and urge him or her to reform." As a fail-safe, Ella cautioned if "after due time there is no appearance of reform the matter should be reported to our parents for consideration."[32] Ella also instructed them about "never speaking to outsiders in regard to anything which is either a personal or family matter."[33] Ella and John insisted they never selected any of their adopted children; instead, "[the children] selected them."

The Residence, home of John Harvey and Ella Kellogg

Perhaps most notable about Ella and John's parenting was the unconditional love they showered on these children.[34]

Married for more than forty-one years, Ella and John, apparently,
never consummated their marriage. Dr. Kellogg was quite open about
their separate bedrooms and his determination to live a life without sexual gratification. Even though he had no scientific evidence to back up
his medical opinions on the matter, John felt that sex sapped vital energy,
harmed health, and was unnecessary except for procreation. There was
also the real risk of contracting incurable sexually transmitted diseases,
all of which he associated with clandestine and impure sexual activities. Over the years, the doctor had seen more than his share of sexual
encounters gone clinically awry, from the infected New York "rakes"
presenting themselves with great embarrassment at Bellevue Hospital to
the well-heeled "playboys" sent by their fathers to the San for a "rest
cure." Ella, too, was a confirmed believer in abstinence and composed a
"Purity Pledge" for girls and boys along with much practical advice on
the pitfalls of adolescence in an 1885 pamphlet, *Talks with Girls,* which
was widely circulated by the Women's Christian Temperance Union.[35]
For years Battle Creekers gossiped about the Kelloggs' sleeping arrangements. Some respected their privacy or simply accepted their chastity as
part of their religious or health reform beliefs. Others whispered that the
doctor had mumps as a youngster resulting in sterility and a nonexistent
libido.[36] Regardless of the precise reason, theirs was a marriage of neither
passion nor convenience, but it was a brilliant working partnership.

At nineteen and two months, Ella became the youngest graduate of
Alfred University, in Alfred Center, New York, in 1872. Her Bachelor
of Arts degree was in nutrition. Ella gave the valedictory address at her
commencement exercises and went on to teach grammar school for the
next four years. In the summer of 1876, she accompanied her sister to
Battle Creek to visit an aunt. The Eaton girls arrived to find a terrible
typhoid fever epidemic brewing in south-central Michigan. Soon after,
Ella's sister became so ill that a Sanitarium doctor named Kate Lindsay
was called in for an emergency consultation.

Today, we know that the causative organism of typhoid fever is *Salmonella typhi,* a bacterium that infects the gut, yielding bloody diarrhea,
high fevers, and dehydration. In the late nineteenth century, when doctors knew neither the cause nor cure for this all too common malady,

typhoid fever often resulted in death. The incubator was incomplete sewage systems and the fecal contamination of drinking water or food. Such conditions and disease spread were hardly restricted to small towns in the Midwest or squalid shanties in poor urban neighborhoods. For example, eight years later, in February of 1884, Theodore Roosevelt's mother, Martha, died of typhoid in the family's posh Manhattan townhouse.[37]

Dr. Lindsay and Ella were successful in nursing her sister back to health. Ella discovered she had a real knack for this type of work and she subsequently volunteered to help Dr. Lindsay nurse many more typhoid victims back to health, including one case so serious that Dr. Kellogg was called in for an emergency visit. John was so impressed by Ella's compassionate nursing skills that he urged her to stay in Battle Creek. He bolstered his pitch by telling her that the patient she was caring for had no chance of survival without her constant attendance. After the epidemic finally burned itself out, Ella delayed her return to New York once again and this time for good. She began studies in nursing and hygiene at the Battle Creek College as well as working alongside the doctor in the editing and composition of his monthly magazine, *Good Health*.[38] The tiny woman, with wavy brown hair parted in the middle and rimless gold spectacles, formed an immediate bond with the dashing young physician, especially after John asked her to join the Sanitarium's staff. For Ella, it turned out to be far more than a professional offer. Although she had other serious suitors, it was John who thrilled her heart the most.

On the evening of George Washington's birthday, February 22, 1879, the Sanitarium guests were instructed to assemble in the parlor. Once there, a band struck up the opening chords of Mendelssohn's "Wedding March." Through the doors entered the doctor and his favorite nurse for a wedding ceremony officiated by the Sanitarium's chaplain, Lycurgus McCoy. After getting the rice out of their hair, they left for a six-week honeymoon in New England, where John spent most of his days and evenings revising new editions of two of his most popular books, *Plain Facts About Sexual Life* and *The Proper Diet of Man*. The former volume contained some of the doctor's harshest warnings against self-abuse, recreational sex, and lascivious activities. It is safe to assume that Ella, who spent her evenings editing John's manuscripts in their honeymoon suite, hardly enjoyed the typical and time-honored wedding night experience.[39]

According to the John Harvey Kellogg scholar Richard Schwarz, Ella may have been a rebound choice for John. His first true love, it seems, was a Battle Creek Adventist named Mary Kelsey, who worked as a proofreader in the *Review and Herald* office. In 1876, she chose to marry Ellen White's son William (John's friend and rival since childhood and who attended the Trall Institute with him). On top of their competition for dominance in the Adventist Church, if true, this triangle may have contributed to the strained relationship between William White and Dr. Kellogg, one that deteriorated with each passing year and would eventually rupture.

Nevertheless, there did exist a deeply loving and mutually admiring relationship between John and Ella, even if modern-day observers might scoff at their chastity. John referred to Ella as his "helpmeet" in eulogy for her in 1920.[40] He admired her "bookishness" and love of learning. He frequently boasted to others how in both her writings and conversations, Ella was able to reel off exact quotations of such diverse social thinkers as Jean-Jacques Rousseau, Friedrich Froebel, Margaret Fuller, and Herbert Spencer.

It was in the kitchen, however, where Ella's light shined the brightest. An excellent cook and creator of many new, healthy dishes, Ella insisted, "the repast [served at the San] must suggest not the handing out of food medicine or medicinal foods, but . . . a good share of life's joys."[41] Well versed on nearly every aspect of modern hygienic homemaking, she was also the chief of the Sanitarium's dietary department, supervised its kitchen, founded and ran the San's School of Home Economics and Cooking, organized the nearby Haskell Home for Orphans—where she helped train foster mothers to prepare nutritious meals—as well as writing scores of magazine articles on food and diet for *Good Health* and some highly regarded tomes, including a 508-page cookbook called *Science in the Kitchen*.[42] Ella was also an active leader in the Women's Christian Temperance Union (WCTU) and a close friend of its president, Frances Willard, who asked her to become the society's national superintendent of hygiene, director of its Social Purity department, and, later, to direct the WCTU's Mothers' Meetings and Child Culture Circles.[43]

Never very physically robust, Ella endured a long battle with neurasthenia, depression, deafness, and what became a semi-invalided state due to colon cancer. As her tumor metastasized, she suffered from an incontinence of stool and urine, debilities rarely mentioned in public then or now. One can only imagine the humiliation the mistress of a medical empire built on intestinal regularity and integrity experienced each time she soiled herself, not to mention her having to wear the adult version of diapers. In 1919, Ella underwent a tumor debulking operation performed by William Mayo at the Mayo Clinic, but it was only palliative; Dr. Mayo found too many deadly metastases to her liver. She "lingered" for a year after the procedure, but needed constant nursing care, before going into a coma and dying on June 14, 1920. The doctor long grieved her death and made sure to note, "without the help derived from this fertile incubator of ideas, the great food industries of Battle Creek would never have existed. They are all direct or indirect outgrowths of Mrs. Kellogg's experimental kitchen, established in the fall of 1883."[44] With the exception of Will, it is safe to state that no one was more important in the corn flake saga than Ella. Especially in the early years of the doctor's food creating, Ella was often at his side, rolling pin in hand. As both always colorfully insisted, it was in her kitchen, and with her "kneading rollers," where boiled wheat dough was rolled out to become the first successful batch of flaked cereal.[45]

THOMAS EDISON FAMOUSLY USED a "hit and miss" process of scientific inquiry while devising the proper filament for his world-changing light bulb but he was hardly alone in such methods.[46] During the winter and early spring of 1894, Dr. Kellogg applied a similar late-nineteenth-century approach of experimental tinkering as he embarked on a series of failures before finally hitting on the precise formula for flaked cereal. In one of his earliest trials, John channeled Henry Perky by forcing the boiled dough through the equivalent of a colander. He, too, succeeded only in making a sticky mess as the dough's wheat bran clogged up all the holes. After several more attempts, Ella suggested rolling out the boiled dough as thinly as possible. This was a critical improvement because the thin sheets facilitated their subsequent scraping the dough off the board with a knife and then turning them into small pieces. John baked these bits of wheat dough in the oven until they were brown, crispy "little pieces of toast."[47] The next advance was a mechanical one. John designed a set of rollers, at Ella's suggestion, turned by a crank just like the old-fashioned "water ringers" used to dry clothing. This allowed for the rapid production of many more flat dough sheets than the few he could roll out by hand on Ella's dough board.

John contended that the precise recipe for flaked cereal was revealed to him in a dream. He had long been fascinated by dreams, and as early as 1892 gave lectures on the topic at the Sanitarium. On a hot, muggy August evening that year he told an audience packing the San's spacious parlor, "we can find a great deal of our true character there. We must not forget . . . that our dreams are made by our daily lives."[48] Dr. Kellogg was hardly a Freudian; in 1910 he compared psychotherapy with heal-ing "cults" such as faith healing, mind healing, and Christian Science.[49] Nonetheless, John did appreciate the power of dreams and visions as an explanatory and convincing medium, most likely a product of his years of devotion to Ellen White and the Adventist cause.

Undoubtedly, the doctor's most famous nocturnal reverie was what he later referred to as the "corn flake dream":

> One night about three o'clock I was awakened by a 'phone call from a patient, and as I went back to bed I remembered that I had been having a most important dream. Before I went to sleep again I gathered up the threads of my dream, and found I had been dream-ing of a way to make flaked foods. The next morning I boiled some wheat, and, while it was soft, I ran it through a machine Mrs. Kel-logg had for rolling out dough thin. This made the wheat into thin films, and I scraped it off with a case knife and baked it in the oven. That was the first of the modern breakfast foods.[50]

A slightly different version involved John working on a batch of dough in his home kitchen in the late evening when the telephone rang. His telephone was one of the few private home lines in Battle Creek at the time. On the other end was the chief surgical nurse at the San calling him to come immediately to perform an emergency operation on a patient *in extremis*. Realizing that he would not likely return home until late the following day, John decided against trashing the raw wheat dough and left it out in the open for the several hours he planned on being gone. Upon his return, he fed the waiting dough through the rollers, just as he did with the many previous batches, scraped it off, and baked the bits. This time, however, when he removed the resultant flakes from the oven, he was astounded to discover that they were perfect, which inspired the doctor to pursue the critical query, What was so different about this particular batch?

It was at this point in the narrative where the collective memory of events takes a series of twists and turns. Ella, of course, vigorously insisted that it was she, not Will, who was John's principal helper on the night flaked cereal was invented. Several years after the event, one of the Kelloggs' adopted children, Dr. Josephine Knapp, and John's brother-in-law, Hiland Butler, each claimed to have held the knife needed to scrape the flakes off the rollers while the doctor fed raw dough into the device on that momentous evening.[51]

IN WILL'S VERSION, the invention of Corn Flakes was an equal partnership. Although he was always careful to defer to the doctor's importance in every telling of the tale over the span of more than fifty years, Will maintained they each contributed important innovations essential to arriving at the perfect recipe. The one person Will rarely mentions in his recounting of the events, however, was his sister-in-law Ella. A generation later, his grandson Norman Jr. also made a point of denying her integral involvement claiming it as a myth. The great moment, Norman Jr. insists, based upon discussions with his grandfather, occurred in the San's experimental kitchen.[52] Yet this version fails to correspond with John's (as well as Ella's, Butler's, and Knapp's) contention that the first batch was made in his wife's home kitchen. There was, however, a long history of animosity between the brother-in-law and sister-in-law. Ella took an almost cruel pleasure in complaining to John about Will's performance at the San and, on several occasions, campaigned for his being fired. It may have been this dynamic that compelled Will to minimize her involvement when retelling the event that underpinned his commercial legacy.

Ironically, when John first recruited him into his cereal-creating schemes, Will looked upon the assignment as one more time-consuming task capriciously assigned by the doctor. Yet with each successive experiment, Will performed the work with more enthusiasm, ingenuity, and precision. It was the first indication—there would be many more during his long career as a food industrialist—that inside Will's increasingly paunchy body existed a man of science always eager to get his hands dirty in order to figure out a particular gastronomic problem.

This brings us to Will's account of reusing the "day-old dough," which remains intriguing, if impossible to prove. In his telling, one Friday night, dog-tired from the fourteen-hours-a-day, six-day workweek that had just ended, the brothers decided to stop and get some much needed sleep. Always careful about the expenditure of every penny, Will put the dough he had just made in a container rather than simply throwing it in the trash. The next day, the Saturday Adventist Sabbath, was a day of rest and the brothers did not return to their experiment until the Sabbath officially ended at nightfall. Upon the close of the concluding service in the San's chapel, Will and John put down their hymnals and raced back to the kitchen where they began kneading and rolling out Friday's dough. During this rolling, however, each detected the distinct odor of mold emanating from the sticky wheat. John and Will shrugged their shoulders, ignored the fact that their dough had turned slightly moldy, fed thin sheets of the stuff through the rollers, scraped off the bits with a big knife, and baked them. A short while later, they contended with a grease fire while the flakes were in the oven that was, fortunately, contained without damage to the batch or the kitchen. A mere fire could not and would not impede the greatest moment of the Kellogg brothers' lives. Consistent with John's account was the discovery, after running the cooked dough through the rollers, "it came out in the form of large, thin flakes, each individual wheat berry forming one flake!"[53]

Regardless of the exact order of events leading up to leaving out the dough for an extended period of time, it was the mold that really made the flakes so good and crunchy. After consulting with several of the bakers at the Sanitarium, the Kellogg brothers learned that by leaving the dough out for so many hours, they were facilitating a process called tempering. Basically, as the mold ferments, the water content of the dough equalizes across the entire mass rather than collecting in specific spots. At the same time, the dough temperature approximates the ambient room temperature. Finally, Will and John learned that thinly rolled, tempered dough baked more evenly and with fewer air bubbles, all of which helped produce perfect flakes.

Will performed countless more experiments to find "the sweet spot" between tempering the dough enough to facilitate equalizing the temperature and water content but not too long so that the dough became too moldy and inedible.[54] With the care and attention of a well-trained scientist, Will kept a detailed record of every batch he produced and every single result in a laboratory notebook. Air-drying, for example, subjected the dough to too much humidity and resulted in flakes that were not sufficiently crunchy or light. Atmospheric conditions, the length of baking time, and, of course, the baking temperature (always within a range of 400 to 480 degrees Fahrenheit), Will discovered, also mattered a great deal.

A major problem that Will had to solve was preventing the boiled dough from sticking to the rollers. The initial rolling apparatus they used was operated by a hand crank device and set up on a tabletop. Dominant John fed the dough into a hopper while standing from above. Subservient Will, crouched directly and uncomfortably underneath the table, essentially catching the flattened dough ejected by the rolls. With a chisel in one hand and a bowl in the other, he scraped off the sticky bits of the wheat dough for toasting. Understandably, Will quickly tired of this painful arrangement and one night he ran over to the Review and Herald Company's production plant. Entering through an unlocked side door into the "finishing room," he borrowed several long knives that the printers used as paper cutters to make individual pages as they came off the press for binding. Once back in the kitchen, Will took out a few screws and nails to firmly affix the long knives to the lower roller. After the blades were nailed in, he weighted them down so that they were as close as possible to the roller. This allowed him to better scrape off the wet dough, while still standing rather than crouching, and produce the optimal tiny thin bits of wheat dough for baking into delicate flakes. Ever the systems expert, Will figured out that the best flakes emerged when they fed carefully measured rolls of dough, 8 inches in diameter and 24 inches in length, through the rollers.[55]

On May 31, 1895, John applied to the U.S. Patent Office for a patent on "Flaked Cereal and Process of Preparing the Same" (No. 558,393).[56] It was granted on April 14, 1896. Clever in protecting his rights, John made sure that the patent covered flakes made of oats, corn, barley, and other grains, as well as wheat flakes. Will should have received a co-credit on the patent application but none was forthcoming from his elder brother. For the rest of his life, Will reasonably insisted that the invention was hardly his brother's alone.[57] In the passive-aggressive manner Will perfected over the years, he always noted that when you looked at Will Kellogg, you were looking at the real creator of flaked cereal: "For some reason," Will quietly added, "the Doctor thought best to take the flakes after they had been nicely formed, put a sieve over a barrel and break the flakes up and rub them to pieces. It was my suggestion that the flakes be allowed to remain whole and be served in that way."[58]

In the summer of 1895, the brothers introduced their wheat flakes as a meal for the General Conference of the Seventh-day Adventists at the Battle Creek Sanitarium. From the buzz in the San's dining room, it was clear that the brothers had hit upon something important. Everyone lined up for bowl after bowl of the flakes and found them especially appealing when splashed with some milk, cream, or yogurt. An added bonus was the regularity of the guests' bowel movements and resolution of their bellyaches following these flaky meals. Dr. Kellogg named the new wheat cereal "Granose," a neologism of grain and the scientific suffix "ose," for metabolism. The brothers sold their cereal at the San and by mail order. A 10-ounce package cost 15 cents. Yet even with this small circle of potential customers, they found that they could not keep up with the demand from the Adventist faithful. It was at this point that Will took on the task of expanding their production methods beyond the tiny setup they had used in Ella's (or the San's experimental) kitchen.

Later that year, Will hired some bakers and workmen to staff a tiny makeshift "factory," which also served as the home of the Sanitarium Food and the Sanitas Nut Food companies. In their first year of production, they sold or served over 113,400 pounds of Granose. By 1898, the business had outgrown the first factory and Will rented a two-story ramshackle building with a basement on Aldrich Street. This structure boasted real ovens and, according to Will, "the business continued to grow under rather mediocre management."[59] Here, the reader must be warned about Will's tendency for modesty; even at this early date his cereal factory was operating twenty-four hours a day while Will was working 118 to 120 hours a week, tending to his responsibilities at the Sanitarium, the publishing house, and ancillary companies.[60] During this same period, Puss and Will Kellogg lost two children. Their son Will Keith Jr. died in 1889 at the age of four and another boy, Irvin Hadley, died in 1895 before he was one year old.

AN OFT-TOLD TALE about the early Kellogg's flaked cereals was that they were manufactured using heavy metal rollers designed to crush the stems off tobacco leaves. This story is only partially true and originates from the fact that the Lauhoff Brothers Company, a Detroit-based firm Will hired to design and manufacture his dough-rolling equipment, manufactured both tobacco rollers for their cigar-making business and the large rollers required for milling flour.[61]

Sometime around 1900, Frank and William Lauhoff made a major contribution to the production of flaked cereal by developing a water-cooled roller, which they hoped to use for manufacturing their own brand of flaked cereal, Crystal Malt Flakes. The original rollers worked at a continuous pace and became quite hot, necessitating stopping them every so often to ice and cool them down, lest the thin dough burn and ruin the batch. Applying his experience with the rolling machines used to separate tobacco leaves from stems, Frank Lauhoff set the individual rollers to move at different speeds, which prevented the doughy, moist flakes from sticking to the rollers, wasting dough, and losing time for frequent cleanings. What's more, when the dough was rolled on a cooled set of rollers going at different speeds, the resulting flakes retained their crispness longer.[62]

As the news spread that the Kelloggs had figured out how to spin 60 cents' worth of wheat into 12 dollars of gold, a phalanx of businessmen, and not a few charlatans, herded themselves to Battle Creek to start their own cereal companies. Unlike John, they had no professional strictures against advertising or how they sold or made their grainy wares. By 1902, Will had instituted a strict policy requiring all employees to sign a legal document promising not to reveal the company's trade secrets to anyone or form competitive cereal firms. Such precautions did little to prevent several employees from breaching this contract, a deceit that, undoubtedly, contributed to the establishment of 101 new cereal companies in Battle Creek between 1888 and 1905.[63] Several of these firms produced some fairly popular cereal products (C. W. Post's being the most sterling example of this success); many others were poorly run and destined for bankruptcy; and some were nothing but clever schemes designed to swindle money from unsuspecting investors.

Failures and bunkum aside, the cereal "gold rush" in Battle Creek made for national news. For example, a front-page article in the September 7, 1902, issue of the *New York World* reported:

> There is not a pauper in Battle Creek, not a hovel home in the town. . . . As for the factories, most of them are running by night and on Sundays in order to keep pace with the demand for their goods. . . . Battle Creek is the greatest cereal food producing city in the world.[64]

John T. McCutcheon, the popular *Chicago Tribune* and Pulitzer Prize–winning cartoonist, presented an even more graphic depiction of the cereal boom. Parodying the flourishing prices and values of cereal stocks and the companies they represented, he portrayed the "Battle Creek Sanitarium Food Co.: The Original and Genuine Battle Creek Food Institution" surrounded by shacks, advertisement signs, and lean-tos and

The cereal "gold rush" in Battle Creek. A cartoon by John T. McCutcheon that appeared in the Chicago Tribune, *circa 1904*

populated by drummers, manufacturers, and con men, each one trying to make a buck off the production of cereal.

Competing with the Kelloggs' wheat flakes were all kinds of cereals with names such as Zest, Vim, Cero-Fruto, Flake-Ho, Per-Fo, and Malta-Vita. One early popular product that presaged the trend toward sugar-filled cereals was Mapl-Flakes, which, as the name implies, was impregnated with loads of maple syrup. Children loved them. A national advertising campaign promised enthusiastic boys and girls across the nation that Mapl-Flakes were the preferred cereal of the University of Michigan football team, coached by the legendary Fielding Yost, and were responsible for the Wolverines' "power and drive" when the team "clobbered Minnesota 23 to 6 on Thanksgiving Day of 1902." In one bold advertisement, the Wolverines' star halfback, Willie Heston, declared he never began a day without a heaping bowl of Mapl-Flakes.[65]

In the midst of the cereal gold rush he helped create, Will pressed the doctor to expand the business even more, develop a national advertising campaign, sell the cereal in grocery stores across the country, and make some real money. Each time Will asked for such permission, John responded with a resounding "No." Everyone in Battle Creek, it seemed, was profiting on Will's hard work and yet his own firm's growth was hamstrung by the doctor's strict orders against any commercialization or advertising that might jeopardize his standing in the medical community. Ironically, the one man who most agreed with Will's vision was the same person who would become his chief rival, a nervous fellow named Charles W. Post who was actively building an enormous food empire of his own.

WHEN CHARLEY POST CAME TO Battle Creek, he was a thirty-six-year-old failed businessman in poor health. He had already suffered, at least, three neurasthenic breakdowns and had long complained of painful indigestion. Emaciated and wheelchair bound, Post first consulted Dr. Kellogg in February of 1891.[66] In the months that followed, Dr. Kellogg analyzed his gastric juices, counted his blood cells, and attempted to alter Post's disordered pattern of bowel movements. The Post coffers, however, were just about empty. Before arriving in Battle Creek, Post's wool mill business in Fort Worth mysteriously burned to the ground and

C. W. Post, circa 1912

he paid some of his San bills with the blankets he was able to rescue from the blaze; other times he and his wife lived off the income from a new type of men's pants suspenders she sold door-to-door. More frequently, Charley Post covered his mounting medical bills by helping out Will and his assistants in the experimental kitchen laboratory, a gig that gave him unfettered access to Dr. Kellogg's most valuable recipes.

Mr. and Mrs. Post never resided in the San because it was too expensive. Instead, they opted for the far cheaper route of rooming across the street in one of the many nearby boardinghouses while spending their mornings and afternoons taking water cures, dining on Sanitarium fare, getting massages, and engaging in calisthenics at reduced "day-patients" rates. In later years, Post complained that Dr. Kellogg's regimes did little to improve his physical health. That may or may not be true, but Charley's stay at the San certainly improved his economic health.

In the spring of 1892, Post settled his account and left the Sanitarium to work with a local Christian Science practitioner. That May, he somehow acquired the funds to buy a ten-acre plot of land some ten miles outside Battle Creek where he opened a "medical boardinghouse" he called La Vita Inn, which offered spiritual and natural remedies.[67] Soon

Postum factory, Battle Creek, Michigan, circa 1900

after, he began to manufacture "health foods" under the brand name "C. W. Post." Post paved the "Road to Wellville" (a utopian ad campaign Post created to hawk his many products) with two wildly popular foods. The first was Postum, a direct steal of Dr. Kellogg's "Minute Brew," a caramelized molasses and roasted bran "coffee substitute," which Charley Post advertised as a health drink with the entirely misleading slogan, "It Makes Red Blood!"[68] Two years later, on January 1, 1895, Post rolled out a cereal he called Grape-Nuts, which contained neither grapes nor nuts of any kind. Instead, they were the same baked wheat crumbs Dr. Kellogg packaged as Granola but sweetened with maltose—the principal sugar in grapes but also found in many other foods. The success of these two foods allowed Post to erect a "White City" of factory buildings in Battle Creek, a name he appropriated from the World's Columbian Exposition of 1893. By 1900, his firm was making a net profit of $3 million a year (or more than $87 million in 2016).

The Kellogg brothers' opinion of Post acidified over the years. Initially, the doctor considered his recipes to be a gift for improving human health rather than a means of making a profit and he appeared not to give Post much attention. Will, on the other hand, constantly carped that the man was stealing their business. The animosity between the two men really bubbled over after 1906, when Post directly copied Will's

*The Road to Wellville, Postum Cereal Company
advertisement, circa early 1920s*

Corn Flake recipe to produce his own corn cereal, originally marketed under the quasi-religious banner of "Elijah's Manna." By 1908, millions of Americans were consuming C. W. Post's corn flakes with the far more appealing brand name, "Post Toasties." A few sales figures from the Post Company easily explain Will's anger over Charley's gastronomic thefts. Between September of 1908 and September of 1909, the C.W. Post Company reported that profits from Post Toasties amounted to $2,185,820.98, from Postum Cereal Coffee, $1.4 million, and from Grape-Nuts, $1.7 million (a total of more than $142 million in 2016).[69] Decades later, Albert Lasker, the successful advertising expert, philanthropist, and public health patron, recalled that Dr. Kellogg "felt that Post was a plagiarist." A seething Will often referred to Post as the "Original Imitator."

Grape=Nuts advertisement, circa early 1900s

A friend of Will's recalled years later, "W.K. never had any love for Mr. Post. He always had the feeling of wanting to surpass the gentleman. . . . They largely hissed at each other over the fence."[70]

C. W. Post never really got over his chronic stomach pain despite his long search for his own Wellville. In the years before the First World War, the Postum palatine encamped at his expansive estate in Santa Barbara, California. By the fall of 1913, he was running out of strength and steam. Scheduled to give a major speech in Philadelphia railing against the policies of Woodrow Wilson in general and, in particular, the ratification of the Sixteenth Amendment to the U.S. Constitution allowing for an income tax, Charley canceled at the last minute.[71] The gastric distress that had plagued him throughout his adulthood became uncontainable. In early March of 1914, Post was rushed from California to Rochester, Minnesota, writhing in pain, for an emergency appendectomy performed by the other fabled pair of Midwestern brothers interested in health matters, Charles and Will Mayo.

Newspapers across the nation ran front-page articles screaming "Michigan Millionaire Races with Death Across the West" and describing the nonstop Pullman car express train specially arranged by Edward P. Ripley, the president of the Atchison, Topeka, and Santa Fe Railway. Mr. Ripley, one account described, ordered "a pilot car . . . sent ahead to side-track through-trains onto spurs in order to speed the special train on its journey. It resulted in the fastest crossing [of the North American continent] ever made up to that time."[72]

Although he valiantly tried to recuperate back in Santa Barbara, Post grew increasingly despondent. On the morning of May 9, 1914, while rummaging through his gun collection, he located a .30–30 Winchester hunting rifle, "placed the muzzle of the weapon in his mouth and pulled the trigger with his toe, blowing off the entire top of his head."[73] Charley was just five months shy of his sixtieth birthday. An elaborate funeral was arranged back in Battle Creek replete with hundreds of mourners, both famous and ordinary, journalists, photographers, and newspaper tributes, but the tragedy failed to sadden or soften the Kellogg brothers.

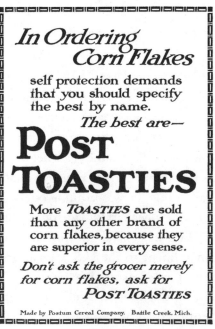

Post Toasties advertisement, circa 1910

John called Post a wreck and gossiped to his friends how much money Charley made off his creations.[74] The passive-aggressive Will made two trenchant observations about Charley's death. Responding to the rumor that in his last years Charley had taken to referring to Will Kellogg as a "dirty yellow dog," Will rejoined, "If so, everyone knows how a dirty yellow dog pays his respects to a Post!"[75] More formally to the press, Will intoned, "I hope when I pass on that I will have done more for the town than Mr. Post ever did."[76]

AT THE SAME TIME C. W. Post was building a cereal empire, Will Kellogg began planning one of his own. Between 1898 and 1905, Will steadily revised and improved the recipe for flaked cereals, including identifying its key ingredients and the precise amounts and ways to cook them. His employees fondly recalled that he had "an unerring judgment" in tasting and selecting the best food samples.[77] It was this talent that turned his attention away from wheat and toward that most American of grains, corn.

No dream inspired Will's switch from wheat to corn. He made a determined and systematic search for flavor and texture, which required years of many trials and even more errors. Although corn was cheap, plentiful, and possessed a sweet, pleasant flavor, it proved especially difficult to tame into flakes. Initially, Will tried using whole corn kernels but the results were neither crunchy nor terribly toothsome. The large amounts of corn oil in the whole kernel ruined the toasting process and, once in the box, the flakes went rancid, especially if stored for long periods of time.

He then experimented with hominy grits, a milled version of corn that typically uses a caustic agent, such as lye, to remove the kernel's hull and germ. This was a definite improvement but it still failed to satisfy Will's discerning palate. Eventually, he took to steaming the corn kernels open over a bubbling boiler of water and after removing and straining them applied a "long blade from a paper cutting machine" to free the corn kernel from its more oily hull and germ. He followed this by "cracking," or grinding, what remained into "flaking grits." To his infinite delight, the dough made from "flaking grits" was far easier to peel off the rollers and, with just the precise amount of "toasting," the resulting flakes were crunchy, crisp, and golden-brown.[78] His advertising men would later glorify Will's flaking grits as "the sweetheart of the corn."

Will's greatest breakthrough, however, was the realization that there were far many more healthy people who would eat and purchase tasty corn flakes for their daily breakfast compared to the relatively small number of invalids who bought and consumed only the blandest of "health foods" to aid their digestion. Unlike the doctor's rather flat and tasteless wheat flakes, Will insisted that his corn flakes had to taste good.[79] After too many bad batches to count, he finally determined the precise sprinkles of malt, sugar, and salt needed to give his flakes that nutty, corny, pleasing, and popular taste. Years later, Will's son John Leonard recalled the argument that occurred right after John found out about Will's culinary tinkering: "The Doctor . . . had a fit. . . . He got after my father, and Mr. W.K. and the Doctor had a row about it, but Mr. W.K. kept on making the flakes with malt, sugar, and salt as the flavoring."[80] The test of time, and the sales of billions of boxes of Corn Flakes, has amply demonstrated that Will was right.

Initially, the annual sales of the Kellogg brothers' Sanitarium cereal products amounted to a tiny fraction of what C. W. Post and the many other imitator cereal firms were selling on a monthly basis. Every time Will tried to do more with the business, his senior partner vetoed his suggestions. On top of the demoralizing work environment Will was forced to inhabit, the doctor vindictively refused to provide the office or factory space Will needed for the food company. Fed up and tired, Will abruptly told John he was leaving the Sanitarium to focus exclusively on the food business, of which he was an agent with a 25 percent ownership rather than merely being the doctor's employee always at his beck and call.[81] In August of 1901, Will cleaned out his desk and packed his few personal belongings with the intention of ending his association with the San.

Although Will was determined to focus on the cereal business, a disastrous event occurred six months after he left his brother's employ. It was a catastrophe of such magnitude that it pulled Will right back into the San. It took another two and a half years before he would finally be free from his brother's daily humiliations, albeit not the psychic scars that irritated his neurons for the rest of his days. That disaster, which made front-page news across the nation, was the destruction of the Sanitarium itself. Nearly fifty years later, Will recalled the morning the Sanitarium burned to the ground with equal parts clarity and indignation:

> The Sanitarium fire of February 18, 1902, occurred six months to the day after I had discontinued working for the institution. Since Dr. Kellogg was not in town and since the sanitarium seemed part of my life work, I met with the members of the boards and offered to come back to work for nothing and board myself as long as my services were needed. The doctor returned late the day of the fire or the following day, and my offer was accepted. . . . During the building of the new sanitarium building, I was given the job, in addition to my other work, of securing the money with which to pay the bills. It frequently happened that on Thursday or Friday the treasury was without funds but in one way or another I secured the funds so that the payroll was never defaulted. These two and one-half years which completed my work of twenty-five years with the San were the hardest years of my life, and no amount of money would tempt me to repeat those years.[82]

7

"Fire!" . . . and Cease-fire

FEBRUARY 18, 1902, began as just another lonely shift for William G. Hall, the San's night watchman. After checking the patient floors, dining room, and main lobby, he wandered down into the labyrinthine tunnels and machinery rooms burrowing beneath the complex's main floor. The only sounds in the dank, steamy byways were the hot air of the hissing boilers and the echo of his leather boots striking the wood-planked floor.[1]

Hall's job that morning, as it was every morning, was to inspect every potential point of unwanted ingress—activities that were exceedingly rare within the borders of Dr. Kellogg's peaceful, medical kingdom. Every thirty minutes, Officer Hall tested the electrical security devices situated along his route. The black metallic boxes, stuffed with wires, bells, and switches, were considered a modern-day wonder in the opening years of the twentieth century. Connected to a series of telegraph wire stations, the devices allowed Hall to communicate urgent messages from anywhere in the San to the "call boy" stationed at the concierge desk in the lobby. That morning, a tall, lanky young man named R. E. Moore was assigned to the desk but for some reason lost to history he did not respond to Mr. Hall's test messages.

At 3:30 a.m., Officer Hall worried that something was amiss with the alarms and ventured into the pharmacy, situated to the rear of the Sanitarium's main building, with the intention of making his way back to the main lobby. As he opened the door to the pharmacy's basement, he "was terrified to hear the crackling of flames." Taking only a few steps down the staircase, he was better able to connect the terrifying dots, a roaring fire consuming everything in its path. Hall ran out of the building and across the lawn, "only a few rods away," to sound the alarm of the Battle Creek Fire Station No. 2.[2]

Less than a minute later, Fire Chief W. Plato Weeks, a long-headed, balding man with intense eyes and jug ears, and Captain George L. Perry, stern in countenance and with close-cropped hair, hurried to the scene accompanied by several firemen. The fire had already spread to the point that flames were bursting out of the pharmacy building's windows and the adjoining bathhouse.[3] Chief Weeks ordered seven hose-men to flood the structures with water. The crew followed his command and soon extinguished what they presumed to be the source of the flames. A satisfied Chief Weeks gave the order to roll up the gear and return to the station with the hope of getting back to sleep.

Before the firemen could put away even one hose, Weeks and Perry felt a violent rumbling beneath the ground on which they were standing. A few minutes after 4:00 a.m., that plot of land gave way to their weight and the two firemen were waist deep in a warm hole. After a bit of digging with his foot, Chief Weeks discovered an underground tunnel containing a tangle of steam pipes originating in the engine room and ending in the main building. The tunnel was five feet wide, eight feet high, and walled by long planks of timber. From the warming temperature of the muddy hole, Weeks realized that the "real" fire was blazing away somewhere in a distant portion of the underground tunnel.

Chief Weeks called in the rest of the firemen in the department to fight what would be the worst conflagration of their careers.[4] As swift as Weeks and his men were, however, the orders came too late. The fire had spread into the bowels of the residence halls, where 307 guests were sleeping. Although a brick veneer sheathed the outer walls, the San's four main buildings were all composed of wood. Making matters worse, the San had recently installed the Otis Elevator Company's newest rope-pulley-operated conveyances to whisk their guests to all six floors of the residence. The airtight, ironclad elevator shafts made for perfect flamethrowers to the upper reaches of the building.

Just as Officer Hall discovered the fire, a "party of 18 or 20 couples" was returning to the Sanitarium from nearby Bedford. Their mode of transportation was a fleet of horse-drawn sleighs. One of the riders, Christo-

The Sanitarium fire, February 18, 1902

pher J. Murphy, recalled hearing someone cry out "Fire!" at about 3:40 a.m. and they turned their sleds in the San's direction to offer help. The men "piled out of the sleighs" to assist "the cripples and others unable to help themselves." Mr. Murphy later told a reporter, "The screams we heard were horrifying. I never want to hear them again, nor see such a fire."[5]

One of those people shouting "Fire!" was Joseph J. Kein. He and his wife, both San patients from Kansas City, Missouri, were slumbering on the east side of the main building's fourth floor. Mr. Kein told a reporter that he first realized something was amiss at exactly 3:48 a.m., when "a peculiar thumping" awakened him and his wife. Upon opening the door to their room, they discovered huge plumes of black smoke wafting their way down the corridor. The Keins pulled their overcoats over their pajamas and bolted down the stairs, leaving all of their valuables behind. Along the way, they pounded on a great many doors, arousing those not already awakened by the clamor.

The Keins were hardly alone in this mission. Nurses, doctors, and attendants worked as a team to get all 307 patients and another 100 staff members safely out of the building. "Here," the *Battle Creek Morning Enquirer* opined, "were to be seen great acts of coolness, on the part of trained men and women, who with their strong hands did deeds never excelled, and as we doubt ever equaled."[6] The *Battle Creek Daily Journal* agreed. "There was no fighting for the escapes. Every person took his or her turn as it came, and the nurses and attendants stood near quieting those who were excited, and assisted them in every way."[7] Dr. Kellogg later explained how he had trained his staff to handle such disasters but even from the distance of more than a century, the calm demeanor displayed by everyone involved is remarkable.[8] That so many "broken-down invalids" suddenly moved like lightning to escape demonstrates both the severity of the threat and the possibility of a psychogenic explanation to a number of these patients' aches and disabilities.

ONLY ONE MAN DIED in the inferno. Abner Case was an eighty-seven-year-old farmer from Bath, New York, suffering from chronic dyspepsia. He had come to Battle Creek, accompanied by his wife and daughter, in search of a cure. When the fire broke out, the Cases were sound asleep in their suite of deluxe rooms on the main building's fourth floor. Mrs. Case tried to stir her husband out of his discombobulated state but even after being awakened, the old man insisted on kneeling at the side of his bed and praying. Mrs. Case and their daughter finally gave up and fled for their own safety. The next morning she sobbed, "The last I saw of him he was sitting at the edge of his bed. Oh I feel so dreadful to think we came and left him. But they kept telling us to come and Mr. Case was crippled and couldn't get on his feet alone . . . we hardly knew what to do."[9]

A San doctor named Howard F. Rand bravely made his way back into the burning building to help Case escape, but upon reaching the exit door the confused man ran back inside, perhaps to retrieve a carpetbag containing $1,100.[10] A few weeks later, on March 5, a nurse and two "call boys" found the charred remains of a human humerus bone (the long bone in the upper arm between the shoulder and the elbow) in the ashen rubble of what was once the San's north wing, near where the Cases were housed.[11] The old man likely died of smoke inhalation and asphyxiation followed by a gory incineration.

By 4:40 a.m., flames were shooting out from a number of windows on all the floors in the main building. One floor above the Cases, Mrs. H. C. McDaniels of Eldorado, Arkansas, awoke to a noisy ruckus outside her room. Her husband was initially too weak to get out of bed, but, unlike Mr. Case, he somehow managed to make his way.[12] Upon opening her door, Mrs. McDaniels saw nothing but darkness as she heard shrieks, shouts, and cries of fear from every direction.[13] This shutdown of electric light may well have saved some lives. An attentive custodian quickly cut off all the power to the San's flammable knob and tube electrical circuits to prevent a secondary source of fire.

Mr. and Mrs. McDaniels, literally, ran into a nurse in the dark corridor. The nurse pointed them toward the rear of the building where they could descend via the fire escape. Mrs. McDaniels and her husband groped along in the pitch-blackness until they reached a window. Directly below, she saw flames shooting toward her. Terrified that she would never be able to hold on to the hot metal fire escape, Mrs. McDaniels jumped to a landing some ten feet below, with the intention of reaching first the rooftop of an adjoining building and, ultimately, the ground. This hastily made plan may have saved her life but it shattered her right femur (thighbone). Fortunately, a fireman named LaVerne Fonda hoisted her over his shoulder and slid "over the edge of the roof to the ladder." Fonda then went back up to retrieve her husband and bring him to the ground as well.[14]

Later that morning, Mrs. McDaniels recuperated in the bedroom of Mrs. Lucy Kelsey, whose home stood a mere two hundred feet from the Sanitarium, across Lincoln Street, but was somehow untouched by the flames. Mrs. McDaniels complained of a sticky attack of catarrh, or post-nasal drip, from the smoke inhalation but freely admitted she was "lucky to have got out of the great fire so cheap as that."[15] A few days later, she added to the price of admission by giving Captain Fonda a $50 reward for saving her life.[16]

With the exception of Mrs. McDaniels's broken leg and the death of Abner Case, the only other injuries involved three Battle Creek firefighters: Fireman Henry Lucas fell from the ladder, wrenched his back, and was badly bruised; Assistant Fire Chief Fred H. Webb also fell from a ladder and suffered bruises but no fractures. Most seriously, Fireman Arthur Robinson fell from a window onto the burning roof. It took more than fifteen minutes to retrieve him. He inhaled too much hot, black smoke and severely scarred his lungs.[17]

Considering the speed with which the fire spread, the wooden complex never really had a chance. The climax of the disaster occurred when the main entrance of the San was engulfed in flames and its seven-story, balconied wooden tower, topped by a copper cupola, plummeted to the ground. Hindered by spotty water pressure, the firemen simply could not get enough water to where it was most needed. Vexing the fire department's every attempt to strategically place their ladders was the tangle of electric and telephone wires surrounding the buildings. By the time the firemen were able to safely move their truck close enough to raise an aerial crow's nest, it was too late.[18]

At 5:20 a.m., the fire spread across the narrow street. Some flaming embers caught wind and set fire to Mrs. Clara F. Salisbury's two-story frame house on the corner of Barbour and Lincoln Streets. Clara was the proprietor of a "hygienic corset firm" and ran a boardinghouse for those San patients on a budget. Next door to the Salisbury house was Mr. and Mrs. Bert Woods's barber and hair dressing parlor. The couple lived above the shop by night and tonsured the heads of San patients by day.[19] The flames spread to their home at 6:00 a.m. and quickly consumed their two-story A-frame bungalow.[20]

By afternoon, the enormity of the devastation was clear. All that stood were a few partial walls here and there, none "larger than ten or twelve feet wide," amid the blackened piles of toppled bricks.[21] Every building of Dr. Kellogg's beautiful Sanitarium was destroyed. Refusing to close down operations, the San's staff opened their homes to house those patients wishing to stay in Battle Creek. In the weeks that followed, the nurses, doctors, attendants, and orderlies worked tirelessly, often without pay, helping the invalids recover and serving breakfast, lunch, and dinner to more than one thousand people. As one employee later recalled: "Houses were mortgaged, savings accounts withdrawn from banks, and every piggy bank emptied, in a magnificent effort to save the Sanitarium."[22]

WHEN THE FIRE BROKE OUT, Dr. John Harvey Kellogg was nowhere near Battle Creek. He was returning home by train after a lecture tour in

What was left of the Sanitarium the day after the fire, February 19, 1902

California. Around midnight, his train made a stop in Chicago's Central
Station. Eager to stretch his weary body before completing his journey to
Battle Creek, he was "met by a newspaper reporter who said 'Dr. Kellogg,
are you going to rebuild?'" To which John replied, "Rebuild what?" The
reporter was incredulous that the doctor was still in the dark and asked
"Don't you know that the Sanitarium burned down last night?" Always
confident on the exterior, John honestly replied, "No, this is the first that
I have heard about it. Of course we are going to rebuild." When told that
the hospital, too, had burned to the ground, he added with a flourish,
"We will rebuild everything." His assistant August Bloese later recalled,
"As soon as Dr. Kellogg entered the train, he called for a table and immediately started to work planning a new building and just before arriving
at Battle Creek was putting the finishing touches on rough plans for a
modern, fireproof sanitarium."[23]

It was just like John to put on a brave front and assume command
in the face of a disaster or emergency. Behind that facade, however, he
struggled to repress overwhelming grief and panic. A few weeks later, the
doctor confessed that immediately upon settling back into his seat in the
train speeding him home:

My heart collapsed as I went back, in thought, over the past history of this Institution and thought of the toil of building up this Institution step by step, and felt that my life had been built into every brick and nail of this institution and I tell you, my friends I felt that something had gone out of my life; I felt as though my best friend had died, and I could not keep back the tears for a moment, and a big lump came into my throat.[24]

Ever resolute, John converted his grief into a swell of excitement and energy. While the embers of the old wooden Sanitarium were still hot and smoking, John realized that the fire was the perfect opportunity to pursue even grander medical dreams. A new San would have to be rebuilt, he reasoned, so why not transform the calamity into a sterling opportunity for constructing the most modern, attractive, and advanced medical center and health resort in the United States? By the time John's train chugged into the Battle Creek station before dawn on February 19, he knew precisely how to proceed. Head held high, he marched off, clutching his sheaf of papers and plans. Meeting him on the platform was the dutiful Will. Before even saying hello or exchanging sympathies over the disaster, John barked at his younger brother to gather together an emergency "mass meeting" of the Sanitarium board and Adventist church Elders, the mayor of Battle Creek and his City Council, clergy from all the other churches in town, and Battle Creek's most prominent and prosperous businessmen and merchants.

A reporter overhearing him cheekily asked the doctor if it would be even possible to rebuild the San given that it "was a great work." The indomitable doctor quickly countered, "I know it is, but in Chicago they build bigger buildings than these will be in sixty days, and if they can do it there we can do it here with the right men." The new San, he insisted, would be ready by the "latter part of the summer."[25] Decades later, Charles MacIvor, another of John's secretaries and, later, food company managers, recalled Dr. Kellogg's enthusiasm that morning as electrifying. The doctor declared to all who would listen:

We have had a fire, all the cockroaches are burned up and now we can have just such a building as we have been dreaming about and planning for so many years. It will be a new modern structure built on the same foundation worthy of the glorious work that is being done here.[26]

THE MASS MEETING Will organized began at 7:00 p.m. in the Seventh-day Adventist Tabernacle, a sprawling red-brick edifice with an ornately arched 108-foot-tall clock tower, topped by a spindly spire. Before the clock struck half-past six, the shellacked oak pews were filled and the auditorium was abuzz.[27] The congregants called it the "Dime Tabernacle" because the entire Battle Creek Adventist community saved and donated their spare dimes toward the church's erection in 1878. When the Tabernacle opened in 1879, at a cost of more than $26,000 (about $637,000 in 2016), the main auditorium seated nine hundred and the gallery accommodated another 1,450. The church also housed a Sunday school with six large classrooms separated by a glass partition, which could be pulled back to seat eight hundred more of the faithful.

The Seventh-day Adventist "Dime Tabernacle,"
Battle Creek

The meeting began with a cavalcade of clergymen offering blessings and prayers followed by the Church Quartette Choir's rousing rendition of Samuel Francis Smith's ode to America, "My Country 'Tis of Thee." One by one, local politicians and prominent citizens ascended the steps leading up to the octagonal stage, framed by two semicircular staircases to the church's gallery. Each man offered his solemn promise to help resurrect Battle Creek's most important economic engine. One was an aged, muttonchopped physician named S. S. French, who regaled the audience with how he had known the San's medical director since his school days. This windbag of a "doc" recited John's impressive medical credentials and boasted about his upright, Christian moral code.

Following Dr. French's oration was the far more entertaining gospel singer and preacher, Ira D. Sankey. The composer of hundreds of hymns and gospel songs, Sankey was nationally known as the "Sweet Singer of Methodism." He was in the middle of a tour of the state of Michigan's Young Men's Christian Association chapters and was spending ten days at the San for rest and relaxation. The gospel singer modestly told the audience tales of his bravery that morning: "The hallway was so full of smoke that I saw it would be risky to attempt to go through it and so I and my wife came down the fire escape. I got her to a place of safety and then went back and helped to get others out of the building." While saving others from the flames, Sankey recounted, "this is only the brick and the pine that is being destroyed, the Institution will arise again and from the ashes I expect to see a more magnificent building than has ever yet stood on this hill."[28] The audience cheered and the Quartette Choir sang, as if on cue, the hymn "It Shall Arise from Its Ashes."[29]

Following this musical interlude, Charles Austin, the program chairman and proprietor of the town's leading produce and grocery store, took the stage and finally introduced the main speaker.[30] Austin's introductory promise for the eagerly awaited comments of Dr. Kellogg was no mere hyperbole: "The more he talks, the more you will want to hear him."

On cue, Dr. John Harvey Kellogg bounded up from his leather-upholstered chair, one of five situated in a semicircle at the center of the Tabernacle's stage, beneath a triptych of stained-glass windows depicting the Ten Commandments. Bouncing off his white suit was the flickering illumination of electric arc lamps suspended from the ceiling two stories above. The dignitaries seated onstage watched with admiration as the doctor slowly and dramatically walked down the stage's orange and brown, diamond-patterned carpet. As he grasped the sides of the ornately carved wooden podium holding his notes, the audience greeted him with a deafening roar of applause and hoorahs. They were articulating the profound empathy they felt for him as a man and their admiration for his important work. Even today, when reading the fading transcript of this "mass meeting," the community's genuine love for Dr. Kellogg during his hour of greatest need remains unmistakable.

The doctor's impassioned speech lasted more than an hour. He reiterated his medical philosophy of biologic living and then spun grand designs for the new San he intended to build. It was to be a modern medical facility rivaling the greatest hospitals of Europe and North America. The new complex would house and heal more patients, generate more curative discoveries, and, because it would attract so many people to the town, accrue mountains of profit for Battle Creek's shopkeepers, merchants, and businessmen. The task would not be easy, Dr. Kellogg warned, the Sanitarium's insurance policy covered only $151,000 ($4.29 million in 2016) in damages. Building the new facility would cost, at least, an additional $100,000 ($2.84 million in 2016) if they were to approach the comprehensive reconstruction he just described. Yet John's confidence, his eagerness to rebuild, and his predictions of success were so infectious that there was not a person in the room who doubted these dreams would come true, no matter what the expense. If John could not raise the capital himself, the audience murmured among themselves, they would find the means to help him and, in so doing, the economic future of Battle Creek.

THE HAUNTING QUESTION THAT LINGERS and refuses to be irrefutably answered is, What started the fire in the first place? Was it merely a random act of chemical combustion and electrical disorder or was the fire sparked on purpose? Over the years, several theories have been suggested, none of them based on much evidence. High on the list, however, is that the blaze was initiated by one or more Adventists acting on the agency of the Whites, or, at least, someone taking too seriously Ellen's ominous sermons of a fire being sent down from heaven to smite the community of Battle Creek.

Long before the San's fire, Ellen White had soured on Battle Creek as the center of all things Adventist. She worried that Battle Creek was in jeopardy of becoming "the Vatican City" of the Seventh-day Adventist denomination. It was a purposeful allusion to Catholicism, still a rather suspect religion in the minds of many Americans, and a connection that she wanted to avoid at all costs. As early as 1882, she recounted a sleepless night in Cooranbong, Australia, during which the Lord advised her to tell her flock to "scatter." She elaborated further, "I have spent hours in agonizing with God over this matter. We need to get ready. It is not God's plan for our people to crowd into Battle Creek."[31]

To bolster her warnings, Mrs. White publicly admonished Dr. Kellogg's imperial ways as a symptom of the greater "Battle Creek problem." For example, in 1897, after learning about the San's new incorporation papers and its state-sanctioned status as a nondenominational institution, Ellen preached that she "not infrequently reminded the Doctor that God had given him the success, which had come to him."[32] Mrs. White again denounced the doctor in March of 1901. Addressing the annual Adventist General Conference in Battle Creek, she offered apocalyptic predictions about the town and its more headstrong inhabitants. Ellen had good reason to be concerned. By this point, John was firmly in control of the most prosperous and famous arm of the entire Adventist movement: the Battle Creek Sanitarium and by extension its nearly fifty San "branches" that had sprouted up in the Midwest, extending to the Rockies and California, all the way to New Zealand, Australia, Egypt, Palestine, India, South Africa, and Japan.[33]

The Whites were equally worried about the rising power of its Battle Creek–based publishing house, the Review and Herald Publishing Association. This enterprise employed more than three hundred people and was sequestering the profits it was generating from publishing popular, secular works, which the Elders deemed to be either sacrilegious or inappropriate. Weirdly, on December 30, 1902, ten months after the Sanitarium burned, the Review and Herald building mysteriously erupted in flames. This building, too, was only partially insured and the losses amounted to more than $300,000 (or $8.5 million in 2016).[34] Electrical wiring was blamed as the cause but many, including John, had their doubts. Writing Ellen White on December 31, 1902, the doctor slyly insinuated, "Last night the main building of the Review and Herald office was burned to the ground and everything in it burned up, an experience exactly parallel to that of the Sanitarium."[35]

Less than a week later, on January 5, 1903, Sister White wrote a letter to "the brethren in Battle Creek" from her winter home in St. Helena, California. In it, she expressed her sympathy for those working at the Review and Herald. Nevertheless, she confessed, she was not surprised by the disaster, just as she was not surprised by the San's fire. She went on to describe a recent vision she had, communicating the Lord's dissatisfaction with the goings-on in Michigan:

> I have seen an angel standing with a sword as of fire stretched over Battle Creek. Once, in the daytime, I lost consciousness, and it seemed as if this sword of flame were turning first in one direction and then another. Disaster seemed to follow disaster because God was dishonored by the devising of men to exalt and glorify themselves.[36]

When it came to which Battle Creeker was dishonoring God by glorifying himself, there can be little doubt that Ellen was referring to Dr. John Harvey Kellogg.

Ellen made her warnings about the sins of Battle Creek even more explicit at the General Conference of the Seventh-day Adventists meeting in Oakland, California, on April 3, 1903:

> The Lord is not very well pleased with Battle Creek . . . and when the Sanitarium there was burned, our people should have studied the messages of reproof and warning sent them in former years and taken heed. That the lives of patients and helpers were spared was a providence for which every one of us should praise God from heart and soul and voice. He gave them an opportunity to live, and to study what these things mean.[37]

Willful as he was, John still considered himself to be a devout Adventist. He could hardly have been pleased to be so soundly denounced in front of the denomination's membership. Ellen White and her son escalated the contretemps by isolating John Harvey in Battle Creek and convincing the General Conference to relocate the Review and Herald publishing house and the church's world headquarters to Takoma Park, Maryland, a suburb six miles from Washington's Capitol Hill.

Perhaps the most troubling speck of evidence suggesting the church Elders were behind the blazes can be found in a letter George Butler wrote to John on January 2, 1905. Long one of the doctor's allies in his many fights against Ellen White, Butler was the director of the Southern Union Conference of Seventh-day Adventists, based in Tennessee. Elder Butler let loose a bomb that is difficult to validate but remains intriguing nonetheless: "I have the testimony of those who heard her say beforehand that she had clearly and plainly stated that those buildings [the San and the Review and Herald] would burn, and they did burn in a most wonderfully rapid way too."[38] That same year, A. G. Daniells, the president of the General Conference and one of John's most virulent foes, groused, "Dr. Kellogg has an imperious will which needs to be broken."[39]

Yet it is precisely this torturous dynamic that has led some retrospective observers to suggest an unstable Adventist congregant interpreted Mrs. White's incendiary testimonies as a message from God to set fire to the San. On the day of the disaster, that rumor took temporary flight when an Adventist bellboy confessed to setting the fire, only to recant an hour later.[40] No solid evidence has yet appeared to corroborate this "confession" or to identify another Ellen White follower as the culprit who burned down the Battle Creek Sanitarium; still, the story—a good one at that—lingers.

IF NOT STRIKING THE MATCH, the doctor fanned the flames of arson allegations during his nonstop spieling in the days after the fire. For example, at the mass meeting on February 19, 1902, John unleashed a stream of consciousness that, in retrospect, can only be described as a kind of Freudian slip:

> I want to tell you, my friends, that when we decided to put up that tinder-box twenty-four years ago this spring, I felt a good many pangs about my heart. You cannot imagine how I wish that I was rich; I wished I had money enough to erect a fire-proof building. I knew what the results might be, of putting so many patients into that building, but, as I have told you, I did the best I could. Some

of you wonder why the patients got out of that building safely. We have been educating certain persons whose duty it was to carry out people from the building when it was burning—for we expected it would be burned, and we have been getting ready for it, because . . . such a building must burn soon or later, and ever since that building has been erected, I have been haunted night and day with the expectation that it would be burned, and that some people burned with it; this thought has been a perfect nightmare to me.[41]

A few days later, February 22, Dr. Kellogg held a "support group" meeting for the patients who refused to leave Battle Creek after the fire. They moved to a smaller building across the street, West Hall, which over the years would house classrooms of the Battle Creek College and the American Medical Missionary Medical College, and, later still, his eugenics-based enterprise, the Race Betterment Foundation. Calling the event an "Experience Meeting," John returned to the topic of the fire's inevitability:

And now we have got a chance to put up a new, safe building, and I am glad—I don't dare say what I think, for fear you will think I set the building on fire,—but I didn't. But I have never doubted but that that [sic] building would burn down at some time, and that it would burn before long, for it has been standing about as long as such buildings do stand.[42]

In almost the same breath, after describing the new, modern safety features he was planning, including spacious hallways and doorways for easier access and exits, call-bells for patients in the event of an emergency, and a safer electrical system, Dr. Kellogg made an even stranger statement of ambiguous culpability: "Deep down in my heart I am glad the building is burned, because now, we will build a better one, and I have been longing for a better building—but I assure you that I didn't set the old building on fire."[43]

IN 1993, the best-selling author T. Coraghessan Boyle proffered the most outlandish theory about the San fire in his brilliant satirical novel

The Road to Wellville, which was adapted into a major Hollywood motion picture in 1994.[44] Ironically, Boyle takes his novel's title from an advertising phrase coined by Will Kellogg's archrival, C. W. Post.[45] The writer uses the San fire as a plot centerpiece and depicts one of John's adopted sons, George, as starting the flames out of some form of misguided revenge. Boyle's George can be best described as a mentally challenged, drunken rogue, partially based on reality and artfully embellished by the author. The real George was the illegitimate child of a Chicago prostitute named Hulda, and the Kelloggs adopted him sometime in 1897 or 1898.[46] In 1901, John wrote a long essay for the *New York Sunday Recorder* telling the story of how he rescued George from the slums of Chicago,

> He was then only four years old, and had been running wild in the streets for a year, receiving practically no care whatever. He picked his living from the garbage boxes and in the gutter, occasionally receiving a crust from some friendly saloon keeper. . . . His heredity was as bad as it could possibly be, and his environment had been up to that time, worse than a savage. . . . He had so little attention that he had not even learned how to talk. He had no ideas. He was covered with vermin. He had practically no hair upon his head, the scalp being one great sore, caused by parasite diseases.[47]

Dr. Kellogg was so moved by the little boy's sorry state that he petitioned a "kind-hearted judge" to let him adopt the tyke. Once the papers were signed, the doctor and "Hulda's Kid" boarded a train for Battle Creek. The doctor brought him home, bathed him in kerosene to kill the vermin, burned his tattered clothing, and nursed his bloody scalp. Within six months, John claimed, the boy, now known as George, was flourishing and sporting a thick crop of curly hair. Enhancing the story even further, Dr. Kellogg concluded, "In three years, he has developed into one of the finest boys of his age that I ever saw—bright, sharp, witty, full of life and energy, rides a bicycle with remarkable skill, swims like a duck, and is an exceedingly promising lad."[48]

The real story was not nearly as wholesome. For years, even after declaring allegiance to the half-baked theories of eugenics, John firmly believed that children could overcome the worst of predestined "natures" by being "nurtured" in an environment of supportive love, healthy routines and diets, Christian faith, and, if needed, discipline.[49] Despite Dr. Kellogg's glowing public descriptions, George was an especially difficult boy to rear. As one Kellogg contemporary recalled, "George Kellogg was one of [John's] adopted kids who didn't pan out. [He was] a drifter and general[ly] no good. [George] later contested [John's] will [and] wanted more from the estate."[50] Poor George's inner demons led him down a path of dissolution, drinking, unemployment, and the constant cadging of loans off his famous father's bankroll.[51]

In the Boyle novel, George's stubborn rebelliousness is nicely captured in a scene where the little boy refuses to hang up his coat on one of the coat hooks in the entry foyer of the Kellogg Residence. Instead, he throws the coat on the floor, much to his adoptive father's chagrin.[52] Each time this occurs, the doctor sternly orders the boy to climb up and down the stairs, reentering the front door each time and hanging up his coat until he correctly completes the required routine. That specific episode, if it happened at all, probably involved a different adopted boy. To be sure, George displayed a definite propensity toward bad behavior and, given his horribly impoverished early childhood, probably exhibited many real, deep-seated psychological issues as well as a plethora of neurological or neurodevelopmental disabilities. The story Dr. Kellogg's colleagues most commonly recounted about George involves the doctor's decree that since the boy was acting like an animal, he would have to sleep in the barn with the animals. George would be allowed to return to the Residence after learning to behave more appropriately. After a few nights, "the little fellow got within a few feet of the doctor, he fairly jumped into his arms and said: 'I don't want to be an animal anymore. I want to be a little boy.'"[53]

Upon the briefest investigation of the 1902 fire, however, the dates of George's adulthood do not at all coincide with Boyle's fictional chronology. In the novel, which mostly takes place during the years 1907 to 1908, George confesses to burning the San down twice, the first time when he would have been about thirteen and, again, as an adult. The motive, Boyle imagines, was out of hatred for his father. In 1902, the real George was still a boy of about eight years old and, of course, the San burned down only once, not twice. Blaming poor George makes for an excellent subplot in a superbly crafted novel but his involvement in the actual fire is most likely fictional.[54] In the end, who or what started the fire, ranging from a deranged Adventist to faulty electrical wiring or a chemical explosion or even John himself, is inescapably lost to the prying eyes of historians and literary rakes alike.

JOHN MAY HAVE OUTWITTED the church elders with the 1897 reincorporation of the San as nondenominational but the Church had its leverage, too. Most of the money invested in the Sanitarium came from Adventist pioneers, including John's father, John Preston. Moreover, a good part of its annual operating budget still came from Adventist coffers. John's lust for expansion had already put the San in debt to the tune of $250,000 (about $7.1 million in 2016). The final estimates on the worth of the destroyed buildings were more than $350,000 (roughly $9.93 million in 2016).[55] The doctor's new plans would easily run more than a full million dollars (a whopping $28.4 million in 2016). This dismal news was not well received by Ellen White, who insisted that no more than $250,000 of Adventist funds would go into the new construction and that this amount was to be generated only by the insurance money and donations, as opposed to new bank loans.

John would have none of that and used the Adventists' monetary rebuke as an opportunity to go directly to the town burghers for the necessary funds. Five weeks later, on March 17, he presented his best case to the right audience. W. R. Wooden, a prize-winning chicken and duck farmer, chaired the second mass meeting, this time at Hamblin's Opera House on West Michigan Avenue.[56] The two-story, red-brick Georgian opera house was not nearly as big as the Tabernacle. There were only 1,200 seats in the down-on-its-heels auditorium and fewer than a quarter of them were filled that night.

The doctor requested a $50,000 bond (or $1.42 million in 2016), an array of tax breaks, and the promise of better fire protection from the city, including a dedicated fire station and water pump directly across the street from the San. In a very different mood from the pep rally held at the Adventist Tabernacle the day after the fire, several of the Battle Creekers present balked and hurled barbed questions at John as to why they should foot the bill for what appeared to be a very profitable medical empire.

Like a well-trained actor responding to his audience, John theatrically took out a huge ledger and, literally, opened the San's books to demonstrate that it was, indeed, a nonprofit organization operating under the laws of the State of Michigan. Fees generated by patients, lodging, dining, and medical treatments went directly into the operating funds needed to run the place, he explained. Any extra money earned was applied to either improving the facility for the next batch of patients seeking help or for charity cases needing medical attention. Dr. Kellogg emphasized that he took no salary for his medical direction of the Sanitarium, save room and board, and that he earned the bulk of his income from the proceeds of his books, public lectures, surgical and medical fees, and burgeoning health food businesses, much of which he also funneled back to the San.

John's flamboyant unfurling of this privileged information infuriated the Adventist leadership. A few months later, at eight o'clock in the morning, on October 19, 1902, the Adventist coterie met at Ellen White's winter home, "Elmshaven," in St. Helena, California. Their discussion centered on the doctor's rebuilding effort and the imperative for him not to "incur large debts." With respect to the money raised at the Hamblin Opera House, Mrs. White was wrong on the figure raised but she, nevertheless, groused, "Twice thirty thousand dollars would have been but a small sum, in comparison with the harm that has been done by allowing this examination [of the San's books] to be made."[57]

Keeping her far-flung Adventist empire solvent, if not profitable, was a concern that weighed heavily upon Ellen's mind, especially after the doctor refused to fully tithe the income he earned from his many health ventures directly to her. John insisted that the money he generated stay in the San's coffers rather than go toward building a church, orphanage, or some other Adventist project Ellen wanted, far from the confines of Battle Creek. Only a few years earlier, on January 25, 1899, Ellen delivered a financially envious sermon and all-points bulletin entitled "To Our Brethren in All Lands." In it, she chastised the Kellogg brothers' nascent health food company as a waste of "precious time." More ominous, she warned that John's avarice presented "great injury to our cause." Offering to resign from the church, John apologetically wrote Mrs. White: "My work has been full of mistakes but I have not been an ambitious schemer. I have been ready to help you, if you had only said the word [at] any moment and with all my might . . . your letter struck me like a thunderbolt and I cannot recover from it. . . . I have gone through the agonies of death over this matter, I have wept until my eyes are dry." He continued the missive by describing his own apparition where he was offered a bicycle to ride across a "very narrow bridge [across a] gulf; it was covered with snow and ice as smooth as glass and arched in the middle." John lost the dream's ending but ultimately interpreted it as a message from God to back away from the Church he had known his entire life.[58]

THE MOST CONVINCING SPEAKER at the second mass meeting was the evening's chairman, W. R. Wooden. The chicken farmer reminded his fellow townsmen that they all profited by the river of misery, illness, and commerce flowing into the San. Moreover, several other communities, stretching from Benton Harbor, Michigan, on the southern shores of Lake Michigan, all the way to Atlantic City, New Jersey, were eager to resettle the San within their city limits. The nearby town of Niles, Michigan, tendered the most serious offer: $200,000 (or $5.68 million in 2016) in cash and forty-five acres of land "beautifully situated on the banks of the St. Joe's River."[59] Charley Post, Wooden declared, was also considering investing some of his many millions into building a competing sanitarium.[60]

The scare tactics worked. Within a week, the Battle Creek bond was fully funded and delivered to the doctor. Unimpressed by this new revenue stream, the San's board and the Adventist Elders urged Dr. Kellogg to stick to their imposed $200,000 limit even though they knew the good doctor would ignore their economic edicts. With each new report detailing how both the bills and plans for building John's new Sanitarium had grown exponentially, Ellen White and her acolytes grumbled and glowered all the more.

Indeed, the fire was the Fort Sumter of the increasingly uncivil war between Dr. Kellogg and the Adventists. Now that the old San was history, the doctor was more determined than ever to strike out on his own and make his lasting mark on the American medical profession. He had outgrown Ellen White's strictures, even if his religious faith and socialization prevented him from actually saying it. And deep down, in the recesses of each of their minds, both John and Ellen knew change was coming.

8

The New San

O N MAY 11, 1902, John Harvey Kellogg hosted a cornerstone-laying
ceremony and announced to all who came that the new San would
not be a "monument" to one man, group of people, or religious creed,
but instead was "a temple to be dedicated to mercy and truth; an institution, the spirit of which shall be all that is noble, sweet, pure, and true, a
practical illustration of good will, beneficence, kindliness, fraternity, and
brotherly helpfulness toward all men."[1] A year later, on May 31, 1903,
the doctor cut a ceremonial red ribbon and gave an even more rousing
speech as he opened the doors to the reconstructed San. The press lauded
his "temple of health" as "great and magnificent."[2]

The new building cost more than a million dollars (or $28.4 million
in 2016) to complete. The Kellogg brothers financed most of it with the
profits earned from the doctor's various book royalties; lecture, medical,
and surgical fees; his food businesses; and a wide network of donations
and loans from the Battle Creek business community, coreligionists, and
former patients across the United States. All of the checks sent by donors
or lenders went directly to Will's accounting office.[3] To each donor, Will
dutifully sent back letters of receipt and news of the fund-raising and
construction process.[4]

THROUGHOUT THE REBUILDING of the new San, the doctor endured
the constant sniping of Ellen White and her increasingly insecure son
William. The real issue, of course, was one of control. The Whites wanted

May 31, 1903. The New San's "Grand Opening" ceremony with
John Harvey Kellogg (right of center) delivering the inaugural speech

to control the San as a subsidiary of the Seventh-day Adventist Church, guided by the precepts of the New Testament as they interpreted them. To John, it was inconceivable that churchmen without a scintilla of medical training would dare tell him how to run his hospital. Fiercely ambitious to join the trailblazers in American medicine, John knew that the San had to be independent of the Adventist Church, even as it remained Christian in spirit. Medical science, he insisted, was to be the authority guiding his empire and practice. Suggesting otherwise meant being disdained, or worse, ignored, by his secular peers making their own great strides in the healing arts. And because he was the San's undisputed star attraction, John insisted on reaping the economic rewards and deciding, without interference, where those riches would be spent. To achieve these ends, John consistently outwitted and circumvented the Adventist leadership's claims of authority, much to their increasing anger. Ellen White, in turn, was not prepared to accept John's haughty claims without a nasty fight replete with complaints, criticisms, and accusations of sinful behavior. The doctor perfectly described his deteriorating relationship with the Whites, on March 30, 1903, when he confided to his friend the Adventist evangelist Stephen Haskell, not without some pride, "I am like a burr in their throats which they can neither swallow nor spew out.

They do not like the taste of me a bit and make wry faces whenever I am around. I seem to be a constant grief to them."[5]

The most serious allegation the Adventist leaders raised against John was supposedly found on the pages of his latest book, *The Living Temple*. He wrote the tome as a vehicle to help fund the construction. In reading this book, buttressed by both the distance of time and objectivity, it appears to be a familiar (if not wholly repetitive) Kelloggian discussion of the structure, function, and care of the body. The book blends his long-held health theories backed by scientific explanations of the day. At several points, the text seems more religious in its tone than his other works but the principal reason for this angle was that the book was addressed to the Adventist faithful willing to pay a dollar a copy, as a donation for rebuilding the San. Throughout *The Living Temple*, Dr. Kellogg emphasized how the human body was a divine creation, which, as Ellen White stated many times, worked in harmony "with the fundamental teachings of both nature and the Holy Writ." The book's title page gives a clearer view of this perspective by quoting Corinthians, Book I (6:19): "Know ye not that your body is the temple of the Holy Ghost?"[6]

Elsewhere in the book, the doctor extended this metaphor to all living things. In other words, Dr. Kellogg explained, the Creator was everywhere and in every living being, extending all the way to the microscopic. This, according to various Adventist theologians, is where John went one step too far. Such a belief, they claimed, iterated that God's will was neither intentional nor providential, that the universe and all of nature was equivalent to the divine, rather than a singular, anthropomorphic deity. Within a few weeks of the book's publication, John's critics charged that it espoused pantheism and, hence, professed the heretical belief there was no singular God in charge of the whole realm of life.[7]

John denied any such claims of being a pantheist. No, no, no, he vehemently protested to Mrs. White and her angry followers. He remained firmly in the camp of the Judeo-Christian monotheists and even offered to remove any passage that offended Sister White or the church Elders. On November 12, 1903, he wrote Ellen an impassioned letter asking forgiveness for his selfish behavior and the promise "to do anything I can to aid in establishing harmony, unity, and peace so that the work may go forward."[8] Disinclined to accept his generous offer, the Adventist leader-ship declared *The Living Temple* to be as inflammatory as the mysterious spark that began the Sanitarium's fire. The book and its author, Sister White commanded, must be extinguished.

Ellen and William White further alleged that the doctor "has united with the arch deceiver in using a hypnotic influence upon souls to deceive them" and that he was inciting "wickedness in Battle Creek."[9] Many Adventists followed suit and took on the task of spreading malicious rumors about John's character both within and widely outside Battle Creek. Others joined in deriding John as a dangerous heretic who was using his position to cast doubt on the veracity of Mrs. White's visions and testimonies. Years later, after the battle finally died down, the doctor would, in fact, question Sister White's claims of being a true prophet, but as late as 1906 he continued to deny such allegations: "I have never denounced Sister White, and never shall. I believe her to be the servant of the Lord, and that the Lord has made her the leader of the Seventh-day Adventist people and movement, and has especially enlightened her mind." On the other hand, even when denying the accusations of his infidelity, he could not help rubbing something caustic into the wound by mentioning in the same breath, "I don't believe her to be infallible."[10]

In spite of such outward signs of bravado, John was emotionally devastated by the Church's attempts to contain his genius and belittle his industry. His "crimes" against the Church included heresy, disloy-alty, slander against the Whites, favoring science over the teachings of the Creator, misappropriation of funds, fraud, and a number of other trumped-up charges. In late 1905, he warned his friend George Butler:

> Don't think I am a screeching fire-eater. If I am wrong in my prog-nostics I shall be happy, but the experience I have had the last six years has taught me a few things. I do not care anything about position. The only thing I am interested in is that I do not want to see you driven out by the same harassing boycotting policy by which they are seeking to drive me out. They have failed in their campaign against me only because they could not do it . . . as far as I am concerned, they have done me all the harm they can; and sizing it all up, it seems they have done me good instead of harm."[11]

The Church's campaign against John reached its zenith in November 10, 1907, when he was unanimously "disfellowshipped" and thrown out of the faith in which he had been reared since birth.[12]

A month later, on December 16, 1907, he wrote "for years I have seen it coming" in an essay entitled "My First and Last Word." John went on to castigate the Church (and especially William C. White) for its attempt to "cripple and destroy the Battle Creek Sanitarium and every work with which I am connected," and defiantly denied the Adventists' charges against him as "whimsical and false."[13] On reflection, John's forced expulsion from the Adventist Church may have been the best thing that happened to his medical career. It freed him to become an independent king of wellness, unshackled by a minority Christian denomination in a world where science was increasingly trumping faith. With respect to his religious beliefs, John remained a Christian in outlook, even if he rarely practiced all its rites or toed the strict line of Adventist theology. His true religion was, and always would be, "biologic living." Nothing, Dr. Kellogg pledged, would get in the way of that crusade. The scriptures he followed most closely now were the articles and books he wrote and the scientific news of the day supporting those writings.

The gentlemen's nurses

The church where he preached his health gospel was the Battle Creek Sanitarium.

FOR A FULL WEEK BEFORE its grand reopening on May 31, 1903, dozens of powerful locomotives and special "excursion trains" arrived at the Battle Creek train station, a Romanesque structure built of rough-hewn Indiana granite and Lake Superior iron-rich brick and topped by a three-story clock tower. A multitude of well-heeled, health-seeking pilgrims exited the trains. They came from all over the world to celebrate the town's new, luxurious Sanitarium. No matter what time of day or night the train arrived, the travelers were greeted by a gaggle of porters, cabbies, and hacks of all shapes and sizes.[14]

On the morning of the opening ceremonies, Dr. Kellogg and Will were warned about a potential dynamite attack on the sparkling new Italian Renaissance building designed by the prominent Dayton, Ohio, architect Frank M. Andrews and erected by the John McMichaels construction firm of Chicago. Fortunately, these threats turned out to be a hoax anonymously sent to a Detroit reporter, who circulated what he thought to be a "scoop" on the Associated Press wire service. Prank or

The ladies' nurses

not, some attendees were frightened enough that Will requested and received an extra large presence of the Battle Creek police force to stand guard during the festivities. By noon, a crowd had congregated on the two-acre front lawn of the San, filling rows of freshly whitewashed seats set up by dozens of staff carpenters earlier that morning. From 1:00 to 3:00 p.m., the building was open for all to tour and promptly closed when the ceremony began "so that the noise of people entering the front doors might not disturb the speakers."[15]

The speakers' platform was "festooned and ablaze with flags and bunting, while upon the flagstaff over the front center [of the building] 'Old Glory' floated proudly in the breeze."[16] A contingent of nurses and distinguished guests began the exercises, led by the redoubtable Dr. Kellogg, to the rousing beat of the Germania Orchestra. As the musicians played marches by John Philip Sousa and W. C. Handy, the speakers and nurses "appeared as well drilled as a body of soldiers. The immense audience gave them a cheer of approval as they took their seats."[17] Patiently standing backstage, Will made sure everyone was in their proper place and that the event unrolled exactly as planned.

There were addresses made by all the usual professional blowhards including Michigan's twenty-fifth governor, the Republican Aaron T. Bliss; Republican congressman Washington Gardner; and a long line of eminent doctors, academics, bankers, and Battle Creek Babbits. The main event, of course, was Dr. Kellogg's keynote address. He did not fail to impress. The new San was dedicated, as Dr. Kellogg asserted that afternoon, "Not as our work, but as God's work, and we ask you to accept it as such."[18] Before closing the ceremony with a benediction by the Reverend Lycurgus McCoy, the longtime Sanitarium chaplain, an army of ushers distributed attractive pamphlets containing congratulatory telegrams from President Theodore Roosevelt, Secretary of War Elihu Root, U.S. Attorney General Philander Knox, and "scores of other high government officials." Later, an evening prayer service, accompanied by an orchestra and a choir singing hymns, was held in the chapel. In the gym, musclemen performed acrobatic drills, and in the parlor the medical staff hosted a "reunion ceremony" for former patients.

The new San's dining room

DR. KELLOGG WAS ESPECIALLY PROUD of the new dining room, "the ceiling and walls of which are adorned with floral designs, fruit pieces, and landscapes."[19] The room's vaulted ceiling and numerous windows were designed to maximize sunlight. A small orchestra played softly in the background during each meal. Prominently painted on the wall on one end of the room, in twelve-inch-high, golden raised letters on a matte black background so everyone could see was the word "FLETCH-ERIZE." The sign was the perfect cue for a ritual that would begin every meal there in the years to come. Dr. Kellogg, or his designate, would lead the diners in the "Chewing Song," memorializing the work of Horace Fletcher, the health advocate who urged his patients to chew each morsel of food forty or more times before swallowing in order to thoroughly mix it with salivary amylase and gently introduce a pre-digested bolus to the stomach and physiological points south. "Chew, chew, chew, that is the thing to do," the song's chorus began, followed by many more verses of musical warnings including, "You may smile when you chew but don't try to talk, too./For perhaps you will choke, and be sorry that you spoke." Ironically, singing the "Chewing Song" probably took longer than the actual "fletcherizing" of the meal itself.[20] Dr. Kellogg was a great admirer of Horace Fletcher's communication skills and often described

Horace Fletcher, circa 1908, a health food faddist, nicknamed "The Great Masticator." He advised people to chew their food forty or more times before swallowing.

him as "a natural born salesman, and when he has a good idea he knows how to present it in such a way that people will accept it and try it."[21]

Although the new dining room had a capacity for eight hundred guests for one meal, even it was too small to house the thousands attending the "grand health banquet" capping the opening day's events.[22] Instead, this meal, the first of many bountiful banquets the San hosted, was held in the gargantuan gymnasium. In the years that followed, scores of medical societies, temperance groups, conventions for teachers, professors, and missionaries, "congresses of nations," Rotarian meetings, and all types of other groups dined there. Six long tables dominated the room to seat the diners, with little alleys between the tables for waiters to scurry back and forth. Dr. Kellogg announced to his guests that all of the food they were about to consume was grown or produced in the San's vegetable greenhouse, farms, dairy, and granary.[23] The subsequent statistics of food consumption at the new San are truly staggering. In 1910, the patients ate "41,319 dozen eggs, 40,282 loaves of bread, 51,206 pounds of butter, 1,600 barrels of apples, 6,000 bushels of potatoes, 1,249 cases of oranges, 1,429 bunches of bananas, and 424 cases of grapefruit," washed down with 19,174 gallons of milk and 27,928 gallons of cream. A decade later, in 1920, "63,816 dozen eggs and 130,814 loaves of bread" were consumed.[24]

FULLY OPEN FOR BUSINESS the following day, a veritable army of health soldiers—twenty attentive physicians, three hundred nurses and bath attendants, and hundreds more masseuses, bakers, waiters, cooks, bellhops, orderlies, and security guards—welcomed guests along the San's stately portico. Upon entering the main doors of the new Sanitarium, the first thing a guest was likely to notice was the clear, fresh air

The San's kitchen

enveloping the place. Air was constantly recirculated with even fresher air from outside by means of an elaborate system of pipes, flues, and fans. On any given day, regardless of the season, the San's ambient temperature was a balmy 70 degrees Fahrenheit by day and a brisk 55 to 60 degrees Fahrenheit by night.

Beyond the heavy brass entry doors was a richly appointed Grand Lobby, anchored by an ornately carved registration desk and topped by

Midwinter vegetables straight from the soil to the San's dining room

The San's vegetable greenhouse

a ceiling decorated "by a world-renowned artist as a token of appreciation." The elaborate ceiling featured geometrical designs in an interlocking fashion and a continuous, molded-plaster chain of wreaths and was held up by a series of majestic columns spiraled by vines of holly.[25] While waiting for their room, newcomers were encouraged to pad around the lobby, arrange for a tour of the place with the friendly concierge, or to take a seat and relax in the finest quarter-sawn oak chairs and sofas available from the Stickley and Sons of Grand Rapids, Michigan, catalog. In the back of the lobby was a fragrant flower balcony featuring ferns, rhododendrons, and hanging plants, atop a brass balustrade, showered by an abundance of light "flooding softly in through the great art-glass windows."[26] One of the windows proclaimed a dictum from Deuteronomy 30:20: "He is Thy Life."[27]

The lobby opened up at its southern end into the Main Parlor where the walls and ceiling were tastefully painted with hues of fresh "cream, and pastel green with touches of gold." Flanked by two smaller private parlors, the focal point of this restive salon was a "big rustic fireplace," where, during the winter, there burned "a real log fire . . . stimulating good cheer and sociability."[28] The main parlor was a welcoming place where "hardly a day or evening passes without a party or entertainment of some kind—a musicale or recital, stereopticon or motion picture, an

The new San's main lobby

address, a pleasant travel talk, a question box lecture by one of the Sanitarium physicians, a concert by the band or orchestra."[29] The wing jutting off the north end of the lobby housed a warren of physicians' offices to examine the male patients and, to the south, several more cubicles and examination rooms for women.

The new Sanitarium's most distinctive feature, however, was a year-round indoor palm garden, topped by a semicircular cone of glass where patients were soothed by sunbeams and "a profusion of growing palms, fruiting bananas and rare exotic plants spread[ing] their luxuriant foliage . . . [and] half hidden by ferns and vines, a gurgling little waterfall find[ing] its way to a limpid pool below."[30] Conveniently placed along the walking paths of this "tropical garden" were benches and chairs, which served as an inviting place of rest and contemplation amid the foliage and the doctor's growing collection of exotic birds and colorful butterflies. In many of the San's advertisements during this period, invalids were invited "to enjoy the restorative rays of Helios" in the Palm Garden while wintering in cold, gray Battle Creek.[31]

Paving the facility's five acres of flooring was an indestructible layer of marble and terrazzo mosaic, in which "germs and vermin can never find a lodging." A stratum of "artificial stone," as concrete was often called at this time, rested directly beneath this impermeable surface, reinforced

*The spectacular Palm Garden, where tropical plants grew and the
sun shined bright, all year round*

by iron cables. Equally important for an institution that had experienced
a total decimation by flames only a year before, Will made certain that
every single wall of this fireproof and frost-proof complex was entirely
constructed of brick, iron, stone, and Portland cement.[32] There were neither wood floors nor wooden partitions. What partitions that did exist
were made of Mackolite, a chemically treated building material, available
in wall form, tiles, and even ceiling beams, composed of ground gypsum
and widely advertised to be "non-combustible" and "vermin proof."[33]
The only wood to be found in the San was the decorative red birch trim
for the windows and doorframes, stained to appear as if it was mahogany,
and golden oak trim in the Grand Parlor. The stairwells were constructed
of iron, slate, and marble; the supporting pillars were constructed of
cement and iron. In all of its promotional brochures, the new San was
heralded as "the only absolutely fire-proof institution of this sort in the
world."[34]

Six steam-operated elevators were at the ready to whisk guests up to
the floors numbered 2 through 5, where four hundred well-appointed
bedrooms and suites were located. Roughly half of these rooms had their
own bathrooms attached, complete with porcelain bathtubs, lavatories,
and the most modern conveniences of plumbing. Those rooms without

private bathrooms offered washstands, basins of water, and ready access to nearby communal toilets, showers, and bathtubs. Each room was furnished with a dresser, mirror, and desk along with a brass bed, which was easier to keep clean than a wooden bed stand. The floors were bare of carpeting. The only exception was a harem of Persian rugs situated around the San's public spaces, but the housekeepers regularly smacked them with rug-beaters to ensure they were dust-free and, thus, harmless to the patients' respiratory health.

Treatment rooms, with space to serve one thousand people in a single day, were located on the fifth and the sixth floors. Surgical patients recuperated on the fifth floor while the operating room suites were on the north end of the sixth floor.[35] At Will's suggestion, the Sanitarium kitchen and dining room were on the sixth floor to prevent the smells of food, which floated upward in the air, from wafting into the guestrooms on the floors below.

Jutting off from the rear of the Sanitarium's main building, like the spokes of a wheel, were three magnificent athletic buildings. The center building housed a fully equipped gymnasium for weight training, volley-ball, badminton, calisthenics, ring and horse gymnastics, and marching drills. The gym also boasted a bank of mechanized exercise contraptions. For example, convinced of the health effects of vibratory movements on both the body organs and circulation, Dr. Kellogg invented a vibrating

Gymnasium drill

machine that connected a jackhammer-like device to a heavy canvas belt to be placed around the waist and buttocks. The theory was that this passive form of vibration ("the machine does all the work," the doctor crowed) melted away unsightly "love handles" plaguing the middle-aged. The machine became a common staple in the "weight reducing" industry of the 1920s and 1930s.

Some of the doctor's other popular exercise devices included vibrating chairs, which were designed to improve circulation to the digestive organs and remove buttocks fat; mechanical kneading machines to stimulate what he called "the crippled colon,"[36] machines that lightly pounded on the back muscles and spine to simulate a "Swedish massage,"[37] tilt tables that ascended and descended eight times a minute to relieve pressure on herniated vertebral discs, revolving ribbed cylinders to stimulate and soothe one's tired feet, a complex series of weights and pulleys,[38] and dynamometers to measure muscle strength.[39] Dr. Kellogg's exercise machines were widely advertised and endorsed by the famous, such as a 1927 advertisement featuring a svelte Barbara Stanwyck, then starring in the Broadway play *Burlesque,* enjoying the benefits of an oscillating "Health Builder" that allowed her to keep fit with only fifteen minutes of "massage-vibratory treatments."[40]

The two other "spokes" housed white-tiled indoor pools and baths of all kinds from Turkish to Russian—and even more attendants and changing rooms; one of the three-story buildings was for men, the other for women.[41] These bathhouses would have made the ancient Romans jealous. Down the hall from the bathrooms was the San's *sanctum sanctorum,* the enema room, stuffed with gleaming "enema machines" that could pointedly deliver fifteen quarts of water per minute into a human colon. Dr. Kellogg advised his patients to produce four or more bowel movements a day, just like the healthy apes he observed while visiting zoos in Chicago, Detroit, and New York.[42] If the water enemas were not enough (a ritual he was said to have engaged in each morning), John ordered his patients to consume a pint of yogurt each day, followed by a yogurt enema, both containing loads of *lactobacilli,* in order to repopulate the bacterial flora of the gut colon with healthy bacteria—a therapeutic aim known today as probiotics and the microbiome of the gastrointestinal tract.[43]

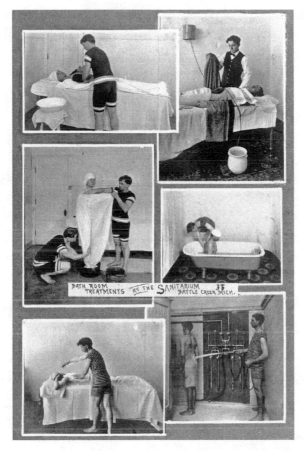

Hydrotherapy at the San

THE NEW SAN WAS ESSENTIALLY a self-contained city. A modern telephone switchboard was built into the basement and connected every room, twenty-four hours a day, seven days a week, with the medical or support staff. Operators were always at the ready to facilitate long-distance lines for guests needing to contact business colleagues or family members during their stays. The massive laundry plant, staffed by sixty-five laundresses, was state-of-the-art. It had to be. Every day the guests went through more than 2,300 towels, 2,000 sheets, 165 tablecloths, and 1,400 napkins. Initially, the facility's ice needs were met by cutting enormous blocks from the frozen Lake Goguac every January, hauled down to the

San by truck, and stored for the remainder of the year in an icehouse. In 1912, the doctor installed modern ice-making machines to replace that antiquated method.[44] Alongside this building was a massive power plant generating the steam and electrical energy required for the Sanitarium's insatiable central heating and cooling, refrigeration, cooking, maintenance, laundry, bathing, electric, and lighting needs.[45]

In 1903, rooms cost $10 to $16 a week ($278 to $444 in 2016) ascending in price with the size of the room and the floor level; suites were $15 to $20 per week ($416 to $555 in 2016). Many medical treatments were included in that price but there were extra charges for a personal nurse, surgeries, and various laboratory examinations. The rates for room, board, and a panel of treatments and exercises would more than double over the next decade as the place became ever more luxurious.[46] Unlike the "average first rate hotel that only offered room and board but no other service except at high charge," the San provided a much fuller package, including "outdoor sports, physical training classes, mechanotherapy [i.e., what we today would call physical and massage therapies], regularly prescribed bath treatments, daily consultations with physicians, health lectures, cooking demonstrations, and the services of trained dieticians." Those on a tight budget registered as "day patients," and took their meals and treatments at the San for approximately $4 to $10 per week ($111 to $278 in 2016). At night, the day patients retired to rented rooms in the cheaper boardinghouses lining the streets near the San. Special rates were offered to physicians, clergymen, and their families, as well as "to worthy objects of charity."[47]

Soon after checking in, a uniformed bellhop escorted the new patient to his room and gave him leave to unpack and settle comfortably into the room. Guests often rested a bit and became acclimated to their new surroundings before making their way upstairs to take their first meal in the dining room. A white-uniformed hostess led them to a special table for newcomers called the "Reception Table," where a dietitian introduced them to the many "dainty and delectable health dishes" served there. Once a week, there was a "Get-Acquainted" banquet so that the patients might meet one another, share experiences, aches and pains, and meet the staff members.[48] As one guest recounted, "everyone seems earnestly interested in the welfare of everyone else—and the workers are kind not only to guests, but to each other."[49] Following this session, the new patients returned to their rooms and were off to bed by 9:00 p.m.

The next morning, at 6:00 a.m., an orderly knocked gently on the new patient's door and escorted him or her downstairs to the bath department for morning sprays, swimming, and "surf baths." Following this was a brisk rubdown and a few minutes under a fan to cool and dry the skin and stimulate the blood flow. Once massage therapy was complete, a prayer service was held in the Chapel for those wishing to attend. And when "breakfast time" was announced by the briskly walking bell-hops clanging their loud bells, everyone "hastened to the big elevators to ascend to the dining room."[50]

After breakfast, a starched young nurse introduced herself to the new patient and escorted him down for the medical examination. A more proper name for this procedure might be a "physical inventory" because the examining doctor carefully went over all one's strengths as well as health weaknesses with the express purpose of "divorcing many people from imaginary ills."[51] Each patient was matched with a physician who was "especially qualified by training and experience to best deal with his particular case."[52]

The wealthiest and most famous patients were typically assigned to the genial Dr. Kellogg, but when any patient requested him, as he routinely announced "all you have to do is leave word," he would arrange an appointment.[53] When John laid on his healing hands and charm, he reliably made each patient feel as if their case was of the utmost importance to him; and it was. A showman at the lecture podium but always a physician in the clinic, he was one of those rare doctors who took a deep interest in all his patients. When a patient spoke with Dr. Kellogg about his health problems, he felt as if he had the doctor's undivided attention; and he did.[54] Even for those who did not see Dr. Kellogg during the initial examination, the San's promotional brochures reassured newcomers that he took great pains to supervise every case admitted to the San and attended a weekly medical staff conference monitoring their progress. In 1897, for example, Dr. Kellogg performed over one thousand operations and personally examined 75 percent of the patients admitted to the San.[55]

A doctor examines a new patient at the San

IN THE EXAMINATION ROOM, both parties sat facing each other
on comfortable chairs. The office was furnished with an examination
table and a small roll-top desk overflowing with instruments and papers.
Directly above the desk was a nine-drawer card catalog of patient files
and a shelf holding a few cherished medical textbooks, including what
many physicians considered to be the bible of medical practice, *The
Principles and Practice of Medicine* by Sir William Osler.[56] The entrance
examination in 1916, for example, cost $25 (about $556 in 2016). Just as
today, the fees for medical examinations and procedures increased with
each passing year.[57]

The doctors, a mix of mostly men and a few women who trained
under the doctor's tutelage at his missionary medical school, began by
launching into a series of queries about the patient's life, social circumstances, physical symptoms, aches and pains, bowel movement and

urination patterns, sexuality, all the way to psychological questions per-
taining to mood, stability, nervousness, and irritability.

After a thorough medical history, the doctor began his physical examination by taking the patient's blood pressure and pulse. It was a gentle
prelude to the patient disrobing as modestly as they felt comfortable.
From there followed a delicate dance of his hands and fingers across
the chest and abdomen and elsewhere to percuss and palpate the organs
for size, shape, consistency and for evidence of chronic constipation.
Women complaining of menstrual disorders, vaginal pain, and other
gynecological complaints underwent a pelvic examination in the presence of a chaperone, whether the examining physician was a man or a
woman. Muscle strength and tone, physique, posture, and neurologic
and reflex responses to the doctor's rubber hammer were recorded on
graph paper and, if found to be abnormal, documented by the San's
medical photography department.[58]

Eager to show off the San's allegiance to modern medical practice, the
doctors tested every patient for evidence of diphtheria, syphilis, gonorrhea, typhoid fever, and trichinosis by means of bacteriological or parasitic cultures. These maladies were discovered or ruled out only after
instructing the patient to deposit a specimen of urine and stool, obtain

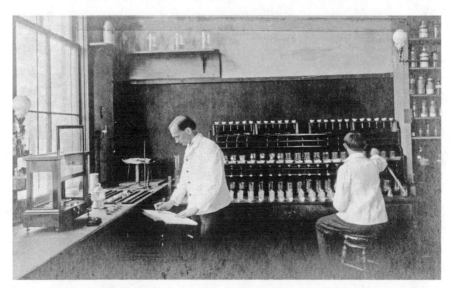

The gastric laboratory, one of many clinical laboratories at the new San

ing a blood sample by means of a sharp needle and rubber tourniquet, and, perhaps most traumatic, snaking a long tube through the nose and down the esophagus, to capture an ounce or two of the stomach's contents. All of these specimens were safely placed in small glass tubes and cups, sealed tightly with wax paper tops, and clearly identified by affixing the patient's name on the container's side in black grease pencil. An orderly appeared out of nowhere and whisked them all away to the basement where they were analyzed in the Sanitarium's ultramodern chemical, bacteriology, and gastroenterology laboratories.

The latter was designed to approximate the laboratory of the famed gastrointestinal physiologist Ivan Pavlov.[59] Dr. Kellogg was so enamored by Pavlov's scientific methods that in 1907 he hired the Russian physiologist's former student, Vladimir Boldyreff, to start up a Pavlovian laboratory of gastroenterology and digestion in Battle Creek. Upon his return, Dr. Kellogg wrote a gushing fan letter to Pavlov and told him that he had hung up a portrait of the Russian scientist in his office.[60] Sixteen years later, in 1923, Pavlov made a grand tour of the United States and insisted on a special trip from Chicago to Battle Creek.[61] Pavlov sought out Dr. Kellogg for more than the mere reunion between old friends. At the age of forty, the Russian physiologist was diagnosed with "neurasthenia or hysteria, but he believed he was suffering from a degenerative disease of the nerves." Hence, the Sanitarium served as a superb place for him to relax in "extraordinary quiet and peace" and, if not to take the waters to, at least, take the enemas offered there every day.[62]

By 1913, every patient at the San underwent a chest X-ray to rule out tuberculosis, and, if he or she complained of stomach or digestive distress, a fluoroscopic examination of the stomach. In all, the doctors had more than thirty radiologic tests to help make a diagnosis.

Upon determining what course of treatment was required, the doctor then handed the patient a prescription booklet bearing his name and case number. Unlike the prescription pads so coveted by today's patients as an "open sesame" to a pharmacopoeia of pills and elixirs, drugs were studiously avoided at the San. Instead, the thickly bound San prescription booklets listed the treatments specifically prescribed for each patient, demonstrating that nothing at the San was cut-and-dry.

A patient undergoing phototherapy. Dr. Kellogg found that bright lights, resembling sunlight, improved one's mood.

Each treatment was "based upon the exact knowledge of the patient's individual needs."[63]

For example, there existed more than two hundred water, or hydriatic, treatments "comprising sprays, douches and baths, each having a different effect and being designed to relieve different conditions of suffering."[64] For obese patients, electrotherapy was used, at low levels of sinusoidal current, to produce muscular contractions, thus allowing the heavyset and sedentary to "passively exercise." For those who were depressed, an electric light cabinet allowed them to spend time under bright "sun lights" that reproduced the naturally occurring phenomenon that was (and is) so rare in southeastern Michigan from late fall to the early spring.[65] Dr. Kellogg was ahead of his time in considering the effects of sunlight on mood, an entity now known as seasonal affective disorder, wherein the gray, sunless winter literally, brings on "the blues."[66] Others underwent diathermy (electrically induced heat) treatments for muscle relaxation, and radium therapies, which were often overused to attack skin conditions like acne and warts and, in some cases, malignant tumors.[67]

Most important was the dietary regime prescribed to each patient. At every meal, the patient found a marked-up menu left by his or her

Counting calories and eating the Dr. Kellogg
way: a typical San dinner menu, May 19, 1916

plate selecting the proper foods complete with a careful calculation of the calories, proteins, carbohydrates, and fats to be consumed during the meal, specially designed, counted, and analyzed for the patient.[68] Well ahead of his colleagues practicing elsewhere, Dr. Kellogg was also certain to remind his dining guests about the importance of portion control as well. "There is a beautiful song," he often told guests sitting down to dinner, " 'Count your blessings, count them one by one.' Somebody has written a parody of it, 'Count your calories, count them one by one.' I think we shall have to have it sung here once in a while to remind you of it."[69]

WHEN THE NEW SAN OPENED, Saturdays were still strictly observed as the Sabbath, a complete day of rest in accordance with the Seventh-day

Adventist Church. This practice continued for several years even after Dr. Kellogg was expelled from the Church because the majority of the San's staff were the Seventh-day Adventist faithful and would not work on Saturday. Dr. Kellogg acquiesced because these former coreligionists worked for relatively low wages, helping his bottom line considerably. The doctor preferred to spend his Saturdays writing, lecturing, experimenting with new foods, and traveling to Chicago for his weekly medical missionary work.

The guests who had no affiliation with the Seventh-day Adventists were less than pleased by the San's shuttering down each and every Saturday. For example, the famed muckraking novelist Upton Sinclair and his often-ill wife, Meta, visited the Sanitarium in 1909, three years after his exposé of the meatpacking industry, *The Jungle,* jolted the U.S. government into enacting food purity laws. Sinclair, a well-known health enthusiast, socialist, and practicing hypochondriac, adopted many of the doctor's dietary, exercise, and lifestyle recommendations. Nevertheless, he complained bitterly about how the place completely closed down every Friday evening all through to Saturday night, out of Adventist piety, only to return back to life on Saturday at sundown with "a little celebration, like Easter's or New Year's, with what I used to call 'sterilized dancing'—the men pairing with men and the women with women."[70]

Dr. Kellogg gradually relaxed this schedule to appease his growing census of non-Adventist guests and maintain the San's status as a tax-exempt, nonsectarian institution. The San held Sunday school classes and chapel services for those practicing other Christian denominations and wishing to observe the Sunday Sabbath. After Ella Kellogg's death in 1920, the doctor grew less enthusiastic about the Saturday services. During the early 1920s, Saturday schedules included recreational events, although Saturday chapel services were still held for Adventists (many of them employees) seeking a place to worship.[71] By the 1930s, the "Saturday Sabbath observance at the San was perfunctory."[72]

FOR THE REST OF THEIR TIME in residence, the San patients rarely had more than a few unscheduled minutes during their day. The mornings after the initial examination were devoted to various exercise or therapy sessions, punctuated by breakfast and optional prayer services. At

Breathing exercises

noon an hour of rest was strictly enforced followed by dinner at 1:30 p.m. Afternoons were devoted to the "fresh air cure and out-of-doors exercise" including tennis, horseback riding, swimming, badminton, croquet, and similar recreations on the San's manicured campus. Also available was an army of bicycles, horse-driven carriages, and sleighs at the ready for rides through the San's labyrinth of wooded trails and deer park. At 4:00 p.m., patients underwent a second treatment session but were back in their rooms to prepare and dress for supper at 6:00 p.m.

Evening activities consisted of a full program of entertainments and diversions ending at the sounding of the "retiring bell" at 8:30 p.m. Each week plays, musicales, and later, motion pictures, were presented in a sumptuous auditorium boasting a state-of-the-art public address system. In the ballroom were nightly dances with a full orchestra. In the men's parlor were billiard tables and, in the basement, a bowling alley. On most nights, at 7:00 p.m., one of the medical staff presented a lecture on a topic certain to draw a crowd. This excitement was especially the case when Dr. Kellogg was in residence.[73]

Perhaps the farthest-reaching activity at the San was the "Grand March" held each evening on the San's rooftop. It was essentially an aerobics and calisthenics session led by Dr. Kellogg to the accompaniment of the San's orchestra brass section. So popular were these exercises

The daily "Grand March" on the San's rooftop

that in 1923 the Columbia Gramophone Company asked Dr. Kellogg to record an album of ten 78-rpm shellac discs (each disc, much like a prizefighting match, was called a "Round"). The album was titled "Dr. John Harvey Kellogg's HEALTH LADDER" and was accompanied by a booklet describing and diagramming dozens of strengthening exercises for the back, abdomen, legs, and arms that the doctor orchestrated every evening at the San. The person at home would play each disc on his or her gramophone, imagine himself in Battle Creek, and work out as the recorded Dr. Kellogg called out a menu of bends, bows, and stretches. To keep the beat, the doctor counted each repetition while the San's brass band played rousing, rhythmic tunes in the background. Dr. Kellogg exhorted his long-distance listeners to work out and keep fit: "sedentary people die from stagnation. . . . They are smothered to death . . . everyone needs exercise. Persons past middle age and chronic invalids (few persons over forty are wholly free from chronic disease) need exercise even more than do persons in health."[74]

Making these records was no easy task and required many takes along with the exasperated assistance of John's secretary, August Bloese:

> Dr. Kellogg acted like a drill sergeant and kept time while I performed the exercises. He invariably forgot to start the watch of [*sic*]

lost track of the number of movements of the exercise. Something usually went wrong, so I had an exhausting time. The exercises were successfully recorded. The company, however, went out of business before the records could be put upon the market. All that Dr. Kellogg received for his trouble was a batch of records.[75]

In fact, the records sold rather well and the Columbia Gramophone Company stayed in business for quite some time after recording the doctor's exercise album. More to the point, decades before Jack LaLanne, Jane Fonda, Richard Simmons, and others made an industry out of exercise tapes and videos, John Harvey Kellogg was toning up thousands of listeners who may have never visited Battle Creek but who joyfully interacted with him daily by playing these inspiring (and expiring) recordings on their phonographs.

PART III

Manufacturing Health

Will Kellogg's cereal factory: the packing room, circa 1920

9

The San's Operations

Biologic living aside, there was a great deal of surgery going on at the San and Dr. Kellogg performed most of those operations. In his earliest days of running the Sanitarium, the young doctor hired moonlighting surgeons from Detroit, Chicago, and Ann Arbor to perform surgery in Battle Creek. John, used to far better outcomes at Bellevue Hospital, was appalled by his hired surgeons' skyrocketing mortality rates. Equally discouraging was the paucity of follow-up care delivered by these per diem blades, who typically beat a fast track out of town shortly after the last stitch was sewn into place. On too many late nights, Dr. Kellogg frantically called these surgeons back to the San's operating rooms to amputate patients' limbs or remove more diseased tissue because the hastily performed procedures went awry with postoperative infections.

Beyond the desire to ameliorate complication rates, John quickly grasped that the fees generated by outside operators represented a lost cash bonanza for the San. By establishing an in-house surgical service, the extra income would help raise the San's bottom line, rather than paying off the proceeds to the outside surgical contractors. Consequently, Dr. Kellogg revised his initial plans to conduct a medical practice that did not include cutting into living human flesh. But because he had no formal training in this delicate craft, he had to learn how to perform surgery all the while he was building and expanding the San, maintaining his ever-growing roster of patients, lecturing around the country, and producing a long written record of his ideas and work.

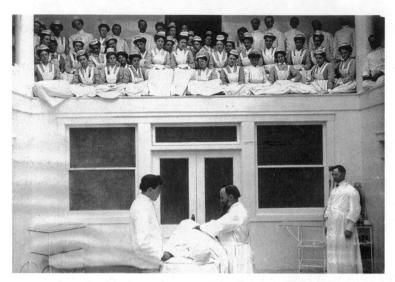

*Dr. Kellogg operating on a patient at the American Medical
Missionary College. In the viewing gallery is a rapt
audience of student nurses.*

Such "postgraduate work" was no easy task. Nearly a decade into his
career as a surgeon, he remained anxious about every procedure he performed and once told Ellen White that he relied upon God's will to tolerate the sight of blood and the anguish of cutting into a living human
being.[1] To satisfy his perfectionism, in the 1880s Dr. Kellogg began a
thorough study of surgical techniques by making a series of observa-
tional trips to Europe's leading hospitals in Vienna, Paris, London, and
Edinburgh, where many of the world's operative masters plied their
trade.[2] Every time John returned from Europe, he came back loaded
with techniques he wanted to replicate in the San's suite of white-tiled,
well-ventilated, and sky-lit operating rooms. Above all, it was John's
attention to detail, his systematic review of the latest surgical journals,
and his constant practice of new methods that made the San's operating
rooms hum with efficiency.[3]

IN 1888, FOR EXAMPLE, Dr. Kellogg visited the Vienna General Hospital (*Allgemaines Krankenhaus*), the leading institution of its kind in the
world. Instead of currying favor with a young Jewish neurologist named
Sigmund Freud, whose psychoanalytic musings on hysteria would have

seemed odd, indeed, to the son of an Adventist broom maker, John spent his days in the operating theater of Theodor Billroth, a pioneer in abdominal surgery.

In the days before antacids and other pharmacological wonders relieved gastroesophageal reflux and "acid indigestion," stomach and intestinal ulcers were commonplace occurrences among many men and women. The pain brought on by a gastric ulcer is so difficult to bear because it feels as if sharp nails are scratching the inner surface of one's stomach. This pain is especially intense after consuming a meal, which stimulates the stomach to secrete loads of scorching hydrochloric acid, further irritating the ulcerated, raw sore. There also existed the very real risk of that ulcer eroding the stomach or intestinal wall so that it perforates entirely through, much like the blow-out of a tire. Such medical emergencies often ended in a bloody, painful death.

To correct these ills, Dr. Billroth devised a series of operations in which large portions of the stomach were entirely removed. This drastic solution obviated the immediate harm of a perforated ulcer but it disrupted one's digestive process long after the surgical wound healed. John was astute enough to know these were procedures he needed to learn, even if he used them only as a last therapeutic resort. The great Billroth was too busy to give John the personal attention he craved but the surgeon's first assistant, Anton Wolfer, privately tutored him on mastering the technique, in return for a healthy stack of Austrian kroners.[4]

Dr. Kellogg also studied under a world-famous gynecological surgeon named Lawson Tait at the University of Birmingham in Great Britain. Women suffering from what were delicately referred to as "female problems," including vaginal tears from childbirth, sexually transmitted diseases often unwittingly contracted from straying husbands, painful uterine fibroids, prolapsing uteruses, ectopic pregnancies, and ovarian, uterine, and cervical tumors, frequently came to the San seeking help. Hence, John was always on the lookout for improved methods to handle such problems. In 1889, when he first visited Birmingham, Dr. Tait was on an unprecedented surgical roll of completing 116 successive operations without a single infection or complication. This was a phenomenal accomplishment in an era where 10 to 20 percent of all surgical procedures ended in death.[5] The number becomes even more striking given Tait's initial opposition to the germ theory of disease and Dr. Joseph

Lister's doctrine of surgical antisepsis, wherein all instruments and the surgical wounds were sprayed with the antiseptic carbolic acid to kill the germs in the operating room and the surgical wound. Nevertheless, Dr. Tait was hardly the dinosaur some medical historians have claimed him to be. He strongly believed in the importance of operating in a scrupulously clean environment, one that today might be classified as "aseptic" or germ-free conditions, even as he eschewed and vigorously debated Lister's harsher chemical approach.[6] Like a surgical sponge, Dr. Kellogg absorbed Dr. Tait's emphasis on operative skill and sanitary precautions. On the same trip, John spent a month at the Samaritan Free Hospital for Women in London observing several Listerian gynecological surgeons practice their craft, so that he might acquaint himself with their techniques, as well.

Incidentally, Lawson Tait's successful operative record was one he substantially increased in the years that followed. The surgeon did have a rather keen competitor in the United States, however, who performed 165 successive operations using the Tait techniques without a single postoperative infection: his name was John Harvey Kellogg.[7] In an era before aseptic surgery and sterile rubber gloves became the gold standard, this record of success is a superb testimony to Dr. Kellogg's operative skills.[8]

At London's famed St. Bart's Hospital in 1907, and again in 1911, Dr. Kellogg studied under Sir William Arbuthnot Lane, one of Great Britain's most prominent gastrointestinal surgeons. Lane, like Dr. Kellogg, was fascinated by the now discarded disease entity known as autointoxication, which was thought to have resulted from chronic constipation. The theory behind this malady was that the poisons emanating from the retained stool (and undigested, putrifying foodstuffs, such as meat) caused problems ranging from anxiety and neurasthenia to depression, chemical imbalances, and far worse. Lane's savage cure was removal of most of the colon, a procedure Dr. Kellogg found too drastic for his taste.[9]

BACK IN BATTLE CREEK, John began each operation by leading his surgical team in prayer, often before the patient was put under the anesthetic. Several patients commented on how much they appreciated this devout touch. John told his patients after they recovered that kneeling in prayer before operating calmed his apprehensions.[10] Always knowing how to play on the doctor's insecurities, Ellen White declared that she had a vision where "heavenly beings" guided Dr. Kellogg as he surgically ventured into the human body. With the passage of time, the doctor grew resentful of such comments, fearing that patients might expect too much from him and, perhaps more pragmatically, diminish the respect of his secular colleagues who routinely took full credit for their own surgical successes.[11]

In fact, Dr. Kellogg took great pride in his dexterity with the scalpels and forceps he routinely manipulated. The doctor modestly attributed these skills to his being a "delicate child" who often stayed indoors with his mother while she taught him to sew. It will also be recalled that as a boy working in his father's broom factory, he was among the best workers at sorting the broomcorn and making brooms. Yet a more cogent reason John was so good at stitching up wounds was that he practiced the craft during any free moment he could find. On many of the long train rides he took for his lectures, meetings, hospital visits, and weekly stints at the Chicago Mission, John would put aside the latest manuscript he was composing to practice making tiny incisions on rough pieces of cloth and elegantly sew them back together. Dr. Kellogg was also quite handy with pen, ink, and paper and often drew his own surgical illustrations to accompany the reports he wrote on the procedures he conducted. Sketching, he insisted, was an important part of his skill building because "the hand is trained to follow the eye," a critical skill for any surgeon.[12]

Many of his surgical colleagues admired his abilities in the operating room. For example, Howard Kelly, the famed gynecological surgeon at Johns Hopkins Hospital and a devoutly evangelical Christian, often visited Battle Creek and assisted John in the San's operating suite. Kelly was said to have "tears in his eyes when he watched" Dr. Kellogg perform surgery. At several public gatherings over the years, Dr. Kelly stated, "John Harvey Kellogg [was] the most skillful surgeon [I] ever saw operate."[13] In recognition of his skills, John was nominated and elected to the prestigious and highly exclusive American College of Surgeons in 1914, only one year after it was founded.

Similarly, Dr. Charles Mayo, of the eponymous Mayo Brothers Clinic, once examined a patient and observed, "I see that Dr. Kellogg has operated on you." The patient confirmed Mayo's assessment and then asked incredulously, "How could you have known who had done the operation?" Dr. Charlie was said to have replied, "That's easy. The scar is small and neat, just like a signature."[14] Dr. Kellogg befriended both Mayo brothers and made many a pilgrimage to their famous surgical clinic in tiny, cold Rochester, Minnesota. A colleague later complained that the Battle Creek Sanitarium did not develop into an enduring Mayo Brothers–type enterprise because John refused to departmentalize and build up specialists and let them run their own practices. "[He] insisted on doing it all himself. [He] was something of an exhibitionist."[15] His biographer, Richard Schwarz, was even more blunt: "loathing self-seeking, John was always concerned lest some colleague or relative try to use association with him for personal advancement. The suspicion often led Kellogg to appear sharp and critical and undoubtedly kept many of his associates from becoming really friendly with him."[16]

ONE OF JOHN'S GREATEST CONTRIBUTIONS to modern surgery, even if he never received due credit for it, was insisting that his surgical patients engage in moving about as soon as possible after the operation. The standard of care at this time was the exact opposite and most surgical patients were strictly confined to a hospital bed for several days to weeks at a time. Today, we know that many of these recumbent patients developed thrombi, or blood clots, which have the power to break off into emboli and clog the arteries wherever they lodge, including the brain, heart, and lungs, often ending in serious disability or death. Many patients also developed bacterial pneumonia as a result of lying too long in bed and breathing in too shallow a manner, allowing mucus and infectious microbes to take root in their chests. Not so on Dr. Kellogg's postoperative ward. Although he stuck to the notion of postoperative bed rest, he ordered his recuperating patients to perform a series of graded physical and deep-breathing exercises while in bed, on the day after surgery and every day thereafter while in the hospital. Today, early ambulation and breathing exercises are a basic (and vital) premise for recovery from nearly every surgical procedure.[17]

Unlike many surgeons of his day, Dr. Kellogg insisted on keeping his patients well hydrated. He encouraged them to drink several large glasses of water before going under the knife and administered water enemas immediately after an operation, while the patient was still anesthetized. Given the high risk of surgical shock from the abrupt loss of body fluids, especially in the years before intravenous fluids were developed, Dr. Kellogg's devotion to "hydrotherapy" likely had a beneficial impact. Another way he mitigated the risk of surgical shock was by inventing an operating table heated with hot water, so as to keep the patient as warm as possible during the procedure. Afterward, he surrounded the patient's body with warm sandbags.[18]

Dr. Kellogg did not quit the operating room until he was eighty-four and performed more than 22,500 operative procedures. During most of his career, he spent two to three days a week in the operating room. On an average day, he performed about twenty-five procedures over an eight- to ten-hour period, many involving the removal of hemorrhoids, ovaries, gall bladders, and appendixes. Most of the surgical fees John generated over this period were donated to the Sanitarium or earmarked for his latest medical crusade rather than lining his pocket.[19] In the first half of 1905 alone, for example, he billed more than $27,000 (or $562,000 in 2016). Approximately one third to one half of the operations he performed were on patients who could not afford surgery and who were not

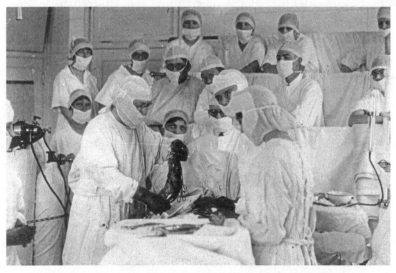

Dr. Kellogg (left) operating on his 75th birthday, February 26, 1927

charged for his services. In a surgical version of Robin Hood, John often charged fees as high as $1,000 on a rich man so that he could afford to operate on a poor one for free.[20]

ODDLY, Dr. Kellogg insisted on dominating all of the gynecological work rather than "assigning it to lady doctors."[21] Over the years, he performed thousands of such procedures with great care and success. One of the most frequent reasons he took a woman into the operating room was for "external and internal massage of the womb." Dr. Kellogg describes this method in his 1883 textbook, *Ladies Guide in Health and Disease: Girlhood, Maidenhood, Wifehood, Motherhood:*

> This new application of massage has won many brilliant successes in the hands of skillful operators. There are three modifications of the treatment; external, internal, and the two combined. Only external massage can be properly employed by untrained persons. The operation consists in grasping the uterus between the two hands, first compressing it and then applying a rolling motion. This should be alternated every minute or two with an upward movement applied with both hands in such a manner as to lift the womb from the pelvis. To facilitate the treatment, the patient should lie with the hips elevated upon a pillow or cushion. The movements should be applied with care and great gentleness at first, and no violence should ever be employed.

The womb massage sessions lasted for ten to thirty minutes and were administered twice a day. The women submitting to them became so exhausted from the sensation that they typically required a half hour's rest, "in a horizontal position . . . after the conclusion of the treatment."[22] Few women complained and many returned for more such treatments over the years, suggesting that there was some amount of pleasure, or, at least, a modicum of strangely positive gain involved in submitting to Dr. Kellogg's healing hands.

At this late date, it is difficult for even the most intrepid medical historian to decipher just what exactly Dr. Kellogg was treating with pel-

vic massages. Unorthodox to the extreme, there developed much talk
and intense curiosity about the practice in Battle Creek and beyond. In
1961, John's longtime colleague, Dr. William Sadler, mused about how
the pelvic massages might give rise to suspicions regarding Dr. Kellogg's
relations with his female patients, but ever faithful to his mentor, Dr.
Sadler insisted that John "was above reproach in all his attitudes toward
women."[23]

DURING THE TWENTY-TWO YEARS Will Kellogg handled and managed the San's more mundane operations in the laundry, greenhouse,
vegetable farm, gymnasium, treatment facilities, dining room, grounds,
and bathhouses, he made certain that the proverbial trains always ran on
time. Will created and supervised all of the San's policies and procedures,
other than the medical ones laid down by the doctor. He was also the
reliably trustworthy keeper of the San's many secrets, including the occasional sexual peccadilloes of the medical staff, as evidenced by a diary
entry he recorded on May 5, 1884:

> I run acrost [sic] a letter from a Miss S to Dr. [J.H.] in which she
> confessed that Dr. F. had seduced her [,] had her for his mistrest
> [sic] for quite a while [.] loved her better than his wife [.] knocked
> her up and performed an abortion on her of a four months kid.[24]

Above all, the San served as Will's business school and it was there
where he learned to run a big complex organization with lots of people,
machinery, specialized facilities, and activities that required his constant attention and upkeep. It is unclear if Will ever read the entirety of
Frederick Winslow Taylor's influential book *The Principles of Scientific
Management,* but he certainly read abridged magazine article accounts
of it. Taylor was the famous engineer who "conducted time and motion
studies during the 1880s and 1890s to reformulate and systematize industrial work tasks" for maximum output by workers supervised by foremen
and executives.[25] From his earliest years working at the San, Will was
fascinated by record-keeping systems and other newly developed means
to make his business run more smoothly. Years later, he made scientific

management a touchstone of his cereal business. As such, he frequently consulted with experts on the latest developments in advertising, marketing, and mass production.[26]

Will often lamented that he never received any "glory" for making the San work so gloriously every day. His days (and nights) were spent accounting for a huge hospital, kitchen, dining room, and hotel, filled with demanding guests. In the Sanitarium, there were countless sheets, towels, and dining linens to buy and launder. Hundreds of bedrooms needed to be made up just so, lest the guests complain. Bathrooms, showers, and changing rooms required constant attending and cleaning as did the gymnasia, swimming pools, lobby, parlor, and the other public rooms and outdoor sporting areas. The dining room was a four-star specialty restaurant serving thousands of meals per day. There was always a raft of bills that needed to be paid, supplies to be purchased and inspected, and a line of new guests to register and please.

Will had his fingers in each and every pot and knew exactly what he was doing at all times. He also had the manager's skill in "manipulating people for maximum advantage," a talent his grandson Norman Williamson Jr. later lamented "was carried over into his relations with his family.[27] Will realized early in his career that supervising these complex enterprises required more than a keen mind, it demanded a routinized and efficient system of management. Will met the embodiment of such a system in 1897. His name was Arch Shaw and their meeting was the result of a cuff link that mysteriously went missing.

Arch Shaw, Will Kellogg's best business consultant and close friend, 1917

ARCH SHAW WAS A YOUNG, handsome, and enterprising man with a vision. Born in Jackson, Michigan, in 1876, Arch was educated at Olivet College but left before receiving a degree. While tutoring a student bound for West Point, he became disenchanted with teaching and, instead, returned to his own education, on his own time, and in his own way. After spending months studying in the reading room of the Jackson Public Library, Arch concluded that because all businesses shared a routine set of practices, executives would benefit from a paper-driven search engine of sorts allowing for easy access to facts, figures, and information related to their firms' operations. The model for information retrieval he developed was based loosely upon the Jackson Public Library's card catalog. Shaw's system facilitated the accurate analysis needed to apply modern standards of work performance for thoughtful planning, ordering, and purchasing, as opposed to the then common practice of merely reacting to each day or crisis as it came along.

In 1899, Shaw founded an office supply and file cabinet business with Lewis Walker in Muskegon, Michigan, and in 1903 he established A. W. Shaw and Company of Chicago, where he helped businesses organize and furnish their offices. His company also published two highly regarded magazines of commerce, *System: The Magazine of Business,* and *Factory,* as well as a long list of books on marketing, sales, and management. Even more lasting a contribution to the business world, Shaw helped create the field of management studies at the Harvard Business School and initiated the concepts of using historical data to plan future ventures, the importance of understanding the culture and practices of businesses, and the central coordination of a firm's activities. Shaw's acumen was so celebrated that Presidents Theodore Roosevelt, William Howard Taft, and Herbert Hoover as well as Thomas Edison, Bernard Baruch, and Robert Taft sought his counsel.[28]

Back in 1897, Shaw was traveling across Michigan in search of clients to purchase his first product, a record-keeping and indexing system. The fourth city he wandered into was Battle Creek. After entering and leaving several stores without a sale, he discovered he had lost one of his cuff links. Shaw found a local jewelry store where he could purchase a new pair. While there, he tried to interest the proprietor in his system but the jeweler declined, explaining that his business was too small for such measures. The jeweler did, however, point Shaw in the direction of the Battle Creek Sanitarium. Arch Shaw had never heard of the San until the jeweler told him it was the biggest business in town. "You go up there and ask for a man named Will Kellogg," the jeweler said. "Maybe he can use your system."[29]

Within a few hours, Shaw sold Will "a buyer's outfit" for keeping quotations from his many suppliers and vendors and a set of ledger systems to keep closer track of the doctor's publishing and food businesses. As good as Will's mind was for figures, business deals, and human resources, he quickly grasped the need for a means of recording all of the San's transactions beyond merely relying on his brainpower or scratch pads. Arch Shaw provided that methodology. Soon after Will founded his cereal company in 1906, Shaw became a crucially important advisor on advertising, sales, and marketing techniques as well as a member of the Kellogg Company's board of directors. Decades later, the always captivating Arch Shaw observed, "Fate makes the wisest decisions."[30] What an understatement. That lost piece of jewelry, a mere hunk of metal used for keeping a single shirt cuff closed, might have been the most valuable cuff link in American business history.

PERHAPS THE BEST WAY to illustrate how central Will was to the daily operations of the Sanitarium is to see how badly it ran after he left. Astonishingly for a man who did not want to be bothered with the dull tasks of running the San's daily operations, John refused to replace Will. Instead, the doctor promoted Will's ineffectual underlings to take over his myriad tasks with the understanding that the lackeys were to report directly to him. Even on their best days, these men performed their jobs in an ineffective manner. There was no one at the San quite like Will who had such a tight grip on every detail, cog, and activity that needed attending to on a daily basis. There was no one who walked up and down the halls looking for problems to fix; no one who came close to caring as deeply about every bed being properly made in each bedroom, every bathroom rendered spotlessly clean, and every meal served as hot and tasty as possible. The inevitable result was that the quality of the Sanitarium experience plummeted. Guests complained about the decline in service and many refused to return; correspondingly, the San's bank ledgers displayed less and less black ink and, in some months, much more of the red variety.

In the summer of 1907, the First National Bank of Chicago requested an audit. John had already borrowed a great deal of money from the bank for his Sanitarium rebuilding efforts and wanted to borrow more. The rumblings of things proceeding poorly at the Battle Creek Sanitarium were so loud, however, that the bankers were less than enthusiastic. To investigate their investment, the bank hired Stephen T. Williams and Staff, Inc., a New York firm renowned for assessing the efficiency of more than four hundred large companies and businesses until 1914 when Mr. Williams committed suicide by shooting himself in the head.[31] The agent assigned to the San was Frederick A. Kerry, a confident man who specialized in advising hoteliers and hospital administrators. After an initial tour of the San, Kerry met with both the Kellogg brothers at John's home on September 26, 1907. Although Will had by now left his brother's employ, John invited him to the meeting as a trusted and knowledgeable advisor.

The news was not good. Kerry collected a huge list of problems after inspecting each department. His first suggestion was to buy better help with better wages. The staff at the San was primarily Seventh-day Adventists from Battle Creek. More than half of the one thousand employees at the San, including nurses, masseuses, orderlies, and patient assistants, worked for room, board, and nominal wages. This was a losing proposition, Kerry argued, because too many of the employees ate too much food, while giving short shrift to their assigned duties. Based upon a complex means of calculation, which Will asked the expert to explain to him and quickly grasped, Kerry estimated it cost 10 to 12 cents a meal (about $2.60 to $3.12 in 2016) to feed the San's staff, representing a substantial loss of income.[32]

Many of the maids and housekeepers were impoverished widows and pensioners who worked for 7 cents an hour (about $1.82 in 2016). Kerry observed that these employees were "tired when they start work in the morning and do not do any work though they put in their time." Instead, the institution would get more work by hiring one young woman at 12 cents an hour (or $3.12 in 2016) doing the work of three elderly maids.[33] "It costs just as much work to do it wrong as it does to do it right," he explained.[34]

Worse, some of the workers interviewed during the audit were surly and rude, representing a huge problem for an institution selling itself as helpful, healthful, and worth shelling out significant amounts of money to visit. Kerry reported that the front desk clerk was "not educated enough to talk decently and politely and diplomatically." Nor was the clerk diligent at collecting initial deposits or final payments from guests, leading many dishonest patients to leave without paying their bill![35]

Kerry identified similar problems in the accounting office, the pharmacy, the stockrooms, and the operating rooms where nurses left work "before they are through for the day." All over the facility, there was furniture in various states of disrepair and too few carpenters were inspecting these pieces, let alone repairing them if loose or broken. The San's carpenters, Kerry wanly observed, spent more time (and money) dodging their work responsibilities than performing them.[36]

At a minimum, Kerry advised, John or his designated manager needed to enforce employee work hours by installing "as many time clocks as necessary" and requiring all employees to "report their time when they come in, when they go to lunch, and when they come back."[37] Another solution Kerry offered was to discharge the least productive employees, even if they had worked there for decades. Both suggestions were unacceptable to the doctor, who saw himself as a benevolent and caring employer. Kerry countered the doctor's hesitance: "You want cheap pay and you give cheap board. That is not good business." To drive his point home, Kerry cautioned, "Don't mix in [with an employee's] private affairs. Ask him what he is worth, and get him as cheap as possible."[38]

By neglecting to document all of the therapeutic and diagnostic services they provided, the medical staff unwittingly created an even greater loss of income. No one was badgering these physicians to complete the paperwork necessary for accurate billing. One modern way of solving this problem, Kerry explained, was to install "teleautograph devices" in every treatment or medical department, which were connected by an electrical wire that went directly to the cashier's office. This novel machine used the principles of a telegraph but featured an electric pen whereby signatures and written orders or messages could be quickly transmitted from one part of the San to another, without ever having to leave one's office. The devices were especially popular in banks. For the San, the machines would provide an up-to-date record of all the treatments a patient underwent, including duration and frequency, and insure that each patient was appropriately charged for every service the San rendered. An electrical engineer named Elisha Gray, the cofounder of the Western Electric Company, invented the device and his company manufactured and leased them out for $50 per month plus a $5 installation fee.[39] Kerry recommended that John lease at least twelve to fifteen teleautographs and place them all around the institution. Dr. Kellogg was noncommittal about installing this modern convenience but it is a safe bet that if Will was still running operations at the San, both the time clocks and the teleautograph machines would have been installed the very next day.

Kerry uncovered several other issues that, in his estimation, required immediate attention. For example, while inspecting the ladies' bathroom and linen room at 7:00 a.m., he found it to be "not very orderly. There were piles of buckets that had been used in washing the feet of the patients, and all kinds of things that had not been scrubbed off as they ought to be, not clean and nice, but with salt left in them, and in some cases, even water that had been used in treatments."[40] The men's bathroom was in a more slovenly condition; the stalls were not cleaned immediately after patients left them and there was, at least, one occasion where Kerry caught some of the help "lying on the couches" in the midst of messy rooms that needed cleaning.[41] While inspecting the laundry plant, he determined that it was run by an abusive supervisor whose employees hated him. In retaliation, many of the laundry staff used the facility for the free washing of all their personal clothes and linens.[42]

In the dining room and kitchen, Kerry noted too much breakage of china and cookware. Kerry acknowledged that broken dishes were part and parcel of any restaurant but he calculated that the San's breakage rate was, at least, 20 percent higher than what should be expected for a large dining facility and, hence, a huge added expense. Kerry suggested a reward system for all the kitchen and table service workers. The employee who broke the least number of dishes each week would receive a 25 cent reward. Dr. Kellogg argued that both the breakage estimate and the reward system were "absurd." As an alternative, Kerry suggested an investment in Carlsbad Chinaware, which was prized by many large restaurants for being "unbreakable."[43] Another potential saving would be to convert the energy source of the kitchen's massive ovens and ranges in the kitchen from gas to coal. Dr. Kellogg remained unenthusiastic about either plan.

The biggest problem was not exactly the clichéd "elephant standing in the room," per se, but, instead, the younger brother seated at the meeting. There was no boss with clear authority running the San. There existed no "walking delegate" to inspect the facility every day, checking every department, making notes of all the problems he encountered, and assigning employees to correct them by a specific time. The doctor, Kerry said, may have been a brilliant inventor, food creator, and physician but he was no manager. Will's only query at this point in the conference was "how much would such a man cost?"[44] Kerry replied $20 a week (about $520 in 2016, and a good deal more than Will's final salary running the San) but Kerry said it had to be the right man:

> You need a mixer, but the right kind of mixer who is diplomatic, who jollies them a little, pats them on the back and gets the work done, and nevertheless who is so close to you that he likes the institution for the institution's sake, and he has to have a time clock everywhere, and he has to have time passes, and has to have records, and he has to have the authority to be the boss. And what he says goes; and he is to have appointments with you, and you are the pope, the king and the emperor who always does not mix with those questions; and this is the way, Doctor, that those fellows—the king, emperor and pope—conduct their affairs. They reserve their great dignity. They do not mix with any mortal being in a usual way. And that is the way you ought to do it.[45]

In other words, Dr. Kellogg needed Will, even if he could not find a way to admit or acknowledge the superb management qualities his younger brother unfailingly brought to the table. All of the problems Kerry discovered at the Sanitarium were directly related to Will's absence. None of them, Will Kellogg must have quietly beamed from within, would have been allowed to occur on his watch.

In typical consultant fashion, Kerry told John that if he accepted all of his suggestions and hired him to get the process rolling, the Sanitarium would save $60,000 a year (about $1.56 million in 2016). John doubted that the savings would amount to more than $25,000 or $30,000 (a respectable $650,000 to $780,000 in 2016) and he chastised the efficiency expert for being so rough and disrespectful of his devoted staff. Nevertheless, Kerry insisted that the intensive work was necessary and it would be well worth his hefty consultant fees. He promised an even more in-depth inspection of all forty-five departments at the San, within a twelve- to fourteen-day period. More enticing, Kerry pledged, "I guarantee that in six months from now you will thank me ten thousand times that I came down here and fixed you up, because I know what a rotten condition it [the San] is in."[46]

In the years to come, John would hire, and just as often fire, several men who administered the complexities of the Battle Creek Sanitarium. He cruelly dominated these employees just as he dominated Will. And yet none of them ever matched the resourcefulness of his brother. In fact, Mr. Kerry's conclusions of how badly the San ran without Will's supervision encapsulated the brothers' lifelong rivalry over which form of operations, the medical type or the managerial kind, was more important. Both enterprises, clearly, needed to be appreciated by each sibling if a successful partnership was to be sustained. Sadly, the brothers were incapable of working together in such a manner. As one former San doctor described their corrosive and competitive relationship, "John Harvey Kellogg and W. K. Kellogg were like two fellows trying to climb up the same ladder at the same time."[47]

10

A *"University of Health"*

FIRST AND FOREMOST, the Battle Creek Sanitarium was a "university of health" and Dr. Kellogg was its mesmerizing dean and professor-in-chief. His student body encompassed the medically curious, the worried well, and the seriously ill. Their coursework centered on biologic living, learning how to preserve, restore, and regain healthy bodies and minds.

The highlight of every week was the Monday night "Question Box Hour," hosted by Dr. Kellogg. In the six days preceding this event, guests were encouraged to write down their most vexing—and potentially embarrassing—health questions on specially printed slips of paper. They then submitted them anonymously into the "Doctor's Question Box," which stood at the head of the dining room. Come Monday at 7:00 p.m., the Sanitarium's sumptuous parlor was overtaken by rows of "Kellogg chairs" filled with enthusiastic and eager patients. Each chair was specially designed by the doctor to promote good posture and the proper care of one's inner organs and spine while seated for long spells of time. Alternatively known as "Perfected Posture chairs," they featured a "chair back" curved in a convex manner to provide lumbar support. Long before the term was coined, Dr. Kellogg taught his patients the importance of ergonomics and the health risks of sitting in a chair too long. "You know sitting is a bad habit that civilization has put upon us," he liked to say, "We are not born attached to chairs. There are no chairs growing on trees."[1]

A few minutes after he was satisfied there was a full house, Dr. Kellogg made his grand entrance, walking briskly down the central aisle,

*One of many Battle Creek Sanitarium advertisements
that ran in the leading national magazines of the day*

acknowledging the faces he recognized, shaking a few hands, and ascending a richly stained, quarter-sawn oak platform placed at the front of the room. On the platform was the same box in which the patients had deposited their burning queries all week. With dramatic flair, Dr. Kellogg reached into it, read the question aloud, sometimes pausing for nervous laughter on particularly sensitive topics, and then proceeded to give an authoritative answer.[2] Many of the questions were written either by Dr. Kellogg himself or by one of his staff. Such planned inquiries emphasized the health messages he especially wanted to strike home to his audience. Impromptu or planned, John enchanted them all with his brilliance and tinny-voiced delivery, which increased in speed as he became especially excited about a particular topic.

On some evenings the doctor dispensed advice on bedwetting: "Faith will sometimes do much toward effecting a cure when other remedies

Dr. Kellogg's weekly "Question Box Hour," circa 1920s

fail."[3] On others he warned parents against trying to change their left-handed children into "righties": "Let him alone is the latest verdict of science. . . . Life is not long enough for the equal training of both hands."[4] Many nights he warned his patients about the risks of fretting, "worry is a veritable demon that gets into you and takes possession of you. . . . Cast it out; flee from worry."[5]

Too frequently, the doctor warned against the sin of masturbation, or "self-abuse," which he described as a scourge afflicting both American boys and girls. It was an all but guaranteed path to disease, diminished vitality, and ruin. During these talks, Dr. Kellogg placed parents on high alert to monitor the activities of once cheerful and pleasant children who suddenly turned into morose, grumpy, and reclusive teenagers. He also advised mothers, when sorting the family's laundry, to check for semen stains on a boy's pajamas and sheets and for vaginal discharges on their daughters' bed clothing.

Over the years, there have been many unsubstantiated claims suggesting Dr. Kellogg invented Corn Flakes as a cure for masturbation. Yet this apocryphal tale simply does not ring true, beginning with the fact that it was Will who created the recipe for Corn Flakes as a tasty breakfast cereal for healthy people and not as a treatment for sexual miscreants; John's original flaked cereals, it will be recalled, were wheat flakes. What the doctor did teach and prescribe was that "to a person struggling to repress evil desires, simplicity in diet and the avoidance of exciting and stimulating foods is of the greatest consequence." Hence, "excitatory" condiments, meat, sugar, candy, tea, coffee, and alcohol should be avoided and the diet "should consist chiefly of fruits, grains, vegetables and milk." The other panaceas Dr. Kellogg prescribed were physical exercise and adequate sleep. This medical advice, incidentally, constituted Dr. Kellogg's chief remedies for almost every condition he treated, from the sexual to the digestive.[6]

For recalcitrant masturbators, Dr. Kellogg offered an armamentarium of medical and surgical procedures. For example, he began treating boys by bandaging their hands and, if that did not work, circumcision. Astonishingly, the doctor performed the latter without anesthetics because the resultant pain tended to have "a salutary effect upon the mind, especially if connected with the idea of punishment, as it may well be in some cases." As an added benefit, the soreness caused by the circumcision lasted for several weeks and "interrupts the practice, and if it had not previously become too firmly fixed, it may be forgotten and not resumed."[7] For the most intractable cases, he performed a barbaric operation where silver sutures or wires were passed "from one side to the other" through the foreskin as it was drawn over the glans penis to prevent erections.[8]

Young women predisposed to self-abuse were equally concerning for the doctor. For masturbating girls (especially those who had sexual orgasms "several times daily") he recommended applying blistering doses of "pure carbolic acid to the clitoris as an excellent means of allaying the abnormal excitement."[9] In the case of the female "nymphomaniac," he advised, "cool sitz baths, the cool enema, a spare diet, the application of blisters and other irritants to the sensitive parts of the sexual organs, the removal of the clitoris and nymphae [i.e., the labia minora of the vulva] constitute the most proper treatment."[10]

What seems most surprising from the distance of more than a century is that the entire audience did not immediately get up and exit the room each time Dr. Kellogg offered such draconian (and excruciating) medical advice. On the other hand, this was a period when many Americans considered sex to be "dirty" and sexually transmitted diseases such as

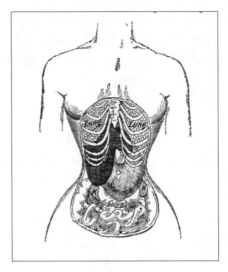

Beware of tight dresses!

syphilis and gonorrhea killed tens of thousands of Americans each year and made hundreds of thousands more miserable with debilitating and embarrassing symptoms.

For the corseted women in the audience, Dr. Kellogg warned against the fashionable, tight-fitting garments of the day. Such strictures, he believed, caused physical decline, lower birth rates, neuralgias, muscle injuries, respiratory problems, poor posture, dyspepsia, and damage to both the reproductive and digestive organs. Dr. Kellogg was particularly concerned about the practice of young women seeking smaller waists by means of "tight bands, corset waists, or corsets." He noted with horror how he had examined hundreds of young girls as early as 9 years of age wearing corsets, resulting in the "young lady's figure [developing] into a mold like a cucumber in a bottle." The solution—and a much more aesthetic look, he insisted— was to wear loose-fitting, comfortable clothing. Unbound garments allowed the female form to develop as God intended. As an added piece of advice on accessorizing, he urged women to avoid earrings, which stretched earlobes out of shape "by the savage habit of weighing them down with wires and stones."[11] Ever the entrepreneur, Dr. Kellogg offered for sale, through one of his side companies, the Sanitary and Electrical Supply Company, "a new system of dress" he had designed, which was "practical, healthful and artistic."[12] Aesthetics aside, John more often encouraged his female patients on the importance of vigorous exercise because "there is no reason why women should regard themselves as the weaker vessel."[13] He was also a strong supporter, along with his wife, Ella, of women's suffrage.[14]

PERHAPS THE LOUDEST, and most famous, medical advice he offered was on avoiding the "death sentence" of meat consumption. In Dr. Kellogg's opinion, meat was poisonous, disease-producing, and nearly impossible for the gut to digest. Although he had proffered this advice since he began practicing medicine, by the early 1900s he was applying the latest bacteriological concepts to illustrate how ingested "animal flesh" putrified in the gut, facilitating the reproduction of dangerous "protein loving bacteria" emitting all kinds of toxins, some of which "possess a degree of virulence or activity surpassing even that of the venoms of poisonous reptiles." The results of a meaty diet, he argued, were severe intestinal stasis, constipation, autointoxication, atherosclerosis, cancer, liver and kidney failure, gallstones, obesity, arthritis, hypertension, and many other dreaded maladies.[15]

The doctor was brilliant at using visual aids to make his points graphic, gross—and lasting. On many evenings, he took out a sharp knife and sliced off a thin piece of beefsteak obtained from Battle Creek's finest restaurant, the Post Tavern. He then carefully stained and affixed it to a glass slide and placed it under the microscope, which was hooked up to a lantern-slide projector for all to see on a large screen. What appeared, he explained, was a sea of disease-yielding microbes, "420 million in a little piece not as big as your thumb."[16] These germs, Dr. Kellogg warned, originated from the guts of the livestock or were parasites, such as trichinosis in pork and tapeworm found in tainted beef.

"What is the difference," he asked a rapt audience in October of 1910, "whether it be beefsteak rotting in the butcher shop, and then you swallow it first, or whether you let it become rotten and decay after you swallow it?"[17] His warnings resonated loudly in an era when health inspections of meat, dairy, and other food products were still rudimentary, at best, and everyone in the room knew someone (if not themselves) who had contracted typhoid fever, cholera, tuberculosis, and any number of diarrheal diseases from ingesting tainted water, meat, eggs, and dairy products.

At other lecture sessions, John ceremoniously removed a white cloth to unveil a Mason jar containing a pickled beefsteak. Dr. Kellogg began using this odd exhibit sometime in 1909. In his laboratory one night, he placed a fresh cut of steak into a jar filled with yogurt buttermilk, screwed on the top tightly, and put it in a cupboard. Over the next several years, he hauled out the jar for a scintillating lecture exhibit. Each time, John sliced off a piece of the beef. Putting this specimen under the microscope he demonstrated that even when properly pickled, the meat still putrefied, giving rise to billions of disease-causing microbes.[18]

By far Dr. Kellogg's most legendary presentation of the principle "you are what you eat" supposedly involved his asking an assistant to wheel in an ironclad cage containing a wolf, snarling and glaring at the alarmed audience. Reassuring the crowd that the bars were solid and secure, he told how he found this wolf as a puppy on the Sanitarium's expansive grounds. He took it home and fed it nothing but vegetables, whole grains, and nuts. The wolf grew so docile that John and Ella Kellogg encouraged their adopted wards to frolic with it in their backyard. Everything changed, however, as soon as the doctor reintroduced the canine beast to a bit of beefsteak. The animal's wolflike and carnivorous instincts kicked in and the doctor had little choice but to imprison the wolf back into a cage.

Making the wolf snarl by holding a piece of red meat tantalizingly close to it yet still out of reach, he warned his audience, those who ate animals soon began to behave like them. Citing his favorite "flesh abstainers of all ages, from Pythagoras and Seneca to Shelley, Lord Byron, Tolstoi and Bernard Shaw," Dr. Kellogg intoned: "flesh-eating, with the slaughter-house and other cruelties which it involves as a part of the civilized man's environments, tends to foster and maintain in him the brutal qualities which are manifested in the barbarities and cruelties of war."[19] Equally compelling, Dr. Kellogg expressed concerns about the wasted energy and resources spent on raising cattle and pork when compared to the energy and costs expended for grain and vegetable production.[20]

MEAT WAS HARDLY Dr. Kellogg's only gastronomic enemy; his most comical foes originated from the sea. For years, John waged war on oysters, be they raw, stewed, fried, or lightly sautéed. With purple prose and bacteriological gore, Dr. Kellogg warned:

> The oyster dwells in the slime and ooze of the ocean bottom. His business is to filter through his beard or gills the filthy water in which he thrives best, collecting and feeding upon millions of germs which swarm in the slime which covers the weeds and stones scattered over the ocean bottom. . . . Oyster juice contains more than one hundred million germs, mostly colon germs, to the ounce . . . it contains more filth germs than does sewage.[21]

In 1931, Dr. Kellogg's hostility to the bivalve proved so damaging to the oyster industry along Chesapeake Bay that the Maryland state legislature formally censured the doctor *and* his brother's cereal company for "libeling the oyster." Dr. Kellogg immediately sent out a press release entitled "A Tempest in an Oyster Pot," which defended his brother's firm as well as "anybody in Battle Creek or Michigan." None of these good people, he declared, had anything to do with his medical declarations. Yet he could not help rubbing more cocktail sauce into the wound:

> To call the oyster a scavenger is no libel. It is merely the statement of a biologic fact; and Maryland legislators, astute politicians although they may be, by resolution or in any other way, cannot change or camouflage the fact. The oyster cannot live without filth.[22]

Parenthetically, one of Will's favorite meals was a heaping dish of oyster stew. On many nights, after a long day toiling in the San, he walked downtown and dropped into Webb's restaurant. After greeting the owner and his waitress, he tied a napkin around his neck and, within minutes of arrival, tucked into a big bowl of the creamy stuff. The doctor's wife, Ella, wanted to fire her brother-in-law for committing the culinary equivalent of a capital offense. Such hostility terrified Will, largely because until he struck out on his own as a cereal maker, he felt entirely reliant on his brother's goodwill for keeping his job. When confronted by John, Will dutifully confessed and resolved to give up the delicacy, which he did for a period of time, followed by a lapse and then a relapse at Webb's. The final act involved enduring still another confrontation over his hunger for seafood and his version of a mea culpa.[23] Will never gave up his fondness for shellfish. For the rest of his life, he told many over the years, he "could hardly wait for months having the letter 'r' so that oysters would be in season."[24]

BEYOND THE LECTURES, activities, and meals, an extra special part of the "San experience" were visits by luminous stars of the American scene now forgotten but whose names and deeds glittered brightly in their day. Celebrity endorsements of the Sanitarium were good for John's business and even better for his professional reputation. Throughout much of his career, he sent out free samples of his health foods along with personally handwritten notes to a long slate of famous authors, politicians, actors, and socialites. In all these letters he made certain to ask after their health, followed by effusive compliments on their recent work, activity, or business success, on which he kept as close a watch as he did the latest advances in the medical literature.

He closed the deal by inviting these celebrities to stay at the San, free of charge, whenever they could spare the time. It was a brilliant marketing tool and the paying guests, of course, ate it up. For example, Eddie Cantor, the popular star of stage, screen, and radio, enjoyed playing golf with Dr. Kellogg while the comedian's wife, Ida, and their five daughters shed pounds in the exercise rooms. Cantor literally sang for his supper as he entertained in the Parlor, gamboling up and down the aisles, warbling "If You Knew Susie (Like I Know Susie!)" and, perhaps to appease his beleaguered wife, the lilting "Ida, Sweet as Apple Cider."

Another frequent guest was Johnny Weissmuller, the Olympic gold medalist (for his swimming) and star of the popular "Tarzan of the Jungle" movies. The actor's legendary jungle yodel opened many a meal in the San's dining room when he was in residence. Dr. Charles E. Welch, the dentist who took over his father's Concord grape juice business, lectured at the San thirty-two times. The Welch family's processed fruit juice, the first of its kind, was sold as a nonalcoholic alternative for churchgoing teetotalers until the dentist introduced it at the 1893 World's Columbian Exposition and grape juice became a wildly popular health drink. Leonard W. Bonney, the pioneering aviator who worked for the Wright brothers, put one of their famous "aeroplanes" through its paces just above the San in 1911, an event that patients spoke about for years.[25] During the late 1920s, Amelia Earhart spent several days at the San as John's personal guest. To show her gratitude, the aviatrix took Dr. Kellogg up in the sky for his first airplane ride. The ten-minute journey afforded the doctor a breathtaking bird's-eye view of the San's campus and Battle Creek.[26]

In March of 1924, Count Ilya Lvovich Tolstoy, the writer and son of the famed Russian novelist of *War and Peace,* entertained the audience with stories about his father's vegetarianism and how his avoidance of alcohol and tobacco led to his literary productivity and ripe old age.[27] Dr. Kellogg revered the novelist and had met him during his 1907 trip to Russia. John loved quoting a letter he once received from Tolstoy stating that "although he didn't have time to read every number of *Good Health,* he always looked at it, and he approved very heartily of its teachings." Tolstoy met and married a beautiful woman in 1907 who loved meat and, as he confessed to Dr. Kellogg, he returned to "flesh-eating" in order to avoid "domestic infelicity and continual contention at home."[28]

Over the years, a parade of luminaries presented lectures in the San Parlor or graced the place with their presence in exchange for their free Battle Creek holidays.[29] This list included the African American educator Booker T. Washington; former first lady Mary Todd Lincoln; botanist Luther Burbank; the Reverend Billy Sunday; national parks chief Gifford Pinchot; tennis star Bill Tilden; Congressman Joseph Cannon; business moguls Harvey Firestone, J. C. Penney, Montgomery Ward, S. S. Kresge, and Alfred duPont; pianist José Iturbi; conductor and composer John Philip Sousa; and broadcaster Lowell Thomas.[30]

The visits of celebrities to the San were reported in the in-house weekly newspaper, *The Sanitarium News,* and the San's monthly magazine, *The Battle Creek Idea.* The arrival of such special guests was widely announced in the dining room and to all the local newspapers and national magazines. More than one wag quipped that Dr. Kellogg's medical specialty was "diseases of the rich and famous." Yet these men and women did far more than add to the cachet or excitement of staying at the Battle Creek Sanitarium. Their medical care at the San provides both a fascinating look at the health of some of America's most prominent citizens and illustrates many of the common ills John diagnosed and treated

36th ANNUAL TOUR

SOUSA AND HIS BAND

Conducted by
Lieut.-Commander JOHN PHILIP SOUSA
SANITARIUM UNION
THURSDAY EVENING, DECEMBER 6th

Like many celebrities, John Philip
Sousa performed at the San in
return for a free stay.

every day at the San. Perhaps the best way to begin such an exploration would be to focus on Dr. Kellogg's "medical partnership" with the greatest industrialist of the day.[31]

HENRY FORD BECAME A lifelong adherent to Dr. Kellogg's "biologic living" beginning in the early 1900s. A resident of Dearborn, Michigan, about 115 miles east of Battle Creek, the "king of the flivvers" and his wife, Clara, were frequent guests at the Sanitarium. Always graceful in his movements, Ford's favorite activity at the San was leading the guests in evening square dances.[32] Ford's vitality, physique, daily diet, and even his exercise regimen were widely reported in the popular press. In an interview with *Redbook* magazine in 1935, Ford opined, "Most wrong acts committed by men are the result of the wrong mixtures in the stomach."[33] Directly channeling Dr. Kellogg, Henry Ford publicly denounced the consumption of sugar, excessive starch, coffee and tea, liquor, and red meat.

Ford prided himself as an outdoorsman who loved nature, exercise, fresh air, and sunshine. He spent each summer from 1915 to 1924 with his fellow self-proclaimed "Vagabonds," Thomas Alva Edison, the tire manufacturer Harvey Firestone, and their guide, the best-selling author and "naturalist" John Burroughs. The first year of their deluxe Ford motor-carriage caravan, the Vagabonds made their way to San Francisco for the Panama-Pacific Exposition of 1915 where John Harvey Kellogg was hosting a conference on eugenics and race betterment. A stop on their subsequent summer sojourns was a week or two at the Battle Creek Sanitarium as John's personal guests.[34]

Like his hero, Thomas Edison, Mr. Ford was so opposed to cigarettes that he forbade smoking in all his plants, an edict held uncontestable at all the Ford plants long after his death.[35] In 1916, Ford published a popular book entitled *The Case Against the Little White Slaver*, which was widely distributed for free in schools and youth clubs, especially for the "boy who expects to make good." It remains an impressive compendium of much of the extant medical and moral evidence on why not to smoke tobacco.[36] In 1918, Ford worked closely with Dr. Kellogg to form the "Committee of Fifty to Study the Tobacco Problem," a consor-

Left to Right: Thomas Edison, naturalist John Burroughs, and Henry Ford. The self-named "Vagabonds" began many a summer cross-country trip with a stay at the San. Circa 1914, at Edison's winter home in Fort Myers, Florida.

tium of scientists, doctors, philanthropists, and successful businessmen focused on the social damages and economic costs of cigarette smoking to society.[37]

When it came to the evils of cigarettes, Ford found a good teacher in John Harvey Kellogg. An opponent of tobacco dating back to his most pious days as a Seventh-day Adventist, John lectured loudly and clearly on tobacco's harms to the body and mind. He was diligent in following the steadily accumulating medical evidence on how smoking was associated with increased incidences of heart disease, lung disease, digestive disorders, infections, and neurological problems.[38] No pun intended but it is breathtaking to review John's grasp of the diseases caused by tobacco and its addictive nature. His prescient thinking on this topic occurred decades before the medical profession and the public came to accepting these facts in the late twentieth century. In 1922, the doctor published a successful book entitled *Tobaccoism, or How Tobacco Kills.*[39] Thousands of copies of *Tobaccoism* were sold and, along with Henry Ford's *White Slaver* books, was an important weapon in a spirited and, ultimately, failed anti-smoking crusade during the Progressive Era.[40]

One reader who took both Henry Ford's and John's anti-smoking warnings especially to heart was Will Kellogg. Will was said to have so despised the habit that when he discovered it in one of his workers, he would either demand they quit or he would discharge them from his

TOBACCO
is a
POISON

DR. JOHN H. KELLOGG, M.D., F.A.
C.S., Etc.
Superintendent of the Battle Creek Sanitarium,

Says:

"Tobacco is a poison. It weakens men physically, mentally and morally. All life processes are impaired by it. Science condemns it. The coming man will discard it."

DR. JOHN H. KELLOGG

Long before the medical profession took to warning about the dangers of smoking tobacco, Dr. Kellogg was sounding the alarm, circa 1922.

employ. Will believed smoking had no place in a food factory dedicated to making nutritious breakfast cereals and that the habit was more dangerous than drinking.[41]

The auto king's and the doctor's favorite topic of conversation, however, revolved around the soybean. Ford made all sorts of plastic parts and knobs for his automobiles out of soybeans. He even took to wearing articles of clothing that came from soy. But it was the nutritional value of soybeans as a food source that most fascinated the doctor. Historians have argued as to which historical figure introduced whom to the soybean and the answer often depends on who is telling the story, "Battle Freaks" or Ford fans. The point is that both these men had the vision to see the industrial and culinary capacities of this legume and persevered, using sound scientific method, in finding more uses for the soybean long before the rest of American society caught on to its importance.

During the periods between the Fords' visits to the Battle Creek Sanitarium, John maintained a steady correspondence with Henry's wife, Clara, and, because Henry rarely put pen to paper, Ford's executive secretary E. G. Liebold.[42] For example, on July 16, 1920, Liebold wrote a letter of introduction for Mr. Ford's cook, Mr. Thomas Satow: "He is very much interested in obtaining information from you as to your methods of preparing food and any courtesies shown will be very much appreciated."[43] On July 20, Dr. Kellogg replied: "I have put [Satow] in the charge of our expert cook and dieticians. . . . He seems a very pleasant young man and we are very glad to help him to increase his efficiency of service to you. Hoping you and Mrs. Ford are in good health and trusting we may sometime have the pleasure of having you with us long enough to be of some service to you."[44]

Ironically, the doctor was a terrible driver who indulged in driving his car very fast through the Battle Creek Sanitarium grounds and was prone to jumping curbs, bouncing into the wrong lane, and ignoring stop signs.[45]

FORD WAS HARDLY the only plutocrat committed to Dr. Kellogg's principles of biologic living. Dyspeptic, constipated, and nervous John D. Rockefeller Jr. came to Battle Creek after a series of disastrous events occurring from September 1913 to December 1914 in Ludlow, Colorado. It was there that the Colorado National Guard and the Rockefeller family–owned Colorado Fuel and Iron Company ended a labor strike by attacking a tent colony of 1,200 coal miners and their families. Referred to as the "Ludlow Massacre," it was a bloody travesty that resulted in the death of between nineteen and twenty-six people, some of them women and children. John D. Rockefeller Jr., who owned 40 percent of the Colorado Fuel and Iron Company's stock, received most of the public's blame for the event.[46]

To calm his jangled nerves and soothe his gurgling stomach, John D. Jr. made several visits to the San. The doctor and "Junior" had much in common, from a hatred of cigarettes to a deep concern about their bowel movements.[47] Writing to another patient, Dr. Kellogg came perilously close to violating his Hippocratic Oath by gossiping about the famous son of the even more famous oil tycoon: "I have often been with young Rockefeller at banquets. He usually sits beside me and I notice he sticks to the biological idea and does not vary a hair."[48]

John D. Rockefeller Jr. soothed his nervous stomach with visits to the San and by adhering to Dr. Kellogg's principles of "biologic living."

John D. Rockefeller Jr. was a fan of Dr. Kellogg's soy acidophilus milk and LD-Lax (a concoction of ground plantago psyllium seeds, lactose, and dextrin designed to gently move the bowels).[49] The regimen, apparently, did the trick. John D. Jr. could be heard boasting to his friends sitting in the posh parlor of the Union Club on New York City's Park Avenue that he was as regular as a clock. For nearly three decades, Dr. Kellogg monitored the tycoon's fragile gastrointestinal health and went as far as to discuss laboratory analyses of Mr. Rockefeller Jr.'s stools.[50] One can only imagine the response of the postmen transporting stool samples from John D. Jr.'s office on the fifty-sixth floor of 30 Rockefeller Center to the gastrointestinal laboratories of the Battle Creek Sanitarium.

Another prominent Battle Creek patient was Samuel S. McClure, the bombastic and muckraking editor of *McClure's Magazine*. McClure first came to Battle Creek in 1909 and made annual pilgrimages thereafter hoping to settle his neurasthenic jitters and unleash the dam of constipation and autointoxication ruining both his mood and health. During one visit, McClure gleefully wrote his wife, "For the last two weeks I've been clean inside, not the slightest odor to my faeces, and I am growing strong."[51] Mr. McClure urged that all the intrepid journalists writing for his pathbreaking periodical take the trip to Battle Creek. Indeed, Sam McClure's vociferous advocacy of John's constipation cures brings new meaning to the term "muckraking."

One of his star reporters, the pioneering investigative journalist Ida Tarbell, took McClure's advice and was a frequent guest at the Sanitarium. It is fascinating to speculate whether or not she or Sam McClure were ever in residence at the same time as John D. Rockefeller Jr. Between 1902 and 1904, Tarbell exposed the monopolistic business tactics of John D.

Rockefeller Sr. and the Standard Oil Company in a spectacular nineteen-part series of articles that first ran in the pages of *McClure's Magazine*. Apparently, Tarbell stuck with Dr. Kellogg's prescriptions for the rest of her life. In 1939, for example, she wrote several letters thanking him for food packages and advice on her Parkinson's disease.[52]

LESS SUCCESSFUL, but a superb example of John's hands-on clinical care for obesity, was the journalist, editor, and publisher Clarence W. Barron. Portly does not begin to describe Barron's girth and weight. The editor's single greatest contribution to American society was to create the modern enterprise of business reporting. He founded the Boston News Bureau in 1887. Soon after, he organized a news exchange

Clarence W. Barron, the president of the Dow Jones Company and guiding light of The Wall Street Journal, could not lose weight despite Dr. Kellogg's best efforts.

with the Dow Jones News Service, which had recently introduced a publication called *The Wall Street Journal*. In 1901, with the financial success
of these enterprises and after starting up a similar business news service
in Philadelphia, Barron acquired control of Dow Jones and Company. A
scrupulously honest journalist, Barron's life mission was to inform stockholders about the soundness of their investments. Over the next twenty
years, he transformed *The Wall Street Journal* from a tiny paper focused
on publishing the New York Stock Exchange's daily stock quotes with
a subscription of a few thousand into the international powerhouse of
commerce and money it has remained ever since.[53]

Weighing in at three hundred pounds, there was not a fine eating
establishment in New York, Boston, or Philadelphia he had not frequented or asked for second helpings. Always properly dressed in a frock
coat and wing collar shirt, with his hair, walrus mustache, and bushy
beard combed and freshly barbered, he could easily have been confused
with Thomas Nast's famous caricature of the Tammany Hall boss, William Marcy Tweed.

Barron struggled with weight issues for most of his adult life. He was
an annual visitor to the Battle Creek Sanitarium where he booked a suite
of rooms with a sunny southern exposure and the goal of "whittling"
himself down to an "ideal" 250 pounds.[54] Dr. Kellogg took Barron's case
on as a special project because of the newspaperman's brilliance, fame,
and his enthusiastic ability to send dozens of wealthy patients to the
San.[55] They became good friends and enjoyed many a long "motoring"
trip together through the Michigan countryside. On one such automobile ride, they passed a peach orchard and bought a bushel of the ripe
fruit directly from the farmer. Barron took to eating the peaches, throwing the pits out the window each time he finished with one. By the time
they returned from their journey, the bushel was half empty.[56]

Their relationship resulted in a great deal of positive press and fresh
"clinical material" for Dr. Kellogg's practice. But there was little that
John could do about the editor's morbid obesity beyond scolding him
when he "backslid" and cheering him on during those rare occasions
when he did not. Barron simply could not stick to the diet he was prescribed, even while in residence at the San. On too many nights in Battle
Creek, Mr. Barron ambled across the road from the Sanitarium to a little
bar and grill called the Red Onion Tavern. There, he inhaled Cuban

Dr. Kellogg loved taking his family and friends on automobile rides even though he was a terrible driver, circa 1910.

cigars, chewed on gargantuan sirloin steaks and pork chops drowned in gravy and onions, and drank tumblers of whiskey before waddling back to his suite to make the San's 11:00 p.m. curfew.

When Barron was not in residence at the San, he and the doctor kept up a steady written correspondence. Sometimes they gossiped about mutual friends, politics, and the character of American presidents. Other times, they discussed financial matters. Barron often chastised the doctor for failing to become one of the richest men in the United States and told one of the doctor's associates, "Think of the millions that Dr. Kellogg has permitted to slip through his fingers too easily." Informed of Barron's observations, Dr. Kellogg explained the difference between him and his capitalistic crony:

> I have been interested in human service, not in piling up money. It requires a great deal of time and effort to make a large amount of money, and in doing so one misses many of the beautiful things in life. That is only the beginning. After one gets it, it is necessary to shut out many more beautiful things because of the effort and time it takes required in taking care of it. During my lifetime I have

done many things that I really wanted to do, so I am glad that I have never had millions to bother with.[57]

The most common topic the two men discussed, however, was Barron's poor health. In early 1923, Dr. Kellogg ominously warned, "You are short-breathed and your lips are blue and you must take time to pull the fat away from your heart or you will find yourself still further pinched in. You should have 350 to 400 cubic inches for expansion of breath in your lungs. (On test found it 200)."[58] On October 31, 1924, he wrote: "You must get down to 250 [pounds]. The record shows that every fat man is predestined to be a diabetic. Avoid candies as you would poison. You can live on dates, nuts and apples."[59]

Barron only succeeded in worsening his precarious health. In March of 1925, the doctor treated the editor for pneumonia.[60] A few years later, on January 21, 1927, Dr. Kellogg demanded better compliance from his famous patient: "We expect you back in a month or six weeks and to stay long enough to get your weight down 40 or 50 pounds."[61] Only a week later, the doctor admonished that while Barron's systolic blood pressure dropped to 175 (still considered to be rather high by modern medical standards), "I am willing to admit that you have an extraordinary mind, almost a super mind, but your body is made of just common, ordinary flesh just like that of the rest of us folks, and there is no way of dodging the things that happen to other people except by removing the cause, and this can only be done by scientific physiologic living."[62] Seven months later, in July of 1927, after still another unsuccessful attempt to right Clarence's weight at the San, Dr. Kellogg wrote a nagging letter that Barron surely ignored. Instead of shoveling fatty food into his mouth, neglecting his health, and allowing the booming stock market to occupy his every waking moment, John begged Barron to "keep walking the straight and narrow road while you are gone and get back without losing any ground."[63]

Unfortunately, neither the treatments nor the cajoling had much effect. In early September of 1928, Barron cut his vacation on Cape Cod short and returned to New York because of a rapidly worsening sense of abdominal discomfort and a loss of his prodigious appetite. When he did eat, he experienced nausea, flatulence, vomiting, and a sharp pain in the right upper quadrant of his abdomen. His stools were a bland gray in color and his urine mirrored the hue of Coca-Cola. His breath began to stink and he had a dry, scaly coating on his tongue. On September 10, his skin and the whites of his eyes had turned neon-yellow and his family put him on the next train to Battle Creek.

Upon Mr. Barron's arrival, Dr. Kellogg ran down the staircase to welcome and examine his old friend. He was shocked to see the editor's debilitated state and quickly diagnosed catarrhal jaundice, a now antiquated term for ascending cholangitis, the formation of gallstones with inflammation of the bile ducts so severe that it obstructs the free flow of bile and often progresses into a raging (and deadly) infection. Many cases of this era were the result of consuming way too much food and alcohol.[64] Such causal descriptions fit Clarence Barron's health profile as tightly as one of his frock coats. Dr. Kellogg recognized that Barron's only chance at survival was an immediate trip to the operating room to resolve the biliary obstruction. John was also astute enough to know that Barron was too weak to withstand the assault of his scalpel and, instead, prescribed a liquid diet of vegetable broth and water in the hope of Barron gaining enough strength to allow for an operation. Despite three weeks of intensive nursing, it was of no use. Barron fell into a coma, most likely from liver failure, on September 30, 1928. His last words before this descent into death was an almost predictable query, "What's the news?" On October 2, at 7:30 p.m., Dr. Kellogg had the unpleasant task of declaring his old friend dead. Barron was seventy-three.[65] It was one of the most painful medical battles that the doctor ever lost.

WHEN IT CAME TO American presidents and presidential candidates, Dr. Kellogg was a physician of choice.[66] In the fall of 1911, he hosted the three-hundred-pound William Howard Taft. President Taft came to Battle Creek to campaign for his failed bid for reelection, thanks to his former boss Theodore Roosevelt's vote-splitting run on the Progressive, or "Bull Moose," Party ticket. After the rally, the doctor coaxed the rotund leader to the Sanitarium and, behind closed doors, diagnosed a number of problems including obstructive sleep apnea (with somnolence so great that Taft fell asleep at state dinners, in the middle of conversations, and, on occasion, while simply standing up). President Taft also suffered from an alarmingly high blood pressure, with a systolic pressure

Dr. Kellogg (center, in white) on the stage as William Howard Taft delivers a campaign speech in Battle Creek. Shortly after Taft's stump speech, the doctor examined the president at the San and told him to lose weight. September 21, 1911.

of more than 200 mm Hg, and evidence of atherosclerosis. Dr. Kellogg counseled him on a number of ways to lose weight and predicted early death if the portly Taft ignored his advice. After Taft lost his presidency that November, he finally had the time to pay attention to his ailing body rather than the body politic. Unlike Barron of Wall Street, however, Mr. Taft, formerly of 1600 Pennsylvania Avenue, shed eighty pounds of his famous girth and lowered his blood pressure by a respectable 50 mm Hg. Taft ultimately became the chief justice of the U.S. Supreme Court in 1921 but his long life of obesity caught up with him; after a series of heart attacks and cerebrovascular strokes affecting his mental faculties, he succumbed at seventy-three, to congestive heart failure in 1930.[67]

Dr. Kellogg crossed to the other side of the presidential aspirant aisle on October 3, 1916, when he had his man drive him down to the train station to meet the thrice-failed Democratic presidential candidate, William Jennings Bryan. The Great Commoner was invited to be a keynote speaker at the San's Golden Jubilee, 50th Anniversary Celebration. As soon as Bryan entered his automobile, John's sensitive nose detected his extremely foul-smelling breath and told him that he was suffering from autointoxication. Bryan reputedly asked, "Is that something that one gets from driving too rapidly in an automobile?"[68] For the remainder of the car trip, Dr. Kellogg proceeded to give his invited lecturer a private oration on the "harm, which results from food residues and body wastes stagnating in the colon." Famously hearty eater that Bryan was (he was especially fond of heaping plates of fried chicken and rare beefsteaks), one can only hope he found something suitably appetizing when he sat down in the San's famous dining room for the meatless Kellogg bill of fare.[69]

Dr. Kellogg diagnosed Warren Harding, then an Ohio state senator, with neurasthenia, twenty-one years before Harding became the 29th president of the United States.

Dr. Kellogg treated Warren G. Harding at least five times. Referred to the San by his physician father and Adventist mother, Harding's first consultation occurred in 1889, when he was twenty-four, and the final visit in 1901, at age thirty-six.[70] On one visit, John diagnosed the then Ohio state senator as a neurasthenic and warned him that his philandering and alcohol consumption might injure his delicate and already damaged heart. Once ensconced in the White House, President Harding took to consulting his wife's homeopathic physician and completely ignored the medical entreaties of Dr. Kellogg, who, no doubt, was offended by the swirling rumors of Harding's sexual proclivities. On August 2, 1923, while resting in a San Francisco hotel during a long campaign trip, President Harding keeled over, fell on his bed, and dropped dead. The cause was a massive heart attack. He was only fifty-eight years of age.[71]

Harding's successor, Calvin Coolidge, was more amenable to the doctor's views on health. Upon assuming the presidency, the athletic and lean Coolidge installed one of Dr. Kellogg's mechanical horses in the White House. "Silent Cal" uncharacteristically boasted about the machine's excellence, a commendation quickly picked up by the White House press corps.[72] John returned the favor of Coolidge's endorsement by sending him several cases of his health foods and natural laxatives. Writing to Clarence Barron on June 17, 1927, he declared, "the President . . . is of a deeply philosophical mind. . . . It is a great satisfaction to have in the presidential chair such a fine character as Coolidge, especially as a successor to Harding, a man of the very opposite type."[73]

In late 1932, Herbert Hoover invited Dr. Kellogg to the White House for a reception held on February 2, 1933, in the final days of that president's administration. John accepted with alacrity, telling Hoover's chief military advisor, Lieutenant Colonel Campbell Hodges, "I highly appreciate the honor of meeting the President personally. I have felt and still feel that he is the ablest man who has ever filled the Presidential chair since Washington."[74]

A few months after Franklin Roosevelt assumed office, John revised his long-held Republican allegiance and courted the new president. Roosevelt was so impressed by the doctor that he invited him to his polio retreat in Warm Springs, Georgia. John promised to do just that the following winter during his annual drive from Michigan down to Florida.

Always promoting his health products, on July 27, 1933, John sent Franklin Roosevelt and his trusted secretary, Marguerite "Missy" LeHand, four portable, lumbar-vertebrae-supporting seat backs, or "posture panels." He invented them to ease the discomfort of automobile seats. "The panel," Dr. Kellogg explained, "permits complete relaxation while the body is held in a physiologic position. It thus prevents weariness. . . . I think Mrs. Roosevelt might also be interested." No response appears to have come from the White House. Only two years earlier, the doctor tried to sell Henry Ford on using the posture panels for his fleet of automobiles. This, too, fell on deaf ears.[75]

The same day John pitched the president's secretary with his new invention, he wrote a cloying tribute to the president about his New Deal:

> May I take this opportunity to express my deep appreciation of the marvelous things you have already done for America and for the world and the still greater things, which the new forces you have set in operation are going to accomplish in the future. This is the first time in all history that science has been so fully summoned to the aid of government and in such a masterly way. . . . I say to you frankly and sincerely that in my opinion your administration marks indelibly the beginning of a third chapter of this great repub-

Eleanor Roosevelt visits the San's world-famous kitchen, circa 1933.

lic, an era which will see greater improving changes in our national life, industrial, civic and social than our most optimistic prophets have envisioned and will develop new standards and methods in government and create a model for the world.[76]

Eleanor Roosevelt visited Battle Creek in 1933 and again in 1940 (she was especially impressed by the San's kitchen and the gymnasium's vast array of exercise machines). The correspondence between the doctor and the president trails off by the end of 1934.[77] There were no more invitations to the Roosevelt White House or Warm Springs. Nor were there any requests for presidential endorsements of John's latest invention. By 1936, John was back in the arms of his father's Grand Old Party. That fall, at a Republican rally in Battle Creek, Dr. Kellogg introduced "the next President of the United States," Alf Landon. On November 3, Roosevelt humiliated Landon. The doctor's candidate carried only Vermont and Maine.[78]

11

Will's Place

A FEW DAYS BEFORE Thanksgiving 1912, Will Kellogg strolled up New York City's Broadway with a sense of purpose and pride. Still embroiled in a bitter fight with his older brother and grieving the premature death of his wife, Puss, on September 2, Will chose to focus on the one prize within his grasp: proving to the world that he was every bit the Titan his brother John purported to be. Bankers without imagination laughed at Will's notion of "cold cereal" and told him he was bound for failure.[1] John Preston Kellogg's youngest son simply found his capital elsewhere. He proved all his naysayers wrong, and within six short years he was America's undisputed "Corn Flake King."

New York City may have been intimidating to most people visiting from small towns like Battle Creek, but not for Will. Walking at a quick clip block after block, he ignored the cacophony of trolley cars clanging and dozens of newspaper boys entreating him to "read all about it." As he crossed 47th Street, he could see inside the lobby of the Palace Theatre, which was being readied for its grand opening as the nation's premier vaudeville Mecca.[2] If he, indeed, looked in that direction, it is safe to assume it was a brief glance, and of minor interest to the determined businessman from Battle Creek. On this afternoon, Will was looking for a different mecca: the Mecca Building, at 1600 Broadway, to be precise.

ERECTED IN 1902 by the Studebaker Brothers to serve as both a showroom and factory for their fleet of all-electric automobiles, the Mecca

Building was triangular in shape. It, therefore, fronted three streets: Seventh Avenue, 48th Street, and Broadway. This lattice of skyscrapers and pavement forms the head of what was once known as Longacre Square, an oddly shaped quadrilateral that extends a full six city blocks. On April 4, 1904, after Adolph Ochs, the publisher of *The New York Times,* moved his operation uptown to the opposite end of the "square," at Broadway and 42nd Street, it was renamed "Times Square." Within a few months, the first of many electric signs was erected, although the famed Times "Zipper," the news ticker illuminating breaking headlines to passersby below, would not be built until 1928.[3] Hyperbolically called the "Crossroads of the World," Times Square was home to "80% of the city's theatres, surrounded by the best hotels the world affords . . . the most frequented restaurants in New York," and "the most advertised section of New York City."[4]

The Mecca Building may well have been the most famous building in the world's most famous neighborhood, even if few who worked outside of its ten stories knew its name. From 1902 until 2004, when it was demolished, almost every recorded image of the "Great White Way," from postcards and photographs to films and television shows, pictured the Mecca Building—even if you could see little of its elaborate red-brick and terra-cotta facade. For decades, the building was covered by a wall of neon and electric light bulb signs featuring animated and brightly colored advertisements, such as the "Good to the Last Drop Cup of Maxwell House Coffee" sign and the "White Rock Soda Water" clock.[5]

In the spring of 1912, Will made the bright blanket of billboards even brighter by signing a five-year lease, at $15,000 per annum (or $378,000 in 2016), giving him the rights to the Mecca Building's rooftop. All summer and through much of the fall of 1912, eighteen construction workers erected an iron scaffold supporting the "largest electric sign ever built." The eighty-ton structure included six "mammoth trusses" to distribute the 106-foot-wide and 80-foot-high sign's weight and the wind stress evenly.[6] The price tag amounted to more than $40,000 (about $1.01 million in 2016). Will was confident that the construction costs and the monthly rental fees were worth every penny.

Electrically rendered on the sign's scaffolding was a boy's smiling face and a box of Kellogg's Toasted Corn Flakes. Both the boy's face and the box measured some forty feet in height. In between them was the now

The World's Largest Electric Sign: "I Want Kellogg's Toasted
Corn Flakes," on the rooftop of the Mecca Building, at the
head of Times Square, New York City, August 17, 1912

familiar red script "Kellogg's." The "K," alone, was sixty-six feet high. A
mechanical device changed the boy's smile into a crying frown. At that
point, electric letters beamed "I Want Kellogg's Toasted Corn Flakes."
When the boy's cry reversed back to a smile, the letters changed to read
"I Got Kellogg's Toasted Corn Flakes." A national magazine and newspaper advertisement campaign proudly announced "the sign portrays a
true story in millions of homes daily."[7] The Mecca Building's display
may have been the largest Kellogg's sign but it was hardly the company's
only glitzy billboard. Between 1906 and 1914, Will erected thousands
more like it across the nation, costing as much as $30,000 (or $756,000
in 2016) each.[8]

WILL'S SUCCESS AT SELLING so many boxes of Corn Flakes was directly tied to the vast changes simultaneously occurring in the United States in the early twentieth century. To begin, his Battle Creek operation was transformed by the rise of the modern mechanized factory, which operated twenty-four hours a day on new forms of power—volts of electricity and the controlled explosion of gasoline, either of which could be started or stopped at the push of a button.[9] The extensive (and competitively priced) railway lines insured both a steady volume of raw grain and other ingredients arriving daily to his Battle Creek factory and his ability to send out carloads of finished product to the far reaches of the nation. His well-cultivated network of food jobbers and brokers made sure the cereal was prominently placed in grocery stores for purchase. The telegram and the telephone further facilitated Will's direct communication with regional markets far away from his Battle Creek headquarters and allowed him to plan and produce accordingly, with close control of his costs. All of these new technologies allowed for "maximum throughput" on a scale of production that both satisfied the hunger of the entire continent and Will's bottom line.[10]

In 1962, Everett Rogers published a seminal book called *Diffusion of Innovations*.[11] Building on the work of several late-nineteenth-century sociologists, Rogers studied why and how new ideas or technologies spread, grew, and became accepted in different cultures and nations. Integral to the process, of course, were the innovators who developed entirely new products and the technologies needed to produce them. Equally important were the early adopters who quickly grasped the importance of what the innovators were coming up with, and extended and magnified their inventions on a grand scale, which was then followed by the diffusion of these methods and products to those who, so to speak, came late to the party and, finally, to the rest of us, the consumers.

To be sure, both Will and John Harvey Kellogg were "ground-floor" innovators in the flaked cereal industry, but Will was also an "early adopter." One example of this adoption process was Will's love of "business systems," such as the ledger and accounting methods he purchased from Arch Shaw while still managing the Sanitarium. Later, at his own company, Will instituted many more improvements both to keep track of his firm's ever-expanding commerce and organizational structure.

Will's most instrumental early adoption, however, was his recognition of the need to create a constant demand for his product. He achieved this goal through the medium of newspapers and magazines and with the sophisticated application of a relatively new profession known as advertising. In concert with the new means of manufacturing and distribution, advertising in the best media outlets of the early twentieth century transformed the Battle Creek–based Kellogg Company into a national, and ultimately a global, brand.

THE MEANS FOR PRINTING newspapers and magazines underwent a technological revolution beginning in the 1880s, thanks to the advent of the linotype machine, which was invented by the German printer Ottmar Mergenthaler and first used by the *New York Tribune* on July 3, 1886. Before this mechanical advancement, printers practiced labor-intensive methods of using lead type and setting each letter of each word into place by hand. Such onerous tasks mandated short issues of newspapers, rarely more than a few pages. With the linotype machine, the printer now entered the letters, words, and sentences of a story onto a keyboard as the machine lined up a "type matrix," in other words, a "line o' type." He then pressed a lever that released molten lead into the casting portions of the type matrix. After it cooled, the type was placed on massive rolling, printing machines. At every stage of these preparations, the printers read each line and proofed the entire article.[12] Consequently, the linotype opened up the newspapers, increased their page count, and thus created enormous amounts of space both for news stories and advertisements. Thomas Edison, the greatest "techie" of the day, described the linotype machine as "the eighth wonder of the world."[13]

Concurrently, newsprint was cheap and plentiful, as paper producers developed far better organized production and distribution methods. Information, the life's blood of any newspaper, also began to flow more freely. The clatter and ring of the rapid, new "typewriter" signaled its dominant role in newsrooms across the nation as the device truly became mightier than the pen. Telephones added to the immediacy of news, reporting, and reach. Information not only traveled long distances at the speed of sound, it was now accessible to everyone whether you knew Morse code or not.

Another simultaneous advancement called half-tone printing freed newspapers and magazines from using only occasional illustrations in the form of woodcuts. The new method, which simulates an image through the elaborate use of dots varying in size and spacing, allowed the presses to rapidly duplicate photographic images, drawings, and graphics, first in black and white and, later, in bright, bold colors. The ability to present beautiful enticing images that captured the public's eye revolutionized the newspaper, magazine, and advertising businesses.

National mechanisms of media distribution advanced during this period as well. In 1863, the U.S. Congress recognized how important mail order subscriptions were to maintaining a "free press" throughout the country, leading them to create a second, and cheaper, postage rate expressly for periodicals. This subvention helped balance a publication's bottom line and stay in print.

Perhaps the most important change was how mass advertising revenues disrupted the subscription-only income model. The economic health of these mass audience publications now became a factor of the number of lines or pages of advertising it sold per issue. Circulation remained a dominant measure both in terms of influence and because the number of readers a magazine or newspaper commanded was directly connected to how much they could charge for advertising space.[14] Regardless of the financial formulae, magazines were devoured by the American public and served as a major form of entertainment and leisure reading, especially in the days before radio and television. The beautifully illustrated advertisements slipped in between the magazine stories influenced millions of people to buy things they might need for daily life *and* achieve the idealized American dream and lifestyle.[15]

Unfortunately, as national magazines and their advertising content gained ground, a wide variety of abuses developed, too. The industry most notable for false advertising and chicanery was the patent medicines and health products business. Both out of self-interest and to protect their readers, "the *caveat emptor* rule was abandoned by the better class of periodicals." In 1904, *The Ladies' Home Journal* made the first major inroad in exposing the most egregious manipulations. The magazine launched a campaign against "Lydia Pinkham's Cure," a popular tonic of herbs and way too much alcohol. At the time, bottles of Lydia Pinkham's were sold by the carload to unsuspecting women, supposedly to allay their menstrual and menopausal complaints and, in reality, leave them in a haze of inebriation.[16] The following year, 1905, *Collier's* magazine published a series of muckraking articles by Samuel Hopkins Adams about the dangerous frauds committed by other American tonic and drug manufacturers. At the same time, Dr. Morris Fishbein, the editor-in-chief of the *Journal of the American Medical Association,* perhaps the most influential medical publication in the United States, exposed quack cures at a relentless rate. And, of course, in 1906, Americans were simultaneously disgusted and fascinated by Upton Sinclair's exposé of the Chicago stockyards and the meat industry in *The Jungle,* which, in turn, inspired enormous political pressure to do something about the health risks of consuming meat. The same year that Sinclair's muckraking novel was published, Theodore Roosevelt led a presidential charge to protect Americans from the fraudulent and dangerous ways employed by the food and pharmaceutical industries in its advertisements and with respect to the purity of the ingredients they used in their goods. The result was the passage of the landmark Pure Food and Drug Act of 1906.[17] Yet even after this landmark regulatory action, there remained an entertaining and exaggerative component to American advertising, especially for "legal" foods, health products, and patent medicines.[18]

THE SAME YEAR he took over the roof of the Mecca Building, 1912, Will invested $1 million (or $25,200,000 in 2016) for advertisements in virtually every major magazine, daily newspaper, and grocery trade paper in the nation. Based upon these periodicals' circulation numbers, over 18 million people saw the Kellogg's advertisements that year.[19]

Only six years earlier, in 1906, Will first dipped his toes into what became a sea of advertising. One such example was a small advertisement he took out in a Dayton, Ohio, newspaper. The cost of the ad was $150 (about $4,070 in 2016) but the price tag included a man wearing an eight-foot papier-mâché ear of corn costume, walking the streets of Dayton and extolling the virtues of Kellogg's Corn Flakes.[20] A few weeks later, Will hired young door-to-door representatives to introduce themselves and hand out boxes of Corn Flakes to Dayton housewives. Indeed, the latter ploy may well have introduced the "free sample."

Some have contended that Will's introduction to mass advertising was through the success of C. W. Post, with his full-color magazine illustrations inviting Post cereal consumers to walk along the "Road to Well-ville" and to drink Postum to "make red blood cells." To some extent, Post's success did influence Will to seek out such sales methods but this explanation tells only part of the story. In fact, Will already had consider-able experience placing national ads for the Battle Creek Sanitarium, as well as its schools of cooking, nursing, and home economics. He super-vised the production of hundreds of enticing, beautifully illustrated bro-chures extolling the charms of the San and was adept at placing bold announcements of Dr. Kellogg's latest tome even as he complained of being shackled by John's strict rule against advertising their health foods.

By July of 1906, Will was ready to make a much bolder statement. Dissatisfied by how many boxes of Corn Flakes he was selling with a

The famous Ladies' Home Journal *advertisement,*
which was an early example of the selling power
of reverse psychology, July 1906

"timid piecemeal policy," Will began plotting his first national advertising campaign. To help the process along, Will implored Arch Shaw, "You understand advertising. How would you like to help us? For a fee of course. We can't pay you in cash, but we could be worth a lot in a short time!"[21] Arch took his remuneration in shares of the Kellogg company's stock and advised Will to bet everything he had on one full-page advertisement in *The Ladies' Home Journal,* which boasted a circulation of over 1 million women across the nation.[22]

With a perfect ear for an effective sales pitch, Arch Shaw designed an unconventional advertisement that launched Kellogg's Corn Flakes into the stratosphere. Using the now time-honored ploy of reverse psychology, Shaw created a demand for what was described as a hard-to-obtain commodity. The advertisement featured a letter from the firm's president under the typewritten heading, "This announcement violates all the rules of good advertising." Will went on to explain that the Battle Creek Toasted Corn Flake Co. was so new it did not yet have a sales force and even if he did, 90% of America's grocers did not yet carry his product:

> We hope by July 1st to be able to fill <u>all</u> orders. In the meantime, the great success of Toasted Corn Flakes will no doubt encourage imitators to take advantage of the situation and endeavor to substitute. There is only one genuine Toasted Corn Flakes. If anything else is offered to you—don't judge the merits of Corn Flakes by the substitute. . . . Toasted Corn Flakes . . . is [the] flavor that won the favor.[23]

Directly below his signature was a coupon for the "exceptional offer" of a "season's supply of Toasted Corn Flakes free" to those housewives willing to storm into their local grocer's shop and demand that he carry Kellogg's Corn Flakes. In so doing, Will enlisted American women to act as his phantom sales force and generate a flood of orders for his cereal. The advertisement did exactly what Will and Shaw hoped it would do. For Will, it set his business trajectory ever upward. For Arch Shaw, the company's second largest individual shareholder after Will, it made him a wealthy man.[24]

As an aside, there was one moment of providence that begs mention. During the very first few weeks of his company's existence, Will wanted to christen his cereal with the entirely corny moniker "Korn Krisp." Providentially, Arch Shaw convinced him to change the name to the more "mouthwatering" and enticing "Toasted Corn Flakes." Still, the name change did come at a cost. Will had already bought 407,176 Korn Krisp cartons, 400,176 of which were never used because of the name change. This created a huge dent in the company's profit margin that year since printing and folding the cardboard cartons represented one of Will's major production expenses. He more than made up for any of the losses by discarding all those boxes emblazoned with such a dud of a name. Within months of the *Ladies' Home Journal* ad, the sensational taste and name of Kellogg's Corn Flakes was on millions of American lips, mouths, and minds.[25]

That first year of business, 1906, Will spent $90,000 (about $2.44 million in 2016) for advertisements. The outlay represented three times the amount of cash the company had on hand.[26] That same year his company sold 178,943 cases of cereal earning $1.00 profit (about $27.10 in 2016) on every case. This success inspired Will to double-down on his bank loans and his advertising campaign in 1907 with an investment of $300,000 (about $7.8 million in 2016) for full-page spreads in more than a dozen leading magazines.

The second sales campaign he mounted might seem tame and old-fashioned today but it was rather daring for its time. In a series of beautifully illustrated advertisements, Will asked American housewives to wink at their grocers on specific days of the week in order to receive a free package of something mysteriously referred to as "K.T.C." The goal was to entice inquisitive women by the droves into grocery stores, either winking or asking what the wink was all about. Initially, Will worried the "wink idea" might prove too salacious. This was still an era when winking at the opposite sex, especially those you did not know and to whom you were not married, engaged, or, at a minimum, formally "keeping company" with, was inappropriate, to say the least. Once American women found out that "K.T.C." referred to Kellogg's Toasted Corn Flakes, they took away as many boxes as they could carry—even if they had to wink at the grocery man to get them. In New York City alone, sales of Corn Flakes skyrocketed fifteen-fold as a result of the "Wink Campaign."[27]

WILL'S CORE AUDIENCE, of course, always consisted of American mothers and especially their children. He was brilliant at slyly marketing his wares to kids who would then beg their moms to buy his cereal, a dynamic that has played itself out in millions of grocery stores, countless times a day, for more than a century. Although Will often lamented that he never really enjoyed his boyhood, he did help create one of the great joys of being a child in twentieth-century America: digging into a box of cereal and finding a wonderful toy.

Beginning in 1909, children all over the nation cut out coupons on the back of their cereal boxes and mailed them to Battle Creek. A week or so later, they were thrilled to receive a colorful book entitled *Kellogg's Funny Jungleland Moving-Pictures*. Richly illustrated and engagingly written, the book featured a series of paper cutout animal dolls, with strips of paper attached that allowed a child to change the animals' appearance and costumes to his or her imaginative content. On the back was a photo of a young girl feeding her stuffed elephant doll a bowl of Kellogg's Corn Flakes with the slogan, "I eat it by the trunk-full too!"[28]

Eventually, Will learned that rather than bother with coupons and the U.S. postal system, there was a significant advantage to stuffing his boxes

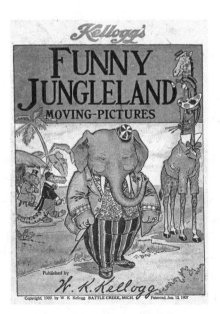

Kellogg's Funny Jungleland *book.*
The first "cereal prize," 1909.

with toys. The "prizes" took up space that would otherwise be filled by cereal, which was still more expensive to produce than the paper books and, later, the buttons, rings, puzzles, games, and other toys he "gave away," much to the delight of every American child who got to them first. Bigger toys meant using less cereal in boxes set at the same price point, which translated into bigger profits.

With each passing year, Will's advertisements became more attractive and clever. By the 1910s, he was employing the best commercial artists in America to paint portraits of beautiful women posing as idealized mothers and wives serving up a bowl of Kellogg's Corn Flakes; others featured children eating, asking for, or thinking about a bowl of the same. All of the advertisements heralded catchy trademarked slogans such as "Won Its Favor Through Its Flavor" and "The Sweetheart of the Corn." From the 1920s well into the 1940s, Will employed cartoon characters such as Mutt and Jeff, Alphonse and Gaston, and the Katzenjammer Kids, whose goofy exploits were avidly followed by tens of millions of American children every Sunday in the funny papers section of their local newspapers. But these cartoon characters were not always used to entice children only. A series of advertisements presented a cartoon character complaining of constipation and another character offering freedom by consuming bowls of Kellogg's All-Bran, Krumbles, and Bran Flakes. Will went one step further in 1933 by commissioning a commercial artist named Vernon Grant to create three new cartoon characters, exclusive to the Kellogg Company, for advertising a new product he introduced in 1928. The cereal was called Rice Krispies. The three gnomes singing the new cereal's praises were, of course, "Snap, Crackle, and Pop," which also reflected the sound a bowl of Rice Krispies were said to make when milk was poured over them.[29] Less savory was a 1930 advertisement featuring the stereotypical African American "Mammy" serving a white boy a bowl of Rice Krispies with the racist slogan, "It Sho Do Crackle."[30]

During the early 1930s, when radio emerged as the major form of mass communication in the United States, the Kellogg Company sponsored what is regarded as the first national show directed at children. Entitled *The Singing Lady* (1931), the show featured the multitalented Ireene Wicker. The "Lady with a Thousand Voices" attracted more than 25 million children a week with stories from the Brothers Grimm, Mother Goose, Hans Christian Andersen, and Rudyard Kipling.[31] Her popular show was just

"The Sweetheart of the Corn,"
Kellogg's Toasted Corn Flakes
advertisement, December 1907

the first of dozens of Kellogg's-sponsored radio and, later, television shows, all showcasing the company's delicious wares at every break.

Will's advertising campaign never really ended and the key to what he was selling rested on the pursuit of wellness. In every communication to the American public, regardless of the medium or the message, Will Kellogg warned the public against unscrupulous imitators and he backed that warning with an unwavering promise that his Kellogg's cereals were the best money could buy.[32] From the earliest days of his company, Kellogg's Corn Flakes were presented as a pure, nutritious, convenient, inexpensive, and essential way to consume the meal Dr. Kellogg had long declared to be the most important meal of the day. Will's brilliant ad men took that phrase one step further in the late 1950s by coining the company's most famous slogan: "The Best To You Each Morning." The constant drumbeat of jingles, print advertisements, giveaways and samples, recipe booklets, and television and radio commercials made "Kellogg's" a household name and a valuable brand. This image of health and nutrition quickly became one of the company's most important tools in the competitive business of selling mass-manufactured foods, one that

Will understood with perfect clarity even if his brother never could. Creative advertising characterized his entire career at the Kellogg Company; between 1906 and 1939, his most active years running the company, Will spent nearly $100 million (more than $1.7 billion in 2016) for advertising.[33] The persuasive messages sent from Battle Creek all over the world have never ceased, even as the media and technology that amplify them have, and continues to, change drastically with each passing year.

UNDOUBTEDLY, the most essential component in making a bowl of Corn Flakes an American icon was milk. Will's talent, hard work, and business acumen facilitated his producing a delicious, cold, ready-to-eat cereal; but he also enjoyed the great good fortune to start his company precisely at the same time fresh, pasteurized, clean, and refrigerated milk was beginning to be produced and nationally distributed.

At the turn of the last century, before the development of effective vaccines and antibiotics, children and infants suffered a great many contagious and deadly diseases. Epidemics of measles, whooping cough, smallpox, and typhus were almost annual events; every summer brought waves of "infantile diarrhea," causing thousands of babies to die of simple dehydration. In 1900, approximately 200 of every 1,000 children born in the United States never saw their first birthdays. The death of an infant or young child was a common tragedy that occurred in almost every American family, including Will Kellogg's.[34]

One of the major causes of infant deaths at the time was dehydration from diarrhea contracted by drinking contaminated milk. Before widespread pasteurization and refrigeration, milk was typically collected at a rural dairy farm on the outskirts of a particular urban center. Some farmers were scrupulous about their handling of milk products; many others were not, and some adulterated their milk with chalk or water, which effectively diminished the quality of what was sold, often at the financial and physical expense of the consumer. For most of the nineteenth century and in the early 1900s, milk was stored in large cans, which may or may not have been set on melting cakes of ice, and transported into town by horse-drawn wagons. Milk was then sold, in bulk, at storefront grocery stores and from pushcarts. Once taken home in a "milk pail," it was often set on a windowsill or on a fire escape to keep cool, unless a consumer was wealthy enough to purchase an icebox. Setting it outside worked far better during the colder months than during the summer. Too many times, when poorly handled or adulterated milk was placed in a bottle for the baby, it was teeming with bacteria and viruses.[35]

By the turn of the last century, a consortium of concerned pediatricians, public health activists, nurses, food chemists, social workers, dairy farmers, milk distributors, politicians, and women's civic groups embarked on a huge national crusade to reduce the alarmingly high infant mortality rates by means of cleaning up the national milk supply. During this same period, the science of proper milk handling, packaging, and spoilage prevention advanced by leaps and bounds.

A major breakthrough in cleansing milk of microbes, of course, was the gentle application of heat, or pasteurization. Ironically, the process bearing Louis Pasteur's name is almost always associated with milk, but it was actually developed by the great microbiologist in 1864 to kill bacteria lurking in wine and beer. In the decades that followed, milk chemists tinkered with Pasteur's findings in order to determine the precise temperature that killed the microbes in cow's milk but did not ruin the taste. Cutting-edge pediatricians played with the composition of cow's milk by adding or subtracting the amount of fats, carbohydrates, and protein to compose custom-made, artificial baby "formulae" for infants. Parents were taught to heat, or sterilize, the formula at home as a means of protecting their babies from milk-borne infections. And philanthropists, such as Nathan Straus, whose family owned the profitable R. H. Macy's department store, funded research and established "milk depots" in the 1890s to distribute clean, inexpensive, or free milk for babies and children of impoverished families.[36]

Another key ingredient in the milk story is the development of refrigeration. Beginning in the late 1870s and extending well into the twentieth century, dairy farmers worked with inventors, engineers, manufacturers, and railroad experts to perfect mechanical refrigeration systems. For example, Gail Borden, who invented a process to "manufacture condensed, canned, and spoil-proof milk" for Union troops during the Civil War, worked with other dairymen to create national distribution systems that reliably delivered safe, clean, refrigerated, pasteurized milk and other dairy products to American mothers and their families.[37] Milk producers and wholesalers, incidentally, were hardly the only food and beverage businesses developing new means to quickly deliver fresh products across the United States. The Anheuser-Busch Brewery of St. Louis made significant investments and progress in pasteurizing their products and developing refrigerated railcars and rail-side icehouses. Chicago meat-packing firms, such as the Swift and the Armour companies, as well as produce, butter, and egg men, baked goods manufacturers, and cheese makers, were also actively involved in the development of refrigerated transportation methods to keep their products fresh for sale in markets far from where they were slaughtered, grown, picked, gathered, or made. By the late 1920s, refrigerated motor trucks were carrying fresh produce and other perishable foods great distances to markets all over the nation.[38]

The ways in which the American public bought groceries was completely transformed during this period, thanks to the creation of large, self-serve markets. No longer did housewives have to request each item they wished to purchase from an imperious clerk who manipulated a long stick with retractable tongs to pull down items placed on the impossibly high shelves. In the twentieth century, American women and men were granted the freedom to inspect and choose whatever food product they desired. For example, between 1912 and 1915, a new A&P (the Great Atlantic and Pacific Tea Company) market opened every three days. The stores were clean, airy, and large, but free of expensive fixtures. Their floor plan was divided into sections specializing in meat, produce, dairy products, and other staples. With the money saved by their no-frills and high-sales-volume approach, A&P passed on its savings to the consumer.[39] In 1916, an entrepreneur named Clarence Saunders advanced the field even further by opening the first Piggly Wiggly grocery store in Memphis, Tennessee. His store featured a floor plan that led customers through turnstiles and into a maze of bountiful shelves, allowing them to see the entire cache of beautifully packaged merchandise before being funneled out through the store's cashier lines and only exit. Grocery stores were never the same since and, thus, began their inexorable march toward the modern mega-supermarket, where most of us purchase our groceries, from the fresh to the frozen.

And, of course, all of these advances and changes in how Americans perceived, purchased, prepared, and consumed food during the opening decades of the twentieth century proved to be extremely beneficial for Will's company.

WILL'S GREAT SUCCESS is even more miraculous when considering the many obstacles John threw in his path.[40] In 1905, the Kellogg brothers' annual gross income from their flaked cereals was a little more than $100,000 (about $2.78 million in 2016). During the same period, C. W. Post bombarded newspapers and magazines with his advertisements, operated three factories working around the clock making Postum cereal coffee and Grape-Nuts, and was generating many millions of dollars a year. Even if Will could drum up additional orders by means of advertising and promotion, which his brother would never allow, his poorly capitalized, makeshift factory could not manufacture much more.

It was not just the vast sums of money Will felt John was leaving for others to collect from the manufacture of "their" cereal foods. Above all, Will firmly believed in the quality, utility, taste, and ultimate success of his Corn Flakes. Just as Mickey Mouse, as social historian Neal Gabler observed, "served as an expression of Walt [Disney]'s personal mythology of trial and triumph," a box of Corn Flakes long served as Will Kellogg's powerful emblem of tribulation, tenacity, and accomplishment.[41] Nearly a half century later, Will recalled a rare moment of moxie in 1898 when he told several Adventist Elders and board members "[that] if given the opportunity, the food company would develop in such a manner that the Sanitarium would be only a sideshow as to the magnitude of the food business. I confess at the time I little realized the extent to which the food business might develop in Battle Creek."[42]

Paltry sales figures aside, in late June of 1905 Will seized his destiny by offering to buy the cereal business outright. His timing could not have been better. The doctor was deep in debt with notes on the Sanitarium for over $180,000 (about $5 million in 2016) and $35,000 (or $971,000 in 2016) in personal debt.[43] Money problems hardly fazed the doctor and he demanded Will hand over a great many shares of stock of his cereal company along with a considerable amount of cash in exchange for his blessing. Legally speaking, Will no longer needed John's permission. The prevailing interpretations of U.S. patent law at the time clearly held that as long as he slightly changed the flaking process, he would not be infringing on the doctor's patents.

Regardless of his legal rights, Will wanted a green light brighter than

Jay Gatsby's as both evidence of his business integrity and to avoid predictable problems down the path given John's habit of contesting virtually every legal agreement he signed. As Will explained years later, "the patent on flaked cereal foods had been declared invalid and all I needed to do, if I wanted, was to start making corn flakes myself. But I wanted to play the game fair and square."[44] On January 22, 1906, after six months of protracted negotiations, John finally sold Will the rights to manufacturing and selling Corn Flakes.[45] The price was $170,000 (about $4.62 million in 2016), broken down into $22,440 in cash (about $450,000 in 2016) and $147,560 (more than $3 million in 2016) in company stock. Even with this rather generous deal the doctor inserted a contentious clause that would soon disrupt Will's path. On one contract, the doctor transferred to Will's company the rights to sell Corn Flakes worldwide. A few weeks later, the doctor insisted on agreeing to transfer only the rights to sell Corn Flakes in the United States, while retaining the rights outside the United States and anywhere in the world. Will, weary of wrangling with John, grudgingly gave in and approved the terms of the second contract.[46] Granting his brother the foreign rights to Corn Flakes represents one of the rare examples of shortsightedness during Will's long business career. To be sure, the U.S. market was where Will was focusing his business during these years and he needed to safeguard his exclusivity of those rights. He may have been more intent on securing an agreement from John that forbade him from divulging the recipe for Corn Flakes; or he may have been blindsided by a desire to get the doctor out of his rapidly thinning hair.

Founding his company placed Will in an almost insurmountable financial hole. He desperately needed large sums of money to increase production *and* pay off his brother. He interested one backer, a former Sanitarium patient named Charles D. Bolin, to pledge $35,000 (about $950,000 in 2016) but Will still needed, at least, another $15,000 (about $407,000 in 2016), to get the firm on its feet. Perhaps too optimistically, he hoped his elder brother would be willing to invest in his future after all his years of hard work and service for the cause of biologic living. This was not to be. After a factory site was finally decided upon, John asked his younger brother to come over to his house to discuss the future of the business. During what started as an ostensibly peaceful meeting, John disabused Will of the suggestion that he would co-sign any bank loans or contribute a dime to the new venture. Will stormed off his brother's property, cursing John the entire way home. Eventually his anger turned into panic when he realized he was entirely obligated to repay the enormous debt. The steady Puss consoled her husband and told Will he needed to go find the money elsewhere.

The next day, Will approached many of his relatives to help him set up the new factory and pay his employees and creditors. He hated begging for money but there were many other Kelloggs in Battle Creek who had great faith in Will's integrity and work ethic. Will told one half-niece "If I don't pay this and my other debts within three months, I will lose everything I have in the world."[47] One way Will retaliated against his brother, incidentally, was by reminding John that he still owned 25 percent of Dr. Kellogg's Sanitas Nut Food Company and, thus, the doctor owed him a quarter of the sale price ($42,500 in stock) and another $30,000 in stock for Will's share in the old Sanitas factory building.

Before long, the doctor was nosing into Will's business and engaging in cruel acts of humiliation and domination. Shortly after the Battle Creek Toasted Corn Flake Company was incorporated on February 19, 1906, Dr. Kellogg complained about Will's $250 weekly salary (roughly $6,790 in 2016). Turning the table on the issue of their 75:25 profit-sharing plan for the Sanitas Company, John demanded he receive Will's paychecks each week in order to "claw back" 75 percent of it, followed by the doctor sending his younger brother a check for $62.50, his 25 percent share (about $1,750 in 2016).[48]

This arrangement, which lasted nearly a year, hardly lessened Will's antipathy for John. Every Friday, when he cashed his discounted paycheck, Will complained to Puss how important it was that he buy out his brother's share of the fledgling firm.[49] At this early stage of the business, however, Will just did not have the capital to both buy John out *and* grow his business. He had to bide his time and carefully plan his attack. For those who knew the quiet Will well, there was little question that he would succeed. As Dr. William Sadler observed in 1960, John Harvey Kellogg and Will Keith Kellogg were "tricky in certain areas [and, if you weren't careful, they] would take advantage of you."[50]

———

W. R. Kellogg's first Corn Flakes factory, 1906.
It burned to the ground on July 4, 1907.

IN EARLY MARCH OF 1906, Will purchased a ramshackle factory on Battle Creek's Bartlett Street, which was formerly owned by the Hygienic Food Company, makers of Mapl-Flakes. The price was $26,340.50 (about $716,000 in 2016) and it included enough production equipment and office space to start making cereal immediately. The factory was near the Grand Trunk Railway Line, which allowed for easy shipping and receiving. Part of the purchase price included a huge, three-story device called a "travelling oven."[51] Like a Ferris wheel, it consisted of a series of moving hoppers, or shelves, which were filled with the raw dough flakes. Exposed to just the right amount of heat from the ovens, the flakes dried and baked perfectly as each hopper moved up and down, closer and away from the heat source. Will's first staff consisted of seven men and women he recruited from his brother's food company. To protect against the thieves trying to make money by making and selling substandard versions of his products, Will ordered a guard to stand watch at the factory's front door, letting in only those who worked for the company. In subsequent years, the outside mechanics he contracted to build and maintain the factory's complex equipment were admitted only after displaying specially endorsed and dated entry passes. All Kellogg's employees had to sign a pledge of nondisclosure against divulging any of the recipes and manufacturing processes.

At the end of his first year of operation, Will's Toasted Corn Flake Company shipped out 178,943 cases of cereal. This is even more impressive considering that during the company's first two months, April and May of 1906, the factory produced only one hundred cases a day and during the last seven months of the fiscal year, more than 170,000 cases (nearly 25,000 per month) were manufactured and shipped.[52]

JUST AS PRODUCTION was humming and the advertising campaigns were corralling new grocers and customers, a tragedy struck that had the potential to put Will out of business. Eerily, on the evening of July 4, 1907, the original wooden corn flake factory burned to the ground.[53] Will recalled the fires that destroyed both the old Sanitarium and the Review and Herald building and worried that a "fire bug was at work" once more in Battle Creek.[54] The conspiracy theory was that a rogue Adventist torched the place in obeisance to Ellen White's allegation that the Kelloggs were agents of Satan. Far more likely a cause was connected to a group of night shift workers seen setting off fireworks, in celebration of the nation's birthday, right near the building.[55]

On July 4, 1907, Will had neither the time nor the luxury to identify a culprit. The new factory owner raced the several blocks from his home on Van Buren Street and arrived at the plant sweating and severely winded but conscious enough to watch his net worth and future security burn to the ground. Will remained calm and climbed up on a wooden box to address the distressed employees who came to the factory hoping to quench the fire. "I want all you men to report here tomorrow morning," Will announced. "You will not be laid off. Some of you will be assigned to our Norka plant and the rest can be used in clean up and construction work." The Norka plant was a nearby four-story former oatmeal factory Will had purchased in late 1906 both for extra capacity to make Corn Flakes and, for a short period, to manufacture an unappealing oat and sugar concoction that was discontinued because it tended to go rancid in the box. The Norka's factory served as its temporary home during the time the new factory was being built.[56]

Twelve hours after the fire, Will met with a Chicago-based architect named M. J. Morehouse to design his new plant. Later that night a determined Will wrote Arch Shaw, "The fire is of no consequence. You can't burn down what we have registered in the minds of the American woman."[57] Three weeks later, he selected a new location on Porter and Stile Streets on the east side of town, equidistant from both the Grand Trunk and Michigan Central lines. A quirk in the Michigan Central's fee schedules brought a smile to Will's face. The railway company categorized boxes of cereal as milled grain, rather than finished manufactured goods, and shipped them at a lower shipping rate. Soon after, the Grand Trunk followed suit to avoid losing business. This break proved to be a boon to Will as well as the Post and Quaker Oats companies, which also had major factories nearby.[58]

The July 4th fire destroyed not only the building but also his custom-made rolling mills. Will had long worked with the Lauhoff Brothers of Detroit, who only a few years earlier developed the water-cooled rollers that flattened corn grit dough and produced perfect flakes. By early 1906, however, the Lauhoffs had signed an exclusive contract with C. W. Post because the "Great Imitator" had designs for his own version of corn flakes. True to form, the wily Post insisted on a clause in his contract that strictly limited access to the special rolling devices for his company but not to any other cereal manufacturer.

Gerald Carson, a social historian of cereal foods in America, claimed that Post called for this stipulation partly as a result of his simmering rage at Will for not lending him the coal a year earlier that Post needed to power his plant.[59] Will's authorized biographer Horace Powell describes Charley Post as the classic robber baron of the day. Post had the resources to buy as many of the intricate rollers as the Lauhoffs produced and so he did. He either put them to use in his factory or simply stored them away for future use, "no doubt laughing heartily at the predicament of the young upstart company. But he hadn't reckoned with the determination and persuasiveness of Will Kellogg."[60]

Will really needed those rollers. They were crucial to his operation. In one account, he traveled to Detroit with "tears in his eyes." Upon arriving at the Lauhoff Brothers factory, he begged the proprietor, "Frank, my plant has burned down. I'm falling behind on my orders. What can you do for me?"[61] Such an open display of emotion on Will's part seems highly unlikely. A more plausible version tells of Will returning to Battle

Creek after his disappointing visit to Detroit. Walking through the ashes of what was once his factory, Will stubbed his toe on a long round metal object. Brushing away the ash, he recognized he had tripped on what was once a water-cooled roller, the very device he had asked the Lauhoff Brothers to design several years earlier and that he now could no longer purchase.

Running to the nearest telephone, Will demanded that the operator drop everything and place a long-distance call to Detroit. The question Will purportedly asked Frank Lauhoff sounds like a perfect example of the legal end-runs Will often played on his competitors: "Does that contract of yours say anything against repairing *broken* machines?" he asked. "You could get around the contract that way, couldn't you?" Before Mr. Lauhoff had a chance to display the slightest hesitation, Will reminded the roller man, "We helped you get started in the cereal roller business. Now you've got to help us."[62]

The ploy worked. Will etched his name with acid on each damaged roller he rescued from the rubble. He then ordered an underling to travel in the freight car carrying them between Battle Creek and Detroit to make sure Post would not appropriate them, as was potentially his contractual right, once they were repaired. Adding to the subterfuge, the Lauhoffs packed the repaired rollers and "flaking mills" in boxes labeled "The Crystal Malt Flakes Company," the name of the Lauhoffs' now defunct cereal company. Even sneakier, the Crystal Malt boxes were not officially listed on the train's bill of lading and the Lauhoffs placed them in the darkest corners of the boxcars transporting the goods. Before each delivery, Will received an advance call from Frank Lauhoff, who would cryptically state, "I am sending you another car load of Crystal Malt Flakes. Unload it at night and you will find a diamond in the corner." Charles Post and his executives did not hear about the scheme until long after. Decades later Frank Lauhoff recalled, "Even after all those years, they gave me hell about it."[63]

Drawing a loan of $55,000 (over $1 million in 2016) against the factory's insurance policy, which was worth $65,000 (more than $1.2 million in 2016), Will threw himself into the construction of his new, brick, fireproof factory. In early September, only a few weeks after he broke ground for the new facility, he realized he would need $50,000 more to complete the structure. Always profiting from his past business experiences, Will applied the know-how he acquired in raising the bonds and loans for the rebuilding of his brother's Sanitarium in 1902. Although the Detroit bankers refused to invest in still another cereal company situated in Battle Creek, Will did find a small Chicago bank, the National Bank of the Republic, willing to loan him $30,000 (roughly $567,000 in 2016) on three ninety-day notes. Will later asked the banker what inspired so much confidence in his firm. The banker replied that he was impressed by Will's character and his attention to detail in both his bookkeeping records and on his loan application. "We have to take chances same as other people," the banker told Will. "Your statement is good." In turn, W. K. Kellogg remained a loyal, and profitable, customer long after far larger and richer financial institutions competed to secure his business. Incidentally, the banker was entirely correct in his assessment of Will's business plan. He paid back the first $20,000 within ninety days and never took out the third installment of $10,000.[64]

The Toasted Corn Flake Company was back in full production by January of 1908. Inside the prosaically named "Building No. 1" were three shifts of white-suited, sanitary workers who made Corn Flakes twenty-four hours a day, seven days a week with trains at the ready to deliver the freshest, toastiest, crispiest cereals across the nation as quickly as possible.[65] It was the first of many modern, technologically driven cereal factories Will Kellogg would erect in the decades that followed. Within six months of reopening, Will was producing many more boxes of Corn Flakes than before the fire. Painted in foot-high letters alongside the factory, so that nearly every passenger on every passing train could

The rebuilt "Factory No. 1," opened in January of 1908

see, was the legend "THIS IS BATTLE CREEK." Upon opening the doors to his new factory in January of 1908, Will told John Leonard Kellogg, his second son and chief assistant, "Now we can turn out 4,200 cases a day and that's all the business I ever want." One year later, August of 1909, Kellogg's was producing and shipping 120,000 cases of Corn Flakes per day.[66]

In these early years of the Kellogg Company, Will improvised each day, learning what worked and discarding what did not. When he began his company there was no handbook or specifically designed machinery that helped Will manufacture cereal. He had to create them.[67] Employing the same attention to detail he displayed at the San, Will worked relentlessly at his task.[68]

He absorbed the best methods of mass production from other industries and shaped them to fit his "cereal assembly line." He worked with steel mills and oven companies to forge and create massive rotary ovens able to toast larger and larger quantities of Corn Flakes. After a batch of flakes was cooled, new and intricate systems of conveyor belts, like the kinds used in auto factories, transported the finished flakes from the "industrial kitchen" into the boxing room, and dumped them into waiting cartons, unsullied by the hands of his employees.[69] Working with printers and packaging experts, he developed machines that folded and glued preprinted pieces of cardboard into cereal boxes. A wonder of modern technology, Will's cereal factory ultimately housed an assembly line where raw grains traveled a distance of over five miles, "from the time they are received as corn until they are shipped as Kellogg's Corn Flakes."[70]

Will and his men worked even harder to develop a national distribution and grocery network. Years later, Will confessed, "I was green when I started the business. I had handled the business affairs of the sanitarium for years, but I did not know the difference between a food broker and a food jobber."[71] (The former is the agent who helps the food manufacturer get his products marketed and sold, typically to food jobbers, who are wholesalers who buy products either from a manufacturer or a food broker and then sell them to grocers for retail sales.) After he opened the second cereal plant, Will traveled around the country, inter-

"The Flaking Department" at Kellogg's, circa 1915

viewing food brokers, food jobbers, and retail grocers about the best ways to get Kellogg's Corn Flakes onto the grocery store shelves and into the American public's stomachs. When he returned to Battle Creek, Will instituted a service department to supply and cultivate relationships with the salesmen along the retail food chain. He formed another to create better means of advertising and marketing. He also kept a close, cold, and calculated eye on the doings of his competitors, from the products they were developing to their monthly sales numbers. And each time Will realized that he had bested his opponent, he indulged in the all too human emotion of *Schadenfreude* by "sit[ting] in his office and chuckl[ing] for minutes at a time."[72]

Like other industrial kings of the era, Will ran his company autocratically, completely, and paternalistically. He suffered few fools gladly and, in every discussion at the plant or in the boardroom, his word was the final one. It was his name on the box and he took that as seriously as if he signed the Declaration of Independence. No deskman ensconced in a fancy paneled office, surrounded by sycophants, Will demonstrated his "ownership" on every level of his ever-expanding business. He loved tackling new challenges that needed to be fixed, revised, or resolved. He routinely walked the factory floors making sure that the conveyor belts, toasting ovens, and other machines were in good working order, and tinkering with them if they were not. He probed his bakers, corn toasters, and boxers about what improvements needed to be made and what procedures needed to be discarded in the cause of profitability. For the men working directly under him in executive capacities, Will quietly demanded to know about every decision and which issues were ignored or dropped and why. When Will asked an employee a question, he retained absolute recall of the query and the employee's answer. He typically returned to that individual a week to ten days later, repeated his question, carefully listened to the response, and measured the progress made. The theme of his "pop" factory tours and unannounced appearances into an executive's office was "How can we do better?"

Will's drive for success might be best described by recalling a company board meeting in the mid-1930s. The featured guest was a prominent business consultant named Robert Updegraff. Much to the chagrin of the executives sitting at the conference table, Updegraff identified a palette of issues requiring attention and change. The Kellogg Company executives' faces fell to the floor as the consultant described his approach to business administration in one bold sentence: "I am never satisfied that anything is being done as well as it should be done." Recognizing a kindred spirit in Updegraff, Will stood up from his perch at the head of

The *"Flavoring Department"*: *"Kellogg's products win their favor through their flavor,"* circa 1915

the table, staring down the seated executives and declared, "Gentlemen, that is what we need in this business—more dissatisfaction."[73]

Will's cereal company was his life's work, his main source of joy, and his most reliable source of fulfillment and identity.[74] For the remainder of his working life, it seems the company occupied his every waking moment, often at the exclusion of his roles as a father and husband. Still, one cannot help but admire his singular resolve to make Kellogg's the best of its kind. In his own fashion, he loved, or at least cared deeply about, his factories, his employees, and those who sold his products extending from the men and women working for him in Battle Creek all the way to every grocer who carried them and, of course, every customer who enjoyed them.[75]

From his early days at the San to his retirement at Kellogg's, Will recognized the importance of human resources to help him achieve his goals. Like many of his cadre of successful industrialists, he was less than enthusiastic about the labor union movement. Corporate paternalism aside, he paid good wages to his factory workers, his executives, and his support staff but he demanded honesty, integrity, hard work, and accountability. He made certain his factories were clean and provided safe working conditions. He built and maintained adequate restrooms and pleasant dining rooms for breakfast, lunch, and dinner breaks. He also instituted a kindergarten, nursery, and day care center for the children of working mothers (free of charge), full medical, dental, and nutritional "attention" to employees and their families, and a ten-acre, well-coiffed garden surrounding the plant for the enjoyment and recreation of the workers. Most important, he listened to his employees' gripes and if he agreed that a problem existed, he fixed it.

Even during the most ominous fiscal threats, such as those set in motion by the long Great Depression, Will remained confident and in charge. Instead of trimming his payroll with layoffs, on December 1, 1930, Will took the novel, and humane, tack of instituting four 6-hour shifts for his factories, rather than three 8-hour shifts, so that his entire work force of more than 1,500 men and women remained employed and able to provide for their families. Will kept this workforce in place because he knew everyone had to eat breakfast. What better and more economical way to do that, he asked, than with a 15 cent box of his nutritious, filling, tasty cereal? And the only way to feed the nation its daily breakfast was to keep manufacturing boxes of Corn Flakes. An impressed President Herbert Hoover, who was contending with a rapidly rising national unemployment rate, invited Will and grandson John Jr. to visit his fishing camp near Winchester, Virginia, for the weekend to discuss the six-hour-shift plan.[76] Will Kellogg's steely resolve, buttressed by his undying faith in his greatest creation—those crispy, toasted, golden Corn Flakes—enabled him to shepherd his company to a gross profit of $6 million (about $110 million today) in 1933, the nadir of the Great Depression, a year when most American companies were struggling to make their payrolls and many others were filing for bankruptcy.

Will learned from his failures as well, such as a sales campaign that almost damaged his beloved Corn Flakes as much as the infamous "New Coke" campaign did to Coca-Cola half a century later. In 1939, when sales of Corn Flakes were stagnating, the Kellogg Company produced a radio show on the National Broadcasting Network about a "club" called "The Circle," presided over by the suave actor Ronald Colman and featuring as "members" the glamorous Carole Lombard, handsome Cary Grant, and sexy Madeleine Carroll, along with the pianist and conductor José Iturbi, and, for laughs, Groucho and Chico Marx. In concert with a parade of national magazine and local newspaper advertisements, the show's commercials pitched "a new way to eat corn flakes"—first by heating a tray of the cereal in the oven, then pouring on hot milk or cream, and eating them "piping hot."[77] The result was a disgusting mess, few Americans took to this unwieldy preparation, and the advertisements were quickly dropped. Despite its stellar cast, the radio show never caught on and barely made it through one season. Never again did Will change the mode of eating a bowl of Corn Flakes (with cold milk), let alone the formula that made his flakes so good in the first place.

WILL KELLOGG STEPPED DOWN from the helm of his company in 1939 at the age of seventy-nine. On April 29 of that year he wrote a letter to his son John Leonard enumerating some twenty-four mistakes he had made over thirty-three years. He ended with a reflective postscript: "Shall be eighty my next birthday and I think it is high time that I get out of business and quit making mistakes."[78] In fact, he had delayed his retirement plans for years because he could not "let go" or find anyone

Manufacturing Kellogg's cereals around the world

he felt was up to the task of running Kellogg's. For almost all of the 1930s, Will interviewed and appointed a string of executives to steer his beloved company, only to become exasperated with each one's failings and, finally, demanding their resignation.[79] In 1939, he successfully lured a former Chicago banker named Watson H. Vanderploeg to assume the helm. That year, the company's profits totaled over $33 million (or $562 million in 2016). Will still kept in close contact with the company and demanded weekly updates on the firm's progress as well as a daily statement of the cash reserves and orders along with a dedicated phone line to question executives when he saw fit. At the time of his retirement, the Kellogg Company controlled "more than 40 per cent of the business in ready-to-eat cereal within the United States and more than 50 per cent of such cereals sold beyond the borders of our nation."[80]

By all metrics, Watson Vanderploeg was a successful chief executive officer and he ran the company with a fierce determination to increase earnings. In 1948, two years after Will finally stepped down from the board of directors, the Kellogg Company reached a record $100 million in sales (about $983 million in 2016) and in 1956 that number doubled (about $1.74 billion today). When Vanderploeg died at age sixty-eight in 1957 while still holding office, the company manufactured food in three gleaming factories in the United States, as well as plants in Canada, Australia, South Africa, Great Britain and Mexico, and three additional contracted factories in Ireland, Sweden, and Holland. [81] In Battle Creek alone, the company maintained a constant grain reserve of 1.5 million bushels, and each day shipped out more than sixty-five train carloads (roughly 6,500 cubic feet of space, or 190,000 pounds) of cereal. Every twenty-four hours, the Battle Creek plant produced six million boxes of the stuff, one million of them filled with Corn Flakes.[82]

In the 1950s, after Will's death, Vanderploeg introduced a succession of sugar-loaded cereals, with unabashed names like Sugar Pops, Sugar Smacks, and, most successfully, Sugar Frosted Flakes. These sweetened grains were aggressively marketed and eagerly consumed, thus initiating a raft of unhealthy practices among all cereal manufacturers and consumers that has only recently begun to diminish because of market demand and a better understanding of the dangerous role processed, sugar-filled foods play in our current obesity epidemic and our overall health.[83] Alas, sugar definitely boosted sales (and waistlines) during these years.

Although many refer to the post–World War II era as the atomic age, and, later, the space age, a more historically correct moniker might be the television age. For several years, the Kellogg's Company licensed Mickey Mouse and Donald Duck from the Walt Disney Studio to hawk their products. In 1949, Watson Vanderploeg took the quantum leap by hiring the Leo Burnett Advertising Agency of Chicago to develop an exclusive line of colorful mascots to sell Kellogg's cereal to children. Burnett had already achieved great acclaim in the advertising world for creating "the Jolly Green Giant" (for the Minnesota Valley Canning Company) and the "Marlboro Man" (for Philip Morris). The frumpy, chain-smoking advertising genius repeatedly hit balls out of the park with a colorful cast of Kellogg characters, including Tony the Tiger ("Sugar Frosted Flakes: They're Gre-e-e-eat!"); a modernization of the Rice Krispies trio of Snap, Crackle, and Pop; Toucan Sam for Froot Loops; and the rooster on Corn Flakes boxes, "Cornelius."

Burnett left nothing to chance in his advertising campaigns. He liked to quote his colleague E. L. Bernays, the "father" of public relations and a nephew of Sigmund Freud, who insisted that what people loved most about Will's cereals was the crunch, which helped people get out their aggressions and angst. Burnett demanded a far more practical approach.

He tested every variable and was a maven of data, from analyzing the type of people who watched the shows best suited for sponsorship by Kellogg's to determining the right colors for the cereal box ("jungle green," for example, was deemed to be "a strong appetite color").[84] Throughout the 1950s and early 1960s, the Leo Burnett Agency kept outdoing itself with new creative Kellogg's advertisements. They included some of the nation's most popular culture figures, such as Norman Rockwell's cherubic, All-American portraits, the swimming queen of the Silver Screen, Esther Williams, silly Andy Devine, and even Groucho Marx rolling his eyes at Tony the Tiger.[85]

The remarkable impact these sales methods had on children and their mothers and fathers cannot be underestimated. In 1949, Kellogg's paid out $12.5 million (or $123 million in 2016) for television advertisements; by 1951, that number jumped to $128 million ($1.26 billion in 2016). During the 1950s, Kellogg's sponsored such hit children's series as the *Adventures of Superman* (starring the ill-fated George Reeves), *The Woody Woodpecker Show,* and *Howdy Doody*. In the 1960s, the company extended its reach by sponsoring the daily children's program *Captain*

TONY THE TIGER SAYS:
"You bet your life they're Gr-r-reat!"

No wonder Groucho's speechless. What if a tiger stole your microphone and your favorite line. But that's Tony for you. And he's all for you when he tells you to try these big, crackly flakes of corn. Because they're the ones with the secret Kellogg's sugar coating all over. Gr-r-reat? You bet your life.

Kellogg's SUGAR FROSTED FLAKES

You bet your life Groucho Marx likes
Sugar Frosted Flakes!

Kangaroo, and every Saturday morning a slate of popular cartoon shows featuring the popular Hanna-Barbera characters Yogi Bear, Huckleberry Hound, and Quick Draw McGraw. And to make sure American mothers and fathers were equally entertained and informed about the cornucopia of Kellogg products, the company sponsored *Art Linkletter's House Party*, *The Garry Moore Show*, and *You Bet Your Life*.[86] The combination of great advertising campaigns and the new medium of television proved to be one of the company's most irresistible, albeit somewhat opportunistic, marketing ploys. Will may not have approved of these methods but he would, undoubtedly, have been gratified to learn that by 1974 Kellogg's enjoyed $1 billion in sales, a number that doubled to $2 billion in 1980. In 2014, the company made sales of over $14.5 billion and employed more than 29,700 people even as it faces serious market shifts in what consumers want to eat for breakfast.[87]

AFTER SUCH A CIRCUITOUSLY TOLD STORY, it seems worthwhile to circle back to that long-ago November day in 1912. One can easily imagine Will Keith Kellogg standing on the Great White Way, looking up into the sky at his gargantuan "I Want Kellogg's" electric billboard atop the Mecca Building. He probably had to catch his breath and steady his bounding pulse. What a grand spectacle: *his* name shining away in big, bright lights on Broadway. For years, he toiled and put all his faith (and future) in his Toasted Corn Flakes. Quietly, and without a hint of conceit, he had even confessed that pending success to a few others, "I sort of feel it in my bones."[88] The giant, electric Kellogg's sign was an important symbol for Will, a trophy of sorts, for the first of many victories in the years that followed. His once daily existence of servitude and humiliation was behind him, even as the bickering between the Kellogg brothers continued to escalate, and he had experienced, and would experience many more, family tragedies and strife. One can only hope that, on the brisk, sunny morning he first fixed his gaze on the largest electric sign ever constructed, Will was able to crowd out thoughts of John, the San, and even his personal demons inaccurately calling him a lackey. By 1912, Will had found his place in the world. And what a remarkable place it was.

PART IV

Battles of Old Age

Woman getting a workout at the San,
circa 1913

12

The Prison of Resentment

IN EVERY LEGAL DISPUTE there exist three truths: the plaintiff's truth, the defendant's truth, and what actually happened. On the battleground where pride, power, and money are challenged, courtroom adversaries care less about discovering that third truth than they do about winning their case. During the long-running war establishing who was the dominant sibling, victory was everything to Will Keith *and* John Harvey Kellogg. That grudge match became codified in the annals of law on August 11, 1910, when Will filed a bill of complaint against John in the Circuit and Chancery Court of Calhoun County, Michigan. His petition requested a permanent injunction against the doctor's food company and a judgment of $100,000 (or $2.57 million in 2016) in damages. It was the opening salvo in what turned out to be a ten-year battle.[1]

Will's personal relationship with John may have been complicated but, from a business standpoint, the reasons undergirding his legal attack were simple. In 1908, shortly after his Battle Creek Toasted Corn Flake Company began to ascend under its new name, "The Kellogg's Toasted Corn Flake Company," the doctor aggressively marketed two of his own "new cereals": rice flakes and "sterilized" wheat bran flakes. Instead of using the old "Sanitas" or "Sanitarium Foods" labels, which he had created and used for more than twenty-five years to avoid charges of self-promotion from the medical profession, John was now selling them under the banner of "The Kellogg's Food Company of Battle Creek." Will charged that John was infringing on *his* brand name by deliberately confusing the public and taking advantage of the investment of labor, advertising, and money he had made in marketing his "Kellogg's cereal." Only a few days later, John filed a countersuit claiming there was no infringement of Will's rights and, in fact, the wrong had been committed against him; to wit, John's lawyers claimed, *John* was the "real" Kellogg known throughout the world as the great healer, dietary expert, and the creator of flaked cereals.[2]

While preparing the lawsuit, Will confided to his son John Leonard that he had an "airtight case" considering he had already paid his brother a great deal of money, both in cash and stock shares in the Battle Creek Toasted Corn Flake Company for "the exclusive right within the United States to manufacture, sell and deal in said certain food products."[3] Never one to leave anything to chance when it came to his business, however, Will instructed his lawyers to enlist scores of housewives, businessmen, grocers, food brokers and jobbers for testimony on how John's strong-arm tactics were hurting Will's company. Will alleged that Dr. Kellogg's flaked cereals were intentionally packaged in boxes nearly identical to those containing his famous "W.K. Kellogg's Toasted Corn Flakes." The confusing packaging resulted in grocers ordering and selling both products, side by side, assuming they were made by the same company. Worse, in Will's estimation, customers too often made the wrong choice by purchasing a box of his brother's tasteless cereal products, which potentially hurt the sales of his tastier brand. Equally compelling were Will's "legal exhibits," a mountain of attractive advertisements for *his* Kellogg's Corn Flakes, which had appeared in hundreds of magazines and newspapers across the nation. Will's superior product backed by intensive sales efforts and a more than $2 million investment (about $51.4 million in 2016) for advertising, his legal brief contended, were the reasons behind the American public's allegiance to products labeled "Kellogg."[4]

EACH BROTHER'S STATE OF MIND merits consideration. Why would two close relatives embark upon such a destructive course? For John, the timing could not have been worse. On November 10, 1907, after years of harmful accusations, deceitful smears of his reputation, and vicious backbiting, he was permanently expelled from the Seventh-day Adventist Church, the faith and guiding light of his spiritual life. John's letters to sympathetic religious brethren throughout the ordeal articulate his depression and anxiety during the traumatic series of events.[5] Historian Richard Schwarz later contended that John "was never his former buoyant, enthusiastic self in the years after his expulsion from the Adventist church . . . [but] the manufacture and promotion of his food creations served, at least in part, to fill . . . these needs."[6] John's pride of authorship over flaked cereals, combined with his envy over Will's success in selling them so profitably, may well have been part of the equation. There exists, however, much evidence to argue against the claim that the doctor was "never his former buoyant, enthusiastic self" after his excommunication. An alternative explanation is that at some deeply rooted level John enjoyed or, at least, thrived on the many conflicts he engaged in and provoked during his long life, especially those involving Will. Fraternal conflict, in a strange way, energized Dr. Kellogg and stimulated his creative juices even if it came at a huge cost to those who loved or worked with him. Fighting with Will was one of the signal constants of his inner, psychic life, from childhood to old age.[7]

In Will's defense, it is easier to understand why he retaliated against his older brother. To use his own words, Will was "sick and tired of this controversy" and, imbued with a newfound confidence, was ready to right what he perceived to be wrongs.[8] Will certainly experienced his brother's hurtful actions on a personal level, but he was far more focused on how the doctor's shenanigans were harmful to his corporate identity. He acted as most modern businessmen do against those trespassing on their profits: he took John to court. In the decades that followed, Will Kellogg rarely, if ever, tolerated slights or attacks against his company. He used the courts, threats of pulling his business from contractors or suppliers, and a wily behavior to decimate and dominate those he considered to be his—or his company's—enemies, which in Will's eyes were one and the same. In retrospect, it is tempting to suggest he saw these foes as psychological straw men representing his older brother. Whatever the battle, from the founding of his company in 1906 until the end of his life, Will usually won.

JOHN HARVEY KELLOGG'S FIRST ENTRÉE into the food business, it may be recalled, began in 1877 with the founding of the Sanitarium Food

Company. The firm initially manufactured Granola, oatmeal, graham- and fruit-based crackers, and whole grain cooked cereals.[9] Sanitarium products were "wholesome" foods free of fillers, additives, animal fat, sugar, or salt preservatives, such as baking soda and sodium chloride. In the years that followed, the doctor, Will, Ella Eaton Kellogg, and a gaggle of assistants created many other new products, all of which were served and sold at the Sanitarium.[10]

In 1880, Will and William S. Sadler, then an eighteen-year-old San employee, urged John to consider marketing the products through individual retail stores, first in the Midwest and subsequently across the nation.[11] Such an enterprise required a larger plant and greater output to meet the additional demand. This suggestion inspired the doctor to ask his Sanitarium board members for funds to build an enlarged food factory and a modern, well-equipped "food laboratory." The San's trustees, already concerned about John's insatiable (and typically expensive) plans for expansion, voted against it. In short, the board "did not think it best to incur the expense of the necessary experimental work."[12] Rebuffed but not defeated, John invested his own funds into the cause. By 1889, Sanitarium Food sold forty-two different health products and appropriated, first, a barn behind the San, and, in 1898, a small freestanding "factory" to manufacture these wares, all under the competent supervision of Will. It was also around this time that John and Will established a separate company, the Sanitas Nut Food Company, which sold a line of nut butters and nut-based meat substitutes. Beginning in 1895, after they discovered how to make flaked cereal, the new Granose wheat flakes were sold under the Sanitas label.[13]

Always too busy with the next conquest to pay attention to the one he had just begun, John was sloppy in his administration of the two food companies (as well as his many other commercial concerns). As a result, there was much crossover in the production, bookkeeping, and marketing activities of these two firms. Less interested in making money for personal gain than he was in promoting biologic living, the doctor viewed both companies as cooperative extensions of the Sanitarium, which were "more or less associated and carried out under a common management."[14]

Dr. Kellogg was, of course, aware of the vast financial opportunities in food production even though he disingenuously told his Adventist

Church commanders that the endeavor was merely a means "to support the entire denominational work." In June of 1896, for example, he told Ellen White that he was "so busy I can do but very little in the way of pushing it . . . my brother, Will, earns the money for me to give away, while I give my time to the Sanitarium."[15] A few years later, in a letter to Ellen in December of 1898, John again downplayed the finances of the food company as he endorsed his brother Will as "one of the most faithful, careful, painstaking persons I have ever met . . . [and someone who] uncomplainingly carries a very heavy load of burdens."[16]

DESPITE JOHN'S CLAIM OF fraternal harmony and benevolent management, Will and John were actively engaged in various food fights. Matters became even more strained when other companies cashing in on the ready-to-eat cereal boom began to subvert John's patent for flaked cereals.[17] By the early 1900s, more than one hundred different companies were making their own version of flaked cereals, many of them earning huge profits that Will thought ought to be flowing into the Sanitarium and Sanitas companies' coffers.

The shaky foundation under John's flaked cereal patent was formally demonstrated in 1903, when the Kellogg brothers filed a lawsuit against the makers of Voigt Cream Flakes, the Voigt Milling Company, and Voigt Cereal Company of Grand Rapids, Michigan. Unfortunately for the Kelloggs, and largely as a function of the highly specific patent laws in the United States, a battery of defense attorneys proved that the Voigt Cream Flakes used a different manufacturing process than the one John filed in 1895. The Voigts eliminated the first step in the Kellogg method, which entailed soaking the grain in a water bath, and proceeded directly to aping the remaining elements of the recipe to produce their "baked, crisp and slightly brown flakes." This distinction made all the legal difference because in order to prove patent infringement, the plaintiff must demonstrate that "the defendant used every element of the patent."[18]

Ironically, the Voigts' key witness was Henry Perky, the creator of Shredded Wheat and the man who walked away from a manufacturing deal with Dr. Kellogg in 1894 to found his own firm. The following year, John and Will developed what many considered to be a better product. Perky, however, saw the Kelloggs' wheat flakes as nothing more than a slightly altered version of *his* creation. The recipes are similar and the main difference between Shredded Wheat biscuits and John's wheat flakes was, essentially, the cereals' distinct shapes. But because John's process did not follow Perky's recipe to the letter, it was not legally considered patent theft. The aggrieved Perky played turn-around on Will and John by demonstrating this very point during the *Kellogg v. Voigt* trial. The court decided in the Voigts' favor in 1903.

After a denied appeal in 1905, Dr. Kellogg concluded he had no exclusivity over flaked cereals as long as others were unscrupulous enough to add or subtract their own alterations to the cooking process. Dr. Kellogg's experience with the Voigt trial convinced him that the flaked bonanza he hoped would accrue to the San was hardly worth the trouble. The doctor shortsightedly resolved to sell his flaked cereal rights because other cereal firms "will pirate them anyhow."[19]

Another reason John wanted to get out of the cereal business was tied to his professional reputation. After his close call of being expelled from the Calhoun County Medical Society in 1885, he had long fretted about being seen as engaging in unethical practices or as an outright quack by the more staid and scientifically based American medical profession. John would later testify under oath that he "thought it was important to do nothing of any sort that would touch even the more sensitive sensibilities or give any occasion . . . for thinking I was actuated by commercial or financial motives."[20] Revisionist historians have incorrectly labeled Dr. Kellogg as a charlatan. The truth of the matter, however, is that while some doctors disagreed with his more outlandish ideas, he was considered by many others to be a fine physician and surgeon, which is exactly the reputation John most desired. Consequently, he was eager to avoid any hint of impropriety, let alone engage in the Barnumesque salesmanship characterizing the cereal trade during the first decade of the twentieth century.

IT WAS IN THIS CONTEXT that Will took the first steps toward changing his life and the way the world eats breakfast. In June 1905, he took a deep breath, summoned up the courage to face his domineering brother, and offered to buy the cereal business outright. Will's timing could not have been better. Aside from the invalidation of his patent for flaked

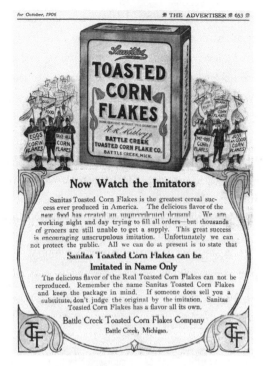

In 1906, Will began pushing the boundaries of John's "Sanitas" brand name by "signing" the cereal boxes and warning customers against "imitators."

cereals, the restrictions placed upon him by the medical profession, and a growing disinterest in the commerce of food, the doctor was deeply in debt and needed money badly to shore up the Sanitarium, his medical school, his mission, and many other ventures.[21] What John's signature on the dotted line did not guarantee, however, was a cease-fire from his constant sniping, interference, and competitive ventures aimed directly at Will and his newborn company.[22]

After signing the deal in January 1906 and resigning from John's Sanitas Foods Company, Will Kellogg worked doggedly to manufacture his cereal, which was, confusingly, still labeled as "Sanitas Toasted Corn Flakes." He realized he needed a better brand name to distinguish his product from all the imitators crowding the market. On March 8, 1906, a few weeks after he changed the name of his cereal from Korn Krisp to Corn Flakes, Will wrote to Arch Shaw:

The following is a matter I would like you to especially consider: What would you think of calling these flakes "Kellogg Corn Flakes" instead of Sanitas Corn Flakes, and then using a signature somewhere on the package similar to the attached? In thinking of this matter, don't take into consideration for a moment that I am ambitious to have my name appear in this way. The only thing I am interested in is the business that will result. I have not spoken to Dr. J.H. about the matter, but I am sure he would object to the plan and he would suggest that the inference would be that it's his corn flakes, but the signature on the package ought to take away this objection. I am exceedingly anxious to do this just right and want the benefit of all the help I can get in making the decision.[23]

By the fall of 1906, Will's boxes of the still confusingly labeled "Sanitas Toasted Corn Flakes" began to include his bold signature and the

A spring 1907 Sanitas Toasted Corn Flakes advertisement (only a few months before changing the name to "Kellogg's Toasted Corn Flakes") boldly featuring Will's signature and promising his customers the "genuine" product

promise, "Beware of imitations. None genuine without this signature."[24] In retrospect, this was not nearly as bold a move as one might suspect at first glance. Beginning in 1903, and with John's permission, the brothers pulled a bit of signatory legerdemain by affixing Will's signature to many of the *other* Sanitas Nut Food products (but not the wheat flakes) under the phrase "None Genuine Without This Signature." This was less a formal acknowledgment of Will's contribution to the products than it was a protective trademark. John egocentrically reasoned that few people would be able to distinguish W.K.'s signature from his, thus affording him the credit he craved and protecting him against inflaming the medical profession.[25]

Around this same time, John learned of still another appropriation of his name in the dietary marketplace, which was far more threatening to his reputation and demanded immediate action. An unrelated quack named Prof. Frank Kellogg opened up a company in Battle Creek to sell "anti-obesity pills." His pills were, at best, useless and, if taken to excess, a potential cause of dehydration and metabolic havoc.[26] As John later declared on the witness stand, with good reason:

> I have suffered much from the advertising of an obesity cure by Frank Kellogg and I was continually receiving letters censuring me because the remedy did not accomplish what it was recommended to do, occasionally personal visits, threatening violence, because they had been badly swindled. I have a stack of letters two or three feet high because of this man's advertising. Sometimes he actually used my initials. Usually he used his own, and I was held responsible for that thing. I appealed to the post office authorities to protect me, but they were not able to do anything, so I thought if I was going to start a food company it would be a little more than I could bear. That was the way I happened to put "Kellogg" into the firm name.[27]

In the early summer of 1907, while John was in Europe, Will took an even bolder step by formally changing the firm's name from the "Battle Creek Toasted Corn Flake Company" to the "Kellogg Toasted Corn Flake Company."[28] Will knew that John's long-distance absence was the only time he could successfully make such a daring motion without suffering the caustic effects of John's obstructionism.[29] The company's board of directors responded enthusiastically and, upon their approval, Will solemnly promised them "there would be no occasion to expect that he would use his name in private enterprises in any way that would be disastrous to the Toasted Corn Flake Co. . . . [and] would therefore operate to his financial detriment."[30] Soon after the meeting ended, Will spread the word to the nation's grocers:

> Don't delay in sending your order to the jobber. See that you get the Corn Flakes with "W.K. Kellogg" [in facsimile] on the package. Kellogg's Corn Flakes was placed on the market as Sanitas Corn Flakes. We're going to drop the word Sanitas and call it Kellogg's Toasted Corn Flakes thereafter. This name protects both you and us better than the old one.[31]

Between the late summer and early fall of 1907, "Kellogg's Toasted Corn Flakes" made its official debut on the American scene with a blizzard of advertisements and many millions of bright green, red, and white boxes of cereal.[32]

August 1907: Finally and forever,
"Kellogg's Toasted Corn Flakes"

In his lawsuit, John described how he was informed of the company's name change, barely after stepping off the transatlantic steamship's gangplank in New York. The doctor also stipulated his angry resolve to block the move, no matter what it took. Repeatedly, John referred to his younger brother as a "rascal." Again, when reviewing all of the legal documents, these matters were not nearly as clear as John claimed. During a subsequent cross-examination, for example, John admitted that when he was first informed of Will's motion to change the firm's name to "Kellogg's," he failed to register a formal objection. From July through September of 1907, John affirmed under cross-examination, he received multiple stock reports, memoranda, and dividend checks with the words "Kellogg's Toasted Corn Flake Company" emblazoned on them and, again, raised no complaints, especially upon cashing his dividend checks. As Will's lawyers battered the doctor with hard evidence over his acquiescence to the name change, John confabulated under oath, "I was informed that—at any rate I was under the belief that there was no use for me to make any protest. . . . I made no protest, no, I mean no formal protest."[33]

Just as the brothers' fight reached a boiling point, Will's son John Leonard and Will and John's nephew Wilfred were still employed by John as supervisors at the doctor's Sanitas Nut Food Company, which continued to make nut and grain products long after John sold the rights to manufacture Corn Flakes to Will.[34] In early 1908, Wilfred left the doctor's Sanitas Nut Food Company to become the secretary of Will's Battle Creek Toasted Corn Flake Company; that same year, Will's son, John Leonard, weary (and wary) of working for his difficult uncle John, left the Sanitarium's food venture to join his father's firm. A few years later, John brazenly exploited this chronology in a countersuit against his brother claiming that John Leonard stole his trade secrets for a "sterilized bran" cereal and handed them over to Will, an allegation that never stuck.

SOMETIME BETWEEN Christmas of 1907 and New Year's Day 1908, the doctor resigned from the board of directors of Will's Toasted Corn Flake Company.[35] John's stated reason was that he needed to focus upon the management duties of his own food firm. This decision was especially ill conceived given that running a complex business was not among his many talents. In early 1908, John escalated matters by informing Will about his intention to trademark the name "Kellogg's" and change the name of *his* Sanitas Nut Food Company to "Kellogg's Food Company." The newly named company would sell his latest creation, flaked rice cereal and the original wheat flakes.[36]

This tactic enraged Will, especially because it was accompanied by an extortionist scheme the doctor offered in exchange for backing away from the name changing. In short, John demanded Will hand over $500,000 worth of stock in Will's company in return for the exclusive rights to making rice and wheat flakes and John's permission for Will to use the family name in his business. Even if Will accepted these outrageous terms, paying John's ransom demand would require him to increase his company's capitalization by an additional $1 million (or about $39 million in 2016); an especially difficult task in that Will had recently announced a 3-for-1 stock split to increase the company's capitalization to $1 million after the July 4, 1907, factory fire and rebuilding effort.[37]

Utterly unaware of the consequences of his hostile actions, John wrote a "letter of peace" on January 20, 1908, reassuring his brother that his intentions were pure and honorable:

> First of all I desire to state that I am not unmindful of the many years of loyal and brotherly assistance that you have given me in my work and the faithful and conscientious manner in which my personal affairs have been looked after. . . . I have been too busy to express to you as I ought to have done my appreciation, but I wish you nevertheless to be sure that my appreciation has been greater and deeper than words ever could have expressed or than I now know how to express. If anything I have ever said or done has led you to feel that there was a lack of appreciation on my part, I sincerely regret and now apologize for the same. . . . I trust that all the business relations between the Sanitas and the Toasted Corn Flake Company will be in every way friendly and amicable. . . . I expect to make some blunders and to suffer for them. But I will do the best I can and will make the best of the consequences. I shall not knowingly permit anything to be done which I consider antagonistic to the legitimate interest of the Toasted Corn Flake Company. . . . Certainly I have no malice in my heart toward any-

one, least of all toward you. I have not intentionally said a word to do you harm or injustice. If anything I have said has seemed to you to have such an intent or purpose, I sincerely hope you will accept this statement as an utter disavowal of any such purpose and a refutation of any statement to the contrary which anyone can make; for what I have written above is a frank and sincere statement of my feeling in reference to our personal and business affairs, and of my appreciation of your personal interest and your valuable service to me and the interests with which I am connected. As Ever, your affectionate brother.[38]

Will responded by taking his elder brother to task. Although his January 29, 1908, letter of response began with the salutation "Dear Brother," it was clear within a few sentences that "Dear" was only an expression of speech rather than a means of describing their relationship:

For twenty-two and one-half years, I had absolutely lost all my individuality in you. I tried to see things with your eyes and do things as you would do them. You know in your heart whether or not I am a rascal. You also know whether or not I would defraud anyone, under any circumstances. The fact that we worked together for so many years, would seem to be a reply to the above inquiry. . . . You have told people that there was no break between you and I, but it begins to look to me as if there [is] going to be a breach, if there was not one already. . . . I think I am justified, under the circumstances, in holding you responsible for the present unpleasant situation. It is unbecoming in either you or myself to allow ourselves to get into a condition of mind where we make uncomplimentary remarks, one of another. . . . Were it not for the fact that I am under obligations to the stockholders of the Toasted Corn Flake Co., I want to assure you that in my present state of mind, I would sell out my holdings in Battle Creek and try some other climate.[39]

John continued to protest (too much) that the name change of his food company was a means to protect his reputation against charlatans like Frank J. Kellogg, the "obesity cure king," as well as a German company, also named Sanitas, which made disinfectants all over Europe and

North America. The doctor claimed that he did not want his health foods to be confused with quacks or smelly chemicals.[40] Will, of course, saw right through his brother's rationale. John's jealousy over Will's success burned brightest in early May of 1908 when he printed the following legend on his cereal boxes: "Sanitas Wheat Flakes is the only flaked product which has a legitimate pedigree."[41]

Will, who was present at the birth of flaked cereals and played a critical role in their development, was offended by John's duplicitous insinuation that *his* Corn Flakes were the nutritional equivalent of a bastard. In early May, Will protested, "It seems to me, Dr., that this puts the Toasted Corn Flake Company in a rather bad light. We have been claiming in all our advertisements originality and I certainly have been laboring under the impression that the Toasted Corn Flakes had a legitimate pedigree, and not an illegitimate one."[42]

Writing to his lawyers on July 6, 1908, Will's bitterness jumps off the page: "It is very apparent the sole purpose in the Dr.'s making this change is that he may be benefitted somewhat by the several hundred thousand dollars the Toasted Corn Flake Company has expended in advertising to make the name Kellogg's of some value." In the same letter, Will explained that he was considering producing a line of wheat flakes to compete with the doctor's version, even though he stood to make little money because Americans overwhelmingly preferred his Corn Flakes.[43] Only two days later, on July 8, Will tried a different tack, solicitously offering to avoid any mention of the Battle Creek Sanitarium and its work on his products and to avoid trespassing on his older brother's domain.[44]

The next day, July 9, Chappell and Earl, the law firm that represented both John and Will in various enterprises for years, withdrew their counsel from Will's company, preferring, instead, to stick with the more famous elder brother. The lawyers closed their letter with some solid advice to Will: "We should regret to see any litigation or controversy between you people. Your interests should be together against the common enemy. You should in the language of Ben Franklin, 'hang together,' or you may, figuratively speaking, hang separately."[45]

JOHN ANTAGONIZED WILL once again at July's end by announcing a grandiose plan to advertise his "Kellogg's Toasted Wheat Flakes" with a series of public events and lectures in New York City and Chicago.[46] Informing Will that he was tired of having his ideas so blatantly commercialized, the doctor insisted that using *his* name on *his* products was the "only way by which they may be protected." John added that his flaked rice and wheat cereals were made from grains not covered in the contract he signed in January of 1906. Acting somewhat like a rascal himself, the doctor claimed he was not violating Will's exclusive rights to sell Corn Flakes in the United States because their contract said nothing about mail order sales and pertained only to grocery stores. And for good measure, the doctor demanded Will remove his signature from his boxes to avoid confusing the public over who was the "real" Kellogg. John ended his missive with a scraggly olive branch: he suggested they settle their differences by consulting a "committee of arbitration."[47]

Will exploded. On July 20, 1908, he wrote John a nine-page letter accusing John of running about Battle Creek telling mutual friends that Will's firm would never succeed and lose bundles of cash for its investors. Will went on to explain the decisions they made together, dating back to 1903, on affixing Will's signature on their various products. He reminded the doctor that in all their years in business together they never received a single complaint as to which Kellogg signed the box nor did his signature in any way sully or take advantage of Dr. Kellogg's medical reputation. Will concluded his declaration of grievance with a slew of reasonable questions and claims:

> If you were the Kellogg who was known to the public through the signature on the package, and feared that bad results would follow from the use of this name, why did you ever consent to my name appearing on the various packages of Sanitas Foods? And if you were harmed by this name appearing on the package, would you not have been likely to have referred to this harm, prior to the organization of the Toasted Corn Flake Co.? . . . In view of the fact that you have refrained for thirty years from allowing your name to be commercialized, it seems to me it is mighty unwise of you, at this late day, to decide to commercialize the name of Dr. J. H. Kellogg. . . . I wish to state that it seems to me I have some claim upon the use of the word "Kellogg's" as applied to cereals. I claim to have worked with you, nights and mornings, and overtime, without

any compensation, in the matter of developing the first Granose flakes . . . for your information [I] will state at this writing, it is my full purpose to organize and get ready immediately for business the W. K. Kellogg Cereal Food Co. I am advised by competent attorneys that I have a perfect right to do this.[48]

Three days later, July 23, John again insisted that the rice and wheat flake cereals were entirely different from Will's Corn Flakes and placing the name "Kellogg" on his cereal boxes was his only means to protect his trade rights against the same charlatans who threatened Will's food business. The doctor added that his actions were "in no way to make war upon the Toasted Corn Flake Company or to do anything which ought to be regarded as hostile or injurious to it. I have taken the best legal advice obtainable in relation to equities and legal rights involved."[49] His only wish, he disingenuously claimed, was for a peaceful accord bound by the ties of fraternity and friendship.[50]

In reply, Will wrote an even longer, and far more exasperated, letter on the evening of July 26:

I am getting very sick and tired of this controversy and thinking it very unprofitable for either you or I. I am awfully busy with various matters and think I will not take the trouble to reply to any more of your communications. Much of your logic and many of your statements seem to me to be erroneous, there seems to be no prospect of our getting together and I think we had best agree to disagree.[51]

Will made one last-ditch attempt at peacemaking only a few days later, on August 7. After a meandering stroll around town to brace his nerves, he finally pointed himself into a direct path to his brother's house. In the stifling summer heat, Will climbed the steps of the Residence's porch, straw hat in hand, ready to plead his case once again. He was not given the courtesy of being invited inside or even offered a cool drink. The porch confab included a hostile John and an even more hostile Ella Eaton Kellogg, who rarely got along with her brother-in-law and often urged her husband to fire him.[52]

Will appealed to his brother about how his chances for a successful career of his own were dissolving with every obstruction John mounted.

The confusion generated by these two competing cereal lines, Will predicted, would be disastrous for his fledgling company as well as for his brother's food firm. Finally displaying a backbone to his domineering brother, Will explained that while he hoped to avoid the costly and potentially embarrassing option of litigation, he was prepared to go down that route if the doctor continued his attacks.[53] The doctor softened a bit at his younger brother's entreaties and the two apparently made a handshake agreement, whereby Will would pay John another $50,000 and more stock in exchange for his "cease and desist." Before pen could be committed to paper, however, the doctor wriggled out of the deal.

The bickering, attacks, and counterattacks escalated for another two full years. Fueling the doctor's angst was how, between 1909 and 1910, Will's business exploded with profits, thanks to an excellent product, savvy marketing and sales techniques, and expenditures of more than $2 million ($51.4 million in 2016) for advertisements shouting about the wonders of Kellogg's Corn Flakes. The only fly in Will's increasingly rich bowl of cereal was his brother's relentless attempts to piggyback on that success with his bland-tasting wheat and rice flakes sold under the same banner of "Kellogg's."[54] By the summer of 1910, Will had had enough and told his lawyers to file their brief against his brother.

WILL'S AND JOHN'S LAWSUITS reached the docket of Calhoun County Circuit Court in mid-August of 1910. The judge hearing the case was Walter North, a slight, round-shouldered, bespectacled man who walked with a stoop even when he was relatively young. Well regarded for his fairness, a facile mind, and an exhaustive knowledge of Michigan's legal precedents, Judge North "worked hard all day and when evening came he always went home with a brief case loaded with briefs and records." He was so dedicated to his judicial tasks that he typically ate lunch at his desk to "gain an extra half-hour to continue his work."[55] After digesting the legal briefs, Judge North denied Will's request for an injunction on the grounds that it carried the potential to bankrupt the doctor's business before the true merits of the case could be heard. He ordered a hearing in a court of equity and he would make his decision after a full declaration of all the facts.[56]

Representing Dr. Kellogg was a well-known attorney named Fred L.

Chappell, a tall, thin man, with a sharp, stern gaze especially useful for staring down uncooperative witnesses during cross-examinations.[57] Assisting Chappell was his partner and brother-in-law, Otis A. Earl.[58] Both experts in patent law, they were members of the local lodge of Free Masons and, like the majority of the Battle Creek community, active members of the Republican Party.[59] Chappell and Earl were the same attorneys who had advised Will to simmer down and warned him that if a lawsuit did arise, they would side with his older brother, which, they insisted, Will would likely lose.

Will scoured the local and New York City bar associations before hiring W. H. Crichton Clarke. Trained in both law and medicine at George Washington University, Clarke was a renowned authority on patent, trademark, and copyright law. [60] Clarke performed so well in the *Kellogg v. Kellogg* trial that Will later appointed him as the Kellogg Company's general counsel. Joining Clarke was John W. Bailey, an imposing man, "with a square jaw that sets like a steel trap when the occasion demands."[61] He was the type of self-made, result-driven man that Will Kellogg admired in others and considered himself to be. After graduating high school, Bailey rose from stoking the engines of Michigan Central locomotives to becoming the railway's chief of freight business. He subsequently went to the University of Michigan Law School and served several terms as Battle Creek's mayor, from 1890 to 1891, 1909 to 1911, 1913 to 1915, and 1927 until his death in 1929, no small feat for a Democrat in a rock-ribbed Republican town.[62]

KELLOGG V. KELLOGG took more than a decade to resolve, beginning with the initial lawsuit filed by Will in 1910; a counterattack by John in 1917; and a final verdict by the Michigan Supreme Court in 1920. Yet even from the distance of a century and across the divide of neatly transcribed and typed words, one can almost hear the brothers' voices, the cadence of their speech, and a shared propensity to shade the truth in a manner that often elided into lies in order to advance their case.

On the witness stand, John was equal parts bombastic, imperious, emotional, passionate, brilliant, and legitimately aggrieved. As his testimony proceeded, the doctor delivered crafty, tricky, and occasionally dishonest answers. Will coached his counsel to push John's psychological buttons and provoke him with sharp questions that challenged the doctor's sense of superiority. To such queries, John reliably lashed back with sarcastic responses. Even more cutting was his talent for mimicking the vocal patterns of his legal adversaries, an unsavory skill he used with Will when he wanted to put his brother in his place. In more reflective moments, John conceded he had a propensity to speak "too strongly," even though he was "quite unconscious of it until afterwards."[63] Admittedly "strong-willed, pugnacious, controversial, and skeptical," the doctor tried to "keep these unpleasant traits under reasonable control [but] when I get worn out they become conspicuous and I appear to very poor advantage."[64] During these legal proceedings, he was often worn out and tired. By all accounts, John was what lawyers routinely refer to as a "bad witness." He consistently antagonized those charged with evaluating the veracity of his version of the events; to use modern parlance, he failed miserably at creating a believable narrative.

John's behavior aside, his legal strategy was compelling and based on a two-pronged defense. First, he sought to demonstrate he was one of the most prominent physicians in the world. His credentials were, in fact, impeccable. The doctor testified he created a system of medicine that had cured or helped thousands of patients; moreover he was an internationally renowned authority on nutrition, exercise, and natural healing, and the founder of a medical school, nursing school, and school of cooking. He lectured on average three or more times a week, around the world, for more than forty years. He personally treated, by his "most conservative estimate," more than 130,000 patients at the Battle Creek Sanitarium. "There is no town of any size in the United States," he proudly stated, "that has not sent people to the Sanitarium, in fact from all parts of the world, Australia, New Zealand, South Africa, all parts of England and South America."[65]

The doctor then unfurled his voluminous curriculum vitae, listing every single one of the hundreds of publications bearing his name, memberships in the most prestigious medical societies, and every other possible credit that testified to the luster of his reputation. He noted the long-distance routes his fame took because his popular monthly magazine, *Good Health,* sold ten to twenty thousand copies per month, amounting to more than five million copies over his forty-year editorship. His book sales were even more phenomenal, netting him $50,000 to $60,000 per year in royalties (about $1.11 million in 2016) and many of these volumes sold in the millions, not only in the United States but also in faraway lands where they were translated into multiple languages, including Swedish, Norwegian, French, German, Spanish, and Chinese.[66] The point of this medical recitative was to demonstrate that when anyone in the world heard or read the word "Kellogg," they immediately thought of John Harvey Kellogg, M.D., whether the name was listed on a box of Corn Flakes or at the bottom of a prescription pad.

The second prong of his defense was to minimize Will's abilities and contributions, not only with the development of flaked cereals but, even more broadly, every culinary achievement made at the San while his younger brother worked there. Dr. Kellogg insisted that he was the sole inventor of a great many food products; the most significant, of course, was his development of flaked cereal, as evidenced by his United States federal patent on the process. The doctor also portrayed Will as mad for money while he was inspired neither by riches nor glory. Prompted by his lawyer Fred Chappell on this very point, the doctor testified that all of his work was guided by his sacred oath as a benevolent and caring physician. His only desire, he insisted, was "to benefit humanity."[67] More wounding, John repeatedly asserted that Will Kellogg was nothing more than his lackey, a dull cipher and order taker who assisted him as he worked toward becoming the inventor of flaked cereal:

> Will K. Kellogg was a bookkeeper and the business manager of the little business that was carried on. He worked for me as a bookkeeper and looking after my private affairs before we began the food business. . . . I usually wrote on a slip of paper or dictated a note giving directions for the experiment and either sent it directly to the laboratory or gave it to my brother, W.K. Kellogg, and he passed it to the laboratory. Very often, I went there myself and assisted and gave verbal directions, sometimes by telephone.[68]

The doctor also attacked Will's practice of "signing" boxes of his Corn Flakes as a blatant means of riding on John's coattails and exploiting his valuable good name.[69] John asserted that by rights he could make formal claim to owning the now famous W. K. Kellogg signature as a trademark. After all, he reasoned, Will's signature appeared first on the labels of many of the doctor's Sanitas Foods Company products, such as Malted Nuts, with the express warning, "Beware of Imitations. None genuine without this signature, W. K. Kellogg." When cross-examined, John descended into a morass of dissembling:

> After we began the Will K. Kellogg signature we made products, which did not bear the signature. Corn Flakes did not carry the signature of Will K. Kellogg at that time. There was nothing wrong with Corn Flakes. I used this "None genuine without the signature Will K. Kellogg," as a means of designation and as a trademark and for this particular article that trademark was adopted, but it was not adopted for certain other articles. I say that that was adopted by the [J.H.'s Sanitas] company. Will K. Kellogg did it while in my employ and I did it because he worked for me and he asked my consent to do it and I agreed to do it because it seemed to be necessary, because imitations were being brought out.[70]

WILL, ON THE OTHER HAND, was a terrific witness.[71] He explained how the doctor deliberately imitated and capitalized on his advertising, marketing, and production, which made Kellogg's Corn Flakes the favorite of millions of Americans. Will also noted that there were millions of dollars at stake in lost sales and market oversaturation that, as the fiduciary of the W. K. Kellogg Company, he could not possibly allow to happen. His quiet reserve and legendary self-control guided his entire testimony and, ultimately, his version of the events carried the day.

In almost every answer he offered, Will shaded the truth to reflect his favor. For example, when asked by Dr. Kellogg's lawyers about the doctor's credentials, Will disingenuously stated under oath "that even to this day [he] didn't know that Dr. Kellogg had any reputation [as] a dietician or as an innovator in food products, health foods, and the improvement of diet." When asked about how many people might confuse his Corn Flakes as a product endorsed by the famous doctor, especially among the Seventh-day Adventist community, Will replied, "Why, Mr. Chappell, I have no way of knowing as to what number of Seventh-day Adventists would say that or know that."[72]

At other points in his testimony, Will feigned absolutely no recollections of key events in his work with his older brother. Will mastered a courtroom version of the boxer Muhammad Ali's famed "rope-a-dope" technique and exhausted (and outsmarted) the opposing lawyers by settling back in his chair and replying, "I couldn't state" or "I don't know" to any question that contained the power to disprove or minimize Will's version of the facts. When queried about the positive statements he made in the past about the doctor's invention of flaked cereals, Will replied, "I think I did [make such a statement] but I am not positive, I couldn't say." Even when directly asked "and is it still true, is it not?" Will calmly replied, "No, at least some matters would be changed I think."

Similarly, when Will was asked questions about his salary compensation at the San, he vaguely replied, "I am unable to state the time. It was so long ago." These answers seem especially suspect given Will's prodigious and near photographic memory for financial facts and figures, from the cost of a bushel of corn to his boxing clerk's weekly salary. After John's lawyers confronted Will with memoranda he wrote to his brother about various food concoctions and products, circa 1906–1907, Will denied their veracity, "I have no recollection in regard to it either as to the note or to the date. It is dated in pencil." John's lawyers then waved pages of company minutes, in which Will first proposed changing his company's name to the Kellogg's Toasted Corn Flakes Company. Will questioned their authenticity, too.

He even denied statements he made in earlier depositions: "I am unable to state positively whether or not this is my testimony. I have not taken the time to read it all through. There are several pages here."[73] The doctor must have squirmed in anger while seated at the defense table, forced to listen to Will's misleading testimony. In reprisal, John ordered his lawyers to expose Will's carefully rehearsed, legalistic trickery by accusing him of perjury. Judge North declined to sustain such objections.[74]

More important to Will's case was establishing that he co-invented flaked cereals with John. At several junctures, Will complained about his brother's domineering and credit-grabbing ways:

> I stated that I did the work as business manager of the Sanitarium and that I got no glory and very little money. . . . I think he [Dr. Kellogg] has been trying to get some glory recently. . . . We were

connected together. We were doing business together and some of
the formulae we worked out and some I did and he made suggestions and I made suggestions and I think he took most of the glory
for the work that I did of that sort. I wrote a great many hundreds
of notes for experiments to be conducted and carried out. . . . The
doctor took all the glory for the invention. I never received any
glory for invention or any credit. Doctor did. . . . I contend now as
I did at that time that I had invented the product [flaked cereals]
with Dr. Kellogg jointly. The process was patented in his name and
he got the credit.[75]

Will stipulated that the original flakes were made of wheat and which
John wanted to grind into crumbs, rather than flakes, until Will stopped
him. To make his sting even sharper, Will testified that the doctor's flakes
were neither terribly tasty nor popular. It was he who discovered that
corn made for a far more appetizing cereal. It was he who, through trial
and error, developed new baking methods and designed new ovens to
toast the flakes to perfection. Most importantly, he was the chef who
added John's forbidden ingredients of sugar and salt to spin out those
deliciously golden flakes of corn, which, as his advertisements heralded,
"won its favor through its flavor." When asked if the doctor had not
helped in this process, Will replied, "He looked the product over and
may have made some suggestions. I don't recall that he made any, though
he may have made some."[76]

ON FEBRUARY 15, 1911, the two legal teams somehow found a third
way to reach an out-of-court settlement. The brothers reconciled and
avoided the inevitable press circus, which they knew threatened their
reputations and commercial interests.[77] In exchange for an acknowledgment that his company was the "sole and exclusive owner of the
trade-name or mark 'Kellogg's' on prepared food products and goods
of a similar character," Will granted his brother's request to continue to
call his company the "Kellogg Food Company," but only on company
letterhead and never conspicuously displayed on his cereal boxes. In the
spirit of a Talmudic truce, Will further consented to the doctor printing
his facsimile signature, "John Harvey Kellogg," on the boxes of his flaked

cereal food cartons, only once per product and in small letters "on the side or end, but not on either face of the carton."[78]

John managed to snatch a bit of victory by insisting on retaining the rights to manufacture and sell a version of Corn Flakes outside the United States. In consideration of his older brother's goodwill, Will agreed to pay John $10,000 in cash (about $257,000 in 2016). Will added more sugar to the deal by allowing John to sell back the remaining 5,704 shares of Will's company stock that his American Medical Missionary College owned at the inflated price of $15 (about $386 in 2016) per share.[79]

Predictably, the accord did not last very long. John continued to alternately compliment Will for his success and then berate him, only to follow such outbursts with written apologies such as one in July of 1911, explaining "the unpleasant word that I used was a slip of the tongue, as I intended another word, which, however, might have been no better."[80] The doctor constantly nibbled around the edges of Will's cereal market. And yet for every round the doctor fired at the W. K. Kellogg Toasted Corn Flake Company, Will retaliated with an even greater force. No assault of Will's was more calculated or better aimed than what John and his legal team deemed as "a vindictive plot to 'get' the older brother." The national press nicknamed this attack "The Battle of the Bran."[81]

IT WAS ALMOST PREDESTINED that a man so fixated on the frequent evacuation of soft, bulky stools would become enamored with one of nature's finest laxatives, wheat bran. In his never-ending war against constipation, John advised his patients to consume large bowls of this hard outer layer of the wheat grain, which is rich in fiber, essential fatty acids, protein, vitamins, and minerals. In 1908, Dr. Kellogg's Sanitas Nut Food Company began manufacturing a product he called "sterilized bran," which capitalized on the public's interest in consuming sanitary, clean foods and a burning desire to cure constipation. Initially, Dr. Kellogg offered his "Battle Creek System Sterilized Bran," and, later, "Kellogg's Sterilized Bran," exclusively to his patients at the Sanitarium. In 1908, he sold fewer than 10,000 boxes; only a year later, in 1909, he sold more than 100,000 boxes.

By 1915, John was employing the same mass advertising techniques pioneered by his brother with full-page advertisements in major magazines such as *Good Housekeeping* and *Ladies' Home Journal.* He also held forth by lecturing at well-heeled department stores across the nation, including J. L. Hudson's of Detroit and Marshall Field's of Chicago. The strategy worked: that year, the doctor sold more than 250,000 boxes of bran, and by 1916 sales climbed to over 600,000 boxes. Of course, Dr. Kellogg insisted that his bran cereal had in no way violated his agreement with Will because that agreement centered on the production of Corn Flakes, which the wheat bran cereal was clearly not, and more cogently because Will's company did not even manufacture bran products at the time.[82] Will still saw this as a worrisome issue. Specifically, of all the health foods John sold (a wide array of cereals, crackers, jams and jellies, laxatives, and nut-based meat substitutes), only the bran cereals boldly proclaimed the name "Kellogg" on the outer label. This marketing move, the doctor insisted, was necessary to assure his customers they were get-ting the original and best bran cereal products rather than imitations made by the "copycat" companies.[83]

Ironically, the "copycat" firm leading the charge in "The Battle of the Bran" was none other than Will Kellogg's Toasted Corn Flake Company. In the fall of 1915, Will began selling "Kellogg's Toasted Bran Flakes" and "Kellogg's Flaked Bran," both of which became instantly popular sellers. The following year, 1916, Will introduced a granulated bran cereal called "Kellogg's All-Bran" (created by his son John Leonard Kellogg) and, in 1920, a crunchy, shredded version known as "Kellogg's Bran Krumbles." In a total turnabout of Will's accusations and John's underhanded meth-ods, it was now Will who was confusing the public by directly competing with his brother's Sterilized Bran products. And so, on August 13, 1916, John filed a restraining order against Will's firm, which led to a trial dur-ing the spring of 1917, again in Judge North's courtroom.[84]

Ever thoughtful about his judicial decisions, Walter North did not make a ruling until late 1917.[85] Much to the doctor's everlasting conster-nation, Judge North ruled in favor of the W. K. Kellogg Toasted Corn Flake Company on every single point. The decision was clear-cut and definitive: "I find that the facts and circumstances established by the proofs in this case are such as entitles the defendants to relief, whereby the plaintiffs and their agents, servants and representatives shall be enjoined and restrained from selling prepared foods as and for the products of the defendants, the Kellogg Toasted Corn Flake Company."[86] North

**Join the "Regulars" with
KELLOGG'S ALL-BRAN**

*Will Kellogg employed well-
known cartoon characters
such as Mutt and Jeff to
offer advice on how to beat
constipation and "Join the
'Regulars.'"*

not only dismissed every one of John's complaints, he also decreed that Will's company
was entitled to all profits earned from John's
cereal products over the past decade and ruled
that the trademark "Kellogg's" was legally
owned by Will's company. John was ordered
to stop "deceiving the public or the trade" and
formally restrained from the use of his own
surname on his foods, with the exception
of being allowed to put the company name
"Kellogg Food Company" in an inconspicu-
ous place on the product's box—as agreed to
by the brothers in their brief peace treaty of
1911. Will's victory seemed to be complete. He
had finally vanquished his older brother.

IF ONLY THE DOCTOR WALKED AWAY
from this decision and returned to his many
medical responsibilities and projects. But he
was incapable of doing so.[87] Before the ink
had a chance to dry on Judge North's ruling,
John foolishly instructed his lawyers to appeal
the case to the Michigan State Supreme
Court.[88]

Handing down their decision on December 21, 1920, the State of
Michigan delivered Will Kellogg the best Christmas gift he could ever
hope for: all eight members of the court voted to uphold every single line
of Judge North's 1917 decision.[89] Will now owned the exclusive right to
the trade name "Kellogg" as well as all the profits his brother had previously made off of his Kellogg-labeled cereals. The court also ordered
that John pay all of Will's legal bills incurred during the drawn-out
contretemps—a sum of more than $225,000 (or at least $2,660,000 in
2016). Will magnanimously told his brother to pay only the legal bills
and that he would forgo the profits earned from John's competing cereal
company. Unwilling to accept even this act of kindness, John fussed,

fumed, and wrote the check for the full amount so Will would have "no excuse for pestering me further."[90]

On January 4, 1921, only two weeks after the State Supreme Court decision, Will decreed that his versions of John's constipation-busting bran cereal were now bona fide W. K. Kellogg Company products. In a memorandum to his sales staff and food brokers, Will could barely contain his glee as he announced, "Dr. Kellogg and the Kellogg Food Co., cannot use the word 'Kellogg' as a trademark or trade name on any articles manufactured by them . . . my company will now start a vigorous Bran campaign and we feel sure of receiving your co-operation in our effort to increase the sale of our Bran product, to the consuming public."[91]

The greatest casualty, of course, was the bond between two brothers. Bitter rivals, they rarely spoke to one another for the remainder of their lives. When they did, Will usually made sure to have someone with him to insure a third party heard exactly what was discussed rather than the version the doctor would later alter in his favor. After the trial, the quiet Will often chastised others who criticized the doctor in his presence but he rarely missed an opportunity to do so himself. Years later, Will met a man who had recently resigned his post at the San and he wryly observed, "Your happiness is just beginning."[92]

13

The Doctor's Crusade Against
Race Degeneracy

CONVINCED OF THE righteousness of his cause, Dr. Kellogg was one of America's great health crusaders. Yet there was an unseemly side to John's enthusiasm and constant attention seeking. Much to Will's distaste, John long exhibited impatience with the slow pace of scientific inquiry and a too ready acceptance (and, at times, exaggeration) of data that served his medical theories, biases, and prejudices. In many cases, such as the diet he recommended, the avoidance of meat, sugar, alcohol, tobacco, and gluttony, and with the health foods he created, the doctor turned out to be stunningly correct, even if the scientific reasoning behind them was not. In other instances, however, he could be just plain wrong and it was those circumstances that have contributed most heavily to his persona non grata status in the pantheon of American medicine.

No single medical misadventure better represents Dr. Kellogg's legacy of being on the wrong side of history than his dauntless support of one of the most popular scientific and social theories of his day. For decades, he subscribed to a prejudiced set of ideas, which were ultimately demonstrated to be a worthless, if not outright racist and harmful, pseudoscience. From the late nineteenth century until his death during World War II, he sounded the alarm over the degeneracy of the white race. In fact, John Harvey Kellogg was one of the most vocal proponents, facilitators, and major financial backers of the American eugenics movement.[1]

BEGINNING IN THE LATE 1890s and reaching its zenith during the first three decades of the next century, a great many "White Anglo-Saxon Protestant," upper-class men (as well as their wives and children) grew increasingly obsessed with the future of the American gene pool.[2] Supporting these fears was a theoretical framework called eugenics, first proposed in 1883 by the British naturalist Sir Francis Galton. The word "eugenics" is taken from the Greek root "*eugenes,* namely good in stock or hereditarily endowed with noble qualities." He used the term to propose the means to improve population health by "giv[ing] to the more suitable races . . . a better chance of prevailing speedily over the less suitable."[3] Before long, Sir Francis's social theories on who was eugenically worthy and who was not spread like wildfire among white intellectuals in almost every Western nation.

In the United States, during what historians now call the Progressive Era (1900–1920), a generation of reformers sought to confront a number of social problems of the day, including urban poverty, assimilating the huge number of immigrants coming to American shores, public health crises ranging from epidemics to alarmingly high infant mortality rates, cultural confusion, and explosive population growth. Many of these reformers applied inappropriate eugenic explanations to their management of those deemed to be socially undesirable: so-called mental defectives (whom doctors and psychologists labeled with newly created clinical terms like "imbeciles," "idiots," and "morons"), the blind, deaf, mentally ill, and "crippled," orphans, unwed mothers, epileptics, Native Americans, African Americans, foreigners, poor residents in the mountains and hollows of Appalachia, and many other outsider groups. All these "inferior races," eugenic theorists concluded, were a drain on the economic, political, and moral health of American life.

The solution of the day was to quarantine, cordon off, and prevent them from contaminating the "superior," dominant white, native-born citizens.[4] Moreover, racial groups deemed "eugenically superior," specifically White Anglo Saxon Protestants, were encouraged to reproduce at greater rates, a concept often referred to as "positive eugenics." Those adjudged to have "inferior genes," however, were to be discouraged from reproducing through the establishment of "negative eugenics" programs, such as state-mandated sterilization for mental defectives, restrictions against who could marry whom in the form of racial or miscegenation laws, and mandatory blood tests for sexually transmitted diseases, birth control policies, harsh adoption laws, and loud nativist calls for laws restricting the entry of swarthy, unkempt, and inassimilable immigrants. In essence, eugenics offered Americans in the majority and in positions of power a seemingly authoritative scientific language to substantiate their biases against those they feared as dangerous.[5]

THE EPICENTER OF THIS MOVEMENT was the Station for Experimental Evolution and the Eugenics Record Office (ERO) in Cold Spring Harbor, Long Island, which was directed by Charles Benedict Davenport, an ambitious, indefatigable, Harvard-trained biologist and member of the prestigious National Academy of Sciences.[6] The ERO was founded in 1910, thanks to a huge bequest from Mary Harriman, the wife of railroad tycoon E. H. Harriman, as well as beneficent donations from the Carnegie Institution of Washington, D.C., John D. Rockefeller Jr., and Dr. John Harvey Kellogg.

Left to right, Harry H. Laughlin, assistant director,
and Charles Davenport, director, of the
Eugenics Record Office, circa 1913

The ERO zealously promoted the observations of Gregor Mendel, a German-speaking Moravian cleric and scientist who in 1865 studied the breeding of pea plants. Most scientists rightly acclaim Mendel for developing the basic scientific foundation of modern genetics. Among other things, Mendel was the first to formally describe recessive and dominant hereditary genes. Yet in a quirk of history, his 1865 paper on this work went largely unnoticed until 1900.[7] In the years following the rediscovery of Mendel, however, his theories generated a maelstrom of discussion, debate, and elaboration. The fruit flies in the proverbial ointment were the eugenicists who incorrectly applied Mendel's basic observations of pea plants to tackling a number of complex human social problems.

Leading this charge was Dr. Davenport, who declared open war on any and all groups he considered a threat to the purity of the American gene pool.[8] At a 1910 meeting of the Committee on Eugenics of the American Breeders Association, he bellowed, "Society must protect itself; as it claims the right to deprive the murderer of his life so also it may annihilate the hideous serpent of the hopelessly vicious protoplasm."[9] At the ERO, he directed an army of social workers, fieldworkers, sociologists, and biologists. This team of "experts" collated thick compendiums of faulty yet highly influential pedigree analyses asserting the hereditary basis for all sorts of behaviors, including lust and criminality, which Davenport claimed were especially common among Italians; the "distinctly Jewish traits" of penuriousness and craftiness in business dealings, neurasthenia, and tuberculosis; feeblemindedness among those living in poverty-stricken Appalachia; nomadism among Gypsies and "hoboes"; and even a love of the sea, or *thalassophilia*, among sailors.

In Davenport's mind, Jews posed an especially grave threat to America. In a starkly candid letter he wrote to his colleague Madison Grant on April 7, 1925, Davenport fulminated: "Our ancestors drove Baptists from Massachusetts Bay into Rhode Island but we have no place to drive the Jews to. Also they burned witches but it seems to be against the mores to burn any considerable part of our population."[10] Indeed, few of Davenport's social eugenics policies had a greater impact than his advocacy for the Immigration Restriction Act of 1924, which blocked the entry of the millions of Jewish, Eastern and Southern European, and Asian immigrants seeking refuge on our shores for the following forty years.[11]

ONE OF THE DIRTIEST REALITIES of the American eugenics movement is that, with relatively few prominent exceptions, it is difficult to
find an Anglo-Saxon Protestant man (or woman) of means who did not
endorse such theories. As the social Darwinist Herbert Spencer famously
opined, it was a matter of the "survival of the fittest."[12] "Race suicide,"
a term introduced in 1901 by the University of Wisconsin sociologist
and best-selling author Edward A. Ross, was a concern that captured the
American conversation all the way up to the White House.[13] Behind his
bully pulpit, President Theodore Roosevelt repeatedly wrung his hands
over the issue.[14]

Other influential eugenicists who fretted over the American protoplasm
included grant makers from both the Rockefeller and Carnegie foundations; U.S. president Calvin Coolidge; David Starr Jordan, the president
of Stanford University; psychologist Henry H. Goddard; Senator Henry
Cabot Lodge (R-MA); Henry Ford; Alexander Graham Bell; Luther Burbank; associate U.S. Supreme Court justice Oliver Wendell Holmes Jr.;
Nobel laureate in physics Robert A. Millikan; novelists F. Scott Fitzger-
ald, Upton Sinclair, and Sinclair Lewis; economist William Z. Ripley;
birth control advocate Margaret Sanger; and, oddly, Helen Keller and
W. E. B. Dubois,[15] to name but a few.[16] Dr. Kellogg, too, had long worried about the degeneration of the white race and actively campaigned to
join the ranks of these eugenics movers and shakers.

As early as 1881, he was complaining, "the human race is growing
steadily weaker year by year. The boys of today would be no match in
physical strength for the sturdy youths of a century ago who are now
their grandparents." Dr. Kellogg's initial diagnosis, however, was that
race degeneracy was caused not by inherited traits but instead by lazy,
inactive boys and girls who rarely exercised or engaged in physical labor
and sapped their strength by indulging in "the secret sin and the kindred
vices," of masturbation.[17]

Beginning in the 1890s, he publicly espoused a mishmash theory combining elements of Lamarckism, Darwinism, biologic living, and Christian faith. John claimed it was possible to "save" the white race, or at
least improve it, by "fixing" the bodies of broken, unhealthy, or behav-
iorally aberrant individuals by means of biologic living. In 1910, the

social reformer, sanitary chemist, and home economist Ellen Richards characterized Dr. Kellogg's approach as *euthenics*, which was, in some sense, an echo of what Francis Galton meant by "nurture" as opposed to nature.[18] Euthenics theorists held that a committed individual (and, thus, the population at large) could acquire a superior set of inheritable traits through healthy living, improved hygiene, and better living conditions. These individuals would then pass their improved traits on to successive generations. Such hereditary plasticity, however, was not widely accepted by the leading lights of the eugenics movement. They insisted vociferously that the expressions of inferior and socially damaging traits were caused by fixed, inherited, Mendelian genes, which would only, to perversely borrow the well-known biblical phrase in Genesis 1:28, "be fruitful and multiply." In order to accommodate the eugenics crowd, John realized he would have to alter and reshape his theories, but he never really let go of the concept of euthenics, a clinical construct that meshed perfectly with his overarching theory of biologic living.[19]

ASIDE FROM HIS predilection for adopting dozens of children whom he hoped to improve by environment and biologic living rather than genetic breeding, Dr. Kellogg's most extended experiments in euthenics occurred at his Chicago Mission.[20] From 1893 until 1913, when he was forced to close the mission down because of insufficient financial support, the doctor devoted his Sundays to offering free medical care for Chicago's great unwashed as well as teaching hundreds of medical students attending his Sanitarium and Chicago-based, biologic living–centered, American Medical Missionary College.[21] Opened to coincide with the heavy traffic generated by the 1893 World's Columbian Exposition, Dr. Kellogg founded the mission on behalf of the Seventh-day Adventist Church.[22] The mission of the mission was to improve, if not save, the spirits, lives, and biological substrate of the downtrodden, indigent, and despondent all crowded into the worst neighborhoods of Chicago and preyed upon by hucksters, criminals, and other unsavory types inhabiting the seamy borders of the "White City."[23]

Every other Saturday, the doctor boarded the evening train bound for Chicago. If he was late because he was operating on a patient or conducting an experiment in the San's kitchen laboratory, one of his assistants ran to the telephone, called the Michigan Central switchboard operator, and ordered her to hold either the Wolverine Special or, if it was later in the evening, the Twilight Limited. The obedient operator and the conductors she informed always did exactly as they were told and delayed the train's departure until the doctor arrived. On one occasion, Dr. Kellogg got to the train station too late and the stationmaster told him, "I'll call ahead, stop the train, and hold it for you. My mother has charge of your linen room and I'm glad to help."[24]

Once ensconced on the train, surrounded by his entourage of secretaries and a full basket of Sanitarium foods, the doctor invariably asked the porter to bring him a few Pullman pillows and a writing table. The conductor would then call out, "The Doctor is on board." Once certain that all were, in fact, aboard, the engineer opened the throttle and began the journey.[25] Four hours later, Dr. Kellogg detrained at the nine-story Romanesque Illinois Central Station. From there, he made his way on foot for the five-minute walk to reach his living euthenics laboratory, the Chicago Medical Mission. It was located at 98–100 Van Buren Street, in the city's skid row on the south end of the Loop, or as Dr. Kellogg described it, "the dirtiest and wickedest place" in the city.[26]

Dr. Kellogg was one of many physicians, social workers, and other reformers hoping to improve the lot of the urban poor. During this period, an ambitious, well-educated cadre of young white professionals created dozens of settlement houses, wherein university students and graduates lived and worked alongside the poor. They were fortified by deeply held political convictions and the nineteenth-century sensibility of noblesse oblige. Many of its participants were simultaneously potent advocates of eugenics and the Social Gospel movement, which held that Christ's teachings were aligned with the aims of socialism and social welfare.[27] The settlement houses and missions they founded and staffed served as social policy incubators spawning new ideas, methods, and approaches to counteract the corrosive changes brought on by the "Modern Age."

Among the notable social reformers working in Chicago at the time were Jane Addams, the founder of Hull House and winner of the 1931 Nobel Peace Prize; Dr. Alice Hamilton, who ran Hull House's "well baby" clinic and later founded the medical specialty of industrial medicine; and Florence Kelley, who fought against sweatshops and child

The Chicago Mission's "Penny Lunch" counter

labor and helped institute the eight-hour workday.[28] According to one of John's favorite students and junior physicians, William Sadler, the doctor approached Jane Addams in 1893 about joining the formidable forces of Hull House with his Seventh-day Adventist–sponsored Chicago Mission. The conversation, apparently, went nowhere because "[she] refused to have anything to do with religion in mission work."[29]

Beyond spiritual nourishment and medical attention, every Sunday at noon the mission fed all comers a nourishing lunch—a hot bowl of bean soup and a hunk of graham bread or a piece of zwieback all for a penny. John insisted on charging this nominal fee in order to preserve his charges' dignity, but if he found someone who did not have a "copper," he gladly reached into his pocket to provide one. Later, he took to printing up books containing "100 penny coupons" for businessmen to distribute to panhandlers knowing that a coupon could be redeemed only at the mission for food as opposed to the handout of a coin, which might be used, instead, for a drink of whiskey. So many poor men came knocking on the mission's doors for food that within a few months the Sunday "Penny Lunch Counter" was opened daily. On a typical day the mission served between five to six hundred men; on busy days it was as high as 1,500.

Equally impressive, during its first three years of operation 38,000 baths were taken (the men could take their ablutions daily, if they desired; women and children could only do so three days a week) and 26,000 medical treatments were provided, from massage and hydrotherapy to mild electrotherapeutics. The mission facilitated 9,000 nurses' home visits and 17,000 penny meals. By 1897, more than 200,000 people used their laundry facilities and 75,000 men and women were given new suits and dresses, thanks to the donations from Adventist church congregations.[30] More than 13,500 gospel tracts were distributed and the Adventist Church expanded the mission to include a dispensary, a lodging house called the Workingman's Home, a larger bathhouse, an employment bureau, and classrooms for teaching carpet weaving and broom making to the destitute men as well as facilities for teaching the students enrolled at John's American Medical Missionary College.[31] It is impossible to determine if the doctor's work had long-term effects but, at the very least, his missionary work did help feed, clothe, and house many poor Chicagoans, rather than merely casting them aside as biologically inferior.

Children's clinic at the Chicago Mission dispensary

The planning committee for the first national Race Betterment conference, 1914. Left, above, Horace Plunkett, the Irish politician and reformer; left, below, S. S. McClure, the muckraking publisher of McClure's Magazine; *right, above, Gifford Pinchot, the first chief of the U.S. Forest Service and, later, governor of Pennsylvania; and right, below, Irving Fisher, professor of economics at Yale; with John Harvey Kellogg (center).*

WHEN IT CAME TO HIS ENTRÉE into the American eugenics movement, John's personal tour guide was a prominent political economist from Yale named Irving Fisher.[32] The Ivy Leaguer and Dr. Kellogg first met a few days after Christmas of 1904. Professor Fisher was in Chicago to speak at the annual meeting of the American Economic Association. On the way back home to New Haven, an exhausted and dyspeptic Fisher stepped off the train at the Battle Creek station, with the intention of spending a week at the Sanitarium. The doctor, acutely aware of Professor Fisher's prestige and professional connections, insisted on personally taking on the economist's case. Conversely, the professor coveted John's medical credentials, wide public following, and financial resources.[33]

Fisher found relief for his many health problems by strictly adhering to Dr. Kellogg's principles of biologic living. A few years into his vegetarian regime, he conducted a study on the influence of flesh eating on endurance. He enrolled forty-nine subjects and divided them into three groups: 1) athletes who ate high-protein meat diets; 2) athletes who consumed low-protein, "flesh-abstaining" diets (but which still included animal products such as milk and eggs); and 3) sedentary "flesh-abstainers." Most of the vegetarians were San employees who had abstained from meat for a period of four to twenty years (the exception being Fisher, who became a vegetarian "two years earlier" but entered himself into the study nonetheless). The athletes were mostly Yale undergraduates. When comparing the two athlete groups, the meatless ones fared far better and even the sedentary group beat out the meat-eating sportsmen for holding one's arms out "horizontally for as long as possible." Ever the careful scholar, Fisher added several "ifs, ands or buts" to the discussion section of his published report and warned against the tendency for those with "vegetarian fanaticism" to overstate the data. That said, he concluded, "there is strong evidence that a low-protein, non-flesh, or nearly non-flesh diet is conducive to endurance."[34] John was thrilled by this study—at least the parts that supported his allegiance to a meatless way of life—and recounted and exaggerated Fisher's conclusions for decades in his lectures and on the pages of his best-selling books.[35]

More germane, Professor Fisher was one of the most powerful intellectual forces in the eugenics crusade. Long before he became the founding president of the American Eugenics Society from 1922 to 1926, he was a committed general in the war to develop a eugenically pure society and "[redeem] the human race."[36] At John's request, Fisher introduced the Battle Creek physician to Charles B. Davenport. The two struck up a correspondence and in 1916 John asked Davenport to deliver the keynote address at the San's grand "Golden (50th) Jubilee Anniversary Celebration." He spoke on "Eugenics as a Religion" and warned the audience, as if he were Moses speaking to the Chosen People:

> From Mount Sinai, God is thundering his commandment against bowing down to idols. . . . God speaks to us again, this time through the microscope, or through the statistics of the notorious Jukes family, thundering again that the iniquity of the fathers rushes on in the blood into the generations following, and curses the children before they ever see the light of day.[37]

After his sermon, Davenport supped on vegetables and grain concoctions with the assembled "Battle Freaks." During the entire meal,
however, the ex–Harvard professor sniffed and
snickered over the doctor's allegiance to frequent bowel movements and his insistence that
inferior traits dissipated with rounds of sit-ups.
Like many of the prominent eugenicists in the
United States, Davenport was all too happy to
take the doctor's money to advance his cause
and "research," even as he ridiculed him behind
his back.

*Madison Grant, author of
the eugenics bestseller* The
Passing of the Great Race

Professor Fisher also facilitated John's meeting Madison Grant, whose best-selling and now
shockingly racist 1916 book, *The Passing of the Great Race,* was employed
as a textbook by a legion of American eugenics enthusiasts. Grant concluded that at least 10 percent of the American public was unfit to reproduce and called for their forced sterilization. The book had an even more
sinister impact in Europe, where Adolf Hitler often referred to it as "my
bible" all the while he was planning his "master race."[38]

Dr. Kellogg admired Grant's work, too, and eventually became the
author's physician. In 1936, for example, the doctor was so worried about
Grant's worsening arthritis and sedentary lifestyle that he demanded
Grant return immediately to the San for some biologic nurturing. John
bluntly admonished the New York socialite, attorney, national park dev-
otee, and trustee of the American Museum of Natural History:

> What your weak muscles need is exercise. If you will dance half an
> hour every day and chop wood for another half hour, your muscles
> will grow apace. But you have been pampered and coddled for so
> many decades that I have no hope you can be persuaded either to
> dance or chop wood.[39]

The doctor's advice hardly helped. Madison Grant died the following
year, 1937, of kidney disease. Oddly for a man obsessed about the future
of his "race," he left no offspring.

As JOHN HARVEY KELLOGG BECAME ever more enmeshed in the net cast by the Eugenics Record Office during the first few decades of the twentieth century, his euthenics creed veered off the rails and merged directly with some of its most restrictive negative eugenics policies. As early as 1903, he wrote, "Heredity is God's method of book-keeping."[40] Seven years later, April 25, 1911, during a highly publicized lecture he delivered to the Connecticut State Conference of Charities and Corrections, the doctor presented reams of evidence on the rise of "degenerative diseases" among twentieth-century Americans, such as vision and hearing defects, mental health maladies, and the rising death rates from cancer, diabetes, alcoholism, tobacco, caffeine, and opium consumption, and "overeating." He cautioned his audience, "The degeneracy and ultimate extinction of the human race is a catastrophe too appalling to consider calmly." On the euthenics side of the equation, the doctor advocated for a national commitment to better (biologic) living to avert such a devastating and downward spiral.[41] After winding down this portion of his lecture, Dr. Kellogg segued and sang the entire eugenics score. His aria climaxed with a call to prevent "the unfit" from reproducing: "We must cultivate clean blood, instead of blue blood. Society must establish laws and sanctions, which will check the operation of heredity in the multiplication of the unfit."[42]

During John's second stint as a member of the Michigan State Board of Health, from 1911 to 1917, he advised Governor Woodbridge Ferris on state-ordered eugenic controls and, especially, the passage of a 1913 state law "mandating the sterilization of mentally defective persons." The greater good had to be protected, Dr. Kellogg urged his fellow Michiganders, even as he acknowledged these hardly benign, and often permanent, surgical procedures were typically performed against the subjects' will and personal liberties.[43]

Such so-called victories in the name of racial purity afforded John many more opportunities to engage the American eugenics elite. Abandoned by the religious faith to which he had devoted much of his working life and still fuming over the ongoing legal contretemps with Will, John seized the opportunity for medical relevance by financially supporting eugenics research with the river of book royalties, magazine subscriptions, surgical fees, health food sales, and Corn Flakes dividends coming his way. In 1914, John closed the accounts of his nonprofit, quasi-religious American Medical Missionary Board, which he had earlier named the "owner" and beneficiary of most of the Kellogg's Corn Flakes shares he extracted from Will in their various business deals. He then redirected these riches by founding and legally incorporating his Race Betterment Foundation.[44] Most famously, the doctor devoted huge sums to support the production of three well-attended and widely publicized national conferences on Race Betterment and eugenics. A glance at the programs of these convocations documents a who's who of many of the most prominent intellectuals, politicos, and social reformers during the Progressive Era.

HUNDREDS OF VESTED, suited, and buttoned-down scientists, physicians, educators, social workers, ministers, insurance company executives, teetotalers, college presidents, *et alia* attended the first National Conference on Race Betterment in Battle Creek. They were all guests of the doctor, and their transportation, first-class accommodations, and bountiful meals, à la Kellogg, were on the house. Of course, John was no fool. He hosted the conference from January 8 to 12, 1914, which coincided with the San's slowest business period because of the arctic blast of cold that descends upon Battle Creek every New Year's Day and lasts until well after the groundhog does or does not see his shadow. At a fraction of the price of the San's high season, John cordoned off the best suites usually reserved for his most monied patients, much to the delight of his Race Betterment conferees.

John welcomed hundreds of distinguished guests into a large assembly room filled with rows of chairs, each with a beautifully printed conference program placed on the seat portion, bearing the foundation's guiding motto on the title page, *Mens sana in corpore sano*. ("A healthy mind in a healthy body").[45] The doctor welcomed his guests with an introductory address, "Needed—a New Human Race," that advocated both his euthenics theories and the ERO's stricter, negative eugenics programs.[46] Over the next four days, he told them, they would listen to lectures on topics ranging from the use of motion pictures, physical education, and classroom techniques to spread the gospel of eugenics, to warnings against the evils of tobacco, alcohol, and "the secret vice" of masturbation.

Despite the grandiloquent speeches and deluxe accommodations, not everyone in attendance was pleased by the conference's message. For example, Jacob A. Riis, the journalist, best-selling author, and photographer of *How the Other Half Lives,* was so offended by several speakers' insistence on improving the heredity of the "children of the slums," rather than arresting the social conditions in which they lived, he stormed off the stage and out of the Sanitarium. Before packing his bags and beating his path back to the train station, Riis gave an interview to the editor, eugenicist, and marriage counselor Paul Popenoe:

> We have heard friends here talk about heredity. The word has rung in my ears until I am sick of it. Heredity, heredity! There is just one heredity in all the world that is ours—we are the children of God, and there is nothing in the whole big world that we cannot do service with it.[47]

Equally uncomfortable was the African American educator Booker T. Washington, who, although a friend of Dr. Kellogg's and a frequent visitor to the San, was forced to sit on the dais while listening to lectures bemoaning the "white man's burden."[48] In his address on "The Negro Race," Dr. Washington thanked Dr. Kellogg for helping to advance his personal health but firmly countered eugenic claims of "Negro inferiority." In measured but emphatic tones, Washington stated:

> These people are worth saving, are worth making a strong, helpful part of the American body politic. The American negro is practically the only race with a dark skin that has ever undergone the test of living side by side of the Anglo-Saxon, looking him in the face and really surviving.[49]

Not surprisingly, Dr. Kellogg's attitudes about and relations with African Americans were complicated. For example, he took into his home seven African American girls from a Chattanooga, Tennessee, orphanage that was having financial difficulties. He later helped that same institution place thirty other African American orphans. He was well regarded among Battle Creek's African American community for the humane, albeit paternalistic, medical treatment he freely offered to many of them. Moreover, John firmly rejected any exclusionary measures or color lines in terms of lodging, medical treatment, athletic activities, and dining arrangements for African Americans at the Sanitarium, admission to his medical school, or visits to his home.[50]

On the other hand, Dr. Kellogg often articulated offensive opinions on the "Negro's fitness as a race." In his 1881 book, *Plain Facts for Old and Young,* he advised against "mixed marriages" between African Americans and whites because "it has been proven beyond room for questions that mulattoes are not so long-lived as either blacks or whites."[51] Two years later, in 1883, in his book *Ladies' Guide in Health and Disease,* he acknowledged that the weights of African American and European male brains were essentially equivalent but he, nevertheless, repeated the then popular trope, "The intellectual inferiority of the negro male to the European male is universally acknowledged."[52] Such racist comments went entirely unchanged in the many reprint editions of these books published well into the first decades of the twentieth century. He also ran numerous squibs and articles detailing the "degeneration of the Negro" in his magazine, *Good Health.*[53]

From the program alone, it is difficult to assess if there were any Jews present at the conference. If there were, they, too, would resent many of the pronouncements made on the unfitness of their "race," especially by the king and prince of the Eugenics Record Office, Charles Davenport and his assistant, Harry Laughlin, who lobbied the U.S. Congress to pass the 1924 Immigration Restriction Act. When it came to "the Chosen people," however, Dr. Kellogg assiduously veered away from the anti-Semitic rhetoric of the eugenics establishment. His philo-Semitism may have emerged out of an admiration many Christians articulate for Judaism as an important source of their own religious faith. John also had a great appreciation for Jewish dietary (kosher) and personal hygiene rituals, which mirrored some of his principles of biologic living. In the years that followed, the doctor was an early voice in defense of Eastern European and German Jews suffering the consequences of Adolf Hitler's anti-Semitic policies. In a 1935 editorial in *Good Health,* he criticized Germany's attempts at race betterment by ejecting "a people (the Jews) whose blood is far superior to their own as indicated by all racial tests."[54]

Five years later, in 1940, and long before most Americans acknowledged Hitler's atrocities, John described *Der Fuehrer,* to his surgical colleague Sir William Arbuthnot Lane, as a "monster."[55]

Nor were there likely many Asians present but Dr. Kellogg had conflicted views about people from that part of the world as well, and often articulated them in public settings. For example, Dr. Kellogg frequently wrote of his admiration of the dietary habits of the Chinese and Japanese people. Yet he frequently referred to the Japanese, especially during World War II, with the then common pejorative "Jap," and as his age advanced he became increasingly concerned about the "yellow peril" ruling the world.[56]

JOHN HARVEY KELLOGG'S second national conference on Race Betterment was based at the far splashier Panama-Pacific International Exposition, which opened in San Francisco on February 20, 1915. The fairgrounds, known as "the Jewel City," was a collection of majestic buildings, exhibits, pavilions, playgrounds, parks, sculptures, and artwork commemorating both the completion of the incredible engineering feat known as the Panama Canal and San Francisco's rebirth after the devastating earthquake of 1906.[57]

John loved visiting world's fairs especially when he could mix such visits with medical business. As a newly graduated medical student he had distributed temperance brochures to fairgoers and marveled at the wonders of the 1876 Centennial International Exposition in Philadelphia. As a Christian missionary doctor, he founded his mission to help some of Chicago's poorest citizens crowded out by the sprawl of the 1893 World's Columbian Exposition. And in 1904 he traveled to St. Louis to staff the Hygienic Reform and Battle Creek Sanitarium exhibits at the Louisiana Purchase Exposition. Not surprisingly, in 1915 he decided that the sparkling Panama-Pacific International Exposition was the perfect place to hold his second national Race Betterment conference during the first week of August.

Again, John assembled an enviable list of speakers including David Starr Jordan, the president of Stanford University,[58] botanist Luther Burbank,[59] and Frederick Ludwig Hoffman, the Prudential Insurance Company's legendary statistician, actuary, and author of a book describing

African Americans as especially prone to illness.[60] Some of the lectures supported Dr. Kellogg's euthenics theories; many others were harsher diatribes declaring the eugenics agenda set out by the ERO to protect the "white race" from ruin.

On August 6, a "playground pentathalon" was held at the exposition's marina between teams of boys from San Francisco, Alameda, and Oakland. The youngsters demonstrated their physical fitness by running hurdles, high jumps and broad jumps, doing push-ups, baseball throwing, and swimming. The event attracted a large and enthusiastic crowd who cheered on the winning team from Oakland.[61]

Perhaps the conference's most dramatic event was, in fact, a drama. On the evening of August 8, the curtain was rung up on a play entitled *Redemption, a Masque of Race Betterment*, written by Sheldon Cheney, directed by Samuel J. Hume, and featuring a cast of over two hundred University of California students. It was presented at the new, "million dollar Civic Auditorium" in Oakland to an audience of over five thousand. The turgid two-act play was billed as an allegory of humankind's struggle with its enemies, disease and war, as it advanced the race "through the ministrations of science and religion."[62]

The Race Betterment Foundation's Eugenics exhibit at the 1915 Panama-Pacific International Exposition in San Francisco

new way
to rest

COME into our Health Studio some
day, tired, nervous, tense and un-
strung. And then see how you feel
after a treatment in our

Battle Creek Vibratory Chair

and you'll scarcely be able to believe
you're the same person.

It's a novel experience. You "rest" in
this combination easy chair while
scientific vibration soothes and quiets
all those tired nerves and revitalizes
every tissue in your body. A wonderful
aid for nerves, irritability, digestive
troubles, constipation or general debility.

Come into the Health Studio and make
arrangements for your first treatment.
You will enjoy it thoroughly.

The Combination
Vibratory Chair. A
comfortable appa-
ratus adaptable both
to general and local
vibratory exercise

*Vibratory Chair
advertisement, circa 1915, one
of many "health products"
John Harvey Kellogg invented
and sold*

Dr. Kellogg and Professor Fisher also introduced a eugenics registry designed to help create "a new and superior race."[63] Although several observers criticized the collection of such data, thousands of fair-goers did sign up for the registry after visiting one of the most popular features of the exposition: John Harvey Kellogg's Race Betterment exhibit. The display was a large and attractive walk-in booth, given pride of place in the exposition's fabulous "Palace of Education." It featured photographs, charts, and visual aids detailing the threat of race suicide, crimes committed by inferior races in America, and statistics on cancer, "mental defectives," and other degenerative diseases. Also on hand was a helpful staff offering recommendations on avoiding race degeneracy through personal hygiene and biologic living (euthenics) and racial hygiene (eugenics).[64]

The most popular attraction of the Race Betterment booth, however, had little to do with eugenics. Dr. Kellogg brought all the way to San Francisco "two batteries of vibrating chairs," which he had invented for his patients at the San. The vibrating chairs "were in constant operation. . . . These chairs," the doctor crowed, "have the faculty of soothing and resting tired, fatigued people and because of this quality they were generously patronized by the visitors who had grown tired through long, weary tramping from building to building."[65] Restful seats aside, and, much to Dr. Kellogg's delight, the second Race Betterment Conference was a stunning success. On its final day, the Panama-Pacific Exposition managers awarded the Race Betterment Foundation a bronze medal of appreciation. Even better, Dr. Kellogg's production garnered a "million words" in newspaper articles and editorials, the majority of which were overwhelmingly positive.[66]

THE THIRD NATIONAL RACE BETTERMENT CONFERENCE of 1928 took somewhat longer to organize because of John's personal health problems, the San's ailing economic health, and World War I. Like the first national conference, it was held at the Battle Creek Sanitarium, again in early January (the 2nd to 6th), when the paying guest census was almost nonexistent. At the opening ceremony, John explained that the conference's purpose was to bring "together a group of leading scientists, educators and others for the purpose of discussing ways and means of applying science to human living in the same thoroughgoing way in which it is now applied to industry—in the promotion of longer life, increased efficiency, and well-being and of race improvement."[67] Afterward, the doctor handed out awards to several Battle Creek residents who won the "Fitter Families Contest." With a great sense of occasion, the white-suited Dr. Kellogg stood on a platform decorated with festive bunting as he congratulated the fit parents and their "well-born" children. They were now members, he told them, of a real "aristocracy, that in this little town of ours, the beginnings of a Better Race are being developed." He also reminded the winning families of the "responsibilities of those who are fit" to maintain their health with regular medical examinations, good diet, and healthful living.[68]

Far less charitable were racist rants by Clarence Cook Little, who was president of the University of Michigan at Ann Arbor from 1925 to 1929 and chairman of the 1928 conference. Professor Little echoed the views he expressed in Battle Creek four years later, in 1932, in an interview he gave on mandatory sterilization laws to *The New York Times*: "When a sink is stopped up, we shut off the faucet. We favor legislation to restrict the reproduction of the misfit. We should treat them as kindly and humanely as possible, but we must segregate them so that they do not perpetuate their kind."[69] Equally offensive was Congressman Albert Johnson, the cosponsor of the eugenics-based Immigration Act of 1924, who spoke on "The Menace of the Melting Pot."[70]

A far less controversial figure on the dais was Fielding Yost, the legendary coach of the University of Michigan football team. Coach Yost, whose "Point a Minute" Wolverines won six national championships (1901, 1902, 1903, 1904, 1918, and 1923), knew from what he spoke when he discussed the importance of "Man Building."[71] The gridiron guru's presence was especially ironic because in 1925 Dr. Kellogg promoted a football team at the Battle Creek College. John had hoped the team would become a shining example of successful athletes who followed his principles of diet and biologic living. The college administrators dismantled the football program after one season, however, because they deemed the sport "too violent to be healthful" and worried that the games might "attract undesirable students." Some locals gossiped that the real reason behind the team's demise was its inability to win games.[72]

The conference's star attraction was Dr. Alexis Carrel, the 1912 Nobel laureate, distinguished scientist, and surgeon of New York City's Rockefeller Institute for Medical Research. One biographer called Dr. Carrel's appearance at the 1928 Race Betterment Conference "the closest he'd [Carrel] yet come to making a public link between his research at the Rockefeller Institute and eugenics." For Carrel, it was a cause that became louder in the years to come, especially with respect to the social burdens of so-called defective individuals, the insane, and criminals. His 1935 book, *Man, the Unknown*, which sold over two million copies, asked, "Why do we preserve these useless and harmful beings?"[73]

*Henry Ford (left of center, with back to the camera, facing a woman in a black hat)
leading a square dance in the Sanitarium Union hall, during Dr. Kellogg's
Third National Race Betterment Conference, January 1928*

Throughout the week, a great many more presentations were centered on the biologic living topics the doctor had long promoted at the San.[74] After dining on several courses of Battle Creek fare served up by smiling Adventist waiters each evening, the guests partook in wholesome, healthy pursuits. On one night, the guests were led in square dancing by the automobile manufacturer and San patient Henry Ford; on another a team of seven children billed as "The Seven Vivacious Vegetarians" entertained them.[75]

DURING THE LATE 1930s, John wrote several bitter letters to Irving Fisher about Charles Davenport's obsessive focus on the inheritance of deleterious traits and flaws. The doctor was especially upset at how Davenport dismissed his euthenics theories on improving "inferior" humans by means of diet, exercise, and a healthy lifestyle. Fisher diplomatically tried to allay the doctor's angst on May 22, 1936, by reporting, "I see that [Davenport] does not deny your contention but he does not admit that within the meaning of 'acquired' as used by biologists you can say that acquired characteristics are inherited." Fisher advised the doctor to stay within the good graces of the powerful ERO director: "Probably it will be better not to use that phrase if something else can be found. Possibly you can make the distinction between characteristics acquired by use and characteristics acquired by trauma or other external, extraneous, sporadic, or whatever else will describe it, causes."[76] Dr. Kellogg held his ground but remained disgruntled. On May 18, 1937, John wrote Fisher insisting, "for complete success in a popular way, eugenics and euthenics or individual hygiene and race hygiene must be pushed together." A week later, Irving Fisher promptly put him down as a relic by replying "I note that you say [the] hereditary influence of habits and environment acting slowly through many generations is now no longer questioned. I do not find this to be the case. I find it is not only questioned but denied." In the end, the two old race warriors had to simply agree to disagree.[77]

In sympathetic accounts of his life, Dr. Kellogg's role in the eugenics movement has been downplayed, especially in light of his milder theories of euthenics; in other versions, they have simply been ignored. The reality is that Dr. Kellogg never completely abandoned many of his most racist beliefs. Like Lady Macbeth's hands, it was a bloody stain on the immaculate white suits he favored, one that can never really be washed clean. In early December of 1941, John began planning a fourth Race Betterment Conference for the late spring of 1942, in commemoration of his ninetieth birthday. That is, he was planning a conference until the December 7, 1941, attack on Pearl Harbor changed everything and the United States entered the Second World War. On December 19, Harry Laughlin, the superintendent of the Eugenics Record Office, wrote Dr. Kellogg a consolation note over the decision to postpone the conference. Laughlin praised John as one of the leading lights of the American eugenics movement, but he could not conclude without refuting the ninety-year-old physician's beloved euthenics: "The basic half [of an individual's character and achievements] which can not be changed in a generation or so is supplied by heredity."[78]

Harry Laughlin's emphasis on nature over nurture must have pained Dr. Kellogg but from a distance it is difficult to offer much sympathy. The rest of the story regarding the fall of the harmful work of Davenport, Laughlin, and others is well documented and need not be repeated here. By the 1930s, a growing cadre of bona fide geneticists, statisticians, and population biologists began developing reproducible laboratory and field methods of study, which formed the basis of a true scientific inquiry on genetics.[79] The ERO was finally closed in 1939.[80] After World War II, when the world discovered the role eugenics played in Hitler's "Final Solution" to cleanse the Third Reich of its unfit, the final nail was hammered into the coffin of the pseudoscience and eugenics became a topic of interest only to a handful of medical historians in search of tenure.

There is one more eugenics tale involving Laughlin and Dr. Kellogg that demands recounting. The great hypocrisy of Harry Laughlin's eugenics policies was his work to create mandatory "eugenical sterilization laws" in the United States for "mental defectives" and the "feeble-minded," a category that included people suffering from insanity, behavioral problems, intellectual disabilities, and epilepsy.[81] Less well known is that Mr. Laughlin long suffered from epilepsy, with frequent grand mal seizures. In 1941, Laughlin wrote Dr. Kellogg that his "local doctor" suggested dosing him with a drug called phenytoin, which was just beginning to be prescribed as an antiseizure drug even though it caused many unpleasant side effects.[82] Falling into the role of patient,

Laughlin complained to John about the new medication, "It seemed to stay off attacks but seemed also to pile up trouble at the end rather than cure it." Instead, Laughlin opted for Dr. Kellogg's prescriptions of "good diet, sound exercise and habits" to help prevent his debilitating seizures.[83] Although Laughlin died in January of 1943 and had no children, there exists no evidence that he consented to undergo a surgical sterilization procedure, in contradiction to the policies and laws he long advocated for other epileptics.

To his dying days, the doctor agonized over the decline of the white race. On November 1, 1943, John wrote to Reginald Atwater, the president of the American Public Health Association, beseeching the organization to take up the cause of Race Betterment: "If the American Public Health Association is indifferent to this matter or lacks the moral courage to give it consideration, it will miss a great opportunity for undertaking a work which may help to solve the world's greatest problem, how to save the human race, or at least the white portion of it."[84] Twenty days later, only a few weeks before he died, John wrote a rambling four-page letter to Henry F. Vaughan, the dean of the University of Michigan School of Public Health, emphasizing that the adoption of his approach to race betterment was "the only hope there is for saving the human race."[85]

In his last will and testament, John Harvey Kellogg left his entire estate to his Race Betterment Foundation. For nearly a quarter of a century, the organization continued under the haphazard direction of several of the doctor's former yes-men, including his loyal amanuensis August Bloese. In 1947, four years after the doctor's death, the Race Betterment Foundation's bankbook bulged with over $687,000 in assets; by 1967, that account had dwindled to a mere $492.87. In April of 1967, Frank J. Kelley, the State of Michigan's attorney general, indicted the trustees for having "completely squandered" the foundation's funds. Attorney General Kelley ordered the foundation into receivership. Although there were attempts by some Seventh-day Adventists to reorganize it under the direction of Kelley's staff, the Race Betterment Foundation, the once loud and proud grand marshal of the American eugenics movement, ultimately closed its books and, finally, its doors.[86] Both the foundation and the spurious cause of Race Betterment, to which Dr. Kellogg devoted so much of his time, reputation, talent, and fortune are dead, gone, and, hopefully, never to be resurrected.

14

A Full Plate

Dr. kellogg's far more enduring and palatable crusade was dietary in nature. To be sure, flaked cereals were his most lasting contribution to the modern breakfast menu but that was just one of the many grain-, vegetable-, fruit-, and nut-based foods John developed over the years.[1] Unfortunately for the doctor's coffers, he was not nearly as good at promoting his food products as his younger brother. Most of his customer base was drawn from current or former San patients, the Adventist faithful, graduates of his cooking school, and his legion of readers, but that hardly approached the millions of people who bought and consumed Will Kellogg's Corn Flakes each day. As John told a large gathering of his Adventist coreligionists in 1897: "You may say that I am destroying the health food business here by giving these recipes. But I am not after the business; I am after the *reform*; that is what I want to see."[2] As a result of his commercial complacency, however, most of John's "health foods" have been either lost to history or altered, reformulated, reshaped, and repackaged so many times as to obscure their true parentage.

John's loudest detractors derided him as a "nut," to which the doctor gleefully countered that he loved nuts of all kinds—from the "true nuts" (a hard-shelled pod containing both the fruit and the seed of the plant but the fruit does not open to release that seed) to legumes

Sanitas Nut Food advertisement, circa 1890s

and beans—as superb sources of healthy protein, fat, and fiber. Indeed, the doctor often urged, "Every highway should be lined with nut trees."[3]

During the late 1880s, John was most enthusiastic about peanuts and, as a result, he introduced dishes of them to the San's dining room menu. One problem he did not predict was that many of his invalided patients had difficulty chewing the roasted peanuts. In 1893, he began experimenting with industrial grinders to crush the nuts into a thick paste that was somewhat easier to swallow but still rather sticky. Later in his life, John often claimed to have invented peanut butter. As with the source of many great ideas, this story is much more complicated.[4] The experimentation of several other historical actors was required before the U.S. National Peanut Board could boast in 2016 that the average American child devours 1,500 peanut butter and jelly sandwiches between kindergarten and the end of high school.[5]

Sanitas Nut Butter label, circa 1900

Dr. Kellogg's earliest peanut butter recipes used roasted peanuts but, much to his consternation, the fat content in the nuts quickly broke down into a rancid, gloppy, oily mess, which both irritated dyspeptic stomachs and tasted awful. By 1897, he discarded the roasting process and, instead, boiled the peanuts at a range of 213 to 230 degrees Fahrenheit (any higher caused them to taste acrid). John's peanut butter was served in the San's dining room and used as a shortening in the kitchen for a variety of baked goods. In the years that followed, John cooked up many tasty nut butters out of almonds, hazelnuts, cashews, and once even used a shipment of macadamia nuts sent to him from a colleague in Hawaii for a more exotic spread.

Family lore claims John never patented this now ubiquitous food product. In 1917, Dr. Kellogg went as far as to assert this claim under courtroom oath that he "let everybody that wants it, have it, and make the best use of it."[6] But between 1894 and 1898, he did apply for and received three U.S. patents for his version of peanut butter.[7] John's methods were later supplanted by other food chemists who used the far tastier roasted peanuts, developed better grinding machinery to make smoother, more spreadable varieties of the stuff, and solved the problems of the peanut butter's solids separating out from the peanut fat with the introduction of partially hydrogenated oils.[8]

Will Kellogg predictably had a very different recollection of how peanut butter was created. In his version, the doctor asked him to "secure a quantity of peanuts, remove the hulls, and put them through the Granose rolls." Left to his own devices in the kitchen, Will claimed to have figured out the best way to roast the nuts and make the "first peanut butter." As the story goes, the doctor again overruled Will by deciding, "roasted peanuts were not wholesome" and ordered the nuts be steamed instead. Decades later, Will recalled that the boiled peanut butter tasted terrible and what "little trade that was developed was lost."[9] Will's grandson Norman Williamson Jr. recounted a similar version in his memoirs, an echo that provides a flavor of how the two brothers' grudge match was handed down to subsequent generations: "Had J.H. climbed on the peanut butter bandwagon," Williamson wrote, "he might have gained a substantial portion of the market, but he simply wouldn't have a younger brother second guess him.[10]

Around the same time he was playing with peanut butter, John created another healthy food he called "Malted Nuts." Malting grains or nuts (a process of germinating grain by soaking it in water and then heating it) converts starches into simple sugars, which makes them easier to digest.[11] Dr. Kellogg's Malted Nuts consisted of a pulverized mixture of peanuts and almonds, which when combined with water became a palatable "substitute milk" drink. He initially developed this product in 1896 for babies whose delicate digestive systems refused to tolerate cow's-milk-based formulae (a problem that many parents and babies contend with to this very day). For example, a full-page advertisement in the July 1901 issue of his *Good Health* magazine boldly declared "Cow's Milk Kills Babies" and, instead, suggested they slurp up bottles of his Malted Nuts. The doctor subsequently prescribed it to adults with dyspepsia, stomach ulcers, and lactose intolerance. Malted Nuts provided these patients with nutritious calories that they could easily digest.[12]

For invalids with especially sensitive stomachs and, as a result, dangerous weight loss, John combined the dry Malted Nuts with predigested, or dextrinized, starch, malt honey, and figs. He served and sold them in the form of small cakes called Bromose. The doctor claimed that it was "the vegetable analogue of malted milk and constitute[d] a perfect food. It was very caloric and helped invalids gain weight [by helping the body to produce] fat and blood." Clara Barton, the founder of the American Red Cross, was one of the product's biggest fans. In 1899, Nurse Barton wrote Dr. Kellogg that she rarely allowed her name to be exploited in any venture other than the Red Cross. In the case of John's Bromose and Nut Butter, which she found to be "choice, appetizing, wholesome foods, very pleasant to the palate, and exceedingly rich in nutritive and sustaining properties," the world-famous humanitarian was only too happy to make an exception. Dr. Kellogg took full advantage of this important endorsement in subsequent advertisement campaigns for his nut foods.[13]

Clara Barton loved John Harvey Kellogg's Bromose and Nut Butter.

GLUTEN (from the Latin, meaning glue) held a special fascination for John but not in the way a modern-day reader might assume. The doctor loved gluten and considered it essential for rejuvenating the wrecked bodies flocking to the San for salvation. He declared gluten to be "one of the most highly valuable elements of the grain. It serves especially to build up brain, bone, nerves, and muscles as well as blood."[14] The bread served in the San's dining room was made from his "Sanitarium Gluten Flour," which contained as much as 44.81 percent gluten. Beginning in 1889 and extending through his long career, John prescribed bags of the stuff for treating the "obese, anemic and the diabetic." In the 1920s, he fortified his gluten flour with casein, a protein found in cow's milk and rich in amino acids, carbohydrates, calcium, phosphorus, zinc, and Vitamin B$_{12}$.[15]

The doctor also used an assortment of chopped nuts thickened with huge amounts of gluten to develop meat substitutes. He shaped the resultant mixes into patties and cooked them in a manner to taste like chicken, beef, and veal. His Sanitarium Food Company manufactured and sold a line of "nut-cutlets," such as Nuttolene, and later, Battle Creek Steaks, Skallops, and Wieners. A similar product called Nuttose was a "nut butter" fortified with gluten and shaped like a square brick of cheese and cut into slices before serving. To accompany these nutty, glutenous entrées, John concocted a yeast extract and garden-vegetable-based powder he called Sativa, which when mixed with a little butter, flour, and water made a delicious "gravy rivaling mushrooms or beef in flavor."[16]

As we confront the confusing epidemic of gluten-intolerance today, it is fascinating to speculate why Dr. Kellogg, the famous healer of the tender gut, saw few, if any, complications with his gluten products during so many years of taking care of so many fragile patients. Several nutrition experts have posited that today's burgeoning "gluten problem" is a result of our species not having suitable time to adapt to consuming grains, in the face of an overconsumption of wheat. Other scientists counter this claim by noting that wheat grains have been a part of the human diet long enough for species adaptation (at least 11,000 years for wheat and closer to 23,000 years for wild wheat and barley). Some have argued that the increase in wheat sensitivities, allergies, and autoimmune diseases may be caused by genetic adaptation (and overadaptation) to increased encounters with disease-causing microbes found in the wheat grains or agents (such as sugar, saturated fats, and the growing number of food additives found in so many twenty-first-century processed wheat products), which can yield inflammatory responses and potential immune dysfunction.

Approximately one percent of the American population suffers from the very real gluten sensitivity known as celiac sprue disease, a genetic and, at times, stress-mediated disorder in which damage is done to the gut after eating wheat grains by means of an autoimmune response. In the United States, the incidence of celiac disease has increased only slightly over the past several decades. In 1950, for example, the incidence was 0.25 percent, despite the same approximate wheat consumption. That said, not a few doctors have privately groused that the current crop of gluten avoiders may have something more wrong with their heads than their intestinal tracts. The short, but unsatisfactory, answer to this multifactorial problem is that it is extremely complicated and its etiology is not yet entirely clear.[17]

THE LAXATIVES OF CHOICE during the late nineteenth and early twentieth centuries were the industrial-strength senna and cascara. John labeled the latter "one of the most vicious of these vile [laxative] substances." These cathartics could "move a mule" but they caused horrible cramping, irritation to the inner lining of the bowels, and, at too high a dose, severe diarrhea, dehydration, and even death.[18] In 1911, while visiting Sicily and North Africa, John was introduced to a gentler laxative: the plantago seed, or psyllium. These mucilaginous seeds are safe for treating constipation because they are not absorbed by the small intestine and, unlike the irritating cascara, cause no harm to the gut. Instead, they proceed through the colon absorbing water and, thus, producing a bulky, soft stool. While on holiday, John drank a glass of the finely ground seeds mixed with water and fruit juice. The next morning, he was impressed by his first evacuation and asked his host for a bag of psyllium seeds. Dr. Kellogg somehow got the seeds through U.S. Customs and home to Battle Creek, where he cultivated them for growing, processing, canning, and sale by his Battle Creek Sanitarium Food Company.

This indigestible fiber remains favored by those intestinally backed up, as well as those with painful hemorrhoids and anal fissures, two ailments the doctor was well acquainted with both professionally and personally.[19] The most popular brand is known as Metamucil, which has

Louis Pasteur

been on the market since 1934, and a host of generic products are also widely available. Recently, psyllium has been found to lower one's serum cholesterol level.[20] Again, Dr. Kellogg demonstrates from the grave how astute many of his nutritional prescriptions could be.

THE DOCTOR'S LONG-STANDING interest in the nutritious properties of milk and substitute milk products led him to explore what we now call probiotics. In 1883, John made the first of many medical pilgrimages to Paris. Soon after arriving at the Gare du Nord railway station, he checked into his hotel room on the Seine and changed out of his wrinkled clothing into a freshly pressed suit. Virtually skipping out of the hotel lobby, he hailed a hansom cab to take him to the famed Pasteur Institute. Once there, the American doctor was welcomed and escorted on a tour by the great Louis Pasteur, an experience that would have been heady for any medical man.

The institute boasted a staff of world-class microbiologists and scientists. One of the most prominent was Élie Metchnikoff, a pioneer

The Pasteur Institute laboratory, Paris, 1890s

in studying the immune system and who shared the Nobel Prize for Medicine or Physiology in 1908 with Paul Ehrlich. Dr. Kellogg visited Metchnikoff's laboratory, where Metchnikoff and his first assistant, Henry Tissier, studied the microbial environment of the gut. In 1907, Metchnikoff assigned Tissier to find scientific evidence supporting his theory that not all germs were pathogenic (disease-causing) or "bad." Such contrary thinking was a hard sell to make during an era when new discoveries about "infectious diseases and their relation to

Élie Metchnikoff, circa 1905

micro-organisms were being announced like corn popping in a pan."[21]

Nevertheless, Metchnikoff and Tissier's work was both sound and revolutionary. The "good" bacteria Tissier worked with the most were *Lactobacillus bulgaricus* and, subsequently, *Lactobacillus acidophilus*. These "healthy" microbes multiplied luxuriously within the intestinal flora of his experimental animals *(in vivo)* and inhibited the growth of many disease-causing germs. The bacilli grew especially well in a culture medium made with milk *(in vitro)*. One way to improve intestinal health, prevent gut infections, and strike down the "putrefactive," disease-causing autointoxication, they reasoned, was to consume *Lactobacillus*-rich milk. Metchnikoff became so enthusiastic about these findings that he invested his considerable influence to hail *Lactobacillus bulgaricus* as a panacea for nearly every human ill and a protection against aging.[22]

This was a medical melody to John's ears and he soon became the American agent for the promotion of *Lactobacilli*. For more than twenty-five years, the doctor continued a dialogue with Tissier by post and subsequent visits to the Pasteur Institute, where "he was shown every courtesy."[23] Dr. Tissier eventually discovered that *Lactobacillus acidophilus* was the better bacterium because it was easier to culture in large volumes, especially after spiking the Petri dish with lactose. In 1911, Dr. Kellogg asked for and received samples of an active strain of *Lactobacillus acidophilus* Tissier had cultured from fermented cow's milk and yogurt.[24] A delighted John immediately put these "good germs" to work at the San dining room.[25]

———

LIKE HIS FAMOUS PATIENT Henry Ford, Dr. Kellogg was fascinated by the soybean.[26] But instead of using them to fashion automobile parts, John wanted to harness their many nutritional properties. The doctor first learned about soy milk, a beverage consisting of pulverized dried soybeans mixed with water, from colleagues in Asia who had long prescribed it for those with sensitive stomachs. John added Tissier's acidophilus to the recipe and called his drink "Soy Acidophilus Milk." Those patients suffering from colitis, duodenal or gastric ulcers, constipation, and excessive flatulence happily found their conditions improved after imbibing soy milk and it soon became one of the San's most popular beverages. For example, in 1935 the San served over two hundred gallons a week; a particular favorite dish was sliced ripe bananas and soy milk.[27]

John backed up his empirical observations of soy milk by studying hundreds of stool specimens in his smelly basement gastrointestinal laboratory. Those who exclusively drank acidophilus soy milk produced the most interesting samples. Like Tissier, as he gazed through the microscope, the doctor was amazed to learn how much the soy milk changed the intestinal flora, from a population of microbes that potentially caused harm to far more health-promoting variants. He was describing, in essence, a powerful probiotic.[28]

Dr. Kellogg's most important discovery in this field came in 1933 after isolating a strain of *Lactobacillus acidophilus* in soy milk, which grew five to ten times more than when it was cultured in cow's milk, was far more temperature resistant, and remained potent for three to four months. Impressed by how well the improved soy milk worked in changing the intestinal flora of adults, he next turned to the hottest topic in pediatrics of the day, the "artificial feeding," or bottle-feeding, of infants with precise formulae of protein, carbohydrates, and fat derived from altered versions of cow's milk. American mothers of this era avidly adopted "artificial feeding" because it was so much more convenient than breast-feeding. That said, not every baby seemed to thrive on the method.[29]

The results of John's infant feeding studies comprise a stunning, if oft ignored, discovery. He found that babies who were exclusively breast-fed had an intestinal flora containing more than 90 percent *Lactobacillus acidophilus*. Sick infants, who were bottle-fed with cow's milk formu-

*The Dionne Quintuplets in January of 1937. The Quints
were thriving, thanks to the attentive care of their physician,
Dr. Allan Dafoe, and plenty of Dr. Kellogg's soy milk.*

lae, produced dark and foul-smelling stools and had 10 to 20 percent
Lactobacillus in their guts. To counteract potential bowel troubles, John
advised that every bottle-fed baby should receive a teaspoonful of his
"Soy Acidophilus Milk" at each feeding. After receiving a patent for his
method of making acidophilus soy milk in 1934, John dreamed about
selling gallons of the soy milk to improve millions of ailing infantile
guts.[30]

To publicize his discovery, John tried to recruit the most
famous babies in the world, Yvonne, Annette, Cécile, Émilie, and Marie
Dionne. Today, the Dionne Quintuplets are an all but forgotten miracle
of human reproduction. Born on May 28, 1934, in the small town of
Callander, Ontario, Canada, these little girls were once the most famous
babies in the world.[31] The hardworking doctor who delivered and cared
for them was a mild-mannered, general practitioner and "country doctor" named Allan Roy Dafoe. He, too, became a renowned celebrity and
his career was dramatized in a string of 20th-Century-Fox films.[32]

Despite the sunny newspaper accounts of their progress, the quintuplets' post-natal course was quite rocky. Among the many problems
the five little girls experienced was a struggle to gain weight and trouble
digesting the cow's milk formula their mother gave them. Breast-feeding
would have, undoubtedly, proved more tolerable to the infants but was

impossible given the ratio of hungry mouths to maternal breasts. Dr. Dafoe was at his wits' end to solve this very real health threat to his young charges.

None of the girls had a more difficult time than Marie Dionne, the youngest and smallest of the babies. At four months of age she developed a severe bowel infection, a not uncommon problem with premature infants. In the decades before modern neonatal intensive care, such infections were often death sentences. After reading about Marie's dilemma, John wired Dr. Dafoe that he was sending a supply of his Soy Acidophilus Milk to help the struggling infant. Within a week and a half of prescribing the soy milk, Dr. Dafoe was amazed to discover that Marie's infection had resolved. The country doctor asked Dr. Kellogg to send the quintuplets as much soy milk as he could deliver.[33] Their earliest ration was just a teaspoonful of soy milk at each feeding, but by 1937 each of the famous Quints was consuming a pint or more per day and all enjoyed good digestive health.

For several years, Dr. Kellogg maintained a solicitous correspondence with Dr. Dafoe. He offered advice on the babies' growth and development and, just as often, sent them crates of soy milk, fresh fruit, and other foods. At the same time, John lobbied David Croll, the Canadian minister of public welfare, who ran the Dionne Trust, which administered the millions of dollars these little girls generated from tourists flocking to Ontario to watch them grow and thrive through a glass-windowed home, movie appearances, product advertisements, postcards, photographs, and even Quint dolls.[34] On many occasions, Dr. Kellogg lobbied Minister Croll for permission to use the names and likenesses of the Dionne girls on advertisements for his soy milk, which was "proving such a boon to babies suffering from bowel trouble." The doctor reported he had no desire to profit from his medical discovery and was only interested in helping humanity, one stomach at a time. All the proceeds, he explained, would go toward his nonprofit Race Betterment Foundation and the Battle Creek College.[35] John long awaited permission from Ottawa for an endorsement or, at least, a photograph of him with the children whose lives he helped save. It never came.[36]

The doctor was, however, free to brag about his success in treating the world-famous Admiral Richard Byrd. The intrepid explorer's once sound digestion was devastated during his first 5-month expedition to the South Pole in 1928–1929. Fortunately, the doctor's prescription of aci-dophilus soy milk quickly restored the admiral's health. As a result, Byrd became a strict adherent of Dr. Kellogg's biologic living diet. When the explorer made a subsequent trip to the South Pole in 1934, John made certain the admiral brought plenty of complimentary cans of his soy milk.[37] The doctor also prescribed Lacto-Dextrin (a product containing milk sugar, or lactose, and dextrose, "to keep *B. Acidophilus* growing well in the colon," as well as reduce the risks of putrefying food left in the colon and to produce odorless stools). And in the event of constipation, the doctor sent along boxes of Paramels (a chocolate-flavored caramel laxative, which combined malt sugar and theobromine, a bitter alkaloid found in the cacao plant, with a dollop of paraffin and mineral oil).[38] In a January 1938 letter to John D. Rockefeller Jr., who funded Byrd's expeditions, John boasted, "Some of our newer methods have certainly done a great deal for him. He looks and acts like another man entirely."[39]

An advertisement for John Harvey Kellogg's "Zo"
cereal, which Admiral Richard Byrd brought with
him on his expeditions to the South Pole

IRONICALLY, the man who paid the closest attention to John's nutritional developments was Will Kellogg. The cereal maker had "long nurtured the dream of combining essential nutrients from different grains to create a concentrated, high protein all-purpose food."[40] Will closely followed the discoveries then being made about protein, carbohydrate, and fat metabolism as well as the importance of vitamins and essential minerals in one's daily diet.[41] During the 1930s, Will introduced PEP, a whole wheat, flaked bran cereal that both stimulated bowel movements and was sprayed with a solution containing all the major vitamins.[42]

Beginning in 1945, Will blended his corn grits with soy-based flakes and turned them into a shredded cereal he called "Corn-Soya Shreds." Each box promised "a fine body—this new protein cereal helps you have it" and the cereal's advertisements featured artistic renderings of muscle-sculpted divers, gridiron heroes, cheerleaders, and gymnasts.[43] The Kellogg Company discontinued Corn-Soya Shreds in the mid-1950s in favor of a low-fat, puffed, flaky cereal made from rice, wheat gluten, wheat germ, powdered skim milk, and brewer's yeast, fortified with phosphorus, copper, iron, folic acid, vitamins B_1, B_{12} and B_6, niacin and riboflavin, and vitamins C and D. The Kellogg's food chemists named this wonder food "Special K" and put it in white boxes labeled with "a big, red K." This cereal is still enjoyed by many millions of consumers around the world.[44]

In 1959, eight years after Will's death, the Kellogg Company introduced an even more potent "perfect food" called "Concentrate." The tiny golden pellets in each box consisted of "defatted wheat germ," wheat gluten, milled rice, corn, and ten minerals and vitamins; it was 40 percent "high-quality protein" and 99 percent fat free. The product was discontinued in 1981 due to poor sales.[45] The great paradox shrouding the W. K. Kellogg Company's search for the perfect food, however, was that it coincided precisely with when the firm was fortifying its more popular cereals with tons of sugar and artificial flavorings.

John Harvey Kellogg would have no truck with such nutritional pandering and, perhaps, it was best that he did not live to see the thick sugar coating of the cereal industry that began in the post–World War II era. Although taste was always a concern in his food endeavors, the doctor would never condone the addition of huge lumps of sugar, salt, and so many other unhealthy ingredients to his products. Speculation aside, the many foods John invented or helped develop constitute his most lasting contributions to human health and nutrition, even if he is rarely recognized for them. In the United States and around the world, health-conscious consumers continue to consume versions of his health food products, from soy milk, psyllium, and bran cereals to fiber bars and nut foods, all to the betterment of their health, digestion, and diet. Unlike the well-deserved stain on his reputation garnered from his work with the American eugenics movement, the virtual ignorance of John's work in developing a healthier diet constitutes a historical shame worthy of both correction and recognition.

15

"Uneasy Lies the Head That Wears a Crown"

W ILL KELLOGG LOVED HORSES. When he was a little boy, his closest companion was Old Spot, the Kellogg family's nag of dubious Arabian origin. That is, until young Will came home from school one day only to learn that his father had sold the beast to a farmer who wanted it to pull his plow. Apparently, this was the moment when the awkward boy vowed he would someday own a collection of prized horses. Slower to pardon than most glaciers used to melt, Will finally settled this childish score with his father at the age of sixty-five. In May of 1925, he bought an eight-hundred-acre horse ranch in Pomona, California, for $250,000 (about $3.38 million in 2016).[1] He could afford it. Will Kellogg was one of America's best-paid men and each year took home a salary of more than a million dollars (over $14,000,000 in 2016).[2]

Soon after his land purchase, Will amassed one of the finest collections of Arabian horses in the world. Unlike John, who spent his last years fearing for the degeneracy of the "white race," Will restricted his theories on breeding strictly to his champion horses, many of which were purchased from the famous Lady Wentworth stables, Crabbet Arabian Stud Farm in Great Britain, and her Sheykh Obeyd Stud Farm near Cairo. Lady Wentworth's savvy horsemen were renowned for their ability to mate their best horses with the Bedouin breeders' sleekest animals. Today, more than 90 percent of the Thoroughbred Arabian horses in the world have descended from Crabbet Stud pedigrees.

Will was especially fond of taking out Antez, a "chestnut stallion with blonde mane and tail," for morning rides around the ranch. At the age of

Will with his twin Arabian colts on their first birthday, February 4, 1940.
Twin foals occur in about one in ten thousand births.

sixty-six, Will nearly died after Antez slipped while climbing a steep hill on a trail wet and muddy from the previous day's rain. Will fell off the saddle, caught his foot in the stirrup, and found himself upside-down and helpless under the horse. As Will proudly recounted, "The trembling horse stood fast in his steps and remained in this position for four or five minutes until the caretaker came back to investigate our delay and then rescued me from the perilous situation."[3] The cereal king ceased riding altogether a few years later. While out with his son John Leonard, Will fell off his horse and broke a rib. Then and there, he decided it was

Antez, the Arabian horse who saved Will's life

best to admire his stallions and mares with his feet on the ground, while walking in the company of one of his German shepherds.[4]

To keep busy, Will built a mansion he called "the Big House," situated on a five-hundred-foot-high hill. Designed to impress, Will's estate cost over $125,000 ($1.67 million in 2016) and was ready for habitation on New Year's Day of 1927. It featured long buildings of a Spanish design, with red-tiled roofs, yawning archways, and a series of courtyards with gurgling, stone-cut fountains.[5] Inside were fourteen rooms, four and a half baths, a fully stocked kitchen, a breakfast room, and a dining room that seated up to twenty guests. The living room was built around a sixty-foot-long picture window, which afforded an excellent view of the Pomona Valley, all the way to the San Jose Hills and, on a clear day, the San Antonio Mountains. Each room was designed to replicate a sense of "early California living." Directly above the lavish furniture was a lattice of ceiling beams made of distressed oak, all bearing the monogram "W.K.K." There were two walk-in dressing closets, several sleeping porches, a Skinner pipe organ in the living room (just like the one he had in his Battle Creek home, costing $25,000, or about $334,000 in 2016), and a chapel-like entry hall with an antique tiled mural depicting St. George slaying the dragon.[6]

Behind the house was a kidney-shaped swimming pool surrounded by a brick and concrete patio, several barns, a seven-car garage to house Will's convoy of Lincoln limousines, and a machine shop. Alongside these structures was a spacious administration building and living quarters for the ranch foreman, ranch hands, and stable boys. The pièce de résistance was a pristine U-shaped stable. Each of the thirty comfortable stalls in this grand structure was equipped with a watering device fed by a million-gallon reservoir activated by the touch of a horse's nose. Surrounding the estate were groves of olive, avocado, grapefruit, orange, pomegranate, and lemon trees and three ponds (two for ducks and one for fish). Completing the picture were several winding roads, horse riding paths, and hiking trails, all leading into a canyon filled with bamboo, eucalyptus, ginger, and one of the world's largest sycamore trees.[7]

EVERY SUNDAY, Will and his staff welcomed nearly three thousand visitors into a grandstand built around a horse ring. Some knew of the

Kellogg ranch from reading the many newspaper and magazine articles describing it; others watched the horses put through their paces every New Year's Day at the annual Rose Bowl Parade in Pasadena. Millions more heard about the ranch in April of 1939, when Will agreed to make his national radio debut on the NBC Blue Network. He did not pitch his cereal, even if the mere mention of his name conjured visions of Corn Flakes. Instead, he spoke about the recent birth of a set of Arabian colt twins, which he heralded as the world's only such pair.[8]

On many of these Sundays, seated right next to the hoi polloi, were members of Hollywood's film royalty, including "America's Sweetheart," Mary Pickford, and her dashing husband, Douglas Fairbanks; Will Rogers, the one comedian who could reliably make Will laugh; the "It" girl, Clara Bow; Tom Mix, the cowboy star of the silent Westerns; a prim and proper Olivia de Havilland; the strong and silent Gary Cooper; Hal Roach's "Our Gang" kids; the always sultry Marlene Dietrich; and the comically crude Wallace Beery. On other occasions he hosted Colonel Charles Lindbergh (for whom Will named one of his horses "Hawaragil," the Arabic word for "airman") and the humanitarian Helen Keller. Like his brother, Will enjoyed hobnobbing with celebrities, both at his ranch and while dining at Hollywood's favorite watering hole, the

VISITORS BEING ENTERTAINED AT STABLES ON W. K. KELLOGG ARABIAN HORSE RANCH, POMONA, CALIF.

*The sumptuous Kellogg horse stable, with a line of visitors on a Sunday
waiting to see Will's horses put through their paces*

*Left to right: W. K. Kellogg, with Carrie Staines Kellogg (Will's second wife),
Hollywood movie star Colleen Moore, Mrs. Elizabeth Selden Rogers
(a leading suffragist and public school reformer), and Mrs. Clara Butler
(Will's sister), circa 1929*

Brown Derby. For example, writing his former daughter-in-law, Hanna,
on March 27, 1929, Will gushed over posing for pictures with the silent
screen star Colleen Moore, who is best recalled today, if at all, for popu-
larizing the bobbed haircut so many women wore during the 1920s.[9]

The weekly horse shows began promptly at 2:00 p.m. and ended at
3:30. Over a loudspeaker system, a seasoned announcer told the fans
about the lineage of each horse and then described the maneuvers the
Arabian jumpers, gaiters, draft, and stock horses were about to perform.
Mounted upon them were trick riders ornately dressed as Bedouin horsemen. The climax of the afternoon was a reenactment of the famous char-
iot race scene from the Metro-Goldwyn-Mayer 1925 blockbuster film,
Ben-Hur, featuring teams of Shetland ponies, elaborate Roman-style
chariots, and several brave charioteers.[10]

Will rarely mingled with his guests, preferring to sit in his Lincoln
limousine, in a reserved slot of the horse ring's parking lot, watching
the crowd watch his horses.[11] Despite the droves of people he invited to
his Pomona estate, he complained that after living there for more than

The finale of Will's weekly horse shows: a mini-chariot race with Shetland ponies, based on the exciting 1925 MGM film Ben-Hur

fifteen years, "I have had only three friends in the whole valley."[12] Even among a throng of grateful visitors, Will was a lonely man.

Will's greatest contribution to the California scene involved the loan of Jadaan, his best Arabian stallion, to Rudolph Valentino, the movie star famously referred to by journalist H. L. Mencken as "catnip to women."[13] On April 16, 1926, Valentino telegraphed Will with the request to borrow Jadaan for his film *The Son of the Sheik*, the sequel to his 1921 smash hit, *The Sheik*.[14] Valentino planned on wearing costumes and jewelry costing more than $11,000 (about $147,000 in 2016) to portray "the best dressed Sheik in all of Araby." For added box office appeal, he cast Vilma Banky, the Hungarian siren discovered by producer Samuel Goldwyn, to play the Sheik's love interest.[15]

In Valentino's mind, the most important actor to cast was of the equestrian variety. As he explained to Will, "I especially ask for Jadaan because I consider him the embodiment of the finest Arab from every standpoint and feel he would be the greatest living example to show people of the world through this picture."[16] Given the value of the animal, Valentino's plan to make Jadaan a "star" was an attractive but risky proposition. Will's eldest son, Karl, objected, fearing for the horse's safety. The next day, April 17, Will overruled Karl and consented to Valentino's request. Will demanded a nonnegotiable return date of May 1, along with Val-

Rudolph Valentino, in Son of the Sheik, *atop Will's best Arabian stallion, Jadaan*

entino's promise to cover all transportation, feeding, and lodging costs, insurance fees of $20,000, and his chief horse trainer's salary. The "Sheik" accepted the terms and enthused to Will via telegram, "Cannot begin to express my thanks for your great courtesy. . . . You may be sure I will give Jadan [*sic*] even more considerate treatment than if he were my own Stop Sincere Regards Rudolph Valentino."[17]

Unfortunately, there were several production delays while shooting the film's desert scenes near Yuma, Arizona. The scorching heat and the angry, biting flies in no way helped the actors, horses, and camels appearing in the film. Way over budget and with too little film in the can, Valentino kept Jadaan longer than the agreed-upon time, a move that was poorly received in Pomona. Both Will and Karl suspected the film star of stalling and secretively using Jadaan for breeding purposes but they could never prove it. In an effort to recall his loan, Will sent reproachful, angry telegrams to the movie set in Yuma. On May 1, for example, Will wired Valentino, "In my business dealings I am not accustomed to treatment of this sort."[18] The horse was eventually safely returned and the film was released to great acclaim and financial success. It grossed more than $1 million in the first year alone (about $13.4 million in 2016), and in the two years that followed it earned more than double that amount.[19]

On the evening of July 9, 1926, Karl Kellogg and his wife, Etta (but not Will), attended the film's premiere at Sid Grauman's famed Los Angeles movie palace the "Million Dollar Theatre." Karl was disappointed to find there was no formal mention of his father in the credits and that Jadaan had relatively few "close-ups." There were, however, some exciting shots of the Sheik in the saddle holding on to Jadaan's reins, as the horse reared up on its hind legs and then raced across the sand dunes, leaving only "a trail of hoof prints."[20]

On August 23, while in New York City during a national tour for the movie, Rudolph suffered a perforated ulcer and died of peritonitis. His funeral, and the crush of fans it attracted, made for one of the biggest spectacles of grief and celebrity ever seen on the streets of Manhattan. H. L. Mencken's tart eulogy for Valentino easily could have been applied to the man who lent the actor a horse, minus the descriptor "young": "Here was a young man who was living daily the dream of millions of other young men. . . . Here was one who had wealth and fame. And here was one who was very unhappy."[21]

AT ODDS WITH WILL'S vast material success was an equal amount of emotional impoverishment and conflict in his personal life. Sadly for the people he loved the most or worked with most closely, Will too often projected the detritus of his inner demons directly onto them. It was a destructive dynamic that refused to die until Will did. "There was in Mr. Kellogg's makeup," his authorized biographer Horace Powell noted, "a high degree of intolerance, as there is in the outlook of many strong men. Few of his executives were ever comfortable in his presence."[22] Behind those thick black glasses was a nest of seething grudges against anyone who crossed him or his company. Will kept his own counsel on almost everything and ran his empire as a "one-man government."[23] "Once his mind was made up," his grandson Norman Williamson Jr. recalled, "there was no changing it through further discussion."[24]

When things did not go the way he demanded or expected, Will could explode with a resounding force, such as the time he attended a vaudeville show with his son John Leonard. The comedian on the bill had the audience laughing hysterically over an improvisational song where he made up lyrics about members of the audience. Will was rolling about and chuckling away until the comedian approached his box singing, "I see a little short, fat man in the box, with a bald head." According to John Leonard, "W.K. got so mad at this, I had to take hold of him and pull him down in his seat."[25]

Will reserved his deepest anger, of course, for his brother, John. Their nonstop enmity placed a great deal of stress on the rest of his family, who had no desire to anger either one of them. Shielding the most sparks from this fraternal feud was their sister Clara. After her divorce from Hiland Butler, Clara lived in John's house, acted as his personal secretary, and, upon Ella Kellogg's death in 1920, took on many of the domestic duties of the Residence. Several years later, Will invited Clara to stay with him at his palatial Tudor Revival home, "Eagle Heights." The house was situated on a bluff comprising thirty acres of land and a view of Battle Creek's picturesque Gull Lake.[26] Clara accepted and enjoyed the luxurious accommodations her brother provided. After a few weeks, however, she pined for the more familiar surroundings she shared with John. Clara wrote the doctor about her desire to "come home." Immediately after reading the letter, John asked his driver to take him to his brother's estate. At the doorstep, a forceful John told Will in no uncertain terms, "She wants to come back." Will responded just as heatedly, "She doesn't need to come home. She is well cared for here." Much to Will's discontent, the doctor won this silly battle and Clara returned to the Residence.[27]

By ALL ACCOUNTS, Will was a cold and inattentive husband to his wife, Puss. Bone-weary after long days at his plant or in the boardroom, Will preferred to eat the dinners she prepared in stony silence. The rare snippets of conversation he did offer almost always centered on the conduct of his company. In fact, the Kelloggs functioned in separate spheres. Puss's life orbited around rearing their children and keeping house even as she struggled with a losing battle against cancer. Will's life was singularly driven by the Kellogg Company. The emotional distance between Puss and Will grew with each passing year and was most poignantly described by a relative recalling family walks on the Saturday Sabbath: "The rest of us went walking with Uncle Will, but his wife never did."[28]

As Puss's cancer progressed, Will did pay closer attention to her but only in his own fashion. He spared no expense in finding the best physicians, consulted with them closely, and sent her on deluxe trips to warm climates so she might recuperate from her latest operation or treatment. The money he spent, however, was not powerful enough to reverse her malignancy. On September 2, 1912, Ella "Puss" Kellogg died. She was only fifty-four. Will found solace by throwing himself deeper into his work even though he knew it could not completely assuage his grief. A relative concerned about Will's prolonged depression after Ella's death suggested that he might want to remarry. Will sadly replied, "I made one woman unhappy. Why should I inflict myself on another?"[29] Will understood the corrosive effects of his brooding silence and how that might negatively impact his inviting another woman to live in his home.[30]

Five years later, Will reversed course by courting Dr. Carrie Staines with quiet suppers and long car trips along the Michigan countryside. Staines, a former schoolteacher from Grand Rapids, went to John's missionary medical school and, for twenty-five years, worked as a physician at the Sanitarium. John told Dr. Staines that he strongly objected to her "keeping company" with Will and threatened to fire her if she continued to see him. When Carrie told Will of her professional dilemma, he "almost impulsively" suggested the solution of marriage. They were wed on New Year's Day of 1918, thus ending her tenure at the San.[31]

For the first few years of their marriage, Will took great pains to make the arrangement work, perhaps as a penitence for his callous treatment of Puss. Carrie, too, tried hard to express her love for Will. Whenever Will traveled, Carrie wrote long letters inquiring after his health and experiences. In return, Will showered her with expensive gifts and displayed an uncharacteristic tenderness. For example, one close friend to both the Kelloggs recalled watching Will "tiptoeing over to the chair in which sat his wife reading a book, there to turn higher a lamp so that she would have more light."[32]

As the years progressed, however, the couple grew increasingly apart. They were far from loquacious and, as one observer noted, "two people who never say anything spontaneously must have found it difficult to communicate orally any feeling toward each other."[33] Carrie was never able to accustom herself to his brooding silence. To Will's disappointment, she was just not the type of wife his intolerant perfectionism demanded.[34] A mutual friend believed that the two truly loved

*Will and his second wife, Dr. Carrie Staines, on a typical evening together
in their Battle Creek mansion, with Rinson, one of Will's Seeing Eye dogs
and the son of Rin Tin Tin*

one another even if Will was unable to express it. Will's quiet rumina-
tions were not rebukes directed at his new wife; they were simply an
instrumental part of his work. "I have to have those times when I can
be alone," he admitted, "when I must have a room to myself where I
can spend some time thinking undisturbed."[35] By the early 1940s, glaucoma and increasing blindness made Will even more withdrawn and
a series of illnesses made Carrie quite frail. Forced to acknowledge the
burden each represented to the other, they mutually agreed "to live their
own lives without impinging too much on the activities of the other."[36]
After several debilitating strokes, Dr. Carrie Staines died in 1948 at the
age of 81.

WILL AND PUSS had five children and three survived infancy: two
sons, Karl (1881–1955) and John Leonard (1883–1950), and a daughter,
Elizabeth Ann (1888–1966).[37] Encumbered by the oppressive duties of
running his cereal empire, the socially awkward Will had little time to
spend with his children. He rarely gave them what every child craves
from their father: loads of unconditional love and silly fun. The man

who "never learned how to play" was incapable of sitting on the floor for a game of jacks with his daughter or venturing out in the backyard to have a catch with the boys.

Most of the time, Will was stiff, reserved, and remote. He insisted that his children refer to him as "Father" and never "Papa" or "Daddy." Their answers to his questions were mandatorily required to begin with a "Yes Sir" or a "No Sir." Will's grandson Norman Williamson Jr. recalled, "If they [the children] misunderstood, they were to query politely, 'Sir?'"[38] He could quiet his boys' most boisterous melees with menacing glares and a snap of his fingers.[39] Will advocated "corporal punishment swift and sure" when "raising his own children and their children as well. He was convinced that at the heart of any behavior problem was an indulgent parent, usually the mother."[40]

The only day of the year his children recalled him being truly jovial was Christmas Eve when the entire family gathered for a sumptuous supper. Will refused to play Santa Claus, even if he had the body habitus to

Three generations of Kellogg "men" at dinner, 1923. Will is at the head of the table and to his right is his grandson Kenneth. On the left side of the table facing the camera are Will's second son, John Leonard, and his two sons, and on the right are Will's eldest son, Karl, and his two sons. At the foot of the table (in sailor suits) are Will's daughter Beth's sons.

fit the iconic red suit with white fur trim. But he did often hire an actor to play St. Nicholas and hand out gifts to the children. Yet, as Will's biographer Horace Powell observed, "Christmases are few and far between, and children need a father on ordinary days of the year."[41] Late in his life, Will wrote a letter of regret over his absentee parenting to one of his children, with a mildly manipulative reminder: "I think, however, I have in some ways tried to indicate to you my interest in your welfare."[42]

KARL HUGH KELLOGG, Will's oldest son, was drawn toward medicine. Not surprisingly, Will refused to allow Karl to enroll at his uncle John's American Missionary Medical College, just down the street. Instead, Karl attended the "regular" Detroit College of Medicine (now Wayne State University School of Medicine). After graduating in 1904, the young physician practiced first in Montana, and in 1905, at age twenty-three, he married a young woman named Etta Landrum, from Stevensville, Montana. A few years later, as Will began expanding his factory's output and workforce, Karl returned to Battle Creek to lead the company's medical staff. In this role, he instituted a number of progressive policies and on-site medical and dental clinics to insure the health of the workers. At home in Battle Creek, Karl and Etta raised their two boys, Karl Landrum and Will Lewis.

By 1925, Karl's poor health forced him to retire from medical practice.[43] For the next two years, he supervised the construction of his father's ranch until the pressures and disagreeableness of working for Will became too great.[44] While not exactly estranged from Will, Karl did his best to avoid squabbling with him. They fought over everything imaginable: the placement of shrubs and fruit trees around the estate, the chauffeur's poor care of Will's cars, the loan of Jadaan to Rudolph Valentino, the profligate spending habits of Will's horse trainer, and especially Will's mean reduction of the budget for a house Karl was building near his father's mansion. Will's false economies led to Karl's house almost burning down, thanks to the installation of a cheaply made and easily overheated furnace.[45] In 1927, Karl and his family left Pomona (and Will) to develop a successful grapefruit and lemon ranch in Chula Vista, near San Diego.[46] A pillar of the Chula Vista community, he died there, at seventy-three, in December of 1955.[47]

JOHN LEONARD KELLOGG (1883–1950), Will's second son, was energetic, mischievous, and robust. The boy especially loved playing practical
jokes, including one Halloween when he hoisted a cow up into the belfry
of the Battle Creek College. Will took to berating John Leonard for all
sorts of infractions, including poor school attendance, failing grades, and
not properly conducting himself as a Kellogg. After the worst of these
paternal dressings-down, the boy wrote his father poorly spelled letters
of apology, which concluded with pledges to do better in the future.
The promises rarely stuck; within a few weeks or months, John Leonard
found a new way to engage in tomfoolery and enrage Will.[48]

Norman Williamson Jr. described him as a "virtual volcano of ideas."[49]
Horace Powell pronounced him to be "the driving, dynamic, indefatigable spark plug of the manufacturing end of the business."[50] Despite
John Leonard's youthful rebellion, his dream was to assume the helm of
his father's firm. To achieve this goal, he invented all kinds of machines
and processes that advanced the quality and sales of Kellogg's products.
Even the reticent Will had to admit, "I do not know the exact number of
patents and trademarks which were taken out by J.L. and assigned to the
Kellogg Company, but with foreign patents, all told, I think they must
have numbered in excess of two hundred."[51]

For example, from 1906 to 1914, Corn Flakes boxes were externally
wrapped with paraffin wax paper to maintain freshness, in the manner
of a Christmas present. This method performed haphazardly, depending on the climate where the boxes were ultimately sold and how long
they sat on the grocer's shelves. In 1914, John Leonard figured out a way
to make a paraffin wax paper bag that fit inside the box. Called "Waxtite," the bag was heat-sealed to preserve the crispness of the cereal,
regardless of the grocery store's ambient temperature or humidity,
and maintain the taste, nutrition, and purity of the product. The new
moisture-and-tamper-proof packaging proved terrifically popular with
consumers.[52] Waxtite had another virtue in that it required two inches
less wax paper than the older, external wrapping method, thus creating
a substantial savings on the company's packaging costs. Over the course
of a few decades, this form of packaging saved the company millions of
dollars.[53] Inside-the-box wrappers became the gold standard for keeping

food products fresh and free from adulteration, thanks to John Leonard Kellogg.

John Leonard was also fascinated by the science of gastroenterology and prided himself on having read "every book extant on the human colon." He even concocted several new cereals of his own, with "a book in one hand, a spoon in the other, a health-giving mixture bubbling on the back of the kitchen range."[54] This work led to the development of a new means to make shredded wheat biscuits, improved versions of "cereal coffee," the creation of corn-soya flakes, and a recipe for wheat bran mixed with the famous Kellogg "malt flavoring," which became the popular "All-Bran."

By 1912, John Leonard was managing the W. K. Kellogg Company's Battle Creek plant, which he had grown to encompass "a huge cluster of buildings extending over 113 acres."[55] Will's response to this expansion was annoyingly contrary: "You're making this plant too big for me. I'm not comfortable in it any more."[56] The son bristled at Will's constant criticism and responded poorly to even the gentlest advice. Yet they were very similar people with respect to their drive, work ethic, and dedication to the firm. After putting in a full day supervising the factory, John Leonard walked across town to the company laboratory where he worked late nights to figure out new ways to improve Kellogg's cereals.

Almost as stern as Will, John Leonard kept a close eye on each employee and every occurrence in his factory. Unfortunately, his explosive temper frightened and antagonized many of those working for him. For example, a foreman recalled the morning John Leonard found an old clock hanging on the wall that was no longer working and beyond repair. John Leonard abruptly ordered the foreman to replace the broken clock. The foreman neglected to do so because he was busy with far more pressing matters. A day later, John Leonard spied the broken clock still hanging and "ripped it off the wall, and let it fall to the floor with a crash" in front of his shocked workers.[57] John Leonard later tried boxing as a form of anger management. His boxing coach grew so weary of John Leonard's constant braggadocio that the instructor finally "decked him," marking the end of his foray into the "sweet science."[58]

John Leonard had many foibles and flaws but he also had to endure the stress of working for a perfectionist father who picked on his every error and minimized his successes. From a medical standpoint, it is interesting to note that John Leonard suffered from digestive problems and eventually developed a duodenal ulcer. At least two other sons of American tycoons experienced gastric distress while working for their famous fathers: Edsel Ford died of stomach cancer at the age of forty-nine and John D. Rockefeller Jr. long endured dyspepsia and stomach ulcers. Will blamed John Leonard's digestive problem on his cigarette smoking and chided his son for overworking even as he placed more and more demands upon him.[59]

The unraveling of John Leonard's career at the Kellogg Company officially began when Will treated himself to a six-month tour of Japan, China, Asia, and the Indian subcontinent. From November 26, 1919, until May 1, 1920, Will left the company in the charge of his son with the expectation that John Leonard would keep him apprised with frequent letters and cables.[60] Inexplicably, the son sent few communiqués to his father and those he did were terse telegrams containing very little information. The paucity of these updates, let alone the fact that his company was running without him, irritated Will to no end. Will's mood only became more hostile after contracting pneumonia. He spent four weeks, including Christmas Day, flat on his back in a Hong Kong hospital. Fortunately, his travel companion, A. C. Selmon, was an accomplished physician (and Adventist missionary) and he helped Will recover.[61] From Hong Kong, Will sailed on to Java, India, Ceylon, Singapore, and the French colony of Cochinchina (now known as the southern portion of Vietnam). He spent his sixtieth birthday in Beijing where he walked along the Great Wall. Imagine his distress when, upon his return to Battle Creek, Will's men informed him that for the first time in its history the company's books were awash in red ink.

In Will's view (and at the Kellogg Company, the only one that really counted), his son had failed his first practical examination at running the firm. With distance and hindsight, it seems that Will's blame was not entirely fair. Some of the responsibility did, of course, rest squarely on John Leonard's shoulders. The scion rashly promised to fill orders for cereal that far exceeded the plant's capacity and committed more money for advertising than the company had in its fungible accounts. But the largest share of the company's financial embarrassment was connected to events far beyond John Leonard's control. Specifically, Will had purchased corn futures contracts at exorbitant wartime prices, which were made only more expensive after the grain market collapsed at the war's end. Will wisely determined to absorb the significant losses generated by his costly supply of corn instead of alienating his consumers by suddenly raising the price for a box of Corn Flakes from what they had been used to paying.[62]

JOHN LEONARD'S RELATIONSHIP with his father made its sharpest descent not in the office but at home. The son lived with his wife, Hanna, and their two sons, Will Keith II (1907–2005) and John Leonard Jr. (1910–1938) right next to Will's house on West Van Buren Street.[63] Looking out his window, Will wondered why his son was returning home so late at night or, on many other evenings, not coming home at all. In fact, there was "another woman" and her name was Helen Eberstein Flanner. John Leonard did not have to go far to find his new love. She worked as a hostess in the company's executive dining room.[64]

By mid-1923, John Leonard was disappearing from the factory for long periods of time. Will's diary on June 1 of that year records, "No one seems to know where he has gone."[65] Ten days later, June 11, Will received a brief letter from John Leonard written on Chicago's Sherman House hotel stationery that "gave no inkling of his plans, merely stating that he was not well."[66] When Helen resigned the following day, June 12, and left for Chicago, Will put one and one together and quickly came up with two lovers. He hired Pinkerton detectives to locate them but it was too late. By summer's end, John Leonard told his father that he was leaving his family for Helen.[67]

Will rushed to Hanna's side and insisted on supporting her and the boys. Disgusted by her husband's actions, Hanna filed a bill of divorcement in early December. Around the same time, Will again contracted the Pinkerton Detective Agency to locate Helen, which they did in California on December 14, 1923. To her credit, Helen resisted Will's attempts to buy her off and send her away. In January of 1924, John Leonard and Helen left California for Reno, then the divorce capital of the United States.[68]

To pass the time while residing in Nevada, John Leonard set up a food laboratory in the garage of the house they were renting. He came up with a new hot oat cereal to compete with the dominant American hot cereal manufacturer, the Quaker Oats Company. Calling his product New-Ota, John Leonard, without a hint of irony, purchased a former Quaker Oats mill in Davenport, Iowa, on the company's dime. Will was strictly a "cold cereal man" and when he was informed of the purchase, he burned up the cross-continental cable wires with scathing telegrams telling his son to STOP.[69] Most of the secondary accounts of this incident agree John Leonard's oat cereal was a flop but disagree on whether Will found another use for the factory or sold it to a competing company.[70]

John Leonard's stack of failures, both personal and professional, outweighed all of the contributions he made to the Kellogg Company. Long a worrier and an insomniac, Will now had many more reasons to stay awake at night.[71] By day, the boss rarely missed an opportunity to express his disappointment whenever he saw John Leonard entering or leaving his office, which adjoined Will's executive suite. On June 22, 1925, the son could take no more and threw down the gauntlet with a hurtful note to his father, which Will dutifully recorded, verbatim, in his diary:

> You have spent your life sticking your nose into other people's business. Why don't you try the experiment of minding your own business and leaving others alone. You will live longer and be happier and the whole world will be a damn sight better off. You certainly have stirred up enough [trouble] for me. Why don't you leave me alone?[72]

Will added no further comment to John Leonard's letter in his diary and the battle between these two proud, strong-willed men smoldered over the next two months. Adding hot milk to this bowl of crackling Rice Krispies, John Leonard and Helen eloped to get married.

It was at this point that Will decreed that his son was unfit to receive the keys to his kingdom.[73] In August, his lawyers drew up an agreement: in exchange for $2 million in Kellogg Company stock (or $27 million in 2016), John Leonard would resign his position at the firm. The acrimony over this transaction rings clearly in the last lines of the resignation letter John Leonard presented to the Kellogg Company board on September 1, 1925:

Upon the express condition that the tendering and acceptance of my resignation shall not at any time or in any manner be construed to be a voluntary withdrawal by me from the service of the Company, I hereby tender my resignation as a member of the Board of Directors of said Kellogg Company.[74]

The unforgiving Will exacted a strict permanence to John Leonard's banishment. Several times in the following years, the son expressed a wish to come back to preside over the family business, but Will promptly rebuffed every request.[75]

Somehow there remained a filial love between them even if they rarely expressed it to each other. In 1930, Will began working on his last will and testament, which gave the bulk of his riches to his proposed W. K. Kellogg Foundation. He told his attorney, Burritt Hamilton, that he had already discussed the issue with John Leonard, who pledged to honor his father's wishes and not to contest the will. Hamilton advised Will to get this promise in writing but Will calmly replied, "No, that is not necessary. John L. has given me his word and his word is good. I prefer to take

Will and John Leonard Kellogg (Will's second son), sitting atop one of his father's prized Arabian horses, circa 1931

it that way without any formality of writing. John L. will never go back on his word."[76]

John Leonard Kellogg never did go back on his word and he never succeeded in righting his once shining career after being fired from Kellogg's. He moved to Chicago where he tried his hand at a number of failed business ventures. Eventually it was Helen who took hold of the family bankbook and stock portfolio.[77] He spent the last month of his life in the California sun. While visiting his brother, Karl, in Chula Vista on April 3, 1950, the sixty-seven-year-old John Leonard suffered a fatal cerebral hemorrhage.[78] The sudden death of his youngest son stunned the ninety-year-old Will. Refusing to shed tears in front of others, Will sequestered himself in his bedroom for several days.[79]

WILL'S DAUGHTER, Elizabeth Ann, known to all as Beth, had the dual burden of looking a great deal like her father and being his most dutiful child. After Puss's death, Beth was unfailingly helpful to Will "even when he tried to dominate her thinking."[80] Her husband, Norman Williamson Sr., hailed from a Seventh-day Adventist family in Toronto and moved to Battle Creek to study pharmacy and work at the San. This connection, along with Norman's inability to find a clear employment track at the Kellogg Company, led Will to suggest she find a more suitable mate. Beth stood her ground and married the man she loved. By all accounts, theirs was a happy and mutually nurturing relationship, even if the father-in-law and son-in-law never succeeded in developing a mutual respect for one another.[81] Norman Jr. recalled with admiration his mother's matrimonial choice and unstinting loyalty to his father. "It took a very strong person indeed to stand up to W. K. Kellogg when he was at the peak of his choler."[82] Beth and Norman gave Will five grandchildren: Kenneth (b. 1912), Eleanor (b. 1913), Norman Jr. (b. 1915), John Harold (b. 1916), and Elizabeth Ann (b. 1920).[83]

Only nine months after Puss's death, tragedy again struck Will's personal life with a resounding force. In May of 1913, a seven-months pregnant Beth dropped off her eldest son, Kenneth, at her father's home while she completed some errands downtown. Ignored by the housekeeper, the toddling one-year-old rambled from room to room, until he climbed out

Will Kellogg, his daughter, Beth Williamson (standing behind him), and his grandchildren (left to right): John, Norman Jr., Elizabeth (in Will's lap), Kenneth (standing; Kenneth was the grandchild who fell out of a window as a toddler and suffered serious injuries), and Eleanor Jane, circa 1923

of a second-story window, fell to the ground, and severely fractured his skull on the concrete driveway below. The grandfather dropped everything and recruited the finest neurosurgeons from Chicago and Detroit to attend to the boy.[84] Comatose for more than three weeks, Kenneth was left with partial blindness in one eye, paralysis of the right arm and leg, and severe cognitive impairment. Kenneth never fully regained his health. Will was inconsolable, both because of the circumstances and the outcome of Kenneth's disabilities. The accident opened up a floodgate of emotions for the buttoned-down Will, who doted on Kenneth and, according to Kenneth's younger brother Norman Jr., enjoyed a "mutually reciprocated relationship that was unique among all W.K.'s grandchildren for it lasted to the end."[85] After the accident, Will constantly worried about the boy's welfare and actively meddled in how his parents dealt with his disabilities. For example, when Kenneth was about six, Will insisted the boy be sent away to a special live-in rehabilitation hospital-school near Chicago, in the hope that some improvement of function might be regained. Instead, the move only succeeded in separating a debilitated and frightened child from his loving parents. Will's overbearing concern, something pediatricians have termed "the vulnerable child syndrome," extended to a hyper-vigilance over all of Beth's children.[86] Norman Jr. later recalled, "W.K. was to propose living arrangements which would take each of Beth's children . . . away from her home at various times for conditions he diagnosed and cures he prescribed, giving his daughter little choice but to go along with his pronouncements."[87]

Beth's unflagging loyalty to her father came at a huge physical toll. During her last decade of life, she suffered a series of debilitating strokes and was eventually confined to long-term care at the Glendale (California) Sanitarium. Beth died on Armistice Day, November 11, 1966, at the age of seventy-eight. Her son Norman Jr. eulogized his mother with the bittersweet observation, "The last several years of her life were far from the joy that she had looked forward to at the time of her father's death."[88]

———

Will and his favorite grandson, John Leonard Jr., circa 1925

Undaunted, Will began grooming John Leonard's youngest son, John Leonard Kellogg Jr. (1911–1938) to take over the firm.[89] Every Saturday, they took long walks along the streets of Battle Creek, always finishing up at the cereal plant where Will mentored the boy on the knotty problems of mass-producing Corn Flakes, the complexities of distribution, advertising, and marketing, and where and how to purchase the best grain. In 1925, Will arranged for a fund of $25,000 (about $338,000 in 2016), with which the fourteen-year-old Junior could learn about investing in the stock market under Will's direct supervision. At Christmas of that same year, Junior accompanied Will to greet the employees. The boss shook the hand of each Kellogg worker and, with the other hand, presented him or her with a life insurance policy in lieu of a bonus check. Next in line to Will, Junior tentatively wished every worker good tidings of cheer. When the boy looked to his grandfather for some reassurance, Will admonished him: "You stand right here now, and do as I say."[90]

Two years later, Will promised the sixteen-year-old John Leonard Jr., "Some day you'll be at the head of this growing business." Not surprisingly, the other grandchildren resented Will's favoritism. An unidentified grandchild griped, "Grandfather was a little obnoxious in holding him up as an example to us other grandchildren. It was a little hard to take, for Grandfather always presented John Jr. as a shining light who was going

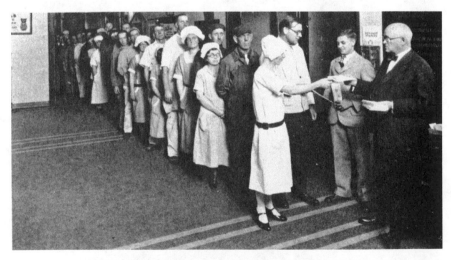

W. K. Kellogg and his grandson John Leonard Jr. greeting
Kellogg Company employees at Christmas, circa 1925

to become a great business leader."[91] One can only wonder how John Leonard Sr. felt while reading a letter from his father praising Junior's business acumen, thus effectively skipping over his own son for the top spot. "He is a wonderful chap," Will wrote John Leonard Sr., "and the more I see him the more I appreciate the foundation that he has for becoming a first-class executive."[92] Will hardly contained his pride for John Leonard Jr. within the family. On October 23, 1929, one day before the stock market crash that ushered in the Great Depression, Will wrote the best-selling author Paul de Kruif how he had just rebuffed another lucrative buyout offer: "We turned down the proposition because we have all the money that we need, and are saving the business for John, my grandson. If my life can be spared to see John develop into a businessman during the next four or five years, it will be worth more than several million dollars to me."[93]

In late 1928, John Leonard Jr. left Battle Creek for Wellesley, Massachusetts, to matriculate into an eighteen-month accelerated business course at the prestigious Babson Institute, a favorite training ground for the scions of American industry. One classmate described the Corn Flake prince as "a flea on a griddle, very intelligent but with more nervous energy than his power plant could accommodate."[94]

Will's plans for his grandson would have been overwhelming for even the most poised of twenty-year-old men, which Junior was not. The boss appointed him as executive vice president, which included a seat on the company's board of directors, the Budget and Merchandising Committees, and the all-important "Control Committee." To round out Junior's training, Will assigned him to investigate how the various departments of the plant might run more efficiently, supervise the advertising and sales departments, watch the foreign exchanges where the company had investment interests brewing, work out new plans for extending sales territories, develop work standards in the factory, and, ultimately, travel to and help coordinate the efforts of the newly built Canadian and Australian factories. Will also asked the long list of temporary Kellogg Company presidents he would hire and fire over the next several years to mentor his grandson so that Junior could take over their job, but none of these men seemed to take this proposition very seriously.[95]

Will's approach to mentoring the young man alternated between avuncular advice and direct orders. For example, Will sent Junior a memorandum on November 11, 1931, entitled "Suggestions for One Who Wishes to Hit the Trail Successfully, Make the Grade, Play the Game, and Win." Although he told the young man these were "fifteen suggestions not commandments," the reality of the communiqué was that Will expected his grandson to heed every one of them.[96] In the missive, Will ordered Junior to get plenty of sleep and recreation so as not to appear tired or work under tension; to avoid looking rushed; have few "irons in the fire at one time"; to finish one job before starting another; "do not scatter your ammunition; concentrate and you may get your bird"; avoid the word "I" in all conversations; lead rather than push others; always exhibit patience; avoid dominating your elders because age often confers a great deal of valuable experience; "do not dictate to your elders; better endure and let the other fellow boss. After all is said and done, we are all striving for results"; consider the feelings of one's employees; be humble; "keep your feet on the earth and your head up"; be kind to all but choose one's friends very carefully; and "remember, it took six days for Jehovah to create the earth. We should not try to reconstruct it in any less time." No matter how hard John Leonard Jr. tried to follow these "suggestions," it was inevitable that he, too, would fail to live up to Will's rigorous, and rigid, standards in running the Kellogg Company. Will craved the idea of retirement but like many powerful men he was unable to release the reins of the company that was the core of his identity. Within a few months of Junior's tenure, the reams of memoranda delivered from the boss's office to his grandson's desk took on an increasingly critical, harsh, and, at times, hurtful tone.

Desperately trying to appear confident and in control, John Leonard Jr. was emotionally insecure. His constant efforts to please his grandfather and real concern over whether he was, to use one of Will's favorite phrases, "making the grade," manifested themselves into chronic indigestion and heartburn, requiring frequent trips to the executive washroom where he was often seen to be "clutching a toilet and retching."[97] To counteract these symptoms, John Jr. guzzled down bottles of Sal Hepatica, a once popular mineral salt laxative that claimed to reduce stomach acidity. He also regularly "dosed" himself with hefty amounts of liquor. After one especially rowdy, alcohol-fueled weekend in Detroit, Junior reported to work "much worse for the wear and clearly hung over." A deadly serious Will "read him the riot act about keeping himself physically in shape."[98]

The once nurturing relationship ruptured in the fall of 1934. While horse riding at the Battle Creek Country and Hunt Club, Junior fell and hit his head hard enough to experience unconsciousness and a brain concussion. He landed at the University of Michigan Hospital for a lengthy stay, followed by an even lengthier period of recuperation at a ranch in Montana. Junior's absence steamed Will more with each passing day. Finally, on July 19, 1935, he wrote his grandson that he was tired of "indirectly aiding and abetting you in these various matters by allowing your salary to be continued while you are on rest cure."[99] Will's solution was to discontinue the young man's sumptuous salary of $10,000 per annum (about $172,000 in 2016). In the same letter, the boss transformed into the grandfather as he reassured his heir that "there is a whole lot of future ahead of you and plenty of time for activities later." Nevertheless, Will believed that "only drastic action would pull John out of a tailspin."[100] The drastic action Will chose was to publicly humiliate Junior by demoting him from high flying vice president to a $50 a week salesman assigned to the grocery stores of rural Wauwatosa, Wisconsin, outside Milwaukee.[101]

After demonstrating little skill in selling cereal to the grocery trade, John Jr. was transferred to the company's food laboratory, with the expectation that he had inherited his father's genius for industrial cookery. There, Junior co-opted a technician's work for puffing corn grits and wheat in a manner similar to that of puffing rice to make Rice Krispies. Junior called the new cereal creation "Pops." The grandfather-owner and grandson-employee relationship metaphorically popped when Junior approached the boss with a proposal to sell the new method to the Kellogg Company. Will chastised the grandson for trying to sell him something that was developed in his company's laboratory on company time. Family history repeated itself and the beleaguered grandson quit the firm in anger.[102] Litigation over cereal being another family trait, Junior sought restitution in the courts for his so-called creation of "Pops." His lawyers were no match for the Kellogg Company's battery of legal bulldogs. Without irony, Will sought help in handling his grandson from his son, John Leonard, who he had forced out of the Kellogg Company only a decade before:

By the way, I received a note from your John [Junior] the other day in which he asked to be relieved from his work with the Kellogg Company. The boy seems to be discouraged and thinks that in some way his grandfather has lost interest in him. . . . I wish you would look John over and see if it is time for him to have a conference with his physician.[103]

In 1937, John Jr. married an airline stewardess named Mary Muensch, moved to Chicago, and started his own company, New Foods, Inc., with the support of his father. The company manufactured a puffed corn cereal he called "Nu-Corn." The product flopped and the company quickly ran out of capital. Worse, the U.S. patent Junior applied for, and which he desperately needed to make the process his own, was denied. On February 26, 1938, a co-worker found John Leonard Kellogg Jr.'s body slumped over his desk in the shuttered Nu-Corn factory. Nearby was a note addressed to his brother, Will Keith II ("Keith"). In the letter, Junior apologized for his business failures and expressed the deluded notion that his wife and unborn child (Mary was seven months pregnant) would be better off without him. After signing the letter and sealing it in an envelope, he put a revolver in his mouth and pulled the trigger. John Leonard Kellogg Jr. was twenty-seven years old.[104]

Will was on a steamship making its way through the Panama Canal when he received the horrific news. Unable to return home in time for the funeral, he made a rare church visit in Panama and knelt in prayer to the memory of his dead grandson. Devastated by John Leonard Jr.'s death, Will obsessed and grieved over his role in the tragedy. Nearly two decades later, Will's biographer, Horace Powell, described Junior's suicide with a bit of well-warranted treacle, "Thus died Will Kellogg's last hope for a dynasty for his business—and forever he was to be haunted by the ghost of a promise made to a young boy."[105]

Will's meddlesome demeanor failed to enchant his other grandchildren. With the exception of John Leonard Jr. (before their falling-out) and the disabled Kenneth, Will was increasingly distant with them, especially as they grew into teenagers and young adults. Will's grandson Norman Williamson Jr. recalled that his grandfather was far more demonstrative and comfortable with his prized horses and dogs, and, to a lesser extent, babies: "From these examples one might deduce that he craved closeness, but he simply couldn't relax his guard with those who might reciprocate, save for pets."[106]

Although Will supported several siblings, cousins, and other family members over the years, he required them to spend their money wisely. When this proved not to be the case, his response was typically harsh. For example, Will gave one unidentified relative $5,000 as a wedding present. He expected the couple to use the money as a down payment for a house even though he stated no stipulations of any kind. Instead, the newlyweds spent all of it on immediate needs and recreational activities. A year later when the couple visited the old man at his ranch in Pomona, Will had his butler seat them in the hallway, on a "hard bench with a stiff, upright back." He left them squirming and staring at his treasured mural of St. George for over an hour before deigning to grace them with his presence. During the meeting, Will articulated his displeasure and told them that they had spent his money "foolishly." Although they had hoped for another check, the couple left the Big House empty-handed and with the impression that they were not welcome to return.[107]

In 1935, Will underwent an operation to resolve his worsening glaucoma, followed by a second procedure in 1937. Both were unsuccessful.[108] The following year, 1938, he took the uncharacteristic step of agreeing to sit for a portrait by Frank O. Salisbury. The British portrait painter was renowned for his renderings of Franklin D. Roosevelt, Harry S. Truman, J. Pierpont Morgan, John D. Rockefeller Jr., Andrew Mellon, Andrew Carnegie, and the coronations of King George VI and Elizabeth II of Great Britain. Salisbury's picture is, to use the cliché,

Portrait of W. K. Kellogg, by artist Frank O. Salisbury, circa 1938

worth many thousands of words. In oil and canvas, Will looks old, world-weary, and unhappy. It hangs to this day in the main lobby of the W. K. Kellogg Foundation offices, eerily following the movements of all who enter.

By 1940 Will was so blind that he could "barely see a hand held close to his face, or recognize an old associate." Along with his sight, he lost one of his few cherished leisure activities: reading the popular works of H. G. Wells and Arnold Toynbee and Mr. Gibbon's scribblings on *The Decline and Fall of the Roman Empire*.[109] Despite Will's enjoyment of the history of other people and places, he did not want his personal history to be written about and expressly sealed his papers to prying eyes. He avoided giving out biographical sketches to universities seeking to grant him an honorary degree or even for a brief entry in the annual edition of *Who's Who*. Railing against all potential biographers from his Pomona perch, the industrialist told one writer, "I am not going to start my memory spinning. I live in the present. Don't ask me questions about what has gone before."[110] He wrote another would-be biographer on August 19, 1940: "From what you write I have no doubt whatever of your ability to write a biography. However it so happens that I am not especially interested in having my biography written."[111]

For the last decade of his life, Will relied upon an elite trio of German shepherd Seeing Eye dogs. The first, Rinson, was the son of the Hollywood canine legend Rin Tin Tin. After Rinson died, Lee Duncan, Rin Tin Tin's owner, sent Rin Tin Tin's other son, Rinson II, to Battle Creek. That dog died prematurely, too, and was replaced by the famous dog's daughter, Rinette, who proved to be Will's favorite and most affectionate canine.[112] One of the few times an associate saw Will smile broadly during this period was when he crowded several of his executives into a small conference room and Rinette "developed a resounding flatulence."[113]

Some afternoons, Will's nurse took him to visit his company's headquarters.[114] Once there, he neither checked on the progress of his successors nor did he enter the toasting or packing rooms. Instead, Will remained in the plant's parking lot, seated in his wheelchair, clutching his white cane and his dog's leash. He enjoyed feeling the heavy machinery as it reverberated through the concrete and listening to the roar of the giant ovens converting the "sweetheart of the corn" into boxes of Corn Flakes. Most of all, he loved the aroma of toasted grains wafting out into the atmosphere blanketing Battle Creek. For Will, it was the scent of accomplishment.

THERE WAS ONE PRESSING ISSUE Will was determined to solve before his improbable run to glory ended. How would he dispose of all the money he had accrued? Where could it be put to the best use and in a manner that would reflect well on his name, family, and values? During the last two decades of his life, Will put his financial affairs together in a manner reflecting the good orderly direction in which he conducted his business.[115] His process was the exact opposite of the scattershot approach his voluble brother John employed with his wealth and energies. As early as 1909, Will discussed his charitable intentions with colleagues, "If I am successful in getting out of debt and become prosperous in my business affairs, I expect to make good use of any wealth that may come to me."[116] Although Will had long dreamed of "aid[ing] humanity in general and America in particular," he later noted, with his not so common sense, "it has been much easier to make money than to know how to spend it wisely."[117] By late 1929, Will had figured out the correct equation and shared it with his friend and advisor, Arch Shaw:

> I know how to invest my money. I'll invest it in people. . . . I want to help those with little or no income. I want to establish a foundation that will help handicapped children everywhere to face the future with confidence, with health, and with a strong-rooted security in their trust of this country and its institutions.[118]

In June of 1930, Will inaugurated the Kellogg Child Welfare Foundation.[119] Two months later, in August, the charity was legally reorganized, its mission broadened, and formally renamed the W. K. Kellogg Foundation for "receiving and administering the funds for the promotion of the welfare, comfort, health, care, education, feeding, clothing, sheltering, and safeguarding children and youth, directly or indirectly, without regard to sex, race, creed, or nationality in whatever manner the Board of Trustees may decide."[120] Writing to his physician, A. R. Dickson, Will recalled how his grandchild Kenneth's severe head trauma, the huge expenses for his medical care, and the paucity of good treatment options motivated his foundation work: "This caused me to wonder what difficulties were in the paths of needy parents who seek help for their children when catastrophe strikes, and I resolved to lend what aid I could to such children."[121]

In recognition of this investment in the nation's youth, President Herbert Hoover invited Will to participate in the "White House Conference on Child Health and Protection." Held on November 19–22, 1930, the summit focused on the welfare of dependent, orphaned, or abandoned children, child labor, children's health issues, and gathered together "3,000 men and women, leaders in the medical, educational, and social fields as they touch the life of the child." Will must have taken some pride that he, and not his brother, was invited to the White House to discuss such nationally important matters.[122]

On December 8, 1930, *Time* magazine headlined the new foundation with the tart observation that Will's philanthropy "belied the general impression that he is a dour moneymaker." The article compared the two Kellogg brothers of Battle Creek. John sold his shares in the cereal business for $250,000 in 1906 and immediately began the Race Betterment Foundation, in the belief that "business should be the servant of society." Will, on the other hand, preferred to let the money amass like Croesus before giving it away, based on his conviction that "business should be the benefactor of society." In the course of their lives, *Time* reported, John "made himself more famous than his business (the Sanitarium) and his benefactions. Brother Will Keith made his business (Kellogg Co.) more famed than himself. The public knows practically nothing about him."[123] All that was about to change. Whenever the name Kellogg is uttered today, most of us instantly think of Will's cereal; but a great many others consider the good works of his wonderful foundation. Either way, it is Will who accomplished both.

By 1934, Will fully endowed his W. K. Kellogg Foundation with more than $66 million (approximately $1.17 billion in 2016). He took to comically griping about the many long-distance telephone calls the foundation staff made or the salaries he paid his professional grant makers. Such jibes were all for show, however, and Will wisely gave them a free hand to conduct their charitable business. Nevertheless, it took many years before he was entirely comfortable with his full name appearing so boldly on the foundation's letterhead. Even as late as 1951, the year Will

died, the founder expressed sincere hesitance over using his initials in the
foundation's formal name. Dr. Emory Morris, a dentist who assumed the
foundation's presidency in 1943, recalled "The only way I could stave off
this suggestion was to tell Mr. Kellogg that to take the initials from the
name of the Foundation would be to leave the public in wonderment
as to which Kellogg (W.K. or John Harvey) was back of the Foundation."[124] It was a convincing argument worthy of a resourceful foundation president.[125] The name, "W. K. Kellogg Foundation," stuck. Since
then, the foundation has donated billions of dollars to support a long
list of worthy and important causes. Today, it remains one of the largest
charitable foundations in the world with assets of over $9.5 billion and
is a major force in advancing the health of children and their families in
Michigan, across the United States, and around the globe.[126]

DURING THE EARLY 1950s, Will's authorized biographer, Horace Powell, took the bold, if clinically unorthodox, step of asking a psychiatrist to
conduct a postmortem, psychological analysis on his subject. Mr. Powell
describes the unnamed mental health professional as a "relative in considerable contact with Will Kellogg through the years." The psychiatrist
in question was almost certainly Dr. William S. Sadler, a former Battle
Creek Sanitarium physician who knew both Kellogg brothers well, was
married to their half-niece Lena, and in 1910, after studying medicine
under John, took an additional year of psychiatric training under Sigmund Freud in Vienna.[127] Whoever the clinician actually was, however,
his diagnostic explanation of what drove Will to do the things he did
remains astute.

To begin, the psychiatrist diagnosed Will with a massive inferiority
complex. "He was going to show his brother, himself, and the world
that he, too, had superior qualities and that only an unfortunate set of
circumstances had prevented him from being as eminent as the Doctor.
Those circumstances he eliminated."[128] The consulting physician was
even more impressed by Will's deep-seated unhappiness and frustration:
"In all my long practice of psychiatry, I don't know of a more lonely, iso-
lated individual. . . . Just a modicum of added extrovertism would have
given him the capacity for an outlet which would have meant much to
his total happiness. . . . Here was a man of great brain power, of practi-

cally photographic memory, who lacked the self confidence needed to complete his being."[129]

An unidentified friend of Will's, most likely Arch Shaw, disagreed and insisted that "he was happy in his own way, with a deep appreciation of living. Concededly, this was a quiet happiness, not exuberant, and only occasionally reflected on Mr. Kellogg's rather impassive countenance. Coming from a religious family, with high, ethical standards, he found real satisfaction in a life-long hobby of helping others."[130] The same friend spoke with admiration of Mr. Kellogg's stoic ability to let nothing interfere with whatever he designated as his "Number One Project," even when facing family tragedies such as the suicide of one grandson and the disabilities of another. As Will stated on those rare occasions he allowed someone into his inner life:

> Now, I can't do anything about what has happened. I can't let this happening interfere with my main project in life, so I must start again and not think about this tragedy any more . . . I could never reach that goal if I let anything interfere with my health, my energies, my strengths, my attitudes.[131]

When asked about these contradictory assessments, Will's daughter, Beth Williamson observed, they were all "partially correct." Her father found a "deep and lasting satisfaction from the accomplishment of so many things of benefit to humanity," Beth noted, but "this quiet joy was almost in conflict with the self that had never had a youth, had never been able to loosen up."[132] Late in his life, it was Will who most succinctly described his warring psychic needs when he confessed to Arch Shaw: "I would give the world to be able to get along with people as well as you do."[133]

It is tempting to suggest that Will's lust for empire building and his generous philanthropy were motivated by his stark childhood. His youth was so bereft of the attention and love every child needs and craves, no matter where he sits in the pecking order of birthdays or how brilliant his other siblings might be. As a boy, his parents' apocalyptic, if not frightening, religious beliefs and their cold child rearing likely emotionally scarred him. As a young man, he was sentenced to nearly twenty-five years of hard labor under the abusive command of his older brother.

Every day of his adult life, long after he left the San, Will grappled with a well of hurt and anger that constantly beat false messages of failure into his every thought and action. His botched relationships with two wives, three children, and many more grandchildren only amplified the negative thoughts swirling about in his head. More than six decades after his death, the historian who will never meet the man, let alone psycho-analyze him, must be guided by compassion as he simply concludes Will was, like so many of us, a damaged soul—even if the precise causes for that damage were uniquely his own.

And yet this extraordinary man refused to be completely oppressed by his damning life experiences. Instead, he applied his executive expertise in creating a lasting structure to make things right, or at least better, for countless children and their families, beneficiaries he would never meet. His famous statement "I never learned how to play" was not a lament; it was a cautionary warning. Will bravely chose to focus his laser-beam intensity and considerable fortune to his "Number One Project," the W. K. Kellogg Foundation. Will's greatness, then, resides not only in how he revolutionized how the world eats breakfast but, more triumphant, in the way he transformed his personal disappointments and tragedies into a charitable trust that advances and benefits humanity in perpetuity. It was a supreme achievement that Will Keith Kellogg was born to do.

The Final Score

DURING THE WINTER of 1918–1919, John contracted bacterial pneumonia followed by a relapse of his long-standing tuberculosis and a painful bout of pleurisy. This triple assault on his scarred lungs forced him to quit Battle Creek for sunny Florida, where he remained critically ill and bedridden for seven and a half months. It was not until late May of 1919 that an out-of-breath and haggard Dr. Kellogg finally made his way back home, determined on returning to a full slate of work activities at the San. For John, the very idea of not being able to doctor, lecture, and hold forth over his medical kingdom was a fate worse than death.[1]

A few weeks later, in June, he hosted the national meeting of the Edward Livingstone Trudeau Society, an association of tuberculosis experts named for the physician who ran the famous sanatorium in Saranac Lake, New York.[2] At John's personal request, several of these distinguished doctors examined his chest. In a pre–Kübler-Ross act of denial and bargaining, John asked if he rested thoroughly for one full year, might he expect to live five more years?[3] His doctors shook their heads, as John must have done countless times when examining hopeless cases. They told him that his pulmonary condition would continue to deteriorate, his breathing would only become more labored, and he would likely be dead from a slow suffocation within three years.[4]

Even though the doctor managed to outwit his doctors by living another twenty-four years, he was never really the same, robust, bombastic John Harvey Kellogg of years gone by. The gossip over his imminent demise only grew louder each year he avoided Battle Creek's harsh winters by spending them in Florida.[5] It also spurred the San's board of directors to plan for his succession.[6] As the 1920s progressed, John grudgingly ceded the day-to-day control of the Battle Creek Sanitarium. His replacement, Dr. Charles Stewart, was a respected physician and vice president of the Sanitarium but the transition was rocky, at best. The San was John Harvey Kellogg and John Harvey Kellogg was the San.

MUCH TO JOHN'S CHAGRIN, the men now running the San forged a different path with new clinical approaches and amenities in the hope of generating a greater profit margin. In 1927, Dr. Stewart announced plans to build a luxurious fifteen-story tower at a cost of more than $4 million (over $54.5 million in 2016). The new building significantly boosted the Sanitarium's guest capacity but it also increased the overhead costs. Replete with carved wooden Corinthian columns, stained glass windows, marble flooring, a grand dining room worthy of royalty, and hundreds of richly furnished guest rooms, the "Tower" was the tallest building between Detroit and Chicago.

John did not like Stewart's expansionism one bit. He railed against what he saw as the board's commercialism and greed. He argued for the

The San Tower

The San Colonnade

San to maintain its patient-centered focus, based not on profits but on the improvement of health through biologic living. John also expressed concern that the San would never be able to pay off the huge loans required for the construction. In the booming economy of 1928, when the American stock market was skyrocketing and the San was packed with patients, his colleagues derided their former boss as out of touch, an old man resistant to new ways and a changing world.[7]

John's gloomy predictions became reality after the stock market crash of 1929. Suddenly, a health facility built and staffed to accommodate a daily census of more than 1,300 patients was attracting fewer than 300. Many of the wealthy people who regularly flocked to Battle Creek no longer had the means to afford such extravagance. The San's debt of over $3 million (about $41.5 million in 2016), not counting interest charges of more than $500 per day (or $6,910 in 2016), translated into drastic layoffs, salary cuts, and plummeting morale. At the end of 1932, the San

Miami Springs–Battle Creek Sanitarium, circa early 1930s

was forced into receivership. Thereafter, neither John nor the trustees controlled the Battle Creek Sanitarium. It was now run by a group of private and city bondholders who demanded a profit on their investment.[8] Thus, John found a new windmill to tilt at and for the next decade he fought bitterly against the "outside interests" controlling the San.[9]

THERE WAS YET ANOTHER enterprise of John's that worried the trustees almost as much as the San's fiscal predicament. On December 1, 1930, Dr. Kellogg announced the opening of the Battle Creek Sanitarium in Miami Springs, Florida. The luxury resort featured a Spanish American architectural design and an interior decorated with Native American motifs, Navajo woven rugs, and bedroom suites made of mahogany. Glenn Curtiss, the airplane pioneer, health enthusiast, and eugenics advocate, offered the hotel to the doctor for the price of $1.00. The seventy-eight-year-old Dr. Kellogg knew a good deal when he saw one but told the multimillionaire, "Mr. Curtiss, I think one dollar is too cheap." Instead, John handed Curtiss a crisp ten-dollar bill to close the deal.[10] The Miami Springs Sanitarium's one hundred rooms remained fully booked during the winter months for the remainder of Dr. Kellogg's life. Everybody seemed to love it save the San's board up in Battle Creek, who only saw the Miami Springs facility as a keen rival and competitor.

The Miami San offered an array of lectures, dietary consultations, exercise programs, and health classes that would be quite familiar to denizens of spa resorts today. It boasted, but barely conducted, a research program centered on extending life spans and improving the lives of the elderly. There was also the temperate Florida climate during the dead of winter. With his impeccable sense of occasion, John invited several marquee names to the new facility, including the best-selling authors Dale Carnegie *(How to Win Friends and Influence People)* and Will Durant *(The Story of Philosophy)*; Nobel laureate and surgeon Alexis Carrel; Gene Tunney, the world's undefeated heavyweight boxing champion from 1926 to 1928; as well as Henry Ford and Thomas Edison (and their wives).[11] When treating the famous, Dr. Kellogg often announced his medical findings to reporters, who then filed their stories on the wire services feeding newspapers across the nation.[12]

One of the doctor's most famous consultations was with the eminent playwright George Bernard Shaw. While on a voyage around the world, Shaw made a special stop at Miami Springs for a vegetable-and-fruit-laden meal with the doctor, followed by an extensive medical examination. "I want to see Dr. Kellogg," he told his host, A. D. H. Fossey, the part-time mayor of Miami and a full-time furniture and upholstery man, "such an opportunity may not come again."[13] At the luncheon table, the two men did their best to ignore the questioning reporters and photographers with their flashing cameras as they sipped freshly squeezed orange juice. Unable to censor his thoughts, Shaw declared Franklin Roosevelt to be a communist even if the president had yet to admit it. Eventually the gaggle of reporters became too annoying for the Irishman. Brandishing his cane at them, Shaw yelled, "I'd like to kill the whole lot of you." Sensing the doctor's distress over such a violent threat, Shaw gently confided to John, sotto voce, "It's all for effect. I have to put on a show. They expect it of me."[14]

The following day, Dr. Kellogg reported Shaw's blood pressure was "remarkably low (106/60 mm Hg) . . . the same which I found in a vigorous North American Indian in Arizona."[15] Shaw's electrocardiogram did show signs of slight muscle deterioration but this was to be expected

*George Bernard Shaw and Dr. John Harvey
Kellogg, February 1936*

in a man of his age and not serious. Nevertheless, he advised Shaw to "avoid any violent straining, such as lifting or doing anything that will embarrass your breathing, or, to use a common phrase, put you out of breath," and to avoid contact with anyone with either influenza or pneumonia, either of which could make him quite ill. The doctor was most concerned about Shaw's low red blood cell count (3,000,000, 40 percent deficient from the normal of 5,000,000) and hemoglobin (71 g/dl, 30 percent deficient from the normal of 100) and his resultant anemia.

These findings, Dr. Kellogg explained, were the result of the writer's not consuming enough iron in his diet. Shaw, a committed vegetarian, simply needed to consume more green leafy vegetables to achieve a normal red blood cell balance and feel better. Shaw's iron deficit was so severe, however, that this prescription translated into his munching of "nearly a pound of spinach" per day. The doctor, of course, had "a better way" to achieve those ends. He prescribed his Food Ferrin, an iron-rich extract of spinach. Three tablespoons equaled Shaw's daily requirement for iron.[16] "I am sending you a bottle of this," Dr. Kellogg wrote Shaw after their visit, "and if you think worth while to make use of it, I will gladly see that you have a larger supply. It can be put aboard your ship at San Francisco when you reach that port or at Honolulu."[17]

Shaw's Miami-San visit was reported in publications ranging from *The New York Times* to the popular magazine *Literary Digest*. In these articles, the doctor stroked Shaw's ego with the prediction that the playwright would easily live to be a hundred. John was off by only a few years; Shaw died in 1950 at the age of ninety-four. John also noted he had no intention of billing Shaw for his medical services. His reward was that his "suggestions may prove of some service to the most distinguished of living Englishmen."[18] Perhaps so, but Dr. Kellogg was equally interested in proving "of some service" to his own celebrity.

JOHN WAS NEVER ABLE to completely sever his connection to the Battle Creek Sanitarium, no matter how angry he was at the men running it. Even though he had predicted the San's financial woes and warned against its expansion, the doctor did everything he could to save the place. He attended humiliating meetings with bankers. He sent desperate letters requesting money from his wealthy patients. He gave public lectures for which admission was charged, all in a futile attempt to raise the necessary capital for putting the San back on a sound and profitable footing.[19]

Perhaps John's most spectacular "Hail Mary" play occurred on May 3, 1937, when he telegrammed Henry Ford requesting a meeting to discuss "a very important matter in which I am sure you will be interested." Two days later, May 5, John received a letter from Ford's general secretary, E. G. Liebold, explaining that Ford was unable to see him. Dr. Kellogg wrote Liebold on May 8 about the dire financial situation of the San and the need to pay off its crushing debt. "I will not surrender control or submit to any changes or ideals or principles of the Sanitarium. The bondholders can take the buildings, but they cannot take the business," he told Liebold. "I am prepared to surrender the property to them and move out and start again." John's entreaties for an appointment with Ford were for naught. The conversation effectively ended on May 12, 1937, when Liebold informed the doctor that "Mr. Ford has been away almost continuously during the last two weeks and for that reason it

"Hello! Merry Christmas 1932." The doctor on the telephone.

has been impossible to arrange an appointment for you." Despite Ford's financial brushoff, Dr. Kellogg remained a loyal admirer.[20]

John subsequently offered to pay off the bankers holding the San's promissory notes or bonds, at 55 cents on the dollar and backed by shares of his food company as collateral. This plan failed, too, because the San's creditors demanded far more money than what John could possibly raise.[21] By mid-1938, all the options had evaporated and the Sanitarium was rapidly approaching bankruptcy. The directors, instead, ended its receivership status and reorganized so that the "new San" had no connection to the man who created it. Losing his monument to biologic living was a harsh blow to John's monumental ego. Making his loss even more painful, John learned that some of the new doctors at the San were now smoking cigarettes and eating meat.[22]

As JOHN REACHED his tenth decade of life, he became less inhibited and more eccentric. He steadily gained weight to the point of becoming rotund, thanks to consuming two enormous meals a day, each of them lasting an "hour and a half at a time."[23] Always proud of his regular bowel movements, he loved bragging how his biologic diet left his stools smelling "as sweet as those of a nursing baby." In the middle of conversations, John would excuse himself to go to the bathroom and emerge with a container of his most recent fecal specimen. He then proudly placed it under the noses of his companions to demonstrate its odorless quality. By 1941, the doctor took to sunbathing and exercising clad only in a thin swath of cotton barely covering his genitalia and bottom. Will was so offended by his brother's erratic behavior that he threatened to file a lawsuit forcing John to dress more appropriately. Fortunately, Will's lawyers convinced him to sit down, take a deep breath, and avoid any legal motions that would only succeed in showering the cereal magnate with far worse publicity than whatever eccentricities his brother could conjure.[24]

In August 1942, the San's main buildings and expansive campus were sold to the U.S. government for $2.25 million (roughly $32.7 million in 2016) and converted into a military (and later a veterans) hospital. Known as the Percy Jones Hospital, it treated soldiers whose bodies were irrevocably damaged by World War II, including three men who would go on to distinguished careers in the United States Senate, Philip Hart (D-MI), Robert Dole (R-KS), and Daniel Inouye (D-HI). The staff of the Percy Jones Hospital treated more than 95,000 soldiers injured during World War II and the Korean War until its closure in 1953 and subsequent conversion into a federal office building in 1954.

After the retirement of the San's debt of $1,519,525 (or $22.1 million in 2016), there remained a profit of roughly $750,000 (or $10.9 million in 2016). John combined his share of this sum with $275,000 (about $3.99 million in 2016) he earned from dissolving his Sanitarium Food Company. The windfall was enough to resume his Sanitarium activities in two smaller buildings he still owned and that housed Dr. Kellogg's Race Betterment Foundation and the Battle Creek College.[25] Despite the reduced circumstances, John told one local businessman in December of 1942: "With the San directly across from the Race Betterment Foundation buildings, we will run there until world affairs have settled down. Then later, I am going out east of town where there is a square mile of lakes and woods and will rebuild the San along the original design." Although John was over ninety years old when he made this pledge and the projected cost of such an ambitious venture was in the many millions of dollars, the businessman later recalled "the uncanny thing was that you did not doubt for a moment that he fully intended to do this thing and that, if his health permitted and he lived a while, it would be done."[26]

———

THE TWO BROTHERS had their last face-to-face meeting on October 3, 1942, a little more than a year after John wrote the conciliatory letter that never elicited a response. Will had his chauffeur drive him to John's home. Ever at odds, John hoped to extract a loan from his millionaire brother while Will wanted to convince his brother to let go of the San's reins. During their five-hour conversation, Will recalled, the doctor admitted the toxicity of his overbearing ways, "I talk too much. I have to overcome it. I talk too much."[27]

Will tried tact and then guile by suggesting if John really wanted to see his work continued, the best plan was to let the Seventh-day Adventist Elders resume the cause. John, who could nurture a resentment even longer than his younger brother, could not, would not, forget the agonizing psychic torture the Adventist Church had put him through nearly forty years earlier as it sought control of his operation and kicked him out of their fold. Suspicious of anything Will suggested or the Church proposed, Dr. Kellogg turned the tables and accused the Seventh-day Adventists of inappropriately trying to seize the money from the sale of the Sanitarium buildings. There was no room for agreement, let alone compromise. The conversation began with both men wary of the other; it was only a matter of time until it became mean and dreadful.

Nine days later, on October 12, Will told Dr. George Thomason, a longtime San physician who was conspiring with the Adventists to take over the San, that his meeting with John was "the most rambling conversation I ever had with anybody in my life." Will also denigrated the doctor's state of mind as "unheard of, unreasonable, and nonsensical" and reported giving his older brother "a tongue chastisement," more severe than any other he had given to anyone "during my rather long life." Most astounding, at least in Will's version, "the Doctor did not resent some of the cutting things I said to him [indicating] very plainly to me that he, in a way, admitted the truthfulness of my remarks."[28]

True to John's allegations, the Adventist Elders did hope to reclaim what they still considered to be one of the Church's most valuable assets. Such enmity was to be expected from his former coreligionists who had long resented John's one-upmanship and knack for goading them into embarrassing situations. What remains appalling, if not outright ugly, was the financial help the Adventists received from the eighty-three-year-old

Will Keith Kellogg in order to pick over the last vestiges of the Sanitarium. Will not only gave them large sums of money to subsidize their mounting legal bills, he also offered the Adventist leaders strategic advice on how to humiliate his ninety-one-year-old brother.[29] For example, on October 18, 1943, Will wrote one of John's most vociferous detractors, Adventist Elder W. H. Branson, about publicly exposing the fetid conditions at the once spotless, hygienic San. After inspecting the premises, Will reported, "the odors in the basement and the elevator shaft are terrific and I am sure that the place is not sanitary."[30]

Some have hypothesized that Will led this attempted coup because he believed his long service to the Sanitarium entitled him to help determine the allocation of its remaining assets. Others have suggested it was out of loyalty to the Seventh-day Adventists, even though it had been many decades since he had actively participated in the Church. Neither explanation seems wholly plausible. More likely, Will seized the opportunity to revise history by obliterating the physical representation of his brother's lifelong work. This was strictly business for Will and, just as he did with the cereal manufacturers, grain producers, grocery chains, railroad executives, and relatives who crossed him, he aggressively used his power to insure that the fight ended in his favor. As he wrote Dr. George Thomason in early 1943, "In view of the fact that the patronage of the Battle Creek Sanitarium . . . has nearly reached the vanishing point, it does not occur to me that it would be desirable to try and perpetuate the institution at this time."[31]

There were more low-grade quarrels between the brothers, as well as backbiting episodes between John and the Seventh-day Adventists. Lawsuits were filed and courtroom tactics implemented but time was clearly running out for the man who created the institution all these other men wanted to control. John knew full well of his brother's treacherous actions to help destroy his legacy but he was too ill and tired to fight back. In the late fall of 1943, he was stricken with Bell's palsy, a viral-induced paralysis of the nerve that controls the facial muscles. The palsy paralyzed the entire left side of his face, causing an unattractive drooping, difficulty in blinking, and severe dryness of the eye's cornea. John also lost his senses of taste and hearing and the ability to swallow his saliva, leading to a great deal of drooling. The illness forced the once proud and extroverted doctor to closet himself in his home, lest others see him in such a debilitated state.[32]

ON DECEMBER 14, 1943, only thirty minutes before midnight, Dr. John Harvey Kellogg drew his final breath. He was ninety-one and nine months old. A few days earlier, he developed a severe bronchial cough, shortness of breath, and a decided heaviness to his chest thanks to a worsening pneumonia. In the hours before he died, John said his final goodbye to his adopted son Richard, who originally hailed from Guadalajara, Mexico. The devoted son, now a successful dentist, was about to leave for service in the war effort.[33] Dr. Kellogg rarely spoke of dying He was all about living life and the ways to enhance and prolong it. As he labored for breath, John worried about the long docket of new patients waiting to see him until he was gently persuaded to cancel all his appointments for the remainder of the week. Approaching the fate he knew came to every living creature, John confessed to his personal physician, James R. Jeffrey. "Well, maybe this is the last time, doctor. " Shortly after this admission, Dr. Kellogg fell into a coma and died.[34]

A few days after the doctor's funeral, Judge Blaine W. Hatch of the local 37th Circuit Court of Calhoun County adjudicated a compromise in which no single party walked away entirely pleased. The Adventist Church received $550,000 in cash (or $7.53 million in 2016) and three farms worth $75,000 (or $1.03 million in 2016) in return for relinquishing any claim on the San. The settlement also allowed a small group of Dr. Kellogg's most loyal acolytes to run John's iteration of the Sanitarium in the buildings his estate owned, across the street from the now government-owned complex of buildings. This shell of what was once the splendid San limped along for over a decade before closing its doors in 1957.[35]

WILL DEEPLY MOURNED his brother's death despite all the years of hostility and avoidance. He even sent a photograph of Dr. Kellogg's tombstone to several of John's friends and admirers.[36] The depth of Will's sorrow might be best explained by returning to that heartfelt letter of reconciliation John wrote Will on September 8, 1941. The mystery of why Will never responded was finally solved six and a half years later. Remarkably, John's assistant who recorded the doctor's dictation of the seven-page letter felt that it was beneath the dignity of the once great man. She was especially worried about alerting Will to John's admission of senility. "I find my memory failing," he wrote, "I thought I had about reached the end of walking and was distinctly doddering."[37] Instead of placing the letter directly in the mail, she sealed the envelope and stuffed it into a file cabinet where it reposed unopened.[38] John's letter was rediscovered and finally delivered to Will on June 22, 1948. Shortly after its arrival, Will's nurse read the communiqué to the blind old man:

> It was the greatest possible misfortune to the work that circumstances arose which led you and me in different channels and separated our interests. I am sure that you were right in regards the food business. . . . Your better balanced judgment has doubtless saved you from a vast number of mistakes of the sort I have made and allowed you to achieve magnificent successes for which generations to come will owe you gratitude. . . . I am making desperate efforts to get all my affairs into such shape as to preserve as much as possible what good they may represent and to mend as many as possible of the errors I have made. I earnestly desire to make amends for any wrong or injustice of any sort I have done to you and will be glad if you will give me a very definite and frank expression of anything I have said or done which you feel should be justly designated unbrotherly or otherwise open to criticism. . . . I hope that this note may find you more comfortable and that you have many years left to promote the splendid enterprises that have given the name you bear a place among the notable ones of our time.[39]

"Magnificent successes." "Amends." "The errors I have made." Sadly, John's sincere good wishes could no longer facilitate a fraternal discourse, an awkward, stiff embrace, or even a handshake. Would the letter have healed the torturous relationship between Will and John had it only arrived more promptly? Such a question generates speculation beyond the ken of the historian. One cannot help but hope the doctor's loving message might have been therapeutic enough for Will to finally find peace and satisfaction. Alas, the words, the sentiments, the thoughtful appreciations were too tardy to do much good.

Had Will Kellogg's life been made into a motion picture, John's letter would have been his "Rosebud," the moment he finally squelched or, at least, better understood his inner demons over the parental and fraternal love denied him. Imagine if he were portrayed in the manner of Charles Foster Kane in Orson Welles and Herman J. Mankiewicz's masterpiece, *Citizen Kane.* The audience would watch a master shot of the nurse reading the letter, dissolving into a close-up of Will's blind eyes tearing up, finally "seeing" the truth. The scene would segue into a medium shot of the old man uttering a plaintive wail and slumping over in his wheelchair. The camera would slowly pan out for one final long shot of the dead man, accompanied by a dramatic swell of music, followed by the closing credits and the familiar: "The End."[40]

Of course, Will's life was no Hollywood movie. He lived another three long years after receiving his brother's posthumous blessing. Almost every day was filled with painful ailments and infirmities. During the summer of 1951, Will developed severe anemia, most likely caused by a chronic form of leukemia. He required frequent, rushed visits to the hospital for blood transfusions, some of which caused severe reactions that threatened his health almost as much as the anemia the transfusions were supposed to correct. Will's last months were mostly confined to the second floor of his home overlooking Gull Lake. The only people he allowed into his bedroom suite were his daughter, Beth, his grandson Kenneth, and his private nurses who attended to his every need.[41]

In mid-September, Will was admitted to the Leila Hospital, which, ironically, was named for its benefactress, Leila Post Montgomery, who was the former private secretary, second wife, and widow of Will's archenemy, C. W. Post. It was there that he spent the final three weeks of his life. Lying uncomfortably in bed and unable to sleep, the old man quietly told his loyal nurse, Elsie Gay Hoatson, "It won't be long now."[42] His last hours were spent in the company of his daughter, Beth, Nurse Hoatson, and his chauffeur, John Elbon. At one point during the vigil, Will appeared to recognize Beth but was "too weak to talk."[43] He fell into a coma and at three o'clock in the afternoon of Saturday, October 6, 1951, Will Keith Kellogg passed away.[44] He was ninety-one and six months of age.

W. K. Kellogg's obituary in The Battle Creek Enquirer and News, *October 7, 1951*

According to Will's wishes, there was no public service. "I do not care to be written up in the paper in the manner in which Mr. ——— was. . . . I do not want any long drawn-out sermon or eulogy of any sort," he said in 1933, "the expenses should not exceed $500. . . . No flowers . . . [and] . . . burial should take place at Oak Hill cemetery after cremation."[45] Much more than $500 was spent on Will's sendoff and, of course, his death was "written up" on the front pages of newspapers, filled the air with radio and television broadcasts, and sparked conversations around the world.

Beginning at 4:00 p.m. on Monday the 8th and lasting until 10 a.m. the following morning, Will's embalmed body was placed on a bier in the Kellogg factory's main lobby so that each shift of employees could pay their respects. Some three thousand townspeople also came and they were ushered by employees who had worked at the plant for twenty-five or more years. All the other Kellogg cereal plants around the world shut down their operations for twenty-four hours on October 9 in honor of the company's founder. United States senators and congressmen; the governor of Michigan, G. Mennen Williams; President Harry Truman; and many other men and women of great distinction all wired their condolences to the Kellogg family. The mayor of Battle Creek, William B. Bailey, declared a week of mourning and ordered all the flags in the city to fly at half-staff. On October 9, the family held a private ceremony at Battle Creek's First Congregational Church. And on October 11, his white, lambskin-leather-aproned and white-gloved "brothers" from the Battle Creek Free and Accepted Mason Lodge No. 12 ceremoniously interred Will Kellogg's ashes.[46]

The two brothers' proximity in death at the Oak Hill Cemetery defies the monumental distance they constructed in life. Decades before, when they were closer allied, or at least worked closely together, the Kellogg brothers purchased matching tombstones, simple small slabs of granite with only enough room to announce their names and years on the planet. Eventually Will ordered his tombstone to be removed and purchased a nearby and much larger plot. There, two black wrought iron gates welcome visitors to a blue-slate-covered burial ground. Each gate bears the famous script "K" that begins the red "Kellogg's" label on every box of Will's cereals. In the center of the double row of grave markers is a bronze sundial featuring a bird's wings with an hourglass in the center. It is inscribed with Will's favorite adage, "The early bird gets the worm." To Will, the virtue of being an "early bird" was clear, especially when it came to realizing the profitability of making ready-to-eat cereals for the masses. Perhaps ten paces away rests the elder brother who never completely appreciated the genius of either his brother or that fundamental point, until it was too late.[47]

Forty-eight years after Will's funeral, his grandson Norman Jr. recalled that few family members wept, "with the possible exception of my mother," who "nevertheless felt a welcome relief from her father's heavy handed paternalism," and "perhaps my brother Kenneth."[48] "On the contrary," Norman Jr. wrote, "most felt a great sense of relief as though a heavy weight had been lifted from them. Now they were free to do as they pleased without a stern patriarch forbidding them."[49] This grandson's belated eulogy articulates, perhaps, the saddest story ever to emerge from the storied town of Battle Creek.

BOTH KELLOGG BROTHERS made a great deal of money during their careers but only one had much to show for it by the time he died. The doctor used his income freely to fund his new food creations, mechanical inventions, book publishing ventures, charitable missions, job training programs, soup kitchens for the destitute, a missionary medical school, various research, eugenics, and public health projects, and his "university of health," the Battle Creek Sanitarium. John Harvey Kellogg may not have always looked before he spent, spoke, or acted but he was generous to a fault. Sadly, the vast majority of his philanthropic, missionary, and medical work, both good and bad, is either extinct or gathering dust in the archives. Too few people today recall the name John Harvey Kellogg and the reverse ought to be true. Those who glibly deride him as a quack have entirely missed the point of his life and work. Although the science, or evidence, underpinning his ideas about "biologic living" have changed, many of his sounder concepts of wellness remain sage prescriptions written out millions of times each day. As narcissistic as he was, it is a safe bet to suggest that Dr. Kellogg would not have minded missing out on the credit for his ideas as long as they were rigorously taught and practiced to the benefit of all humankind. Perhaps one day they will.

Will Kellogg proved to be as shrewd a philanthropist as he was an industrialist. Laboriously amassing his fortune as the years passed, he meticulously designed the W. K. Kellogg Foundation. That it is dedicated to the welfare of children is as much a testimony to his divining the best possible use for his wealth as it was to his loveless youth. His dream of a Kellogg dynasty never came to be because he tended to either fire or discourage each succeeding generation from spending much time at his company or his foundation. As his grandson Norman Jr. noted, his greatest enterprises have been "perpetuated without benefit of his heirs."[50] Nevertheless, it was Will Keith Kellogg, and not his charismatic and once more famous brother, John Harvey Kellogg, who achieved a certain kind of immortality.

What remains indisputable, even if Will and John had great difficulty admitting it, is that their remarkable success was mutually dependent if not outright synergistic. John needed Will to administer and expand his empire of health. He required a businessman to manage the business he found so boring. Even after they acrimoniously dissolved their partnership, Will's stunning success in the cereal business spurred John to create many other foods and health innovations. Will, in turn, needed John to launch his career as a manager, executive, and business visionary. Perversely, this once subservient bookkeeper used his older brother's rough turns to drive his relentless hunger for achievement and, of course, introduce him to the possibilities of those toasted flakes of corn.

Equally indisputable, but far more heartrending, is how much these brothers hurt and, at times, hated each other. Theirs was a rancorous disequilibrium that impoverished their lives, diminished their piece of mind, and spilled over onto their relations with friends, colleagues, and family. Such dysfunction was a striking contrast to their mutual quest to achieve a balance of health through sound digestion and diet. They could see the other's foibles clearly even if they were incapable of contemplating their own. One is tempted to bleat the old English proverb, "great men's faults are never small."[51] But John and Will's sister, Emma, explained the dynamic even better when she observed, "the Kellogg men can be *mean*."[52] In fact, they were human with all the possibilities of failure that membership in our species implies. The psychic costs their flaws imposed upon each other were every bit as dear as their outsized talents, imagination, and lasting impact on the world. All told, this volatile brew constitutes the tragedy and the triumph of the Brothers Kellogg.

Acknowledgments

THIS BOOK HAS A FEW of its roots in a journey I made as a six-year-old boy growing up in suburban Detroit. My first-grade class took a field trip to Battle Creek to tour the Kellogg's factory. I still have the Tony the Tiger cereal bowl we were each given as souvenirs but the small box of Sugar Frosted Flakes I also received that day was consumed before our school bus turned onto the highway to take us home. If you grew up in Michigan, you could not help but be aware of the Kellogg's Cereal Company or the beneficence of the Will Keith Kellogg Foundation. Years later, as a medical student at the University of Michigan, I skimmed many of Dr. John Harvey Kellogg's entertaining health tomes as respite from cramming still another medical textbook into my memory bank. I recall thinking at the time that someone ought to tell the tale of these two extraordinary brothers, never imagining I might be that person.

Personal history aside, there are many people and institutions who helped pave my literary journey to Battle Creek and back. At the University of Michigan in Ann Arbor, Francis J. Blouin, the former director; Terrance McDonald, the current director of the Bentley Historical Library; and the Bentley's medical archivist, Brian Williams, were instrumental in helping me navigate the vast collection of the John Harvey Kellogg papers and sharing their wealth of historical knowledge with me. The University of Michigan's library staff was critical in helping me obtain hundreds of other documents and reports cited within this book. I am equally grateful to Garth "Duff" Stoltz of the Adventist Heritage Village and Museum in Battle Creek; the archival and library staffs of the

Michigan State University Archives in East Lansing; the State of Michigan Archives in Lansing; the Center for Adventist Research, Andrews University, Berrien Springs; George Livingstone and his colleagues at the Willard Public Library of Battle Creek; the Benson Ford Center of the Henry Ford Museum, in Dearborn; the Library of Congress, Washington, D.C.; the National Library of Medicine, Bethesda, Maryland; and the New York Public Library, New York City. For every query and request I made of these superb librarians, there was always a helpful answer that went above and beyond the call of their collective duties. At the University of Michigan Center for the History of Medicine, Dr. J. Alexander Navarro, Heidi Mueller, and Brendan Flynn ably assisted me in too many ways to enumerate and I hope my thanks on these pages will suffice to demonstrate my indebtedness for their generosity and support.

Navigating the stormy, and often shark-infested, waters of academia is no easy task. Having done so for more than three decades without yet drowning, I was fortunate in having several true friends and colleagues who were always present for advice, counsel, and simply to listen. I thank Michael Schoenfeldt, John R. Knott Jr., and Arthur J. Vander at the University of Michigan; Martin Cetron of the U.S. Centers for Disease Control and Prevention; Catherine D. Deangelis of Johns Hopkins University; Daniel M. Fox of the Milbank Memorial Fund; William Richardson, president emeritus of the W. K. Kellogg Foundation; David Rosner of Columbia University; and Drs. Sheldon F. Markel and Andrew P. Metinko. They were all thoughtful readers of this book *in utero* and, more broadly, have enriched my life simply by my knowing them.

My literary agents, Glen Harley and Lynn Chu, of Writers Representatives, remain steadfast and superb shepherds of the publishing process. I am fortunate, indeed, to be represented by such able professionals who are true "book people."

This is the third book I have completed with my wonderful editor, Victoria Wilson, associate vice president and associate publisher of Alfred A. Knopf/Penguin Random House. Tough, savvy, and uncompromising in the pursuit of good writing and storytelling, her constructive advice and attention to detail has made this volume far better than it might have otherwise been. I would also like to thank her editorial assistant,

Ryan Smernoff, for his cheerful help and professionalism; copy editor Fred Chase, for his superb attention to questions of language, grammar, and factual detail; Josephine Kals of the Publicity Department; and to the entire staff at Pantheon who performed their jobs with great ability and insight.

I am proud to acknowledge the assistance of the John Simon Guggenheim Memorial Foundation. Beyond the incredible honor of being named a Guggenheim Fellow for 2015, the award afforded me the funds, time, and concentration necessary to complete this book. In 2017, the Rockefeller Foundation awarded me an academic writing residency at their Bellagio Center in Italy, a signal distinction that greatly helped me crystallize my ideas and thoughts about the amazing Kellogg brothers.

Finally, I thank my daughters, Bess and Sammy, for their support and encouragement during the process of writing this book. Authors in the throes of composition tend to be preoccupied when the writing is going well and downright ornery when it is not. Nevertheless, my wonderful girls have never flagged in their support and love for or their belief in me, both during pleasant times and emotional maelstroms, and for that I am both fortunate and grateful.

Howard Markel
Ann Arbor, Michigan
August 2017

Notes

ABBREVIATIONS AND SHORT CITES USED IN THE NOTES

A. S. Bloese Manuscript   August S. Bloese, "Manuscript of an unfinished biography of John Harvey Kellogg," Charles MacIvor Collection, No. 251, Center for Adventist Research, Andrews University, Berrien Springs, Michigan

Carson   Gerald Carson, *Cornflake Crusade: From the Pulpit to the Breakfast Table* (New York: Rinehart, 1957)

Center for Adventist Research   Center for Adventist Research, Andrews University, Berrien Springs, Michigan

J. H. Kellogg Papers, MSU   John Harvey Kellogg Papers, Michigan State University, East Lansing, Michigan

J. H. Kellogg Papers, U-M   John Harvey Kellogg Papers, Bentley Historical Library, University of Michigan, Ann Arbor, Michigan

Powell   Horace B. Powell, *The Original Has This Signature: W. K. Kellogg* (Englewood Cliffs, NJ: Prentice Hall, 1956)

Schwarz, *John Harvey Kellogg*   Richard W. Schwarz, *John Harvey Kellogg, M.D.* (Nashville: Southern Publishing Association, 1970)

Schwarz, PhD thesis   Richard W. Schwarz, "John Harvey Kellogg: American Health Reformer" (PhD thesis in Modern History, University of Michigan, 1964)

Williamson Jr., *An Intimate Glimpse*   Norman Williamson Jr., *An Intimate Glimpse of a Shy Grandparent, W. K. Kellogg* (Privately printed, 1999), copy in Bentley Historical Library, University of Michigan, Ann Arbor, Michigan

INTRODUCTION:
THE CAIN AND ABEL OF AMERICA'S HEARTLAND

1. All told, more than 128 billion bowls of Corn Flakes are consumed each year. The Kellogg Company produces more than 65 million boxes of Corn Flakes annually. See The Kellogg Company, *2014 Annual Report. Letters to Shareowners and SEC Form 10-K. Fiscal Year End: January 3, 2015* (Battle Creek, MI: Kellogg Company, 2015).

See also "Kellogg's to Laser-Brand Individual Corn Flakes," *The Telegraph* (Great Britain). October 13, 2009, accessed July 1, 2015, at http://www.telegraph.co.uk/news/uknews/6316425/Kelloggs-to-laser-brand-individual-Corn-Flakes.html.

2. Dr. Kellogg's books include: J. H. Kellogg, *The Household Manual of Domestic Hygiene, Foods, and Drinks, Common Diseases, Accidents and Emergencies and Useful Hints and Recipes* (Battle Creek, MI: The Office of the Health Reformer, 1875); *Practical Manual of Health and Temperance Embracing the Treatment of Common Diseases, Accidents, and Emergencies, the Alcohol and Tobacco Habit, Helpful Hints and Recipes* (Battle Creek, MI: Good Health Publishing Co., 1885); *Plain Facts for Old and Young: Embracing the Natural History and Hygiene of Organic Life* (Burlington, Iowa: Senger and Condit, 1881, 1886, 1887; Battle Creek, MI; Modern Medicine Publishing Co., 1910); *Sunbeams of Health and Temperance: An Instructive Account of the Health Habits of All Nations With Interesting Information on All Subjects Relating to Health and Temperance Affording Both Instruction and Entertainment for Young and Old* (Battle Creek: MI: Good Health Publishing Co., 1888); *Man, the Masterpiece* (Burlington, Iowa: Senger and Condit, 1886; Battle Creek, MI: Health Publishing Co.; 1891); *Colon Hygiene: Comprising New and Important Facts Concerning the Physiology of the Colon and an Account of Practical and Successful Methods of Combating Intestinal Inactivity and Toxemia* (Battle Creek, MI: Good Health Publishing Co., 1916); *The Itinerary of a Breakfast: A Popular Account of the Travels of a Breakfast Through the Food Tube and of the Ten Gates and Several Stations Through Which It Passes, Also of the Obstacles Which It Sometimes Meets* (Battle Creek, MI: Good Health Publishing Co., 1918); *The Crippled Colon: Causes, Consequences, Remedies* (Battle Creek, MI: The Modern Medicine Publishing Co., 1931); *Why the "Blues"? "Nerves," Neuralgias, and Chronic Fatigue or Neurasthenia* (Battle Creek, MI: Modern Medicine Publishing Co., 3rd edition, 1921); *The New Dietetics: A Guide to Scientific Feeding in Health and Disease* (Battle Creek, MI: The Modern Medicine Publishing Co., 1921, 1927). Will Durant, the best-selling author of *The Story of Philosophy,* insisted that *The New Dietetics* merited inclusion "among the 100 best books ever published." Will Durant to J. H. Kellogg, February 20, 1929, Reel 3, John Harvey Kellogg Papers, Michigan Historical Collections, Bentley Historical Library, University of Michigan, Ann Arbor, Michigan (hereinafter J. H. Kellogg Papers, U-M).

3. Richard W. Schwarz, *John Harvey Kellogg, M.D.* (Nashville: Southern Publishing Association, 1970), p. 90 (hereinafter Schwarz, *John Harvey Kellogg*); Richard W. Schwarz, "John Harvey Kellogg: American Health Reformer" (PhD thesis in Modern History, University of Michigan, 1964), p. 236 (hereinafter Schwarz, PhD thesis); Henry T. Finck to J. H. Kellogg, October 5, 1922, Reel 2, Images 615–617, J. H. Kellogg Papers, U-M.

4. Glenville Kleiser, "Who's Who–1932," *Sarasota Tribune,* March 24, 1932, Clippings File, Reel 32, Image 234, J. H. Kellogg Papers, U-M. (Also included in file is a copy of the same article that ran in the *West Palm Beach Tropical Sun,* March 18, 1932.)

5. The Kellogg Company, *2014 Annual Report for 2014: Letter to Shareholders and SEC Form 10-K, Fiscal Year End: January 3, 2015* (Battle Creek, MI: Kellogg Company, 2015).

6. Schwarz, *John Harvey Kellogg*, p. 238.

7. "Are We Too Civilized," February 23, 1911, Reel 12, Image 669 (page 13 of the typescript), J. H. Kellogg Papers, U-M. Marshall Field and Company of Chicago was also his brother Will's favorite department store. Norman Williamson Jr., *An Intimate Glimpse of a Shy Grandparent, W. K. Kellogg* (Privately printed, 1999), copy in the Bent-

ley Historical Library, University of Michigan, Ann Arbor, p. 54 (hereinafter William-son Jr., *An Intimate Glimpse*).

8. Charles MacIvor, manuscript of "The Lord's Physician," Addendum to Chapter 40: "Tributes to His Memory," Charles MacIvor Collection, Box 10, File 12, Chapters 31–40, Center for Adventist Research, Andrews University, Berrien Springs, Michigan. Among the many tributes that arrived included telegrams from John D. Rockefeller Jr., Dale Carnegie, Will Durant, and Senator Arthur Vandenberg (R-MI).

9. "Obituary: J. H. Kellogg Dead at 91," *Battle Creek Enquirer and News,* Decem-ber 15, 1943, p. 1, Reel 34, Images 585–87; Funeral Program, John Harvey Kellogg, Reel 31, Image 333, J. H. Kellogg Papers, U-M; Charles MacIvor, Manuscript of "The Lord's Physician," Chapter 40: "The End Time," p. 8, Charles MacIvor Collection, Box 10, File 12, Chapters 31–40, Center for Adventist Research.

10. Gerald Carson, *Cornflake Crusade: From the Pulpit to the Breakfast Table* (New York: Rinehart, 1957), pp. 12–13 (hereinafter Carson).

11. Ibid., p. 174.

12. In the Calhoun County death records, Ella's cause of death on June 14, 1920, is listed as "carcinoma of the colon." Elizabeth Neumayer, *"Mother": Ella Eaton Kellogg* (Battle Creek, MI: Heritage Battle Creek, 2001), p. 16; "Battle Creek. Points of Inter-est, Oak Hill Cemetery," Writers' Program of the Works Project Administration in the State of Michigan, *Michigan: A Guide to the Wolverine State* (New York: Oxford University Press, 1941), pp. 195–97; J. H. Kellogg, "In Memoriam, Ella Eaton Kellogg." (Originally appeared in *Good Health,* July 1920. Reprints from the Collections of the University of Michigan Center for the History of Medicine, Ann Arbor, Michigan).

13. Horace B. Powell, *The Original Has This Signature—W. K. Kellogg* (Englewood Cliffs, NJ: Prentice Hall, 1956), pp. 285–87 (hereinafter Powell); "W. K. Kellogg, 91, Dead in Michigan," *New York Times,* October 7, 1951; "Will Keith Kellogg. Memorial Announcement. October 6, 1951" (Battle Creek, MI: Kellogg Company, 1951), Collec-tions of the University of Michigan Center for the History of Medicine.

14. Powell, p. 78.

15. Ibid., p. 117.

16. "Community to Mourn W. K. Kellogg for Week," *Battle Creek Enquirer and News,* October 7, 1951, p. 14. Similarly, a memorial issue of the company newspaper for W. K. Kellogg, 1860–1951, *The Kellogg News,* October 1951, Collections of the Willard Library of Battle Creek, Michigan, cites this same figure on page 7.

17. Carson, p. 87. The italics for emphasis are Carson's (or Emma Kellogg's), not the present author's. Carson does not indicate the authorship of this emphasis in his book.

18. Kadish Millet, "What's More American," recorded by Bing Crosby (with the "Bugs" Bower Orchestra), 45 RPM Single, PIP 8940-A (Long Island City, NY: Pickwick International Productions, 1968); Anne Kadet, "The Neighborhood Report: Brooklyn Up Close—City People: A Song in His Heart, But It's Falling on Deaf Ears," *New York Times,* July 16, 2000, accessed July 16, 2015, at http://www.nytimes.com/2000/07/16/nyregion/neighborhood-report-brooklyn-up-close-citypeople-song-his-heart-but-it-s-falling.html.

19. Schwarz, *John Harvey Kellogg,* pp. 138–39.

20. August S. Bloese, "Manuscript of an unfinished biography of John Harvey Kel-logg," Charles MacIvor Collection, No. 251, Box 1, Folder 14, p. 250, Center for Adven-tist Research, Andrews University, Berrien Springs, Michigan (hereinafter A. S. Bloese Manuscript); J. H. Kellogg, "Lecture: Clinical Dietetics. (For members of Domestic Science, Physical Culture, and Nurses Classes)," January 17, 1911, Reel 12, Image 397,

J. H. Kellogg Papers, U-M; University of Michigan Lecture by J. H. Kellogg to Junior Medical Students, October 9, 1906, pp. 12–13, Reel 10, Images 595–96, J. H. Kellogg Papers, U-M.

21. Dr. Kellogg describes a visit to the Chicago stockyards, which were near the Chicago Mission. "Question Box Hour Lecture," June 11, 1906, Reel 10, Images 310–16 (pages 14–20 of the typescript), J. H. Kellogg Papers, U-M.

22. J. H. Kellogg, *Tobaccoism, or How Tobacco Kills* (Battle Creek, MI: Modern Medicine Publishing Co., 1922).

23. "Sugar," July 29, 1909, Reel 11, Images 659–75, J. H. Kellogg Papers, U-M.

24. Schwarz, *John Harvey Kellogg*, p. 244.

25. J. H. Kellogg, *The Household Manual of Domestic Hygiene, Foods, and Drinks, Common Diseases, Accidents and Emergencies and Useful Hints and Recipes* (Battle Creek, MI: The Office of the Health Reformer, 1875), pp. 36–37.

26. James C. Whorton, *Inner Hygiene: Constipation and the Pursuit of Health in Modern Society* (New York: Oxford University Press, 2000).

27. Lecture, "The Old Way and the New," July 5, 1906, Reel 10, Image 410 (page 24 of the typescript), J. H. Kellogg Papers, U-M.

28. Carson, p. 87. Carson observed: "the busy doctor dictated while seated in his *cabinet de nécessité* with humble Will taking notes and instructions." Carson goes on to explain on the same page that Dr. Kellogg made Will follow him as he rode his bicycle "in wide circles in front of the San while Will trotted beside him with a notebook. It was a neat combination of exercise, business conference and brotherly hazing. No wonder, then, when *his* turn finally came at the wheel of fortune, W.K. was as short as a butter cake with his brother." Lyndon B. Johnson long enjoyed inviting aides into his bathroom while defecating to record his orders and thoughts. See Robert A. Caro, *Master of the Senate: The Years of Lyndon Johnson* (New York: Alfred A. Knopf, 2002), pp. 121–23. John bought his first bicycle in 1879. "Gus Bell Bought First High Bicycle in Town," unidentified clip, circa 1879, Reel 32, Image 18, J. H. Kellogg Papers, U-M.

29. Powell, p. 76.

30. Ibid.

31. Frederick Winslow, *The Principles of Scientific Management* (New York: Harper Brothers, 1911). The development and advancement of the Ford Motor Company assembly line is described in Henry Ford, with Samuel Crowther, *My Life and Work* (Garden City, NY: Doubleday and Page Co., 1923); Allan Nevins and Frank Ernest Hill, *Ford: Expansion and Challenge, 1914–1933* (New York: Charles Scribner's Sons, 1957); Alfred D. Chandler Jr., *The Visible Hand: The Managerial Revolution in American Business* (Cambridge: Belknap Press of Harvard University Press, 1977).

32. The phrase was coined in 1917, not by Dr. Kellogg but by Lenna Cooper, the longtime director of the Sanitarium's School of Home Economics. Her article was titled "August Breakfasts" and appears in *Good Health*, 1917; 52: 389–90. The phrase "breakfast is the most important meal of the day" appears on page 389.

33. Benjamin K. Hunnicutt, *Kellogg's Six-Hour Day* (Philadelphia: Temple University Press, 1996), pp. 13–45.

34. Rea Irvin, "Historic Moments in the Annals of American Industry," *The New Yorker*, August 22, 1936; 12(27): 21. Cartoon is used with the permission of his literary executor, Molly Rea (Copyright, Molly Rea, 1916). See also Powell, p. 175.

35. The three major collections are the John Harvey Kellogg Papers housed at the Bentley Historical Library at the University of Michigan in Ann Arbor; an equally large collection of John Harvey Kellogg papers at the Michigan State University Archives

in East Lansing; and a superb collection of the papers of his associates and the Battle Creek Sanitarium at the Center for Adventist Research of Andrews University in Berrien Springs, Michigan. There is a smaller collection of materials in the Archives of the State of Michigan, Lansing, Michigan, which is especially rich in copies of Dr. Kellogg's published books, magazines, and journals, materials related to the Battle Creek College, and a number of other documents that complement the archival collection.

36. The authorized biography of W. K. Kellogg, published in honor of the Kellogg Company's fiftieth anniversary, is Horace B. Powell, *The Original Has This Signature— W. K. Kellogg* (Englewood Cliffs, NJ: Prentice Hall, 1956); the memoir by his grandson is Norman Williamson Jr., *An Intimate Glimpse of a Shy Grandparent, W. K. Kellogg* (Privately printed 1999), copy in Bentley Historical Library, University of Michigan. The archives of the Kellogg Company, which contain corporate documents extending to those covering the founding of the company is also, sadly, restricted to "outside researchers."

37. Henry R. Luce, "The American Century," *Life,* February 17, 1941; 10: 61–65.

I.

"GO WEST, YOUNG MAN"

Chapter title: Often ascribed to Horace Greeley, there exists a great deal of controversy among historians as to who actually coined the axiom "Go west, young man." For an engaging explanation of the saying's provenance, see Thomas Fuller, " 'Go West, young man!'—An Elusive Slogan," *Indiana Magazine of History,* 2004; 100(3): 231–42.

1. Judd Sylvester and Lucius Boltwood, *History of Hadley, Including the Early History of Hatfield, South Hadley, Amherst, and Granby, Massachusetts* (Northampton, MA: Metcalf and Co., 1863), p. 17.

2. Ibid., pp. 228–33.

3. Merritt G. Kellogg, "A Bit of Family History" (typescript dated July 6, 1914), J. H. Kellogg Papers, U-M, Reel 1, Images 17–44, Mary Ann Call Kellogg's birthdate was October 1, 1811. John Preston Kellogg was born on February 14, 1807.

4. Brian C. Wilson, *Dr. John Harvey Kellogg and the Religion of Biologic Living* (Bloomington: University of Indiana Press, 2014), p. 143; Note on Genealogy of the Kellogg Family, Reel 1, University of Michigan, Bentley Historical Library.

5. Timothy Hopkins, *The Kelloggs in the Old World and the New,* Volume 1 (San Francisco: Sunset Press, 1903), pp. 1–5, quote is from p. 3.

6. H. A. Allerd, "Chicago, a Name of Indian Origin, and the Native Wild Onion to Which the Indians May Have Had Reference as the 'Skunk Place,'" *Castanea,* March 1955; 20(1): 28–31.

7. The principal treaties, in which the U.S. purchased land at stunningly low rates, included the Treaty of Detroit, 1807 (southeastern Michigan including what are now Wayne and Washtenaw counties), the Treaty of Saginaw, 1819 (the "thumb" area of the lower peninsula), the Treaty of Chicago, 1821 (west Michigan), the Treaty of Washington, 1836 (much of the upper portion of the lower peninsula and parts of the upper peninsula), and the Treaty of La Pointe, 1842 (the entirety of the upper peninsula). Willis F. Dunbar and George S. May, *Michigan: A History of the Wolverine State* (Grand Rapids, MI: William B. Eerdmans, 1995; 3rd revised edition), pp. 119–20, 146–54.

8. Dollar translations from the nineteenth century into twenty-first-century values

are challenging to even the most accomplished economic historians. I have used the online economic historical calculator MeasuringWorth.com to approximate these figures to provide the reader with a sense of the value of the investments being made by the protagonists in this book between 1833 and 1951.

9. "A Michigan Emigrant Song. From the *Detroit Post and Tribune,* February 13, 1881," in *Michigan Historical Commission. Pioneer Collections. Report of the Pioneer Society of the State of Michigan,* Volume 3 (Lansing, MI: W. S. George, 1881), p. 265; Powell, pp. 6–7.

10. "The Erie Canal was in embryo a matter of national survival, and in realization a miracle of national growth." Dorothie Bobbe, "Erie Canal," in James Truslow Adams and R. V. Coleman, eds., *Dictionary of American History,* Volume 2 (New York: Charles Scribner's Sons, 1940), pp. 225–26.

11. New York Governor DeWitt Clinton managed to navigate a large sum of money toward its construction, for which he endured the gibes and sneers of his political opponents, who nicknamed the venture "Clinton's Ditch." Gouverneur Morris gave the canal its nickname, "the artificial river." For those investors who did have financial faith, the Erie Canal turned out an amazing stream of profits. By 1882, the canal had generated revenues amounting to $121 million (about $2.89 billion in 2016), or a profit of over $41 million ($979 million in 2016). Gerald Koeppel, *Bond of Union: Building the Erie Canal and the American Empire* (New York: Da Capo, 2009), pp. 395–96.

12. Peter L. Bernstein, *Wedding of the Waters: The Erie Canal and the Making of a Great Nation* (New York: W. W. Norton, 2006), pp. 325–55; Carol Sherriff, *The Artificial River: The Erie Canal and the Paradox of Progress, 1817–1862* (New York: Hill & Wang, 1997); Koeppel, *Bond of Union.*

13. W. S. Tyron, ed. *A Mirror for Americans: Life and Manners in the United States, 1790–1870, as Recorded by American Travelers,* Volume 1 (Chicago: University of Chicago Press, 1952), p. 113.

14. Merritt G. Kellogg, "A Bit of Family History" (typescript dated July 6, 1914), Reel 1, p. 1 (Images 17–44), J. H. Kellogg Papers, U-M; A. S. Bloese Manuscript (Chapter 1, "Early Days," unpaginated), Box 1, File 13.

15. Frances Trollope, *Domestic Manners of the Americans* (London: Whittaker, Treacher and Co., 1832), Chapter 32, in R. W. Hecht, ed., *The Erie Canal Reader, 1790–1950* (Syracuse, NY: Syracuse University Press, 2003), p. 63.

16. Bela Hubbard, *Memorials of a Half-Century* (New York: G. P. Putnam's Sons, 1887), quote is from p. 13, population data circa 1835 is found on page 115; Dunbar and May, *Michigan: A History of the Wolverine State,* pp. 139–62. For a superb pictorial and descriptive history of Early Detroit, see Brian Leigh Dunnigan, *Frontier Metropolis: Picturing Early Detroit, 1701–1838* (Detroit: Wayne State University Press, 2001).

17. Hubbard, *Memorials of a Half-Century,* p. 118.

18. R. Alan Douglas, *Uppermost Canada: The Western District and Frontier Detroit, 1800–1850* (Detroit: Wayne State University Press, 2001), pp. 224–26; Silas Farmer, *The History of Detroit and Michigan: Or, the Metropolis Illustrated; a Chronological Cyclopaedia of the Past and Present, Including a Full Record of Territorial Days in Michigan, and the Annals of Wayne County* (Detroit: Silas Farmer, 1884), pp. 48–49; Arthur Woodford, *This Is Detroit, 1701–2001* (Detroit: Wayne State University Press, 2001); Howard Peckham, *The Making of the University of Michigan, 1817–1992* (Ann Arbor: Bentley Historical Library, 1994); Howard Markel, *When Germs Travel: Six Major Epidemics That Invaded America and the Fears They Unleashed* (New York: Vintage/Random House, 2005), pp. 181–82; Richard Adler, *Cholera in Detroit: A History* (Jefferson, NC: McFar-

land, 2013); Charles Rosenberg, *The Cholera Years: The United States in 1832, 1849, and 1866* (Chicago: University of Chicago Press, 1987, 2nd edition).

19. Dunbar and May, *Michigan: A History of the Wolverine State*, p. 339.

20. Hubbard, *Memorials of a Half-Century*, pp. 374–76; Dunbar and May, *Michigan: A History of the Wolverine State*, pp. 139–62, 338–51; William Barillas, "Michigan's Pioneers and the Destruction of the Hardwood Forest," *Michigan Historical Review*, 1989; 15(2): 1–22; L. D. Watkins, "Destruction of the Forests of Southern Michigan," *Michigan Pioneer and Historical Collections*, 1900; 28: 148–50; John R. Knott Jr., *Imagining the Forest: Narratives of Michigan and the Upper Midwest* (Ann Arbor: University of Michigan Press, 2012).

21. Merritt G. Kellogg, "A Bit of Family History" (typescript dated July 6, 1914), Reel 1, p. 1, J. H. Kellogg Papers, U-M; A. S. Bloese Manuscript (Introductory Chapter, unpaginated), Box 1, File 13; Dunbar and May, *Michigan: A History of the Wolverine State*, pp. 160–62; Payson J. Treat, *The National Land System, 1785–1820* (New York: E. B. Treat and Company, 1910); Powell, pp. 7–8.

22. For an excellent description of "Michigan Fever," see Caroline M. Kirkland, *Western Clearings* (New York: Wiley and Putnam, 1846). Kirkland also wrote a popular novel about life in the woods of territories such as Michigan; see Caroline M. Kirkland, *Forest Life* (New York: C. S. Francis and Co./Boston: J. H. Francis, 1844, in two volumes).

23. Dunbar and May, *Michigan: A History of the Wolverine State*, p. 164.

24. The estimated amount of destroyed timber on a plot of land in southeastern Michigan measuring 320 acres circa 1834 as well as the methods of clearing trees in this era can be found in Barillas, "Michigan's Pioneers and the Destruction of the Hardwood Forest," pp. 1–22; William Nowlin, *The Bark Covered House: Being a Graphic and Thrilling Description of Real Pioneer Life in the Wilderness of Michigan* (Detroit: E. W. De La Vergne, 1876).

25. Powell, pp. 8–10.

26. Hubbard, *Memorials of a Half-Century*, p. 486. See also Nowlin, *The Bark Covered House*.

27. Powell, p. 9.

28. A. S. Bloese Manuscript (Introductory Chapter, unpaginated), Box 1, File 13; Schwarz, *John Harvey Kellogg*, pp. 9–10.

29. Edgar W. Martin, *The Standard of Living in 1860: American Consumption Levels on the Eve of the Civil War* (Chicago: University of Chicago Press, 1942), p. 220.

30. Madge E. Pickard and R. Carlyle Buley, *The Midwest Pioneer: His Ills, Cures and Doctors* (New York: Henry Schuman, 1946), p. 13; Edgar W. Martin, *The Standard of Living in 1860: American Consumption Levels on the Eve of the Civil War* (Chicago: University of Chicago Press, 1942), p. 226.

31. R. H. Shryock, *Medicine and Society in America, 1660–1860* (New York: NYU Press, 1960), pp. 44–81; R. H. Shryock, *Medical Licensing in America, 1650–1965* (Baltimore: Johns Hopkins University Press, 1967), pp. 3–76; Martin, *The Standard of Living in 1860*, pp. 220–47.

32. The doctor's therapeutic armamentarium, circa 1840, changed very little since the age of Hippocrates (c. 460 to 370 BC). There were, of course, a few notable exceptions: during the seventeenth century, Western physicians and Jesuit missionaries began prescribing cinchona or Peruvian bark and, later, quinine for malaria. In 1785, the British physician William Withering began using an extract of a flowering plant called foxglove, or digitalis, as a treatment for "dropsy," or congestive heart failure. By

the early 1800s, Edward Jenner's smallpox vaccine was well known, but it remained a controversial technique that many avoided as assiduously as the disease it was developed to prevent.

33. Charles Rosenberg, "The Therapeutic Revolution: Medicine, Meaning and Social Change in 19th Century America," in M. Vogel and C. E. Rosenberg, eds., *The Therapeutic Revolution: Essays in the Social History of Medicine* (Philadelphia: University of Pennsylvania Press, 1979), pp. 1–25.

34. Pickard and Buley, *The Midwest Pioneer*, pp. 103–8; LeRoy G. Davis, "Frontier Home Remedies and Sanitation," *Minnesota History*, 1938; 19(4): 369–76.

35. *Vis medicatrix naturae* is the Latin translation of this Greek aphorism. Max Neuberger, "An Historical Survey of the Concept of Nature from a Medical Standpoint," *Isis*, 1944; 35(1): 16–28; W. F. Bynum, "Nature's Helping Hand," *Nature*, 2011; 414:21; G. M. A. Grube, "Greek Medicine and the Greek Genius," *Phoenix*, 1954; 8(4): 123–35.

36. J. C. Whorton, *Crusaders for Fitness: The History of American Health Reformers* (Princeton: Princeton University Press, 1982), pp. 22–24, 35–37; Stephen Nissenbaum, *Sex, Diet and Debility in Jacksonian America: Sylvester Graham and Health Reform* (Westport, CT: Greenwood Press, 1980).

37. As a point of comparison, in 2000 the U.S. infant mortality rate was about 5.3 per 1,000 live births for non-Hispanic white babies, 12.2 per 1,000 live births for non-Hispanic black babies, and 5.4 per 1,000 live births for Hispanic babies; most of these babies died of complications related to prematurity. Table Ab1–10: Fertility and Mortality, by Race, 1800–2000, in S. B. Carter, S. S. Gartner, M. R. Haines, A. L. Olmstead, R. Sutch, and G. Wright, eds., *Historical Abstracts of the United States. Earliest Times to Present. Millennial Edition.* Volume 1. Part A, *Population* (New York: Cambridge University Press, 2006), pp. 1–391.

38. Irvine Loudon, "The Measurement of Maternal Mortality," *Journal of the History of Medicine and Allied Sciences*, 1999; 54: 312–29. See also Robert J. Gordon, *The Rise and Fall of American Growth* (Princeton: Princeton University Press, 2016), pp. 35–36, 50–51.

39. Pickard and Buley, *The Midwest Pioneer*, 110–11.

40. Schwarz, *John Harvey Kellogg*, p. 10.

41. The discussion of trachoma is drawn from Markel, *When Germs Travel*, pp. 86–87.

42. Calomel chemically transforms the bile pigment bilirubin into biliverdin, which in turn changes the stool from its typical brown color into an emerald green. Herman Sahli, Francis P. Kinnicutt, and Nathanial B. Potter, *A Treatise on Diagnostic Methods of Examination* (Authorized Translation from the 4th Revised and Enlarged German Edition) (Philadelphia: W. B. Saunders Co., 1909), pp. 424–25; "Influence of Calomel Upon the Decomposition of Bile," *American Journal of Pharmacy*, 1887; 59: 444.

43. This discussion of tuberculosis is drawn from Markel, *When Germs Travel*, pp. 24–31.

44. Merritt G. Kellogg, "A Bit of Family History" (typescript dated July 6, 1914), Reel 1, Image 20, p. 4, J. H. Kellogg Papers, U-M; James Copland, *The Forms, Complications, Causes, Prevention and Treatment of Consumption and Bronchitis Comprising Also the Causes and Prevention of Scrofula* (London: Longman, Green, Longman and Roberts, 1861), pp. 415–16.

45. Powell, pp. 11–12, quote is from p. 11.

46. Merritt G. Kellogg, "A Bit of Family History" (typescript dated July 6, 1914), Reel 1, Images 17–44, page 7, Image 23, J. H. Kellogg Papers, U-M.

47. Powell, pp. 11–12.

48. Ibid.; Schwarz, *John Harvey Kellogg,* p. 10; Merritt G. Kellogg, "A Bit of Family History" (typescript dated July 6, 1914), Reel 1, pp. 6–7, J. H. Kellogg Papers, U-M.

49. The story of Mr. Kellogg's foot injury, including all the quotations from the conversations he recalled, is drawn from Merritt Kellogg, "A Bit of Family History," Reel 1, pp. 17–19 (Images 34–35). Merritt also suffered an ax wound to the foot, which resulted in "being laid up three weeks with this cut." Ann Janette cared for him as "if I had been her own son," Reel 1, p. 11, Image 27.

2.

THE CHOSEN ONE

1. For extended genealogies of the Kellogg family, see Timothy Hopkins, *The Kelloggs in the Old World and the New,* Volume 1 (San Francisco: Sunset Press, 1903), p. 636; and in Volume 2, pp. 1315–20.

2. Merritt G. Kellogg, "A Bit of Family History" (typescript dated July 6, 1914), Images 17–44. See, especially, Reel 1, Image 41, p. 25, J. H. Kellogg Papers, U-M.

3. Ibid., p. 25, Image 41.

4. "Dedication of the Portrait of Ann J. Kellogg. The Life and Influence of Ann J. Kellogg," Reel 31, Images 461–76, J. H. Kellogg Papers.

5. Merritt G. Kellogg, "A Bit of Family History" (typescript dated July 6, 1914), Reel 1, Images 17–44, J. H. Kellogg Papers, U-M. At various times, the well's bucket rope would break and have to be retrieved. Mr. Kellogg took the treacherous step of going down into the well, much to Ann Janette's discomfort and fear (pp. 26–27, Images 42–43).

6. Schwarz, *John Harvey Kellogg,* pp. 10–11.

7. Merritt G. Kellogg, "A Bit of Family History" (typescript dated July 6, 1914), Reel 1, Images 17–44, p. 27, Image 43, J. H. Kellogg Papers, U-M.

8. "Dedication of the Portrait of Ann J. Kellogg. The Life and Influence of Ann J. Kellogg," Reel 31, Images 461–76, J. H. Kellogg Papers, U-M.

9. Merritt G. Kellogg, "A Bit of Family History" (typescript dated July 6, 1914), Reel 1, Image 27, p. 11, J. H. Kellogg Papers, U-M.

10. William G. McLoughlin, "Revivalism," in Edwin S. Gaustad, ed., *The Rise of Adventism: A Commentary on the Social and Religious Ferment of Mid-Nineteenth Century America* (New York: Harper & Row, 1974), pp. 119–50, quote is from p. 138.

11. Everett M. Dick, "The Millerite Movement, 1830–1845," in Gary Land, ed., *Adventism in America* (Berrien Springs, MI: Andrews University Press, 1998), pp. 1–28.

12. Henry David Thoreau, "Economy," in Henry David Thoreau, edited by Michael Meyer, *Walden and Civil Disobedience, and Other Essays* (New York: Penguin, 1983), p. 50. Regarding the term "Burnt-over District," Charles Grandison Finney, the minister and later president of Oberlin College, found it difficult to find people to evangelize, especially while traveling through central and western New York after the occurrence of the "Great Disappointment." In his memoirs, Finney referred to the region as a "burnt district" because "there had been, a few years previously, a wild excitement, which they called a revival of religion but which turned out to be spurious." Charles G. Finney, *The Memoirs of Rev. Charles G. Finney* (New York: A. S. Barnes and Co., 1876), p. 78.

13. Timothy L. Smith, "Social Reform," in Gaustad, ed., *The Rise of Adventism,* pp. 18–29.

14. Carson, p. 88; Richardson L. Wright, *Hawkers and Walkers in Early America:*

Strolling Peddlers, Preachers, Lawyers, Doctors, Players, and Others. From the Beginning to the Civil War (Philadelphia: J. B. Lippincott, 1927), p. 64.

15. Washington Gardner, *The History of Calhoun County, Michigan: A Narrative Account of Its Historical Progress, Its People, and Its Principal Interests,* Volume 1 (Chicago and New York: The Lewis Publishing Company, 1913), pp. 82–93, 311–52. John H. Kellogg was an associate editor of this book and a long chapter is devoted to the Battle Creek Sanitarium, pp. 369–93.

16. Powell, p. 16.

17. Schwarz, *John Harvey Kellogg,* p. 13.

18. Merritt G. Kellogg, "A Bit of Family History" (typescript dated July 6, 1914), Reel 1, Images 17–44, J. H. Kellogg Papers, U-M; A. S. Bloese Manuscript, Chapter 1, "Early Days," unpaginated, Box 1, File 13; Schwarz, *John Harvey Kellogg,* p. 11; Gardner, *The History of Calhoun County, Michigan,* pp. 82–93. Gardner, a member of the Republican Party, was the U.S. congressman for the 3rd District of Michigan from 1889 to 1911. The history of the Underground Railroad that John H. Kellogg would have likely read would be Wilbur Siebert, *The Underground Railroad: From Slavery to Freedom* (New York: The Macmillan Co., 1898), Appendix E, p. 412, where, interestingly, John Preston is *not* named as one of the "operators" in Calhoun County, Michigan, in the alphabetical listing that ends this book.

19. For example, in 1847, a runaway slave named Adam Crosswhite from nearby Marshall made national headlines. Crosswhite and his family had been living there openly since fleeing Kentucky in 1843. Their former master, Francis Giltner, discovered his whereabouts and, in January 1847, hired a team of slave hunters to seize Mr. Crosswhite. More than two hundred enraged townspeople, led by a banker named Charles T. Gorham, gathered together, freed Crosswhite from his pursuers, and helped him, his wife, and their children escape to Canada (although in 1878, they returned to settle in Marshall). The people of Marshall went one step further by demanding that the slave hunters be arrested for assault and breaking and entering. In turn, the aggrieved slave owner filed a lawsuit against Gorham, who was subsequently ordered by the court to pay Giltner $4,800 (about $142,000 in 2016). Many historians of American slavery ascribe the congressional passage of the restrictive 1850 Fugitive Slave Act to the Crosswhite case. Others have suggested this sorry episode made its way onto the pages of Harriet Beecher Stowe's influential 1852 novel, *Uncle Tom's Cabin,* and that the character George Harris (Eliza's husband and a runaway slave) was loosely based on Adam Crosswhite. Writers Program of the Works Projects Administration in the State of Michigan, *Michigan: A Guide to the Wolverine State* (New York: Oxford University Press, 1941), pp. 401–2; Harriet Beecher Stowe, *Uncle Tom's Cabin, Or Life Among the Lowly* (New York: Modern Library, 1938); Willis F. Dunbar and George S. May, *Michigan: A History of the Wolverine State* (Grand Rapids, MI: William B. Eerdmans, 1995, 3rd revised edition), pp. 304–5.

20. Charles E. Barnes, "Battle Creek as a Station on the Underground Railway," in Gardner, *The History of Calhoun County, Michigan,* pp. 82–87, quote is from p. 83.

21. Writers Program of the Work Projects Administration in the State of Michigan, *Michigan: A Guide to the Wolverine State* (New York: Oxford University Press, 1941), p. 193.

22. *Battle Creek News and Enquirer,* June 12, 1932, p. 1. For a similar account, see Charles MacIvor, "The Lord's Physician," manuscript of an unpublished biography of J. H. Kellogg, Chapter 37, "Sojourner Truth," pp. 2–3, Charles MacIvor Collec-

tion, No. 251, Box 10, File 12, Chapters 31–47, Center for Adventist Research (hereafter Charles MacIvor, "The Lord's Physician").

23. Nell Irvin Painter, *Sojourner Truth: A Life, a Symbol* (New York: W. W. Norton, 1996), pp. 148, 254; *Battle Creek News and Enquirer,* June 12, 1932, p. 1; Sojourner Truth, edited by Nell Irvin Painter, *Narrative of Sojourner Truth* (New York: Penguin, 1998), pp. 156, 228–43.

24. Maintaining a public face of humility, Dr. Kellogg concluded that he did not amount to much. "Helpers Meeting, September 2, 1908, Full Meeting Minutes," Reel 11, Images 118–37; see Image 125, J. H. Kellogg Papers.

25. Letter from J. H. Kellogg to H. C. Sherman, June 4, 1935, Reel 3, Images 945–54, quote is from p. 4, Image 949, J. H. Kellogg Papers, U-M.

26. A. S. Bloese Manuscript, p. 55, Box 1, Folder 13.

27. Bound Scrapbooks of J. H. Kellogg, Student Notebooks in German, Mathematics, Poetry and Literature, Reel 37, Images 984–1261, J. H. Kellogg Papers, U-M.

28. Schwarz, *John Harvey Kellogg,* p. 14.

29. A. S. Bloese Manuscript, p. 37, Box 1, Folder 13.

30. Ibid., pp. 36–37, Box 1, File 13.

31. Ibid., p. 52, Box 1, File 13; Schwarz, PhD thesis, p. 12.

32. A. S. Bloese Manuscript, p. 49.

33. MacIvor Manuscript, Chapter 5, "Early Influences"; Schwarz, *John Harvey Kellogg,* pp. 9–16; A. S. Bloese Manuscript, "Early Days," Box 1, File 13.

34. "Sugar," July 29, 1909, Reel 11, Images 659–75, J. H. Kellogg Papers, U-M.

35. A. S. Bloese Manuscript, pp. 21–43. Box 1, File 13. Schwarz, PhD thesis, p. 12.

36. Ronald Numbers, *Prophetess of Health: A Study of Ellen G. White* (Grand Rapids, MI: William G. Eerdmans, 2008, 3rd edition), pp. 276–90. Numbers provides a useful appendix of the physical and psychological experiences of Ellen G. White, "related in her own words," pp. 291–319.

37. Ibid., pp. 175–83; Harvey Green, *Fit for America: Health, Fitness, Sport* (New York: Pantheon, 1986), p. 135.

38. Carson, p. 28. See also Andrew F. Smith, *Eating History: Thirty Turning Points in the Making of American Cuisine* (New York: Columbia University Press, 2009), pp. 141–54.

39. Mose Velsor (Walt Whitman), "Manly Health and Training, with Off-Hand Hints Toward Their Conditions," ed. Zachary Turpin, *Walt Whitman Quarterly Review,* 2016; 33: 184–310. (Velsor was one of Whitman's favorite pen names.) Although Whitman thought meat was an important component of a healthy diet, he was, like John Harvey Kellogg's mother, an avid reader of Russell Trall's *Water Cure Journal.*

40. Carson, p. 31.

41. Robert. J. Gordon, *The Rise and Fall of American Growth* (Princeton: Princeton University Press, 2016), pp. 39–40.

42. Carson, pp. 28–42, quote is from p. 37. See also W. O. Huston, "The American Disease," *Columbus Medical Journal,* 1896; 16: 1–6; J. C. Whorton, *Crusaders for Fitness: The History of American Health Reformers* (Princeton: Princeton University Press, 1982); J. H. Baron and A. Sonnenberg, "Hospital Admissions for Peptic Ulcer and Indigestion in London and New York in the 19th and Early 20th Centuries," *Gut,* 2002; 50: 568–70.

43. Merritt G. Kellogg, "A Bit of Family History" (typescript dated July 6, 1914), Reel 1, Image 22 (page 6 in typescript), J. H. Kellogg Papers, U-M.

44. A. S. Bloese Manuscript, pp. 48–49, Box 1, File 13.

45. Carson, p. 37.

3.

NEW BROOMS SWEEP CLEAN

1. William Alexander Alcott (1798–1859) recommended diets of simply prepared vegetables and unleavened bread, accompanied only with water. He stressed the importance of personal and sexual cleanliness through daily baths and vows of abstinence. See William Alcott, *Vegetable Diet as Sanctioned by Medical Men and by Experience in All Ages* (Boston: Marsh, Capen and Lyon, 1838); William Alcott, *The Young Man's Guide* (Boston: Perkins and Marvin, 1838, 12th edition); William Alcott, *Tea and Coffee* (Boston: G. W. Light, 1839); William Alcott, *The Laws of Health; or the Sequel to "The House I Live In" Designed for Families and Schools* (Boston: John P. Jewett and Co., 1859).

2. Ronald Numbers, *Prophetess of Health: A Study of Ellen G. White* (Grand Rapids, MI: William B. Eerdmans, 2008, 3rd edition), pp. 95–126; Ellen G. White, *Health, or How to Live* (Battle Creek, MI: Steam Press, 1865).

3. A. S. Bloese Manuscript, pp. 67–68, Box 1, File 13.

4. Sylvester Graham, *A Treatise on Bread and Bread-Making* (Boston: Light and Stearns, 1837); Sylvester Graham, *A Lecture to Young Men on Chastity: Intended Also for the Serious Consideration of Parents and Guardians* (Boston: Light & Stearns, Crocker & Brewster, 1837); Sylvester Graham, *Lecture on Epidemic Diseases Generally and Particularly the Spasmodic Cholera* (Boston: David Campbell, 1838); Sylvester Graham, *Lectures on the Science of Human Life* (London: Horsell, Aldine Chambers, 1849). See also A. E. Foote, *A Defence of the Graham System of Living, or: Remarks on Diet and Regimen, Dedicated to the Rising Generation* (New York: W. Applegate, 1835). For several superb secondary accounts of Graham and his colleagues, see Richard H. Shryock, "Sylvester Graham and the Popular Health Movement, 1830–1870," *Mississippi Valley Historical Review,* 1931; 18(2): 172–83; H. E. Hoff and J. F. Fulton, "The Centenary of the First American Physiological Society Founded at Boston by William A. Alcott and Sylvester Graham," *Bulletin of the History of Medicine,* 1937; 5(8): 687–722; M. V. Naylor, "Sylvester Graham," *Annals of Medical History,* 1942; 4(3): 236–40; J. C. Whorton, *Crusaders for Fitness: The History of American Health Reformers* (Princeton: Princeton University Press, 1982), pp. 38–61; J. C. Whorton, *Nature Cures: The History of Alternative Medicine in America* (New York: Oxford University Press, 2002), pp. 85–89; Charles Rosenberg, "Piety and Social Action: Some Origins of the American Public Health Movement," in Charles E. Rosenberg, *No Other Gods: On Science and American Thought* (Baltimore: Johns Hopkins University Press, 1976), pp. 109–22; Jonathan Gunther Penner, "Public Speaking in the Health Reform Movement in the United States, 1863–1943," PhD thesis in Speech and Theatre, Purdue University, 1962; Kare Iacobbo and Michael Iacobbo, *Vegetarian America: A History* (Westwood, CT: Praeger, 2004), pp. 15–70 ("Sylvester Graham, Grahamism and Grahamites"), 71–88 ("The American Vegetarian Society"), and 89–106 ("The Water Cures, Seventh-day Adventists and the Civil War").

5. James Whorton, *Nature Cures: The History of Alternative Medicine in America* (New York: Oxford University Press, 2002), p. 88.

6. A. S. Bloese Manuscript, p. 61, Box 1, File 13.

7. Schwarz, *John Harvey Kellogg,* p. 27; *Catalogue of the Officers and Students of the*

Michigan State Normal College for 1870–1871 (Ypsilanti: Michigan State Normal College, 1871); *Catalogue of the Officers and Students of the Michigan State Normal College for 1871–1872 and Register for Students* (Ypsilanti: Michigan State Normal College, 1872), Burton Historical Collections, Detroit Public Library, Detroit, Michigan. This college is now known as Eastern Michigan University.

8. Schwarz, PhD thesis, pp. 17–22, 113–14.

9. Russell T. Trall, *The New Hydropathic Cookbook, with Recipes for Cooking on Hygienic Principles: Containing Also a Philosophical Exposition of the Relations of Food to Health* (New York: Fowler and Wells, 1857); Russell T. Trall, *The Hydropathic Encyclopedia: A System of Hydropathy and Hygiene in Eight Parts. Designed as a Guide to Families and Students and a Textbook for Physicians* (New York: Fowler and Wells, 1851). See also J. H. Kellogg, *Rational Hydropathy: A Manual of the Physiological and Therapeutic Effects of Hydriatic Procedure, and the Technique of Their Application in the Treatment of Disease, in Two Volumes,* 2nd edition (Philadelphia: F. A. Davis Company, Publishers, 1903).

10. At his father's insistence, Merritt (1832–1922) earned his bachelor's degree in 1851 at the abolitionist-minded and spiritually compatible Oberlin College (as did Smith Kellogg). He had attended Trall's school during the winter term of 1867 and was working as a missionary in California. In 1878, he directed a Rural Health Retreat in the Napa Valley and in 1893 he worked on missionary and health reform work in the South Pacific and Australia, where he established the Seventh-day Adventist Sanitarium in Sydney. He returned to California in 1903 when health problems forced him to retire. Numbers, *Prophetess of Health*, pp. 172–73; Merritt Kellogg, *The Bath: Its Use and Application* (Battle Creek, MI: Office of the Health Reformer, 1873); Merritt Kellogg, *The Hygienic Family Physician: A Complete Guide for the Preservation of Health, and the Treatment of Sick Without Medicine* (Battle Creek, MI: Office of the Health Reformer, 1874); Gary Land, "Kellogg, Merritt Gardner (1832–1922)," *Historical Dictionary of the Seventh-Day Adventists,* 2nd edition (Lanham, MD: Rowman & Littlefield, 2014), p. 159.

11. Numbers, *Prophetess of Health,* pp. 173–74. The witness Professor Numbers is referring to is the Elder John Loughborough in *The Great Second Advent Movement: Its Rise and Progress* (Washington, DC: Review and Herald Publishing Association, 1909), pp. 364–65. Dr. Numbers cautions his readers on the reliability of this witness. See also J. N. Andrews and Others, "Lectures by Dr. Trall," *Advent Review and Sabbath Herald,* May 26, 1868; 31: 360; Russell T. Trall, "Visit to Battle Creek, Michigan" and "Dress Reform Convention," *The Health Reformer,* September 1869; 4: 14 and 57.

12. Russell Trall, *An Essay on Tobacco-Using. Being a Philosophical Exposition on the Effects of Tobacco on the Human System* (Battle Creek, MI: Office of the Health Reformer, 1872), pp. 47–48. The italicized "prepense" is Trall's; the term "malice prepense" means deliberate malice.

13. Whorton, *Nature Cures,* p. 91.

14. Ibid.

15. Russell Trall, *Sexual Physiology and Hygiene, or The Mysteries of Man,* 28th edition (New York: Fowlers and Wells, 1881), pp. xi, 201, 244–45, 248, 257; Whorton, *Nature Cures,* pp. 93–94.

16. Trall, *Sexual Physiology and Hygiene,* pp. 244–45.

17. Schwarz, *John Harvey Kellogg,* pp. 27–28.

18. Merritt G. Kellogg, Dictated Memories to Clara K. Butler, October 12, 1916, Reel 1, Images 132–39 (page 3 of the typescript), J. H. Kellogg Papers, U-M.

19. Ibid., pp. 6–7 of the typescript.

20. Ibid., p. 2 of the typescript; A. S. Bloese Manuscript, p. 55, Box 1, File 13.

21. Merritt G. Kellogg, Dictated Memories to Clara K. Butler, October 12, 1916, p. 5 of the typescript; William H. Brock, *Justus von Liebig: The Chemical Gatekeeper* (New York: Cambridge University Press, 2002), pp. 72–93, 215–49.

22. Numbers, *Prophetess of Health,* pp. 176–77; Schwarz, *John Harvey Kellogg,* pp. 28–29, 91.

23. Merritt G. Kellogg, Dictated Memories to Clara K. Butler, October 12, 1916, quote appears on Images 135–36, or pp. 4–5 of the manuscript copy.

24. Numbers, *Prophetess of Health,* p. 177.

25. James White, "She Sleeps in Jesus," *Advent Review and Sabbath Herald,* March 11, 1880; 55(11): 169. Typhoid pneumonia is an infection of the lungs caused by the same bacillus, *Salmonella typhii,* that causes typhoid fever. "Typhoid Pneumonia," *Journal of the AMA,* 1901; 37(20): 1322.

26. *15th Census of the United States: 1930, Volume 1: Population. Number and Distribution of Inhabitants* (Washington, DC: Government Printing Office, 1931). The 1870 population data for Battle Creek and Ann Arbor appears on page 512. The Pioneer Society, *History of Washtenaw County, Michigan: Together with Sketches of its Cities, Villages and Townships, Educational, Religious, Civil, Military and Political History; Portraits of Prominent Persons and Biographies of Representative Citizens* (Chicago: Chas. C. Chapman & Co., 1881); O. W. Stephenson, *Ann Arbor: The First Hundred Years* (Ann Arbor: Ann Arbor Chamber of Commerce/Alumni Press of the University of Michigan, 1927).

27. By 1877, however, the University of Michigan could no longer ignore the glaring deficits in their lesson plans and the Regents ordered the Medical School to increase its annual session from two six-month semesters to two terms lasting nine months each. In 1880, a new three-year, graded course introduced a sequence of basic science courses, followed by pathology and therapeutics, and then clinical work; and in 1890 a four-year calendar. Abraham Flexner, *A Report on Medical Education in the United States and Canada: A Report to the Carnegie Foundation for the Advancement of Teaching,* Bulletin No. 4 (New York: Carnegie Foundation, 1910); Horace W. Davenport, *Not Just Any Medical School: The Science, Practice and Teaching of Medicine at the University of Michigan, 1850–1941* (Ann Arbor: University of Michigan Press, 1999), pp. 1–20.

28. "University of Michigan Department of Medicine and Surgery. Examination of Candidates for Admission. 6th October, 1875" and "University of Michigan Department of Medicine and Surgery. Examination of Candidates for Admission. September 30, 1876," Michigan Historical Collections, Bentley Historical Library, University of Michigan.

29. *Calendar of the University of Michigan for 1876–77* (Ann Arbor: Published by the University, 1873), p. 100. Michigan Historical Collections, Bentley Historical Library, University of Michigan, Ann Arbor, Michigan.

30. Steward's Ledger of Medical Students, for 1873–1874, University of Michigan, Department of Medicine and Surgery, Michigan Historical Collections, Bentley Historical Library, University of Michigan, Ann Arbor, Michigan.

31. Victor C. Vaughan, *A Doctor's Memories* (Indianapolis: Bobbs-Merrill Co., 1926), pp. 197–98.

32. William Osler, "Books and Men," *Aequanimitas with Other Addresses to Medical Students, Nurses and Practitioners of Medicine* (Philadelphia: P. Blakiston's Son and Company, 1904), pp. 217–25, quote is from p. 220; Davenport, *Not Just Any Medi-*

cal School, pp. 1–20; Wilfred B. Shaw, ed., "The Medical School and the University Hospital," *The University of Michigan: An Encyclopedic Survey,* Volume 2 (Ann Arbor: University of Michigan Press, 1951), pp. 773–1015.

33. "Practice of Surgery," Notebook for 1873–1874, J. H. Kellogg, University of Michigan Medical School Notes, Box 16, J. H. Kellogg Papers, U-M.

34. Vaughan, *A Doctor's Memories,* p. 202.

35. In the late 1880s, Dr. Maclean tried to block the medical school's request to the governor of Michigan for a university hospital in Ann Arbor, much to Dean Vaughan's chagrin. The surgeon was either forced to resign or was fired from the Medical School in 1889. He then focused on his surgical practice in Detroit and explained to others that he left because he could not keep his fingers nimble enough in a village with so few patients. Davenport, *Not Just Any Medical School,* pp. 19–22.

36. Vaughan, *A Doctor's Memories,* pp. 184–212; Rueben Peterson, "Edward Swift Dunster: A Biographical Sketch," *The Michigan Alumnus,* June 1905, pp. 417–25. For a history of the Long Island College Hospital, see Jack E. Termine, *SUNY Downstate Medical Center* (Mount Pleasant, SC: Arcadia, 2000), pp. 9–48. For a history of science as practiced on Long Island, see Arnold H. Eggerth, *The History of the Hoagland Laboratory* (Brooklyn: Long Island College Hospital, 1960).

37. Sanitarium Minutes, May 11, June 18, August 4, 1873; August 17, 23, 24, 30, 1874; Collection 234, Box 4, File 5, Center for Adventist Research.

38. A. S. Bloese Manuscript, p. 91, Box 1, File 13.

39. *Eagle Heights: The W. K. Kellogg Manor* (Hickory Corners, MI: Michigan State University/Kellogg Biological Station, 2015), p. 11.

40. Powell, pp. 24–25.

41. Daniel Drake, *Malaria in the Interior Valley of North America. A selection by Norman D. Levine from a systematic treatise, historical, etiological, and practical, on the principal diseases of the interior valley of North America, as they appear in the Caucasian, African, Indian, and Esquimaux varieties of its population* (Urbana: University of Illinois Press, 1964); E. H. Ackerknecht, *Malaria in the Upper Mississippi Valley, 1760–1900* (Baltimore: Johns Hopkins University Press, 1945); Sok Chul Hong, "The Burden of Early Exposure to Malaria in the United States, 1850–1860: Malnutrition and Immune Disorders," *Journal of Economic History,* December 2007; 67(4): 1001–35.

42. Powell, p. 29.

43. Williamson Jr., *An Intimate Glimpse,* p. 7.

44. Powell, p. 26.

45. Ibid., p. 33; Steven Watts, *The People's Tycoon: Henry Ford and the American Century* (New York: Alfred A. Knopf, 2005), pp. 10–13.

46. Powell, p. 32.

47. Ibid., p. 220.

48. Ibid., p. 130. The friend was Arch Shaw.

49. Ibid., p. 32.

50. Ibid., p. 37.

51. The foundation funded two institutes at the University of Michigan, the W. K. Kellogg Foundation Institute for Graduate and Postgraduate Dentistry (1938) and the W. K. Kellogg Eye Center (1976).

52. See David Nasaw, *Children of the City: At Work and at Play* (New York: Anchor, 2012).

53. W. K. Kellogg, "In His Own Words," in "A Battle Creek Celebration: W. K. Kellogg 150 Years," *Scene Magazine,* 1997; 34(1): 14–15, quote is from p. 15.

54. Quote is from Powell, p. 24; Carson, p. 89.
55. Powell, pp. 34–35.

4.

LONG-DISTANCE LEARNING

1. Austin Flint, *A Treatise on the Principles and Practice of Medicine Designed for the Use of Practitioners and Students of Medicine* (Philadelphia: Henry C. Lea, 1873, 4th Edition, Carefully Revised). I used the 4th edition as a source while composing this chapter because it best corresponds with the medicine that was taught at Bellevue Hospital Medical College during the years John Harvey Kellogg went to school there. After Flint's death in 1886, Dr. Frederick P. Henry of the Women's Medical College of Philadelphia "thoroughly revised" and authored a 7th edition of the textbook, which was published by Lea Brothers of Philadelphia in 1894; see also Austin Flint, *A Practical Treatise on the Diagnosis, Pathology and Treatment of Diseases of the Heart* (Philadelphia: Blanchard and Lea, 1859).

2. *Seventeenth Annual Announcement of the Bellevue Hospital Medical College, Sessions of 1877–1878, with the Annual Catalogue for 1876–77*, p. 3, Lillian and Clarence de la Chapelle Medical Archives, New York University Health Sciences Libraries, New York, N.Y. See also Frederick A. Castle, *Second Decennial Catalogue of the Trustees, Faculty, Officers and of the Alumni of the Bellevue Hospital Medical College of the City of New York, 1861–1881* (New York: Alumni Association of the Bellevue Hospital Medical College, 1884), pp. 7–51.

3. *Seventeenth Annual Announcement of the Bellevue Hospital Medical College, Sessions of 1877–1878, with the Annual Catalogue for 1876–77*, p. 15.

4. "Bellevue Medical College Matriculation Ticket, 1875–1876," made out to Ezra W. Homiston and endorsed by Isaac E. Taylor, President, and Austin Flint, Secretary, Collections of the University of Michigan Center for the History of Medicine.

5. The New York City sewage system would not be unified, let alone built upon modern sanitary methods, until the 1870s during the reign of the Tammany Hall boss, William Marcy Tweed. Edwin G. Burrows and Mike Wallace, *Gotham: A History of New York City to 1898* (New York: Oxford University Press, 1999), pp. 930–31, 991; George E. Waring Jr., *Street-cleaning and the Disposal of a City's Wastes* (New York: Doubleday and McClure Co., 1897).

6. Much of this section is drawn from my book: Howard Markel, *An Anatomy of Addiction: Sigmund Freud, William Halsted and the Miracle Drug Cocaine* (New York: Pantheon, 2011), pp. 38–43; H. M. Silver, "Surgery in Bellevue Hospital Fifty Years Ago," *Medical Journal and Record*, 1924; 120: 551–57; Robert J. Carlisle, ed., *An Account of Bellevue Hospital with a Catalogue of the Medical and Surgical Staff from 1736 to 1894* (New York: Society of the Alumni of Bellevue Hospital, 1893); Page Cooper, *The Bellevue Story* (New York: Thomas Y. Crowell, 1948); Salvatore R. Cutolo, with Arthur and Barbara Gelb, *This Hospital Is My Home: The Story of Bellevue* (London: Victor Gollancz, 1956); John Starr, *Hospital City: The Story of the Men and Women of Bellevue Hospital* (New York: Crown, 1957); David Oshinsky, *Bellevue: Three Centuries of Medicare and Mayhem at America's Most Storied Hospital* (New York: Doubleday, 2016).

7. *Report of the Special Committee of the Medical Board of the Bellevue Hospital on Erysipelas and Pyaemia* (New York: Bellevue Press, Department of Public Charities and Correction of the City of New York, 1872).

8. This quote is from the Old Testament, Book of Amos, 4:12. See "The Bellevue of Today: Sights in the Wards of the Great Charity Hospital," *New York Times,* November 23, 1884, p. 6; W. H. Rideing, "Hospital Life in New York," *Harper's New Monthly Magazine,* July 1878; 57: 171–89; J. W. Roosevelt, "In the Hospital," *Scribner's Magazine,* October 1894; 16(4): 472–86; A. B. Ward, "Hospital Life," *Scribner's Magazine,* June 1888; 3(6): 697–716; A. B. Ward, "The Invalid's World: The Doctor, the Nurse, the Visitor," *Scribner's Magazine,* January 1889; 5(1): 58–73; H. M. Silver, "Surgery in Bellevue Hospital Fifty Years Ago," *Medical Journal and Record,* 1924; 120: 551–57; Helen Campbell, "Hospital Life in New York, Chapter 13," *Darkness and Daylight, or, Lights and Shadows of New York Life: A Pictorial Record* (Hartford, CT: Hartford Publishing Co., 1898), pp. 279–304; C. F. Gardiner, "Getting a Medical Education in New York City in the Eighteen-Seventies," *American Bookman,* 1955; 8(2): 3–12.

9. Charles E. Rosenberg, *The Care of Strangers: The Rise of America's Hospital System* (New York: Basic Books, 1987); David Rosner, *A Once Charitable Enterprise: Hospitals and Health Care in Brooklyn and New York, 1885–1915* (New York: Cambridge University Press, 1982).

10. Rosner, *A Once Charitable Enterprise;* Rosenberg, *The Care of Strangers,* p. 36; Howard Markel, "When Hospitals Kept Children from Parents," *New York Times,* January 1, 2008, p. F6.

11. Austin Flint adopted the use of the binaural (two ears) stethoscope in 1866 but prior to that he preferred Laënnec's original monoaural model. Howard Markel, "The Stethoscope and the Art of Listening," *New England Journal of Medicine* 2006; 354(6): 551–53. See also P. J. Bishop, "Evolution of the Stethoscope," *Journal of the Royal Society of Medicine* 1980; 73: 448–56; L. T. H. Laënnec, *A Treatise on the Diseases of the Chest,* J. Forbes, translator (London: Underwood, 1821); Henry E. Sigerist, *The Great Doctors: A Biographical History of Medicine* (New York: W. W. Norton, 1933), pp. 283–90; Sherwin B. Nuland, *Doctors: The Biography of Medicine* (New York: Vintage, 1995), pp. 200–37; Jacalyn Duffin, *To See with a Better Eye: A Life of R. T. H. Laennec* (Princeton: Princeton University Press, 1988).

12. Samuel D. Gross, *Autobiography of Samuel D. Gross with Sketches of His Contemporaries in Two Volumes* (Philadelphia: George Barric, 1887), 2: 161–62.

13. In 1882, for example, after reading the news that the German bacteriologist Robert Koch had proven the tubercle bacillus to be the cause of the "white plague," Flint ran down the street and up the stairs into the brownstone where William Henry Welch made his home. Welch was a pathologist and bacteriologist at Bellevue who in 1884 moved to Baltimore where he helped found and direct the Johns Hopkins Hospital and Medical School. Welch was still slumbering in his long nightshirt and nightcap when Dr. Flint was said to have burst through the doors of his bedchamber. Flint shook the younger man awake with the joyful squeals, "I knew it! I knew it!" See Alfred S. Evans, "Austin Flint and His Contributions to Medicine," *Bulletin of the History of Medicine* 958; 32: 224–41; quote is from page 238; H. R. M. Landis, "Austin Flint: His Contributions to the Art of Physical Diagnosis and the Study of Tuberculosis," *Bulletin of the Johns Hopkins Hospital* 1912; 23: 182–86. See also Austin Flint, "Logical Proof of the Contagiousness and Non-Contagiousness of Diseases," *New York Medical Journal* 1874; 19: 113–33; Austin Flint, *Medicine of the Future: An Address Prepared for the Annual Meeting of the British Medical Association in 1886* (New York: D. Appleton and Co., 1886); Austin Flint, *Medical Ethics and Etiquette: The Code of Ethics Adopted by the American Medical Association* (New York: D. Appleton and Co., 1883).

14. Flint, *Medicine of the Future.*

15. On February 23, 1875, John received a certificate for his taking twenty-five private lessons on physical diagnosis under Flint and Janeway. On April 7, 1875, he received a similar certificate for twenty-five private lessons in microscopy and normal and pathological histology under Janeway and J. W. S. Arnold at the Bellevue Hospital Laboratory. Scrapbook No. 1, Diploma Collection, J. H. Kellogg Papers, U-M. Dr. Janeway was also a learned scholar of anatomy and *materia medica* and, from 1875 to 1881, served as New York City's commissioner of health. See "Edward Gamaliel Janeway," in Dumas Malone, ed., *Dictionary of American Biography*, Volume 9 (New York: Charles Scribner's Sons, 1932), pp. 607–8; Schwarz, *John Harvey Kellogg*, p. 31.

16. *Seventeenth Annual Announcement of the Bellevue Hospital Medical College. Sessions of 1877–1878, with the Annual Catalogue for 1876–1877*, pp. 6–7, Collections of the University of Michigan Center for the History of Medicine.

17. Schwarz, PhD thesis, pp. 31–32; Schwarz, *John Harvey Kellogg*, pp. 31–33.

18. *Seventeenth Annual Announcement of the Bellevue Hospital Medical College. Sessions of 1877–1878, with the Annual Catalogue for 1876–1877*, p. 7, Collections of the University of Michigan Center for the History of Medicine. John Harvey Kellogg also studied under Lewis Sayre, an orthopedic surgeon, early proponent of the germ theory of disease, and advocate of compulsory vaccination; and the pediatrician Job Lewis Smith, who is credited with writing one of the first American textbooks on the diseases of childhood. Lewis A. Sayre, *Lectures on Orthopedic Surgery and Diseases of the Joints: Delivered at Bellevue Hospital Medical College During the Winter Session, 1874–1875* (New York: William Wood and Co., 1876); "Lewis A. Sayre," in Dumas Malone, ed., *Dictionary of American Biography*, Volume 16 (New York: Charles Scribner's Sons, 1935), pp. 403–4; "Job Lewis Smith," in Dumas Malone, ed., *Dictionary of American Biography*, Volume 17 (New York: Charles Scribner's Sons, 1935), pp. 293–94; J. Lewis Smith, *A Treatise on the Diseases of Infancy and Childhood* (Philadelphia: Henry C. Lea, 1869).

19. Proceedings of Societies, American Public Health Association, 3rd Annual Meeting (3rd Day, Morning Session); Frederic R. Sturgis, "How Does Syphilis Affect Public Health?," *Medical Times and Register*, November 28, 1874; 5: 140; William W. Sanger, *The History of Prostitution: Its Extent, Causes and Effects Throughout the World* (New York: The Medical Publishing Co., 1913), p. 686.

20. Venereal Diseases, March 13, 1874, Medical School Notes, Images 196–206, quote is from Reel 38, Image 198, J. H. Kellogg Papers, U-M.

21. See Fordyce Barker, *The Puerperal Diseases: Clinical Lectures Delivered at Bellevue Hospital* (New York: D. Appleton and Co., 1874, 3rd edition), Preface, pp. iii–v, pp. 464–67, 516; John H. Kellogg's notes, "Puerperal Fever, February 25, 1874," Medical School Notes, Reel 38, Images 406–13, J. H. Kellogg Papers, U-M; Sherwin B. Nuland, *The Doctors' Plague: Germs, Childbed Fever and the Strange Story of Ignac Semmelweis* (New York: W. W. Norton, 2004); Irvine Loudon, *The Tragedy of Childbed Fever* (Oxford: Oxford University Press, 2000); Oliver Wendell Holmes Sr., "The Contagiousness of Puerperal Fever," in *Medical Essays, 1842–1882* (Boston: Houghton, Mifflin Co., 1883, 2nd edition), pp. 103–72; Ignac Semmelwers (translated by K. Codell Carter), *The Etiology, Concept and Prophylaxis of Childhood Fever* (Madison, WI: The University of Wisconsin, 1983).

22. Perhaps even more inspiring to John was Smith's success as the popular author of *The City That Was*, in which Smith proposed several important municipal, state, and national regulations related to public health. See "Stephen Smith," in Malone, ed., *Dictionary of American Biography*, Volume 17, pp. 348–49; Stephen Smith, *The*

City That Was (New York: Frank Allaban, 1911); typescript of "The Battle Creek Idea," Stereo-opticon Lecture at the Sanitarium Parlor, September 15, 1910, Reel 12, Images 546–50, J. H. Kellogg Papers, U-M.

23. Carson, p. 93; Howard Markel, *Quarantine! East European Jewish Immigrants and the New York City Epidemics of 1892* (Baltimore: Johns Hopkins University Press, 1997).

24. Medical School Notes, Reel 38, Images 192–317, 318–405, J. H. Kellogg Papers, U-M.

25. Ibid., Reel 38, Images 812–43.

26. Carson, p. 118; Schwarz, PhD thesis, pp. 33–34.

27. Testimony of J. H. Kellogg, *Kellogg v. Kellogg, State of Michigan Supreme Court Record*, Volume 2, p. 362, J. H. Kellogg Papers, Michigan State University Archives, East Lansing, Michigan (hereinafter J. H. Kellogg Papers, MSU); Schwarz, PhD thesis, p. 34.

28. Lawrence Veiller, "Tenement House Reform in New York City, 1834–1900," in Robert W. DeForest and Lawrence Veiller, *The Tenement House Problem, Including the Report of the New York State Tenement House Commission of 1900* (New York: The Macmillan Co., 1903), pp. 71–118, quote is from p. 94. See also Richard Planz, *A History of Housing in New York City: Dwelling Type and Social Change in the American Metropolis* (New York: Columbia University Press, 1990), pp. 1–20. In his *Model Housing Law*, first published in 1914, Lawrence Veiller urged legislating the removal and disinfecting of all privy vaults in the city. Lawrence Veiller, *A Model Housing Law* (New York: Russell Sage Foundation, 1920, revised edition), pp. 246–48.

29. Veiller, "Tenement House Reform in New York City, 1834–1900," p. 78; C. A. Mohr, "Tenement Evils as Seen by an Inspector," in DeForest and Veiller, *The Tenement House Problem*, pp. 421–43, quote is from p. 434.

30. Schwarz, PhD thesis, p. 34; *Seventeenth Annual Announcement of the Bellevue Hospital Medical College. Sessions of 1877–1878, with the Annual Catalogue for 1876–1877*, pp. 16–18.

31. J. H. Kellogg, "What Is Disease?," MD thesis for Graduation, Bellevue Hospital Medical College, February 14, 1875, Reel 6, Images 269–284, "Lectures, Speeches and Related, 1875–1943," J. H. Kellogg Papers, U-M.

32. *Seventeenth Annual Announcement of the Bellevue Hospital Medical College. Sessions of 1877–1878, with the Annual Catalogue for 1876–1877*, p. 16.

33. Ibid., pp. 16–17. For a review of these "irregular" systems of medicine, see Norman Gevitz, ed., *Other Healers: Unorthodox Medicine in America* (Baltimore: Johns Hopkins University Press, 1988); John S. Haller Jr., *Medical Protestants: The Eclectics in American Medicine, 1825–1939* (Carbondale and Edwardsville: Southern Illinois University Press, 1994).

34. Schwarz, *John Harvey Kellogg*, p. 32.

35. The same critic found "every other aspect" of the building—its overall design and architecture, the decor and the too closely spaced seats—to be a "decided failure." "Opening of the Academy of Music," *New York Times*, October 3, 1854.

36. Henry E. Krehbiel, *The Philharmonic Society of New York: A Memorial Published on the Occasion of the Fiftieth Anniversary of the Founding of the Philharmonic Society, April, 1892, by the Society* (New York: Novello, Ewer & Co., 1892); Howard Shanet, Henry Edward Krehbiel, James Huneker, and John Erskine, *Early Histories of the New York Philharmonic* (New York: DaCapo, 1979); Howard Shanet, *Philharmonic: A His-*

tory of New York's Orchestra (Garden City, NY: Doubleday, 1975); H. Wiley Hitchcock and Joseph Horowitz, *Grove Music Online* (New York: Oxford University Press, April 2015).

37. Graduating Exercises: Bellevue Medical College, Fourteenth Annual Commencement, Order of Exercises, List of the Graduates and Prizes, Judge Brady's Address, *New York Times,* February 26, 1875; "Bellevue Hospital Medical College Commencement," *Medical Record,* 1875; 10: 175–76.

38. Schwarz, *John Harvey Kellogg,* p. 33.

39. Schwarz, PhD thesis, p. 36.

40. Ibid., p. 37.

41. Ibid., p. 37, citing Certificate of Instruction signed by George M. Beard, April 5, 1875, Scrapbook No. 1, J. H. Kellogg Papers, U-M.

42. Dr. Beard testified that Guiteau was a "hereditary monomaniac" in a then novel effort to prove the assassin "not guilty by reason of insanity." C. E. Rosenberg, *The Trial of the Assassin Guiteau* (Chicago: University of Chicago Press, 1968), p. 227. For a popular account of the trial, see Candice Millard, *Destiny of the Republic: A Tale of Madness, Medicine and the Murder of a President* (New York: Doubleday, 2011).

43. Charles M. Beard, *American Nervousness: Its Causes and Consequences. A Supplement to Nervous Exhaustion* (New York: G. P. Putnam's Sons, 1881), quotes are from pp. 96, 176; George M. Beard, "Neurasthenia or Nervous Exhaustion," *Boston Medical and Surgical Journal* 80 (1869): 217–21; George M. Beard, *A Practical Treatise on Nervous Exhaustion (Neurasthenia): Its Symptoms, Nature, Sequences, Treatment* (New York: William Wood and Co., 1880). See also Tom Lutz, *American Nervousness, 1903: An Anecdotal History* (Ithaca, NY: Cornell University Press, 1991), pp. 1–30; H. A. Bunker, "From Beard to Freud: A Brief History of the Concept of Neurasthenia," *Medical Review of Reviews,* 1930; 36: 108–14; Charles E. Rosenberg, "The Place of George Miller Beard in American Psychiatry," *Bulletin of the History of Medicine,* 1962; 36: 245–59; Edward Shorter, *A History of Psychiatry: From the Era of the Asylum to the Age of Prozac* (New York: John Wiley & Sons, 1997), pp. 129–30; Harvey Green, *Fit for America: Health, Fitness, and American Society* (New York: Pantheon, 1986), pp. 137–66; F. G. Gosling, *Before Freud: Neurasthenia and the American Medical Community, 1870–1910* (Urbana: University of Illinois Press, 1987).

44. Charles E. Rosenberg, "George M. Beard and American Nervousness," in Charles E. Rosenberg, *No Other Gods: On Science and American Social Thought* (Baltimore: Johns Hopkins University Press, 1978), pp. 98–108, quote is from p. 108.

45. George M. Beard and A. D. Rockwell, *The Medical Uses of Electricity* (New York: William Wood and Co., 1867). For a useful synopsis of the medical uses of electricity during this period, see Green, *Fit for America,* pp. 167–80.

46. John subsequently invented shocking devices that he marketed, sold, and employed on his patients at the Battle Creek Sanitarium. J. H. Kellogg, *Light Therapeutics; a Practical Manual of Phototherapy for the Student and the Practitioner, with Special Reference to the Incandescent Electric-Light Bath* (Battle Creek, MI: The Good Health Publishing Co., 1910).

47. The Seventh-day Adventist Battle Creek College was founded in 1874, primarily as a Christian-based school for young Adventist students. In 1901, after Ellen White began making predictions of the destruction of sinful Battle Creek, it was moved to Berrien Springs, Michigan, as the Emmanuel Missionary College and later Andrews University. John ran a smaller-scaled Battle Creek College from 1902 to 1938. It supported itself with tuition dollars, grants from the Race Betterment Foundation, the

proceeds of his food companies, and occasional gifts from donors. See *The Battle Creek Schools: Professional, Academic, Biblical, Technical, Industrial. Announcement for 1905–1908. Incorporated Under the Statutes of the States of Michigan and Illinois* (Battle Creek, MI: Battle Creek Schools, 1905).

48. Schwarz, *John Harvey Kellogg,* pp. 60–61.

49. J. S. Ingram, *The Centennial Exposition Described and Illustrated* (Philadelphia: Hubbard Brothers, Publishers, 1876), p. 5.

50. "Healds' Hygeian Home of Wilmington, Delaware in successful operation since January 1, 1871, with 500 patients from 35 States, Territories and the Canadas. Terms Reduced for 1875" (advertisement), *The Herald of Health Devoted to the Culture of Body and Mind* (New York: Wood and Holbrook, 1875), Volume 59, p. 232.

51. See, for example, Stephen Smith, "Alcohol: Its Nature and Effects," in *Centennial Temperance Volume: A Memorial of the International Temperance Conference Held in Philadelphia, June, 1876* (New York: National Temperance Society and Publication House, 1877), pp. 251–57.

52. For excellent guides of the exhibits that J. H. Kellogg saw in 1876, see U.S. Centennial Commission, *International Exhibition, 1876: Official Catalogue, Complete in One Volume* (Philadelphia: John R. Nagle and Co., 1876), pp. 92 (Special Buildings), 120, 129 (Department II, Manufacturers), 255 (Classification, Department III, Science and Education); 67, 284–85 (U.S. Government Building); Carson, pp. 94–95; *A Facsimile of Frank Leslie's Illustrated Historical Register of the Centennial Exposition of 1876* (New York: Paddington Press/Two Continents Publishing Group, 1974), pp. 154, 236, 239, 319; Robert C. Post, *1876: A Centennial Exhibition* (Washington, DC: National Museum of History and Technology, Smithsonian Institution, 1976), pp. 75–100, 153–57. For an engaging study on health exhibits at the world's fairs of this era, see Julie K. Brown, *Health and Medicine on Display: International Exhibitions in the United States, 1876–1904* (Cambridge: MIT Press, 2009), pp. 11–41.

53. Charles M. Gilmore, *The Herald Guide Book and Directory to the Centennial Exposition* (Philadelphia: Herald Guide Books, 1876), p. 8.

54. Howard Markel, "From Eakins's Canvas, 1800s Version of Medical Docudrama," *New York Times,* August 13, 2002, p. D5.

55. James D. McCabe, *The Illustrated History of the Centennial Exhibition* (Philadelphia: The National Publishing Co., 1876), p. 585.

56. The Zander Institute, *Mechanical Exercise, A Means of Cure: Being a Description of the Zander Institute, London, Its History, Appliances, Scope and Object* (London: J. & A. Churchill, 1884), p. 5.

57. J. H. Kellogg, "A Hygienist Abroad," *Good Health,* August 1883, pp. 246–49. John visited Europe again in 1899, 1907, 1911.

58. Powell, p. 38. Ann Janette died at the age of sixty-nine in 1893 of heart failure. In 1932, Will endowed a school in her name. It was designed to teach disabled children right alongside other children, a pioneering educational advance now called "mainstreaming" but at the time was anything but mainstream in the American educational system.

59. Ibid., pp. 37–38.

60. Ibid., p. 37.

61. Carson, p. 90.

62. Ibid., p. 91; Powell, p. 35.

63. Carson, p. 91.

64. Powell, p. 40.

65. Will Kellogg's diary for this period is excerpted and quoted in ibid., pp. 41–45.

66. Powell, pp. 41–42.

67. Ibid., p. 42.

68. Will's grandson Norman Williamson Jr. reported, "his teeth were very bad. He wrote of frequent toothaches and subsequent extractions. By the time he got to Battle Creek, he had lost all of his molars. He was to depend on store teeth [dentures] for most of the seventy odd years remaining in his life." Williamson Jr., *An Intimate Glimpse*, p. 11.

69. Powell, p. 42.

70. Ibid., p. 43.

71. Ibid.

72. Ibid., p. 44.

73. Ibid., pp. 44–45.

74. Ibid., p. 43.

75. Williamson Jr., *An Intimate Glimpse*, p. 155.

76. Powell, p. 43.

77. Ibid., p. 45.

78. Ibid., p. 47.

79. Ibid., p. 46. Will's "graduation certificate" is reproduced in Powell's book.

80. Ibid., p. 69.

81. Williamson Jr., *An Intimate Glimpse*, p. 14.

82. Powell, p. 259.

83. Ibid., pp. 265–66. By the 1930s, Richards's show, *The Voice of Prophecy*, broadcast his evangelism in thirty-six languages on more than 1,100 stations.

84. Ibid., p. 265.

85. Brian Wilson, *Dr. John Harvey Kellogg and the Religion of Biologic Living* (Bloomington: Indiana University Press, 2014), p. 132.

5.

BUILDING THE SAN

1. Map of the New York Central and Hudson River Railroad, "Water Level Route," Map Collections of the University of Michigan Libraries; T. J. Stiles, *The First Tycoon: The Epic Life of Cornelius Vanderbilt* (New York: Vintage, 2010), p. 334; New York Central and Hudson River Railroad Company, *Railway Timetable* (New York: American Bank Note Co., 1885).

2. Charles MacIvor, "The Lord's Physician," Chapter 11, "Dr. Kellogg—a Wise Decision," p. 1, Charles MacIvor Collection, No. 251, Box 10, File 12, Chapters 11–20, Center for Adventist Research.

3. The Friday Sabbath service was actually held on June 5, 1867, but because the sun had already set, the new day was considered to have begun, in keeping with the Hebrew method of dating events; hence, in many Adventist writings, both dates for the vision are given, Friday the 5th and Saturday the 6th. Since Ellen White states it was the 6th, in her recollection of the event for the Adventist newspaper, I used the latter. See Ellen White, "Questions and Answers," *Advent Review and Sabbath Herald*, October 8, 1867; 30(17): 260–61. See also *Testimonies for the Church*, Volume 1, pp. 485–95, 552, 553–67; www.gilead.net/egw/books/testimonies/Testimonies_for_the_Church_Volume

_One/; MacIvor, "The Lord's Physician," Chapter 12 ("A Noble Experiment"), Charles MacIvor Collection, No. 251, Box 10, File 12, Chapters 11–20, Center for Adventist Research. And see also E. G. White, *Christian Temperance and Bible Hygiene* (Battle Creek, MI: Good Health Publishing Co., 1890), p. 219; Harold M. Walton and Kathryn J. Nelson, *Historical Sketches of the Medical Work of the Seventh-Day Adventists* (Washington, DC: Review and Herald Publishing Association, 1948), p. 31; John Skrzypaszek, "The Heart of the Seventh-day Adventist Health Message," *Ministry: The International Journal for Pastors,* December 2014, accessed January 21, 2016, at https://www.ministrymagazine.org/archive/2014/12/.

4. Ellen G. White, *Testimonies,* Volume 1, No. 87, pp. 485–95. See also Nos. 88, 89, 90, 91, 100, 101 102, 112, 117, accessed June 23, 2015 at www.gilead.net/egw/books/testimonies/Testimonies_for_the_Church_Volume_One/.

(John Harvey Kellogg used May 20, 1866, as the founding date of the San and in 1916 held a fiftieth "Golden Jubilee" anniversary convocation in Battle Creek to commemorate the event.)

5. Ronald Numbers, *Prophetess of Health: A Study of Ellen G. White* (Grand Rapids, MI: William B. Eerdmans, 2008, 3rd edition), p. 156; D. E. Robinson, *The Story of Our Health Message* (Nashville: Southern Publishing Association, 1965 revised and enlarged edition), pp. 144–52; The Western Health Reform Institute, *Advent Review and Sabbath Herald,* June 19, 1866; 28(3): 24; J. N. Loughborough, "Report from J. N. Loughborough," *Advent Review and Sabbath Herald,* September 11, 1866; 28(15): 117.

6. Schwarz, *John Harvey Kellogg,* pp. 59–61; Western Health Reform Institute/Battle Creek Sanitarium Minutes for May 17, July 22, 1867; September 11, 1867; October 1 and 11, 1880, Center for Adventist Research; *Battle Creek Daily Journal,* September 10, 1872, p. 1.

7. Charles MacIvor, "The Lord's Physician," Chapter 12, "A Noble Experiment," p. 2, Charles MacIvor Collection, No. 251, Box 10, File 12, Chapters 11–20, Center for Adventist Research; J. N. Loughborough, *Rise and Progress of the Seventh-Day Adventists* (Battle Creek, MI: Herald and Review Publishing Co, 1892), p. 262.

8. Charles MacIvor, "The Lord's Physician," Chapter 12, "A Noble Experiment," p. 3, Charles MacIvor Collection, No. 251, Box 10, File 12, Chapters 11–20, Center for Adventist Research.

9. Ellen G. White, *Testimonies,* Volume 3, pp. 165–85, quote is from p. 181, accessed June 24, 2015, at www.gilead.net/egw/books/testimonies/Testimonies_for_the_Church_Volume_Three/index.htm?http&url=www.gilead.net/egw/books/testimonies/Testimonies_for_the_Church_Volume_Three/1_THE_TIMES_OF_VOLUME_THREE.htm.

10. Schwarz, *John Harvey Kellogg,* pp. 59–61; Carson, pp. 69–70, 82–83.

11. Ellen G. White, *Testimonies,* Volume 3, pp. 165–85, quote is from p. 175, accessed June 24, 2015, at: http://www.gilead.net/egw/books/testimonies/Testimonies_for_the_Church_Volume_Three/index.htm?http&url=www.gilead.net/egw/books/testimonies/Testimonies_for_the_Church_Volume_Three/1_THE_TIMES_OF_VOLUME_THREE.htm.

12. James White, "Eight Weeks in Battle Creek," *Advent Review and Sabbath Herald,* June 1, 1876; 47(22): 172.

13. J. H. Kellogg, The American Medical Missionary College, *Medical Missionary,* October 1895; 5: 291.

14. Numbers, *Prophetess of Health,* p. 183.

15. Charles MacIvor, "The Lord's Physician," Chapter 12, "A Noble Experiment," pp. 7–8, Charles MacIvor Collection, No. 251, Box 10, File 12, Chapters 11–20, Center for Adventist Research.

16. *Battle Creek Enquirer and Evening News,* April 21, 1921, p. 1.

17. A. S. Bloese Manuscript, p. 102a; Box 1, File 13.

18. For a history of the American Medical Association, see James G. Burrow, *A.M.A.: Voice of American Medicine* (Baltimore: Johns Hopkins University Press, 1963).

19. It should be noted that the phrase "First, do no harm" (translated into Latin as "*Primum non nocere*") is often mistakenly ascribed to the Hippocratic Oath, although it appears nowhere in that venerable pledge. Hippocrates came closest to issuing this directive in his treatise *Epidemics,* in an axiom that reads, "As to diseases, make a habit of two things—to help, or at least, to do no harm." Hippocrates, *Epidemics I,* Volume 1, Loeb Classical Library (Book I, Section 11, 5), W. H. S. Jones, translator (Cambridge: Harvard University Press, 1995), p. 165; Howard Markel, "I Swear by Apollo—On Taking the Hippocratic Oath," *New England Journal of Medicine,* 2004; 350: 2026–29.

20. Schwarz, PhD thesis, p. 156; Schwarz, *John Harvey Kellogg,* p. 35.

21. See "The Battle Creek Sanitarium: For Profit and Pleasure, a Trip to Battle Creek," circa 1910–1915. Other advertisements of this era include "Are You in Search of Health? The Battle Creek Sanitarium," *Country Life,* circa 1906; "Where Should an Invalid Spend the Winter," promotional booklet, 1903–1904; "The Battle Creek Sanitarium: Seven Acres of 'Florida Sunshine,'" *McClure's Magazine,* circa 1909; "A New Interest in Life: The Battle Creek Sanitarium," *Outlook Magazine,* circa 1910; "Here the Very Air Inspires New Health: The Battle Creek Sanitarium," *Hamptons Magazine,* circa 1910; "Rest Two Weeks in One: The Battle Creek Sanitarium," unidentified magazine, circa 1915. Collections of the University of Michigan Center for the History of Medicine. There exist hundreds more advertisements for the San, dating from the 1880s through the 1930s, most of them identifying John as the medical director.

22. A year later, a few of John's critics attempted to prefer charges against him to the Michigan State Medical Board but the charges went nowhere and were soon dropped. Schwarz, *John Harvey Kellogg,* pp. 35–36; *Battle Creek Daily Journal,* June 27, 1877, December 5, 1877, December 4, 1878; Schwarz, PhD thesis, pp. 155–56.

23. Schwarz, *John Harvey Kellogg,* p. 138.

24. Typescript of "The Question Box Hour," Lecture at the Sanitarium Parlor, February 6, 1911, Reel 12, Images 545–46 (pages 11–12 of the typescript), J. H. Kellogg Papers, U-M. See also Carson, pp. 99–100.

25. Numbers, *Prophetess of Health,* pp. 179–83.

26. "The Sanitarium Buildings," *Health Reformer,* 1877; 12: 257–61, quote is from p. 261; Patsy Gerstner, "The Temple of Health: A Pictorial History of the Battle Creek Sanitarium," *Caduceus,* 1996 (Autumn); 12(2): 12–14.

27. Schwarz, *John Harvey Kellogg,* pp. 61–72.

28. Ibid., p. 62.

29. This tale has been told to the author several times over the years while conducting research for this book but he can find no evidence of its truth, hence the term "legend."

30. Schwarz, PhD thesis, p. 183.

31. Carson, pp. 98–101; Schwarz, *John Harvey Kellogg,* p. 66.

32. Fannie Sprague Talbot, "The Sanitarium Kindergarten," *Battle Creek Sunday Journal-Record,* June 7, 1908, Reel 32, Image 70, J. H. Kellogg Papers.

33. Gerstner, "The Temple of Health: A Pictorial History of the Battle Creek Sani-

tarium," pp. 8–23, quote is from p. 15; *Description of the Medical and Surgical Sanitarium Located at Battle Creek, Michigan* (Battle Creek, MI: Battle Creek Sanitarium, 1888), p. 14.

34. Gerstner, "The Temple of Health: A Pictorial History of the Battle Creek Sanitarium," pp. 8–23; Carson, p. 101; Schwarz, *John Harvey Kellogg,* p. 66.

35. Carson, p. 103.

36. Schwarz, *John Harvey Kellogg,* pp. 66–69.

37. Ibid., p. 68.

38. Ibid., pp. 69, 174–92. In late December of 1905, Dr. Kellogg delivered a lecture to his patients at the San going over in great detail the contretemps between him and the Seventh-day Adventist Church, the Sanitarium's ownership issues, as well as how the Sanitarium was a nondenominational institution open to all who desired to come. See "Talk. Thursday, December 28, 1905 in the Sanitarium Chapel," Reel 9, Images 1298–1358, J. H. Kellogg Papers, U-M.

39. Powell, p. 57; Schwarz, PhD thesis, pp. 47–48, Chapter 2; Richard Schwarz interviews with Kellogg secretaries Roy V. Ashley, November 6, 1958, and A. S. Bloese, October 16, 1958, Richard Schwarz Collection, No. 157, Box 33, Folder 1, Center for Adventist Research; A. S. Bloese Manuscript, pp. 255–56, 284, Box 1, Folder 14.

40. Over the years, the doctor created more than thirty companies, including the Michigan Sanitarium and Benevolent Association, Sanitary Supply Company, Sanitarium Health Food Company, the individual periodicals *Health and Temperance Beacon, Modern Medicine Journal, Bacteriological World, Modern Medicine and Bacteriological Review, Health Reformer,* as well as the American Health and Temperance Association, Good Health Publishing Company, Good Health Publishing Association, Sanitas Nut Food Co. Ltd., Sanitas Food Co., Modern Medicine Publishing Co., Modern Medicine Co., Race Betterment Foundation, Social Purity Association, Battle Creek Food Co., Kellogg Food Co., Noko Co., Electric Light Bath Co., the Kellogg Rice Flake and Biscuit Co., in addition to the many schools making up the Battle Creek College. See Powell, p. 60.

41. Ibid., pp. 57–66.

42. Ibid., p. 51.

43. George Howe Colt, *Brothers: On His Brothers and Brothers in History* (New York: Scribner, 2012), p. 124.

44. Powell, p. 59.

45. Ibid.

46. Ibid., p. 66.

47. Ibid., p. 64.

48. Schwarz, *John Harvey Kellogg,* p. 142.

49. Powell, p. 61.

50. Ibid., pp. 59–60.

51. Ibid., p. 61.

52. Ibid., p. 50.

6.

"WHAT'S MORE AMERICAN THAN CORN FLAKES?"

Chapter title: Kadish Millet, "What's More American," song recorded by Bing Crosby (with the "Bugs" Bower Orchestra), 45-RPM Single PIP 8940-A (Long Island

City, NY: Pickwick International Productions, 1968). The first chorus announces: "What's more American than Corn Flakes? / The Fourth of July and Uncle Sam. / What's more American than Baseball? / I am, I am, I am!"

1. Joe Musser, *The Cereal Tycoon: Henry Parsons Crowell, the Founder of the Quaker Oats Company* (Chicago: Moody Press, 1997), pp. 82–84.

2. Ibid., pp. 88–95.

3. Testimony of J. H. Kellogg, *State of Michigan Supreme Court Record*, Volume 2 (*Kellogg v. Kellogg*, p. 362), Box 21, File 3, J. H. Kellogg Papers, MSU; Carson, p. 93.

4. Carson, p. 118.

5. Ibid., pp. 36–37. See also W. O. Huston, "The American Disease," *Columbus Medical Journal*, 1896; 16: 1–6; J. C. Whorton, *Crusaders for Fitness: The History of American Health Reformers* (Princeton: Princeton University Press, 1982); J. H. Baron and A. Sonnenberg, "Hospital Admissions for Peptic Ulcer and Indigestion in London and New York in the 19th and Early 20th Centuries," *Gut*, 2002; 50: 568–70. In the 1850s, 1860s, and 1870s, the English novelist George Eliot's lover and domestic partner, G. H. Lewes (1817–1878), was a best-selling author of popular books on the physiology of digestion and indigestion. See, for example, G. H. Lewes, *The Physiology of Common Life, in Two Volumes* (Edinburgh and London: William Blackwood and Sons, 1859). Ivan Pavlov was a great admirer of Lewes's studies on digestion.

6. Michael Foster, *Lectures on the History of Physiology During the Sixteenth, Seventeenth, and Eighteenth Centuries* (Cambridge: University of Cambridge Press, 1901); Owsei Temkin, *Galenism* (Ithaca, NY: Cornell University Press, 1973); Galen, *A Translation of Hygiene (De Sanitate Tuenda)*, translated by R. M. Green (Springfield, IL: Charles C. Thomas, 1951); L. J. Rather, "The Six Things Non-Natural: A Note on the Origins and Fate of a Doctrine and Phrase," *Clio Medica*, 1968; 3: 337–47; Jack W. Berryman, "Motion and Rest: Galen on Exercise and Health," *The Lancet*, 2012; (380): 210–11; Nicholas Bauch, *A Geography of Digestion: Biotechnology and the Kellogg Cereal Enterprise* (Berkeley: University of California Press, 2017).

7. For a précis of Dr. Kellogg's admiration and understanding of Dr. Beaumont's work, see "Question Box Hour Lecture," September 24, 1908, Reel 11, Images 171–204 (Beaumont story is told on Images 172–78, pp. 2–7 of typescript), J. H. Kellogg Papers, U-M; J. H. Kellogg, *The Health Question Box, or A Thousand and One Health Questions Answered* (Battle Creek, MI: Modern Medicine Publishing Co., 1920), pp. 881–86.

8. Jerome J. Bylebyl, "William Beaumont, Robley Dunglison, and the 'Philadelphia Physiologists,'" *Journal of the History of Medicine and Allied Sciences*, 1970; 25(1): 3–21; J. S. Myer, *Life and Letters of William Beaumont* (St Louis: C. V. Mosby & Co.; 1912), p. 289; R. L. Numbers, W. J. Orr Jr., "William Beaumont's Reception at Home and Abroad," *Isis*, 1981; 72(264): 590, 612; George Rosen, *The Reception of William Beaumont's Discovery in Europe* (New York: Schuman, 1942).

9. Ivan P. Pavlov, *The Work of the Digestive Glands*, translated by W. H. Thompson (London: Charles Griffin and Co., 1902); Daniel Todes, *Pavlov's Physiology Factory: Experiment, Interpretation, Laboratory Enterprise* (Baltimore: Johns Hopkins University Press, 2002).

10. Pavlov, *The Work of the Digestive Glands*, pp. 45, 65–66, 152–53; Ivan Pavlov, *Conditioned Reflexes: An Investigation of the Physiological Activity of the Cerebral Cortex*, translated by G. V. Anrep (Oxford: Oxford University Press: Humphrey Milford, 1927); Horace W. Davenport, *Physiology of the Digestive Tract* (Chicago: Yearbook Medical Publishers, 1982, 5th edition), pp. 103–12.

11. Carson, p. 118.

12. Candida J. Rebello, William D. Johnson, Corby K. Martin, Wenting Xie, Marianne O'Shea, Anne Kurilich, Nicolas Bordenave, Stephanie Andler, B. Jan Willem van Klinken, Yi-Fang Chu, and Frank L. Greenway, "Acute Effect of Oatmeal on Subjective Measures of Appetite and Satiety Compared to a Ready-to-Eat Breakfast Cereal: A Randomized Crossover Trial," *Journal of the American College of Nutrition*, 2013; 32(4): 272–79. Both the glycemic index and glycemic load of Corn Flakes are among the highest of common or representative foods; see David S. Ludwig, "The Glycemic Index: Physiological Mechanisms Relating to Obesity, Diabetes and Cardiovascular Disease," *JAMA*, 2002; 287(18): 2414–23.

13. A. S. Bloese Manuscript, p. 70d, Box 1, File 13; Carson, p. 124.

14. Ronald Numbers, *Prophetess of Health: A Study of Ellen G. White* (Grand Rapids, MI: Eerdman's Publishing Co., 2008, 3rd edition), pp. 127–55; James J. Jackson, "Diphtheria, Its Causes, Treatment and Cure," *Advent Review and Sabbath Herald*, February 17, 1863; 21: 89–91; James C. Jackson, *Hygiene and the Gospel Ministry* (Dansville, NY: F. Wilson Hurd and Co., 1859); James C. Jackson, *Hints on the Reproductive Organs: Their Diseases, Causes, and Cure on Hydropathic Principles* (New York: Fowler and Wells, 1852); James C. Jackson, *The Sexual Organization and Its Healthful Management* (Boston: B. Leverett Emerson, 1862); James C. Jackson, *Consumption: How to Prevent It, and How to Cure It* (Boston: B. Leverett Emerson, 1862); James C. Jackson, *How to Beget and Rear Beautiful Children* (Dansville, NY: F. Wilson Hurd and Co., 1866); James C. Jackson, *American Womanhood: Its Peculiarities and Necessities* (Danville, New York: Austin, Jackson and Co., 1870); James C. Jackson, *How to Treat the Sick Without Medicine* (Danville, New York: Austin, Jackson and Co., 1877).

15. Today's granola, of course, is a very different entity but the name is a Kellogg creation. Schwarz, *John Harvey Kellogg*, p. 209; Hilary Greenbaum and Dana Rubenstein, "Who Made That Granola?," *New York Times Magazine*, March 23, 2012, p. MM22.

16. Powell, p. 90.

17. Carson, pp. 119–22; Schwarz, *John Harvey Kellogg*, pp. 117–18.

18. Jim Holechek, *Henry Perky: The Shredded Wheat King* (New York: iUniverse, 2007), pp. 176–77. Based upon a handwritten agreement the two drew up in October of 1892, Ford took credit as the co-inventor of this manufacturing process for many years to come.

19. Carson, p. 120.

20. Carson, p. 120. In Holechek's version (*Henry Perky*, pp. 181–83), Perky came to Battle Creek carrying "a wooden box containing his Shredded Wheat machine under one arm" and demonstrated the machine to Dr. Kellogg and, later, to Charley Post.

21. Powell, p. 147.

22. Carson, p. 121.

23. "The Wonders of Niagara: Scenic and Industrial," promotional booklet for the Shredded Wheat Company (Niagara Falls, NY: The Shredded Wheat Co., 1914), Collections of the University of Michigan Center for the History of Medicine; "Henry Perky Is Dead. He Was an Advocate of Vegetarianism—End Hastened by Fall," *New York Times*, June 30, 1906, p. 7; Holechek, *Henry Perky*, pp. 231–53.

24. Jill Jonnes, *Empires of Light: Edison, Tesla, Westinghouse, and the Race to Electrify the World* (New York: Random House Trade Paperbacks, 2004), p. 329.

25. Carson, p. 121.

26. Powell, p. 90.

27. See *Kellogg Company v. National Biscuit Company*, 305 U.S. 111 (1938), Supreme Court of the United States, Nos. 2, 56; argued October 10, 1938; decided November 14,

1938. For a legal history of the case, see Graeme B. Dinwoodie, "The Story of Kellogg Co. v. National Biscuit Co.: Breakfast with Brandeis," in Jane Ginsburg and Rochelle Dreyfuss, eds., *Intellectual Property Stories* (Foundation Press, 2005), pp. 220–58, accessed online on June 22, 2015, at http://works.bepress.com/graeme_dinwoodie/28.

28. Carson, pp. 219–20.

29. Elizabeth Neumeyer, *"Mother": Ella Eaton Kellogg* (Battle Creek, MI: Heritage Battle Creek, 2001).

30. Schwarz, *John Harvey Kellogg*, p. 151. The address was 202 Manchester Street. *Battle Creek, Michigan City Directory* (Detroit: R. L. Polk Co., 1921), p. 581.

31. Interview with Mary Lamson, conducted by Richard Schwarz, May 17, 1959. B9, File 8, Lamson. Richard Schwarz Collection, Center for Adventist Research. Lamson later became the dean of women at Andrews University.

32. Neumeyer, *"Mother": Ella Eaton Kellogg*, p. 54. Neumeyer does an excellent job of tracing the lives of the adopted Kellogg children in her book.

33. A. S. Bloese Manuscript, p. 108h, Box 1, Folder 13.

34. On Christmas night 1906, for example, John touchingly wrote his eighteen-year-old former foster daughter Cecile, who had recently left the home to continue her education in Philadelphia: "You are just as dear to me as though born in our house and you must not allow yourself to feel any less a member of our family and our home than if you were adopted. You have no other home and you need to be anchored somewhere." Twelve years later, after a series of calamitous family events, he wrote the adult Cecile, "Be sure and let me know if you get into any serious trouble. I am always glad to come to your rescue." Letter from John H. Kellogg to Cecile May Hatch-Kellogg, Christmas night 1906; Letter from J. H. Kellogg to Cecile May Hatch-Kellogg, November 3, 1918, Collection of Dr. Kenneth Woodside and Mrs. Kathleen D. Woodside of Battle Creek, Michigan. Dr. Broadside's great-grandmother Cecile married a man named Clarence Parrish who worked at the San, first as a bellhop; later, he was in charge of the photography shop. The marriage ended in divorce. She subsequently married a man named Harry Pickard and lived on a farm outside Battle Creek. At the end of her life, she lived in a Kellogg-funded building called the Sunshine Center. I am grateful to Dr. Woodside for sharing his family heirlooms and history with me.

35. Ella E. Kellogg, *Talks with Girls: An Address on the Social Purity Pledge* (Battle Creek, MI: Good Health Publishing Co., 1889). John wrote a companion piece called *Social Purity*. See Neumeyer, *"Mother": Ella Eaton Kellogg*, pp. 68–69, 74. Ella also wrote a book entitled *Studies in Character Building. A Book for Parents* (Battle Creek: Good Health Publishing Co., 1905).

36. Carson, p. 111. Carson states: "In the days of his youth, [John] said, a young buck was almost expected to contract a venereal infection as proof of his manhood."

37. Martha B. Roosevelt died at the age of forty-eight from typhoid fever on the same day, February 14, 1884, and in the same house as Theodore's young wife, Alice Lee Roosevelt, who died from Bright's disease or kidney failure. See William H. Harbaugh, *The Life and Death of Theodore Roosevelt* (New York: Collier, 1963), pp. 50–52.

38. A. S. Bloese Manuscript, pp. 108b–108i, Box 1, File 13; *In Memoriam, Ella Eaton Kellogg* (Originally appeared in *Good Health*, July 1920).

39. Carson, pp. 110–11; Schwarz, *John Harvey Kellogg*, p. 149.

40. J. H. Kellogg, "My Helpmeet," in "In Memoriam, Ella Eaton Kellogg" (originally appeared in *Good Health*, July 1920). Reprints from the Collections of the University of Michigan.

41. Carson, pp. 111–12.

42. "Recollections" (unpublished memoir of Ella Kellogg), Reel 1, Images 55–117, J. H. Kellogg Papers, U-M; "Mrs. Kellogg Succumbs to Long Illness. Wife of Dr. J. H. Kellogg and One of the Best Known Women in the Community" (obituary), *Battle Creek Moon-Journal*, June 14, 1920, Reel 32, Images 99–100 (obituaries from the *Detroit Free Press*, June 15, 1920, and *Detroit Evening News* are clipped on Images 101–3, Reel 32, J. H. Kellogg Papers, U-M; Mrs. E. E. Kellogg, *Science in the Kitchen: A Scientific Treatise on Food Substances and Their Dietetic Properties Together with a Practical Explanation of Healthful Cookery and a Large Number of Original, Palatable, and Wholesome Recipes* (Battle Creek, MI: Health Publishing Co., 1892); Ella E. Kellogg, *Healthful Cookery: A Collection of Choice Recipes for Preparing Foods, with Special Reference to Health* (Battle Creek, MI: The Modern Medicine Publishing Co., 1904); "In Memoriam, Ella Eaton Kellogg," originally appeared in *Good Health*, July 1920. Reprints from the Collections of the University of Michigan; Neumeyer, *"Mother": Ella Eaton Kellogg*.

43. Schwarz, *John Harvey Kellogg*, p. 156.

44. Carson, p. 112. See also "In Memoriam, Ella Eaton Kellogg," originally appeared in *Good Health*, July 1920, reprints from the Collections of the University of Michigan.

45. Testimony of J. H. Kellogg, *State of Michigan Supreme Court Record*, Volume 2 (*Kellogg v. Kellogg*, p. 365), Box 21, File 3, J. H. Kellogg Papers, Michigan State University.

46. Edison's famous search for a proper filament to create illumination in his light bulb is nicely described in Matthew Josephson's classic *Edison: A Biography* (New York: Francis Parkman Prize Edition/History Book Club, 2003) in a chapter entitled "The Breakthrough," pp. 205–27.

47. Carson, p. 122.

48. Dreams, Sanitarium Lecture, August 19, 1892, Reel 6, Images 641–67. J. H. Kellogg Papers, U-M. I discuss Freud's interpretation of dreams in my book *An Anatomy of Addiction*, pp. 157, 218.

49. "Divine Healing," Lecture by J. H. Kellogg, April 10, 1909, Reel 11, Images 383–89, Bentley Historical Library, University of Michigan. Interestingly, Dr. William Sadler, who knew both Freud and Dr. Kellogg, claimed they had one thing in common in that "both hung on tightly to basic ideas they had started with." William Sadler Interview with Richard Schwarz, September 22, 1960. Box 6, File 11, Sadler 6. Richard Schwarz Papers, Center for Adventist Research.

50. Carson, p. 124. See also A. S. Bloese Manuscript, "Founded a New Industry," pp. 68–70H, Box 1, File 13.

51. Carson, p. 123. Butler was married to John's sister Clara, who was divorced from him sometime in 1907. Clara was entirely devoted to her brother, lived in his house for most of the remainder of her life, and often served as his secretary and boon companion. See Schwarz, PhD thesis, p. 87; see also Schwarz, *John Harvey Kellogg*, p. 148.

52. Norman Williamson Jr., too, denies the "romantic account" that flaked cereals were invented in Ella's kitchen. More likely, it was the San's experimental kitchen where "in his [Will's] unrelenting search for nutritious substitutes for meat he burned the midnight oil." See Williamson Jr., p. 25.

53. Powell, p. 91. Williamson Jr. contends that Will did this work on his own and then told the doctor of the events concerning the moldy dough. Given the closeness of the relationship between the chronicler and the subject, as well as the stakes in telling this particular version, it is probably somewhat of an exaggeration and, more likely, *both* brothers were involved in the seminal discovery of the value of "tempered dough." See Williamson Jr., pp. 25–26.

54. Carson, pp. 124–25; Powell, pp. 90–91.

55. Powell, p. 91.

56. J. H. Kellogg, "Flaked Cereal and Process of Preparing the Same," U.S. Patent 558,393, April 14, 1896, Reel 5, Box 6, File 4, J. H. Kellogg Collection, Michigan State University; Charles MacIvor, MS of "The Lord's Physician," Chapter 9: "A Man of Many Talents" (page 6 of typescript). MacIvor Collections, Center for Adventist, Box 10, File 12.

57. Deposition of W. K. Kellogg, May 5, 1917, *Kellogg Food Company v. Kellogg's Toasted Corn Flake Company,* Box 20, File 2, pp. 22–24 of the typescript, J. H. Kellogg Papers, MSU; Carson, p. 125.

58. Powell, p. 92.

59. Ibid., p. 93.

60. Ibid.; Carson, p. 125.

61. *Michigan State Gazetteer and Business Directory, 1897,* Volume 13 (Detroit: R. L. Polk and Company, 1897), pp. 643, 685, 2276.

62. Carson, p. 127.

63. Over the years, different secondary historical accounts have estimated between forty and fifty such firms, but research conducted by Garth "Duff" Stoltz, using the records of the Corporations and Securities Bureau of the Department of Commerce of the State of Michigan, numbers 101 companies. See Garth "Duff" Stoltz, "101 Cereal Manufacturing Companies in Battle Creek, Michigan," *Adventist Heritage,* Fall 1992; 15(2): 10–13. See also Garth "Duff" Stoltz, "A Taste of Cereal," *Adventist Heritage,* Fall 1992; 15(2): 4–9.

64. *New York World,* September 7, 1902, p. 1, quoted in Powell, p. 101.

65. Carson, p. 182; "Willie Heston, 85, Football Star at Michigan Under Yost, Dies." *New York Times,* September 11, 1963, p. 43. Heston, considered one of college football's all-time greatest halfbacks, scored 93 touchdowns during the seasons of 1901–1904. *The New York Times* reported that Heston was the first player outside of the Ivy League to "make All-America."

66. Nettie Leitch Major, *C. W. Post—The Man and the Hour: A Biography with Genealogical Supplement* (Washington, DC: Press of Judd and Detweiler, Inc., 1933), pp. 38–63.

67. Post was hardly the only businessman to compete with the Battle Creek Sanitarium. From 1907 to 1909, muscleman and body trainer Bernarr Macfadden took over the former Phelps Sanitarium in Battle Creek and operated his Institute of Physical Culture. A Barnumesque promoter of health foods, exercise, and many of the same pursuits espoused by Dr. Kellogg, Macfadden also founded the famed *Physical Culture,* several other magazines, and the rather racy tabloid newspaper, *The New York Graphic.* See Robert Ernst, *Weakness Is a Crime: The Life of Bernarr Macfadden* (Syracuse, NY: Syracuse University Press, 1991).

68. In later years, Dr. Kellogg ordered his laboratory men to feed rabbits Postum and then measure their red blood cell counts in comparison to the rabbits that were fed normal diets. The doctor was pleased to learn that Post's claim was bunkum. See Helen S. Mitchell, *Popular Survey. Animal Experiments Conducted at the Nutrition Laboratory, Battle Creek Sanitarium,* 1927 (reprint). See also canister of "Battle Creek Sanitarium Minute Brew" ("A Table Beverage with Bran, Malt, Starch, Rye and Calcium Carbonate Dissolves Instantly in Hot Water"), Battle Creek Food Co., Battle Creek, MI. Both in Collections of the University of Michigan Center for the History of Medicine.

69. Charles Goodrum and Helen Dalrymple, *Advertising in America: The First 200 Years* (New York: Harry Abrams, 1990), p. 68.

70. Powell, p. 172.

71. Major, *C. W. Post—The Man and the Hour,* pp. 144–45; John Milton Cooper Jr., *Woodrow Wilson: A Biography* (New York: Alfred A. Knopf, 2009), pp. 188–89.

72. Major, *C. W. Post—The Man and the Hour,* pp. 145–46, quote is from p. 145; Nancy S. Rubin, *American Empress: The Life and Times of Marjorie Merriweather Post* (New York: Villard, 1995), pp. 89–94.

73. "C. W. Post a Suicide in California Home," *New York Times,* May 10, 1914, p. 12.

74. Letter from J. H. Kellogg to C. W. Barron, September 23, 1919, in Arthur Pound and Samuel T. Moore, eds., *More They Told Barron: Conversations and Revelations of an American Pepys in Wall Street* (New York: Harper and Brothers, 1931), p. 281.

75. Norman Williamson Jr., *An Intimate Glimpse,* p. 18.

76. Carson, pp. 154–56.

77. Powell, p. 94.

78. Deposition of W. K. Kellogg, May 5, 1917, *Kellogg Food Company v. Kellogg's Toasted Corn Flake Company,* Box 20, File 2, pp. 3–4, J. H. Kellogg Papers, MSU; Powell, p. 102; Carson, p. 184.

79. Schwarz, *John Harvey Kellogg,* p. 120.

80. Powell, pp. 110–11; Carson, p. 184.

81. Powell, p. 98.

82. The length of Will's tenure at the San varies with different tellings. He began in 1880 and resigned in August 1901. He took on the task of raising capital for the new San, after the old one burned down in mid-February 1902, for about two and one half years but was primarily focused on building his food business. Will often dated his San tenure as twenty-two and a half years, but at other times he used the number twenty-five years to date his tenure. Ibid., p. 99.

7.

"FIRE!" . . . AND CEASE-FIRE

1. The Battle Creek Sanitarium Fire was widely reported across the United States; see, for example, "Wild Panic in Sanitarium Fire," *Chicago Tribune,* February 19, 1902, p. 2; "Fire Imperils 400 Lives," *Washington Post,* February 19, 1902, p. 2; "Many Escape from Fire," *New York Times,* February 19, 1902, p. 3; "The Sanitarium Burned!," *Battle Creek Daily Moon,* February 18, 1902, p. 2. See also "In Days Gone By," unidentified clipping about the fire on the Sanitarium's twenty-fifth anniversary, circa 1927, Reel 33, Image 452, J. H. Kellogg Papers, U-M.

2. "Battle Creek Sanitarium in Ruins," *Battle Creek Daily Journal,* February 18, 1902, p. 1.

3. "Will Rebuild the Sanitarium," *Battle Creek Daily Journal,* February 19, 1902, p. 2.

4. "In Days Gone By."

5. "Battle Creek Sanitarium in Ruins," p. 1.

6. "Now in Ruins! Kellogg Sanitarium," *Battle Creek Morning Enquirer,* February 18, 1902, pp. 1, 8.

7. "Battle Creek Sanitarium in Ruins," p. 1.

8. Ibid., p. 6.

9. "The Sanitarium Burned!," *Battle Creek Daily Moon,* February 18, 1902, p. 1.

10. "In Days Gone By."

11. Carson, p. 133; "In Days Gone By."

12. "Battle Creek Sanitarium in Ruins," p. 1.

13. Ibid.

14. "The Sanitarium Burned!," p. 1.

15. Ibid.

16. "In Days Gone By."

17. "Battle Creek Sanitarium in Ruins," p. 1.

18. "The Sanitarium Burned!," p. 1. In the "In Days Gone By" account written twenty-five years later it is claimed that while there was poor water pressure, it was "not due to the pumping station as the standpipe was kept filled." Whatever the precise cause, there were problems in getting enough water out to extinguish the flames.

19. "Battle Creek Sanitarium in Ruins," p. 1.

20. "The Sanitarium Burned!," p. 2.

21. Ibid.

22. "Disastrous Fire and Great Tribulation," A. S. Bloese Manuscript, Box 1, File 13.

23. Ibid., p. 110.

24. Typescript, "Mass Meeting of the Citizens of Battle Creek at the Tabernacle, February 19, 1902," p. 19, Reel 8, Images 333–65, J. H. Kellogg Papers, U-M.

25. The new San was actually not completed until May of 1903. "Will Rebuild the Sanitarium," p. 2.

26. Charles MacIvor, "The Lord's Physician." Manuscript Biography of Dr. Kellogg. "Fire! Fire! Fire!," Chapter 14 (p. 3 of typescript), Box 10, File 12, Charles MacIvor Papers, Collections of the Adventist Research Center; J. H. Kellogg, *The Battle Creek Sanitarium Fire* (pamphlet), Reel 33, Image 279, J. H. Kellogg Papers, U-M; "The Fire," manuscript dated October 31, 1907, Reel 10, Images 1101–2, J. H. Kellogg Papers, U-M.

27. "Mass Meeting of the Citizens of Battle Creek at the Tabernacle," February 19, 1902," Reel 8, Images 333–65, J. H. Kellogg Papers, U-M.

28. "Will Rebuild the Sanitarium," p. 2. See also *The Standard* (Chicago), March 1, 1902; 49: 30. And also see I. D. Sankey, *My Life and the Story of the Gospel Hymns and of Sacred Songs and Solos* (New York: Harper & Brothers, 1907); I. D. Sankey, *Welcome Tidings: A New Collection of Sacred Songs for the Sunday School* (with Robert Lowry and Howard Doane) (New York: Biglow & Main, 1877); I. D. Sankey, *Gems of Song for the Sunday School* (with Hubert Main) (Chicago: The Biglow & Main Co., 1901).

29. Interestingly, this phrase is also the city of Detroit's motto. The French Roman Catholic priest Father Gabriel Richard, who was, at the time, the assistant pastor at St. Anne's Church, is credited for uttering it. On June 11, 1805, "a fire destroyed nearly the entire city, weeks before the Michigan Territory was established." It was this fire that led Father Richard to write: "*Speramus meliora; resurget cineribus,*" the Latin for "We hope for better things; it will arise from the ashes." Kate Linebaugh, "Rising from the Ashes: The Origins of Detroit's Motto," *Wall Street Journal,* July 19, 2013.

30. "Entry on the Hon. Charles Austin," *Portrait Biographical Album of Calhoun County, Michigan Containing Full-Page Portraits and Biographical Sketches of Prominent and Representative Citizens of the County* (Chicago: Chapman Brothers, 1891), pp. 211–12. In 1876, Austin was mayor of Battle Creek, and in 1880 he was elected to the state legislature.

31. Carson, p. 129.

32. Ibid., p. 130.

33. Ibid. There were San branches in St. Helena, Los Angeles, and San Diego, California; Boulder and Colorado Springs, Colorado; Spokane, Seattle, and Tacoma, Washington; Lincoln, Nebraska; Chicago, Peoria, and Moline, Illinois; Detroit, Jackson, and Grand Rapids, Michigan; as well as locations in Mexico, Switzerland, England, New Zealand, Australia, Egypt, Palestine, India, South Africa, and Japan. For a detailed description of Dr. Kellogg's far-flung health reform empire and the church's growing missionary activities around the world, see *Year Book of the International Medical Missionary and Benevolent Association. Origin and Development of Medical Missionary and Other Philanthropic Work Among Seventh-day Adventists* (Battle Creek, MI: International Medical Missionary and Benevolent Association, 1896), Reel 28, Images 1009–1228; Articles of Incorporation of the Guadalajara Sanitarium, May 28, 1898, Images 414–17, 424–25; "The Guadalajara Mission, 1894–1897," Reel 30, Images 478–80. See also Articles of Association of the Michigan Sanitarium and Benevolent Association, December 1897, and "Minutes of the Annual Meeting of the Michigan Sanitarium and Benevolent Association, March 9, 1899," Reel 30, Images 488–509, 513–37; all in J. H. Kellogg Papers, U-M.

34. "Review and Herald in Ashes," *Battle Creek Daily Moon,* December 31, 1902, p. 1. There were two suspicious "accidental," and ultimately unsolved, fires in town that occurred prior to the San's disaster: John's Sanitarium Food Company factory burned to the ground on July 19, 1898; another fire destroyed his Sanitas Nut Food Company factory on July 21, 1900. Additionally, Will's first Corn Flakes factory burned down on July 4, 1907, and the Haskell Memorial Home, an orphanage actively supported by Ella Kellogg, burned down on February 5, 1909.

35. Letter from J. H. Kellogg to Ellen White, December 31, 1902, Reel 1, Images 206–8, Correspondence with Seventh-day Adventist Members on Rebuilding the Sanitarium, J. H. Kellogg Papers, MSU.

36. Ellen G. White, *Testimonies for the Church,* Volume 8, p. 97, Chapter 18, "The Review and Herald Fire." Letter to the Brethren of Battle Creek," January 6, 1903, accessed July 24, 2015, at http://text.egwwritings.org/publication.php?pubtype=Book&bookCode=8T&pagenumber=97.

37. Ellen G. White, "Our Duty to Leave Battle Creek. Talk by Mrs. E. G. White, Friday Morning, April 3, 1903," *The General Conference Bulletin. Thirty-Fifth Session,* April 6, 1903; 5(6): 84–91. In this sermon, she heatedly criticized Dr. Kellogg's imperious ways in Battle Creek. John made his own impassioned defense of his plans for the new San, its branches, and the realities of "ownership" of a nonprofit, nondenominational medical center in Michigan under existing state laws at the same conference that same morning, pp. 71–84.

38. Letter from George Butler to J. H. Kellogg, January 2, 1905, Reel 2, Box 2, File 6, Images 615–25 (page 5 of the typescript), J. H. Kellogg Papers, MSU.

39. Carson, p. 132.

40. Ibid., p. 134.

41. "Mass Meeting of the Citizens of Battle Creek at the Tabernacle, February 19, 1902," Reel 8, Images 333–65 (p. 28 of the typescript), J. H. Kellogg Papers, U-M.

42. "Experience Meeting (Patients) in the West Hall, February 22, 1902," Reel 8, Images 367–88 (p. 3 of the typescript), J. H. Kellogg Papers, U-M.

43. Ibid., p. 7.

44. T. C. Boyle, *The Road to Wellville* (New York: Viking, 1993); *The Road to Wellville*, Columbia Pictures, 1994, screenplay by T. C. Boyle and Alan Parker, based on T. C. Boyle's book, directed by Alan Parker and starring Anthony Hopkins as Dr. Kellogg. The film can be seen online, on YouTube, accessed July 20, 2015, at https://www.youtube.com/watch?v=5-vv7V8URe8.

45. C. W. Post, *The Road to Wellville* (Battle Creek, MI: 1910). In 1925, his company was still advertising his products in popular magazines with slogans such as "Follow this Road to Wellville!," Postum Cereal Company Advertisement, *Saturday Evening Post*, November 28, 1925, p. 62, Collections of the University of Michigan Center for the History of Medicine. Mr. Boyle, of course, knows the origin of this slogan and duly notes in the text that "the Road to Wellville" was C. W. Post's sales pitch (p. 118).

46. "Hulda's" real name is lost to history. The spelling of her name varies in different primary and secondary accounts, such as "Hildah" and "Huldah." I use "Hulda" because that is how Dr. Kellogg refers to her in an account he wrote on the child in the *New York Sunday Recorder*, August 4, 1901, pp. 1 and 7. William Sadler claimed Dr. Kellogg paid "Hilda" $50 for the child and added, in a 1960 interview, "Hilda's kid turned out to be a disappointment after a promising start, later blackmailed JHK, and brought him much sorrow." William Sadler interview by Richard Schwarz, September 22, 1960, Box 11, File 1, Sadler A, Card VII-B-1,2,4; IX-B-2, Richard Schwarz Papers, Center for Adventist Research. See also Elizabeth Neumayer's *"Mother."* Neumayer does a yeoman's job of collecting birth records, government and court records, journal entries and letters to document the list of the Kelloggs' forty-two adoptees. She calls the chapter in which this table appears "Work in Progress" because there may be slight discrepancies in what she found. She cites the year of George's adoption as 1897, but it could have been 1898.

47. "Unique Experiments in the Training of Slum Children by Dr. J. H. Kellogg," *New York Sunday Recorder*, August 4, 1901, pp. 1 and 7, Reel 35, Images 12–14 (quote is from p. 7), J. H. Kellogg Papers, U-M.

48. Ibid., p. 7. Kerosene baths were then a common treatment for skin infestations such as ringworm and body or head lice.

49. Brian Wilson, *Dr. John Harvey Kellogg and the Religion of Biologic Living* (Bloomington: Indiana University Press, 2014), pp. 150–51. See also a series of clippings in the J. H. Kellogg Papers, U-M: "Adopts 22 Children to Make 'Gentlemen' in One Generation," *North American*, April 13, 1902; "Educating Slum Children: Dr. Kellogg's Experiments in Proving That Environment Is Greater than Heredity," *New York Tribune*, August 3, 1901 (all these clips on Reel 32, Image 25); "Environment Wins Against Heredity in Famous Family," *Detroit Tribune*, March 31, 1912 (Reel 33, Image 496); George T. B. Davis, "The Father of Forty Children: The Story of Dr. J. H. Kellogg and His Unique Philanthropy," *The Quiver*, February 1908, pp. 259–64 (Reel 35, Images 4–9); untitled clipping on the Kelloggs' twenty-two adopted children, *"Charlotte Tribune*, August, 1898" (Reel 36, Images 211–12). See also J. H. Kellogg, "What Must Be Done for the Street Waif" (an account of his "adoption" of Hulda's child, or George), *Life Boat*, February 1902; 5: 26–28. Richard Schwarz goes into great detail on Dr. Kellogg's adoption of children and his changing views over nurture versus nature in his PhD thesis, pp. 88, 92, 303–9, and in his biography, *John Harvey Kellogg*, pp. 147–56. For a complete list of the children the Kelloggs adopted, in deed or by law, see Neumayer, *"Mother": Ella Eaton Kellogg*, p. 49.

50. Interview with Emil Storkaw, conducted by Richard Schwarz, June 5, 1962 (Card VII-B-2,4), B9, F8, Storkaw, Richard Schwarz Collection, Center for Adventist

Research; unidentified clipping, "Dr. Kellogg Will to Be Contested," February 18, 1944 (Image 464); "Kellogg Will Suit Date Set," *Detroit Times,* February 26, 1944 (Image 471), both clips in Reel 32, J. H. Kellogg Papers, U-M.

51. Wilson, *Dr. John Harvey Kellogg and the Religion of Biologic Living,* pp. 149–50; Schwarz, *John Harvey Kellogg,* pp. 147–56.

52. Boyle, *The Road to Wellville,* pp. 46–48.

53. A. S. Bloese Manuscript, pp. 108h-108i, Box 1, Folder 13; Schwarz, *John Harvey Kellogg,* pp. 147–56.

54. Boyle, *The Road to Wellville,* pp. 380–82, 448–63.

55. Schwarz, *John Harvey Kellogg,* pp. 70–71.

56. This creaky firetrap of an opera house was built in 1868 for $40,000 (or $687,000 in 2016). "Mass Meeting, March 17, 1902 at Hamblin's Opera House," Reel 8, Images 389–428, J. H. Kellogg Papers, U-M; advertisement for Wooden's Buff Wyandotte chickens and Indian Runner ducks, in *Michigan Poultry Breeder,* May 1904, 19(5) (Battle Creek: George S. Barnes, 1904).

57. "Report of a portion of a council meeting held at Mrs. E. G. White's home, 'Elsmhaven,' St. Helena, Cal., 8 a.m., October 19, 1902. Present: Mrs. E. G. White, elders A. G. Daniells, W. C. White, W. T. Knox, E. R. Palmer, A. T. Jones, J. O. Corliss," Reel 1, Images 155–60; Correspondence with SDA Members on Rebuilding the Sanitarium, J. H. Kellogg Papers, MSU.

58. Letter from J. H. Kellogg to E. G. White, March 8, 1899, Images 34–37; Mrs. White's sermon and letter "To Our Brethren in All Lands," January 25, 1899, Reel 1, Images 43–47, Correspondence with SDA Members on Rebuilding the Sanitarium, J. H. Kellogg Papers, MSU.

59. "Mass Meeting, March 17, 1902 at Hamblin's Opera House," p. 5, Reel 8, Images 389–428, J. H. Kellogg Papers, U-M. See also "A Great Philanthropic Enterprise. (Report of the Citizen's Committee Investigating the Sanitarium's Finances)," March 17, 1902, Reel 33, Images 365–68, J. H. Kellogg Papers, MSU.

60. "Remarks Made at the Laying of the Cornerstone, May 11, 1902 by Dr. J. H. Kellogg," Reel 8, Images 442–47, J. H. Kellogg Papers, U-M. Sixteen months later, on May 31, 1903, he would dedicate and open the new sanitarium. "New Sanitarium Dedication Exercises. May 31, 1903," Reel 8, Images 1040–67, J. H. Kellogg Papers, U-M.

8.

THE NEW SAN

1. "Remarks Made at the Laying of the Corner Stone, May 11, 1902 by Dr. J. H. Kellogg," Reel 8, Images 442–47, J. H. Kellogg Papers, U-M.

2. The New Sanitarium's dedication ceremony is discussed in detail in "New Sanitarium Dedication Exercises, May 31, 1903," Reel 8, Images 1040–67, J. H. Kellogg Papers, U-M. See also "Battle Creek's New Temple of Health," *Battle Creek Daily Moon,* June 1, 1903, p. 1; "A Grand Temple of Health. The Battle Creek Sanitarium Arises from Its Ashes, Stands Forth Today the Largest and Best Appointed in the World," *Battle Creek Morning Enquirer,* June 1, 1903, p. 1.

3. See, for example, letter from W. K. Kellogg to William Janney, January 15, 1903, which documents Janney's loan of $1,500 to the rebuilding project. Reel 1, Images 242–43, Box 1, File 1; Letter from W. K. Kellogg to Caroline S. Cowels, February 14, 1903, Reel 1, Images 217–18, Box 1, File 1. J. H. Kellogg Papers, MSU. W. K. Kellogg

sent out hundreds of such requests and was quite successful in generating the necessary funds through appeals to Adventist "brothers and sisters across the nation." He also kept these donors up to date on the battles between the Adventist elders and the doctor, defending John's methods of operation and tamping down the whispering campaign orchestrated by William White and his cronies. Many examples of such letters can be found on this same file of archival materials. See also Schwarz, *John Harvey Kellogg*, pp. 71, 174–92.

4. One notice announces a capital campaign for $2 million to fund the new San and states the insurance policy was for $154,900. "Note for the Review," undated, circa 1902–1903, Reel 28, Images 192–93, J. H. Kellogg Papers, U-M.

5. Letter from J. H. Kellogg to S. N. Haskell, March 30, 1903, Reel 1, Images 537–39, Box 1, File 4, J. H. Kellogg Papers, MSU. Stephen N. Haskell was an Adventist missionary and one of Dr. Kellogg's loyal friends during the battles between him and the Whites.

6. J. H. Kellogg, title page, *The Living Temple* (Battle Creek, MI: Good Health Publishing Company, 1903). Dr. Kellogg abbreviates the line from the King James version: "What? know ye not that your body is the temple of the Holy Ghost which is in you, which ye have of God, and ye are not your own?"

7. Letter from J. H. Kellogg to Sarah McEnterfer. January 28, 1906, Reel 3, Images 355–68, Box 3, File 6. See also Letter from George Butler to J. H. Kellogg, December 8, 1905, Reel 3, Images 175–79, Box 3, File 4; Letter from J. H. Kellogg to S. N. Haskell, December 27, 1905, Reel 3, Images 215–16, Box 3, File 4; Letter from J. H. Kellogg to G. Butler, January 1, 1906, Reel 3, Images 245–49, Box 3, File 5, all in J. H. Kellogg Papers, MSU. For nuanced analyses of this battle as well as the theological and semantic tangles it involved, see Richard H. Schwarz, "The Kellogg Schism: The Hidden Issues," *Spectrum* 1972 (Autumn); 4:23–39; Schwarz, *John Harvey Kellogg*, pp. 174–208; Wilson, *Dr. John Harvey Kellogg and the Religion of Biologic Living*, pp. 82–132. See also Norman Young, "The Alpha Heresy: Kellogg and the Cross," *Adventist Heritage*, 1972; 12(1): 33–42.

8. Letter from J. H. Kellogg to Ellen White, November 12, 1903, Battle Creek Sanitarium Collection No. 234, Box 9, File 18, Center for Adventist Research.

9. Letter from William White to A. G. Daniells, December 20, 1906. This letter quotes Ellen White in long passages, especially with respect to Dr. Kellogg's supposed pact with the devil. Reel 3, Images 1096–1102, Box 4, File 3, J. H. Kellogg Papers, MSU.

10. Letter from J. H. Kellogg to G. I. Butler, April 1, 1906, Reel 3, Images 678–81, Box 3, File 9, J. H. Kellogg Papers, MSU.

11. Letter from J. H. Kellogg to G. I. Butler, November 5, 1905, Reel 3, Images 135–40, Box 3, File 3, J. H. Kellogg Papers, MSU.

12. The back-and-forth accusations between Adventist Elders and Dr. Kellogg, the controversies raised by his book, and his anguish over the controversy are preserved in the doctor's papers at Michigan State University, Reel 1, Files 3–9. His excommunication proceedings are on Reels 3 and 4; there also is an interview with Dr. Kellogg, conducted by Elders George Amadon and A. C. Bordeau, October 7, 1907, wherein Dr. Kellogg gives his views and notes that the controversy over his book was largely a political affair generated by allegations that he doubted the primacy of Mrs. White and her teachings, as well as her "direct connection to God." See also *An authentic interview between Elder G. W. Amadon, Elder A. C. Bordeau and Dr. John Harvey Kellogg in Battle Creek, Michigan on October 7th, 1907* (Battle Creek, MI, 1907).

13. J. H. Kellogg, "My First and Last Word," December 16, 1907, Reel 4, Images 324–29, Box 4, File 10, J. H. Kellogg Papers, MSU. He also defended his Sanitarium as an independent institution that drew no funds from the Adventists that were not fully paid back with interest, and defended his honor and faith.

14. Daily Programme and Expenses, circa 1903, Battle Creek Sanitarium, Collections of the University of Michigan Center for the History of Medicine.

15. "Battle Creek's New Temple of Health," *Battle Creek Daily Moon,* June 1, 1903, p. 1.

16. "A Grand Temple of Health," *Battle Creek Morning Enquirer,* June 1, 1903, p. 1.

17. "Battle Creek's New Temple of Health," p. 1.

18. "New Sanitarium Dedication Exercises. May 31, 1903," Reel 8, Images 1040–67, J. H. Kellogg Papers, U-M. See also "Dedication of the New Main Building of the Battle Creek Sanitarium" (typescript program of the event), Reel 28, Images 30–33, J. H. Kellogg Papers, U-M.

19. "A Grand Temple of Health," *Battle Creek Morning Enquirer,* June 1, 1903, p. 4. See also *The Battle Creek Sanitarium* (undated patient pamphlet and promotional brochure), Shaw Printing Co., Battle Creek, MI, p. 2, Collections of the University of Michigan Center for the History of Medicine.

20. "A Chewing Song. Dedicated to Horace Fletcher by One Who Chews." J. H. Kellogg wrote the lyrics to this song. (Battle Creek, MI: Good Health Publishing Co., 1903), Reel 31, Images 214–17; J. H. Kellogg Papers, U-M. For more on Horace Fletcher, see Horace Fletcher, *Fletcherism, What It Is or How I Became Young at Sixty* (New York: Frederick A. Stokes, 1913, 3rd edition); James C. Whorton, " 'Physiologic Optimism': Horace Fletcher and Hygienic Ideology in Progressive America," *Bulletin of the History of Medicine,* 1981; 55: 59–87; Patsy Gerstner, "The Temple of Health: A Pictorial History of the Battle Creek Sanitarium." A photograph of the "Fletcherize" sign in the dining room can be found on p. 45.

21. See, for example, typescript of "Stereopticon Lecture, November 3, 1910 at 8 pm," Reel 12, Image 111, J. H. Kellogg Papers, U-M.

22. "A Grand Temple of Health," *Battle Creek Morning Enquirer,* June 1, 1903, p. 1; Patsy Gerstner, "The Temple of Health: A Pictorial History of the Battle Creek Sanitarium, *Caduceus: A Humanities Journal for Medicine and the Health Sciences,* 1996 (Autumn): 12(2): 33.

23. Powell, p. 56; "Battle Creek's New Temple of Health," *Battle Creek Daily Moon,* June 1, 1903, p. 1; "The Great and Magnificent New Battle Creek Sanitarium: Fire Proof," *Battle Creek Morning Enquirer,* June 1, 1903, p. 1.

24. Gerstner, "The Temple of Health: A Pictorial History of the Battle Creek Sanitarium," pp. 1–99, quote is from p. 33. See also: *Battle Creek Idea,* January 21, 1910, pp. 3–4.

25. *The Battle Creek Sanitarium* (n.d., patient pamphlet and promotional brochure), Battle Creek, MI: Shaw Printing Co., p. 2. Collections of the University of Michigan Center for the History of Medicine, Ann Arbor, MI.

26. Ibid., pp. 1–2. See also Gerstner, "The Temple of Health: A Pictorial History of the Battle Creek Sanitarium," p. 31.

27. When the Israelites were gathered together by Moses, they swore allegiance to their God with this phrase. I am indebted to Mr. Timothy Hoyle, Public Affairs Specialist, U.S. Department of Defense Logistics Agency, Hart-Dole-Inouye Federal Center, Battle Creek, MI (formerly the Battle Creek Sanitarium) for pointing this window out to me during a tour of the facility.

28. *The Battle Creek Sanitarium* (n.d., patient pamphlet and promotional brochure), p. 2.

29. Ibid.

30. Ibid., p. 4.

31. Advertisements: "The Battle Creek Food Idea Is the Health Food Idea Today. We Are the Originators," *Review of Reviews,* circa 1903; "Make an Investment This Summer Which Will Pay Dividends in Lengthened Life in the Years to Come . . . Come to the Battle Creek Sanitarium. The Greatest and Pleasantest Health Resort in the World," *Literary Digest,* July 14, 1906, p. 63; "The Battle Creek Sanitarium: Come to Battle Creek," *Review of Reviews,* circa 1913; "Where Should an Invalid Spend the Winter?," Battle Creek Sanitarium brochure, circa 1908; "Sun Baths All Winter at Battle Creek Sanitarium," Battle Creek Sanitarium Brochure, circa 1929; "Winter at the Battle Creek Sanitarium," n.d.; "Sun Baths All Winter at Battle Creek," circa 1915; "Battle Creek for Rest," circa 1929–1930; Collections of the University of Michigan Center for the History of Medicine.

32. Letter from W. K. Kellogg to Mrs. Caroline S. Cowels, January 14, 1903, Reel 1, Images 217–18, J. H. Kellogg Papers, MSU.

33. J. H. Kellogg, *The Battle Creek Sanitarium: History, Organization, Methods* (Battle Creek, MI: The Battle Creek Sanitarium, 1908), pp. 23–24; *Sweet's Indexed Catalogue of Building Construction* (New York: Architectural Record Company, 1906), pp. 112–16; Letter from W. K. Kellogg to Mrs. Caroline S. Cowels, January 14, 1903, Reel 1, Images 217–18, J. H. Kellogg Papers, MSU.

34. Gerstner, "The Temple of Health: A Pictorial History of the Battle Creek Sanitarium," p. 31.

35. J. H. Kellogg, *The Battle Creek Sanitarium,* pp. 67–106.

36. J. H. Kellogg, *The Crippled Colon: Causes, Consequences, Remedies* (Battle Creek, MI: The Modern Publishing Co., 1931).

37. J. H. Kellogg, *The Art of Massage: A Practical Manual for the Nurse, the Student and the Practitioner* (Battle Creek, MI: Good Health Publishing Co., 1895).

38. Dr. Kellogg appears to have developed many, if not all, of his exercise machines directly based on the work of Gustav Zander in Sweden. The doctor always gave due credit to its originator but insisted that his versions were much improved and more beneficial, an ironic stance for someone who often railed against those who "copied" his more original inventions. Schwarz, *John Harvey Kellogg,* pp. 33, 124, 127. See also J. H. Kellogg, *Good Health,* August 1883, pp. 246–49, and J. H. Kellogg, "A Hygienist Abroad," *Good Health,* February 1884, 19: 50–52; "Mechanical Exercise," *Good Health,* January 1896, 31: 10–12; February 1896, 31: 42–44; and March 1896, 31: 74–75; T. J. Hartelius, translated by A. B. Olsen, with Introduction and Notes by J. H. Kellogg, *Swedish Movements of Medical Gymnastics* (Battle Creek, MI: Modern Medicine Publishing Co., 1896).

39. These dynamometers were used by the U.S. Navy for twenty-five years to measure the muscle strength, before and after training, of cadets matriculating into and graduating from the Naval Academy at Annapolis, Maryland. Schwarz, *John Harvey Kellogg,* pp. 76–77, 125.

40. "Health and Beauty in 15 Minutes a Day . . . That's what Barbara Stanwyck . . . says about the Battle Creek Health Builder . . . The Health Builder Keeps You Fit, Sanitarium Equipment Company, unidentified clipping, circa 1927. Collections of the University of Michigan Center for the History of Medicine; Richard Schwarz, *John Harvey Kellogg,* pp. 123–24.

41. J. H. Kellogg, *The Battle Creek Sanitarium,* pp. 23–25.

42. Dr. Kellogg frequently wrote zookeepers around the world asking about the bowel habits of their gorillas. On October 23, 1939, he received a fecal analysis, with respect to *Lactobacillus acidophilus* growth in chimpanzees, orangutans, and gorillas. They were considered low. Nicholas Kepeloff, Ph.D., Consulting Bacteriologist to Battle Creek Food Company, Attn: Dr. J. H. Kellogg, October 23, 1939, Reel 5, Image 767, J. H. Kellogg Papers, U-M. See also Letter from Leonard J. Goss, DVM, Laboratory and Hospital of New York Zoological Park, to J. H. Kellogg: "The primates frequently evacuate within two hours of feeding time." They also occasionally develop constipation which was relieved by altering the diet by decreasing rice and cereal and increasing fruits. Goss also reports trying the doctor's soy acidophilus on sick animals, including a dying monkey and, more successfully, dogs with diarrhea. Letter from Leonard J. Goss to J. H. Kellogg, November 28, 1939, Reel 5, Images 818–19, J. H. Kellogg Papers, U-M. On August 14, 1940, J. H. Kellogg wrote to Mary L. J. Ackley, wife of a professor who worked at the New York Museum of Natural History, "The stools were not in the least degree offensive . . . the gorilla is the cleanest thing I have encountered." Letter from J. H. Kellogg to Mrs. Mary Ackley, August 14, 1940, Reel 5, Images 1251–52, J. H. Kellogg Papers, U-M.

43. "In very chronic cases and when rapid results are desired, the culture should be used both by enema and by mouth, thus planting the protective germs where they are most needed and may render the most effective service." J. H. Kellogg, *The Health Question Box, or A Thousand and One Health Questions Answered* (Battle Creek, MI: Modern Medicine Publishing Co., 1920), pp. 437–38, quote is from p. 438.

44. Gerstner, "The Temple of Health: A Pictorial History of the Battle Creek Sanitarium," p. 34; "Laundering for the Sanitarium," *Battle Creek Idea,* March 10, 1911, p. 4; "The Icehouse," *Battle Creek Idea,* January 23, 1908, p. 3.

45. J. H. Kellogg, *The Battle Creek Sanitarium,* pp. 23–27.

46. Battle Creek Sanitarium, pamphlet, "Rate Schedule, Battle Creek Sanitarium, effective January 1, 1916." Room, board, and treatment in the main building was $30 to $60 per week and about $20 to $40 per week in the annex and depending on treatment options. Collections of the University of Michigan Center for the History of Medicine.

47. Daily program and expenses, circa 1903, Battle Creek Sanitarium, pamphlet, "Rate Schedule, Battle Creek Sanitarium, effective January 1, 1928."

48. "What I Found at Battle Creek by a Guest," Battle Creek Sanitarium Brochure, n.d., Collections of the University of Michigan Center for the History of Medicine, p. 21.

49. Ibid., p. 5.

50. Ibid., pp. 3–4.

51. Ibid., p. 5.

52. J. H. Kellogg, *The Battle Creek Sanitarium,* p. 31.

53. See, for example, "Question Box Hour Lecture," November 26, 1906, Reel 10, Images 753–74 (quote is on Image 769 or p. 16 of the typescript); and "Question Box Hour Lecture," November 29, 1910, Reel 12, Image 274, J. H. Kellogg Papers, U-M. In each lecture, he invites anyone who wants to see him to make an appointment through the medical office.

54. Schwarz, *John Harvey Kellogg,* p. 142.

55. "Living Leaders: Dr. J. H. Kellogg Performs Prodigies of Hard Work. How Does Dr. J. H. Kellogg Labor Day and Night to Advance Christ's Kingdom—The Secret

of His Power," *Ram's Horn,* December 17, 1897, Reel 36, Images 207–9, J. H. Kellogg Papers, U-M.

56. Postcard Image of a doctor examining a patient at the Battle Creek Sanitarium, circa 1909, Collections of the University of Michigan Center for the History of Medicine.

57. The Battle Creek Sanitarium. "Rates for board, treatment, etc., January 1, 1916, Collections of the University of Michigan Center for the History of Medicine. By 1928, an entrance physical examination, which included a "physical inventory," X-ray (fluoroscopic) examination of the heart and lungs, alveolar CO_2 tension test, urinary, fecal, and blood analyses, blood pressure, examination of colon, mouth, teeth, and tonsils, test of vision, and strength test cost $75. "The Battle Creek Sanitarium. Weekly Rates, effective June 1, 1928," Reel 33, Images 229–48, J. H. Kellogg Papers, U-M.

58. The examination protocol can be found in J. H. Kellogg, *The Battle Creek Sanitarium,* pp. 31–66.

59. J. H. Kellogg, "A Visit to Pavlov's Laboratory"; and V. N. Boldyreff, "Ivan Pavlov as a Scientist," in *Special Issue in Honor of the 80th Birthday of Professor Ivan P. Pavlov. The Bulletin of the Battle Creek Sanitarium and Hospital Clinic,* October 1929; 24(4): 203–11 and 212–29; T. Joe Willey, "Kellogg and Pavlov: Portrait of a Friendship," *Spectrum,* 1983; 14(2): 16–19.

60. Daniel Todes, *Ivan Pavlov: A Life in Science* (New York: Oxford University Press, 2014), pp. 316–17.

61. "A Great Scientist Visits the Sanitarium," *Battle Creek Sanitarium Idea,* August 1923, p. 10, Reel 33, Image 636, J. H. Kellogg Papers, U-M; W. Boldyreff, "Academician I. P. Pavlov," *American Journal of Digestive Diseases,* 1934; 1(9): 747–54.

62. Todes, *Ivan Pavlov,* pp. 3, 456–57.

63. "What I Found at Battle Creek by a Guest," Battle Creek Sanitarium Brochure, n.d., Collections of the University of Michigan Center for the History of Medicine, p. 11.

64. Ibid., p. 11; J. H. Kellogg, *Rational Hydropathy: A Manual of the Physiological and Therapeutic Effects of Hydriatic Procedure, and the Technique of Their Application in the Treatment of Disease, in Two Volumes, Second Edition* (Philadelphia: F. A. Davis Company, Publishers, 1903).

65. "Phototherapy and Electrotherapy as Employed at the Battle Creek Sanitarium," *Good Health,* July 1909; 44: 565–68. Kellogg goes into much greater depth on his theories about the therapeutic uses of light and electricity in J. H. Kellogg, *Light Therapeutics: A Practical Manual of Phototherapy for the Student and Practitioner* (Battle Creek, MI: The Modern Medicine Publishing Co., 1927, 2nd edition). For an advertisement of the sunlamps Dr. Kellogg invented and sold, see "Use Sunlight to Build Vigorous Health. The Battle Creek Sunarc Bath Company," *Literary Digest,* March 23, 1929, p. 57. Collections of the University of Michigan Center for the History of Medicine. For all therapies and exercise regimens at the San, see J. H. Kellogg, *The Battle Creek Sanitarium,* pp. 73–116.

66. N. E. Rosenthal et al., "Seasonal Affective Disorder: A Description of the Syndrome and Preliminary Findings with Light Therapy," *Archives of General Psychiatry,* 1984; 41: 72–80.

67. J. H. Kellogg, *The Health Question Box, or A Thousand and One Questions Answered* (Battle Creek, MI: Modern Medicine Publishing Co., Second edition, 1920), pp. 535–67.

68. J. H. Kellogg, *The Battle Creek Sanitarium,* pp. 117–38; "What I Found at Battle Creek by a Guest," p. 8; Menu, Battle Creek Sanitarium, Dinner, May 19, 1916, J. H. Kellogg Papers, U-M.

69. "Question Box Hour Lecture," February 15, 1911, Reel 12, Image 604, J. H. Kellogg Papers, U-M.

70. Upton Sinclair, *The Profits of Religion: An Essay in Economic Interpretation* (Self-published by Upton Sinclair in Pasadena, CA, 1918), p. 237; Lauren Coodley, *Upton Sinclair: California Socialist, Celebrity Intellectual* (Lincoln: Bison Books/University of Nebraska Press, 2013), pp. 52, 86.

71. Schwarz, *John Harvey Kellogg,* p. 190.

72. Schwarz, PhD thesis, p. 411; Wilson, *Dr. John Harvey Kellogg,* p. 136.

73. "Pointers for Patients: A Few Helpful Hints to Aid in the Climb Healthward," Battle Creek Sanitarium Pamphlet, circa 1916. Collections of University of Michigan Center for the History of Medicine.

74. J. H. Kellogg, *The Battle Creek Sanitarium Health Ladder: A Series of Twenty Health Promoting Exercises,* album and instruction booklet (New York: Columbia Gramophone Co., 1923). Quote is from the album's instruction booklet, p. 4.

75. A. S. Bloese, "Anecdotes and Interesting Episodes in the Life of Dr. John Harvey Kellogg," p. 4, A. S. Bloese Manuscript, Box 1, File 12.

9.

THE SAN'S OPERATIONS

1. Schwarz, PhD thesis, p. 266.

2. For archival information on Kellogg's European trips, see "A Hygienist Abroad," Scrapbooks, Reel 36, Images 311–52, J. H. Kellogg Papers, U-M; and Notes of Meeting Brown-Sequard of Paris, c. 1884–85 (Images 1018–19); Notes of Europe trip for 1911, Billroth of Vienna (Images 994–96); Notes of meeting with Arbuthnot Lane (Images 1232–33); Operative notes while observing Lawson Tait (Images 1280–84), Reel 38, J. H. Kellogg Papers, U-M; J. H. Kellogg, "Lawson Tait" (obituary), in *Surgery, Gynecology and Obstetrics,* circa 1927, in Reel 40, Images 892–910, J. H. Kellogg Papers, U-M; for a published version of Dr. Kellogg's 1883 trip, see J. H. Kellogg, "A Hygienist Abroad," *Good Health,* August 1883, Vol. 18, pp. 246–49.

3. Schwarz, *John Harvey Kellogg,* pp. 110–14.

4. Theodor Billroth, translated by William H. Welch, *The Medical Sciences in the German Universities: A Study in the History of Civilization* (New York: Macmillan, 1924); H. Engel, "Billroth, Christian Albert Theodor," *Dictionary of Scientific Biography,* Volume 2 (New York: Charles Scribner's Sons, 1970), pp. 129–31. For a description of Wolfer's work, see Howard Markel, *An Anatomy of Addiction: Sigmund Freud, William Halsted and the Miracle Drug Cocaine* (New York: Pantheon, 2011), pp. 25, 31, 44, 107–8.

5. Schwarz, *John Harvey Kellogg,* p. 111; L. M. Jackson, S. J. Dudrick, and B. E. Sumpio, "John Harvey Kellogg: Surgeon, Inventor, Nutritionist, 1852–1943," *Journal of the American College of Surgeons,* 2004; 199(5): 817–21. See also "Operative notes while observing Lawson Tait," Reel 38, Images 1280–84, J. H. Kellogg Papers, U-M; J. H. Kellogg, "Lawson Tait," in *Surgery, Gynecology and Obstetrics,* circa 1927, Reel 40, Images 892–910, J. H. Kellogg Papers, U-M.

6. Anna Greenwood, "Lawson Tait and Opposition to Germ Theory: Defining Science in Surgical Practice," *Journal of the History of Medicine and Allied Sciences,* 1998; 53(2): 99–131; Lawson Tait, "An Experimental Research on the Value of Listerism in Abdominal Surgery," *British Medical Journal,* 1882; 1: 543; Lawson Tait, "One Hundred Consecutive Cases of Ovariotomy Performed Without Any of the Listerian Details," *British Medical Journal,* 1882; 2: 830–32; Lawson Tait, "An Account of Two Hundred and Eight Consecutive Cases of Abdominal Section Performed Between Nov. 1st, 1881, and December 31st, 1882," *British Medical Journal,* 1883; 1: 300–304; Lawson Tait, "Abstract of an Address on One Thousand Abdominal Sections," *British Medical Journal,* 1885; 1: 218–20; Lawson Tait, "One Hundred and Thirty Nine Consecutive Ovariotomies Performed Between January 1st, 1884, and December 31st, 1885, Without a Death," *British Medical Journal,* 1886; 1: 921–24; Lawson Tait, "An Address on the Present Aspect of Antiseptic Surgery," *British Medical Journal,* 1890; 2: 728–32; Lawson Tait, "Skepticism and Asepticism," *British Medical Journal,* 1890; 2: 925; U. Tröhler, "Statistics and the British Controversy About the Effects of Joseph Lister's System of Antisepsis for Surgery, 1867–1890," *James Lind Library Bulletin: Commentaries on the History of Treatment Evaluation,* 2014, accessed August 1, 2015, at http://www.jameslindlibrary.org/articles/statistics-and-the-british-controversy-about-the-effects-of-joseph-listers-system-of-antisepsis-for-surgery-1867–1890/.

7. Schwarz, *John Harvey Kellogg,* p. 111.

8. I discuss the development of the rubber surgical glove in my book *An Anatomy of Addiction,* pp. 193–94.

9. Reel 38, Images 674–99, J. H. Kellogg Papers, U-M; J. H. Kellogg, "Should the Colon Be Sacrificed or May It Be Reformed?," *Journal of the AMA,* June 30, 1917; 68(26): 1957–59. (Kellogg wanted to avoid such drastic surgery except for the "extremely rare and exceptional cases."); J. H. Kellogg, "Surgery of the Ileo-Cecal Valve: A Method of Repairing an Incompetent Ileocecal Valve and a Method of Constructing an Artificial Ileocolic Valve" reprint from the November 1913 issue of *Surgery, Gynecology and Obstetrics,* Collections of the University of Michigan Center for the History of Medicine. See also William Arbuthnot Lane, *The Operative Treatment of Chronic Intestinal Stasis* (James Nisbet and Co., 1915, 3rd edition). Previous editions of this book were titled *Chronic Constipation.* For biographical information on Dr. Lane, see T. B. Layton, *Sir William Arbuthnot Lane, Bt., C.B., M.S.: An Enquiry into the Mind and Influence of a Surgeon* (Edinburgh: E. and S. Livingstone, 1956); Robert P. Hudson, "Theory and Therapy: Ptosis, Stasis, and Autointoxication," *Bulletin of the History of Medicine,* 1989; 63: 392–413; E. Ernst, "Colonic Irrigation and the Theory of Autointoxication: A Triumph of Ignorance over Science," *Journal of Gastroenterology,* 1997; 24(4): 196–98; John Leonard Smith, "Sir Arbuthnot Lane, Chronic Intestinal Stasis, and Autointoxication," *Annals of Internal Medicine,* 1982; 96: 365–69.

10. Schwarz. *John Harvey Kellogg,* p. 114.

11. Schwarz, PhD thesis, p. 275.

12. A. E. Wiggam, "The Most Remarkable Man I Have Ever Known," *American Magazine,* December 1925, p. 120; A. S. Bloese Manuscript, pp. 365–66, Box 2, Folder 1; Schwarz, PhD thesis, p. 271.

13. Schwarz, *John Harvey Kellogg,* p. 113; Schwarz, PhD thesis, p. 266; Interview with Dr. William Sadler conducted by Richard Schwarz, September 22, 1960, Richard Schwarz Papers, B8, F12, Sadler 2 (card V-B), Center for Adventist Research. See also Howard Markel, "Onward Howard Kelly, Marching as to War," *JAMA,* 2011; 306(22):

2513–15; Audrey W. Davis, *Dr. Kelly of Hopkins: Surgeon, Scientist, Christian* (Baltimore: Johns Hopkins University Press, 1959).

14. Carson, p. 95; Schwarz, *John Harvey Kellogg*, pp. 111–12; Schwarz, PhD thesis, p. 271.

15. Interview with Dr. William Sadler conducted by Richard Schwarz, September 22, 1960.

16. Schwarz, *John Harvey Kellogg*, p. 142.

17. A. S. Bloese Manuscript, pp. 154–55, Box 1, File 13; Schwarz, PhD thesis, p. 272. For modern approaches to preventing deep venous thrombosis postoperatively, including early ambulation after a procedure, see Michael R. Cassidy, Pamela Rosenkranz, and D. McAneny, "Reducing Postoperative Venous Thromboembolism Complications with a Standardized Risk-Stratified Prophylaxis Protocol and Mobilization Program," *Journal of the American College of Surgeons*, 2014: 218(6): 1095–1104.

18. L. M. Jackson, S. J. Dudrick, and B. E. Sumpio, "John Harvey Kellogg: Surgeon, Inventor, Nutritionist, 1852–1943," *Journal of the American College of Surgeons*, 2004; 199(5): 817–21.

19. "The Story of the Miami-Battle Creek," p. 12, Reel 33, Images 559–69, J. H. Kellogg Papers, U-M; Charles MacIvor, "The Lord's Physician," Chapter 24, "A Day in the Operating Room," pp. 1–8, Center for Adventist Research.

20. Schwarz, *John Harvey Kellogg*, pp. 110–14.

21. Interview with William S. Sadler, by Richard Schwarz, December 28, 1961 (card VIII-H), Bio, F6, Richard Schwarz Collection, Center for Adventist Research.

22. J. H. Kellogg, *Ladies' Guide in Health and Disease: Girlhood, Maidenhood, Wifehood, Motherhood* (Des Moines, Iowa: W. D. Condit, 1883); both the longer and the short quote appear on p. 611. This book went through several editions and was largely unchanged from the original volume, although more figures and illustrations appear in each successive edition. The same passage appears on page 643 of the 1905 edition, which by then was published by John's publishing company, the Modern Medicine Publishing Company of Battle Creek.

23. Interview of William S. Sadler by Richard Schwarz, December 28, 1961. For a study of Sadler's work and life, see Vonne G. Meussling, "William S. Sadler: Chautauqua's Medic Orator," PhD thesis in Speech, Bowling Green State University, 1970.

24. Norman Williamson Jr. quoting from his grandfather's diary for May 5, 1884, in Williamson Jr., *An Intimate Glimpse*, pp. 17–18.

25. Steven Watts, *The People's Tycoon: Henry Ford and the American Century* (New York: Alfred A. Knopf, 2005), quote is from page 153. See also Frederick W. Taylor, *The Principles of Scientific Management* (New York: Harper and Brothers, 1911).

26. Williamson Jr., *An Intimate Glimpse*, p. 15.

27. Ibid., pp. 15–16, quote is from p. 16.

28. Melvin T. Copeland, "Arch W. Shaw," *Journal of Marketing*, 1958; 22(3): 313–15; Robert Cuff, "Edwin F. Gay, Arch W. Shaw, and the Uses of History in Early Graduate Business Education," *Journal of Management History*, 1996; 2(3): 9–25. See also, for example, Arch W. Shaw, *An Approach to Business Problems* (Cambridge: Harvard University Press, 1920); Arch W. Shaw, *Some Problems in Market Distribution* (Cambridge: Harvard University Press, 1915). When McGraw-Hill Publishing Company purchased the Shaw Company in 1928, it changed the name of *System* magazine to *Business Week*.

29. Powell, pp. 105–6.

30. Ibid., p. 106.

31. "Efficiency Expert a Suicide," *Chicago Daily Tribune,* January 21, 1914, p. 1.

32. An Interview Between Dr. J. H. Kellogg and W. K. Kellogg, and Frederick A. Kerry of 1744 First National Bank Building, Stephen T. Williams and Staff, 546 Broadway, New York, NY, at the Residence of Dr. J. H. Kellogg, Thursday, September 26, 1907, 12:30–4 pm, p. 17, Reel 5, Images 3050–3460, J. H. Kellogg Papers, MSU.

33. Ibid., p. 4.

34. Ibid., p. 1.

35. Ibid., p. 30.

36. Ibid., p. 22.

37. Ibid., p. 10. Will was quick to adopt time clocks in his cereal factory, beginning around 1906–1907.

38. Ibid., quotes are from pp. 15 and 18.

39. Nicholas Bakalar of the *New York Times* (October 27, 2015, p. D5) has reported that some historians dispute it was not Alexander Graham Bell who invented the telephone; rather, it was Elisha Gray. See also the following articles in *The New York Times:* "Telegraphy," July 10, 1874, p. 2; "Audible Speech by Telegraph," October 21, 1874; "Prof. Bell's Telephone," May 12, 1877.

40. An Interview Between Dr. J. H. Kellogg and W. K. Kellogg, and Frederick A. Kerry of 1744 First National Bank Building, Stephen T. Williams and Staff, 546 Broadway, p. 1.

41. Ibid., p. 19.

42. Ibid., p. 27.

43. Ibid., pp. 12–13.

44. Ibid., p. 11.

45. Ibid., p. 22.

46. Ibid., p. 12.

47. Powell, p. 75.

10.
A "UNIVERSITY OF HEALTH"

1. Quote is from "Question Box Hour," February 6, 1911, Reel 12, Images 534–67; quote is from Image 536 (page 3 of the typescript), J. H. Kellogg Papers, U-M. See also, for example of Kellogg chairs, U.S. Patent Office, J. H. Kellogg, Chair, U.S. Patent No. 1,576,613, filed July 21, 1924, and patented March 16, 1926, Chair, U.S. Patent No. 509,316, filed January 17, 1931 and July 11, 1933.

2. The manuscripts to many of Dr. Kellogg's lectures and "Question Box Hour" sessions are on Reels 10 and 11 in the J. H. Kellogg Papers, U-M. See also a compilation of the best of the "Question Box Hour" sessions: J. H. Kellogg, *The Health Question Box, or A Thousand and One Questions Answered* (Battle Creek, MI: Modern Medicine Publishing Co., 2nd edition, 1920). Although the "Question Box Hour" lectures tended to be held on Mondays, Dr. Kellogg would lecture occasionally on other days and, at various points, deliver "Question Box Hours" on other weeknights when it suited or complied with his busy travel schedule. See also A. S. Bloese Manuscript, chapter on the "Question Box Hour," pp. 283a–297, Box 1, Folder 14.

3. J. H. Kellogg, *The Health Question Box,* p. 37.

4. Ibid., pp. 35–36.

5. "Lecture: Question Box Hour," October 24, 1910, Reel 12, Images 54–83, quote is from Image 61 (page 8 of the typescript), J. H. Kellogg Papers, U-M.

6. An excellent example of the recommendation of the "non-excitatory" grain diet prescribed by Dr. Kellogg, see J. H. Kellogg, *Man, the Masterpiece: Or, Plain Truths Plainly Told About Boyhood, Youth and Manhood* (Battle Creek, MI: Health Publishing Co., 1891), pp. 399–400, quotes are from p. 399. The Corn Flakes–masturbation myth may have originated in the work of the pioneering sexologist and professor of pediatrics at Johns Hopkins Medical School, John Money, especially in his book, *The Destroying Angel: Sex, Fitness and Food in the Legacy of Degeneracy Theory, Graham Crackers, Kellogg's Corn Flakes and American Health History* (Buffalo, NY: Prometheus Books, 1985), pp. 17–27.

7. J. H. Kellogg, *Plain Facts for Old and Young* (Burlington, Iowa: I. F. Segner, 1886), p. 295.

8. "The prepuce, or foreskin, is drawn forward over the glans, and the needle to which the wire is attached is passed through from one side to the other. After drawing the wire through, the ends are twisted together and cut off close. It is now impossible for an erection to occur, and the slight irritation thus produced acts as a most powerful means of overcoming the disposition to the practice." J. H. Kellogg, *Plain Facts for Old and Young* (Burlington, Iowa: I. F. Segner, 1886), see also pp. 231–61 and pp. 293–97 for his discussions on the solitary vice and cures for it. This book went through sequential editions well into the 1900s even though each edition was essentially the same text. See also J. H. Kellogg, *Plain Facts for Old and Young* (Battle Creek, MI: Health Publishing Co., 1910), pp. 267–364; J. H. Kellogg, "Sexual Sins and Their Consequences," in *Man, the Masterpiece*, pp. 367–440. Inserted discreetly into the back cover of this thick hardbound volume is an Appendix on venereal diseases.

9. J. H. Kellogg, *Plain Facts for Old and Young*, p. 296.

10. J. H. Kellogg, *Ladies' Guide in Health and Disease: Girlhood, Maidenhood, Wifehood, Motherhood* (Des Moines, Iowa: W. D. Condit, 1883). The quote describing the treatments for women engaging in the solitary vice, including removal of the clitoris, is on page 546, but he also discusses the problems of "vicious habits" such as "the secret vice" of "self-abuse" on pp. 144–70.

11. See, for example, John H. Kellogg, "The Influence of Dress in Producing the Physical Decadence of American Women," Annual Address Upon Obstetrics and Gynecology delivered before the Michigan State Medical Society at the Annual Meeting Held at Saginaw, June 11–12, 1891 (Provo, Utah: Repressed Publishing, 2012, reprint edition), pp. 5, 11.

12. *The Battle Creek Sanitarium Dress System* (Battle Creek, MI: The Sanitary and Electrical Supply Company, 1898), p. 17, Collections of the University of Michigan Center for the History of Medicine.

13. "Talk to Women," July 31, 1906, Reel 10, Images 413–35, quote is from image 418, page 6 of the typescript, J. H. Kellogg Papers, U-M.

14. "Ella Eaton Kellogg," in John W. Leonard, ed., *Woman's Who's Who of America: A Biographical Dictionary of Contemporary Women in the United States and Canada, 1914–1915* (New York: American Commonwealth Co., 1914), p. 449; "Dr. Kellogg on Suffrage," unidentified newspaper clipping, March 29, 1913, Reel 35, Image 34, J. H. Kellogg Papers, U-M. John states in this editorial: "Women possess these inalienable rights as truly as do men, and no sound reason for the possession of the right to vote by men can be offered which does not apply with equal force to women."

15. J. H. Kellogg, *Autointoxication or Intestinal Toxemia* (Battle Creek, MI: The

Modern Medicine Publishing Co., 1919), pp. 22–23, 56–83, quote is from page 22. See also stereopticon lecture for November 17, 1910: "The Conventional Beefsteak," Reel 12, Images 169–91, quote is on image 189, J. H. Kellogg Papers, U-M. He says in this talk, "Non-flesh eaters rarely ever have cancer in any form."

16. Typescript of "Some Features of Race Degeneracy," May 15, 1911, Reel 12, Images 981–1003. Bacteria quote is on Image 999 (p. 19 of the typescript), J. H. Kellogg Papers, U-M.

17. J. H. Kellogg, lecture, "Why Flesh Eating Is Wrong," April 14, 1910, Reel 11, Images 990–1019, J. H. Kellogg Papers, U-M.

18. "Question Box Hour," January 23, 1911, Reel 12, Images 458–81, J. H. Kellogg Papers, U-M. (He discusses the pickled beefsteak in this lecture, on Images 458–65; pp. 1–7 of the typescript.) "Why Eat Flesh?," February 16, 1911, Reel 12, Images 643–56, J. H. Kellogg Papers, U-M.

19. J. H. Kellogg, *The Health Question Box,* pp. 146–47, quote is from 147. With respect to this eulogy on the ills caused by the slaughterhouse, Dr. Kellogg is quoting the work of a London physician named Harry Campbell. Dr. Kellogg told many variants of the wild animal turning tame story, using a number of different animals, many times over the years. See, for example, the Bloese memoir. On page 206, Bloese notes, "To prove the truth of his contention he collected a number of meat-eating creatures and fed them on essentially the same food he ate himself. With the exception of a stubborn eagle, which refused the meatless fare, the animals did not seem to object to this radical change in their dietary [*sic*] and it produced no ill effects. On the contrary, it improved the appearance as well as the disposition of these creatures." On p. 207a, Bloese tells an alternate story of Kellogg visiting a zoo in Switzerland where the bears were fed a vegetarian diet since being cubs. The zookeeper played with the bears "without the slightest danger." The keeper went away for a week on vacation, and during this period the other zookeepers fed the bears meat, with the result that they soon became ferocious and "bear-like." When the zookeeper returned, he went into the same cage to play with the bears. The meat-eating bears almost killed him because "they had been transformed from lumbering, harmless comedians into savage snarling death-dealing brutes." After changing the diet back to a vegetarian one, "they regained their good dispositions and were as harmless as kittens." A. S. Bloese Manuscript, pp. 206–207a, Box 1, Folder 14.

20. See, for example, typescript of "Stereopticon Lecture, October, 6, 1910 at 8 pm.," Reel 12, Images 19–53, J. H. Kellogg Papers, U-M. See also "Lecture: Why Eat Flesh?," February 16, 1911, Reel 12, Images 643–56, J. H. Kellogg Papers, U-M.

21. J. H. Kellogg, "Fletcherizing the Oyster" (Battle Creek, MI: Good Health Extension Bureau, undated pamphlet, Box 7, "Lectures, Speeches, and Related Materials, 1923–1933" (p. 3 of the pamphlet), J. H. Kellogg Papers, U-M. See also J. H. Kellogg, *The Health Question Box,* pp. 144–45. Dr. Kellogg reported that oyster juice, based on laboratory analyses in the Battle Creek Sanitarium bacteriology laboratory, had the same composition as urine and the oyster carried the germ of typhoid fever.

22. J. H. Kellogg, "A Tempest in an Oyster Pot," typescript dated April 12, 1931, Box 7, "Lectures, Speeches, and Related Materials, 1923–1933," J. H. Kellogg Papers, U-M.

23. Williamson Jr., *An Intimate Glimpse,* pp. 14–15.

24. Powell, p. 45.

25. Postcard: "Aviator Bonney with Wright Aeroplane No. 2 at Battle Creek, Mich.

July 3, 1911," Collections of the University of Michigan Center for the History of Medicine.

26. Carson, pp. 241–42.

27. "Transcript of conversation with Count Tolstoy," March 16, 1924, Reel 26, Images 631–46, J. H. Kellogg Papers, U-M.

28. "Lecture: Some Features of the New Hygiene, December 8, 1910," Reel 12, Images 286–307, quote is on Images 296–97, pp. 11–12 of the typescript, J. H. Kellogg Papers, U-M; "Lecture: The New Hygiene," November 3, 1910, Reel 12, Images 111–41, J. H. Kellogg Papers, U-M.

29. Schwarz, *John Harvey Kellogg*, pp. 75–77.

30. Ibid.

31. Carson, pp. 242–43; Powell, p. 83.

32. Mary Butler, Frances Thornton, and Garth "Duff" Stoltz, *The Battle Creek Idea: Dr. John Harvey Kellogg and the Battle Creek Sanitarium* (Battle Creek, MI: Heritage Publications/Historical Society of Battle Creek, 1994), pp. 44–45. When the San's grand new "Tower" was opened in 1928, Henry Ford was the first patient to sign the guest register.

33. Norman Beasley, "The Commonest Thing We Do, We Know Least About," *Redbook*, May 1934, pp. 59, 164; Steven Watts, *The People's Tycoon: Henry Ford and the American Century* (New York: Vintage, 2006), pp. 326–31.

34. John Burroughs discusses these summer trips of the group self-named the "Vagabonds" and which included Thomas Edison, Henry Ford, Harvey Firestone, Alexis Carrel, and Charles Lindbergh in *Under the Maples: The Writings of John Burroughs, Volume 22* (Boston: Houghton Mifflin and Co., 1921), pp. 109–26. See also James Newton, *Uncommon Friends: Life with Thomas Edison, Henry Ford, Harvey Firestone, Alexis Carrel, and Charles Lindbergh* (San Diego: Harcourt, 1987); Edward J. Renhean Jr., *John Burroughs: An American Naturalist* (Hensonville, NY: Black Dome Press, 1998).

35. Edison hated smokers and fired anyone working in his company suspected of smoking, Letter from Thomas Edison to Henry Ford, April 26, 1926, Acc. 1, Box 113, Anti-Smoking-Edison Letter, 1914, 113–19, Benson Ford Research Center; Watts, *The People's Tycoon*, pp. 306–9.

36. Henry Ford, *The Case Against the Little White Slaver*, Volumes 1, 2, 3, 4 (Dearborn, MI: Henry Ford, 1914, 1915, 1916).

37. In 1923, the committee issued a fascinating report written by M. V. O'Shea, a professor of education at the University of Wisconsin who wrote several health textbooks with Dr. Kellogg. Some of the committee's other prominent members included Sir William Osler, the Regius Professor of Medicine at Oxford, Dr. Howard Kelly of the Johns Hopkins Hospital, naturalist John Burroughs, Yale economist Irving Fisher, and the businessman and philanthropist George Foster Peabody. M. V. O'Shea, *Tobacco and Mental Efficiency* (New York: The Macmillan Company, 1923).

38. Elizabeth Fee and Theodore M. Brown, "J. H. Kellogg, MD: Health Reformer and Antismoking Crusader," *American Journal of Public Health*, 2002; 92(6): 935; Schwarz, *John Harvey Kellogg*, p. 107; Allan Brandt, *The Cigarette Century: The Rise, Fall, and Deadly Persistence of the Product That Defined America* (New York: Basic Books, 2007), pp. 49, 61.

39. J. H. Kellogg, *Tobaccoism, or How Tobacco Kills* (Battle Creek, MI: Modern Medicine Publishing Company, 1922). Kellogg had been writing and lecturing on

these harms decades before publishing this book. See, for example, J. H. Kellogg, "The smoke nuisance," *Good Health,* 1886; 21: 257–58.

40. Efforts by famous reformers like Dr. Kellogg and Henry Ford did lead to a bill introduced by Senator Reed Smoot (R-UT) in 1929 that called for cigarettes to be regulated under the Pure Food and Drug Act of 1906. Although many favored this bill, including the American Public Health Association, it never saw its way out of Congress. Association News, *American Journal of Public Health,* 1929; 19: 1240; Fee and Brown, "J. H. Kellogg, MD: Health Reformer and Antismoking Crusader," p. 935; Schwarz, *John Harvey Kellogg,* p. 107.

41. Powell, p. 174.

42. This correspondence can be found at the Benson Ford Research Center, Henry Ford Museum, Dearborn, Michigan, Fairlane Papers, Box 113, Acc 1, Letter from J. H. Kellogg to Clara Ford, November, 14, 1922. See also Letter from J. H. Kellogg to Clara Ford, February 21, 1932, Acc. 1, Box 59, Correspondence-"Kellogg," 59–4. Other Ford correspondence can be found in the J. H. Kellogg Papers at the University of Michigan, such as J. H. Kellogg to Clara Ford, February 21, 1940, Reel 5, Images 977–98.

43. Letter from E. H. Liebold to J. H. Kellogg, July 16, 1920, Henry Ford Office, 1920, Acc. 284, Correspondence I-K, Box 17, Folder 8, Benson Ford Research Center.

44. Letter from J. H. Kellogg to E. H. Liebold, July 20, 1920, Henry Ford Office, 1920, Acc. 284, Correspondence I-K, Box 17, Folder 8, Benson Ford Research Center.

45. A. S. Bloese, "Anecdotes and Interesting Episodes in the Life of Dr. John Harvey Kellogg," p. 6, A. S. Bloese Manuscript, Box 1, File 12.

46. Ron Chernow, *Titan: The Life of John D. Rockefeller, Sr.* (New York: Vintage, 2004), pp. 571–90.

47. Letter from John D. Rockefeller Jr. to J. H. Kellogg, May 7, 1938, Reel 5, Image 239, J. H. Kellogg Papers, U-M.

48. Letter from J. H. Kellogg to Clarence W. Barron, April 8, 1927, Reel 3, Images 81–82, J. H. Kellogg Papers, U-M.

49. Can of Battle Creek LD-Lax, Battle Creek Food Company. Artifact in the Collections of the University of Michigan Center for the History of Medicine.

50. Letter from J. H. Kellogg to John D. Rockefeller Jr., May 17, 1939, Reel 5, Images 250–53, J. H. Kellogg Papers, U-M. Dr. Kellogg also asked the tycoon for help in fighting tobacco use and reports that it causes cardiovascular disease. He wrote, "The cigarette habit has been spreading so rapidly the last few years among women as well as men it is becoming a monster evil which should be vigorously combated."

51. Peter Lyon, *Success Story: The Life and Times of S. S. McClure* (Deland, FL: Everett/Edwards, 1967), p. 345.

52. Letters from J. H. Kellogg to Ida Tarbell, July 20, 1939, Images 632–36; Ida Tarbell to J. H. Kellogg, July 28, 1939, Images 638–40; J. H. Kellogg to Ida Tarbell, August 3, 1939, Images 644–48, in which he states, "Old age is a disease"; Ida Tarbell to J. H. Kellogg, December 6, 1939, Images 827–28; J. H. Kellogg to Ida Tarbell, January 5, 1940, Images 895–96, all on Reel 5, J. H. Kellogg Papers, U-M. Tarbell had Parkinson's disease around this time and thanked him for sending various health foods to her as well as, accidentally, thanking him for sending Postum—a C. W. Post product. In her December 6, 1939, letter she notes, "Mine is an annoying case of *paralysis agitans* [now called Parkinson's disease]. And they tell me nothing can be done for it. Now that is what I want to get at in this particular study I have in mind. And anything that your institution has done that would help or direct me I should be very glad of." For Tarbell's famous exposé of John D. Rockefeller and the Standard Oil Company, see

Ida M. Tarbell, *The History of the Standard Oil Company* (New York: McClure, Phillips and Co., 1904).

53. Kevin J. Hayes, "Clarence W. Barron," in J. A. Garraty and M. C. Carnes, *American National Biography,* Volume 2 (New York: Oxford University Press, 1999), pp. 239–40; "Clarence W. Barron, Publisher Is Dead. Head of the *Wall Street Journal* a Victim of Catarrhal Jaundice at 73 in Battle Creek," *New York Times,* October 3, 1928, pp. 1–2, and October 5, 1928, p. 25. See also Arthur Pound and Samuel T. Moore, eds., *They Told Barron: Conversations and Revelations of an American Pepys in Wall Street* (New York: Harper and Brothers, 1930); Arthur Pound and Samuel T. Moore, eds., *More They Told Barron: Conversations and Revelations of an American Pepys in Wall Street* (New York: Harper and Brothers, 1931).

54. See, for example, Letters from C. W. Barron to J. H. Kellogg, June 26, 1927, Images 103–4; C. W. Barron to J. H. Kellogg, July 11, 1927, Image 106; C. W. Barron to J. H. Kellogg, September 28, 1927, Images 116–17; J. H. Kellogg to C. W. Barron, September 30, 1927, Images 118–19, all on Reel 3, J. H. Kellogg Papers, U-M; Pound and Moore, eds., *They Told Barron,* pp. xxxi–xxxii.

55. Letter from C. W. Barron to J. H. Kellogg, March 23, 1927, Reel 3, Image 75, J. H. Kellogg Papers, U-M. In this letter, for example, Barron referred to the famed coloratura soprano opera Amelita Galli-Curci, the Populist U.S. senator from North Carolina, Marion Butler, and Calvin Coolidge's eldest son, John.

56. A. S. Bloese Manuscript, p. 325, Box 1, Folder 14.

57. Ibid. See also Schwarz, PhD thesis, p. 85; A. E. Wiggam, "The Most Remarkable Man I Have Ever Known," *American Magazine,* December 1925, pp. 14–15, 117–18.

58. Letter from J. H. Kellogg to C. Barron, February 1, 1923, in Pound and Moore, eds., *They Told Barron,* p. 175.

59. Letter from J. H. Kellogg to C. Barron, October 31, 1924, in Pound and Moore, eds., *They Told Barron,* p. 231.

60. "Clarence Barron Ill," *New York Times,* March 26, 1925, p. 23.

61. Letter from J. H. Kellogg to C. W. Barron, January 21, 1927, Reel 3, Image 63, J. H. Kellogg Papers, U-M.

62. Ibid., Image 66.

63. Ibid., Image 105.

64. A. O. J. Kelly, "Acute Catarrhal Cholangitis (Catarrhal Jaundice)," in William Osler and Thomas McCrae, eds., *Volume 5: Diseases of the Alimentary Tract. Modern Medicine: Its Theory and Practice* (Philadelphia: Lea and Febiger, 1908), pp. 807–11.

65. "Clarence W. Barron, Publisher, Is Dead. Head of the *Wall Street Journal* a Victim of Catarrhal Jaundice at 73 in Battle Creek. Noted Financial Figure. A Writer on World Fiscal Topics—Body Will Be Taken to His Old Home in Boston," *New York Times,* October 3, 1928, pp. 1, 2; Pound and Moore, eds., *They Told Barron,* xxxii.

66. "LBJ Will Be Battle Creek's Fourth Presidential Visitor. McKinley, Taft Here. FDR Didn't Stop, Visit Held Secret," *Battle Creek Enquirer and News,* September 4, 1966, p. 3, Reel 33, Image 419, J. H. Kellogg Papers, U-M. The number of presidential visits in the newspaper is slightly off, if you count former presidents, presidential candidates or future presidents. William McKinley made a whistle-stop visit in 1900; William Howard Taft visited in 1911 as described above and actually visited the San; former president Teddy Roosevelt came in 1916 campaigning for Republican presidential candidate Charles Evans Hughes but was only there briefly to speak at a rally. Warren Harding's visits are described in the text. Herbert Hoover came to visit with

Will Kellogg in 1930 and again in 1941. Senator Harry Truman spent the night in Battle Creek after inspecting local army bases in December of 1930. Franklin Roosevelt's train secretly went through Battle Creek en route to Detroit in September of 1942. After Dr. Kellogg's death in 1943, Adlai Stevenson made brief campaign stops in Battle Creek during the 1952 and 1956 elections as did John Kennedy and Richard Nixon in 1960. Lyndon Johnson visited in 1966 and in his speech, in front of the old Sanitarium, he made several references to Dr. Kellogg. Lyndon B. Johnson, 36th President of the United States, 1963–1968. "433-Remarks at the Battle Creek Sanitarium, Battle Creek, Michigan," September 5, 1966, *American Presidency Project,* accessed July 26, 2015, at http://www.presidency.ucsb.edu/ws/?pid=27830. In the speech LBJ stated "From what Mrs. Johnson has told me of Dr. Kellogg, he was my kind of man. He started early, he stayed late. He worked to fulfill his ambition, and I quote him, 'to spend my entire life in human service.'"

67. "Ex-President Dies at Capital, Succumbing to Many Weeks Illness, Five Hours After Justice Sanford," *New York Times,* March 9, 1930, pp. 1, 26. Supreme Court Justice Edward T. Sanford died in his home that day, of uremic poisoning and kidney failure. His obituary appears on the same page of this issue.

68. Scott Bruce and Bill Crawford, *Cerealizing America: The Unsweetened Story of American Breakfast Cereal* (Boston and London: Faber and Faber, 1995), p. 17.

69. A. S. Bloese Manuscript, p. 353a, Box 2, Folder 1.

70. Francis Russell, *The Shadow of Blooming Grove: Warren G. Harding in His Times* (New York: McGraw-Hill, 1968), p. 80.

71. Ibid.; Robert K. Murray, *The Harding Era: Warren G. Harding and His Administration* (Newtown, CT: American Political Biography Press, 1969), p. 438; Howard Markel, "The Strange Death of Warren G. Harding," PBS Newshour.org, August 2, 2015, accessed August 3, 2015, at http://www.pbs.org/newshour/updates/strange-death-warren-harding/.

72. "Iron Nag's Inventor Defends Hobby," unidentified clipping about Coolidge's mechanical horse by the United Press Reel 36, Image 18, J. H. Kellogg Papers, U-M.

73. Letter from J. H. Kellogg to C. W. Barron, June 17, 1927, Reel 3, Image 95, J. H. Kellogg Papers, U-M.

74. Letters from Lt. Col. Hodges to J. H. Kellogg, December 28, 1932, Reel 3, Image 506; J. H. Kellogg to Lt. Col. Hodges, January 2, 1932, Reel 3, Image 508, J. H. Kellogg Papers, U-M.

75. Letter from J. H. Kellogg to Marguerite Le Hand, July 27, 1933, Reel 3, Images 564–65; Letter from J. H. Kellogg to Henry Ford, February 21, 1932, Reel 3, Images 421–22, J. H. Kellogg Papers, U-M.

76. Letter from J. H. Kellogg to Franklin D. Roosevelt, July 27, 1933, Reel 3, Images 566–67, J. H. Kellogg Papers, U-M.

77. Letter from J. H. Kellogg to Franklin D. Roosevelt, May 12, 1934, Reel 3, Images 667–69, J. H. Kellogg Papers, U-M. Dr. Kellogg writes the president about the health benefits of outdoor gardening, especially in Florida; Mary Butler, Frances Thornton, Garth Stoltz, *The Battle Creek Idea* (Battle Creek, MI: Heritage Publications, 1994), p. 45; Eleanor Roosevelt, "My Day" (newspaper column for April 16, 1940), accessed March 12, 2017, at https://www2.gwu.edu/~erpapers/myday/display doc.cfm?_y=1040&_f=.

78. Schwarz, *John Harvey Kellogg,* p. 143.

II.

WILL'S PLACE

1. Powell, p. 105.

2. "Palace, New Year's," *Variety,* November 1, 1912; 28(9): 6.

3. Susan Tifft and Alex S. Jones, *The Trust: The Private and Powerful Family Behind the* New York Times (Boston: Little, Brown, 1999), pp. 69–73; Donald L. Miller, *Supreme City: How Jazz Age Manhattan Gave Birth to Modern America* (New York: Simon & Schuster, 2014), pp. 287–88. The first New Year's "ball drop" was organized by Ochs in 1908.

4. "Mecca Building," *The Economist* (Chicago), December 27, 1919; 62(26): 1310; Christopher Gray, "Streetscapes: The Studebaker Building," *New York Times,* January 1, 1989, p. R4; David W. Dunlap, "Change, as It Does, Returns to Times Square," *New York Times,* November 8, 2004.

5. Among the building's many uses, from 1939 to 1941, Robert Ripley, of "Believe It or Not" fame, rented out the first two floors for his "Odditorium." Neal Thompson, *A Curious Man. The Strange and Brilliant Life of Robert "Believe It or Not!" Ripley* (New York: Crown Archtype, 2013). It is interesting to note that in 2016 the Kellogg Company announced the opening of a new Kellogg's "breakfast boutique store" in Times Square at the site of the former Mecca Building, 1600 Broadway. Jonah E. Bromwich, "$7 for Corn Flakes? Cereal Gets Makeover at Kellogg's Store in Times Square," *New York Times,* June 30, 2016, accessed July 19, 2016, at http://www.nytimes .com/2016/07/01/nyregion/7-for-corn-flakes-cereal-gets-makeover-at-kelloggs-store -in-times-square.html?_r=0.

6. Powell, p. 138.

7. "The Largest Electric Sign Ever Built," advertisement for Kellogg's Corn Flakes, *Saturday Evening Post,* August 17, 1912 (back cover), Collections of the University of Michigan Center for the History of Medicine. In 1915, Will tried to default on his lease agreement because the building owners erected other signs that, he felt, obstructed the view of his sign. He won the case. See Appellate Division of the Supreme Court of New York, First Department, *Mecca Realty Co. (Appellate) v. Kellogg Toasted Corn Flake Co. (Respondent),* February 11, 1915; "A Skeleton Structure Is a Building Under the Law," Appellate Division of the Supreme Court of New York, First Department, 166 App. Div. 74 (New York App. Div. 1915); *Printer's Ink,* February 25, 1915; 90(8): 92.

8. *State of Michigan Supreme Court Record,* Volume 3, *Kellogg v. Kellogg,* Box 21, File 3, Exhibit No. 525, pp. 984–85, J. H. Kellogg Papers, MSU.

9. Powell, p. 119.

10. Francis X. Blouin, "Not Just Automobiles: Contributions of Michigan to the National Economy, 1866–1917," in Richard J. Hathaway, ed., *Michigan Visions of Our Past* (East Lansing: Michigan State University Press, 1989), pp. 151–61, quote is from p. 155; Alfred D. Chandler Jr., *The Visible Hand: The Managerial Revolution in American Business* (Cambridge: Belknap Press of Harvard University Press, 1977), pp. 79–82, 195, 299.

11. Everett Rogers, *The Diffusion of Innovations* (New York: Free Press of Glencoe/ MacMillan, 1962).

12. Frank Luther Mott, *American Journalism: A History, 1690–1960* (New York: Macmillan, 1962, 3rd edition), pp. 495–513. See also Richard Kluger, *The Paper: The Life and Death of the* New York Herald Tribune (New York: Alfred A. Knopf, 1986), pp. 151–52.

13. John Hendel, "Celebrating Linotype, 125 Years Since Its Debut," *The Atlantic,* May 20, 2011, accessed August 29, 2015 at http://www.theatlantic.com/technology /archive/2011/05/celebrating-linotype-125-years-since-its-debut/238968/.

14. Roland Marchand, *Advertising the American Dream: Making Way for Modernity* (Berkeley: University of California Press, 1986); Juliann Sivulka, *Soap, Sex, and Cigarettes: A Cultural History of American Advertising* (Boston: Wadsworth Cenage Learning, 1998); Stephen R. Fox, *The Mirror Makers: A History of American Advertising and Its Creators* (Urbana: University of Illinois Press, 1997); Susan Strasser, *Satisfaction Guaranteed: The Making of the American Mass Market* (Washington, DC: Smithsonian Books, 1989); Charles Goodrum and Helen Dalrymple, *Advertising in America: The First 200 Years* (New York: Harry N. Abrams, 1990), pp. 56–68; Larry Tye, *The Father of Spin: Edward L. Bernays and the Birth of Public Relations* (New York: Henry Holt, 1998).

15. T. Jackson Lears, *Fables of Abundance: A Cultural History of Advertising in America* (New York: Basic Books, 1994), p. 1.

16. James Harvey Young, *Toadstool Millionaires: A Social History of Patent Medicines in America Before Federal Regulation* (Princeton: Princeton University Press, 1961), pp. 205–46; James Harvey Young, *The Medical Messiahs: A Social History of Health Quackery in Twentieth-Century America* (Princeton: Princeton University Press, 1975); James Harvey Young, *Pure Food: Securing the Federal Food and Drug Act of 1906* (Princeton: Princeton University Press, 1989).

17. Frank Luther Mott, *A History of American Magazines, 1885–1905* (Cambridge: Belknap Press of Harvard University Press, 1957), Chapter 2, "The Counting Houses," pp. 15–35; Chapter 13, "Newspapers and Advertising," pp. 243–49; Chapter 21, "Women's Activities," 354–70. W. K. Kellogg, incidentally, was a great supporter of the Pure Food and Drug Act of 1906. He was especially supportive of the first chief administrator of what became the Food and Drug Administration (FDA), Harvey W. Wiley, an activist chemist and reformer many food manufacturers resented because of the regulations he imposed and the investigations he conducted. See Williamson Jr., *An Intimate Glimpse,* p. 35.

18. Samuel Hopkins Adams, "The New World of Trade, II. The Art of Advertising," *Collier's,* May 22, 1909; 43: 13–15.

19. *State of Michigan Supreme Court Record,* Volume 3, Kellogg v. Kellogg, Box 21, File 3, Exhibit No. 525, pp. 977–91, J. H. Kellogg Papers, MSU.

20. Powell, pp. 132–33.

21. Williamson Jr., *An Intimate Glimpse,* p. 34.

22. *State of Michigan Supreme Court Record,* Volume 3, pp. 977–90; File 3, Box 21, J. H. Kellogg Papers, MSU.

23. The underlining of the word "all" is in Kellogg's letter and is his (or Arch Shaw's) emphasis. Powell, pp. 132–34. This July 1906 advertisement still carries the "Sanitas" label; so, too, does an advertisement called "The Lady and the Grocer: Two Minds with a Single Thought," *Ladies' Home Journal,* November 1906; 23(12): 55. An advertisement in an early 1907 issue of the *Delineator* continues with the Sanitas label but does have Will's signature prominently displayed under the banner "But they can't use this signature." An advertisement in the February 1907 (Volume 69, No. 2), *Delineator,* p. 327, still uses the brand Sanitas but does show Will's signature on a box. By late summer, 1907, Sanitas disappears as a label and the product is known as Kellogg's and made by the Battle Creek Toasted Corn Flake Company, which soon after simply becomes the

Kellogg's Toasted Corn Flake Company. These advertisements are from the Collections of the University of Michigan Center for the History of Medicine.

24. N. Williamson Jr., *An Intimate Glimpse*, pp. 34–36. Will owned 70 percent of the company's stock at this point in time.

25. Powell, p. 123; *Michigan State Supreme Court Record*, Volume 3, p. 971, File 3, Box 21, J. H. Kellogg Papers, MSU.

26. Powell, pp. 134–35.

27. Ibid., 134–35; Letter from J. R. Smith, Food Broker for Kellogg's Toasted Corn Flakes, to Grocers on the "Wink Campaign," June 10, 1907 (Images 3970–80), Box 20, File 6, J. H. Kellogg Papers, MSU.

28. *Kellogg's Funny Jungleland Moving-Pictures*, pamphlet (Copyright 1909; Patent 1907), Collections of the University of Michigan Center for the History of Medicine.

29. See, for example, All-Bran advertisement featuring the Captain and the Kids, *Women's Home Companion*, circa 1940; All-Bran advertisement featuring Alphonse and Gaston, *Literary Digest*, circa 1939; All-Bran advertisement featuring Mutt and Jeff, *Life* magazine, circa 1939. Collections of the University of Michigan Center for the History of Medicine. Throughout the years, Kellogg's would use numerous cartoon characters to advertise their cereals to children, ranging from Disney's Mickey Mouse, Donald Duck, and Goofy to Hanna-Barbera's Yogi the Bear and Huckleberry Hound and, most famously, their own cartoon stars such as Tony the Tiger, introduced in the early 1950s, and Snap, Crackle, and Pop, who date back to the 1930s. See, for example, "Boys! Girls! Get Your Walt Disney Character 'Joinies,'" Kellogg's Raisin Bran and Rice Krispies advertisement appearing in syndicated Sunday color funnies section, circa 1949, Collections of the University of Michigan Center for the History of Medicine. For the origins of Snap, Crackle, and Pop, see Kellogg's Rice Krispies website, accessed January 27, 2016, at http://www.ricekrispies.com/snap-crackle-pop.

30. "It Sho Do Crackle. Kellogg's Rice Krispies," advertisement in *Good Housekeeping*, September 1930, unpaginated, Collections of the University of Michigan Center for the History of Medicine. An earlier Kellogg's Toasted Corn Flakes ad circa 1908 features an African American bellhop wheeling a giant box of cereal, with the slogan "Everywhere they go—everywhere they know—the original—the genuine—the kind with the flavor."

31. Nan Robertson, "Ireene Wicker Hammer Dies, 86; Storyteller to Millions of Children," *New York Times*, November 18, 1987, accessed June 16, 2015, at http://www.nytimes.com/1987/11/18/obituaries/ireene-wicker-hammer-dies-86-storyteller-to-millions-of-children.html.

32. Carson, p. 212; "Kellogg's Krumbled Bran for Better Health," advertisement, *The Literary Digest*, November 15, 1919; 63(7): 85. The ad carries a message from W. K. Kellogg: "Don't be constipated. Eat our bran every morning as a cereal. You'll like its looks, enjoy its taste, and value its benefits. Each package is identified and guaranteed by my signature." Collections of the University of Michigan Center for the History of Medicine.

33. Powell, p. 142; Carson, p. 225.

34. Much of this section is drawn from earlier papers I wrote for the academic, peer-reviewed press: Howard Markel, "Caring for the Foreign Born: The Health of Immigrant Children in the United States, 1890–1925," *Archives of Pediatrics and Adolescent Medicine*, 1998; 152: 1020–27; Howard Markel, "For the Welfare of Children: The Origins of the Relationship Between U.S. Public Health Workers and Pediatricians,"

American Journal of Public Health, 2000; 90: 893–99; Howard Markel, "'When It Rains It Pours': Endemic Goiter, Iodized Salt and David Murray Cowie, MD," *American Journal of Public Health,* 1987; 77: 219–29; Howard Markel, "Academic Pediatrics: The View from New York City a Century Ago," *Academic Medicine,* 1996; 17: 146–51; Howard Markel, "Henry Koplik, MD, the Good Samaritan Dispensary of New York City, and the Description of Koplik's Spots," *Archives of Pediatrics and Adolescent Medicine,* 1996; 150: 535–39; Howard Markel, *Quarantine!: East European Jewish Immigrants and the New York City Epidemics of 1892* (Baltimore: Johns Hopkins University Press, 1997); Howard Markel and Frank A. Oski, *The H. L. Mencken Baby Book: Comprising the Contents of H. L. Mencken's What You Ought to Know About Your Baby, With Commentaries* (Philadelphia: Hanley and Belfus, 1990).

35. Manfred J. Wasserman, "Henry L. Coit and the Certified Milk Movement in the Development of Modern Pediatrics," *Bulletin of the History of Medicine,* 1972; 46: 359–90.

36. Richard Meckel, *Save the Babies: American Public Health Reform and the Preservation of Infant Mortality, 1850–1929* (Ann Arbor: University of Michigan Press, 1990), 62–91; *The Mellin's Food Method of Percentage Feeding* (Boston: The Press of Mellin's Food Company, 1908).

37. Markel, "For the Welfare of Children," pp. 893–99; Thomas R. Pegram, "Public Health and Progressive Dairying in Illinois," *Agricultural History,* 1991; 65(1): 36–50; J. B. Frantz, *Gail Borden: Dairyman to a Nation* (Norman: University of Oklahoma Press, 1951); Daniel Boorstin, *The Americans: The Democratic Experience* (New York: Random House, 1973), pp. 312–16.

38. Boorstin, *The Americans,* pp. 109–10, 115, 316–22, 327. See also Susanne Freidberg, *Fresh: A Perishable History* (Cambridge: Belknap Press of Harvard University Press, 2010); Aaron Bobrow-Strain, *White Bread: A Social History of the Store-Bought Loaf* (Boston: Beacon Press, 2013); John H. White Jr., *The American Railroad Freight Car: From the Wood-Car Era to the Coming of Steel* (Baltimore: Johns Hopkins University Press, 1993). And also see: John Harvey Young, *Pure Food: Securing the Federal Food and Drugs Act of 1906* (Princeton: Princeton University Press, 1989).

39. Mark Levinson, *The Great A&P and the Struggle for Small Business in America* (New York: Hill & Wang, 2012); Avis H. Anderson, *A&P: The Story of the Great Atlantic and Pacific Tea Company (Images of America)* (Charleston: Arcadia Publishing, 2002); William I. Walsh, *The Rise and Decline of the Great Atlantic & Pacific Tea Company* (New York: Lyle Stuart, 1986); Guru Madhavan, *Applied Minds: How Engineers Think* (New York: W. W. Norton, 2015), pp. 59–61; Mike Freeman, *Clarence Saunders and the Founding of Piggly Wiggly: The Rise and Fall of a Memphis Maverick* (Mount Pleasant, SC: The History Press, 2011); John Brooks, "A Corner in Piggly Wiggly: Annals of Finance," *The New Yorker,* June 6, 1959; 25(16): 128–60.

40. Williamson Jr., *An Intimate Glimpse,* p. 29.

41. Neal Gabler, *Walt Disney: The Triumph of the American Imagination* (New York: Alfred A. Knopf, 2006), pp. 111–64, quote is from p. 155.

42. Powell, p. 93.

43. Schwarz, *John Harvey Kellogg,* p. 212.

44. Powell, p. 111.

45. Schwarz, *John Harvey Kellogg,* pp. 211–12; Powell, pp. 111–13.

46. Powell, pp. 111–12.

47. Ibid., p. 98.

48. Ibid., pp. 111–14.

49. Ibid., pp. 113–14.

50. Interview of William S. Sadler by Richard Schwarz, November 13, 1960 (Card IX-A-3), B10, F14, Sadler, Richard Schwarz Collection, Center for Adventist Research.

51. In W. K. Kellogg's obituary, it states he bought this plant from the Hygienic Food Company, where it made "Maple Flakes," for $26,340.50, half of which was in cash. "Community to Mourn W. K. Kellogg for Week," *Battle Creek Enquirer and News*, October 7, 1951, p. 12. The entire obituary appears on pp. 1, 12, 13, and 14.

52. Powell, p. 123.

53. Ibid., p. 117.

54. Carson, p. 205.

55. Norman Williamson Jr. gives this explanation, too, in his *An Intimate Glimpse*, p. 30.

56. Powell, p. 118. The Norka plant was later abandoned and it burned down in 1912.

57. Ibid., p. 135. Morehouse would later design an "annex"—which was actually a fifteen-story patient tower—for the Battle Creek Sanitarium in 1928. Laura R. Ashlee, ed., *Traveling Through Time: A Guide to Michigan's Historical Markers* (Ann Arbor: University of Michigan Press, 2005).

58. Williamson Jr., *An Intimate Glimpse*, p. 34.

59. Carson, p. 206.

60. Powell, pp. 124–25.

61. Carson, p. 205.

62. Powell, pp. 125–26. The italics are Powell's.

63. Carson, p. 206.

64. Powell, p. 125; Williamson Jr., *An Intimate Glimpse*, p. 33; "Community to Mourn W. K. Kellogg for Week," *Battle Creek Enquirer and News*, October 7, 1951, p. 14. The entire obituary appears on pp. 1, 12, 13, and 14.

65. Williamson Jr., *An Intimate Glimpse*, pp. 30–31.

66. "Community to Mourn W. K. Kellogg for Week," p. 14; similarly, a memorial issue of the company newspaper, *The Kellogg News*, for October 1951, Collections of the Willard Library of Battle Creek, Michigan, cites this same figure on page 7. Powell, however, lists a far lower figure on p. 126 of only 24,000 cases per day for 1920, which is clearly too low for this late date and success of the company.

67. Powell, p. 182.

68. Ibid., pp. 181–82.

69. Robert Froman, "Here's the Latest Exciting Chapter in the Cereal Story," *Collier's*, April 12, 1952; 129: 28, 78–81, Reel 34, Images 525–30, J. H. Kellogg Papers, U-M; photographic postcards of the W. K. Kellogg Toasted Corn Flake Company employees, circa 1908, and of the process of making Corn Flakes, circa 1920s, Collections of the University of Michigan Center for the History of Medicine.

70. The Kellogg Company, postcards of the manufacturing process, circa 1920s, Collections of the University of Michigan Center for the History of Medicine.

71. Powell, p. 121.

72. Ibid., p. 162.

73. Ibid., pp. 161–63, quote is from p. 163. Robert Updegraff was the author of numerous books and articles on business and marketing as well as a valued advisor to the top management of several major companies including the Aluminum Company of America, American Brake Shoe Company, General Foods Corporation, W. T. Grant Company, John Hancock Mutual Life Insurance Company, Hart Schaffner and Marx,

Lever Brothers, and Westinghouse Electric. He was a frequent contributor to *System*, a trade magazine published by Arch Shaw's company, and was likely introduced to W. K. Kellogg through Shaw.

74. Powell, p. 115.

75. Carson, p. 217; Powell, pp. 157, 161–62.

76. Benjamin K. Hunnicutt, *Kellogg's Six-Hour Day* (Philadelphia: Temple University Press, 1996); Williamson Jr., *An Intimate Glimpse,* pp. 140–42.

77. "You Won't Believe It Until You've Tried It. Delicious! Kellogg's Corn Flakes Served Piping Hot with Hot Milk or Cream," 1939 advertisement, *Ladies' Home Journal,* Collections of the University of Michigan Center for the History of Medicine.

78. Powell, p. 279.

79. Williamson Jr., *An Intimate Glimpse,* pp. 128–29, 153, 169–73. Among the interim (and in Will's view unsuccessful) chief executives of the Kellogg Company during this period were Lewis J. Brown and Walter Hasselhorn.

80. Powell, pp. 210–11, quote is from p. 209.

81. "Watson Vanderploeg Dies at 68; President of Kellogg Company; Head of Cereal Concern Since 1939. Previously Had Been a Banker in Chicago," *New York Times,* May 29, 1957, p. 21. The three U.S. plants were in Battle Creek; San Leandro, California; and Omaha, Nebraska. By 1955, Kellogg's operated plants in London, Ontario, Canada; Sydney, Australia; Manchester, England; Quarétaro, Mexico; Springs, South Africa; along with the three contracted plants in Ireland, Sweden, and Holland. By the early 1960s, according to a company promotional brochure, that number increased to plants in sixteen countries: Australia, Brazil, Canada, Columbia, Denmark, Finland, Great Britain, Holland, Ireland, Mexico, New Zealand, Norway, South Africa, Switzerland, the United States, and Venezuela and more than "100 countries enjoy Kellogg's Corn Flakes for breakfast!" See promotional postcard, "Kellogg's Company Plants," circa 1955; and brochure, "Let's Take a Peek at Kellogg's of Battle Creek (featuring Yogi Bear as your tour guide)," circa 1960. Kellogg's cereals are currently sold in over 180 countries around the world. Collections of the University of Michigan Center for the History of Medicine.

82. Powell, p. 210.

83. Scott Bruce and Bill Crawford, *Cerealizing America: The Unsweetened Story of American Breakfast Cereal* (Boston and London: Faber and Faber, 1995), pp. 103–13. The current public health problem of obesity, of course, is much more multi-factorial and complicated than indicting the cereal companies alone. See, for example, K. M. Flegal, M. D. Carroll, B. K. Kit, and C. L. Ogden, "Prevalence of Obesity and Trends in the Distribution of Body Mass Index Among US Adults, 1999–2010," *Journal of the American Medical Association,* 2012; 307(5): 491–97; C. L. Ogden, M. D. Carroll, B. K. Kit, and K. M. Flegal, "Prevalence of obesity and trends in body mass index among US children and adolescents, 1999–2010." *Journal of the American Medical Association,* 2012; 307 (5): 483–90; A. S. Singh, C. Mulder, J. W. Twisk, W. van Mechelen, and M. J. Chinapaw, "Tracking of Childhood Overweight into Adulthood: A Systematic Review of the Literature," *Obesity Reviews,* 2008; 9(5): 474–88.

84. Bruce and Crawford, *Cerealizing America,* pp. 137–41.

85. "Tony the Tiger Says 'You Bet Your Life They're Gr-r-eat. No Wonder Groucho's Speechless," Kellogg's Sugar Frosted Flakes advertisement, *Life* magazine, February 21, 1955; "Boys! Girls! Get Your Walt Disney Character 'Joinies,'" Kellogg's Raisin Bran and Rice Krispies advertisement appearing in syndicated Sunday color funnies section (undated and not sourced, circa 1949); "Howdy Doody's Favorite Treat—9-minute

Marshmallow 'Crispy Squares,' " Kellogg's Rice Krispies and marshmallows recipe and advertisement (undated and not sourced, circa 1951); "Two Don't Forgetters," Kellogg's Corn Flakes advertisement, illustrated by Norman Rockwell (undated and not sourced, circa 1950s); Kellogg's Variety Package advertisement, featuring Uncle Sam: "U.S. Needs US Strong. Eat Nutritional Food" (undated and not sourced, circa 1942); Rice Krispies Marshmallow Crispy Treats recipe advertisement, featuring Woody Woodpecker, "Now Appearing on TV for Kellogg's Exclusively" (not sourced, 1957), "The Self-Starter Breakfast Keeps Me on My Toes, says Esther Williams," Kellogg's Corn Flakes advertisement (not sourced, 1941); "Reach for It Andy—They're Gr-r-eat," Tony the Tiger and Andy Devine, Kellogg's Sugar Frosted Flakes advertisement (not sourced, 1955); Garry Moore and Tony the Tiger, "Won't They Even Tell You, Tony?" (*Life* magazine, October 3, 1955; 39[14]: 133), Collections of the University of Michigan Center for the History of Medicine.

86. Art Linkletter and Tony the Tiger, "Tony the Tiger Says: I'm Having My Own House Party with Sugar Frosted Flakes," *Life* magazine, undated, circa 1955, Collections of the University of Michigan Center for the History of Medicine.

87. Bruce and Crawford, *Cerealizing America*, pp. 114–25; The Kellogg Company, *2014 Annual Report, Letters to Shareowners and SEC Form 10-K, Fiscal Year End: January 3, 2015* (Battle Creek, MI, 2015).

88. Powell, p. 117.

12.
THE PRISON OF RESENTMENT

1. Powell, pp. 145–56; *Battle Creek Enquirer,* August 12, 1910, p. 1. For the detailed court papers, including the bill of complaint and various testimonies and affidavits in this case, see *Kellogg Toasted Corn Flake Co. (Complainant) v. J. H. Kellogg, the Kellogg Food Company and the Kellogg Toasted Rice Flake and Biscuit Company (Defendant),* State of Michigan in the Circuit Court for the County of Calhoun, in Chancery, filed August 11, 1910, Box 19, File 3, Items 260–70, 280–90, 300–40, 350–90, 680–1010), J. H. Kellogg Papers, MSU. See also additional affidavits in opposition to temporary injunction, filed by J. H. Kellogg, September 1, 1910, State of Michigan in the Circuit Court for the County of Calhoun, in Chancery, Box 19, File 4, Items 1040–50, 1140–70, 1250–1760, Box 19, File 5, Items 1800–3690; Box 19, File 6, Items 3720–4470, 4480–4750, J. H. Kellogg Papers, MSU.

2. Schwarz, *John Harvey Kellogg,* p. 216.

3. *Kellogg Toasted Corn Flake Co. (Complainant) v. J. H. Kellogg, the Kellogg Food Company and the Kellogg Toasted Rice Flake and Biscuit Company (Defendant),* State of Michigan in the Circuit Court for the County of Calhoun, in Chancery, filed August 11, 1910, Items 680–1010, Box 19, File 3, J. H. Kellogg Papers, MSU.

4. *Kellogg Toasted Corn Flake Co. (Complainant) v. J. H. Kellogg, the Kellogg Food Company and the Kellogg Toasted Rice Flake and Biscuit Company (Defendant),* State of Michigan in the Circuit Court for the County of Calhoun, in Chancery, Complainant's Application for Temporary Injunction and Further Supporting Affidavits, filed September 1, 1910, Box 19, File 3, Items 350–90, J. H. Kellogg Papers, MSU.

5. The schism between John and the Church is nicely summarized and explained in Richard Schwarz, "The Kellogg Schism: The Hidden Issues," *Spectrum,* 1972 (Autumn); 4(4): 23–39. For an extensive collection of the correspondence between

J. H. Kellogg and various Adventist authors between 1904 and his expulsion from the Church in 1907, including the controversy over his book *The Living Temple,* see Reels 1, 2, 3, and 4, J. H. Kellogg Papers, MSU. There is also the transcript of an eight-hour interview, just before his formal expulsion, conducted by Elder A. C. Bourdeau and in the presence of Dr. James T. Case, a San physician, at John's home on October 7, 1907, that delves in great detail into Dr. Kellogg's side of the story, his disagreements with Ellen White and others, and many other issues. Accessed July 30, 2015, at http://text .egwwritings.org/publication.php?pubtype=Book&bookCode=IJHK&lang=en& collection=6&section=all&pagenumber=1.

6. Schwarz, PhD thesis, p. 418. See also J. H. Kellogg, *Biologic Living: Rules for Right Living* (Battle Creek, MI: Health Information Bureau, 1920); Interview with Dr. W. S. Sadler by R. Schwarz, September 22, 1960, Box 10, Files 8 and 16, Sadler 10 (Cards VIII-A-4, VII-E; VII-D, Box 9, F18, Sadler 3, B9, F15, Sadler; B9, F18, Sadler 5; B10, F2, Sadler 2; B9, F18, Sadler A and B; B9, F6, Sadler 8A; B8, F1 and 3; B9; F10, B9, 16; B11, F1, B6, F11, B7, F1, Richard Schwarz Collection, Center for Adventist Research.

7. There was a "Question Box Hour" on September 26, 1910, where a card read "What is the difference between W. K. Kellogg and J. H. Kellogg?" The doctor explained they were brothers and not twins but they were in a legal dispute over naming rights and that "it does not obtain between the brothers at all." "Question Box Hour Lecture," September 26, 1910, Reel 11, Image 1463 (page 9 of the typescript), J. H. Kellogg Papers, U-M.

8. Letter from W. K. Kellogg to J. H. Kellogg, July 26, 1908, *State of Michigan Supreme Court Record (Kellogg v. Kellogg),* Volume 2, Box 21, File 3, J. H. Kellogg Papers, MSU.

9. Schwarz, *John Harvey Kellogg,* p. 209.

10. *Yearbook of the International Medical Missionary and Benevolent Association for 1897* (Battle Creek, MI: International Medical Missionary and Benevolent Association, 1897), pp. 135–36, 137–38.

11. Schwarz, PhD thesis, p. 420.

12. Powell, p. 89.

13. J. H. Kellogg testimony, *State of Michigan Supreme Court Record,* Volume 2, pp. 367, 371–72; Powell, p. 89.

14. Powell, p. 89.

15. Letter from J. H. Kellogg to E. G. White, June 10, 1896; Letter from J. H. Kellogg to E. G. White, December 6, 1898, Ellen White Papers, Ellen G. White Estate, General Conference of Seventh-day Adventists, Silver Spring, Maryland, quoted in Schwarz, PhD thesis, p. 421.

16. Ibid., p. 421.

17. U.S. Patent No. 558,393, "Flaked Cereals and Process of Preparing Same," Applicant: John H. Kellogg, M.D., May 31, 1895, Issued April 14, 1896, Reel 5, Box 6, File 4, J. H. Kellogg Papers, MSU.

18. *Sanitas Nut Food Company, Limited v. Carl G. A. Voigt, Elizabeth Voigt, Frank A. Voigt, M.P. and Charles Perkins, d/b/a The Voigt Milling Company and the Voigt Cereal Company,* in the Circuit Court of the United States for the Sixth Circuit of the Western District, Southern Division of Michigan, 1903, J. Wanty Presiding. See also appeal case in 1905, 139 F. 551, 553; 1905 U.S. App. 1905; James A. Mitchell, *The Journal of the Historical Society of the United States District Court for the Western District of Michigan,* 2003; Volume 1, Issue 3: 1–9; *Sanitas v. Voigt, Federal Reporter. Cases Argued and*

Determined in the Circuit Courts of Appeals and Circuit and District Courts of the United States, permanent edition, Volume 139, September to December 1905 (St. Paul, MN: West Publishing, 1906), pp. 551–56.

19. Schwarz, *John Harvey Kellogg,* p. 211. See also Powell, pp. 111–14.

20. J. H. Kellogg cross examination testimony, *State of Michigan Supreme Court Record,* Volume 2, p. 549.

21. Schwarz, *John Harvey Kellogg,* p. 212.

22. The price broke down into $22,440 in cash (about $450,000 in 2016) and $147,560 (more than $3 million in 2016). See Powell, pp. 111–12.

23. Ibid., p. 109.

24. Ibid., pp. 109, 134. Memorandum on changing the name from Sanitas to Kellogg's Corn Flakes, W. K. Kellogg to Wilfred Kellogg, September 24, 1907, Box 20, File 6 (Image 3950), *State of Michigan Supreme Court Record,* Volume 2, pp. 595–620, J. H. Kellogg Papers, MSU.

25. *State of Michigan Supreme Court Record,* Volume 2, pp. 370–76, 471–78, 630–40; Letter from J. H. Kellogg to the Toasted Corn Flake Company, July 17, 1908, Box 20, File 6, Images 4360–80, J. H. Kellogg Papers, MSU.

26. Frank Kellogg sold a "fat cure," under the name "F. J. Kellogg's Rational Treatment for Obesity." His slogan was "Makes Fat People Lean" and he based his operations in Battle Creek. He sold his useless product, which contained ground toasted bread, thyroid extract, and the harsh laxative poke root for $10 a package, which came with a booklet of instructions. His obesity food "compels the proper and perfect assimilation of food nutriment, and sends it where it belongs, into bone, brain, muscle, nerves and food." Useless as it was dishonest, the Kellogg brothers could do nothing to stop this unrelated charlatan from advertising and using their good name to confuse innocent dupes. See Letter from F. J. Kellogg to Kate Kering, October 20, 1905, J. H. Kellogg Papers, Reel 3, Image 89, Box 3, File 2, and Letter from F. J. Kellogg to Mrs. Kate Kling, November 1, 1905, Reel 3, Images 119–20, Box 3, File 3, J. H. Kellogg Papers, MSU. See also pill canister for "Professor F. J. Kellogg's Obesity Food Tablets. Turns Fat into Muscle. Not a Drug, But a Digestive That Reduces the Weight and Increases the Strength, When Used with Prof. F. J. Kellogg's System of Muscular Improvements." Will should have been more concerned by "Prof. Kellogg" in that the latter took to putting his signature on the back of his pill canisters with the tagline "And None Are Genuine Without His Signature." Collections of the University of Michigan Center for the History of Medicine.

27. J. H. Kellogg testimony, *State of Michigan Supreme Court Record,* Volume 2, pp. 374–75; quote is from p. 375, J. H. Kellogg Papers, MSU.

28. J. H. Kellogg, "A Visit to Pavlov's Laboratory"; W. N. Boldyreff, "Ivan Pavlov as a Scientist." Both articles appear in "Special Issue in Honor of the 80th Birthday of Professor Ivan P. Pavlov," *Bulletin of the Battle Creek Sanitarium and Hospital Clinic,* October 1929; 24(4): 203–11 and 212–29.

29. Testimony of W. E. Goff, *State of Michigan Supreme Court Record,* Volume 2, p. 633–34; J. H. Kellogg testimony, pp. 401–23, 545–67, *State of Michigan Supreme Court Record,* Volume 2; John R. Smith Testimony, pp. 509–13, *State of Michigan Supreme Court Record,* Volume 2, J. H. Kellogg Papers, MSU. See also Memorandum from W. K. Kellogg to Wilfred Kellogg, September 24, 1907, Memorandum to develop a limited partnership of Battle Creek Sanitarium Foods with Kellogg Food Company, September 1, 1908, Box 20, File 6; Minutes of the Regular Weekly Meeting of the Board

of Directors of the Toasted Corn Flake Company, July 6, 1908; July 13, 1908; July 14, 1908; July 20, 1908; January 18, 1909; May 3, 1909; Box 20, File 6, all in the J. H. Kellogg Papers, MSU.

30. Minutes of Regular Weekly Meeting of the Board of Directors of the Toasted Corn Flake Company, July 12, 1909, Box 20, File 6, J. H. Kellogg Papers, MSU.

31. Memorandum from J. R. Smith, June 10, 1907, Box 20, File 6, J. H. Kellogg Papers, MSU. In 1915, Will Kellogg took the formal step of trademarking a facsimile of his signature with the U.S. Patent Office. U.S. Patent Office, No. 105,213, July 13, 1915, "Kellogg Toasted Corn Flake Company of Battle Creek, Michigan. Trademark for certain foods." ("This trademark is a copy of the signature of Will K. Kellogg, president of this applicant company.")

32. "The Sweetheart of the Corn: Kellogg's Toasted Corn Flakes," advertisement, copyright 1907. This advertisement appeared in a 1907 issue of *Technical World Magazine* but is one of hundreds of advertisements that began running in major magazines after Will's decision to change the name of the company. Collections of the University of Michigan Center for the History of Medicine.

33. *State of Michigan Supreme Court Record,* Volume 3, pp. 757–60, quote is from p. 758, J. H. Kellogg Papers, MSU.

34. Letter to J. H. Kellogg from Jesse Arthur, Attorney, re: John's sale of Sanitas Nut Food Company's rights to manufacture and sell Corn Flakes to Will's company, October 8, 1906, Reel 6, Images 614–20, J. H. Kellogg Papers, MSU.

35. Dr. Kellogg's resignation was formally accepted by the board of directors of Will's company on March 30, 1908. Wilfred Kellogg to J. H. Kellogg, April 6, 1908, Reel 7, Image 555, J. H. Kellogg Papers, MSU.

36. Powell, p. 147.

37. Ibid., pp. 147–48. The previous 1907 capitalization and stock split increased John's Toasted Corn Flake Company's holdings to 11,420 shares, or about $114,200, about $2.97 million in 2016.

38. Letter from J. H. Kellogg to W. K. Kellogg, January 20, 1908, *State of Michigan Supreme Court Record,* Volume 2, pp. 614–21, Box 21, File 3, J. H. Kellogg Papers, MSU.

39. Letter from W. K. Kellogg to J. H. Kellogg, January 29, 1908, Reel 4, Box 4, File 11, J. H. Kellogg Papers, MSU.

40. Testimony of J. H. Kellogg, *State of Michigan Supreme Court Record,* Volume 2, p. 460, J. H. Kellogg Papers, MSU.

41. Schwarz, PhD thesis, p. 428.

42. Letter from W. K. Kellogg to John H. Kellogg, May 5, 1908, Reel 7, Image 558, J. H. Kellogg Papers, MSU.

43. Letter from W. K. Kellogg to Chappell and Earl Law Firm, July 6, 1908, Images 4560–90, Box 20, F6, J. H. Kellogg Papers, MSU.

44. Letter from W. K. Kellogg to J. H. Kellogg, July 8, 1908. Box 20, F6, Image 4610, J. H. Kellogg Papers, MSU.

45. Letter from Chappell and Earl to W. K. Kellogg, July 9, 1908, Image 810, Reel 5, J. H. Kellogg Papers, MSU.

46. Schwarz, PhD thesis, p. 430, citing Letter from J. H. Kellogg to W. K. Kellogg, July 20, 1908, and July 23, 1908, Reel 7, J. H. Kellogg Papers, MSU.

47. Schwarz, PhD thesis, citing Letter from J. H. Kellogg to Will K. Kellogg, July 17, 1908, J. H. Kellogg Papers, MSU.

48. Letter from W. K. Kellogg to J. H. Kellogg, July 20, 1908, Reel 18, Box 20, File 6, Images 4260–4350, J. H. Kellogg Papers, MSU.

49. Testimony and Deposition of J. H. Kellogg taken by Mr. Bailey, *State of Michigan Supreme Court Record,* Volume 2, Box 21, File 3, pp. 592, 596, 599, quote is from p. 599, when he was asked to read the letter from J. H. Kellogg to W. K. Kellogg, July 23, 1908, J. H. Kellogg Papers, MSU.

50. Testimony/Deposition of J. H. Kellogg by Mr. Bailey, citing letter from J. H. Kellogg to W. K. Kellogg, July 23, 1908, *State of Michigan Supreme Court Record,* Volume 2, Box 21, File 3, pp. 600–601, J. H. Kellogg Papers, MSU.

51. Testimony/Deposition of J. H. Kellogg taken by Mr. Bailey, citing letter from W. K. Kellogg to J. H. Kellogg, July 26, 1908, *State of Michigan Supreme Court Record,* Volume 2, Box 21, File 3, p. 591, J. H. Kellogg Papers, MSU.

52. Williamson Jr., *An Intimate Glimpse,* pp. 14–15.

53. "Notice to Desist from Infringement of Trade-marks, and from Other Unfair Competition, Given by Kellogg Toasted Corn Flake Company of Battle Creek, Michigan to Kellogg Toasted Rice Flake and Biscuit Company, Kellogg Food Company, and J. H. Kellogg, December 20, 1909," Box 19, F3, Images 300–40, J. H. Kellogg Papers, MSU.

54. J. H. Kellogg Testimony, *State of Michigan Supreme Court Record,* Volume 2, Box 21, File 3, pp. 419–21, J. H. Kellogg Papers, MSU; *State of Michigan Supreme Court Record,* Volume 3, Exhibit d-380, Letter from J. H. Kellogg to W. K. Kellogg, August 8, 1908, pp. 778–79, J. H. Kellogg Papers, MSU. (n.b., Vol. 3 of this trial is missing in the MSU collection. The xerox of this volume was given to me by Garth "Duff" Stolz, of the Historic Adventist Village in Battle Creek, MI.)

55. Michigan Supreme Court History Society, Biographies: Walter North, accessed September 9, 2014, at http://www.micourthistory.org/justices/walter-north/.

56. "Denies Injunction in Kellogg's Case," *Battle Creek Enquirer,* September 20, 1910.

57. Born in upstate New York in 1865, Chappell's parents moved westward to Kalamazoo after the Civil War. Chappell went on to graduate with a Bachelor of Science degree from Michigan Agricultural College in 1885, whose class motto declared, "Activity is Life; Idleness is Death." Michigan Agricultural College, *Album of the Class of 1885 of the Michigan Agricultural College* (Lansing: Casey and Whitney, 1885), p. 21.

58. Charles A, Weissert, *An Account of Kalamazoo, MI County* (Dayton: National Historical Association, 1928), pp. 244, 253–54.

59. T. W. Day, *Michigan Federation of Labor Official Year Book, 1906–7* (Detroit: Houghton-Jacobson Printing Co., 1907), p. 140. A junior partner, named Ira Beck, also helped in the case. Beck was well regarded as "a counselor well fortified in knowledge and material judgment." Washington Gardner, *The History of Calhoun County, Michigan: A Narrative Account of Its Historical Progress, Its People, and Its Principal Interests,* Volume 1 (Chicago and New York: The Lewis Publishing Company, 1913), pp. 850–51.

60. "W. H. C. Clarke, 59; A Law Councilor. Advisor to Senate Committee on Study of Small Business Enterprises Dies Here. Ran for Congress in 1919. Sought Office in Fifth District of New Jersey—Ex-Head of Fair Trade Council, Inc.," *New York Times,* January 3, 1942, p. 19.

61. Gardner, *The History of Calhoun County,* pp. 1226–28.

62. Bailey's 1909–1911 term was especially notable because "more sidewalks were built, more pavement put in, more sewers were built, more water pipe laid than in any previous two years in the city's history." One of those repaired roads was Porter Street, where the new Kellogg factory was situated. Powell, pp. 168–69.

63. Richard Schwarz, *John Harvey Kellogg,* p. 139.

64. Charles MacIvor, "The Lord's Physician," Chapter 7, "This Man Kellogg," p. 5, Charles MacIvor Collection, No. 251, Box 10, File 12, Center for Adventist Research.

65. *State of Michigan Supreme Court Record,* Volume 2, Box 21, File 3, pp. 368–79, quote is from page 369, J. H. Kellogg Papers, MSU.

66. *State of Michigan Supreme Court Record,* Volume 2, Box 21, File 3, pp. 376–77, J. H. Kellogg Papers, MSU.

67. *State of Michigan Supreme Court Record,* Volume 2, Box 21, File 3, p. 368, J. H. Kellogg Papers, MSU.

68. Ibid., quote is from page 371 and after the ellipsis, page 377.

69. Ibid., p. 431.

70. Ibid., p. 466.

71. Powell, p. 149.

72. Deposition of W. K. Kellogg, in the Circuit Court for the County of Calhoun, State of Michigan, *The Kellogg Food Company vs. the Kellogg Toasted Corn Flake Company,* before Hon. Walter H, North of the Circuit Court, Friday, May 4–5, 1917, 9:00 a.m., J. H. Kellogg Papers, Box 20, File 2, pp. 25 of typescript.

73. Ibid., p. 35.

74. State of Michigan in the Circuit Court for the County of Calhoun, in Chancery, *John Harvey Kellogg et al. v. Will K. Kellogg et al.*, Brief for Plantiffs, June 5, 1917, claims of Will's perjury appear on p. 7 of the typescript; Schwarz, *John Harvey Kellogg,* p. 17.

75. Deposition of W. K. Kellogg, in the Circuit Court for the County of Calhoun, State of Michigan, *The Kellogg Food Company v. the Kellogg Toasted Corn Flake Company,* before Hon. Walter H. North of the Circuit Court, Friday, May 4–5, 1917, 9:00 a.m., quotes are from pp. 21 and 26 of typescript, J. H. Kellogg Papers, MSU, Box 20, File 2, pp. 22–24.

76. Ibid.

77. Schwarz, *John Harvey Kellogg,* p. 216.

78. Michigan Reports, *Cases Decided in the Supreme Court of Michigan, from September 30, 1920 to December 21, 1920,* Volume 212 (Chicago: Callaghan and Co., 1921), pp. 95–118, quote is from p. 98.

79. Schwarz, PhD thesis, pp. 432–33; Memorandum of Agreement made February 15, 1911, between J. H. Kellogg, the Kellogg Food Company and the Kellogg Toasted Rice Flake and Biscuit Company and the Kellogg Toasted Corn Flake Company, Box 19, File 10, J. H. Kellogg Papers, MSU.

80. Letters from J. H. Kellogg to W. K. Kellogg, July 27, 1911, and September 15, 1911, in *State of Michigan Supreme Court Record,* Volume 3, File 3, Box 21, pp. 1044–46, J. H. Kellogg Papers, MSU. The quote is from the letter written on September 15.

81. Schwarz, *John Harvey Kellogg,* p. 217.

82. Powell, p. 149; *State of Michigan Supreme Court Record,* Volume 2, Box 21, File 3, pp. 725–28, J. H. Kellogg Papers, MSU.

83. Testimony of J. H. Kellogg, *State of Michigan Supreme Court Record,* Volume 2, Box 21, File 3, pp. 387–90, 395–401, 638–48.

84. R. Schwarz. *John Harvey Kellogg,* p. 217.

85. Horace Powell erroneously states that the North decision was handed down in November of 1919, but the archival and court papers are quite clear that Judge North delivered his decision on November 19, 1917. Judge Walter North Decision, State of Michigan in the Circuit Court of Calhoun, in Chancery, November 19, 1917, in the matter of *Kellogg v. Kellogg,* Box 20, File 34, J. H. Kellogg Papers, MSU.

86. "Sweeping Decision in Kellogg Case," *Journal of Commerce and Commercial Bulletin*, clipping, November 30, 1917, Box 20, File 4, J. H. Kellogg Papers, MSU.

87. John engaged in other failed attempts to tie the case up in the court system, including an appeal to the U.S. Court of Appeals in Washington, DC, with respect to Will trademarking the name Kellogg, the U.S. Patent Office, and even a case in the Canadian courts over his sales of Corn Flakes in that country. Ultimately, they all failed, too. See *Kellogg Food Company v. Kellogg Toasted Corn Flake Company*, Patent Appeals No. 1110 and 1111, June 2, 1917; U.S. Patent Office, *Kellogg Food Company v. Kellogg Toasted Corn Flake Co.*, Opposition No. 2140 petition, September 20, 1917, and Memorandum for Opposers, Oppositions Nos. 2139 and 2140, September 26, 1917; in Box 20, File 3, J. H. Kellogg Papers, MSU.

88. The majority of the *State of Michigan Supreme Court Record*, in five volumes, is preserved in the J. H. Kellogg Papers, Michigan State University Collection, with the exception of Volume 3. Fortunately, Duff Stoltz, the historian and curator of the Adventist Heritage Village and Museum in Battle Creek, Michigan, was most generous in locating a copy of that volume for my review. These proceedings include all the affidavits, exhibits, and testimonies of the First Circuit Court case presided over by Judge Walter North of Battle Creek.

89. Richard Cooper (court reporter), *Michigan Reports. Cases Decided in the Supreme Court of Michigan from September 30, 1920 to December 21, 1920*, Volume 212 (Chicago: Callaghan and Co., 1924), pp. 95–118.

90. Letter from J. H. Kellogg to Dr. Percy T. Magan, June 28, 1921, Percy T. Magan Papers, Vernier-Radcliffe Memorial Library, Loma Linda University, Loma Linda, California, cited in Schwarz, PhD thesis, p. 437.

91. Letter from W. K. Kellogg to E. D. Henderson, January 4, 1921, Box 20, File 5, 1921, Image 3300, J. H. Kellogg Papers, MSU.

92. George Howe Colt, *Brothers: On His Brothers and Brothers in History* (New York: Scribner, 2012), p. 143.

13.

THE DOCTOR'S CRUSADE AGAINST RACE DEGENERACY

1. See, for example, the proceedings of the national eugenics conferences he underwrote and hosted between 1914 and 1928: E. F. Robbins, ed., *Proceedings of the First National Conference on Race Betterment, January 8, 9, 10, 11, 12, 1914* (Battle Creek, MI: Race Betterment Foundation, 1914); *Official Proceedings of the Second National Conference on Race Betterment, August 4, 6, 7, 8, 1915, Held in San Francisco, CA in connection with the Panama-Pacific International Exposition* (Battle Creek, MI: Race Betterment Foundation, 1915); *Proceedings of the Third Race Betterment Conference, January 2–6, 1928* (Battle Creek, MI: Race Betterment Foundation, 1928).

2. Howard Markel, "*Di Goldene Medina* (The Golden Land): Historical Perspectives of Eugenics and the East European (Ashkenazi) Jewish-American Community, 1880–1925," *Health Matrix*, 1997; 7: 49–64; Howard Markel, "The Stigma of Disease: The Implications of Genetic Screening," *American Journal of Medicine*, 1992; 93: 209–16.

3. Galton also coined the term "Nurture vs. Nature." See Francis Galton, *Inquiries into Human Faculty and Its Development* (London: Macmillan and Co., 1883), pp. 17, 24–25, 44. Francis Galton, *Hereditary Genius: An Inquiry into Its Laws and Consequences*

(London: Macmillan and Co., 1869); Francis Galton, "On Men of Science: Their Nature and Their Nurture," *Proceedings of the Royal Institution of Great Britain,* 1874; 7: 227–36. Galton and Charles Darwin shared the same grandfather, Erasmus Darwin.

4. Howard Markel, *Quarantine! East European Jewish Immigrants and the New York City Epidemics of 1892* (Baltimore: Johns Hopkins University Press, 1997), pp. 179–82; Howard Markel, *When Germs Travel: Six Major Epidemics That Invaded America Since 1900 and the Fears They Unleashed* (New York: Pantheon, 2004), pp. 34–36; Kenneth M. Ludmerer, *Genetics and American Society: A Historical Appraisal* (Baltimore: Johns Hopkins University Press, 1972), pp. 87–119; Mark H. Haller, *Eugenics: Hereditarian Attitudes in American Thought* (New Brunswick, NJ: Rutgers University Press, 1963), pp. 50–57.

5. John Higham, *Strangers in the Land: Patterns of American Nativism, 1860–1925* (New York: Atheneum, 1963), p. 152. See also Barbara M. Solomon, *Ancestors and Immigrants: A Changing New England Tradition* (Cambridge: Harvard University Press, 1956).

6. Charles E. Rosenberg, "Charles Benedict Davenport and the Irony of American Eugenics," in *No Other Gods: On Science and American Social Thought* (Baltimore: Johns Hopkins University Press, 1976), pp. 89–97; Garland E. Allen, "The Eugenics Record Office at Cold Spring Harbor, 1910–1940: An Essay in Institutional History," *Osiris* (Second Series), 1986; 2: 225–64; Oscar Riddle, "Biographical Memoir of Charles B. Davenport, 1866–1944," *Biographical Memoirs,* 1947, Volume 25—Fourth Memoir (Washington, DC: National Academy of Sciences of the United States of America, 1947), accessed July 4, 2015, at http://www.nasonline.org/publications/biographical-memoirs/memoir-pdfs/davenport-charles.pdf.

7. J. G. Mendel, "Versuche über Pflanzenhybriden," *Verhandlungen des natur-forschenden Vereines in Brünn,* Bd. IV für das Jahr, 1865 Abhandlungen (Papers 1866): 1–47. For the English translation, see William Bateson, "Experiments in Plant Hybridization," *Journal of the Royal Horticultural Society,* 1901; 26: 1–32. A PDF copy, originally published in the February 6, 1965, issue of the *British Medical Journal,* 1965; 1(5431): 368–74, honoring the centenary of Mendel's paper, published both in the original German and in English, can be accessed at http://www.ncbi.nlm.nih.gov/pmc/articles/PMC2165333/pdf/brmedj02380-0068.pdf.

8. Rosenberg. *No Other Gods,* p. 91.

9. Charles B. Davenport, "Report of the Committee on Eugenics," *American Breeders Magazine,* 1910, 1: 129.

10. Letter from C. B. Davenport to Madison Grant, April 7, 1922, Charles B. Davenport Papers, American Philosophical Society, Philadelphia, Pennsylvania, cited in Rosenberg, *No Other Gods,* pp. 95–96.

11. Markel, *Quarantine: East European Jewish Immigrants and the New York City Epidemics of 1892,* pp. 1–12, 66–67, 75–98, 133–52, 163–78, 181–85; Markel, *When Germs Travel,* pp. 9–10, 35–36, 56, 87–89, 96–97, 102–3; Gerald Sorin, *A Time for Building: The Third Migration, 1880–1920* (Baltimore: Johns Hopkins University Press, 1992), pp. 57–58; John R. Commons, *Races and Immigrants in America* (New York: Macmillan, 1907), pp. 63–106; R. Daniels, "No Lamps Were Lit for Them: Angel Island and the Historiography of Asian American Immigration," *Journal of American Ethnic History,* 1997; 17: 2–18; Nayan Shah, *Contagious Divides: Epidemics and Race in San Francisco's Chinatown* (Berkeley: University of California Press, 2001); Allen, "The Eugenics Record Office at Cold Spring Harbor, 1910–1940," 2: 225–64; John F. Kennedy, *A*

Nation of Immigrants (New York: Harper & Row, 1964). Also see President Lyndon B. Johnson, "Remarks at the Signing of the Immigration Bill, Liberty Island, New York, October 3, 1965," accessed from the LBJ Presidential Library in Austin, Texas, on June 4, 2015, at http://www.lbjlib.utexas.edu/johnson/archives.hom/speeches.hom/651003.asp.

12. Herbert Spencer, *The Principles of Biology*, Volume 1 (New York: D. Appleton, 1864); Herbert Spencer, *The Principles of Biology*, Volume 2 (New York: D. Appleton, 1886); Herbert Spencer, *The Study of Sociology, in Three Volumes* (New York: D. Appleton, 1898); Richard Hofstadter, *Social Darwinism in American Thought, 1860–1915* (Philadelphia: University of Pennsylvania Press, 1944).

13. Edward A. Ross, "The Causes of Race Superiority," *Annals of the American Academy of Political and Social Science*, July, 1901; 18: 67–89, quote is from p. 88.

14. Letter from Theodore Roosevelt to Marie Von Horst, October 18, 1902, in Mrs. John (Bessie) Van Horst, *The Woman Who Toils: Being the Experience of Two Ladies as Factory Girls* (New York: Doubleday and Page, 1903), pp. vii–ix. Roosevelt states on p. vii, "What is fundamentally infinitely more important than any other question in this country—that is the question of race suicide, complete or partial." See also Theodore Roosevelt, "On American Motherhood" (a speech given by President Roosevelt in Washington on March 13, 1905, before the National Congress of Mothers), in William Jennings Bryan, *The World's Famous Orations in Ten Volumes*, Volume 10 *(America III)* (New York: Funk and Wagnalls, 1906), pp. 253–62; Thomas G. Dyer, *Theodore Roosevelt and the Idea of Race* (Baton Rouge: Louisiana State University Press, 1980), pp. 143–67.

15. The complex adoption of eugenics and "racial uplift" among members of the "New Negro" movement, including W. E. B. Du Bois, is superbly discussed in Shantella Y. Sherman, "In Search of Purity: Popular Eugenics and Racial Uplift Among New Negroes, 1915–1935," PhD diss., University of Nebraska at Lincoln, 2014.

16. Edwin Black, *War Against the Weak: Eugenics and America's Campaign to Create a Master Race* (New York: Basic Books, 2003); Upton Sinclair, *Unseen Upton Sinclair: Nine Unpublished Stories, Essays, and Other Works,* ed., Ruth C. Engs (Jefferson, NC: McFarland, 2009), pp. 91–104, 149–71; Margaret Sanger, *The Pivot of Civilization* (New York: Brentano's, 1922).

17. John Harvey Kellogg, *Plain Facts for Old and Young: Embracing the Natural History and Hygiene of Organic Life* (Burlington, Iowa: Senger and Condit, 1887), quotes are from pp. 345–46.

18. Lamarckism, named for the French biologist Jean-Baptiste Lamarck, proposed that a living being passes on characteristics it has acquired during life to subsequent generations. Ellen H. Richards, *Euthenics: The Science of Controllable Environment. A Plea for Better Living Conditions as a First Step Toward Higher Human Efficiency* (Boston: Whitcomb and Barrows, 1910); Lester F. Ward, "Eugenics, Euthenics and Eudemics," *American Journal of Sociology*, 1913; 18(6): 737–54.

19. John H. Kellogg, "Tendencies Toward Race Degeneracy," *New York Medical Journal: A Weekly Review of Medicine (Incorporating the Philadelphia Medical Journal and the Medical News)*, September 2, 1911; 94(10): 461–67, and September 9, 1911; 94(11): 526–29 (New York: A. R. Elliott Publishing Co., 1911). For examples of Dr. Kellogg's lectures on the topic of race degeneracy, see "Lecture: Race Degeneracy," April 16, 1911, Reel 12, Images 917–46, and "Lecture: Are We Too Much Civilized," February 23, 1911, Reel 12, Images 657–88, both in J. H. Kellogg Papers, U-M.

20. "The Workingman's Home," *Medical Missionary*, October, 1896; 6: 299–302.

Medical Missionary was the publication of the Seventh-day Adventist–operated American Medical Missionary and Benevolent Association—the social welfare arm of the denomination.

21. "Announcement for the Battle Creek Sanitarium Medical Missionary Training School, 1898–99," Reel 29, Images 166–227; as well as similar annual announcements for 1900–1901, 1901–1902, 1902–1903, 1903–1904, 1907–1908, and 1908–1909, and John H. Kellogg, "Commencement Exercises (Speech) of the American Medical Missionary College (AMMC)," June 23, 1903, Reel 27, J. H. Kellogg Papers, U-M. See also *Year Book of the International Medical Missionary and Benevolent Association for 1896: Origin and Development of Medical Missionary and Other Philanthropic Work Among Seventh-Day Adventists* (Battle Creek, MI: American Missionary and Benevolent Association, 1896), Reel 28, Images 1009–1248, J. H. Kellogg Papers, U-M.

22. Jonathan Butler, "Ellen G. White and the Chicago Mission," *Spectrum,* 1970 (Winter); 2: 41–51.

23. J. H. Kellogg, "Successful Self-Supporting City Missions," which details the history and practice of the Chicago Mission, founded by J. H. Kellogg in 1893 and staffed by two of Dr. Kellogg's closest medical associates, Drs. David Paulson and William Sadler. Reel 28, Images 381–425, J. H. Kellogg Papers, U-M. The rest of this reel (Images 426–670) contains a wealth of materials, mission statements, magazine and newspaper articles on the work of the mission.

24. A. S. Bloese Manuscript, pp. 339–40, Box 2, Folder 1.

25. Carson, p. 239.

26. Richard Schwarz, "J. H. Kellogg: Adventism's Social Gospel Advocate," *Spectrum,* Spring 1969; 1: 15–28. Schwarz notes that when searching for a place to settle his missionary work, Dr. Kellogg asked the Chicago chief of police to direct him to "the dirtiest and wickedest place" in the city (p. 18); Schwarz, *John Harvey Kellogg,* p. 165.

27. For discussions on the Social Gospel movement, see Schwarz, PhD thesis, 296–466; Schwarz, "J. H. Kellogg: Adventism's Social Gospel Advocate," 1: 15–28; Richard Schwartz, "J. H. Kellogg as Social Gospel Practitioner," *Journal of the Illinois State Historical Society,* 1964; 57(1): 5–22. The classic texts on this movement include Richard T. Ely, *Social Aspects of Christianity* (New York: T. Y. Crowell & Co., 1889); and Walter Rauschenbusch, *Christianity and the Social Crisis* (New York: Macmillan, 1907). See also Charles H. Hopkins, *The Rise of the Social Gospel in American Protestantism, 1865–1915* (New Haven: Yale University Press, 1940), pp. 319–22; Sidney Fine, *Laissez Faire and the General Welfare State* (Ann Arbor: University of Michigan Press, 1956), p. 179; Angie G. Kennedy, "Eugenics, 'Degenerate Girls,' and Social Workers During the Progressive Era," *Affilia: Journal of Women and Social Work,* 2008; 23(1): 22–37. Christine Rosen, *Preaching Eugenics: Religious Leaders and the American Eugenics Movement* (New York: Oxford University Press, 2004), pp. 75–77; "Jane Addams on Clothes," *Boston Evening Transcript,* September 26, 1913, p. 11 (in this article Addams is quoted as stating, "I favor strict eugenic laws and woman's suffrage"); "No Loveless Eugenics Declares Jane Addams," *Milwaukee Sentinel,* December 15, 1914.

28. Howard Markel, "Exploring the Dangerous Trades with Dr. Alice Hamilton," *JAMA,* 2007; 298(23): 2802–4. See also Jane Addams, *Twenty Years at Hull-House, with Autobiographical Notes* (New York: Macmillan; 1912); Louise W. Knight, *Citizen: Jane Addams and the Struggle for Democracy* (Chicago: University of Chicago Press; 2006); Allen F. Davis, *Spearheads for Reform: The Social Settlements and the Progressive Movement, 1890 to 1914* (New Brunswick, NJ: Rutgers University Press, 1985). And also see

A. S. Bloese Manuscript, chapter on missionary work in Chicago, pp. 240–48, Box 1, Folder 14.

29. Interview with William Sadler, MD, by Richard Schwarz, November 13, 1960 (Card VII-E-1). Richard Schwarz Collection, B9, F10, Sadler 8, Center for Adventist Research.

30. Schwarz, *John Harvey Kellogg*, pp. 164–71.

31. Abraham Flexner found the American Medical Missionary College too irregular for his model of a modern medical school. Specifically, Flexner worried that "the Sanitarium is devoted to the application of certain ideas rather than to untrammeled scientific investigation. Disciples rather than scientists are thus trained." Soon after the publication of the Flexner Report of 1910, John's academy closed its doors and its Chicago assets and property were taken over by the University of Illinois Medical School. See Abraham Flexner, *Medical Education in the United States and Canada. A Report to the Carnegie Foundation for the Advancement of Teaching,* Bulletin No. 4 (New York: Carnegie Foundation, 1910), pp. 244–45; *American Medical Missionary College. Thirteenth Annual Announcement, 1907–1908,* Reel 27, Images 1437–91; J. H. Kellogg, "Commencement Exercises of the American Medical Missionary College, June 23, 1903," Reel 27, Images 815–19; and "Qualifications of the Christian Physician," Reel 27, Images 1165–75, J. H. Kellogg Papers, U-M. The Annual Announcements of American Medical Missionary College for 1900–1901, 1901–1902, 1902–1903, 1903–1904, and 1908–1909 are also on Reel 27. See also "The Opening Exercises of the American Missionary College," *Medical Missionary,* October 7, 1908, Volume 17, pp. 802–6; "The American Medical Missionary College," *Medical Missionary,* May 1910, Volume 19, pp. 135–40.

32. Robert L. Allen, *Irving Fisher: A Biography* (Cambridge, MA: Blackwell, 1993), pp. 87–89; Robert W. Dimand and John Geanakoplos, eds., *Celebrating Irving Fisher: The Legacy of a Great Economist* (Malden, MA: Blackwell, 2005); Nathaniel Comfort, *The Science of Human Perfection: How Genes Became the Heart of American Medicine* (New Haven: Yale University Press, 2012), pp. 32–35, 47–56. For primary sources on the copious Fisher-Kellogg correspondence, see Reels 2, 3, 4, 5, J. H. Kellogg Papers, U-M.

33. J. H. Kellogg, "The Eugenics Registry," *Official Proceedings of the Second National Conference on Race Betterment. August 4, 5, 6, 7, and 8, 1915. Held in San Francisco, CA in Connection with the Panama-Pacific International Exposition,* pp. 76–87.

34. Irving Fisher, "The Influence of Flesh-Eating on Endurance," *Yale Medical Journal,* March 1907 (Reprinted by the Modern Medicine Publishing Co., Battle Creek, Michigan, 1908). For an example of the doctor's imprecise citing of Fisher's research, see J. H. Kellogg, *The Natural Diet of Man* (Battle Creek, MI: The Modern Medicine Publishing Co., 1923), pp. 42–44. A year earlier, Fisher studied the effects of Fletcherizing, or chewing one's food thoroughly, on endurance. See Irving Fisher, "The Effect of Diet on Endurance, Based on an Experiment in Thorough Mastication, with Nine Healthy Students at Yale University, January to June, 1906, *Transactions of the Connecticut Academy of Arts and Sciences,* 1907; 13: 1–46.

35. In 1915, Professor Fisher founded the Life Extension Institute, a nonprofit group that encouraged Americans to maintain their health across the entire life span by means of a "eugenic health registry" to determine who was healthy and who was not. See Irving Fisher and Eugene Lyman Fisk, *How to Live: Rules for Healthful Living Based on Modern Science* (New York: Funk and Wagnalls, 1915).

36. Irving Fisher, "Eugenics—Foremost Plan of Human Redemption," *Official Pro-*

ceedings of the Second National Conference on Race Betterment. August 4, 5, 6, 7, and 8, 1915. Held in San Francisco, CA in Connection with the Panama-Pacific International Exposition (Battle Creek, MI: Race Betterment Foundation, 1915), pp. 63–69, quote is from page 63; Comfort, *The Science of Human Perfection*, pp. 29–66.

37. "Eugenics as a Religion," paper read at Golden Jubilee Celebration of Battle Creek Sanitarium, ten-page manuscript, Sermon 43, ID 743, *The Golden Jubilee of the Battle Creek Sanitarium: October 3, 4, and 5, 1916, in Celebration of the Fiftieth Anniversary of its Founding in 1866* (American Philosophical Society, American Eugenics Society, 575.06: Am3), accessed July 27, 2015, at http://www.eugenicsarchive.org/html/eugenics/static/images/791.html. See also Christine Rosen, *Preaching Eugenics: Religious Leaders and the American Eugenics Movement* (New York: Oxford University Press, 2004), pp. 92–94; Wilson, *Dr. John Harvey Kellogg*, p. 162.

38. The Jukes were a "hill family" studied by the eugenicist Richard Dugdale in the late nineteenth and early twentieth centuries. They, along with the Kalikak, the Zeros, and the Nams, were followed to link one's environment to determining risks of criminality, disease, and poverty. Madison Grant, *The Passing of the Great Race, or The Racial Basis of European History* (New York: Charles Scribner's Sons, 1916); Jonathan P. Spiro, *Defending the Master Race: Conservation, Eugenics, and the Legacy of Madison Grant* (Burlington: University of Vermont Press, 2009); David Oshinsky, "No Justice for the Week" (review of *Imbeciles: The Supreme Court, American Eugenics, and the Sterilization of Carrie Buck* by Adam Cohen, and *Illiberal Reformers: Race, Eugenics and American Economics in the Progressive Era* by Thomas C. Leonard), *New York Times Book Review,* March 20, 2016, pp. 1, 22, 23.

39. For example, on June 12, 1936, Kellogg offered some hostile medical advice to Grant urging him to come to the Sanitarium. Letter from J. H. Kellogg to Madison Grant, June 12, 1936, Reel 4, Images 210–11, J. H. Kellogg Papers, U-M.

40. John H. Kellogg, *The Living Temple* (Battle Creek, MI: Good Health Publishing Company, 1903), p. 450.

41. John H. Kellogg, "Tendencies Toward Race Degeneracy," *New York Medical Journal: A Weekly Review of Medicine (Incorporating the Philadelphia Medical Journal and the Medical News),* September 2 1911; 94 (10): 461–467 and September 9, 1911; 94 (11): 526–29 (New York: A.R. Elliott Publishing Co., 1911), quote is from page 461.

42. John H. Kellogg, "Tendencies Toward Race Degeneracy," *New York Medical Journal: A Weekly Review of Medicine (Incorporating the Philadelphia Medical Journal and the Medical News),* September 2, 1911; 94(10): 461–67, and September 9, 1911; 94 (11): 526–29, the quote appears on p. 528. For examples of Dr. Kellogg's lectures on race degeneracy and eugenics, see "Lecture: Race Degeneracy," April 16, 1911, Reel 12, Images 917–46, J. H. Kellogg Papers, U-M; "Lecture: Are We Too Much Civilized," February 23, 1911, Reel 12, Images 657–88, J. H. Kellogg Papers, U-M; A. S. Bloese Manuscript, chapter on the Race Betterment Foundation, pp. 268–82, Box 1, Folder 14.

43. The State of Michigan has a rather checkered past with respect to parental fitness and laws mandating the forced sterilization of "unfit parents," including the insane, mentally retarded, and others until 1960. As early as 1897, the state government proposed forced sterilization of criminals and "degenerates," a law that enjoys the dubious distinction of being one of the first such laws proposed in the nation. While this law was found to be unconstitutional by the Michigan State Supreme Court, later sterilization laws against the "mentally defective" and the insane, among others considered eugenically "unfit," were enacted in 1913 and 1923, with amendments over the years. See the excellent history by Jeffrey A. Hodges, "Dealing with Degeneracy: Michigan

Eugenics in Context" (PhD thesis, Michigan State University, 2001), p. III. See also Jeffrey A. Hodges, "Euthenics, Eugenics and Compulsory Sterilization in Michigan, 1897–1960" (Master of Arts thesis, Michigan State University, 1995), pp. 151–54. For Dr. Kellogg's advocacy of these laws and how they conflicted with the issue of personal liberty, see J. H. Kellogg, "Argument for Sterilization of the Unfit," *Good Health*, February 1913; 48(2): 106; J. H. Kellogg, "Testing Eugenics," *Good Health*, January 1916; 51(1): 7–8; J. H. Kellogg, "The Perils of Personal Liberty," *Good Health*, April 1919; 54(4): 191–93. Dr. Kellogg's conclusion in this last but very revealing piece is that personal liberty does not give one the right to harm society and quotes Galatians 6:7: "Whatever a man soweth, that he shall also reap." See also Jacob H. Landman, *Human Sterilization: The History of the Sexual Sterilization Movement* (New York: Macmillan, 1932); Harry H. Laughlin, *Eugenical Sterilization in the United States* (Chicago: Municipal Court of Chicago, 1932). For a broader study of sterilization laws within the context of the famous U.S. Supreme Court case *Buck v. Bell*, in which Associate Justice Oliver Wendell Holmes Jr. infamously concluded in the majority opinion holding up the legality of such laws, "Three generations of imbeciles are enough," see Paul Lombardo, *Three Generations, No Imbeciles: Eugenics, the Supreme Court, and Buck v. Bell* (Baltimore: Johns Hopkins University Press, 2010); Adam Cohen, *Imbeciles: The Supreme Court, American Eugenics and the Sterilization of Carrie Buck* (New York: Penguin, 2016).

44. See Wilson, *Dr. John Harvey Kellogg and the Religion of Biologic Living*, p. 158. This move finalized Dr. Kellogg's shift from funding medical missionary work toward the cause of race betterment. On July 22, 1914, Dr. Kellogg held a meeting of the American Missionary Medical Board to make this change and the newly reconstituted charity began meeting officially as the Race Betterment Foundation on October 3, 1914. Dr. Kellogg informed the board that the name change was approved by the State of Michigan on February 21, 1916. See "Race Betterment Foundation, Articles of Association Filed with the State of Michigan, changing the name of the American Medical Missionary Board to the Race Betterment Foundation," January 4, 1917, Collection 234, Box 2, File 4; and "Instrument of Trust, Race Betterment Foundation to J. H. Kellogg et al., Trustee, December 11, 1923," Collection 234, Box 2, File 1–1, Adventist Research Center. See also J. H. Kellogg, "Finis," *Medical Missionary*, 1914; 23(12): 354; J. H. Kellogg, "The Race Betterment Foundation," *Good Health*, December 1914, 49(12): 609–10.

45. E. F. Robbins, ed., *Proceedings of the First National Conference on Race Betterment, January 8, 9, 10, 11, 12, 1914* (Battle Creek, MI: Race Betterment Foundation, 1914), p. 22. The Latin phrase is from Juvenal's *Satires*, 10: 356.

46. See J. H. Kellogg, "Needed—A New Human Race," in E. F. Robbins, ed., *Proceedings of the First National Conference on Race Betterment, January 8, 9, 10, 11, 12, 1914* (Battle Creek, MI: Race Betterment Foundation, 1914), pp. 431–50.

47. Jacob A. Riis's lecture was entitled "The Bad Boy," in ibid., pp. 241–50. Shortly after leaving the dais, he spoke to Paul Popenoe, who quoted Riis in his May 1915 editorial for the *Journal of Heredity*. Paul Popenoe, "From the Editor: Nature or Nurture?: Actual Improvement of the Race Impossible Except Through Heredity—Facts on Which the Eugenicist Bases His Faith—The Attitude of Eugenics Toward Social Problem," *Journal of Heredity*, 1915; 6(5): 227–40. Riis's quote about heredity is on p. 227. Popenoe disagreed with Riis and stated that "*heredity is not only much stronger than any single factor of the environment, in producing important human differences, but is stronger than any possible number of them put together.*" (Italics are Popenoe's emphasis and appear on p. 238.) For superb and tempered accounts of Popenoe's work on eugen-

ics, see Wendy Kline, *Building a Better Race: Gender, Sexuality, and Eugenics from the Turn of the Century to the Baby Boom* (Berkeley: University of California Press, 2001); Molly Ladd-Taylor, "Eugenics, Sterilization and Modern Marriage in the U.S.A.: The Strange Career of Paul Popenoe," *Gender and History,* 2001; 13(2): 298–327.

48. Washington was friendly with Dr. Kellogg and first met him as a Sanitarium patient in 1910, a visit that was enthusiastically announced in the Sanitarium's magazine for patients and former patients, *The Battle Creek Idea.* Another visit, including Washington's delivery of a major lecture, occurred a year later in 1911. "News and Personals," *Battle Creek Idea,* Volume 4, No. 14, March 10, 1911; 4(14): 8; "News and Personals," *Battle Creek Idea,* March 17, 1911; 4(15): 8; "News and Personals," *Battle Creek Idea,* March 24, 1911; 4(16): 8; "The Progress of a Race," *Battle Creek Idea,* March 24, 1911; 4(16): 1–5; Wilson, *Dr. John Harvey Kellogg,* p. 145.

49. Booker T. Washington, "The Negro Race," in Robbins, ed., *Proceedings of the First National Conference on Race Betterment, January 8, 9, 10, 11, 12, 1914,* pp. 410–20.

50. Wilson, *Dr. John Harvey Kellogg,* p. 145; Schwarz, PhD thesis, p. 340.

51. J. H. Kellogg, *Plain Facts for Young and Old* (Burlington, Iowa: Senger and Condit, 1881), p. 164. This same passage appears on p. 151 of the 1887 Senger and Condit edition as well as on p. 182 in the 1910 reprint edition under the doctor's imprimatur, the Modern Medicine Publishing Company of Battle Creek, Michigan.

52. J. H. Kellogg, *The Ladies' Guide in Health and Disease: Girlhood, Maidenhood, Wifehood, Motherhood* (Des Moines, Iowa: W. D. Condit and Co, 1883), p. 193. This book went through successive reprint editions under the doctor's imprimatur, the Modern Medicine Publishing Company of Battle Creek, Michigan, in 1896 and 1902, with the sentence about the Negro's inferiority unchanged and intact, on the same page 193. His discourse on heredity, pedigrees, eugenics, euthenics, the importance of good child rearing, race deterioration, and illustrations of the adages "like father, like son" and "like mother, like daughter" appear on pp. 383–96.

53. Unsigned piece, "The Degeneration of the Negro," *Good Health,* October 1908; 43(10): 588. See also Reynold Spaeth, "Eugenic Aspects of the Negro," *Good Health,* October 1919; 54(10): pp. 590–93; Interview with William Sadler, by Richard Schwarz, Card VII-H, B9, F11, Sadler, Richard Schwarz Collection, Center for Adventists Research.

54. J. H. Kellogg, "Germany's Futile Effort at Race Betterment," *Good Health,* October 1935; 71(10): 307.

55. In 1940, Kellogg worried to his British friend, Sir Arbuthnot Lane, about what "that monster, Hitler, is going to try to do to your lovely island, which for so many years has held up the banner of our advancing Christian civilization." J. H. Kellogg to Arbuthnot Lane, July 20, 1040, Reel 5, Images 1220–21, J. H. Kellogg Papers, U-M.

56. J. H. Kellogg, "Japs Didn't Require Meat," *Good Health,* October 1908; 43(10): 558; Wilson, *Dr. John Harvey Kellogg,* pp. 142, 213.

57. There are several superb studies of Panama-Pacific International Exposition of 1915, including William Lipsky, *San Francisco's Panama-Pacific International Exposition (Images of America)* (Charleston, SC: Arcadia Publishing, 2005); Laura A. Ackley, *San Francisco's Jewel City: The Panama-Pacific International Exposition of 1915* (Berkeley: Heyday, 2014), discusses the Rare Betterment Foundation exhibit on pp. 167–68; Donna Ewald and Peter Clute, *San Francisco Invites the World: The Panama-Pacific International Exposition of 1915* (San Francisco: Chronicle Books, 1991), discusses the Palace of Education on pp. 72–73; Abigail M. Markwyn, *Empress San Francisco: The Pacific Rim, the Great West and California at the Panama-Pacific International Exposition*

(Lincoln: University of Nebraska Press, 2014), discusses the role the RBF played in the fair on pp. 24, 56–57.

58. David Starr Jordan, "Eugenics and War," in *Official Proceedings of the Second National Conference on Race Betterment. August 4, 5 ,6, 7, and 8, 1915. Held in San Francisco, CA in Connection with the Panama-Pacific International Exposition* (Battle Creek, MI: Race Betterment Foundation, 1915), pp. 12–26.

59. Luther Burbank, "Evolution and Variation with the Fundamental Significance of Sex," in ibid., pp. 45–51.

60. Frederick L. Hoffman, "Statistics of Race Betterment," pp. 27–33; A. J. Rccd, "Discussion; Longevity vs. Life Expectancy" (with comments by J. H. Kellogg, I. Fisher, C. F. Ballard), pp. 34–44, both in ibid. For Hoffman's views on African Americans and disease, see Frederick L. Hoffman, *Race Traits and Tendencies of the American Negro. Publications of the American Economics Association*, Volume 11, Nos. 1, 2, and 3, pp. 1–329 (New York: Published for the American Economics Association by the Macmillan Company, 1896).

61. "The Playground Pentathalon," in *Official Proceedings of the Second National Conference on Race Betterment. August 4, 5, 6, 7, and 8, 1915. Held in San Francisco, CA in Connection with the Panama-Pacific International Exposition* (Battle Creek, MI: Race Betterment Foundation, 1915), pp. 143–44.

62. "Morality Masque," in ibid., pp. 138–43. A synopsis of this play is included in the proceedings. For John's short summation of the play, see J. H. Kellogg, "Michigan: National Conference on Race Betterment. American Association for the Study and Prevention of Infant Mortality," *Transactions of the Sixth Annual Meeting, Philadelphia, November 10–12, 1915* (Baltimore: Franklin Printing Co., 1916), p. 398.

63. J. H. Kellogg, "The Eugenics Registry," in *Official Proceedings of the Second National Conference on Race Betterment. August 4, 5, 6, 7, and 8, 1915. Held in San Francisco, CA in Connection with the Panama-Pacific International Exposition* (Battle Creek, MI: Race Betterment Foundation, 1915), pp. 76–87, 144; Schwarz, *John Harvey Kellogg*, p. 222.

64. "The Race Betterment Exhibit," *Official Proceedings of the Second National Conference on Race Betterment. August 4, 5, 6, 7, and 8, 1915. Held in San Francisco, CA in Connection with the Panama-Pacific International Exposition* (Battle Creek, MI: Race Betterment Foundation, 1915), p. 145.

65. Ibid.

66. A. S. Bloese Manuscript, p. 275, Box 1, Folder 14.

67. John H. Kellogg, *Proceedings of the Third Race Betterment Conference, January 2–6, 1928* (Battle Creek, MI: Race Betterment Foundation, 1928), p. ii.

68. J. H. Kellogg, "The Responsibilities of Those Who Are Fit," *Proceedings of the Third Race Betterment Conference, January 2–6, 1928* (Battle Creek, MI: Race Betterment Foundation, 1928), pp. 118–19; Steven Selden, "Transforming Better Babies into Fitter Families: Archival Resources and the American Eugenics Movement, 1908–1930," *Proceedings of the American Philosophical Society*, 2005; 149(2): 199–225.

69. William L. Laurence, "Sees a Super-Race Evolved by Science: Dr. C. C. Little Tells Ithacans Laws to Weed Out Misfits Are 'Just Around the Corner.' Heredity an Iron Law. Knowledge of It Must Be Used for Nation's Good, He Says—Geneticists Gather for Congress," *New York Times*, August 25, 1932, p. 40; "Educators from Many Parts of the Country Coming . . . President Little of the University of Michigan Selected Chair of the Conference," *Battle Creek Enquirer*, November 18, 1927, p. 1, Reel 33, Images 409–10, J. H. Kellogg Papers, U-M.

70. Congressman Albert Johnson (R-WA), "The Menace of the Melting Pot," *Proceedings of the Third Race Betterment Conference, January 2–6, 1928* (Battle Creek, MI: Race Betterment Foundation, 1928), 200–201; Howard Markel et al., "The Foreignness of Germs: The Persistent Association of Immigrants and Disease in American Society," *The Milbank Quarterly,* 2002; 80(4): 757–88.

71. Fielding H. Yost, "Man Building," *Proceedings of the Third Race Betterment Conference, January 2–6, 1928* (Battle Creek, MI: Race Betterment Foundation, 1928), pp. 715–20.

72. Schwarz, *John Harvey Kellogg,* p. 102.

73. At the outbreak of World War II, he returned to Paris and spent his last years as the regent of the French Foundation for the Study of Human Problems *(Fondation Française pour l'Etude des Problèmes Humains),* created by the pro-Axis Vichy regime in 1941. There, Carrel helped implement a menu of eugenics and health policies. Alexis Carrel, "The Immortality of Animal Tissues and Its Significance," *Proceedings of the Third Race Betterment Conference, January 2–6, 1928* (Battle Creek, MI: Race Betterment Foundation, 1928), pp. 309–14; David M. Friedman, *The Immortalists: Charles Lindbergh, Dr. Alexis Carrel and Their Daring Quest to Live Forever* (New York: Harper Perennial, 2008), pp. 46, 86–94; Alexis Carrel, *Man, the Unknown* (West Drayton, Middlesex, England, and New York: Pelican, 1945; originally published by Harper in 1935), p. 290.

74. *Proceedings of the Third Race Betterment Conference, January 2–6, 1928* (Battle Creek, MI: Race Betterment Foundation, 1928), pp. iii–xix.

75. Wilson, *Dr. John Harvey Kellogg,* p. 160.

76. Letter from Irving Fisher to J. H. Kellogg, May 22, 1936, and Letter from Charles B. Davenport to Irving Fisher, May 18, 1936, Reel 4, Images 193–96, J. H. Kellogg Papers, U-M.

77. Letter from J. H. Kellogg to Irving Fisher, May 18, 1937, Reel 4, Images 833–36; Irving Fisher to J. H. Kellogg, May 28, 1937, Reel 4, Images 844–46, J. H. Kellogg Papers, U-M. In the latter letter, Fisher noted gleefully "how the Eugenics Society helped get through the restrictions on immigration on eugenics grounds," referring to the Immigration Restriction Act and National Origins Act of 1924.

78. Letter from Harry Laughlin to J. H. Kellogg. December 19, 1941, Reel 5, Images 1409–10, quote is on image 1410, J. H. Kellogg Papers, U-M. For an account of the role Harry Laughlin played in public policy issues (especially immigration restriction), see Ludmerer, *Genetics and American Society.*

79. See, for example, T. H. Morgan, A. H. Sturtevant, H. J. Muller, and C. B. Bridges, *The Mechanism of Mendelian Heredity* (New York: Henry Holt and Co., 1915); Raymond Pearl, *Modes of Research in Genetics* (New York: The Macmillan Co., 1915); Raymond Pearl, "The Biology of Superiority," *The American Mercury,* 1927; 12: 257–66.

80. Comfort, *The Science of Human Perfection;* Daniel Kevles, *In the Name of Eugenics: Genetics and the Uses of Human Heredity* (New York: Alfred A. Knopf, 1985); Ludmerer, *Genetics and American Society,* pp. 87–119; Mark Haller, *Eugenics: Hereditarian Attitudes in American Thought* (New Brunswick, NJ: Rutgers University Press, 1963); Ruth Schwarz Cowan, *Heredity and Hope: The Case for Genetic Screening* (Cambridge: Harvard University Press, 2008); Stefan Kühl, *For the Betterment of the Race: The Rise and Fall of the International Movement for Eugenics and Racial Hygiene* (London: Palgrave Macmillan, 2013); Paul Lombardo, *A Century of Eugenics in America: From the Indiana Experiment to the Human Genome Era* (Bloomington: Indiana University Press, 2011); Allen, "The Eugenics Record Office at Cold Spring Harbor, 1910–1940," 1986;

2: 225–64; Garland E. Allen, "The Role of Experts in Scientific Controversy," in Hugo Tristram Engelhardt and Arthur Leonard Caplan, eds., *Scientific Controversies: Case Studies in the Resolution and Closure of Disputes in Science and Technology* (New York: Cambridge University Press, 1987), pp. 169–202.

81. After careful study of state laws regarding mandatory sterilization of the mentally ill and finding many to be badly written or easily challenged as unconstitutional, Laughlin designed a "model eugenical sterilization law," which led to a number of programs and the sterilization of more than 64,000 mentally ill and disabled people well into the 1960s. See Harry H. Laughlin, *Eugenical Sterilization in the United States* (Chicago: Psychopathic Laboratory of the Municipal Court of Chicago, 1922).

82. Grand mal seizures, in modern medical parlance, are known as generalized tonic-clonic seizures. They are caused by abnormal electrical activity throughout the brain and are among the most severe seizures seen with epilepsy and brain injuries. Symptoms can include a loss of awareness or consciousness and striking, sudden, and involuntary muscular contractions. Phenytoin was synthesized in 1908 by a German chemist named Heinrich Biltz, who sold the rights to the drug to the Detroit pharmaceutical firm Parke-Davis. Its antiseizure properties were not elucidated until 1938 and the U.S. Food and Drug Administration approved its general use for the treatment of epilepsy in 1953. W. J. Friedlander, "Putnam, Merritt, and the Discovery of Dilantin," *Epilepsia*, 1986; 27, Supplement 3: S1–20.

83. Letter from H. H. Laughlin to J. H. Kellogg, December 19, 1941, Reel 5, Image 1408, J. H. Kellogg Papers, U-M. Laughlin misspells the drug's trade name as "dilltin" even though he meant "Dilantin," which was manufactured by the Parke-Davis Company of Detroit.

84. Letter from J. H. Kellogg to Reginald Atwater, November 1, 1943, Reel 6, Images 78–82, quote is on image 81, J. H. Kellogg Papers, U-M.

85. Letter from J. H. Kellogg to Henry Vaughan, November 21, 1943, Reel 6, Images 84–87, the quote appears on Image 87, or page 4 of the letter. J. H. Kellogg Papers, Michigan Historical Collections, Bentley Historical Library, University of Michigan.

86. "Kelley Files Race Betterment Suit," *Battle Creek Enquirer and News*, April 18, 1967, pp. 1–2; "Fund Faces Charges of Wasting $687,000," *New York Times*, April 19, 1967, p. 42; "Foundation Accused of Squandering," *Arizona Republic*, April 19, 1967, p. 68; "Charge Foundation's Funds Squandered," *Chicago Tribune*, April 19, 1967, p. A1; "Foundation Wasted Funds, State Says," *Detroit Free Press*, April 19, 1967, p. 10; "Says Foundation Squandered Half Million Dollars! Only $498 Left, Kelley Charges," *St. Joseph* (Michigan) *Herald-Press*, April 18, 1967, p. 1; "Race Betterment Group Denies Squander Claims," *Battle Creek Enquirer and News*, September 28, 1968, p. 2; Wilson, *Dr. John Harvey Kellogg*, pp. 169–70. Some of the foundation's money funded scholarships for children of two of the directors; another $200,000 was transferred to a "supposed non-profit entity" in Florida, and other assets were transferred to another director.

14.

A FULL PLATE

1. For a complete listing of all the doctor's foods for sale and consumption, see *Healthful Living: Fundamental Facts About Food and Feeding* (Battle Creek, MI: Battle Creek Food Company, undated, circa 1925), Collections of the University of Michi-

gan Center for the History of Medicine. A copy from the Michigan State University Archives can be found online at https://archive.lib.msu.edu/DMC/sliker/msuspcsbs_batc_battlecree10/msuspcsbs_batc_battlecree10.pdf.

2. J. H. Kellogg, "Health Principles," *General Conference Daily Bulletin,* March 1, 1(12): 185–89, quote is from p. 189, the italics on the word "reform" is Kellogg's. He delivered this address at the general conference on February 18, 1897.

3. J. H. Kellogg, *The New Dietetics: A Guide to Scientific Feeding in Health and Disease* (Battle Creek, MI: Modern Medicine Publishing Co., revised edition, 1923), p. 371. (First edition published in 1921.)

4. Ibid., pp. 382–83. This is not to say John Harvey Kellogg has singular claim to having invented peanut butter, per se. It has probably been around since the days of the ancient Aztecs. Contrary to popular belief, however, peanut butter was not invented by George Washington Carver, who cultivated peanuts and was a great advocate of peanuts, soybeans, and many other nuts and legumes. A Canadian chemist named Marcellus G. Edson patented a process to mill and make a peanut paste in October 21, 1884 ("Manufacture of Peanut-Candy," U.S. Patent 306,727). This concoction, which included sugar, was said to have the consistency of lard.

5. U.S. National Peanut Board. "Fun Facts," accessed July 7, 2015, at http://nationalpeanutboard.org/the-facts/fun-facts/.

6. For quote, see J. H. Kellogg's testimony in the Supreme Court case, *Kellogg v. Kellogg, State of Michigan Supreme Court Record,* Volume 2, p. 369; in J. H. Kellogg, "Good and Bad Foods," *General Conference Daily Bulletin,* March 5, 1899; 8(15): 151–52, he discusses peanut butter on p. 152. See also Schwarz, *John Harvey Kellogg,* pp. 120–21.

7. John Harvey Kellogg, U.S. Patents for peanut butter: "Food Compound" (U.S. Patent 567,901), application on November 4, 1895, and dated September 15, 1896; "Process for Preparing Nutmeal (U.S. Patent 580,787), application filed on November 4, 1895, and dated April 13, 1897; "Process of Producing Alimentary Products" (U.S. Patent 604,493), application filed on February 16, 1897, and dated May 24, 1898.

8. In 1922, Joseph Rosefield developed the process in which smooth peanut butter is made by keeping the oil from separating using partially hydrogenated oil. Rosefield sold the licensing rights to this process in 1928 to the Peter Pan Peanut Butter Company, and in 1932 made his own product under the brand name Skippy. For the history of this tangle of peanut primacy, see John E. Buchmeier, "A Sticky Subject," *Adventist Heritage,* Fall 1992; 15(2): 16–17; Bernice Lowe, *Tales of Battle Creek* (Battle Creek, MI: Robert L. and Louise B. Miller Foundation, 1976), p. 81; "Who Really Invented Peanut Butter?" *Battle Creek Enquirer,* March 29, 1990; Jon Krampner, *Creamy and Crunchy: An Informal History of Peanut Butter, the All-American Food* (New York: Columbia University Press, 2013).

9. Powell, pp. 94–95.

10. Williamson Jr., *An Intimate Glimpse,* p. 25.

11. The name Malted Nuts was actually a play on another popular health drink, Malted Milk, which was concocted in 1887 by James and William Horlick. The Horlick brothers' product, a mixture of malted barley, wheat flour, and evaporated whole milk, was widely sold as "a healthful, invigorating food drink for everybody, from infancy to old age." "Horlick's Malted Milk," advertisement, circa 1906, Collections of the University of Michigan Center for the History of Medicine; Rima Apple, *Mothers and Milk: A Social History of Infant Feeding, 1890–1950* (Madison: University of Wisconsin Press, 1987); Richard Meckel, *Save the Babies: American Public Health Reform and the*

Prevention of Infant Mortality, 1850–1929 (Ann Arbor: University of Michigan Press, 1998).

12. Sanitas Nut Food Advertisement, "The Food That's All Food. Delicious, Wholesome, Tempting. Prepared in many forms to suit many palates, One pound of Sanitas Nut Foods contains three times the combined nutriment, blood-making and flesh-building value of a pound each of BEEFSTEAK AND BREAD. The most easily digested food made. The perfect food for children. Assorted box of delicious Nut foods, 12 two-cent stamps. Our new Nut Food Booklet Free. Sanitas Nut Food Co., Ltd., 67 Washington St., Battle Creek, Mich," Collections of the University of Michigan Center for the History of Medicine. See also Schwarz, *John Harvey Kellogg*, p. 121; J. H. Kellogg, "Nut Butter and Nut Meal," *Good Health*, February 1896; 31(2): 56–57.

13. Clara Barton to the Sanitas Nut Food Company of Battle Creek, April 12, 1899, J. H. Kellogg Scrapbook, Volume 1, Box 16, J. H. Kellogg papers, U-M; Schwarz, *John Harvey Kellogg*, p. 121. An example of the Sanitas Nut Foods advertisements with Barton's endorsement appears in *The Vegetarian Magazine*, February 1900; 4(5): 26. For biographical information on Barton and the American Red Cross, see Howard Markel, "Clara Barton's Crusade to Bring the Red Cross to America," *PBS NewsHour*, May 22, 2014, accessed April 23, 2016, at http://www.pbs.org/newshour/updates/clara-barton -founding-american-red-cross/.

14. J. H. Kellogg, *Life, Its Mysteries and Miracles: A Manual of Health Principles* (Battle Creek, MI: Modern Medicine Publishing Co., 1910), p. 115.

15. Sanitarium Gluten Flour 44.81% Battle Creek Food Company advertisement, circa 1910, University of Michigan Center for the History of Medicine; J. H. Kellogg. *The New Dietetics*, pp. 801–3.

16. Sativa, which came in the form of bouillon cubes, was also frequently prepared and served as a consommé soup. Advertisement, "Foods that Build Health can be Palate-Tempting," Battle Creek Sanitarium Health Food, undated; "Good Eating for Health. 95 Delicious Recipes, 36 Appetizing Menus," The Battle Creek Sanitarium Food Company, booklet, undated; "Recipes for Everybody," Battle Creek Sanitarium Food, booklet, undated. Collections of the University of Michigan Center for the History of Medicine.

17. Moises Velasquez-Manoff, "The Myth of Big Bad Gluten," *New York Times*, July 4, 2015, p. SR6.

18. J. H. Kellogg, *The Health Question Box, or A Thousand and One Questions Answered* (Battle Creek, MI: Modern Medicine Publishing Co., 2nd edition, 1920), pp. 859–60.

19. V. Vuskan, A. L. Jenkins, D. J. A. Jenkins, A. L. Rogovik, J. L. Sievenpiper, and E. Jovanovski, "Using Cereal to Increase Dietary Fiber Intake to the Recommended Level and the Effect of Fiber on Bowel Function in Healthy Persons Consuming North American Diets, *American Journal of Clinical Nutrition*, 2008; 88(5): 1256–62.

20. J. W. Anderson, N. Zettwoch, T. Feldman, J. Tietyen-Clark, P. Oeltgen, and C. W. Bishop, "Cholesterol-Lowering Effects of Psyllium Hydrophilic Mucilloid for Hypercholesterolemic Men," *Archives of Internal Medicine*, 1988 (February); 148(2): 292–96; H. Lipsky, M. Gloger, and W. H. Frishman, Dietary Fiber for Reducing Blood Cholesterol," *The Journal of Clinical Pharmacology*, 1990 (August); 30(8): 699–703.

21. Harvey Cushing, *The Life of Sir William Osler* (Oxford: Oxford University Press, 1925), Volume 1, pp. 215–16.

22. See J. H. Kellogg, *Autointoxication or Intestinal Toxemia* (Battle Creek, MI: Modern Medicine Publishing Co., 1922, 3rd edition), pp. 30–48, 85–106, 306–13. Dr. Kellogg later chided Metchnikoff as someone who eats "a pound of meat and lets it rot in his colon and then drinks a pint of sour milk to disinfect it." This meaty diet, the doctor asserted, caused Metchnikoff's premature death at seventy-one years of age (p. 86). See also Élie Metchnikoff, *The Nature of Man: Studies in Optimistic Philosophy,* translated by Peter Chalmers Mitchell (New York: Putnam and Sons, 1903); Scott Podolsky, "Cultural Divergence: Élie Metchnikoff's *Bacillus bulgaricus* Therapy and His Underlying Concept of Life," *Bulletin of the History of Medicine,* 1998; 72(1): 1–27.

23. A. S. Bloese Manuscript, p. 178a; No. 251, Box 1, Folder 14.

24. Alexandre Mikhailovich Besredka, translated by J. H. Kellogg, "Doctor Tissier and His Work at the Pasteur Institute," reprinted from the *Bulletin of the Battle Creek Sanitarium and Hospital Clinic,* April 1929; 24(2): 73–82, Reel 40, Images 925–37, J. H. Kellogg Papers, U-M. John always gave the primary credit for discovering what we now call probiotics to Tissier, rather than Metchnikoff. On September 2, 1937, Kellogg wrote Tissier's widow about the preparation of this paper, which he planned to present at the annual meeting of the American Public Health Association. "Dr. Tissier's discovery has been of very great service to me and I want to make the world acquainted with the great services which he rendered," Reel 4, Images 998–99, quote is from Image 998, J. H. Kellogg Papers, U-M.

25. At first, John enlisted a cohort of "old ladies" to help him make capsules containing acidophilus-rich sour milk, vinegar, and corn starch. Unfortunately, the vinegar destroyed the yogurt's ability to ferment, thus rendering the pills medicinally useless for improving the intestinal flora. Nevertheless, for a brief period, the pills were hugely popular, thanks to a great deal of promotion in the doctor's *Good Health* magazine. With each passing year, despite serving tons of acidophilus-spiked milk, yogurt, and cheese at the San, the doctor grew increasingly disenchanted with cow's milk. "Cows' milk is good for calves," John advised to his patients in 1910, "but it is not really good food for human beings. "Lecture: Question Box Hour," November 21, 1910, Reel 12, Images 192–223, quote is from Image 210, J. H. Kellogg Papers, U-M.

26. John extolled soybeans as especially useful for a diabetic's diet. *The New Method in Diabetes: The Practical Treatment of Diabetes as Conducted at the Battle Creek Sanitarium Adapted to Home Use, Based Upon the Treatment of More than Eleven Hundred Cases* (Battle Creek, MI: Good Health Publishing Co., 1917), p. 65. His enthusiasm continued in subsequent editions of that work and he devoted four pages to soy, including a detailed discussion of tofu, in his 1920 omnibus volume, *The Health Question Box, or A Thousand and One Questions Answered,* pp. 350–53. One of his most popular books increased that coverage with seven pages discussing the joys of soy sauce, soy milk and soy sprouts; J. H. Kellogg, *The New Dietetics,* pp. 322–29. In the 1920s, Henry Ford ordered the farmers working for him to devote more than eight thousand acres of his farmland to growing soybeans. Although Ford expressed some interest in the nutritional aspect of soybeans, the butter, biscuits, meat substitutes, ice cream, and artificial dairy products his engineers produced simply did not taste all that good. Nor did the soy-based cloth his engineers produced yield much more than a collection of oddly textured neck ties Ford took to wearing. Instead, the auto magnate used the beans to develop paints, oil products, and plastics his factory fashioned into "the gearshift knobs, dash controls, door handles, window trim, accelerator pedals and horn buttons" for his automobiles. See Steven Watts, *The People's Tycoon: Henry Ford and the American*

Century (New York: Vintage, 2006), pp. 483–86. See also William Shurtleff and Akiko Aoyagi, eds., *Henry Ford and His Researchers: History of Their Work with Soybeans, Soyfoods, and Chemurgy, 1928–2011: An Extensively Annotated Bibliography and Sourcebook* (Lafayette, CA: SoyInfo Center, 2011).

27. William Shurtleff and Akiko Aoyagi, "Dr. J. H. Kellogg and Battle Creek Foods: Work with Soy: A Chapter from the unpublished manuscript," "History of Soybeans and Soyfoods, 1100 B.C. to the 1980s" (Copyright 2004, SoyInfo Center, Lafayette, California), accessed November 6, 2014, at http://www.soyinfocenter.com/HSS/john_kellogg_and_battle_creek_foods.php.

28. "Soy Acidophilus Milk: The New Acidophilus Therapy, pamphlet, circa 1930s, The Battle Creek Food Co., Reel 40, Images 629–31, J. H. Kellogg Papers, U-M.

29. Howard Markel, "For the Welfare of Children: The Origins of the Partnership Between Public Health Workers and Pediatricians in the United States," *American Journal of Public Health,* 2000; 90: 893–99.

30. Method for Making Acidophilus Milk, U.S. Patent 1,982,994, applied for June 13, 1933, issued on December 4, 1934.

31. Pierre Berton, *The Dionne Years: A Thirties Melodrama* (New York: W. W. Norton, 1977). On page 159, there is a description of W. K. Kellogg driving six hundred miles to see them. Alexander Woollcott and Bette Davis went to see them, as did Amelia Earhart. The aviatrix saw them on April 23, 1937, five weeks before she vanished into thin air.

32. Two of the Dionne films, starring the venerable Jean Hersholt as a version of the Canadian doctor, are available on DVD: *The Country Doctor,* released by 20th Century Films, 1936 (Beverly Hills: Twentieth Century Fox Cinema Archives, DVD, 2014); *Five of a Kind,* released by 20th Century Fox in 1938 (Beverly Hills: Twentieth Century Fox Cinema Archives, DVD, 2012). A short film, *Reunion,* was made between these two motion pictures and was released in 1937 but is not available on DVD. See Paul Talbot, *The Films of the Dionne Quintuplets* (Albany, GA: Bear Manor Media, 2007); Willis Thorton, *The Country Doctor,* based on the 20th Century Fox Photoplay (New York: Grosset and Dunlap, 1936). See also A. J. Liebling and Harold Ross, "Miss Rand," in Lillian Ross, *The Fun of It: Stories from the Talk of the Town,* The New Yorker (New York: Modern Library, 2001), pp. 89–90.

33. Clipping from an unidentified Battle Creek newspaper, which describes the Soy Acidophilus treatment for the Dionne quintuplets. Dated in pencil, July 11, 1935, "Quintuplet Doctor Thanks Dr. Kellogg for Treatment Which Helped Save Babies," Reel 32, Image 307, J. H. Kellogg Papers, U-M.

34. See letters from J. H. Kellogg to Allen Roy Dafoe, November 8, 1936, Images 435–36; J. H. Kellogg to David Croll, November 13, 1936, Image 443; David Croll to J. H. Kellogg, November 23, 1936, Image 462; J. H. Kellogg to Allan Roy Dafoe, November 26, 1936, Images 467–69; J. H. Kellogg to A. R. Dafoe, November 27, 1936, Image 470; J. H. Kellogg to David Croll, Minister of Public Welfare, Canada, November 27, 1936, Images 475–76; A. R. Dafoe to J. H. Kellogg, December 1, 1936, Image 480; David Croll to J. H. Kellogg, December 3, 1936, Image 483; Dr. Kellogg to David Croll, December 6, 1936, Images 487–90; J. H. Kellogg to A. R. Dafoe, December 9, 1936, Images 492–94; J. H. Kellogg to A. R. Dafoe, December 20, 1936, Images 508–10; A. R. Dafoe to J. H. Kellogg, December 22, 1936, Image 512; J. H. Kellogg to A. R. Dafoe, January 29, 1937, Images 605–6; J. H. Kellogg to David Croll, January 29, 1937, Images 608–9; J. H. Kellogg to A. R. Dafoe, February 11, 1937, Images 643–45, all on Reel 4, J. H. Kellogg Papers, U-M.

35. Letter from J. H. Kellogg to David Croll, November 27, 1936, Reel 4, Images 475–76, quote is from Image 475, J. H. Kellogg Papers, U-M.

36. Letters from A. R. Dafoe to J. H. Kellogg, March 25, 1936, Reel 4, Image 116, J. H. Kellogg Papers, U-M; W. J. Morse to J. H. Kellogg, April 4, 1936, Reel 4, Image 127, J. H. Kellogg Papers, U-M; A. R. Dafoe to J. H. Kellogg, June 24, 1936, Reel 4, Image 235; J. H. Kellogg to A. R. Dafoe, September 21, 1936, Reel 4, Images 316–17, J. H. Kellogg Papers, U-M.

37. Letters from J. H. Kellogg to R. E. Byrd, October 21, 1936, Images 404–6; J. H. Kellogg to Admiral R. E. Byrd, November 11, 1936, Images 440–41; R. E. Byrd to Battle Creek Food Co., November 17, 1936, Image 450; R. E. Byrd to J. H. Kellogg, November 18, 1936, Image 451; J. H. Kellogg to Byrd, November 23, 1936, Images 463–64, all on Reel 4 (1936–1938 Correspondence), J. H. Kellogg Papers, U-M. See also "Miami Scientist Aids Byrd Antarctic Expedition" and Cecil Warren, "Noted Miami Doctor Prescribes Diet for New Byrd South Pole Expedition," both in *Miami News,* November 5, 1939, Reel 32, Images 400–401, J. H. Kellogg Papers, U-M. For the life and times of Admiral Byrd, see Lisle A. Rose, *Explorer: The Life of Richard E. Byrd.* (Columbia: University of Missouri Press, 2008); Vincent P. Morris, "Richard E. Byrd," in John A. Garraty and Mark C. Carnes, eds., *American National Biography,* Volume 4 (New York: Oxford University Press, 1999), pp. 133–35. Byrd's first trip to the South Pole began in late 1928 and extended, off and on, until June 1930. This was a brief trip that was followed by a second, longer trip on January 17, 1934, that lasted until May of 1935. He made subsequent trips there in 1939, 1946 to 1947, and in December 1955–February 1956. Interestingly, the W. K. Kellogg Company was another provider of provisions for at least one of the Byrd expeditions and sent packaged cereals in a special container to retain their fresh taste under the harsh conditions of Antarctica. See Williamson Jr., *An Intimate Glimpse,* p. 180.

38. Letter from J. H. Kellogg to John D. Rockefeller Jr., January 24, 1938, Reel 4 (1936–1938 Correspondence), Images 1293–94. In this letter, John invites Rockefeller back to Battle Creek. J. H. Kellogg Papers, U-M. Another fan of the Battle Creek Soy *Acidophilus* Milk was the Johns Hopkins gynecologist Howard A. Kelly. Letter from Howard A. Kelly to J. H. Kellogg, April 21, 1936, Reel 4, Image 138; J. H. Kellogg to Kelly, April 24, 1936, Reel 4, Image 140, J. H. Kellogg Papers, U-M. For a description of Paramels, see Schwarz, *John Harvey Kellogg,* p. 123. For a description of Lacto-Dextrin, see "Lacto-Dextrin," promotional brochure, circa 1930s, Battle Creek Food Company, Battle Creek, Michigan, Collections of the University of Michigan Center for the History of Medicine.

39. Letter from J. H. Kellogg to John D. Rockefeller Jr., January 24, 1938, Images 1293–94, quote is on Image 1293, J. H. Kellogg Papers, U-M.

40. Scott Bruce and Bill Crawford. *Cerealizing America: The Unsweetened Story of American Breakfast Cereal* (Boston and London: Faber and Faber, 1995), p. 112.

41. Howard Markel, "'When It Rains It Pours': Endemic Goiter, Iodized Salt, and David Murray Cowie, M.D.," *American Journal of Public Health,* 1987; 77(2): 219–29. See also E. V. McCollum, *The Newer Knowledge of Nutrition: The Use of Food for the Preservation of Vitality and Health* (New York: Macmillan, 1922, 2nd edition); Apple, *Vitamania.*

42. Advertisement for Kellogg's "PEP Toasted Wheat Flakes Plus Extra Bran. Ready to Eat," circa 1934, featuring Detroit Tigers Hall of Fame catcher Mickey Cochrane, Collections of the University of Michigan Center for the History of Medicine.

43. Kellogg's Corn-Soya Shreds advertisements, unidentified magazine clipping, circa 1949, Collections of the University of Michigan Center for the History of Medicine.

44. Bruce and Crawford, *Cerealizing America,* pp. 112–13.

45. Two of the cereal's biggest fans were the film actress Claudette Colbert and Ohio State University football coach Woody Hayes. Bruce and Crawford, *Cerealizing America,* p. 113; advertisement for Kellogg's Concentrate: "The Little Gold Box: How it helps you balance your diet every day without a single chart," unidentified and undated magazine clipping, circa 1967, Collections of the University of Michigan Center for the History of Medicine.

15.
"UNEASY LIES THE HEAD THAT WEARS A CROWN"

Chapter title: William Shakespeare, *Henry the Fourth, Part 2,* Act 3, Scene 1, line 31.

1. Powell, p. 259.

2. During much of the 1920s, Will also occupied himself by building his Pomona ranch, a mansion on Gull Lake outside Battle Creek, and a luxury apartment building in Battle Creek, where he combined four apartments on the top floor for his own personal residence. See Williamson Jr., *An Intimate Glimpse,* p. 83.

3. Powell, p. 241.

4. Ibid., pp. 239–42.

5. The ranch was designed by the architect Charles Gibbs. Mary Jane Parkinson, *The Kellogg Arabian Ranch, The First Fifty Years: A Chronicle of Events, 1925–1975* (Anaheim: The Arabian Horse Association of Southern California, 1975), pp. 1–191.

6. Williamson Jr., *An Intimate Glimpse,* pp. 107–8. Nearby, Will built a house for his daughter Beth's family and his eldest son, Karl.

7. Powell, p. 229. In 1932, W. K. Kellogg donated his ranch, the land it occupied, and his beloved collection of horses to the state of California and its university system, where it became the W. K. Kellogg Institute of Animal Husbandry and the campus of California State Polytechnic University at Pomona. Will resided at "the Big House" until 1942. Parkinson, *The Kellogg Arabian Ranch,* pp. 177–85; Williamson Jr., *An Intimate Glimpse,* pp. 131–37.

8. Powell, p. 237.

9. Powell, pp. 237–38, 281.

10. Powell, p. 237. For descriptions of the 1925 M-G-M film *Ben-Hur,* see Scott Eyman, *Lion of Hollywood: The Life and Legend of Louis B. Mayer* (New York: Simon & Schuster, 2005), pp. 99–110; Mark A. Vieria, *Irving Thalberg: Boy Wonder to Hollywood Prince* (Berkeley: University of California Press, 2010), pp. 48–58.

11. Williamson Jr., *An Intimate Glimpse,* p. 137.

12. Powell, pp. 260–61.

13. H. L. Mencken, "Valentino," in Alistair Cooke, ed., *The Vintage Mencken* (New York: Vintage, 1955), pp. 170–74, quote is from p. 174. (Originally appeared in the August 30, 1926, issue of the *Baltimore Evening Sun.*)

14. *The Sheik* (1921) and *The Son of the Sheik* (1926), DVD, Blackhawk Films Collection (Los Angeles: Image Entertainment, 2002).

15. A. Scott Berg, *Goldwyn: A Biography* (New York: Alfred A. Knopf, 1989), pp. 105, 129–32, 161.

16. Parkinson, *The Kellogg Arabian Ranch,* pp. 67–89; Walter H. Roeder, "Jadaan, the Sheik and the Cereal Baron," *The Cal Poly Scholar,* 1988 (Fall); 1: 99–103; Powell, pp. 228–43.

17. Parkinson, *The Kellogg Arabian Ranch,* pp. 70–72, quote is from Valentino's reply telegram to W. K. Kellogg on p. 72.

18. Parkinson, *The Kellogg Arabian Ranch,* p. 76.

19. Tino Balio, *United Artists: The Company Built by the Stars, Volume I: 1919–1950* (Madison: University of Wisconsin Press, 2009), p. 56.

20. Emily W. Leider, *Dark Lover: The Life and Death of Rudolph Valentino* (New York: Farrar, Straus & Giroux, 2003), p. 369.

21. H. L. Mencken, "Valentino," in Alistair Cooke, ed., *The Vintage Mencken* (New York: Vintage, 1955), p. 174. (Originally appeared in the August 30, 1926, issue of the *Baltimore Evening Sun.*)

22. Powell, p. 172.

23. Ibid., p. 185.

24. Williamson Jr., *An Intimate Glimpse,* p. 50.

25. Powell, p. 196.

26. *Eagle Heights: The W. K. Kellogg Manor House* (Hickory Corners, MI: Michigan State University/Kellogg Biological Station, 2015). W. K. Kellogg spent nearly $750,000 (about $10 million in 2016) building this sumptuous Tudor Revival mansion between 1925 and 1926. It featured a grand oak staircase, Rookwood tile flooring, rooms with seven (his favorite number) windows and wooden panels, rare Flemish tapestries, and a Skinner pipe organ. In early 1942, he donated Eagle Heights to the federal government as a convalescent center for wounded soldiers who had graduated from staying at what was once his brother's Battle Creek Sanitarium but still required additional therapy. Will moved a few doors down the street.

27. Powell, p. 252.

28. Ibid., p. 152.

29. Ibid., p. 155.

30. Ibid., p. 249.

31. Ibid., pp. 214–15. The quote "almost impulsively" appears on page 214.

32. Ibid., p. 249.

33. Ibid., p. 215.

34. Ibid., p. 249.

35. Ibid., p. 250.

36. Ibid.

37. Will and Puss also had two boys who died very young. They were Will Keith Jr. (1885–1889) and Irvin Hadley (1894–1895). Williamson Jr., *An Intimate Glimpse,* p. 22.

38. Ibid., p. 23.

39. Powell, pp. 72–73.

40. Williamson Jr., *An Intimate Glimpse,* p. 7.

41. Powell, p. 152.

42. Ibid., p. 151. The letter was to his eldest son, Karl. There was one other child in the household who merits a footnote. A red-haired Canadian girl named Pauline was taken into the Kellogg home, to play with and watch the other children, but her behavior was disruptive and combative. She left the Kellogg home to take up nursing around 1920, training at the White Memorial Hospital in Los Angeles. See Powell, pp. 154–55. In Powell's version, Pauline joined the family at the age of three years. In Norman Williamson Jr.'s version, she came to the family as a teenager, during Puss's illness. Wil-

liamson Jr. notes that Pauline's behavior was so unruly that Will "finally packed her off once again; this time to a hospital in Chicago." Later, Pauline was institutionalized in the 1930s in a mental health hospital in Guelph, Ontario, and lived there until 1978. Will Kellogg took care of her financial needs. Williamson Jr.'s version seems to be the one that is more accurate given his claim that he visited her when she was seventy-eight and was a trustee of the trust fund Will left in her name. See Williamson Jr., *An Intimate Glimpse,* pp. 23–24.

43. For a listing of Karl's many maladies, including tuberculosis, malaria, and chronic ulcerative colitis, see Williamson Jr., *An Intimate Glimpse,* p. 186. At one point, Karl even fractured several vertebrae while working on Will's mobile "Ark," which was built in 1923 upon the chassis of a White truck and contained sleeping berths, a galley kitchen, ice maker, shower bath, toilet, intercom, radio, and a sixteen-foot folding boat. See Powell, p. 220.

44. Williamson Jr., *An Intimate Glimpse,* p 186.

45. Ibid., p. 110.

46. Chula Vista Diamond Anniversary Committee, *Chula Vista Heritage, 1911–1986* (Chula Vista, CA: City of Chula Vista, 1986), pp. 1–32, 51; Williamson Jr., *An Intimate Glimpse,* p. 186.

47. Williamson Jr., *An Intimate Glimpse,* pp. 186, 201–2. Karl was a member of the local school board and an elementary school in Chula Vista is named for him.

48. Letter from John L. Kellogg to his father Will Kellogg, October 3, 1897. See Powell, pp. 153–54.

49. Williamson Jr., *An Intimate Glimpse,* p. 67.

50. Powell, p. 193.

51. Ibid.

52. Wednesday, February 4, 1914, U.S. Patent for Waxtite, by W. K. Kellogg Co. (trademark serial number 71075679); Powell, pp. 194–95; "The Most Important Announcement I Ever Made," *Saturday Evening Post,* May 23, 1914; 186(47): 74.

53. Carson, p. 223. Carson estimated a savings of at least $250,000 per year.

54. Ibid.

55. Powell, p. 173.

56. Ibid., p. 160.

57. Ibid., p. 195.

58. Williamson Jr., *An Intimate Glimpse,* pp. 68–69.

59. Ibid., p. 195.

60. Ibid., pp. 53–65.

61. Dr. Selmon's medical skills and diplomatic tact so impressed Will that, in 1930, he appointed Selmon the first president of the W. K. Kellogg Foundation. *"I'll Invest My Money in People": A Biographical Sketch of the Founder of the Kellogg Company and the W. K. Kellogg Foundation* (Battle Creek, MI: W. K. Kellogg Foundation, 1990), pp. 65–66.

62. Williamson Jr., *An Intimate Glimpse,* p. 67.

63. Will lived at 256 West Van Buren and John Leonard's home was at 250 West Van Buren. *Battle Creek, Michigan City Directory, 1921* (Detroit: R. L. Polk and Co., 1921), p. 581.

64. Helen came from an impoverished background. Her father was an alcoholic who stayed home in a stupor while demanding his young daughter run to the local saloon to fetch him tankards of beer. Despite her awful childhood, Helen was smart, ambitious, and eager to leave all of it behind. She had one son with her late husband, a boy named

Thomas. According to Williamson Jr., "The death of her husband set back her plan for self-advancement a bit but the Kellogg Company executive dining room opened up a fascinating new opportunity." See Williamson Jr., *An Intimate Glimpse,* p. 69.

65. Ibid., p. 71.

66. Ibid.

67. John Leonard's wife, Hanna (whom W.K. always wrote to as "Hannah"), emigrated from Sweden in her teens in 1900 to help an ailing Puss with taking care of the children and home. Beautiful, tall, and blond, Hanna was irresistibly alluring to the adolescent and hormonal John Leonard. In 1901, when they were both eighteen, they eloped to Hastings, Michigan. Williamson Jr., *An Intimate Glimpse,* pp. 22, 67–75; Carson, pp. 222–23; Powell, p. 196.

68. Williamson Jr., *An Intimate Glimpse,* pp. 71–75.

69. Ibid., pp. 77–81; Carson, p. 223.

70. Gerald Carson reports W.K. sold it at a loss to the Ralston Company, p. 223; Norman Williamson Jr. claims it became the first domestic Kellogg cereal plant outside Battle Creek, *An Intimate Glimpse,* pp. 77, 81.

71. Powell, pp. 195, 220–21.

72. Williamson Jr., *An Intimate Glimpse,* p. 89, quoting from Will's diary for June 22, 1925.

73. Ibid., p. 90.

74. Powell, p. 196.

75. Williamson Jr., *An Intimate Glimpse,* p. 186.

76. Powell, p. 197.

77. Williamson Jr., *An Intimate Glimpse,* p. 93. At the time of Helen's death in 1978, the John L. and Helen Kellogg Foundation had assets worth nearly $50 million; much of it went to Northwestern University and the University of Notre Dame.

78. Ibid., p. 186.

79. Carson, pp. 223–24.

80. Powell, p. 154.

81. Williamson Jr., *An Intimate Glimpse,* pp. 42–43.

82. Ibid., p. 40.

83. Ibid., pp. 41–42.

84. Ibid. Kenneth Williamson died at age sixty-eight in Laguna Hills, California, after choking on a piece of food. "Kellogg Heir Dies," *Spokane Daily Chronicle,* June 10, 1980, p. 10.

85. Williamson Jr., *An Intimate Glimpse,* pp. 42, 45–46, 49; Powell, p. 156.

86. M. Green and A. J. Solnit, "Reactions to the Threatened Loss of a Child: A Vulnerable Child Syndrome," *Pediatrics,* 1964; 34: 58–66. This dynamic commonly occurs after a child's close call with death. The parents believe the child (or all of their children) to be especially vulnerable to illness and injury and overreact to any hint of a problem.

87. Williamson Jr., *An Intimate Glimpse,* pp. 45–46, quote is from p. 46. When Norman Jr. and Eleanor were discovered to have scoliosis of the spine, Will arranged for an orthopedic surgeon to resolve this condition. Norman Jr. recalled that he, Eleanor, and John Harold suffered "severe nutritional deficiencies," which seems odd given the family's wealth and access to plenty of nutritional food. John Harold also suffered from pyloric stenosis as an infant, which required surgery.

88. Ibid., pp. 106–7, 202–3. Norman Williamson Sr. died on Christmas Day 1967.

89. Ibid., p. 73.

90. Powell, p. 201.

91. Ibid., quotes are from pages 198 and 199.

92. Ibid., p. 199.

93. Ibid., p. 200. The stock market crash of 1929 began on October 24, "Black Thursday," when the Dow Jones Industrial average lost 11 percent in value at the opening bell. The following Monday, the 28th ("Black Monday"), margin calls facilitated another 13 percent loss, and on Tuesday the 29th ("Black Tuesday"), the Dow lost another 30 points or 12 percent.

94. Ibid., p. 201.

95. Williamson Jr., *An Intimate Glimpse,* pp. 115–18, describes the tenures of several executives who were hired as president of the company, including an efficiency expert named Walter Hasselhorn from the consulting firm then known as McKinsey-Wellington and now McKinsey and Company.

96. This entire memorandum is reproduced in Powell, p. 203.

97. Williamson Jr., *An Intimate Glimpse,* p. 158.

98. Powell, p. 204.

99. Letter from W. K. Kellogg to J. L. Kellogg Jr., July 19, 1935, quoted in Powell, p. 204.

100. Powell, p. 205.

101. Williamson Jr., *An Intimate Glimpse,* pp. 158–61.

102. Powell, pp. 205–6.

103. Letter from W. K. Kellogg to John L. Kellogg, undated, quoted in ibid., p. 206.

104. Williamson Jr., *An Intimate Glimpse,* pp. 160–63; "W. K. Kellogg's Grandson Found. Shotgun and Note to His Brother Nearby," *Chicago Tribune,* February 7, 1938, p. 7. John Jr.'s son, John Leonard Kellogg III, was born on April 4, 1938, one day before his great-grandfather returned to New York from his cruise.

105. Powell, pp. 206–7, quote is from page 207; Carson, p. 224.

106. Williamson Jr., *An Intimate Glimpse,* pp. 22–23, quote is from p. 23.

107. Powell, pp. 253–54.

108. Carson, p. 215.

109. Ibid.; Powell, p. 342.

110. Carson, p. 225.

111. Powell, p. 287.

112. Other proud owners of Rin Tin Tin's progeny included the M-G-M screen legends Greta Garbo and Jean Harlow. See Carson, p. 215; Powell, pp. 278, 346; Susan Orleans, *Rin Tin Tin: The Life and the Legend* (New York: Simon & Schuster, 2012), p. 72.

113. Carson, pp. 215–16.

114. Williamson Jr., *An Intimate Glimpse,* photo insert between pages 106 and 107. Photograph of Will's chief nurse, Elsie Gay Hoatson. Another one of his nurses in this photograph is Mrs. Louise Gardner. There were several other nurses and aides who took care of Will Kellogg in his last years, including his longtime secretaries Bessie Young and Helen Abbott, but Ms. Hoatson was Will's chief caregiver from 1939 to his death in 1951. See Powell, pp. 262–63.

115. Powell, p. 263.

116. Letter from W. K. Kellogg to Charles N. Crittenton, October 5, 1909, quoted in Powell, p. 293. Crittenton's principal charity was directed at "rescue homes" for young unwed mothers, prostitutes, and "wayward girls." "Charles N. Crittenton Dead.

Wealthy Druggist Founded 73 Rescue Homes in Daughter's Memory," *New York Times,* November 17, 1909, p. 9.

117. Powell, p. 293 ("humanity" quote), p. 297 ("spend it wisely" quote).

118. Powell, pp. 303–4. In early 1930, hardly dreaming his life would extend to nonagenarian status, Will wrote his attorney, Burritt Hamilton, "I want you to draft a will for me. It will contain about thirty trusts. It must be carefully drawn. It will dispose of property of the estimated value of $50,000,000" (over $709 million in 2016). In actuality, Will's lawyer created more than fifty trusts, twenty-six of which took care of the financial needs of his living children, his grandchildren, unborn great-grandchildren, a few old friends, and needy relatives and employees. Another twenty-four trusts were created for various colleges, universities, an animal husbandry institute at Pomona to care for his beloved Arabian horses, the donation of his homes in Palm Springs and Florida, a bird sanctuary and biological station, and his mansion on Gull Lake just outside Battle Creek. Williamson Jr., *An Intimate Glimpse,* p. 193. The twenty-six family trusts amounted to more than $5 million, an amount greater than $70.9 million in 2016. See also Powell, pp. 298–311. The "draft a will" quote appears on p. 298.

119. Letter from W. K. Kellogg to L. J. Brown, Eugene McKay, and A. C. Selmon, June 7, 1930, reproduced in Powell, p. 301.

120. Powell, p. 306.

121. Ibid., p. 305.

122. *White House Conference, 1930: Addresses and Abstracts of Committee Reports. White House Conference on Child Health and Protection Called by President Hoover* (New York: The Century Co., 1931), pp. v–vii.

123. "Medicine: Breakfast Food Men," *Time,* December 8, 1930; 16(23): 30, 32.

124. Powell, pp. 308–9.

125. "Emory Morris, Obituary," *Toledo Blade,* July 9, 1974, p. 5.

126. For the history and impact of the W. K. Kellogg Foundation, see *W. K. Kellogg Foundation: The First Eleven Years, 1930–1941* (Battle Creek, MI: W. K. Kellogg Foundation/Lakeside Press, R. R. Donnelly and Sons, Chicago, 1942); *W. K. Kellogg Foundation: The First Twenty-Five Years: The Story of a Foundation* (Battle Creek, MI: W. K. Kellogg Foundation, 1955); *W. K. Kellogg Foundation: The First Half-Century, 1930–1980: Private Approaches* (Battle Creek, MI: W. K. Kellogg Foundation, 1980); *"I'll Invest My Money in People"* (Battle Creek, MI: The W. K. Kellogg Foundation, 1979).

127. "Dr. Sadler, 93, Dies; Services Are Scheduled," *Chicago Tribune,* April 28, 1969, p. B18.

128. Powell, p. 182.

129. Ibid., p. 289.

130. Ibid., pp. 289–90.

131. Ibid., p. 290.

132. Ibid., pp. 258, 290.

133. Ibid., p. 291.

16.

THE FINAL SCORE

1. Schwarz, *John Harvey Kellogg,* pp. 133–34; Schwarz, PhD thesis, p. 55.

2. For the history of Trudeau's sanatorium, see E. L. Trudeau, *An Autobiography*

(Garden City, NY: Doubleday, Page, 1916); Robert Taylor, *Saranac: America's Magic Mountain* (New York: Paragon House, 1986).

3. Elisabeth Kübler-Ross, *On Death and Dying: What the Dying Have to Teach Doctors, Nurses, Clergy and Their Own Families* (New York: Macmillan, 1969). She famously described the five steps of death and dying as denial, anger, bargaining, depression, and acceptance.

4. Schwarz, PhD thesis, p. 55; Schwarz, *John Harvey Kellogg*, pp. 133–35.

5. Every late autumn, Dr. Kellogg wrote an "open letter to the people of Battle Creek" announcing his "enforced winter sojourn in the South," which was published in the Battle Creek newspapers. See, for example, "A Letter from Dr. J. H. Kellogg," *Battle Creek Enquirer and News*, October 25, 1936, Reel 4, Images 410–11, J. H. Kellogg Papers, U-M.

6. Schwarz, PhD thesis, pp. 464–68.

7. Ibid., p. 466.

8. "Seek to Avert Sale of Sanitarium. File Action to Prevent Auction Sale," *Battle Creek Moon-Journal*, May 24, 1929, p. 1, Images 43–44, "Sanitarium Fights Taxes. Million Involved in Legal Action," *Battle Creek Enquirer and the Evening News*, May 24, 1929, pp. 1–2, Images 45–46; "City Commission Proceedings, Battle Creek Michigan," *Battle Creek Moon-Journal*, May 27, 1929; *Battle Creek Moon-Journal*, May 28, 1929, pp. 13–14, Images 47–48; "City to Hire Expert Talent in Tax Action," *Battle Creek Enquirer*, May 28, 1929, Image 49; "Mayor Urges Counter Suit Against San," *Battle Creek Moon-Journal*, May 28, 1929, Images 50–52; "Tax Sale Held by City Clerk," *Battle Creek Moon-Journal*, May 31, 1929, Image 52; all on Reel 36, J. H. Kellogg Papers, U-M.

9. Schwarz, PhD thesis, pp. 468–69.

10. Schwarz, *John Harvey Kellogg*, pp. 79–80; Carson, p. 244. The property was worth at least $200,000, or about $2.84 million in 2016.

11. See, for example, letters from Mrs. Thomas A. Edison, February 8, 1931, Reel 3, Images 350–52; Will Durant to J. H. Kellogg, November 8, 1939, Image 801, J. H. Kellogg to W. Durant, November 10, 1939, Reel 5, Images 803–5, W. Durant to J. H. Kellogg, November 16, 1939, Reel 5, Images 811–12; J. H. Kellogg to W. Durant, November 20, 1939, Reel 5, Image 813; W. Durant to J. H. Kellogg, November 28, 1939, Reel 5, Images 817–18, Reel 5, Images 831–32; J. H. Kellogg to Alexis Carrel, January 30, 1939, Reel 5, Images 509–10; Dale Carnegie to J. H. Kellogg, April 5, 1938, Reel 5, Image 180; J. H. Kellogg to Dale Carnegie, April 12, 1938, Reel 5, Images 198–201; J. H. Kellogg to Clara Ford, December 2, 1937, Reel 5, Images 1184–85; J. H. Kellogg to Clara Ford, February 21, 1940, Reel 5, Images 977–78; Lt. Commander Gene Tunney to Dr. Kellogg, March 6, 1942, Reel 6, Images 23–24, all J. H. Kellogg Papers, U-M.

12. Letter from J. H. Kellogg to John D. Rockefeller Jr., May 17, 1938, Reel 5, Images 250–53, J. H. Kellogg Papers, U-M.

13. A. S. Bloese Manuscript, pp. 316–18, quote is from p. 316; Box 1, Folder 14.

14. Ibid., p. 316.

15. Letter from J. H. Kellogg to George Bernard Shaw, February 7, 1936, Reel 4, Images 36–39, J. H. Kellogg Papers, U-M.

16. "Food Ferrin Is a Modern Source of Assimilable Iron," brochure, circa 1941, Battle Creek Food Company, Battle Creek, Michigan, Collections of the University of Michigan Center for the History of Medicine.

17. Letter from J. H. Kellogg to George Bernard Shaw, February 7, 1936, Reel 4, Images 36–39, J. H. Kellogg Papers, U-M.

18. "Predicts Noted Playwright Will Be Active When 100," *Miami Herald,* February 10, 1936; "G. B. Shaw Asserts Roosevelt Is a Red. President Beginning to Realize He is a Communist, Says Writer, Now in Cuba," *New York Times,* February 8, 1936, p. 17; "Shaw Bounces His Wit into Miami," *Literary Digest,* February 15, 1936, p. 29, all in Reel 32, Images 328–31, J. H. Kellogg Papers, U-M.

19. "Transcript of Telephone Call Between J. H. Kellogg and Bankers, April 6, 1933," Reel 26, Images 1072–94, J. H. Kellogg Papers, U-M.

20. Telegram from J. H. Kellogg to Henry Ford, May 3, 1937; Letter from E. G. Liebold, General Secretary to Henry Ford, May 5, 1937; Letter from J. H. Kellogg to E. H. Liebold, May 10, 1937; E. G. Liebold to J. H. Kellogg, May 12, 1937; J. H. Kellogg to E. G. Liebold, May 15, 1937; E. G. Liebold to J. H. Kellogg, June 10, 1937, Accession 285, Box 2041, 1937–593-Kello-Kelly (Correspondence), Benson Ford Research Center, Henry Ford Museum and Greenfield Village, Dearborn Michigan. It is interesting to note that on September 10, 1937, J. H. Kellogg wrote Henry's wife, Clara Ford, "You have both shown so much interest in our work here that I am sure you will be glad to know that the embarrassment which distressed us considerably a few months ago is being satisfactorily adjusted," Reel 4, Image 1006, J. H. Kellogg Papers, U-M. A few years later, in 1940, he wrote to Clara: "I esteem Mr. Ford as one of the greatest men this country has produced. His contributions to industry and especially to the welfare of the average man are inestimable, and most of all I admire his sound philosophy and broad vision and unbiased common sense attitude toward fundamentals." J. H. Kellogg to Clara Ford, February 21, 1940, Reel 5, Images 977–98, J. H. Kellogg Papers, U-M.

21. "Reorganization Petition Mailed," *Battle Creek Enquirer and News,* June 4, 1937, Reel 32, Image 363; "Sanitarium Conferees Continue Discussions," *Battle Creek Enquirer and News,* August 26, 1938, Reel 32, Image 384; "San Policies Discussed at Board Meeting," *Battle Creek Enquirer and News,* November 24, 1938, p. 12, Reel 32, Image 389; "San Creditors Will Get Part Cash This Week," *Battle Creek Moon-Journal,* January 29, 1939, Reel 32, Image 390, J. H. Kellogg Papers, U-M.

22. Schwarz, PhD thesis, pp. 469–72.

23. Interview with Leslie Sargent, conducted by Richard Schwarz, August 8, 1962, Box 5, File 16, Sargent, Richard Schwarz Papers, Center for Adventist Research.

24. George Howe Colt, "Brother Against Brother: John and Will Kellogg," *Brothers: On His Brothers and Brothers in History* (New York: Scribner, 2012), pp. 162–63; Schwarz, *John Harvey Kellogg,* p. 238; J. H. Kellogg, "The Simple Life in a Nutshell," in *Dr. Kellogg's Lectures on Practical Topics,* Volume 1 (Battle Creek, MI: Good Health Publishing Co., 1913), pp. 61–80.

25. Schwarz, *John Harvey Kellogg,* pp. 233–34.

26. Powell, p. 285.

27. Schwarz, *John Harvey Kellogg,* p. 140.

28. Ibid., p. 238. Here Schwarz is quoting a letter from W. K. Kellogg to Dr. George Thomason, October 12, 1942, and the "Deposition in the matter of the Estate of John Harvey Kellogg," February 8, 1945, Schwarz PhD thesis, p. 482. This document exists in the now restricted files of the W. K. Kellogg Foundation Archives, to which I did not have access.

29. For details on Will's extensive letter-writing campaign against his brother to various Seventh-day Adventist officials, see letters from W. K. Kellogg to Elder W. H. Branson, October 18, 1943; April 16, 1943; November 19, 1943, Collection 234, Box 8,

File 17, as well as letter from George Thomason, M.D. to W. E. Nelson of the General Conference of the Seventh-day Adventist Church, January 17, 1943, which quotes a letter from W. K. Kellogg to George Thomason guaranteeing the Adventist Church "against financial loss," Collection 234, Box 9, File 2, Center for Adventist Research. See also earlier letters from W. K. Kellogg to Elder J. F. Wright, September 10, 1942, September 11, 1942 (in which he reports that John has "notified Seventh-day Adventist helpers at the Sanitarium work Saturdays, the same as other days"), September 18, 1942; September 16, 1942; October 24, 1942 (in which W.K. complains about John's purported attempts to ruin the U.S. government's plan to buy the San and reporting on his work to contain his brother's "wild and expensive plans" and "spending spree"). On November 19, 1943, Will wrote W. H. Branson about how badly his brother presented himself on the witness stand. "Knowing from past experiences that Dr. Kellogg is a very evasive witness, it occurs to me that the unfavorable impression that he is almost sure to make on the Court would make a wonderfully good witness for the defense." All these letters are in Collection 234, Box 9, F 20, Center for Adventist Research.

30. W. K. Kellogg to Elder W. H. Branson, October 18, 1943, Collection 234, Box 9, F 20, Center for Adventist Research.

31. Letter from George Thomason, M.D. to W. E. Nelson of the General Conference of the Seventh-day Adventists, January 17, 1943, Collection 234, Box 9, File 2, Center for Adventist Research. This letter attaches a copy of a letter Will Kellogg wrote to Thomason, undated. The quote is from page 4 of the letter.

32. Schwarz, *John Harvey Kellogg*, pp. 238–40.

33. Elizabeth Neumayer, *"Mother": Ella Eaton Kellogg* (Battle Creek, MI: Heritage Battle Creek, 2002), p. 49. This page has a table listing all forty-two of the Kelloggs' adopted or foster children.

34. "Dr. Kellogg Is Dead at 91," *Battle Creek Enquirer and News*, December 15, 1943, Page 1; "Funeral Program for John H. Kellogg," Reel 31, Image 333, J. H. Kellogg Papers, U-M; Schwarz, *John Harvey Kellogg*, pp. 240–41; Brian Wilson, *Dr. John Harvey Kellogg and the Religion of Biologic Living* (Bloomington: Indiana University Press, 2014), p. 173.

35. What remained of the San, now called the Sanitarium Association, was absorbed by a group of Seventh-day Adventist physicians and reopened in 1959 as the Battle Creek Health Center, which focused on mental health and substance abuse treatment and acute care. Long-term sanitarium services ended in 1972 and, two years later, in 1974, the facility was absorbed into the Seventh-day Adventist Hospital System. In 1993, the entire facility was sold to the secular Battle Creek System, which is now defunct. See Wilson, *Dr. John Harvey Kellogg*, p. 173; Carson, pp. 251–53; Schwarz, *Dr. John Harvey Kellogg*, pp. 239–41; *Battle Creek Enquirer and News*, December 15, 1943, p. 1.

36. Powell, pp. 285–86.

37. Ibid., p. 286.

38. Ibid.

39. Ibid., pp. 286–87.

40. Pauline Kael, Herman J. Mankiewicz, and Orson Welles, *The Citizen Kane Book: Raising Kane by Pauline Kael and the Shooting Script* (Boston: Little, Brown, 1971).

41. Powell, pp. 350–51.

42. Ibid., p. 351. Hoatson later married Elbon. Williamson Jr., *An Intimate Glimpse*, p. 203.

43. Powell, p. 351.

44. "W. K. Kellogg, 1860–1951," *The Kellogg News,* October 1951, Collections of the Willard Library of Battle Creek, Michigan.

45. Powell, p. 345.

46. "Community to Mourn W. K. Kellogg for Week," *Battle Creek Enquirer and News,* October 7, 1951, p. 1. The obituary appears on pp. 1, 12, 13, and 14.

47. Also buried in this plot are Will's first wife, Elmira (Ella) Osborn Davis Kellogg, their two sons who died in childhood, Irvin Hadley and William Keith Jr., his sister Hester, his niece Gertrude, and a cousin, Sarah E. Kellogg. Deb Stanley, "W. K. Kellogg Rests Here," in "A Battle Creek Celebration: W. K. Kellogg 150 Years," *Scene Magazine,* 1997; 34(1): 57; Colt, *Brothers: On His Brothers and Brothers in History,* p. 166.

48. Williamson Jr., *An Intimate Glimpse,* pp. 186–87, 190.

49. Ibid., p. 190.

50. Ibid., p. 187.

51. William Carew Hazlitt, *English Proverbs and Proverbial Phrases Collected from the Most Authentic Sources, Alphabetically Arranged and Annotated with Much Matter Not Previously Published* (London: Reeves and Turner, 1907), p. 173. The author of the proverb is unknown but it appears in John Clarke's 1639 proverb collection *Paroemiologia Anglo-Latina in Usum Scholarum Concinnata; Or proverbs English, and Latine, methodically disposed according to the common-place heads, in Erasmus his adages. Very use-full and delightful for all sorts of men, on all occasions. More especially profitable for scholars for the attaining elegancie, sublimitie, and varietie of the best expressions* (London: Imprinted by Felix Kyngston for Robert Mylbourne, and are to be sold at the signe of the Vnicorne neere Fleet-bridge, 1639).

52. Carson, p. 87.

Index

A NOTE ON THE TYPE

This book was set in Adobe Garamond. Designed for the Adobe Corporation by Robert Slimbach, the fonts are based on types first cut by Claude Garamond (ca. 1480–1561). Garamond was a pupil of Geoffroy Tory and is believed to have followed the Venetian models, although he introduced a number of important differences, and it is to him that we owe the letter we now know as "old style." He gave to his letters a certain elegance and feeling of movement that won their creator an immediate reputation and the patronage of Francis I of France.

Composed by North Market Street Graphics,
Lancaster, Pennsylvania

Printed and bound by Berryville Graphics,
Berryville, Virginia

Designed by M. Kristen Bearse